Southern India
A Guide to Monuments Sites & Museums

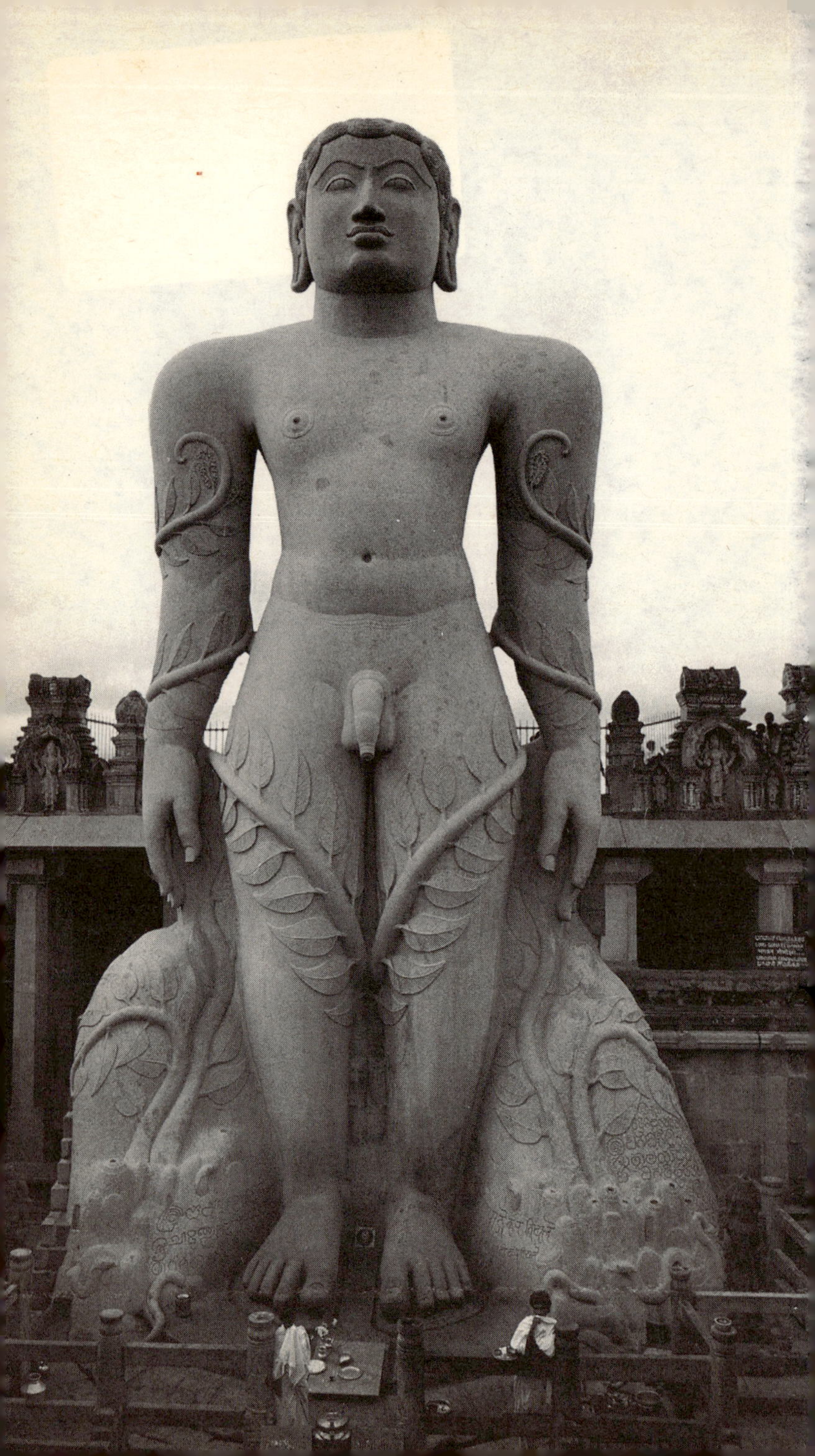

Southern India
A Guide to Monuments Sites & Museums

George Michell

LOTUS COLLECTION
ROLI BOOKS

PHOTO CREDITS

American Institute of India Studies: 37, 42-43, 70, 78, 91, 106, 113, 168, 188, 223, 238, 298, 332, 343, 357, 359, 371, 410, 414, 433, 465, 488, 510-511, 540
Corbis: 54 (From *100 Wonders of India*, Roli Books)
Dinodia: 2 (From *100 Wonders of India*, Roli Books)
George Michell: 385, 388-89
India Picture: 10-11, 131, 179, 289, 481, 524
Iramuthusamy/ Wikimedia Commons: 160-161
Roli Collection: 194-195, 281
Sanjay Acharya/ Wikimedia Commons: 98
Toby Sinclair: 304-305 (From *Forts & Palaces of India*, Roli Books)
Vijayshankar Munoli/ Wikimedia Commons: 139

Lotus Collection
© George Michell, 2013

All rights reserved. No part of this publication may be reproduced or transmitted, in any form or by any means, without the prior permission of the publisher.

The Lotus Collection
An imprint of Roli Books Pvt. Ltd.
M-75, G.K. II Market, New Delhi 110 048
Phone: ++91 (011) 4068 2000. Fax: ++91 (011) 2921 7185
E-mail: info@rolibooks.com; Website: rolibooks.com
Also at Bengaluru, Chennai, & Mumbai

Frontispiece: Gommateshvara Monolith, Sravana Belgola, Karnataka.
Cover design: Bonita Vaz-Shimray
Layout: Sanjeev Mathpal
Production: Shaji Sahadevan & Jyoti De

ISBN: 978-81-7436-920-8

Printed in Polykam Offset, New Delhi.

Contents

Foreword	7
Maps	8-9

Introduction

History	12
Architecture	20
Art	31

Maharashtra

1. Mumbai	45
2. Around Mumbai	61
3. Pune	73
4. Nasik	87
5. Aurangabad	94
6. Ahmadnagar	123
7. Mahabaleshwar	128
8. Kolhapur	137
9. Sholapur	145
10. Nagpur	154

Goa

11. Central Goa	165
12. North Goa	181
13. South Goa	187

Karnataka

14. Bengaluru	196
15. Mysore	206
16. Kodugu	217
17. Mangalore	219
18. Chikmagalur	230
19. Shimoga	236
20. Hampi	243
21. Hubli	263
22. Badami	267
23. Bijapur	279
24. Gulbarga	287
25. Bidar	296

Andhra Pradesh

26. Hyderabad	307
27. Around Hyderabad	323
28. Warangal	330
29. Vijayawada	336
30. Rajahmundry	346
31. Visakhapatnam	351
32. Kurnool	358
33. Anantapur	366
34. Cuddapah	374
35. Tirupati	380

Tamil Nadu
36. Chennai — 391
37. Around Chennai — 406
38. Vellore — 422
39. Puducherry — 429
40. Thanjavur — 441
41. Tiruchirapalli — 462
42. Salem — 473
43. Coimbatore — 477
44. Madurai — 483
45. Tirunelveli — 498

Kerala
46. Thiruvananthapuram — 513
47. Kochi — 520
48. Kozhikode — 543

Glossary — 551
Index — 573

Foreword

In recent years Southern India has attracted ever growing numbers of travellers, scholars, students and pilgrims from other parts of India, as well as from abroad. Yet until now there has been no comprehensive, handy reference to the region's major historical monuments and sites and principal museum collections. Hence the present volume, which is conceived as a series of itineraries based in and around a city or town where visitors may expect to find adequate accommodation and other essential facilities. The itineraries cover more than 500 monuments and sites, far more than visitors could expect to reach in a single tour, no matter how extended. These places are all included here in the hope that visitors will consider returning to Southern India on more than one occasion so as to explore a region that is unusually richly endowed with ancient buildings, remains, and objects and artefacts spanning more than 2,000 year of history.

In preparing this volume, I have benefitted from inputs offered by friends and colleagues. They include Andrew Bauer, Henry Brownrigg, John Copland, Anna L. Dallapiccola, John M. Fritz, Sandhya Harendra, Helen Philon, Klaus Rötzer and Bob Simkin. Priya Kapoor, together with her team at Roli Books in Delhi, has offered encouragement and editorial and design skills. To all these individuals I offer my sincere thanks.

George Michell
Goa, January 2013

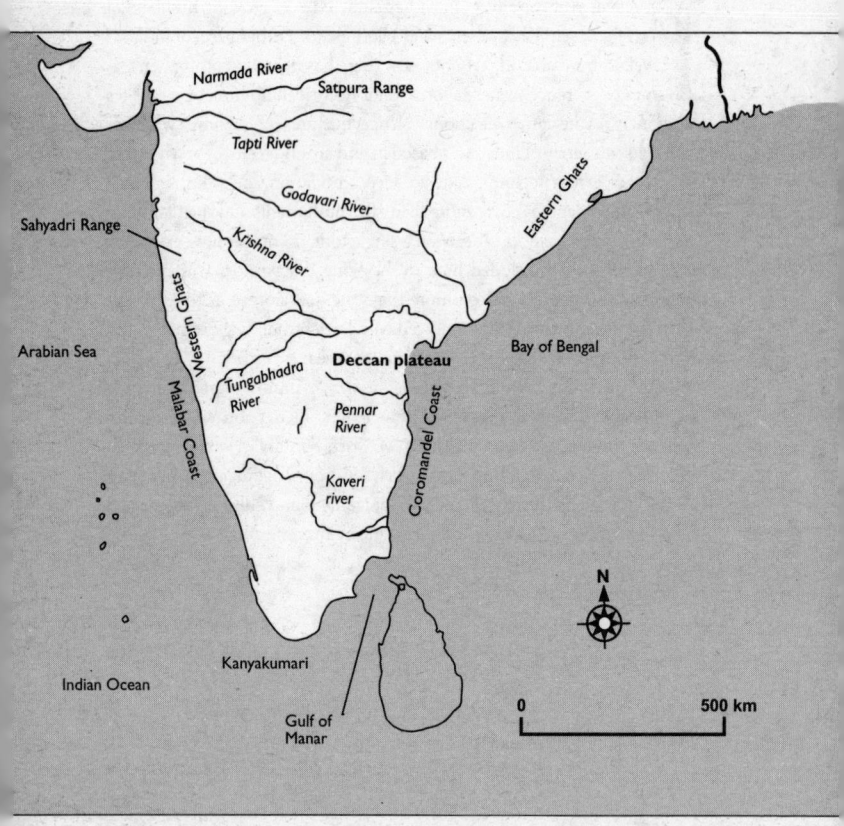

Southern India, Physical.

Southern India, Political.

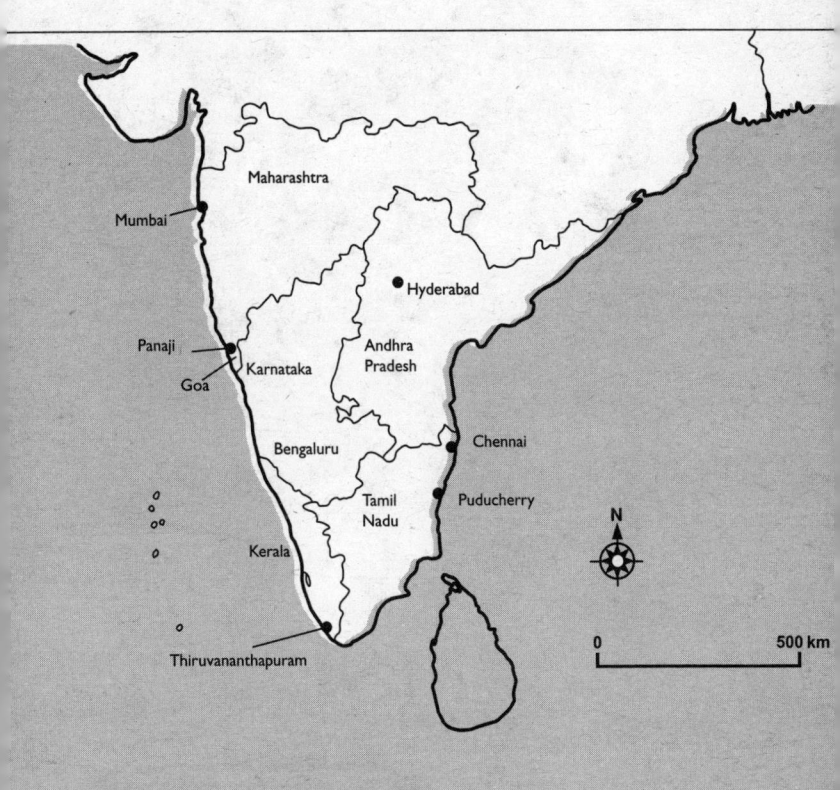

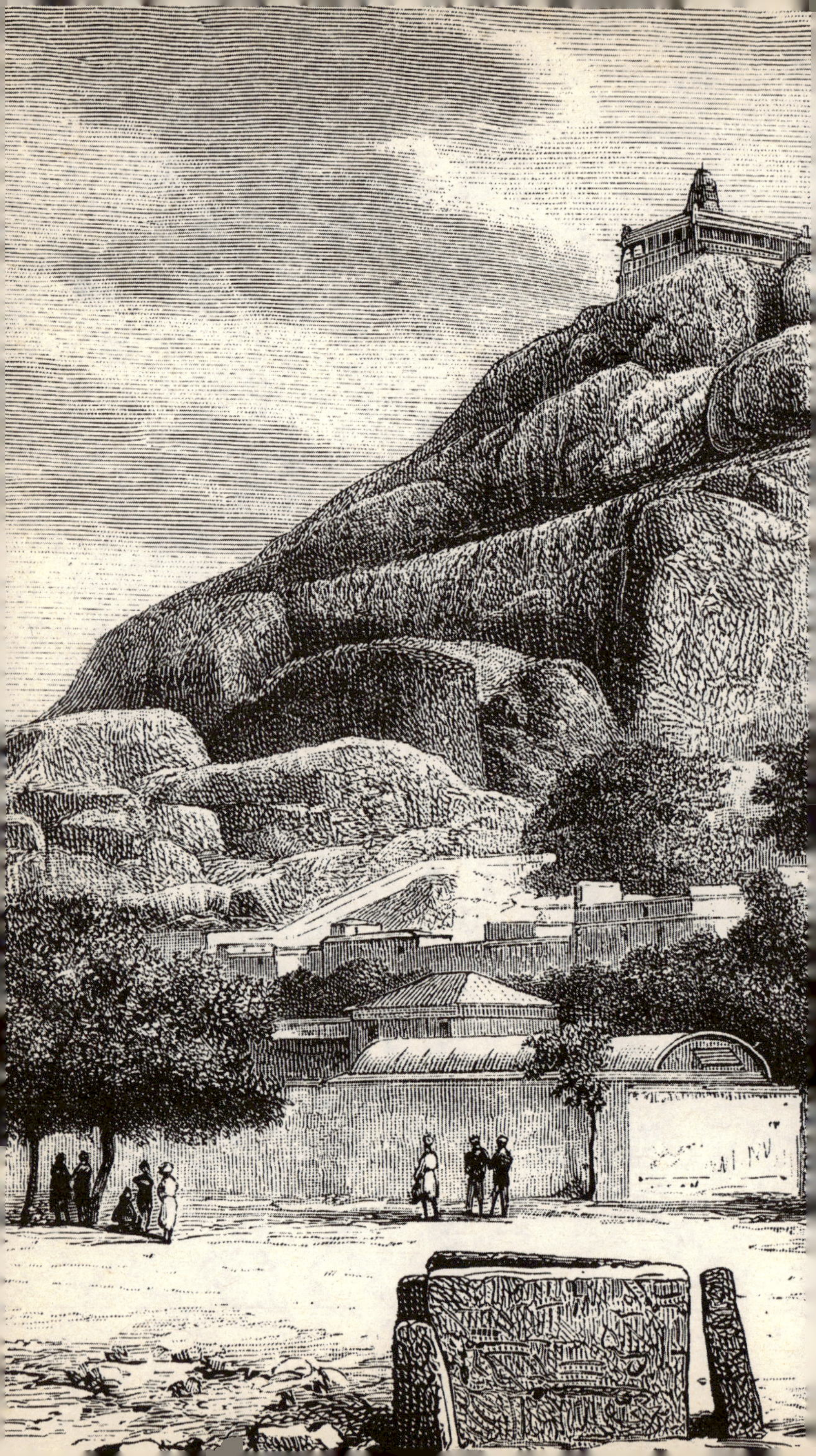

Rock Fort, Tiruchirapalli, Tamil Nadu

INTRODUCTION

History

The dense array of monuments and sites that forms the subject of this volume is a testament to the historical complexity of Southern India over more than 2,000 years. Never during this long period was the region unified into a single state.

THE FIRST KINGDOMS

While the presence of Ashokan edicts at Brahmagiri [20L] and Maski [20M] in Karnataka indicate that this part of Southern India formed part of the Maurya empire of Northern India in the 3rd century BCE, it is not until the following century that the region emerges as a historical entity, under the Satavahanas of Paithan [5L] in southern Maharashtra. From this centre the Satavahanas spread their influence throughout the region, and even beyond, into central India, conquering a vast territory that encompassed much of the peninsula. The Satavahanas were responsible for inaugurating Buddhist architecture in Southern India: the rock-cut sanctuaries at Ajanta [5F] and Pandu Lena [4B], as well as the free-standing complexes at Amaravati [29K] and Guntupalle [30B], are among the many monuments assigned to their reign. Some sites, like Ter [9D], are rich in coins, terracottas and ivories.

Though the Satavahanas were challenged on their western flank by the Shakas of Middle Eastern origin in the 1st century CE, they retained their independence until the end of the 2nd century, when they were supplanted by the Ikshvakus. Though this line of rulers was not so long-lived, they managed to wrest control of much of Andhra Pradesh in the 3rd-4th centuries, selecting Nagarjunakonda [27H] on the Krishna River as their capital. At about the same time, the Tamil country came under the sway of the Pallavas of Kanchipuram [37E], but only fragmentary evidence is available for the first kings of this dynasty.

The Vakatakas of central India held an important place in politics and culture in the 4th-5th centuries, and their influence extended into Maharashtra.

Nandivardhana [10B] served as one of their capitals, and vestiges of their presence are still seen on nearby Ramtek Hill [10B]. It is, however, for their patronage of rock-cut Buddhist shrines and monasteries at Ajanta and Aurangabad [5B] that these rulers and their subordinates are best known. Harishena (460-78) is the outstanding personality of the era; the painted depiction of a king receiving gifts from a foreign delegation in Cave 1 at Ajanta is sometimes thought to be his portrait.

EARLY HINDU DYNASTIES

The next phase of Southern Indian history is marked by the growth of simultaneous lines of kings who sponsored Hindu monuments. The Mauryas and Kalachuris, who were active in Maharashtra in the 6th century, derived their wealth from the trade routes that led from the Arabian Sea Coast, known as the Konkan, to the Deccan plateau of the interior peninsula. Their cave-temples at Elephanta [2A] and Ellora (Caves 21 and 29) [5E] are the most elaborate of the era. These rulers were to some extent displaced by the Early Chalukyas of Badami [22A], who controlled most of Karnataka as well as parts of Andhra Pradesh. It was under these kings that structural architecture first appears in the region, as can be seen at Badami and nearby Pattadakal [22D] and Aihole [22E]. As they expanded southwards, the Early Chalukyas came into conflict with their rivals further south, the Pallavas. Pulakeshin (609-54), one of the prominent Early Chalukya kings, attained renown by defeating Harsha of Kanauj, the most powerful ruler of Northern India at the time, and executing raids on the Pallava capital of Kanchipuram. The Pallavas retaliated, and in 654 occupied Badami. Struggles between the two kingdoms continued into the 8th century, but the career of the Early Chalukyas came to an end in 753 with the invasion of their domains by the Rashtrakutas. These rulers brought a large part of Maharashtra, Karnataka and Andhra Pradesh under their sway. An idea of their considerable resources may be had from the colossal monolithic temple known as the Kailasa (Cave 16) at Ellora, begun by Krishna I (756-73).

The Pallavas established themselves as the leading power part in the northern part of Tamil Nadu during the 7th-9th centuries. Their earliest monuments are rock-cut or monolithic, as at Mamallapuram [37A] and Mandagapattu [39E], but later developments at their capital, Kanchipuram, and Panamalai [39G] demonstrate a shift towards structural building techniques. The Pallavas were restrained on their southern flank by their contemporaries, the Pandyas of Madurai [44A], masters of the southern part of Tamil Nadu, who also extended their influence into neighbouring Kerala.

In the 10th-13th centuries, central Karnataka and southern Andhra Pradesh came under the sway of the Nolambas and Gangas, who ruled from Hemavati [33G] and Talkad [15E] respectively. The latter kings were the first patrons of

Sravana Belgola [15F], the preeminent Jain site in Southern India. At this time northern Karnataka and parts of Andhra Pradesh were dominated by the Late Chalukyas of Basavakalyan [25D], so-called to distinguish them from their predecessors of the same name, to whom they were only vaguely related. The Late Chalukya temples at Ittagi [20G] and Dambal [21D] give an idea of the remarkable architectural achievements of the era. Meanwhile, the remainder of Andhra Pradesh was controlled by another line of the Badami family, known for convenience as the Eastern Chalukyas. These kings built extensively throughout the Bay of Bengal provinces, as at Bikkavolu [30E] and Samalkot [30H].

The rise of the Cholas signals a new period in the history of Southern India. These kings first established their supremacy in the Tamil zone in the 9th-10th century, before invading tracts of Karnataka and Andhra Pradesh, absorbing the Nolamba and Ganga territories, and progressing up the eastern coast as far as Orissa. Chola naval campaigns even reached Sri Lanka and Southeast Asia. Under forceful personalities like Rajaraja (985-1016) and Rajendra I (1012-44), the Chola state took on the dimensions and apparatus of a grand empire. Thanjavur [40A] served as their principal capital, supplanted for a time by Gangaikondacholapuram [40J]. Magnificent temples at both these sites testify to the impressive ambitions of the Cholas in the 11th century, a situation that continued into the 12th century, judging from the large-scale projects at Chidambaram [39H] and Tribhuvanam [40H].

Chola expansion was resisted towards the end of the 12th century by the Hoysalas, based at Halebid [18B] in southern Karnataka. These kings set about to conquer Tamil Nadu, but were checked by the resurgent Pandyas in the extreme south of the peninsula. Even so, the Hoysalas managed to bring all of Karnataka under their control, subduing the Late Chalukyas. They also sponsored a uniquely ornate style of religious architecture, as can be seen in temples at Halebid and nearby Belur [18A]. As the Hoysalas were consolidating their hegemony, the Kakatiyas of Hanamkonda [28B] and Warangal [28A] emerged as the prevailing power in Andhra Pradesh. Their domains encroached on those of the East Chalukyas, who were steadily absorbed into the Warangal kingdom.

The dissolution of Rashtrakuta power during the 10th century was hastened by the rise of their successors, the Yadavas. Basing themselves at the great rock citadel of Devagiri [5C], the Yadavas consolidated their gains in the 11th-12th centuries, bringing peace and prosperity to much of Maharashtra. Though they built extensively, only a few of their monuments survive intact. The temple at Sinnar [4D] shows stylistic influence from Northern and Western India, with which the Yadavas had commercial contact. Like the Hoysalas and Kakatiyas, the Yadavas continued to rule until the invasion by the Delhi army at the end of the 13th century.

The Delhi Conquest and its Aftermath

The first intrusion into Southern India by the forces of the Khalji sultans of Delhi occurred in 1296. This was followed by a series of campaigns that eventually dislodged all the previous ruling houses of the region, bringing to an end the Yadava, Kakatiya, Hoysala and Pandava lines. By 1323, the commanders of the Delhi Tughluq army were firmly established at Madurai in the far south. In an effort to control this newly won part of the country, Muhammad Tughluq shifted his capital to Devagiri in 1327, rebuilding the fortifications and renaming it Daulatabad. Soon after, in 1334, Muhammad Tughluq recalled the army to Delhi to assist in wars elsewhere. The results were twofold: the Muslim governors of Madurai and Daulatabad proclaimed their independence, and an obscure line of Hindu chiefs known as the Sangamas, based in Hampi [20B] on the Tungabhadra River in Karnataka, set about reclaiming the lands lost to the Tughluqs. These events led to the creation of the Bahmani and Sangama kingdoms, the latter known as Vijayanagara, after the name of their newly founded capital near Hampi.

After securing their autonomy in 1347, the Bahmanis shifted from Daulatabad to Gulbarga [24A], remaining there until the early 15th century, when they relocated to Bidar [25A]. The Bahmanis ruled over an extensive territory encompassing all of Maharashtra and large tracts of northern Karnataka and Andhra Pradesh. The influx of Persians, Arabs and Turks into Southern India introduced a new language, culture and religion. This was accompanied by an equally novel architecture that reconciled imported Islamic forms and decorative devices with indigenous practice. Amongst the most powerful Bahmani figures were Tajuddin Firuz (1397-1422), Ahmad I (1422-36) and Mahmud Gawan, Prime Minister under Muhammad III (1468-82). The Bahmanis established great circular citadels, inside which they erected sumptuous palaces. Royal tombs were situated on the outskirts, as were the graves of saintly figures who bolstered the prestige of these kings. Among the fortified outposts that effectively guarded their kingdom are the citadels at Purandhar [3J], Sholapur [9A] and Raichur [20N].

The first task of the Sangamas of Vijayanagara was to liberate the lands lost to the Delhi forces; this they achieved with astounding swiftness. By 1371 the Sangamas had reached the southern tip of Tamil Nadu, extinguishing the line of Madurai sultans, and thereby earning the allegiance of the lesser chiefs and governors of the region. At the turn of the 15th century the Sangamas were in command of almost all of the peninsula south of the Tungabhadra and Krishna Rivers; only parts of the Malabar Coast lay beyond their grasp. The centralised government of the Sangamas rapidly assumed the authority of an empire, with all the resources of this vast territory being siphoned off to the capital. Under Bukka I (1354-77) and Devaraya II (1423-56), two of the most influential

Sangama kings, Vijayanagara was built up into a showpiece of imperial magnificence, furnished with impressive military, ceremonial and religious structures [20C].

Bahmani-Vijayanagara conflict in the 14th-15th centuries mainly concentrated on control of the richly irrigated triangle of land lying between the Tungabhadra and Krishna Rivers. In spite of repeated wars, sieges and raids, the two kingdoms coexisted uneasily until the end of the 15th century, when both were subjected to internal forces of disruption.

RISE OF THE SUCCESSOR STATES

Rivalry between immigrants from the Middle East and local Muslims contributed to the break-up of the Bahmani kingdom. By the beginning of the 16th century, the region had fragmented into smaller states, each founded by a former provincial governor. The three most significant figures of the era were Yusuf Adil Khan (1490-1510), who established the Adil Shahi dynasty, which ruled from Bijapur [23A], in northern Karnataka; Ahmad Nizam Shah, who performed a similar role for the Nizam Shahis of Ahmadnagar [6A] in Maharashtra; and Quli Qutb al-Mulk (d. 1543), originator of the Qutb Shahi line at Golconda [26E] in Andhra Pradesh. Lesser personalities were Qasim Barid (1488-1504), first of the Baridi rulers of Bidar, capital of a much smaller dominion, and Fathullah Imad Shah (d. 1510) of Achalpur [10D] in Berar, in the northern extremity of Maharashtra. A review of the simultaneous careers of these Deccan states reveals a history of shifting alliances that effectively prevented any one of these kingdoms from attaining supremacy in the region. Only when these rulers perceived Vijayanagara on their southern flank as a common enemy was a consortium formed that led to the battle of January 1565, in which the Vijayanagara forces were finally vanquished.

With the removal of the immediate threat of Vijayanagara, Bijapur and Golconda emerged as the two most prosperous Deccan states, the former eventually engulfing the territories of the Baridis. The Nizam Shahi kingdom was the first to bear the impact of the Mughals, who began intruding into Southern India in the last years of the 16th century. Ahmadnagar was lost to the Mughals in 1636, but it took another 50 years of constant warring before Bijapur and Golconda capitulated. In the meantime, both states were able to achieve a high degree of affluence and cultural sophistication. This is clear from the grand building programmes initiated by Ibrahim II (1580-1627) and Muhammad Adil Shah (1627-56), both of whom erected imposing mausoleums at Bijapur. Equally influential was Muhammad Quli (1580-1611), the ruler responsible for shifting the Qutb Shahi capital to the newly planned city of Hyderabad [26A].

Further south in the first half of the 16th century, the Tuluva emperors of Vijayanagara ruled with unprecedented splendour. Investment in large-scale

Hindu complexes was sustained at the capital and at religious sites like Ahobilam [32F] and Tirumala [35B]. Local governors under Vijayanagara also acted as sponsors of temple projects, as at Tadpatri [33B] and Lepakshi [33F]. Krishnadevaraya (1510-29) made extensive tours of his dominions, as well as embarking upon warring campaigns against his neighbours to the north. His expedition to Orissa in 1516 was marked by the capture of Udayagiri [34D], the premier fortress guarding the Bay of Bengal coastal strip. Achyutaraya (1529-42) sustained this aggressive policy, but courtly intrigue under his successor, Sadashiva, gave Ramaraya, commander of the imperial forces, an excuse to seize control. In the process, Ramaraya antagonised the kings of Bijapur, Golconda and Ahmadnagar, with fateful results for Vijayanagara.

After the abandonment of the Vijayanagara capital in 1565, a new line of rulers, known as the Aravidus, who were descended from Ramaraya, retreated southwards to Penukonda [33D], before settling permanently at Chandragiri [35C]. In consequence of losing much of their lands in Karnataka and Andhra, the Vijayanagara emperors were greatly reduced in prestige and influence. This situation encouraged the governors of Tamil Nadu to assert their independence in the second half of the 16th century. Known as Nayakas, these figures gradually emerged as independent rulers based at Gingee [39F], Thanjavur and Madurai. Conflicts between the Nayakas and the Aravidus led to the civil war in which the Vijayanagara emperor Venkata patideva (1586-1614) lost his life. The later Aravidus were of minor significance.

The 17th century coincides with the ascendancy of the Nayakas in the Tamil zone. Raghunatha (1614-34) and Vijaya raghava (1634-73) were among the greatest of the Thanjavur Nayakas, though the latter was killed in battle against the Madurai forces. Tirumala Nayaka of Madurai (1623-59) was the outstanding statesman and warrior of the era. His grandiose building projects are evident at Madurai, Srirangam [41B] and Alagarkoil [44C].

The pattern of provincial figures emerging as autonomous rulers in the wake of Vijayanagara's decline also occurred in Karnataka. The Nayakas of Keladi [19B] and Ikkeri [19C] were the first in this region to stake their claim to sovereignty, governing freely over the forested tracts in the western part of the state. The somewhat later Wodeyars of Mysore [15A] and Gowdas of Bengaluru [14A] came into competition over the territories further south, with the Wodeyars eventually triumphing over the Gowdas.

The 16th-17th centuries also witnessed the arrival of the first Europeans in Southern India. Vasco da Gama landed on the Malabar Coast in 1498, and by 1510 the Portuguese had founded Goa [11B] as the headquarters of their seaborne Asian empire. Forging alliances with the rulers of Kerala they became involved in local affairs at Kochi [47A] and Kozhikode [48A]. The Portuguese were followed in the 17th century by the Dutch, who managed to wrest several ports from them, including Kochi. The English arrived not long after, and by the end of the 17th century the newly formed East India Company had established lucrative trading posts at Mumbai [1C] and Chennai [36A], known at that time as Bombay and Madras.

THE MUGHALS AND MARATHAS

The Mughal conquest of Southern India occupied all of the later years of the emperor Aurangzeb's reign (1658-1707). After absorbing the Bijapur and Golconda kingdoms into the Deccan provinces of the Mughal empire, Aurangzeb's forces swept southwards into Tamil Nadu. They were, however, impeded in their progress by daring raids executed by the Maratha forces under Shivaji (1674-80) and his successors. Mughal-Maratha skirmishes became a constant feature of warfare, continuing into the 18th century. By this time large portions of Southern India were firmly in Maratha hands, including Thanjavur, which became the seat of an independent line of rulers that lasted into the 19th century. Aurangabad and Hyderabad, on the other hand, remained with the Mughals. Under the command of Nizamul Mulk (1723-48), first of the Asaf Jahi line, the Mughal Deccan provinces separated from Delhi to become the independent state of Hyderabad. The Asaf Jahis, known better by their title of Nizam, survived into the middle of the 20th century.

The 18th century witnessed the remarkable expansion of Maratha power beyond Southern India. This rapidly growing empire was directed by the Peshwas, Prime Ministers of Shivaji's descendants, based in Pune [3A]. Wars between the Asaf Jahis and the Marathas continued throughout the era, with the British and French contributing troops to Hyderabad in return for trading rights on the Bay of Bengal, known to Europeans as the Coromandel Coast. The outstanding event of the second half of the 18th century was the rise to power of Haidar Ali, former Mughal governor in Karnataka. After usurping the Wodeyar throne of Mysore, Haidar pursued a series of aggressive campaigns throughout Southern India, a policy that was successfully continued by his son, Tipu Sultan. Only in 1799, after the Maratha, Asaf Jahi and English armies joined forces, was Tipu finally vanquished in the siege of Srirangapattana [15C]. The Maratha state thereafter disintegrated into civil war, prompting the English to intervene. By 1818 the Maratha factions were defeated, and the English were in charge of all their former territories in Southern India.

The 18th century also witnessed struggles between different European powers for control of the coastal trade. The Portuguese maintained their hold on Goa, while the English and French came into conflict over commercial control of the Coromandel Coast. The French raided Madras on several occasions, but in the end retired to a minor position from their headquarters at Puducherry [39A].

FROM EMPIRE TO INDEPENDENCE

Comparative peace and prosperity returned to Southern India in the 19th century. More than half the region was absorbed into the Bombay and Madras Presidencies, the two major British provinces, while the remainder was divided among princely realms such as those of Hyderabad, Mysore and Travancore, the last based at Thiruvananthapuram [46A]. The rulers of these states, as well as of lesser kingdoms of Kolhapur [8A] and Pudukkottai [41G], were under the firm control of British Residents. Revenues previously used to finance private armies were redirected towards building programmes, with the result that princely capitals were furnished with handsome palatial and civic buildings. Meanwhile, Bombay and Madras now Mumbai [1] and Chennai [36], developed into manufacturing and shipping centres of global significance. Grandiose public monuments in both cities expressed the wealth and confidence attained in the second half of the 19th century.

Though only a minor disturbance in Southern India, the Uprising of 1857 led inexorably to demands for self-rule. The Indian National Congress was founded in Bombay in 1885, and was followed by other parties. From 1915 Mahatma Gandhi was the major focus for the independence movement, and many decisions of national importance were taken from his retreat near Wardha [10C] in rural Maharashtra. Independence was finally achieved in 1947, two years after the end of World War II. The former British Presidencies and princely domains of Southern India were thereupon dismantled and reorganized along linguistic lines into the modern states of the Indian Union.

FURTHER READING

Bayly, Susan, *Saints, Goddesses and Kings: Muslims and Christians in South Indian Society 1700-1900*, Cambridge 1989.

Eaton, Richard, *A Social History of the Deccan, 1300-1761*, Cambridge 2005.

Gordon, Stewart, *The Marathas, 1600-1818*, Cambridge 1993.

Hall, Maurice, *Window on Goa: A History and Guide*, London 1995.

Howes, Jennifer, *The Courts of Pre-Colonial South India: Material Culture and Kingship*, London 2002.

Joshi, P.M. and G. Yazdani, eds., *History of Medieval Deccan (1295-1724)*, Hyderabad 1973-4.

Keay, John, *India: A History*, London and New Delhi 2000.

Nilakanta Sastri, K.A., *A History of South India From Prehistoric Times to Fall of Vijayanagara*, Delhi 1975.

Pearson, M.N., *The Portuguese in India*, Cambridge 1987.

Stein, Burton, *Vijayanagara*, Cambridge 1989.

Architecture

WOODEN TRADITIONS

Stone imitations of timber and thatch buildings offer convincing evidence for a lost wooden tradition in Southern India. Chaitya halls at Karla [3C] and Ajanta [5F], dating from the 2nd-1st century BCE, for example, have horseshoe-shaped openings derived from flexible bamboo construction. Masonry stupas from the 2nd-4th centuries CE are surrounded by stone posts and railings that copy wooden originals, such as those at Amaravati [29K]. Timber and thatch buildings are also the source for vaulted and domical roof forms in Hindu temple architecture, but only the hut-like, linga shrine at Chidambaram [39H] actually preserves its wooden framework, renewed through the centuries. Hut-like roofs and parapet elements were fashioned in stone for the first time in the 7th century at Badami [22A] and Mamallapuram [37A], and remain a constant feature of Southern Indian architecture thereafter.

Stone temples in Karnataka and Andhra Pradesh display open halls with intricately worked circular columns that reproduce lathe-turned, wooden originals. Peripheral supports are sheltered by eaves that angle or curve outwards in the semblance of thatch, supported by timber-like, stone rafters and ribs. The sloping stone roofs of the 8th century Early Chalukya temples at Aihole [22E], for instance, have their joints covered with log-like strips, a feature that also occurs in temples of the west coast of Karnataka, as at Mudabidri [17C].

Kerala architecture has always retained sloping roofs to shed the heavy rains of the region. Frameworks of timber beams and rafters support pyramidal and conical roofs, often rising in multiple tiers, clad in copper or terracotta tiles. Finely worked wooden screens, beams and ceilings are typical of this tradition, as can be seen in temples at Ettumanur [47G] and Kaviyur [47K]. Mosques in Kerala employ the same multi-tiered wooden roof structures, but with the exception of examples at Kozhikode [48A], these have now mostly disappeared. Palaces display a similar preference for timber construction. The complex at Padmanabhapuram [45O] is composed largely of wooden columned pavilions with slatted screens, sheltered by sloping tiled roofs with decorated gables.

Royal structures in other parts of Southern India must have also employed timber columns and tiled roofs, but these have vanished, leaving only stone foundations and footing blocks, as in the royal enclosures at Vijayanagara [20C]. An exception is the 16th century Rangin Mahal in the palace at Bidar [25A], which preserves its ornately carved wooden columns, brackets and beams. Similar timber elements may be seen in the 19th-20th century mansions on the Chettinad area of Tamil Nadu [44K].

CUTTING INTO ROCK

Monumental stone architecture in Southern India begins with excavation rather than construction. The basaltic plateau of Maharashtra is punctuated by escarpments and deep gorges that offer ideal sites for cutting into rock. Chaitya halls and monasteries were created for Buddhist communities as early as the 2nd-1st centuries BCE, as can be seen at Karla and Bhaja [3D]. Apsidal-ended halls are divided into three aisles by double rows of columns, creating horseshoe-shaped arched openings in the front. Interiors are dominated by monolithic stupas raised on cylindrical drums. Chaitya halls of the 5th-6th century CE, Vakataka and Early Chalukya eras, such as those at Ajanta (Caves 19 and 26) and Ellora (Cave 10) [5E], add screen walls with doorways and arched windows. Viharas, or monasteries, at these sites follow a standard pattern, with sleeping cells opening off central halls. The end shrine rooms generally accommodate Buddha images. The 2nd century BCE monasteries at Pandu Lena [4B] have octagonal columns standing in pot-like bases. These imitate the brass vessels in which actual timbers would have been placed. Balcony seating is adorned with relief representations of wooden railings. (That these halls and monasteries had structural equivalents is indicated by salvaged structures at Nagarjunakonda [27H], and brick shrines at Ter [9D] and Cherzala [29N], all assigned to the 3rd-4th century CE, Ikshvaku period.)

Cutting into rock was also the preferred technique for early Hindu sanctuaries. The 6th century Early Chalukya cave-temples at Badami, excavated into red sandstone cliffs, consist of verandahs fronting columned halls, or mandapas, with small shrines cut into the rear walls. Such schemes are amplified at Ellora in the 7th-8th centuries (Caves 11 and 15). The 6th century cave-temple at Elephanta [2A] has a linga sanctuary positioned in the middle of an extensive mandapa. Granite outcrops in Tamil Nadu were also exploited by the Pallavas and Pandyas in the 7th-8th centuries, as can be seen at

Mamallapuram and Tiru pparankunram [44B]. Excavated shrines here have verandahs overhung by curved eaves, with small arch-shaped windows in shallow relief.

The habit of fashioning monolithic temples in the semblance of actual structures was also popular at this time, as can be judged from the 'rathas' at Mamallapuram, which present a full range of contrasting roof typologies. This tradition reaches a climax in the 8th-9th centuries under the Rashtrakutas. The stupendous monolithic Kaliasa (Cave 16) at Ellora reproduces the features of an actual built complex, such as those at Pattadakal [22D]. The Indra Sabha (Cave 32) at Ellora brings this phase to an end.

EARLY TEMPLES

It was not until the 7th-8th centuries that structural techniques in Southern India were sufficiently developed for temple architecture to advance. Experiments of the Early Chalukyas at Aihole and Badami show simple tripartite arrangements of porch, mandapa and sanctuary. Such schemes were further developed at nearby Pattadakal and the Pallava capital at Kanchipuram [37E]. The outer walls of temples at these sites are divided into pilastered projections framing sculpture niches, topped with parapets of miniature roof forms. These features are repeated at diminishing scales to create the multi-storeyed superstructures that are typical of the Dravida style. Influences from Northern and Western India also had an impact: temples at Alampur [32B] employ towers with curving surfaces covered with miniature arch-shaped motifs and topped by circular ribbed elements.

The Late Chalukya period temples at Ittagi [20G] and Dambal [21D] show slender pilasters and split-arched motifs on walls and towers. Lathe-turned and multi-faceted columns enhance the interiors of porches and halls. These elements become the hallmark of later architecture in Karnataka and Andhra Pradesh. The 12th-13th century Hoysala temples at Halebid [18B] and Somnathpur [15D] have multiple shrines laid out on complex, star-shaped plans, with a profusion of angles carried up into the towers. Attached mandapas have projecting porches with balcony seating, as do those in contemporary Kakatiya temples at Hanamkonda [28B] and Palampet [28C].

A rather different style was developed at the same time under the Yadavas in Maharashtra. Temples at Amarnath [2J] and Sinnar [4D] demonstrate architectural influence from Central India and Gujarat. The curving towers present complex designs, with tiers of miniature elements on the central shafts. Bands of tapering ornament in the middle of each side lead to crowning circular elements, surrounded by deeply cut ribs.

Beginning in the 9th century with modest shrines like the Nageshvara at Kumbakonam [40G], the Cholas went on to commission great projects at Thanjavur [40A] and Gangaikondacholapuram [40J] in the early 11th century.

Temple sanctuaries at these sites are crowned with imposing pyramidal towers that rise to unprecedented heights. As previously, ascending storeys of sanctuary towers are defined by pilastered wall projections and parapets of model roof forms. That Chola builders were able to sustain this achievement in the 12th century is evident at Darasuram [40F], but by this time the emphasis had shifted from sanctuaries to towered entrance gateways, known as gopuras. The quartet of gopuras at Chidambaram, the finest of the Chola era, have steeply pyramidal, brick and plaster towers that are divided into multiple storeys, and capped by vaulted roofs with arched ends.

LATER TEMPLES

The next phase of religious architecture in Southern India coincides with the revival of temple building after the disruption caused by the conquest of the region by the Delhi forces. The 15th century Hazara Rama shrine at Vijayanagara, for example, shows a dependence on Chola models, with its pilastered wall surfaces and multi-storeyed, brick and plaster tower. 16th century temples at the same site are developed into spacious complexes, with rectangular walled compounds entered through gopuras on one or more sides. Mandapas attached to shrines have columns transformed into complex piers with cut-out, slender colonnettes. Other halls have internal podiums for ritual ceremonies or performances of sacred dance. The Garuda subshrine in the Vitthala temple at Hampi [20B] is treated like a chariot, complete with wheels. The Anantashayana temple at nearby Hospet [20A] is roofed with a unique brick vault.

Religious architecture at Vijayanagara inspired developments throughout Southern India in the 16th-17th centuries. Temples at Tadpatri [33B] are densely ornamented, with carved detail almost obscuring basement and wall mouldings. Free-standing gopuras at Tirupati [35A] and Sri Kalahasti [35F] demonstrate the monumental possibilities of the Vijayanagara style. Their steeply pyramidal brick towers are divided in usual fashion into ascending and diminishing storeys. Mandapas at Vellore [38A] and in the Varadaraja complex at Kanchipuram have their outer supports transformed into vigorous sculpted compositions. Similarly treated columns line the aisles of interior mandapas leading to the sanctuaries.

Variant temple forms evolved in the forested tracts of western Karnataka at the same time. The 16th century temple at Sringeri [19H] blends revived Hoysala features with contemporary Vijayanagara elements. In contrast, the temple at Ikkeri [19C] fuses Hoysala styled porch seating and columnar forms with arch profiles and parapet details derived from contemporary Adil Shahi mosques and tombs (see below).

17th century Hindu architecture under the Nayakas in Tamil Nadu represents the climax of the Dravida temple style. The outstanding development of this period is the outward expansion of the religious complex, achieved by multiplying the quadrangular walled enclosures containing the focal shrine. Gopuras are axially aligned, with the largest and highest gates generally at the peripheries, dwarfing the shrines in the middle. Even so, there is considerable variation. The Ranganatha temple at Srirangam [41B] has seven concentric compounds, while that at Tiruvannamalai [38E] has only four, though these are extended eastward to create a sequence of spacious open courts. The outermost quartet of gopuras is here aligned with the central linga sanctuary in four directions. The temple at Tirukkalukkundram [37B] is framed by four perfectly matched gopuras. The great religious monument at Madurai [44A] has twin shrines with colonnades and corridors disposed along parallel axes. Single gopuras in the outermost enclosure walls have lofty slender towers with slightly concave profiles. These are exceeded in height only by the tower at Srivilliputtur [44G], reputedly the highest in Southern India.

18th century religious architecture in Maharashtra under the Marathas draws on diverse traditions to achieve novel forms. Temples sponsored by the Peshwas of Pune and their subordinates at Sasvad [31] and Wai [7F] have domed interiors imitating mosques and tombs; characteristic 12-sided towers incorporate Mughal styled niches. Larger temples at Trimbak [4C] and Ellora revive earlier Yadava schemes, complete with curving towers displaying clustered elements on the shafts, and spacious porches with balcony seating.

Temples in Goa adapt Christian Baroque traditions to Hindu ritual needs. Examples at Manguesh [11G], Mardol [11H] and Quelem [11K], for instance, have octagonal towers crowned with domes. Free-standing, multi-storeyed lamp towers, enlivened with Neo-Classical pilasters and round-headed windows, recall belfries on contemporary Christian churches.

Mosques and Tombs

The first Muslim religious buildings in Southern India show a dependence on contemporary architecture in Delhi, with its emphasis on sloping walls, battlemented parapets, arched openings and flattish domes. The 14th century Jami mosque at Daulatabad [5C], the earliest and largest in the region, has a vast square courtyard overlooked by a colonnaded prayer hall fronted by a trio of arched portals. In contrast, the Jami mosque at Gulbarga [24A] dispenses with any court; its interior is entirely roofed with vaults and domes carried on broad arches with angled profiles. Mausoleums of the Bahmani kings at Gulbarga tend to be simple domed chambers, sometimes joined together as double tombs, but decorated with fine plasterwork. 15th century Bahmani architecture at Bidar [25A] reveals increasing Persian influence, the madrasa here being a unique architectural transplant from Central Asia, complete with brilliantly coloured tile mosaic. The court within had portals with pointed arches in the middle of each side. Tombs at nearby Ashtur [25B] show a preference for arcaded facades topped with ornate parapets. The Chaukhandi here is a modest domed chamber contained within an unusual, octagonal screen wall.

Mosques and tombs developed variant forms in the 16th-17th centuries. The Nizam Shahis were responsible for a distinctive style that specialised in carved decoration and perforated stone screens. The finest examples include small but exquisite Damri mosque at Ahmadnagar [6A], and the tomb of Malik Ambar at Khuldabad [5D]. The Adil Shahis built on a grander scale, as is obvious from the Jami mosque at Bijapur [23A], the first monument to exploit intersecting arches to support a dome. This ingenious structural device was perfected some years later in the Gol Gumbaz at Bijapur, the largest domed chamber to be erected in Southern India. Its austere exterior is relieved by octagonal staircase towers, while the dome itself is raised on a petalled frieze.

That the Adil Shahi architects were also capable of a more ornate manner is demonstrated in the Ibrahim Rauza, a paired tomb and mosque complex at Bijapur. Both structures present pyramidal arrangements of minarets and domical pinnacles, surmounted by three-quarter spherical domes on petalled bases. Intricately worked reliefs with calligraphic designs adorn the walls of the tomb chamber. A similar fascination with carved detail is seen in the multi-storeyed gateway to the Mihitar Mahal, and the mosque of Malika Jahan Begum, both at Bijapur.

Plaster was the primary medium of decoration in Qutb Shahi architecture, as demonstrated in the ornate Mushirabad and Toli mosques on the outskirts of Hyderabad [26C, F]. The emphasis here is on richly treated overhangs, arcaded galleries and parapets; flanking minarets have shafts covered with boldly incised patterns. The royal tombs outside Golconda [26F] present pyramidal compositions of arcaded storeys topped with imposing bulbous domes. Such schemes were the inspiration for later funerary architecture in Southern India, as in the 18th century mausoleum of Haidar Ali and Tipu Sultan at Srirangapattana [15C].

Mughal architecture in Southern India is mostly concentrated in and around Aurangabad [5A-B]. Lobed arches and rooftop pavilions are typical features of the many mosques and tombs erected here by Aurangzeb and his governors in the second half of the 17th century. The grandest Mughal monument is the Bibi-ka-Maqbara (fully hyphenated according to the ASI), outside the city. Though modelled on the Taj Mahal at Agra, the tomb incorporates an unusual raised gallery that overlooks the grave below. Like its prototype, the maqbara stands in the middle of a formal garden.

The final phase of Muslim religious architecture is represented by the austere Wallajah mosque in Chennai [36F] and the dargah at Nagore [40O], the latter provided with five slender square minarets.

FORTS

The earliest surviving, complete example of defensive architecture in Southern India is the remarkable circular city of Warangal [28A], capital of the Kakatiya rulers in the 13th century. This is surrounded by triple rings of fortifications, the innermost walls being of finely jointed granite blocks reinforced with quadrangular bastions, and protected by a broad moat. Shielded by barbicans with massive ramparts, the gateways have entrances requiring two changes of direction. Vestiges of Kakatiya fortifications at other sites include the inner circuit of walls at Raichur [20N].

The strongly defended core of Vijayanagara was first laid out in the 14th century. Though irregular in configuration, the walls and gateways are comparable to those at Warangal. That this system of fortification was widespread in Southern India is revealed by the 15th-16th century outposts of the Vijayanagara domains at Chitradurga [20K] and Penukonda [33D]. These formidable citadels have granite walls climbing up and over the rugged hills against which they are built. Gingee [39F], the greatest stronghold in Tamil Nadu, encompasses three distinct mountain citadels, each encircled by ramparts, with a vast triangular walled zone in between. The fort at Vellore displays round bastions with curved battlements, interspersed with projecting guardrooms. These features derive from Bahmani military architecture.

The Delhi army developed Daulatabad into the greatest stronghold of peninsula India. Double lines of sloping ramparts strengthened with round and polygonal bastions, crenellated parapets and projecting guard rooms fan outwards in part-circular formation from the focal rock citadel. The preference for circular configurations was maintained in the 15th-16th centuries by the Bahmanis at Gulbarga and Bidar, as well as by their successors at Ahmadnagar, Bijapur and Golconda. Quadrangular forts are also known during this period, as a Sholapur [9A] and Parenda [9G]. Gateways in all these forts have arched openings capped with bold parapets and shielded by barbicans. Massive outworks defining passageways with multiple changes of direction are standard devices for deflecting cavalry attacks. Nor are these entrances devoid of ornamentation: heraldic animals in stone or plaster adorn the forts at Bidar and Golconda. The triple west gate of the Adil Shahi citadel at Panhala [8B] is unsurpassed for its carved decoration. A significant aspect of all these strongholds is the elaborate hydraulic works with which they were furnished: aqueducts, channels, and ventilation towers to regulate water pressure are still operational at Bijapur and Aurangabad, as are the large storage tanks.

A new phase of military architecture was inaugurated by the Marathas in the second half of the 17th century. Shivaji was responsible for establishing an impregnable series of hill forts that exploited the rugged terrain of the Sahyadri Ranges of western Maharashtra. The ramparts at Rajgad [3M] and Pratapgad

[7B] follow the edges of cliffs in continuous undulations, reinforced by round bastions. The same system was employed in the forts on the Konkan Coast, as can be seen at Sindhudurg [8D]. Gates shielded by curving massive outworks are a particular feature of Maratha military works, as in the mountain citadel at Raigad [7C].

Military building was sustained in the 18th century. Janjira [2I], the finest island fort on the Konkan Coast, is the work of the Sidi admirals. The walls, which rise sheerly from the Arabian Sea, have curving battlements alternating with arched openings for cannons. Forts with more regular layouts were preferred for cities. The Peshwa citadel at Pune [3A] is a simple rectangle of high walls with corner round bastions, the main entrance being flanked by polygonal outworks.

A completely different tradition of military architecture was introduced in Southern India by the Europeans. The Portuguese were the first to build European styled forts in the 16th-17th centuries, as can be seen in Goa. The stronghold at Aguada [12A] consists of a quadrangle of sloping walls with sharply attenuated corners, guarded by a moat and an earthen embankment. Corner towers at Chapora [12D] have circular chambers with domical tops. The French and Dutch were also active fort builders, but few examples have survived. Of the Danish enterprise, there is only the enclosure at Tarangambadi [40Q] on the Coromandel Coast. The British were also concerned with providing adequate protection for their commercial outposts. Fort St George at Chennai [36A] is the most elaborate to be preserved. Laid out as an irregular pentagon facing the Bay of Bengal, its massive sloping walls are reinforced by triangular bastions that protrude into the moat.

Palaces

The reception halls, pleasure pavilions, bath-houses, stores and stables in the royal compounds at Vijayanagara constitute the earliest and most complete record of palace architecture in Southern India. Many of these buildings have pointed and lobed arches carrying domes and vaults, often of imaginative designs, decorated with geometric and arabesque patterns in finely worked plaster. These features, which obviously derive from Bahmani architecture, contrast with the curving eaves and multi-storeyed towers borrowed from contemporary temple architecture. This hybrid idiom was invented specially for the Vijayanagara court. Its royal associations were maintained in later times, as is apparent in the Raja Mahal at Chandragiri [35C], residence of the Aravidu emperors.

The Vijayanagara courtly style continued to evolve under the Nayakas, as can be seen in the courtly pavilions at Gingee. Granaries, with lofty curved vaults, are the most remarkable structures at this site. This royal idiom reaches a climax in the spacious audience hall and dance chamber at Madurai, where massive circular columns support broad arches with pointed and lobed profiles; lofty domes and vaults elevated on clearstoreys rise above.

Courtly architecture of the Bahmanis and their successors reflects the influence of Persian and Central Asia models. This is illustrated by the formal arrangement of ceremonial portals, audience halls and private apartments. The Bahmani remains at Firuzabad [24D], a city founded in 1400, incorporate palaces grouped in a palace zone, outside which stands a vaulted ceremonial reception hall. The vaulted and domed hammams nearby are the earliest in Southern India. The slightly later complex at Bidar consists of a formally planned ensemble of audience halls and residential suites. The apartments face into courtyards surrounded by high walls. The imposing arched gateways include one example with royal lions and sunburst emblems in coloured tiles.

The impact of Iranian architecture is most evident in Farah Bagh, on the outskirts of Ahmadnagar [6B]. This large pavilion has monumental portals in the middle of four sides, framing half domes plastered with multiple facets. The double-height chamber in the middle is roofed with a flattish dome. Audience halls with lofty central arches facing onto assembly courts are a particular feature of the walled citadel of Bijapur. Such halls probably also formed part of the extensive walled complex at Golconda, but are no longer extant; even so, the progression from public to private zones is apparent, and individual structures, such as the royal bath, armoury and barracks, can still be identified. Of the original Qutb Shahi residence at Hyderabad, only the quartet of free-standing arches that define the central square in front of the parade grounds still stand. The adjacent Char Minar, intended as a ceremonial urban marker at the intersection of the two main bazaar streets, continues to dominate the city.

Overgrown ruins are all that can now be seen of Shah Jahan's palace at Daulatabad: the hammam outside the walls is better preserved. Residences of the Asaf Jahis and their nobles in Hyderabad combine revived Qutb Shahi features with Neo-Classical architecture, with the latter predominating from the end of the 19th century onwards. Falaknuma is an imposing Palladian mansion that rivals any European project of the day. Other princely palaces present imaginative stylistic hybrids, often devised by British architecture for Indian patrons, such as Charles Mant's New Palace at Kolhapur [8A], and Henry Irwin's Amba Vilas in Mysore [15A].

Churches and Civic Buildings

The appearance of European architecture in Southern India coincides with the arrival of the Portuguese. The 16th-17th century Baroque churches of Old Goa [11B] make extensive use of Neo-Classical columns defining doorways and windows. Facades with pedimented tops framed by volutes are flanked by towers; naves are roofed with coffered vaults that shelter ornate carved and gilded wooden altars. Italianate influence is most obvious in the Church of St Cajetan, which has a dome rising over the interior crossing. The majestic church at Santan [11D] and the ruined cathedrals at Vasai [2E] and Chaul [2H] testify to the spread of the Baroque idiom to lesser sites in the region. 18th century churches in Goa tend to be smaller, and to employ altarpieces decorated in an intricate Rococo manner, as at Calangute [12C] and Moira [12E]. Baroque architecture was by no means restricted to Portuguese possessions, as is clear from churches at Kaduthuruthi [47F] and Palai [47H] in Kerala. Churches in Puducherry [39A] confirm the popularity of the Baroque idiom under the French.

A more severe Neo-Classical mode was generally preferred by the British for their religious and civic buildings in the 18th-19th centuries. Churches were provided with colonnaded porticos, steepled towers and vaulted interiors. The examples in Chennai are the finest, especially St Andrew's Kirk, which has an unusual circular domed nave [36C]. The Neo-Palladian style was also adopted for ceremonial projects such as the Banqueting Hall (Rajaji Hall) in Chennai [36E], and the British Residency (University College for Women) in Hyderabad [26C], the latter with a dignified Corinthian colonnade topped by a pediment containing the East India Company's coat-of-arms. A more severe, Neo-Greek manner was preferred for the Town Hall in Mumbai [1C], and Pachaiyappa's College in Chennai [36B].

By the middle of the 19th century a fashion for Neo-Gothic architecture had asserted itself. The Afghan Memorial Church in Mumbai [1F], the first such stone building in Southern India, employs an attenuated steepled tower as well as pointed arched windows filled with stained glass. Its richly appointed interior contrasts with the somewhat bleak style of later churches, such as the starkly unadorned St Thomé Basilica in Myapore [36G]. This ecclesiastical style continued into the 20th century, as can be seen at Mysore and Medak [27C]. An unusual adaptation of this style for Jewish liturgical purposes in seen in the synagogue at Pune [3B].

The application of Neo-Gothic to public buildings inspired considerable creativity on the part of local architects, as well as practitioners like George Gilbert Scott, who sent out designs from London. Mumbai preserves a unique ensemble of impressive High Victoria public monuments, built in a striking mixture of revived Gothic, Venetian and Mughal modes. Frederick William Stevens's Victoria Terminus (Chhatrapati Shivaji Terminus) [1E], the masterpiece of the series, is unsurpassed for its immense scale, symmetrical and dramatic arrangement of arcades, turrets and domes, and richly decorated surfaces. Scott's Bombay University, including the Rajabai Tower next to the library, is another fine example of this unique variant of the Neo-Gothic manner. Architects at the same time also took their inspiration from indigenous building traditions, which were better appreciated by the end of the 19th century. George Wittet's Prince of Wales Museum and Post Office in Mumbai are based on careful studies of mosques and tombs at Bijapur; his Gateway of India was modelled on ceremonial portals in Ahmedabad in Gujarat. The High Court and Art Gallery in Chennai [36B, D], both designed by Henry Irwin, are closer to the Mughal tradition of Northern India, though with considerable improvisation. Neo-Mughal schemes were also adopted by Vincent Esch for the public buildings sponsored by the Nizams of Hyderabad. The work of Robert Fellowes Chisholm reveals a more original approach. His Senate House of Madras University blends Middle Eastern Islamic forms with Neo-Mughal detailing [36F], while his Art Museum in Thiruvananthapuram presents an equally inventive synthesis [46A]. That this revivalist mode survived into the Independence era of Southern India is illustrated by the grandly conceived Vidhana Soudha a Bengaluru [14B].

FURTHER READING

Branfoot, Crispin, *Gods on the Move: Architecture and Ritual in the South Indian Temple*, London 2007.

Fritz, John M. and George Michell, *Vijayanagara Hampi*, Mumbai 2011.

London, Christopher W., *Architecture in Victoria and Edwardian India*, Mumbai 1994.

----, *Bombay Gothic*, Mumbai 2002.

Michell, George, *Architecture and Art of Southern India. Vijayanagara and the Successor States*, Cambridge 1995.

---- ed., *Temple Towns of Tamil Nadu*, Mumbai 2003.

---- ed., *Kanara: A Land Apart*, Mumbai 2012.

Michell, George and Indira Viswanathan Peterson, **The Great Temple at** *Thanjavur: One Thousand Years, 1010-2010*, Mumbai 2010.

Michell, George and Mark Zebrowski, *Architecture and Art of the Deccan Sultanates, 14th-18th Centuries*, Cambridge 1999.

Philon, Helen, ed., *Silent Splendour: Palaces of the Deccan*, Mumbai 2010.

---- ed., *Gulbarga, Bidar, Bijapur*, Mumbai 2012.

Tadgell, Christopher, *The History of Architecture in India: From the Dawn of Civilization to the End of the Raj*, London 1990.

Wolwahsen, Andreas, *Splendours of Imperial India: British Architecture in India in the 18th and 10th Centuries*, Munich 2003.

---- ed., **Kanara:** *A Land Apart*, Mumbai 2012.

---- *Gulbarga, Bidar, Bijapur*, Mumbai 2012.

Art

EARLY TRADITIONS

Sculptural art in Southern India can be traced back at least 2,000 years, the earliest examples being the 2nd-1st century BCE, Satavahana period reliefs in the Buddhist rock-cut sanctuaries of western Maharashtra. Wall panels at Bhaja [3D] show celestial deities riding majestically through the heavens; stately donor couples in affectionate embrace, and riders on animals, appear at Karla [3C]. All these figures are modelled in robust relief, with finely etched jewellery and costumes.

Another school of early sculpture in Southern India flourished under the Ikshvakus in Andhra Pradesh. Limestone posts and curved drum panels from 2nd-4th century CE stupas at Amaravati and Nagarjunakonda, now on display in the Archaeological Museum on the island at Nagarjuna Sagar [27H], and the Government Museum, Chennai [36D], are enlivened with friezes showing scenes from the life of Buddha and episodes from the Jataka stories. Some panels depict the stupa being worshipped by celestials; others show fully open lotus flowers. Certain compositions and figures recall Roman art, suggesting that artistic influences accompanied commercial contacts between this part of India and the Mediterranean at this time. Classical traits are especially evident in the three-dimensional Buddhas clad in flowing fluted costumes, such as those displayed in the Salar Jung Museum, Hyderabad [26B], and Archaeological Museum, Amaravati [29K]. That Hindu cults also occasionally resorted to stone carving in these early centuries is evident from the linga under veneration in the shrine at Gudimallam [35E]. Dated to the 1st century BCE, this unique Shiva emblem incorporates a worshipper carrying a slaughtered deer.

ROCK-CUT SCULPTURE

Buddhist art was much developed under the Vakatakas in the 4th-5th centuries CE. Rock-cut monasteries and chaitya halls at Ajanta [5F] are embellished with fully modelled figures of Buddha seated in teaching posture, usually flanked by Bodhisattva attendants in symmetrical swaying poses. Cave 26 is of outstanding interest for its expressive rendition of the Parinirvana, with the recumbent Buddha being mourned by disciples. Flying couples, serpent deities, musicians and amorous maidens are carved onto columns shafts, brackets and doorways. These themes are further developed in Cave 10 (Vishvakarma) at Ellora [5E].

During the 6th-7th centuries, Hindu mythological themes find graphic expression in grandly conceived compositions. Large tableaux cut into basalt at Elephanta [2A], for instance, illustrate all the major aspects of Shiva. The panels are dominated by the colossal, triple-headed bust of the god in the middle of the rear wall. This sculptural masterpiece presents a central introspective face of Shiva between a side female face and a fierce male face. A contemporary, but contrasting tradition of rock-cut art is found at the Early Chalukya capital of Badami [22A]. Cave 3 at this site has bracket figures fashioned as lyrical couples embracing beneath trees. Imposing panels at the ends of the verandah show Vishnu seated on the coil of Ananta, and as Trivikrama, kicking one leg up high. The vitality of these compositions is matched by the deep modelling of the figures in dark red sandstone.

Rock-cut carving reaches a climax in the 8th century at Ellora. Wall panels in Cave 15 (Dashavatara) illustrate Shiva and Vishnu in diverse mythological appearances, all characterised by energetic postures. Cave 21 (Rameshvara) is of particular interest for the sensuous beauty of the maidens on the brackets, and the river goddesses at the end panels. These sculptural tendencies are fully realised in Cave 16 (Kailasa), where friezes illustrating Ramayana and Mahabharata episodes are combined with icons of the major deities. One celebrated scene portrays Shiva seated with Parvati on Kailasa, disturbed by multi-headed Ravana beneath.

A quite separate sculptural tradition evolved in Tamil Nadu during these centuries. Here Hindu themes achieved a gentle plastic expression in smoothly rounded granite, as in the 7th century, Pallava period cave-temples and rock reliefs at Mamallapuram [37A]. Two large-scale compositions, Krishna lifting up Govardhana Mountain to shield the herd of cows, and Arjuna's penance, in which the hero is rewarded with Shiva's magical axe, are characterised by an outstanding naturalism and vitality. The same vigour is expressed in Pandya cave-temples, such as the savage depiction of Narasimha disembowelling his victim, in the 8th century cave-temple at Namakkal [42D].

Monolithic granite sculpture is the only aspect of rock-cut art to continue into later times. The 10th century colossus at Sravana Belgola [15H], no less than 17.7 m. high, shows naked Gommateshvara standing immobile, his legs and arms overgrown with vines. Later copies of this image are found at Karkala [17D] and Venur [17E]. The 16th century monoliths of Ganesha and of

Narasimha seated in yogic postures are sculpted out of boulders near Hampi [20B]. The finest of several richly decked Nandis of the same period is that at Lepakshi [33F].

STONE TEMPLE CARVINGS

Temple facades are encrusted with sculptures that cover basements, walls, cornices and towers. Carved monsters, such as makaras and yalis, are common on basements, sometimes combined with miniature panels illustrating narrative scenes, as at Darasuram [40F], where the stories of all the Nayanmars are depicted. The basement of this Chola temple is distinguished by leaping horses and spoked wheels, suggesting an actual wooden temple chariot. The grey-green schist basements of 11th-13th century Hoysala monuments are more ornate. The temple at Halebid [18B] displays superimposed friezes of meticulously rendered elephants, lions, horses, scrollwork, narrative epic scenes, makaras and geese with foliated tails.

Sculpted wall panels in early Hindu monuments illustrate the full range of Hindu divinities and attendant figures. The 8th century Virupaksha temple at Pattadakal [22D] has major icons of Shiva and Vishnu set into niches either side of the main entrance; the contemporary 'Durga' temple at Aihole [22E] presents images of both gods, as well as of Durga, in the curving passageway that runs around the sanctuary. Panels in Tamil Nadu temples focus on a more restricted range of icons. Shiva as Dakshinamurti, Ardhanarishvara and Brahma appear on three sides of sanctuary walls in the 9th century Nageshvara temple at Kumbakonam [40G]. The refinement of the carvings, with the figures angled slightly to the wall plane, is unsurpassed. The emphasis on wall sculptures reaches a climax at Thanjavur [40A] and Gangaikondacholapuram [40J] in the 11th century. Here, double tiers of wall panels represent all the important aspects of Shiva, including Natesha, Bhikshatanamurti and Dakshinamurti. That the emphasis in 12th century Chola sculptural art shifts from the sanctuary to the lower walls of gopuras, is demonstrated by the profusion of icons in the gopura niches at Chidambaram [39H]. Here, too, female dancers in different poses adorn the jambs within the passageways.

Somewhat variant sculptural styles were also developed in Karnataka and Andhra Pradesh at this time. The walls of the Hoysala period temple at Halebid consist entirely of carved panels set at angles to each other. Hindu divinities with richly decorated costumes and headdresses stand beneath luxuriant scrollwork or foliage. A similar sculptural density is achieved in 15th-16th century Vijayanagara temples, as can be seen in the Chennakeshava shrine at Pushpagiri [34B] and the gopuras at Tadpatri [33B]. The walls of the Hazara Rama temple at Vijayanagara [20C] are covered with Ramayana reliefs, repeated on the inner face of the enclosure walls of the compound. In contrast, the outer face of these walls portray an array of contemporary royal scenes: processions of elephants and horses, parades of militia, and lines of dancing girls and female musicians. Similar subjects enhance the enclosure walls of the temple at Srisailam [32C], though here combined with Shaiva topics.

Stone towers of Southern Indian shrines are also enlivened with carvings of divinities. Dancing Shiva is a popular icon on 8th-9th century monuments, as on the frontal panels of towers rising over the sanctuaries at Alampur [32B] and Pattadakal, and the splendid image of the same deity set into the tower of the main shrine at Kodumbalur [41D]. Temple towers from the 13th century onwards tend to be fashioned out of brick and plaster, thereby introducing the art of polychrome stucco. Successive storeys of sanctuary and gopura superstructures are embellished with a profuse imagery, all brightly painted. Nowhere is this better illustrated than at Madurai [44A], where the towers of the 17th century gopuras present a dizzying assemblage of vividly painted divinities, guardians, attendants and animals. Horseshoe-shaped arches at the ends of the capping vaulted roofs are transformed into fierce monster masks surrounded by flaming tufts, all rendered in deeply modelled plaster.

Temple interiors are equally sculptural. Mandapa and porch columns in Pallava architecture generally have seated or rearing lions carved onto the shafts. This theme is elaborated in later times, as in the columns in the 16th century mandapa addition to the Virupaksha temple at Hampi [20B], which display rearing yalis with riders. A similar preference for fantastic animals with riders, together with female attendants bearing offerings, is found in the temples at Tadpatri. Columns in the outer mandapas at Vellore [38A] and Srirangam [41B] are fashioned with remarkable virtuosity into leaping yalis and richly bridled horses bearing armed warriors; lesser figures beneath struggle with wild panthers and other animals. Various deities, including Manmatha and Rati riding parrots, carved almost in the round, animate piers in the free-standing mandapa in the outermost enclosure of the Varadaraja temple at Kanchipuram [37E].

The column as a vehicle for three-dimensional sculpture continued to evolve in Tamil Nadu under the Nayakas. Temples at Madurai and Alagarkoil [44C] have larger than human-size divinities and heroes projecting outwards from the supports lining the central aisles of mandapas and corridors. The Pudu Mandapa at Madurai serves as royal gallery, in which all the Madurai rulers up to Tirumala, the major patron of the monument, are portrayed. The figures are shown with swelling limbs, richly adorned with jewelled costumes, crowns and daggers. A comparable gallery is seen at Srimushnam [39I], where the Gingee Nayakas are depicted on the mandapa columns in front of the sanctuary. A later example of this theme is seen in the outer corridor of the temple at Rameswaram [44J], in which effigies of the Setupati rulers are found on the piers. Meanwhile, the emphasis on corridors lined with yali columns continues, as at Srivilliputtur [44G]. Columns with divinities and heroes carved in almost three dimensions are also found in temples in Tenkasi [45J] and Thiruvananthapuram [46A].

Other parts of temple interiors are also subjected to ornate sculptural treatment. Angled brackets in the porches and halls of Hoysala and Kakatiya monuments are fashioned as maidens and embracing couples beneath trees, a theme familiar from Early Chalukya times. Exquisitely modelled females adjusting their hair, admiring themselves in mirrors, and playing with parrots adorn brackets in the temples at Belur [18A] and Palampet [28C]. The carvings at Palampet have unusually elongated bodies and sinuous postures.

Ceilings of temples in Karnataka are often elaborate compositions, generally with deeply cut lotuses surrounded by flying figures or sets of dikpalas. The Aihole temples show trios of divinities, one set now removed to the Chhatrapati Shivaji Vastu Sanghralaya, Mumbai [1B]. The refinement of the Natesha image on the ceiling of the remotely located temple at Aralaguppe [18F] is unique; so too the textile patterns and double-headed eagle motif incised onto the ceiling of the temple at Keladi [19B].

BRONZES

The larger temples in Southern India are repositories of high quality, metal images. Elaborately dressed and jewelled bronzes receive worship in sanctuaries, as well as serving as processional icons on festival occasions. Many of the finest bronzes are now on display in the Government Museum, Chennai, and the Art Gallery, Thanjavur. These constitute the largest and most comprehensive collections of metallic art in Southern India.

Bronze figures from the 11th-12th century Chola period are admired for their elegant postures and gentle facial expressions. The smoothly modelled bodies of males and females and their finely detailed jewellery, costumes and headdresses represent the highest achievement of the bronze casters. Representations of Shiva include the celebrated Nataraja icon, which shows the god with one foot raised, his hair flying outwards, surrounded by a fiery halo. The example from Tiruvelangadu in Chennai is justly celebrated for its poised majesty. The image of Shiva as Ardhanarishvara from Tiruvengadu, in the same collection, perfectly combines male and female bodies into a single composite figure. Shiva also appears with Parvati, sometimes with the infant Subrahmanya in Somaskanda family groups. Vishnu is usually accompanied by a pair of consorts, while Rama appears together with Sita and Lakshmana. Saints such as Sundarar and Manikkavachakar are represented as youthful devotees of Shiva, the palms of their hands brought together in adoration.

That Chola art was not restricted to Hindu imagery is demonstrated by the Buddhist bronzes from Nagapattinam [40M], now in Chennai, which depict the Master standing within an ornate frame, or seated beneath a tree. The spectacular bronzes in the temple at Kadri on the outskirts of Mangalore [17A], most likely shipped from a Tamil Nadu workshop, depict Buddha as Manjushri and Lokeshvara.

16th-17th century bronzes produced in Vijayanagara and Nayaka times rival their Chola predecessors in quality, such as the seated icon of Kali with flame-like hair, in Thanjavur, and the image of Krishna dancing on the serpent, now in the Mumbai museum. Effigies of Krishnadevaraya and his two queens in the temple at Tirumala [35B] testify to the development of royal portraiture during this period. Another fine portrait is that of Vijayaraghava Nayaka, in the Thanjavur Art Gallery.

Images produced for Jain worship illustrate a further aspect of bronze art in Southern India. The Jain matha at Sravana Belgola houses a large collection Tirthankara icons, some dating back to the 9th century. The most elaborate examples are furnished with ornate frames. Other fine pieces are displayed in the Chandranatha Basti at Mudabidri [17C].

Wood and Ivory Carvings

Wood carving was evidently widespread throughout Southern India but only a fraction of this tradition survives. In Tamil Nadu and parts of Karnataka and Andhra Pradesh, great wheeled chariots are parked outside temple gopuras, waiting for festival occasions when they are pulled through the streets. Only then are they decked with bamboo and cloth to shelter metal images of gods and goddesses. Chariots are entirely wooden in construction: protruding beams carved with beasts and monster heads provide a framework for tiers of panels that cantilever outwards. That the panels are sculpted with a full range of divinities and accessory figures is evident from the trio of chariots parked in the main street at Chidambaram. The small chariot in front of the Ramaswami temple at Kumbakonam present an unusual selection of Ramayana subjects.

Kerala preserves the most extensive range of wood carving in Southern India. Temples at Ettumanur [47G], Kaviyur [47K] and Chengannur [47L], for instance, have sanctuaries surrounded by timber screens framed by panels carved with mythological subjects. Wooden struts, angled beneath roof overhangs, are fashioned as three-dimensional figures, generally female musicians and dancers, as well as yalis. Struts on shrines at Peruvanam [47U] and Taliparamba [48H] show figures in twisting postures holding bows and arrows in illustration of the story of Arjuna fighting Shiva disguised as kirata, the hunter. Entrance porches and pavilions in front of sanctuaries have miniature brackets fashioned as characters from the Ramayana and the Arjuna story; beams show narrative friezes. Ceilings here are divided into compartments filled with divinities and lotus flowers; a common arrangement shows Brahma with the dikpalas, as in the temple at Thiruvanchikulam at Kodungallur [47S].

Narasimha Temple, Chengannur.

Church art also exploited the skills of Southern Indian wood carvers. The richly sculpted and gilded altarpieces in the cathedrals and churches of Old Goa [11B] portray polychromed figures of Christ and saints accompanied by winged angels. The swaying figure of St Francis Xavier in the cathedral of Bom Jesus is a typical example of the ecstatic manner that was perfected by Goan artists. Pulpits have their sides and canopies covered with saints in the company of angels; the same subjects line chancel walls, as at Rachol [13D].

That this exuberant figural style was not confined to Christian art in Goa is demonstrated by the church at Kaduthuruthi [47F] in Kerala, which preserves highly ornate altarpieces.

Ivories often imitate wooden figures. Goa is celebrated for delicate images of the Christ Child, the Crucifixion, and Christ at the Good Shepherd, fine examples of which are displayed in the Mumbai museum, and the Museum of Christian Art in Old Goa. Ivory carving produced elsewhere in Southern India tended to favour Hindu themes. Figurines, furniture panels and combs manufactured at Nayaka workshops in Tamil Nadu show divinities, embracing courtly couples, and even Europeans with dogs, as in the Art Museums of temples at Srirangam and Madurai.

MURALS AND CEILING PAINTINGS

Pictorial traditions in Southern India date back to the 2nd-1st centuries BCE, as indicated by fragmentary compositions in rock-cut chaitya halls at Ajanta; more complete cycles from the 5th century CE survive in viharas at the same site. The Ajanta murals are of the greatest significance for the wide range of subjects and the assured mastery of the medium. Buddhist divinities and incidents from the life of the Master appear together with scenes from the Jatakas. Depicting life in the court, town, hermitage or forest of the day, these Jataka episodes are crowded with princes, consorts, attendants, musicians and servants. Never again did Southern Indian painting exhibit such virtuosity and freedom, nor such convincing, perspective-like effects. The colours are harmoniously blended, with ochres, browns and greens predominating; the linework is sinuous and sensitive throughout.

Except for tantalizing traces at Badami (Cave 3), Ellora (Cave 16) and Kanchipuram (Kailasanatha temple), dating from the 6th-8th centuries, and the inaccessible murals in the 11th century Brihadishvara temple at Thanjavur there is a dearth of mural art in Southern India until the Vijayanagara and Nayaka periods. The first great cycle of paintings to be preserved from this later era is that at Lepakshi. Frescoes on the ceiling of this 16th century temple show the donors of the monument in the company of male and female retinues, all dressed in diversely patterned costumes. Other compositions here include Virabhadra, the fierce form of Shiva to whom the temple is dedicated, and the boar hunt of Arjuna in the company of terrified sages.

17th century ceiling painting on temples in Tamil Nadu are generally supplied with identifying labels. One of the most complete cycles is that in the Shivakamasundari shrine at Chidambaram. The compositions here are characterised by a fluid linework and bright red, ochre and green tones, mostly on white backgrounds. Arranged in narrow registers, the panels depict the story of Bhikshatanamurti and Mohini seducing the wives of the sages, as well as the long and eventful life of the saint Manikkavachakar. Animated scenes on red backgrounds, depicting temple festivities, appear on the ceiling of an outer mandapa within the complex at Tiruvarur [40L]. The story of Mukunda, another Shaiva saint, here forms the subject of a set of animated episodes.

Jain narratives are painted onto the ceiling of the temple mandapa at Tiruparuttikunram [37E], on the outskirts of Kanchipuram. The stories of Rishabhadeva and Vardhamana, two popular Jain saviours, follow a standard pattern, with courtly scenes crowded with parades, and contrasting with forest episodes. A fascinating cycle of murals is seen in the upper chambers of the entrance gopura at Tiruppudaimarudur [45K]. Here varied mythological subjects alternate with scenes of boats transporting merchants and soldiers, all executed in a bold linear style.

The Ramalinga Vilasa at Ramanthapuram [44H], residence of the Setupati rulers, is worth a visit for its extensive murals, executed in brilliant reds, ochres and blues. In addition to stories from the Hindu epics, and depictions of shrines within the Setupai kingdom, these 18th century paintings show courtly receptions, hunting expeditions and battles.

18th-19th century paintings in Karnataka belong to a different tradition that was partly revived under Tipu Sultan. The Daria Daulat Bagh in Srirangapattana [15C] has murals depicting military victories over the British. Royal pastimes are shown on the walls of the upper chamber of the Chamrarajendra Art Gallery in Mysore [15A]. An engaging but little-known cycle of paintings of the same era is preserved on the ceiling of the temple at Sibi [14D]. Here, mythological topics are combined with courtly scenes and parades of troops in European dress. One large composition portrays flute-playing Krishna in a rocky landscape. A comparable ceiling composition is found in the Virupaksha temple at Hampi.

A contrasting, but equally lively mural tradition is preserved in Kerala, most examples dating from the 17th-19th centuries. The Kerala pictorial style is distinguished by paintings that extend without interruption across the walls of temples and palaces. Panels are crowded with figures with exaggerated expressions, dressed in elaborately jewelled costumes and crowns; the vigorous linework is enhanced by the deep red, green, ochre and yellow colours. Murals at Vaikom [47E], for example, show Vishnu riding on Garuda, and Rama battling with Ravana. Wall panels at Ettumanur juxtapose Vishnu reclining on the serpent with dancing Shiva surrounded by celestials. In contrast, the compositions at Triprayar [47T] concentrate on Ramayana combat scenes and the story of Narasimha.

Similar mythological themes appear in the murals of royal complexes in Kerala. Representations of Vishnu reclining on the multi-headed cobra cover the walls of the shrine room in the Padmanabhapuram palace [45O], while Ramayana scenes decorate the king's bedroom in the Dutch Palace at Mattancheri in Kochi [47A].

FINE ARTS

Southern India is celebrated for the diversity of its decorative arts, abundant examples of which are on display in museums in Mumbai, Hyderabad and Chennai. Miniature painting was much favoured in the courts of Ahmadnagar [6A], Bijapur [23A] and Golconda [26E] in the 16th-17th centuries. Brilliantly coloured compositions show royal, military and saintly personalities in formal postures, as well as animated hunting expeditions and animal fights and languishing maidens and youths. In the 18th century this tradition came under the sway of provincial Mughal art, as practiced in workshops in Hyderabad, Shorapur [24H] and Kurnool [32A]. New schools also appeared in the 19th century at the Maratha and Wodeyar courts of Thanjavur and Mysore. Paintings on wood and glass produced at these centres illustrate traditional Hindu mythological themes, as well as courtly subjects. Thanjavur paintings are recognised by their encrusted textures and mirrored surfaces.

Southern Indian metalwork attained technical perfection at Bidar [25A], after which an inlaid technique known as bidri became widely known. 17th-18th century ewers, basins, bowls and huqqa bases exhibit delicately inlaid silver and brass designs with stylised floral and arabesque motifs. Ornate weapons constitute another dimension of Southern Indian metalwork. The largest assemblage, which comes from the Thanjavur armoury and is now exhibited in Chennai, includes innumerable pattar swords, katar daggers and ceremonial ankushas, or elephant goads. Many of these have perforated metal hilts and handles incorporating fantastic animals and birds.

Brightly painted and dyed cotton textiles, called kalamkaris, produced at workshops on the Coromandel Coast, were exported in bulk to Southeast Asia and Europe from the 16th century onwards. (This explains why some of the best preserved, oldest examples are now in museums in London, Paris and New York.) Temple cloths and canopies used for display on festival occasions are divided into strips and bands, sometimes surrounding enlarged central panels, exactly as in ceiling paintings. However, the only cloths now to be seen in Southern India temples are mostly of modern manufacture.

FURTHER READING

Behl, Benoy K., *Ajanta Caves*, London 1998.

Dallapiccola, Anna L., *South Indian Paintings: A Catalogue of the British Museum's Collections*, London 2010.

Dehejia, Vidya, *Art of the Imperial Cholas*, New York 1090.

Harle, J.C., *The Art and Architecture of the Indian Subcontinent*, London 1986.
Huntington, Susan L., *The Art of Ancient India, Buddhist, Hindu, Jain*, New York 1985.
Michell, George, ed., *Living Wood: Sculptural Traditions of Southern India*, Bombay 1992.
----, *Elephanta*, Mumbai 2002.
----, *Badami, Aihole, Pattadakal*, Mumbai 2011.
Nagaswamy, R., *Masterpieces of Early South Indian Bronzes*, New Delhi 1983.
Seth, Mira, *India Painting: The Great Mural Tradition*, New York 2006.
Zebrowski, Mark, *Deccani Painting*, London 1983.

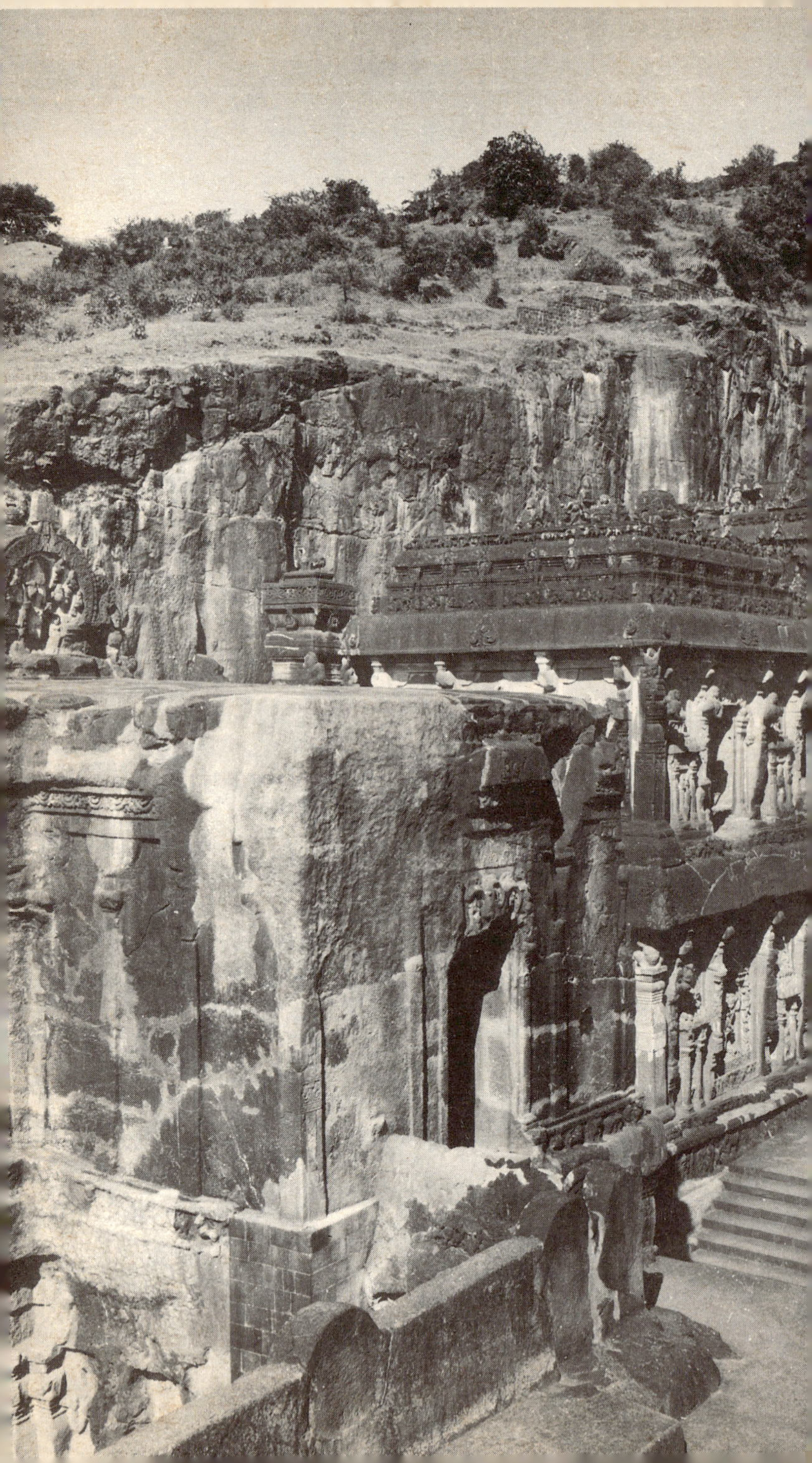

Kailasa Temple, Ellora

MAHARASHTRA

Maharashtra

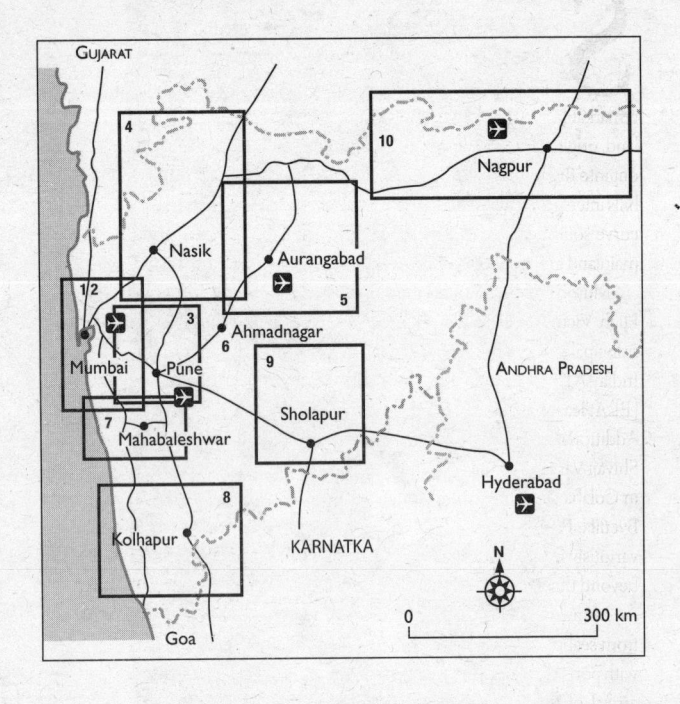

1. Mumbai

Still commonly referred to as Bombay, its original British name, Mumbai is the capital of Maharashtra and Southern India's largest and most cosmopolitan city. Though it suffers from overcrowding, traffic jams and pollution, these ever worsening problems have not obscured the remarkable beauty of its natural setting. Mumbai occupies a long thin piece of land, originally a string of seven islands separated by lagoons and creeks, jutting out into the Arabian Sea. The ocean frontage on the west is marked by tree lined hills interspersed with sandy stretches, such as Back Bay, which sweeps in a broad curve south from Malabar Hill. Mumbai Harbour separates the city from the mainland to the east, beyond which rise the Western Ghats.

Mumbai preserves a splendid architectural heritage. Its noble ensemble of High Victorian period monuments being the finest in Southern India. The principal examples are located in the busy downtown area, near the Gateway of India [A], the Fort Area [C], Maidan [D] and Chhatrapati Shivaji Terminus [E]. At least one full day will be required to cover the buildings described here. Additional time will be required to explore the collection of the Chhatrapati Shivaji Vastu Sanghralaya [B]. Other notable historical monuments are located in Colaba [F] to the south, and in the residential districts of Malabar Hill [G], Byculla, Parel and Mahim [H] to the north. These zones may be combined variously into one or more half-day tours. Recommended full-day excursions beyond the metropolitan limit are described in the following itinerary [2].

Mumbai's strategic location explains its unique commercial history, profiting from seaborne links with Gujarat to the north and Kerala to the south, as well with ports on the Persian Gulf, the Red Sea and Swahili Coast of East Africa. The arrival of the Portuguese in the beginning of the 16th century marked the beginning of the European domination of the Arabian Sea trade. In 1535 the Portuguese concluded a treaty with Bahadur Shah of Gujarat that granted them the trading rights of Mumbai and nearby Vasai [2E] and Chaul [2H]. Even so, Mumbai was little developed at first. The most celebrated European to live here in the late 16th century was Garcia Orta, a physician and botanist. His Manor House, at the time the largest residence in the city, later became the residence of the Portuguese governors. Meanwhile, Parel and Mahim, two of the northern islands of Mumbai, were taken over by the Franciscans.

By the turn of the 17th century Mumbai had emerged as a lively port. Its growing wealth attracted the English, who landed here in 1626, burning down the Manor House, but this raid did little to curb Portuguese activities. Competition with the Dutch merchants in the area persuaded the Directors of the newly formed East India Company in London to establish trading stations on the Arabian Sea coast. Diplomatic negotiations with Portugal culminated in the marriage agreements of 1668 between Charles II and the Infanta Donna Catherina, by which the islands of Mumbai passed into the possession of the English crown.

Mumbai under the English developed steadily into a lucrative trading centre. General Aungier, Governor in 1669-77, did much to improve the settlement, remodelling the Manor House, thereafter known as the Castle, establishing the first church, and building forts on rocky promontories. Mumbai became a haven for oppressed communities, mostly notably the Parsis, who arrived after 1670, and later the Jews. In 1708 Mumbai displaced Surat in Gujarat as the principal headquarters of the East India Company on the Arabian Sea coast. The area around the Castle, known as the Fort, was strengthened with earthen ramparts to shield British fleets from attacks by the Marathas, the dominant power on the mainland in the 18th century. Under William Hornby, Governor in 1771-84, the ramparts were replaced by stone walls and gates.

Mumbai grew rapidly in the 19th century, mainly due to private enterprise, which was much stimulated by the abolition of the Company's trade monopoly. This era witnessed the rise in the fortunes of Parsi and Jewish families, such as the Wadias, Jeejeebhoys, Tatas, Jehangirs and Sassoons. The first railway in India was completed in 1854, connecting Mumbai (then Bombay) to Thane (then Thana) on the mainland; other lines followed. With the disruption of cotton deliveries from the United States to Europe due to the American Civil War of 1861-65, Mumbai boomed as an alternative source of supply, with textile mills springing up all over the city. The opening of the Suez Canal in 1868 brought Mumbai closer to Europe. The increased volume of shipping necessitated a new dockyard with extensive shipbuilding facilities, which was laid out on the harbour side of the city.

Mumbai's expansion was led by dynamic figures like Governors Mountstuart Elphinstone (1819-27) and Bartle Frere (1862-67). These Governors were responsible for ambitious reclamation schemes that transformed Mumbai into a continuous peninsular by draining the lagoons and joining together the islands. Additional land was gained by demolishing the walls and gates surrounding the Fort. This provided a setting for a new and imposing series of municipal, educational and commercial monuments designed in an exotic variation of the Victorian Neo-Gothic style. Many of these survive to give the city its distinctive architectural personality.

Mumbai's development has been sustained in recent years, with new residential and commercial complexes crowding the reclaimed land fringing Back Bay. Though much of the city's heavy industry has now shifted beyond the old metropolitan limits, the port continues to benefit from the largest and busiest dockyard in Southern India. In addition, a thriving film industry lends the city a certain glamour and notoriety. The enormous garish posters and hoardings advertising new 'Bollywood' films are to be seen everywhere in Mumbai.

A. GATEWAY OF INDIA

The tour of downtown Mumbai described here begins at the *Gateway of India*, a prominent landmark overlooking the harbour. Erected in 1927 on Apollo Bunder (a corruption of local words meaning 'fish quay'), the gateway was designed by George Wittet to commemorate the visit of George V and Queen Mary on their way to the Delhi Darbar of 1911. It was the point of departure for the last British regiment to leave India in 1948. In spite of these British associations the gateway is inspired by the ceremonial architecture of Ahmedabad, capital of Gujarat. Its triple arches lead to a central hall with side chambers, all domed. The wider and higher arches in the middle are flanked by part-octagonal buttresses, capped with tiers of domical finials. The narrower side arches contain doorways framed by pierced stone screens with varied geometric patterns. The bold eaves carried on curved brackets unify the whole scheme. The small garden in front forms part of a civic improvement scheme and is now a favourite picnic spot. An equestrian statue of Shivaji was placed here in 1961. Launches for Elephanta [2A] and Alibag [2G] leave from the jetty behind the gateway.

The statue of Shivaji is overshadowed by the tower of the *Taj Mahal Hotel* annex. This adjoins the original block built by Jamsetji Nusserwanji Tata, a prominent Parsi businessman, who is supposed to have suffered the humiliation of being asked to leave Watson's Hotel on the grounds that he was a native. Completed in 1904 at a cost of half a million pounds, the hotel faces the Mumbai Harbour. Its facade presents a busy but symmetrical assemblage of arcades and balconies, gabled turrets and domical towers. The composition is flanked by a quartet of smaller domes that roof an interior staircase bounded by cast-iron balconies. The newly refurbished residential wings on either side have corridors originally open to the sky for natural ventilation.

Just behind the statue of Shivaji is the *Yacht Club* of 1880-83. Its pleasant clutter of arcades and gables is offset by a rounded corner tower. A short street passing to one side of the club leads to the spacious S.P. Mukharji Chowk (formerly Wellington Circle), with *Wellington Fountain* in the middle. This was erected in 1865 in honour of the Duke of Wellington, who visited Mumbai in 1801 and 1804.

A varied ensemble of buildings surveying the traffic that circulates around the fountain. On the east side of Mukharji Chowk is the *Maharashtra State Police Headquarters* (permission required to visit). This was built as the Royal Alfred Sailors' Home and then used by the legislature of the Bombay Presidency, later the state of Maharashtra. The home marks the beginning of the career of Frederick William Stevens, one of Mumbai's most talented architects. Conceived in the Neo-Gothic manner, with arcades headed by polychrome stonework, the building has a central four-storey wing. Relief compositions in the upper gable depict Neptune with nymphs and dolphins, an obvious tribute to Mumbai's seaborne trade.

Commercial and residential blocks on the south side of the Chowk echo the Neo-Gothic style of the Sailors' Home, though with the occasional addition of Mughal derived portals and turrets. They contrast with the *Royal Institute of Science*, a vast Neo-Classical pile occupying the west side of the Chowk at the bottom of Mahatma Gandhi Road. The institute owes its foundation to Parsi and Jewish benefactors, who commissioned Wittet to design a new building in 1910. The yellow basalt facade is dominated by a portico with solid Ionic columns leading to a domed hall. The National Gallery of Modern Art occupies part of the present building.

On the north side of Mukharji Chowk is the *Chhatrapati Shivaji Vastu Sanghralaya*, the largest museum in Mumbai. The building stands in a well maintained garden, in the middle of which, partly hidden by trees, is a bronze portrait by Leonard Jennings of George V as Prince of Wales. The museum, designed by Wittet in 1908, shows the same knowledge of Indian traditions that characterises his Gateway of India. Here, however, the model is that of Bijapur [23A], as is clear from the large central dome and smaller end domes, surrounded by finials with petalled domical tops. The entrance porch has a balcony with an unusual curving vault framed by slender minarets. The portal rising above contains an imposing arch flanked by balconied windows filled with stone screens. Arcaded wings open off to the sides. The large dome over the central chamber rises on a petalled frieze; internally it is carried on intersecting arches, exactly as in Bijapur's larger monuments. (The collections are described below.)

St Andrew's Kirk stands just behind the museum, within what was once the Fort area. This simple Neo-Classical building with a severe Doric portico dates from 1818; the steeple was added in 1827. A circular structure on a site next door, now demolished, served as a store for blocks of ice shipped from Massachusetts.

From Mukharji Chowk visitors have a choice of walking in three directions: Mahatma Gandhi Road to the north will take them into the Fort, with Victoria Terminus beyond; Madam Cama Road runs west to the Maidan; Shahid Bhagat Singh Road, traversing Maharji Chowk, proceeds south to Colaba.

B. CHHATRAPATI SHIVAJI VASTU SANGHRALAYA

Still known by its old name as the Prince of Wales Museum, this collection is the most important in Mumbai (closed Mondays). A Domed Hall occupies the ground floor of the triple-height space in the middle of the museum. Among the items shown here are 16th-17th century miniature paintings, jade bowls and jade-handed daggers from the Mughal period, and wooden and ivory figures, including those of the infant Christ from Goa [11B]. Buddhist fragments from 5th-6th century sites, now in Pakistan, include stucco heads and figurines from Gandhara and terracotta figures from Mirpur Khas. A gracefully posed nymph from a 12th century Karnataka temple is placed in the middle.

The *Sculpture Gallery* to the right of the domed hall is crowded with fine Buddhist, Jain and Hindu images. They include rare 1st century CE sculptures from Pitalkhora [5G], as well as a set of 7th century ceiling panels from Aihole [22E] that depict a trio of Hindu divinities. A plaster cast of the gigantic Shiva figure at Parel and a fragmentary Durga and image of Brahma from Elephanta give a good idea of artistic traditions in the vicinity of Mumbai in the 6th-9th centuries. Among the other carvings on display here are a remarkable 6th century panel from Samalaji in Gujarat, showing Shiva with trident and snakes against a background of rocks, and a 5th century seated dwarf attendant with curly hair from Koh in Madhya Pradesh.

A staircase ascends through a mezzanine gallery with showcases crammed with prehistoric pots, beads, tools and toys. The *Octagonal Gallery*, on the first floor beneath the central dome, is surrounded by a wooden arcade. Glass showcases here contain inlaid metalwork and beaten silver trays, mostly 19th century work, as well as ivory pieces. Miniature paintings adorn the walls. The painted cloth compositions include a mandala and a set of Buddhist scenes, both from Nepal.

The *Painting Gallery*, the finest of any museum in Southern India, represents all the major Indian schools, ranging from 14th-15th Jain manuscripts to 16th-17th century Mughal and Rajput miniatures. Paintings from the Deccan include a large composition showing a procession of Abdullah Qutb Shah of Golconda [26E], hung at the end of the gallery. Among the most charming miniatures are an elephant scene from Bundi in Rajasthan, a depiction of Rama with Sita from Aurangabad [5A], and, from Shorapur [24H], a portrayal of Krishna dallying with gopis.

The adjacent *Fine Arts Gallery* presents Mughal items, especially glass huqqa bowls, gold jewellery, enamelwork and ivory figurines. A unique copper bowl dated 1591 is engraved with hunting scenes on its underside. The collection is overlooked by an ornate wooden facade removed from a house in Gujarat. The *Bronze Gallery*, which opens off to one side, has a variety of figures spanning the 9th-17th centuries. Notable are Krishna dancing on Kaliya, and Vishnu standing in an ornate frame, as well as the small but delicately modelled icon of the Jain saviour Bahubali.

Stairs lead to the second floor of the museum, which is mostly reserved for non-European art. The *Octagonal Gallery* beneath the dome houses Chinese and Japanese porcelains, jades and ivories, as well as European crystal and china. Painting galleries on both sides are hung with European oils from the collection of Sir Ratan Tata, whose statue is also on display. The landscapes and portraits are of indifferent quality, with the exception of two seascapes by Eugène Boudin. The nearby *Textile Gallery* has a dazzling selection of shawls from Kashmir, ikat cloths from Gujarat, and saris from Kanchipuram and Thanjavur in Tamil Nadu [37E and 40A]. Swords with animal hilts and daggers with ornate blades may be viewed in the adjacent *Weapons' Gallery*. A brass shield with zodiac signs and an inscribed breast plate are supposed to have been used by the Mughal emperor Akbar.

C. FORT AREA

Though the defensive walls and gates of the original British settlement were demolished after 1862, this area is commonly known as the Fort. The original outline of the ramparts on the west can still be made out by following Mahatma Gandhi and Dadabhoi Naroji Roads, which create an arc, some 1.5 km. from north to south, facing east towards Mumbai Harbour. The crowded commercial streets of this zone constitute the business heart of Mumbai. Here stand many traditional buildings, with upper storeys cantilevering outwards on angled wooden struts.

The route described here proceeds north along Mahatma Gandhi Road from Mukharji Chowk. Passing beside the museum, visitors arrive at the *Jehangir Art Gallery*, one of the city's principal venues for contemporary painting and sculpture. In Forbes Street nearby, just off Mahatma Gandhi Road, stands the *Knesseth Eliyahoo Synagogue*, the finest in Mumbai, erected in 1884 by David Sassoon. (This prominent Jewish benefactor of the city died in Pune, where he is buried [3B].) The synagogue is distinguished by its brightly painted, blue and white Neo-Classical facade. Steps from a side entrance climb to the prayer hall at the upper level. Here, cast-iron columns supporting galleries on three sides have Star of David motifs incorporated into the brackets. Stained-glass windows are positioned over the Ark in the rear wall.

Elphinstone College stands on Mahatma Gandhi Road, diagonally opposite the Jehangir Art Gallery. The impressive Neo-Gothic college has triple storeyed arcades on either side of a central rectangular tower, crowned by a pyramidal roof and framed by turrets at two levels. The porch at ground level, also with turrets, incorporates a bust of Sir Cowasjee Jehangir, nicknamed 'Readymoney', patron of the college. The *David Sassoon Library* next door displays a gabled portico, repeated in the pediment that caps the facade. The basalt columns on the upper level of the library carry polychrome arcades. A marble portrait of the patron dominates the stairwell.

Mahatma Gandhi Road arrives at Hutatma Chowk, a broad circle with *Flora Fountain* in the middle. This coincides with the site of Church Gate, the original west entrance to the Fort, after which the station beyond the Maidan is named. The much loved fountain shows a marble figure of Flora standing upon a quartet of dolphins, with shells beneath. The monument is the work of James Forsyth in 1869, in honour of Governor Frere.

On the north side of Hutatma Chowk are the *Oriental Buildings*, completed by Stevens. These occupy the triangular plot at the junction of Mahatma Gandhi and Dadabhoi Naoroji Roads. The angled Neo-Gothic facade of the complex culminates in a five-storeyed corner tower framed by slender circular turrets and crowned by a pyramidal tiled roof. A shorter tower at the north end of the buildings has an octagonal steeple.

Other Neo-Gothic monuments face each other across Vir Nariman Road (formerly Churchgate Street), immediately west of Hutatma Chowk. The *Public Works Department* on the south was erected in 1869, according to a design by General Henry St Clair Wilkins. The central rectangular tower has a pyramidal roof with twin turrets. The side wings are terminated by end bays with arcaded storeys enriched with polychrome stonework. The *Telegraph Office* opposite, originally the General Post Office, dates from the same year. Its handsome facade is punctuated by twin towers with steeply pitched roofs rising over arcaded galleries with finely worked decoration. A two storeyed-porch marks the entrance in the middle.

Vir Nariman Road continues west across the Maidan towards Churchgate Station but the tour described here returns to Hutatma Chowk before proceeding east along the same route into the middle of the Fort area. The first building of importance to be seen is *Readymoney Mansion*, home of the Parsi philanthropist. Its superimposed arcaded balconies in carved wood echo local architectural traditions.

Further east along Vir Nariman Road stands the *Cathedral Church of St Thomas*. Begun in 1672 by General Aungier, but not completed until 1718, this is the oldest Christian structure still in use in Mumbai. The two-storeyed battlemented tower replaced the original belfry in 1839. The interior is spacious but simple, with double rows of plain Doric columns carrying shallow masonry vaults. The stained glass in the chancel dates from the reconstruction of 1869. A rich assortment of carved memorials is found here. One of the earliest commemorates Jonathan Duncan, Governor of Mumbai in 1795-1811; another shows Lieutenant Colonel Charles Burr surrounded by Indian officers. The most remarkable tomb is the full marble reclining figure of Thomas Carr, first Bishop of Mumbai. The delicately sculpted Neo-Gothic fountain outside the west entrance to the cathedral is the work of Sir George Gilbert Scott, the famous Victorian architect, who never visited India.

Immediately east of St Thomas is *Horniman Circle*, laid out in 1860 as Elphinstone Circle, on the site Bombay Green, the original open space within the

Fort. The circular garden in the middle is ringed by cast-iron railings with four orate gates flanked by lanterns. The circle is overlooked by Italianate styled buildings with deep arcades at street level. At the corner of Vir Nariman Road on the west fringe of the circle stands *Elphinstone Building*, a splendid Neo-Gothic mansion of 1870. Its triple-arcaded storeys in golden sandstone are enlivened with basalt and granite inlays. The top level has intersecting arches in the Venetian manner.

The east side of Horniman Circle is dominated by the *Town Hall*, an accomplished Neo-Greek scheme designed in 1821 by Thomas Cowper, and finished by others after his death in 1833. The central portico, with eight Doric columns, is approached by a broad flight of steps. This side and end porticos preserve wooden louvres; together with the wooden shuttered doors and curving sun shades, these are original features shipped from England. Corinthian and Ionic columns adorn the interior chambers. Marble statues of Elphinstone and other Mumbai Governors, executed by Francis Chantrey, are displayed in the lobby and stairwell. The Asiatic Society of Mumbai occupies one end of the Town Hall. Founded in 1804, its library stocks more than 100,000 volumes, as well as antiquities, such as those discovered at the Buddhist site of Sopara [2F].

Vestiges of Mumbai's earliest structures are engulfed by the dockyards behind the Town Hall (permission required to visit). The only portion that survives of the *Castle*, the original Manor House, is an entrance gate in the bastion wall. This is surmounted by a coat-of-arms flanked by reliefs of Portuguese soldiers. The *Old Customs House*, south of the Town Hall, incorporates a Portuguese barracks block of 1665. The Mint to the north dates partly from 1824.

D. THE MAIDAN

Mumbai is justly famous for the magnificent group of High Victorian buildings that overlooks the great open space in the middle of the downtown area. Partly created by dismantling the walls of the Fort, the *Maidan* was originally intended for civic ceremonies and military parades; it is now mostly used for recreation, cricket matches being particularly popular. The panorama of Back Bay, one enjoyed by the Neo-Gothic monuments that face west onto the Maidan, is now blocked by apartments and offices built on reclaimed land.

The tour of this zone of Mumbai begins at the south end of Karmavip Bhaurao Patel Marg, the road that skirts the east side of the Maidan. The *Secretariat* of the Government of Mumbai, built in 1867-74 by Wilkins, has a 140 m. long Neo-Gothic facade. The wings with verandahs are enriched with polychrome arches on four levels. The 52 m. high square tower in the middle is dominated by an arched recess framing a circular window. The tower above is crowned with a tiled pyramidal roof.

Next comes the *Mumbai University Complex* of 1869-74, Scott's most important contribution to the city's architecture. The *Senate Hall* was financed by 'Readymoney', to whom there is a statue of Thomas Woolner in front. The south end of the hall is apsidal, in the manner of a church; the rose window above the arcaded north porch is flanked by square towers with slender colonettes and octagonal steeples. Open spiral staircase towers provide access to the side verandahs. A carved timber gallery carried on cast-iron brackets encloses a two-storeyed structure with arcaded galleries, stained-glass windows, pierced parapets and delicately carved stonework. The circular corner towers, with tapering spires on the west, contain spiral staircases.

The vaulted entrance porch to Senate Hall serves as the base for the magnificent, 79 m. high *Rajabai Tower*, the loftiest Neo-Gothic edifice in Mumbai. Added in 1878, the tower is named after the mother of the benefactor, Premchand Raichand. The lowest stage exhibits large pointed arches containing windows filled with stained glass. Sculpted figures set in corner niches and part-octagonal buttresses also appear at this level. The topmost stage is marked by clock faces framed by steep gables. The tower is capped by an intricately worked octagonal lantern with figures at the corners and at the summits of the turrets.

The *High Court*, the next monument on this side of the Maidan, was begun in 1869 under the direction of John Augustus Fuller. Its immense bulk is lightened through extravagant use of Neo-Gothic detail. The central tower has a steeply pyramidal roof with side gables, attaining an overall height of 53 m. The corners of the tower are enlivened by octagonal steeples, repeated at a lower level on the front, where they are topped by figures of Justice and Mercy. The tower contains a staircase reserved for judges. Octagonal towers mark the northern and southern extremities of the building.

Crossing the Maidan by proceeding west along Vir Nariman Road, visitors will arrive at the *Railway Offices*, designed by Stevens in 1894 for what was then known as the Bombay, Baroda and Central Indian Railway. The offices have an almost Byzantine appearance due to the bands of red sandstone and white plaster set into basalt, and the cluster of domes at different levels that rises above. Each facade has a gabled centrepiece flanked by projecting wings and topped by pairs of domes. A female statue on the west gable, representing the Spirit of Progress, grasps a locomotive body and wheel. The whole composition is crowned by a domed tower rising in diminishing square and octagonal stages.

The *Railway Offices* flank the ugly modern block of Churchgate Station, principal hub of Mumbai's extensive suburban network. Opposite, on the south side of Vir Nariman Road, is the former *Eros Cinema*, one of the city's most striking Art Deco schemes. Its painted concrete facade, culminating in a circular tower, punctuates the corner of the Maidan. The cinema blends with the nearby apartments that line the streets running from the Maidan to Back Bay. Many of these were designed by European architects who settled in

Mumbai in the years just before and during the World War II. The apartments have curving balconies with cast-iron grilles in the fashionable Art Deco manner. Similarly styled residences line the great curve of *Marine Drive*, completed in 1940, now renamed Netaji Subhash Road. This grand thoroughfare terminates in Nariman Point, created out of landfill, marked by the lofty towers of the Air India Offices and the Hilton and Oberoi Hotels. Beyond is the *National Centre for the Performing Arts*, Mumbai's largest auditorium, designed in 1975 by the American architect Phillip Johnson in an International Modernist style, and which opened in 1981.

E. From Chhatrapati Shivaji Terminus to Crawford Market

The tour of Mumbai continues from Flora Fountain or the Maidan northwards to a traffic circle on Dadabhai Naoroji Road, the site of the original north gate of the Fort. The circle is dominated by *Chhatrapati Shivaji Terminus*, formerly Victoria Terminus, abbreviated to just VT, the chief landmark of the downtown area. Designed by Stevens in 1887-88, this is arguably the city's greatest Neo-Gothic building, surpassing in grandeur of conception St Pancras Station in London, on which it was partly modelled.

Chhatrapati Shivaji Terminus, Mumbai.

In spite of its huge scale the workmanship of the terminus is of the finest quality: its symmetrically organised arcades are enhanced by polychrome stonework, intricate ironwork, marble and ceramic inlays, and vigorous relief carving. The west frontage displays side wings with gabled ends and corner towers topped with squat octagonal spires. The dome above, lined with eight ornamental ribs, is crowned with a 4 m. high figure of Progress by Thomas

Earp. Other carved motifs fill the rounded and triangular tympanums over the porches and windows. Busts in medallions portray civic worthies of the era; coats-of-arms represents the railway company. The interior of the booking hall in the left wing is conceived as a church nave, complete with tiled floor and painted ribbed vault. A majestic staircase is positioned beneath the dome.

The *General Post Office* stands a short distance east of the terminus. Like the museum, it too is influenced by the architecture of Bijapur. Wittet was also involved, and together with John Begg supervised its construction in 1904-10. Its long facade has a central portal distinguished by an ornate parapet running between octagonal finials. The framing towers, including those at the ends of the side wings, are topped with domes on petalled fringes. The intermediate bays are defined by part-octagonal buttresses rising above the roof as domical finials. The central booking hall is roofed with a flattish dome carried on pointed intersecting arches. Beyond the General Post Office lie the regularly laid out blocks of *Ballard Estate*, a commercial development dating from the first decade of the 20th century.

Returning to the west front of Chhatrapati Shivaji Terminus visitors will note the *Municipal Buildings* opposite, designed by Stevens in 1893. This confident Neo-Gothic edifice dramatically exploits its corner location at the junction of Mahapalika Marg and Dadabhoi Naoroji Road. The building is dominated by an impressive 7 m. high corner tower capped with a bulbous dome. The gabled facade beneath the dome is crowned with a winged figure labelled 'Urbs Prima in India'. Flanking towers repeat the domed theme. The porch is animated by winged griffins at the corners of the roof; similar beasts crown the gables and porches of the wings extending along the side streets.

A further series of fine buildings line Mahapalika Marg. The first to be seen is the *Magistrates Court* of 1884-89, designed by John Adams. Its central porch is punctuated by an unusual part-circular balcony with decorated corbels. A slender spire is placed to one side. The adjacent *Cama and Abless Hospital* has a central square tower enlivened by circular corner buttresses with smoothly tapering spires. Next comes *St Xavier's College* and the *Elphinstone Technical High School* of 1872-79, the latter at the corner of Lokmanya Tilak Road. The triple-arcaded entrance to the school, filled with cast-iron gates, is approached by a broad flight of steps. The towers flanking the central wing and marking the corners have octagonal pavilions crowned with tiered pyramidal roofs.

The tour returns to Chhatrapati Shivaji Terminus before proceeding north along Dadabhoi Naoroji Road. Just after the *Times of India* Offices on the left is the *Tyebji High School*, built in a revivalist Islamic manner with a prominent domed tower. Next comes the *Sir Jamsetji Jeejeebhoy School of Art*, Mumbai's oldest such institution, founded in 1854. John Lockwood Kipling was

Principal here when his son Rudyard was born in 1865. Carvings by students of the school adorn many buildings in the city, notable Chhatrapati Shivaji Terminus. The School of Art, built in the Neo-Gothic style by Wittet in 1874-78, has an entrance porch with bracket figures of local craftsmen. The later Architecture School next door has unusual semicircular windows interrupted by Ionic colonettes.

The intersection of Dadabhai Naoroji and Lokmanya Tilak Roads is commanded by *Crawford Market*, now renamed Phule Market, designed by William Honour and named after Arthur Crawford, Commissioner of Mumbai in 1865-71. Its triple-arched entrance has reliefs designed by Kipling in the tympanums depicting local occupations of the city. The octagonal clock tower above is capped with a small lantern. A small Neo-Gothic fountain inside the market is almost totally concealed by food stalls.

The busy area north of Crawford Market is characterised by narrow lanes crowded with shops, including the celebrated *Chor Bazaar*. This zone is also home to the notorious 'Cages', the red-light district of the city. Javeri Bazaar, just off Muhammad Ali Road, is overlooked by the *Jumma Mosque*. Its prayer hall and minarets, raised high above the surrounding streets, are executed in a Neo-Mughal manner, with lobed arches and domed pavilions picked out in bright green and white. The nearby *Minar* and *Baydari* mosques are built in a similar idiom.

Shaikh Menon Street, west of the Jumma mosque, leads directly to *Mumbadevi Temple*, recognised by its curving tower, which soars above the rooftops. The temple is dedicated to the goddess worshipped by the original inhabitants of the islands and lagoons of Mumbai; the city's new name was chosen in response to the even growing popularity of Mumbadevi. The present temple is a 19th century replacement on an earlier shrine that occupied a site near Chhatrapati Shivaji Terminus. It is entered through a mandapa with Neo-Classical pilasters and shutters. The tower is built in the Gujarat manner, with clustered elements and superimposed balconies on the sides, and a gleaming brass finial at the summit.

F. COLABA

The southern extremity of Mumbai was once a separate island joined to the Fort by a causeway. Known as Colaba, this part of the city preserves a peaceful atmosphere, with spacious houses and apartment blocks lining leafy streets. The principal historical feature is the *Afghan Memorial Church*, consecrated to St John the Baptist, commemorating those who fell in the First Afghan War of 1838-43. The church was built by Henry Conybeare in 1858 in a sombre Neo-Gothic manner, the earliest stone example of this style in Southern India. Its steeply gabled facade is dominated by a square corner tower with a tapering octagonal spire rising a total of 58 m., completed in 1865. The interior is divided into triple aisles by pointed arches. Stained-glass windows in the chancel depict the Crucifixion and seated Christ; mosaic patterns adorn arched recesses in the walls beneath. The tiled pavement and ironwork screen in the choir partly follow designs sent out to Mumbai by William Butterfield.

G. Malabar Hill

The peninsula formed by Malabar Hill provides a spectacular backdrop to Back Bay. Surrounded on three sides by the Arabian Sea, this part of Mumbai was once the setting for extravagant villas, with imposing Neo-Classical facades and grand staircases set in gardens furnished with European statuary. One of the few such residences to survive the onslaught of recent development is *Mount Nepean* on the road of the same name (permission required to visit). This imposing pile is raised high on a balustraded terrace, reached by curving flights of steps. The corner tower is capped with a Mughal styled dome; similar half-domes top the curving balconies. Today's business barons and film personalities prefer the modernist high-rise apartments clustered on the steeply rising ground of the hill. Benefitting from fine ocean views and refreshing sea breezes, the apartments present a brightly lit mass at night.

Hanging Gardens, built on the tanks that supply Mumbai with water, skirt the south flank of Malabar Hill, offering sweeping panoramas of downtown Mumbai. The *Towers of Silence* nearby are where Parsis, who do not practice burial or cremation, expose their dead to vultures and other birds of prey (only Parsis admitted). The towers are secluded in a garden intended foster contemplation and repose. The *Bhulnatha Temple* nearby dates from 1900. A mechanical lift transports worshippers from S.S. Patkar Road beneath. *Mani Bhavan Gandhi Sanghralaya*, at 19 Laburnum Road a short distance away, is where Gandhi stayed on his visits to the city. The house is converted into a museum and research library dedicated to the life of the Mahatma (closed Mondays).

A small *Jain Temple* is located on B.G. Kher Marg that runs along the south flank of Malabar Hill. Dating from 1904 and dedicated to Adinatha, the ornate white marble structure is built in the Gujarat style. Its walls are covered with paintings of the lives of the Jain saviours.

Raj Bhavan, the official residence of Mumbai's Governors since 1884, occupies beautifully maintained grounds at the extreme point of Malabar Hill (permission required to visit). The house has a pitched roof and pleasant verandahs with tiled roofs. A short distance north is the sacred tank of *Banganga*, overlooked by shrines and traditional wooden houses. Stray stone blocks from the 10th-11th century suggest an early history for Banganga, the name of which refers to Rama's magical bow. The *Walkeshwar temple* facing the tank, near its southwestern corner, dates from 1715, when it was built to replace an earlier shrine dismantled by the Portuguese. Its curving plastered tower is divided into clustered elements, with carved images of sages and musicians beneath. A stone tortoise and Nandi are placed in front of the linga sanctuary. A pair of stone lamp columns marks the southeastern corner of the tank.

A popular place of worship in Mumbai is *Mahalakshmi Temple*, near the northern tip of Malabar Hill. This stands with its back to the ocean, on a promontory just off Bhulabhai Desai Road (formerly Warden Road). The temple has been completely renovated in recent years, and is now cloaked in marble and topped with a massive but plain curving spire. Images of Lakshmi, Sarasvati and Kali receive worship within the same sanctuary.

Haji Ali Mosque nearby occupies an islet in the watery shallows of the bay separating Malabar Hill from Worli, reached by a causeway at low tide. The prayer hall and slender minarets commemorate a local saint who was drowned here. Lala Lajpatrai Marg, the road that skirts the bay, follows the course of Hornby Vellar, the sea wall erected by Governor Hornby as one of Mumbai's first great land reclamation projects. *Mahalaxmi Racecourse* opposite is the largest in Southern India.

An unusual edifice in the Malabar Hill is the *Opera House* on Vithalbhai Patel Road. The setting of lavish productions after its inauguration in 1924, it has now been tastefully restored, and is now mostly used as a cinema. Its Neo-Classical facade has tapering Corinthian pilasters alternating with shuttered windows. Statuary fills the pediment above.

H. Byculla, Parel, Mahim and Bandra

Further historical features are located in Byculla and Parel in central Mumbai. These densely populated districts are dotted with textile museums with high circular chimneys many dating from the 19th century, but now no longer in use. The *Magan David Synagogue* on Sir Jamsetji Jeejeebhoy Road was erected by David Sassoon in 1861 and renovated by his son Jacob in 1910. The church-like east facade has a lofty Neo-Classical portico topped by a four-stage clock tower. A raised women's gallery runs around three sides of the cream and white interior. The Ark is accommodated in apsidal recess.

Christ Church of 1934 stands a short distance away on Mirza Ghalib Street (formerly Clare Road). The quartet of Doric columns in its west porch belongs to the batch imported for use in the Town Hall. The triple-stage tower above has Greek styled palmettes at the corners. The interior is enhanced by well formed Corinthian columns. The earliest of the memorials that line the walls is the grave of Robert Grant, Governor of Mumbai in 1835-38.

Further north, beyond Byculla Station on Dr Bahasheb Ambedkar Road, is the newly restored *Dr Bhau Daji Lad Museum*, (closed Wednesdays), founded as the Victoria and Albert Museum by Sir George Birdwood in 1857. The present building, which dates from 1871, has pedimented windows set between fully formed Corinthian columns. This heavy Neo-Classical scheme contrasts with the light-weight cast-iron columns and brackets that support the balustraded gallery and painted wooden ceiling of the interior. The lower level of the museum is home to an exhibition of local crafts. The display is dominated by a marble portrait of Albert, Prince Consort, executed by Mathew Noble in 1869. The upper level, paved with Victorian tiles, has a selection of maps, watercolours, models and coins illustrating the history of Mumbai. Among the displaced statuary deposited in the garden at the rear of the museum is a worn sculpture of an elephant shipped from Elephanta island, as well as a large but defaced portrait of Queen Victoria of 1872. An ornate metal fountain nearby is dated 1867.

The museum stands next to the beautifully planted *Victoria Gardens* on 1861, now a popular zoological park known as Veermata Jijabai Bhonsle Udyan. This is entered through an ornate Italianate gate with triple arches. The tropical planthouse within has an attractive curvilinear cast-iron frame; the Oriental Garden is a donation by the Japanese Government.

The curious *Clocktower* in front of the museum on Dr Bahasaheb Ambedkar Road was a gift from David Sassoon in 1865. The arched openings at the base are decorated with polychrome tiles and allegorical heads portraying Morning, Noon, Evening and Night. The *Railway Hospital* opposite was built in 1871 as a college by 'Readymoney'. Its arcaded range has a lofty central tower topped with a pyramidal metal roof.

Parel lies north of Byculla. The *Haffkine Institute*, within the medical complex on Acharya Dhonde Road, is one of the city's most ancient structures (permission required to visit). The site was first occupied by a Franciscan chapel in 1673. In 1719 it was taken over by the English, who converted it into a government residence, using it as an alternative to the Castle in the Fort. The banqueting hall and ballroom built within the shell of the original chapel survive, though much altered. The accompanying park and lake are, however, lost. The building was transformed into a medical institution at the end of the 19th century, a role it continues to fulfil.

About 350 m. east of the institute, in a somewhat obscure side lane, stands the *Baladeva Shrine*, of interest for its remarkable 6th century sculpture. Discovered only in 1931 and now under veneration, this 3.5 m. high image represents Shiva in cosmic form, expanding outwards through multiple figures that extend upward and outward to both sides.

Mahim, one of Mumbai's northern suburbs, is best known for the *Shrine of Makhdum Ali Mahimi*, a Muslim saint born in Mahim in 1372, during the period when much of the Konkan came under the domination of the Delhi sultans, and dying there in 1431. An influential Sufi teacher, Makhdum's treatises and doctrines are still widely read. The brightly painted green and white shrine, just a few metres from the Arabian Sea, dates from 1748. The tomb chamber has a central dome surrounded by a quartet of lesser domes. The complex is entered through a lofty gateway portal of more recent construction. The anniversary of the saint's death celebrated over a period of ten days in December each year is the occasion for a lively fair.

Nearby *Mahim Fort* on a rocky point overlooking Mahim Creek is a vestige from the early period of Portuguese occupation. Little is preserved other than battlemented walls rising directly out of the water.

The *Basilica of Our Lady of the Mount*, commonly known as Mount Mary, tops a small rise in Bandra in the extreme north of Mumbai. The church is one of the city's most popular Roman Catholic places of worship, especially in September when the birth of the Virgin Mary is celebrated here. Founded in 1760, it was subsequently rebuilt in a High Victorian, Neo-Gothic style with sharply pointed steeples.

2. Around Mumbai

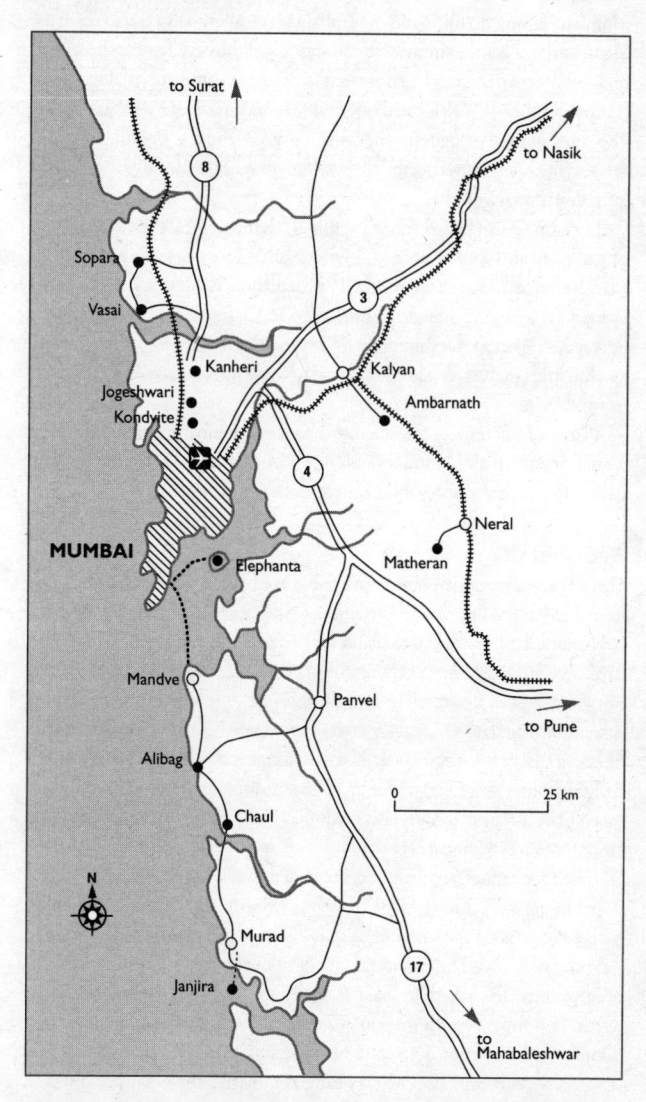

Mumbai's situation on a long narrow peninsular, joined to the mainland at its northern end, means that road or rail trips beyond the metropolitan area are

61

unavoidably tedious. The exception is the pleasurable boat trip across Mumbai Harbour to the island of Elephanta [A]. Allow half a day to reach the island and inspect the impressive carvings in its the cave temple there. This rock-cut monument may be compared to others at Kondvite [B], Jogeshwari [C] and Kanheri [D], all located on Salsette Island, north of Mumbai's airport. The ruins of the Portuguese sea fort at Vasai [E] and the Buddhist stupa at Sopara [F] lie yet further north. All these sites may be reached by suburban rail from downtown Mumbai.

Ports on the Arabian Sea coast south of Mumbai reveal the varied history of the Konkan Coast. Alibag [G] is accessible by boat from Mumbai via Mandve, but can also be approached by road, though this takes much longer. From Alibag it is possible to continue on to Chaul [H], with its decaying Portuguese period monuments, and the island fortress of Janjira [I], headquarters of the Sidi admirals. A visit to these three sites will occupy a full day and more.

Places of interest on the mainland east of Mumbai include the ruined temple at Amarnath [J] and the hill resort of Matheran [K] in the Western Ghats. These are also accessible from the rail line to Pune [3].

A. ELEPHANTA

This attractive wooded island in Mumbai Harbour, a one hour launch ride from the Gateway of India [1A], is famous for its cave temple (closed Mondays). No historical information is available for this rock-cut monument, which may have been excavated in the 6th century by the Mauryas who controlled the Konkan Coast at this time. (Note that this line of rulers is unrelated to the earlier but more famous dynasty of the same name based in Northern India). Elephanta Island is known locally as Gharapuri, but its European name is derived from a stone carving of an elephant discovered here in Portuguese times. (The damaged piece is now on display in the garden of the Dr Bhau Daji Lad Museum in Mumbai [1H].)

The Elephanta *Cave Temple* is excavated into a basalt cliff, approached from the jetty by a long flight of steps. The principal shrine, flanked by rock-cut courts on the east and west, is entered through openings scooped out on three sides. The ingenious layout of the temple combines two axial progressions: from east to west towards the linga sanctuary; and from north to south towards the majestic triple-headed bust of Shiva that dominates the interior. The columns have squat tapering shafts and fluted cushion-shaped capitals; ceiling beams emphasise the east-west aisles. A square linga sanctuary detached from the walls is entered through four doorways, each framed by a pair of gigantic guardian figures in symmetrical swaying poses.

Large-scale mythological scenes are deeply recessed into the walls of the cave temple. The damage to the figures, partly inflicted by the Portuguese, in no way diminishes the artistic impact of the carvings, which are among the greatest masterpieces of Hindu art in Southern India. The compositions portray different aspects of Shiva. The north entrance, which serves today as the main entrance, is flanked by images of the god seated in yogic posture as Lakulisha (left), and vigorously dancing as Nataraja (right). Coupled images of Shiva and Parvati seated on Kailasa are seen at either side of the east entrance. The god and his consort gamble at dice (left), or sit unperturbed by multi-headed Ravana, who shakes their mountain home (right). Shiva violently spearing the demon Andhaka (left), contrasts with a peaceful scene of the marriage of Shiva and Parvati (right) at the west entrance.

Three panels are set into the rear (south) wall of the cave temple. To the left, Shiva and Parvati are joined in the composite figure of Ardharnishvara; to the right, Shiva assists in the descent of the goddess Ganga, observed somewhat warily by Parvati. These complex male-female, husband-wife relationships are also embodied in the immense triple-headed bust of Shiva in the middle. The god emerges only partly from the mountain, his fourth head turned unseen into the rock. The two side profiles contrast a feminine aspect (left) with a fierce masculine aspect (right); the central head is introspective and serene.

Other carvings are found in the small side courts. On the south side of the east court is a porch with chambers adorned with images of Karttikeya, Ganesha and the Matrikas, now damaged. The porch leads to a small linga shrine. Another smaller sanctuary opens off the west court. Its porch has unfinished images of Shiva as the yogi and as the dancer. The adjacent cistern is rock-cut.

1.5 km. to the south is a second cave temple, with a 36 m. long facade supported by a row of columns. Except for the decoration of the shrine doorway within there are no carvings.

B. Kondvite

This little visited Buddhist site is located 6 km. east of Andheri station on the main suburban line, 22 km. north of downtown Mumbai. Some 18 cave temples here are arranged on the sides of a small rocky hill. Two excavations are of particular interest.

Cave 9 is a plain chaitya hall dating from the 2nd century. It has an unusual circular sanctuary cut into the rock at the rear. This is fashioned in imitation of a thatched hut, with a door placed between trellis windows, and overhung by curving eaves. Its domical interior is almost entirely filled with a monolithic hemispherical stupa raised on a circular drum. A dedicatory inscription is seen beside one of the windows. Reliefs of the Buddha on the right wall of the hall are later additions.

Cave 13, fashioned as a vihara, is assigned to the 5th-6th century. This comprises a columned verandah, a hall with four central pillars, off which open eight small cells, some with rock-cut beds, and a central shrine with a vacant pedestal.

C. JOGESHWARI

The large *Cave Temple* at this site is located 24 km. north of Mumbai's centre, about 1.5 km. east of Jogeshwari railway station. Though this 6th century monument is now badly eroded and encroached by slum dwellings, it is worth visiting for its unusual layout. The cave temple is approached from the east and west by long flights of steps deeply cut into the rock. The east doorway is flanked by guardian figures; the lintel above shows Nataraja and a scene of Shiva and Parvati playing dice. The columned hall within has a sanctuary standing freely in the middle, entered through four doorways. The verandah on the north has windows and doorways in the rear walls.

D. KANHERI

More than 100 Buddhist rock-cut monuments are dotted around *Krishnagiri Upavana National Park*, an attractive wooded site situated about 10 km. from Borivili, a station on the main suburban line, 35 km. north of downtown Mumbai. The park is notable for its many reservoirs, including Tulsi Lake, 3 km. north.

Kanheri was occupied from the 1st century CE onwards by a large Buddhist community that was supported by local merchants for over a millennium. Most of the features are modest excavations with frontal verandahs and adjacent cisterns. Some are adorned with carvings of Buddhas, Bodhisattvas and naga deities. The caves are numbered haphazardly, not all the labels being visible.

Cave 3, the most impressive at Kanheri, is easily found by following the trail that leads to the main group. This 2nd century monument is a chaitya hall that appears to imitate that at Karla [3C]. Its exterior is concealed by a rock-cut wall, partly restored, flanked by columns with sculpted bases and capitals. The facade has three doors with carvings of donor couples in between. The semicircular window above lacks carved ornamentation, but the side walls of the verandah are covered with 5th-6th century reliefs of standing Buddhas. The apsidal ended hall within is divided into three aisles by two lines of octagonal columns, several with pot bases and bell-shaped capitals. Carved brackets show animal riders and Buddhist motifs, such as worship of the stupa and footprints beneath the bodhi tree. The vaulted roof was once provided with wooden ribs, now lost. The hemispherical stupa at the rear is unadorned. Several structural stupas stand outside the hall; when excavated, they yielded urns with relics, one dated 495.

Caves 1 and 2 are located south of Cave 3, but are of little interest. Further along the same path is *Cave 41*. This has an unusual image of Avaloki-teshvara with four arms and eleven heads.

A circuitous path following the south side of a forested ravine leads to *Cave 11*. This 5th-6th century vihara is approached through a verandah with eight octagonal columns. Three doorways lead into a hall with columned aisles and small cells on three sides. A central shrine housing Buddha images is located to the rear. Two low benches cut out of the floor were probably intended for eating or reading.

Other important rock-cut monuments are located on the opposite side of the ravine. *Cave 90* has a carving of Avalokiteshvara between female deities. The surrounding miniature scenes show the Bodhisattva delivering his devotees from the Eight Great Perils. The terrace beyond is occupied by commemorative stupas, both rock-cut and brick built.

E. Vasai

The ruined *Portuguese Fort* of Vasai overlooks a small river at a point where it flows into the Arabian Sea. The site is most easily reached from Vasai Road, 8 km. distant, a station on the suburban network, 53 km. north of downtown Mumbai. The massive ramparts and grandiose churches and convents constitute the most impressive Portugese remains in Southern India after those in Old Goa [11B]. Though now mostly decayed, these buildings are picturesquely cloaked in vines and bushes, and set in groves of mango trees and palms.

Originally known as Bassein, the port has a similar origin to Mumbai itself, having been granted to the Portuguese in 1535 by Bahadur Shah of Gujarat. The Portuguese developed Bassein into a flourishing city, renowned for its wide streets, luxurious mansions and impressive churches, monasteries and public buildings. Apparently only Christians were permitted to live inside its walls. Francis Xavier visited Bassein four times, and after his death was adopted as the patron saint of the city. Bassein survived an attack of plague in 1695, which decimated one third of its population, but its fortunes declined after 1738 when it was besieged by the Marathas, who took the city in the following year. The Marathas were expelled in 1780 by the British, who heavily bombarded the ramparts and buildings. The city was virtually abandoned in 1818 when it was absorbed into the Bombay Presidency; it is now partly inhabited by local fishermen.

Vasai is contained by comparatively well preserved *Ramparts*. These define an irregular elliptical zone, almost 1 km. along its greater east-west axis, extending up to the water on the east and south. Nine massive bastions of triangular shape, originally named after Christian saints, protrude outwards from the walls. Round headed openings in the walls are for cannon; angled bastions line the walkway on top. Visitors arriving from Vasai Road enter the city through the *Land Gate* on the west, shielded by a barbican wall. The inner portal has an upper arched opening flanked by colonettes with crudely fashioned leaf like capitals.

Immediately south of the Land Gate are the remains of the *Church of St Paul*, a Franciscan foundation. The church is entered through an unusual triple-arched portal framed by Doric columns. The imposing nave within is roofless, except for the coffered vault in the chancel and the broad arch of the gallery. Tombstones are set into the floor. Several columns of the adjacent cloister still stand.

A short distance further south is the *Church of St Anthony*, associated with the Jesuit order, founded in 1548 by Francis Xavier. The facade, the finest at Bassein, has pairs of Corinthian columns on either side of an arched doorway. A rectangular pedimented window flanked by volutes and pinnacles and a smaller circular window are seen above. The composition is topped with a rounded pediment. Panels set into the facade are carved with 'IHS', the Jesuit motto. Other than the coffered vault in the chancel nothing remains of the interior roof. The dilapidated cloister next door frames a spreading mango tree.

The *Citadel* to the east, standing roughly in the middle of the fort, is a quadrangular walled zone with prominent corner bastions. Access is from the east, through a gate with the Portuguese coat of arms over the arched door. No structures are preserved inside.

Bassein's cathedral, known as the *Matriz of St Joseph*, was founded in 1546 a short distance further east, beside the city walls. The entrance is marked by a triple-staged tower with pot finials at the summit, dating from the rebuilding of 1601. The interior is reduced to a mere shell. The *Seat Gate* to the rear of the cathedral, at the eastern extremity of the city, consists of two arched doorways. The outer one preserves its iron-clad doors, framed by massive round buttresses. The gate leads directly to the port, with its small fleet of fishing boats.

The tour of Vasai continues by returning through the Sea Gate and proceeding through the city towards a small 19th century *Shiva temple*. This stands on the edge of a pond and is recognised by its fluted dome. North of the temple stands the *Church of the Dominicans*, the largest in Vasai. The interior is mostly ruined, but the decorated door leading to the side cloister is worth noting. A four-stage tower marks the southeast corner. The south door of the nave has side volutes framing dogs, an unusual motif. A sort distance in front (west) of the church are the remains of civic buildings. The include the *Camera*, or Town Hall, with an arcaded porch. A carved panel over an interior doorway show a royal coat-of-arms and an armillary sphere.

F. Sopara

This peaceful town is most conveniently reached from Nola Sopara station on the main line, 8 km. north of Vasai Road. Sopara is identified with the ancient emporium of Shurparaka, which traces its history back to the 3rd-2nd centuries BCE. This early date is confirmed by the discovery of stone fragments inscribed with edicts of Ashoka, the Maurya emperor of Northern India. Sopara seems also to have been known in the 2nd century CE to Ptolemy, who refers to it as Supara.

The most important feature that can be seen at Sopara today is the *Stupa Mound*, which stands in a pleasant mango grove some 500 m. west of the railway station. The mound is almost 90 m. in circumference, with steep earthen sides on a brick base, rising more than 5 m. The stupa is surrounded by brick and stone foundations that define a rectangular enclosure entered on the east and south. Small mounds indicate votive stupas. A pile of 11th-12th century Hindu carvings is seen on the east. Excavations here in the 1880s revealed a brick chamber set into the base of the mound. A circular stone coffer within the chamber disclosed a remarkable sequence of caskets of different materials, one placed inside the other. The outermost casket, of copper, contained almost 300 tiny gold flowers, as well as semiprecious stones, stone beads, a small gold plaque showing Buddha preaching, and an unworn silver coin of a 2nd century Satavahana king. Eight bronze images of about the 8th-9th centuries were arranged around the casket. The innermost casket, of gold, contained pottery fragments, believed to be pieces of the begging bowl of Buddha. These finds are now in the collection of the Asiatic Society in Mumbai's Town Hall [1C].

A path from the stupa mound at Sopara leads for about 750 m. to a small lake overlooked by the Chakreshvara temple, a recent construction. Among the 11th-12th century panels strewn about is an extraordinary 2 m. high *Image of Brahma*, and a charming composition showing a maiden holding a parrot.

G. Alibag

This port lies about 90 km. south of Mumbai, via Panvel on NH17. More conveniently, it may be reached by catamaran from the Gateway of India in the city, which transports visitors to Mandve, from where a road runs to Alibag. It is difficult now to imagine that this small town, nestling peacefully in palm groves overlooking the estuary of Sakhar Creek, was once a busy naval station.

In 1662 Shivaji made Alibag the chief port for the Maratha fleet, and in the following years it became the headquarters of the Angres. These skilled admirals earned a reputation for piracy, disrupting shipping to and from Mumbai, until the port was taken by the British in 1840.

The principal feature of interest of Alibag is *Hirakot*, or Diamond Fort, a short distance northwest of the town. Erected by Kanhoji Angre in 1820, Hirakot is built of massive basalt blocks, and is entered from the south by a steep flight of steps. A small shrine dedicated to Maruti is built into the gate. Cells for prisoners and a small treasury stand within the enclosure.

Kanhoji Angre is also associated with the more impressive fort of *Kolaba*, which occupies a narrow rocky island in the middle of Alibag harbour. Kolaba consists of a quadrangular arrangement of basalt walls, punctuated by 17 round towers. The main entrance, at the northeast corner, is shielded by an outwork with a long causeway. The pointed arched doorway is flanked by towers; the teak doors within preserve iron spikes. Immediately inside the fort are two domed storerooms and a dilapidated shrine consecrated to Padmavati and Bhavani. The ruined lines of buildings to the south have been identified as granaries and stables. The remains of a residence built by the younger Raghoji Angre in 1816 are seen further south, in the vicinity of a large reservoir. The *Ganapati Panchayatana Temple* opposite is the work of the elder Raghoji Angre before 1793. The jail and guardrooms lie beyond.

The *Magen Aboth Synagogue* southeast of Alibag, erected in 1848, testifies to the presence here of an ancient Bene Israel community. Its plain exterior, with windows at two levels, conceals a spacious whitewashed hall dominated by an arched wall riches accommodating the Ark. The synagogue stands in a walled compound entered through a bright blue-painted iron gate.

H. CHAUL

The remains of this fortified Portuguese port overlook the mouth of the Roha River, 18 km. south of Alibag. This verdant and tranquil site gives little indication of the vigorous commerce of former times.

The history of Chaul goes back to the 15th century when the port came under the control of the Bahmanis of Gulbarga [24A]. It was the Portuguese, however, who developed Chaul into an international emporium: their first factory was established here as early as 1516. In spite of repeated raids on Chaul by the forces of Ahmadnagar [6] and Bijapur [23A], commerce flourished, especially with Gujarat and the ports of the Persian Gulf and Red Sea. Merchants from different parts of India settled in Chaul, where they traded in rice, precious stones and locally manufactured cottons and silks. In 1592 Burhan Nizam II established a fort a Korle on the opposite side of Chaul harbour, but was expelled soon after by the Portuguese. Business declined after the establishment of Mumbai. The port passed into the hands of the Marathas in 1740, but was virtually abandoned by the time it was occupied by the British in the early 19th century.

The overgrown *Fortifications*, containing dense palm groves, picturesquely border the Roha on the south and west. Basalt walls define an approximately circular zone, more than 500 m. across, reinforced by massive triangular bastions on the landward side. Their sloping flanks can still be seen, though the moat which protected them is now filled in. The road from Alibag passes through a small gate in the northern arc of the walls. Instead of continuing south, however, visitors should take the path immediately to the right. This leads to the *Church of the Augustinians* of 1587, now a collapsing pile of masonry.

The *Church of the Franciscans*, a short distance southwest, was begun in 1535 and dedicated to St Barbara. It preserves a 30 m. high, six-storey tower, the loftiest in the city. The *West Gate* of Chaul, which lies beyond, has an arched entrance surmounted by a royal coat-of-arms and two crosses flanked by saints. The *Church of the Dominicans*, to the south, retains a portion of its coffered vault over the chancel. Fragments of other vaulting with fanciful designs cover the side chapels. The ruins of St Francis Xavier's chapel lie to the east.

The path continues until it joins the main road from Alibag that runs through the city. Here can be seen the collapsing enclosure of the fortified residence of the governor of Chaul, known as the *Castle*, and the site of the original Portuguese factory. The entrance has an arched door surmounted by royal arms and a cross. A path passing by the walls of the Castle arrives at the *Matriz*, now much overgrown. The arched portals and decaying walls of this large cathedral date from 1534. The only other building of interest is the *Church of the Jesuits*, situated on the main road. This is represented by a single facade with an arched doorway. The *Sea Gate*, south of the Castle, is protected by a small outwork. A slab carved with a figure of a warrior wearing the insignia of the Order of Christ is set into the walls. An inscribed panel to the right records that the walls along the water were completed in 1577.

The Sea Gate gives onto a modern bridge that crosses the Roha River, beyond which is situated *Korle Fort*. This citadel consists of a fortified ridge, almost 100 m. high, shielding the estuary from the ocean. On the river side of the ridge is the village of Korle, with a well maintained church, partly dating from Portuguese times.

Upper Chaul, known also as *Revdanda*, is reached by returning to the Alibag road, and proceeding 2.5 km. north. This small settlement has quite different history, since it was under Maratha control for a longer period. Thickly wooded and well watered, the village is built beside a row of ponds at the foot of a hilly ridge. A domed 18th century tomb is built on a rise overlooking Bhavle pond to the west. The *Dancing Girls' House*, consisting of a domed hall and a mosque within a walled enclosure, occupies a pass in the hall 500 m. north of the village. Simple excavations dating back to the 1st-4th centuries dot the southeast face of the ridge. The temple of Hinglaj at the summit is reached by a flight of steps.

I. Janjira

The town of Murad lies 33 km. south of Chaul; 5 km. further south is the fishing village of Rajapuri, from which boats can be hired to transport visitors to Janjira. This remarkable island citadel commands the mouth of a tidal creek that gives access to the Konkan hinterland.

Island Fort, Janjira.

Janjira was founded in 1511 by the Sidis, Muslim Abyssinian admirals in the service of the Adil Shahis. The Sidis gradually affirmed their autonomy from Bijapur, and by 1618 were virtually independent, partly financed by the armed escorts that they provided for pilgrims bound for Mecca. Shivaji attacked Janjira in 1659, followed some years later by his son, Sambhaji. But neither the Marathas, Portuguese nor British were able to capture Janjira. The Sidis even raided Mumbai on several occasions between 1672 and 1690. The rulers of this virtual island kingdom survived into modern times, but abandoned their citadel after it was burnt in 1860. A fanciful mansion with domical turrets erected on the hill above Murad in the early 20th century is the residence of the modern descendant of the Sidi line.

Janjira presents a formidable appearance, due to the carbuncled basalt blocks of its *Fortifications* that rise 15 m. vertically out of the ocean. Begun in 1694, the walls were completed in 1707 by Sirul Khan. They have battlements with angled tops, separated by arched openings for cannon, some still in place. The walls are strengthened by massive circular bastions positioned at regular intervals. Lead is used in the joints between the lower blocks to avoid the corroding effects of salt water.

Janjira is entered through a single *Gate* on the north side of the island, facing towards Rajapuri. The arched opening is surmounted by a frieze of battlements flanked by lions with curling tails. The guardroom on top has a balcony carried on lotus brackets. Steps lead up to a domed chamber, the walls of which are embellished with carvings of lions clutching captive elephants.

The interior of the island is crowded with overgrown ruins that are attractively grouped around two tanks, one elliptical the other circular, both partly scooped out of the rock. A Mosque with plain arches and a mihrab with faintly Neo-Classical details faces the elliptical reservoir. On the north of the circular reservoir stands the *Darbar Hall*. This four-storeyed mansion has bold cornices running between square corner towers. The central doorways display lobed arches; the windows above are round headed. The Magazine is situated on the highest point of the island, more than 60 m. above the Arabian Sea.

The tour continues by returning by boat to Rajapuri. The *Jami Mosque* here has an arcaded prayer chamber flanked by corner buttresses with cut-out curved brackets. Windows are placed in both the side and rear walls. Of greater interest are the *Sidi Tombs*, next to the road about 1.5 km. upstream from the village. The largest mausoleum is that completed by Sirul Khan before his death in 1733. It is raised on a double terrace and surrounded by ditch. The prayer chamber is surrounded by an arcade and surmounted by large but flattish dome a frieze of boldly moulded petals. Two smaller tombs are associated with earlier rulers.

J. AMARNATH

This town lies on the main line to Pune, 6 km. south of Kalyan, an important railway junction. Amarnath derives its name from the *Ambaranatha Temple*, 1 km. to the east. Together with the example at Sinnar [4D], this is the finest religious monument of the Yadava era, in spite of the fact that most of the sculptures are damaged and the tower is now incomplete.

Dedicated to Shiva, the Ambaranatha temple preserves an inscription that mentions its repair in 1016. Both the sanctuary and adjoining mandapa with triple porches expand outwards in multiple projections. The walls have moulded basements, carved panels and prominent overhangs; axial niches are sheltered by angled eaves. The curved tower that rises over the sanctuary displays a cluster of miniature elements that repeat the overall form of the central shaft, while continuing the wall projections beneath; bands of mesh-like ornament adorn the middle of each side. The roof over the mandapa is a pyramid of recessed capping elements. Among the better preserved sculptures are those depicting Nataraja, Harihara, Brahma and Bhairava on the south wall. Graceful female figures are placed in the intervening recesses.

K. Matheran

Spreading over a flat-topped spur of the Sahyadri Ranges, little more than 50 km. directly inland from Mumbai, Matheran is most easily reached by train from Neral, a station on the main line 86 km. from Mumbai, or about 120 km. from Pune. Road access from Neral ends at a car park 4 km. from the centre of Matheran, no motor transport being permitted on top.

At more than 750 m. above sea level, Matheran offers considerable climatic relief to the citizens of Mumbai and has been a popular retreat since the middle of the 19th century. The first European house was erected in 1851, and in 1858 Lord Elphinstone, Governor of Bombay, constructed a road leading to his private lodge. Thereafter, Matheran became much frequented with Mumbai's elite. The *Church* completed in 1865 soon came to be surrounded by civic buildings and private bungalows.

The chief attraction of Matheran is its natural setting. Sensational views may be had on all sides of the Sahyadri Ranges, dropping more than 500 m. to the plains below. The topmost scarp consists of a central block and two small side ridges. Lookouts are dotted along the main headland; Porcupine Point is a popular sunset spot, while Louisa Point, 3 km. away, offers prospects of the ruined hill forts of *Prabal* and *Vishalgarh*. The extreme southwest flank of the hill, 4 km. distant, is marked by Chowk Point.

3. Pune

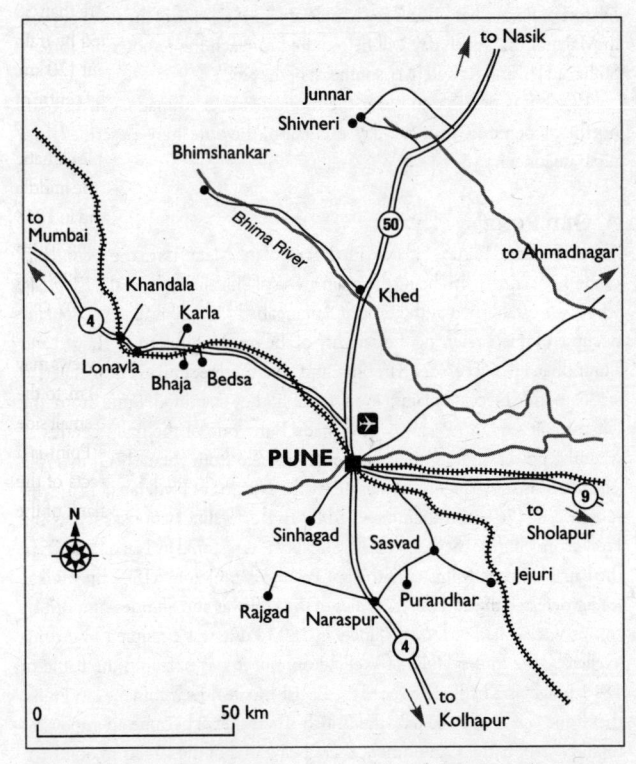

Pune is a thriving, industrial, commercial and educational centre in Maharashtra, second in importance only to Mumbai [1]. Pune is situated on the Deccan Plateau at an altitude of 580 m. beneath the Sahyadri Ranges of the Western Ghats. The civic and religious monuments of Old Pune [A] are mostly associated with the Peshwas, Prime Ministers of the Maratha royal line. Vestiges of the British period are mostly confined to New Pune [B]. One day should be sufficient to tour both parts of the city.

The Pune region is rich in historical localities, on or beneath the rugged crests of the Sahyadri Ranges. The rock-cut Buddhist shrines at Karla [C], Bhaja [D] and Bedsa [E] may be combined in a single day tour to the east, perhaps en route to Mumbai. Similar excavations in the vicinity of Junnar and the adjacent hill fort of Shivneri [H] to the north may be visited together with the mosque and tomb at Khed [F], and the pilgrimage shrine at Bhimshankar [G].

A trip southeast of Pune can take in the charming town of Sasvad [I], the hill fort of Purandhar [J] and the temple at Jejuri [K], one of the most popular in Maharashtra. A full day will be required to reach the remoter hill forts of Sinhagad [L] and Rajgad [M], southeast of the city.

While it is possible to cover the monuments at Ahmadnagar, 116 km. northeast of Pune, in a full-day excursion, they are here described as a separate itinerary [6].

A. OLD PUNE

The area around Pune is linked with the rise of the Marathas in the second half of the 17th century, this being the main arena of Shivaji's raids on the Mughals, who were established at the time at Aurangabad [5A]. Shivaji never actually occupied Pune, preferring the security of the nearby hill forts of Rajgad and Purandhar. His successors, Sambhaji and Shahu, were similarly disinclined to settle in the Deccan plains, even though they captured Pune from the Mughals. It was the Peshwas who made Pune one of the main centres of Maratha power, shifting their headquarters here from Satara [7G] in 1750. The city was subsequently contested by the Nizams of Hyderabad [26] who raided it in 1763, and then disputed by rival Maratha factions, such as the Holkar and Shinde (Scindia) chiefs. Stability was restored by Nana Phadnavis, the capable Prime Minister of the last Peshwas. In October 1802 the Holkar forces defeated the combined armies of the Peshwas and Shindes, and British troops were called in for assistance. In 1803 Pune was occupied by Arthur Wellesley, the future Duke of Wellington. But it was not until the battle of 1818, fought at Khadki (Kirkee to the British), a site now within the city limits, that Pune was finally taken by the British. Thereafter, it became an important military station, the Cantonment there being one of the largest in Southern India. Commerce flourished once peace was restored, and Pune attracted industrialists from Mumbai, including Parsis and Jews. Benefactions of the Sassoon family dot the city.

The 18th century Peshwa capital is situated on the south bank of the Mutha River, near to its confluence with the Mula River. The heart of Old Pune consists of crowded streets and lanes lined with traditional brick houses with timber frames and sloping tiled roofs, punctuated by Hindu shrines with brightly painted spires.

The great fort of *Shanwar Wada*, immediately south of Shivaji Bridge marks the core of Old Pune. This was the chief residence of the Peshwas from 1727 until 1808, when the palace inside was destroyed by fire. The agreement between the East India Company and the Peshwas to combat Tipu Sultan at Srirangapattana [15C] was signed here in 1790. Shanwar Wada is contained by a rectangle of high walls of stone (beneath) and brick (above), some 170 by

150 m. Prominent round bastions occur at the corners and in the middle of three sides; polygonal bastions flank the Delhi Gate on the north, its arched entrance being surmounted by a timber balcony with a wooden roof. The palace that stood inside has now vanished, except for the masonry foundations of its various halls and courts. The present landscaping draws attention to the formal arrangement of water channels and differently shaped pools. The open space in front of Shanwar Wada, now mostly used for recreation, has an equestrian statue that serves as a memorial to the soldiers that fell in World War I. A short distance south is *Vishram Bagh*, a Peshwa mansion with an ornate wooden facade, for a time used as a Post Office.

Only a selection of Pune's numerous Hindu shrines is described here. The *Omkareshvara Temple*, built by the second Peshwa, Bajirao I, in 1736, stands in the middle of a compound beside Shinde Bridge over the Mutha. The compound is entered from the east through an arched gate, outside which is a stone lamp column. The temple within has nine arcaded bays roofed with alternating flat domes and pyramidal vaults. The linga shrine that occupies the central bay is topped with a square tower. Double tiers of lobed arches sheltering plaster figural reliefs are surmounted by a small lotus dome.

Other shrines are tucked away behind crowded shops in the commercial heart of Old Pune. *Tulsi Bagh* is the name given to a tree-filled court surrounded by traditional timber dwellings. The *Rama Temple* in the middle, dating from 1761, was a favourite of Nana Phadnavis. It consists of an unadorned cube topped by a lofty decorated spire some 45 m. high. This has a lower square storey adorned with lobed niches filled with plaster figures; turrets are positioned at the corners. The tower rises in five diminishing stages, each with 12 niches, and is crowned with double lotus domes on petals. The front of the temple is partly obscured by a wooden arcaded hall with a decorated ceiling.

The nearby *Bel Bagh Temple*, founded in 1765 by Nana Padhis, presents a similar scheme, with 12-sided towers, painted in bright colours, but devoid of sculptures. The shrine, which is dedicated to Krishna, can be approached through a Mughal styled, triple arcade with stone columns. Paintings of divinities cover the flat ceiling of the antechamber. An open wooden hall stands in front. Opposite stands *Mahatma Phule Market*, the busiest in Pune. Dating from 1886, it is named after a 19th century social reformer. Its eight wings fan outwards in regular formation.

The *Raja Dinkar Kelkar Museum* (no closed days), south of Mahatma Phule market, occupies a Peshwa period mansion. The museum houses a vast collection of items from all parts of India, including architectural fragments, sculptures and paintings, as well as innumerable small objects associated with everyday life, such as ivory and wooden combs, kumkum boxes, and even ornamental foot-scrubbers. The first-floor galleries display brass and ceramic pots and dishes, papier-mâché utensils, and wooden kitchen wares, such as decorated noodle-makers. A variety of textiles is presented in the second floor galleries. The embroidered children's clothing is particularly delightful. There is also a remarkable range of brass lamps. Musical instruments and painted textiles are seen in the extension of the galleries in the other half of the museum. The ground floor galleries, which are visited only at the end of the tour, are stocked with ivory games, pen boxes, chess sets, and carved wooden doors from Peshwa houses.

Additional religious monuments of interest are located in the northeast sector of Old Pune, not far from the Mula River. Here stands the *Trishund Ganapati Temple*, completed in 1770, the only Peshwa shrine to be built entirely in stone. The temple is entered through an elaborate doorway flanked by guardian figures. Side niches have carvings of Englishmen, a rhinoceros and fighting elephants. Bracket figures appear beneath the cornice that runs around the building. Carvings are also seen on the interior doorway leading to the main shrine. An unusual feature is the underground chamber beneath the domed hall, intended for yogic instruction. The nearby *Nageshvara Temple* presents a small octagonal sanctuary capped with a brightly painted lotus dome. The adjoining hall has a decorated flat stone ceiling. There is the usual open wooden hall in front. The entrance gate to the temple compound is surmounted by a chamber for musicians.

No tour of Old Pune would be complete without a visit to the *Parvati Temple*, on the summit of the small hill to the south of the city. This popular shrine was begun in 1748 by the third Peshwa, Balaji Balajirao. It stands within a polygonal walled compound that gives the appearance of a fortress. Indeed, the complex served occasionally as a lookout; from here the last Peshwa viewed the defeat of his forces by the British in 1818. A long flight of steps ascends to the temple. The goddess shrine is recognised by its polychromed tower with a central spire surrounded by four lesser pinnacles. The copper pot-shaped finials are replacements of the gilded originals stolen by the Nizam, when he raided Pune in 1763. A golden image of Parvati is worshipped within. Not far from the base of the hills is *Lal Bagh*, is the largest garden in Old Pune. A shrine to Ganapati stands on a small rise in the middle.

B. NEW PUNE

British period Pune, known at that time and since as Poona, extends across both the Mutha and Mula Rivers to the north and west. Much of this area was laid out as a Cantonment, with basalt barracks and service buildings for army contingents, and verandahed bungalows set in spacious grounds for officers. Civic and religious monuments line the broad shady streets in this part of the city. *Viddhant Bhavan*, built as the Council Hall in 1879, stands in a well maintained garden on Manekji Mehta Road. The rectangular red brick block has an entrance porch on the west, surmounted by an Italianate styled tower, 25 m. high, topped with an arcaded loggia and a pyramidal tiled roof. The double-height hall within is surrounded by a gallery carried on cast-iron brackets. Painted portraits of 19th century worthies line the walls. **St Pauls' Church** stands nearby. Begun in 1863 this somewhat severe Neo-Gothic building is relieved by an arcaded porch with animated gargoyles and an octagonal spire. Stained-glass windows frame the marble altar inside.

Of greater architectural interest is the *Othel David Synagogue* on Laxmi Road, the largest Jewish place of prayer in Southern India. Constructed in 1863, it presents a plain red brick exterior, with fine carved stone columns and Neo-Gothic windows. The solid square tower is topped in church-like fashion with a pyramidal spire. Interior arcades carry wooden columns and a flat wooden ceiling. The Ark has finely finished wooden doors, while the central podium is surrounded by a polished brass balustrade. David Sassoon's tomb in front is conceived as a Neo-Gothic chapel, with an octagonal pyramidal roof surrounded by corner turrets.

Another foundation of the Sassoon family, in a similar Neo-Gothic style, is the complex of *Sassoon Hospitals*, founded by Sir Jacob Sassoon in 1867, on Dr Ambedkar Road. This thoroughfare leads to leads to Wellesley Bridge, opened in 1875, which crosses the Mutha River. Vidyapeth Road, on the other side, is lined with the Neo-Gothic Engineering College and District Court.

A short distance south, on Jangali Maharaj Road, is the rock-cut *Pathaleshvara Temple*, the only pre-Maratha period monument within Pune. Assigned to the 8th-9th century Rashtrakuta period, the temple consists of an open rectangular court excavated into a basalt outcrop. The free-standing circular pavilion in the middle is entirely monolithic; it faces an unadorned colonnaded hall containing three shrines. The temple was reinvested for worship in the 18th century.

Further along Vidyapeth Road is the *College of Agriculture* of 1911, designed by George Wittet. The campus of *Pune University* beyond occupies the grounds of former Government House. The original building is recognised by the high water tower capped by an open iron dome. Other British period buildings stand in Khadki Cantonment, near the Mula River. *All Saints Church*, consecrated in 1841, is worth visiting for the tablets and brasses commemorating the officers who died in service.

Holkar Bridge, which crosses the Mula leads to the *Deccan College*. The original buildings of this institution, designed by Henry St Clair Williams in 1864, present battlemented facades and arcaded ranges. The *Gandhi National Museum*, 1 km. east of the college, was originally a palace of the Aga Khan. Mahatma Gandhi was held here under house arrest in 1942, during which time his wife Kasturba died. Her memorial stands in the spacious grounds.

Pune achieved a certain notoriety in the 1980s when Bhagawan Rajneesh, the controversial spiritual teacher, returned from the United States to set up his ashram here. Known as the *Osho Commune International*, the ashram continues to attract international visitors, even though its founder died in 1990. It is situated at 17 Koregaon Park, in the eastern part of New Pune.

C. Karla

Karla lies 10 km. south of Lonavla, a popular hill resort 64 km. northwest of Pune. The site overlooks a forested valley in the Sahyadri Ranges through which runs NH4 and the Mumbai-Pune railway line.

The rock-cut monument for which Karla is famous is reached by a steep climb of more than 350 steps from a car park. This consists of a Buddhist *Chaitya Hall* assigned to the 1st century CE, Kshatrapa period, the largest and best preserved such monument in Maharashtra, comparable to examples at Kanheri [2D] and Ajanta [5F]. The hall is approached through an excavated court, on the left side of which stands a monolithic column with a quartet of lion torsos forming the capital. A small Hindu shrine to the right, dedicated to the goddess Ekvira, is probably built over the base of a similar matching column, but this can no longer be observed. Though lacking in antiquity, the shrine is the chief attraction for most visitors to Karla today.

Chaitya Hall, Karla.

The facade of the chaitya hall is dominated by a large horseshoe-shaped window, complete with imitation wooden ribs. Panels depicting stately pairs of donors are positioned between three doorways headed by arched motifs. The foreparts of three elephants support reliefs of vaulted buildings with arched windows and railings. The magnificent apsidal-ended interior of the hall is divided into three aisles by two rows of columns, most of which have octagonal shafts with pot-shaped bases and fluted cushion-like capitals. Pairs of seated elephants ridden by embracing couples are carved onto the blocks above. The curved vault over the central aisle has original teak ribs set into the rock. The monolithic stupa at the end of the hall is raised on a double circular drum carved with railing friezes. The hemispherical dome is topped with an inverted stepped finial and a unique wooden umbrella, its underside carved with delicate petalled patterns.

D. BHAJA

The Buddhist antiquities at this site are cut into the cliff face on the other side of the valley to Karla. The Bhaja excavations date back to the 2nd century BCE, Satavahana period, making them among the earliest rock-cut monuments in Maharashtra. Most of the 20 viharas consist of a verandah and a hall lined with small cells provided with sleeping benches. Many of these monasteries are associated with cisterns. One excavation has 14 rock-cut stupas bearing the names of religious teachers.

Cave 12 at Bhaja is possibly the oldest known chaitya hall, the dependence on wooden models being particularly noticeable throughout. Socket holes indicate that a wooden facade was originally inserted into the horseshoe-shaped opening over the entrance. The interior is divided into the usual three aisles by two lines of octagonal columns, which incline slightly inwards. The roof over the central aisle is fashioned as a curved vault, with notches for teak beams, now lost. An unadorned hemispherical stupa stands at the end.

Cave 19, a short distance south, is an irregularly shaped hall approached through a columned verandah. Two doors are flanked by guardian figures; the pierced stone window above admits additional light. The verandah roof has an unusual half-vault, complete with timber-like ribbing. Supporting columns have part-octagonal shafts. Sculptural compositions are seen on either side of the doorway leading to the cell at the right end of the verandah. The left panel depicts a figure, possibly Surya, attended by two women driving an aerial chariot. The four horses pulling the chariot trample a demon beneath. The right panel represents a majestic figure, probably Indra, riding a mighty elephant in the company of an attendant holding banner and spear. Dancers, a man and a horse-headed woman appear beneath. The hall interior has four side cells with doorways headed by horseshoe-shaped motifs.

A path with steps ascends for 1.5 km. to *Lohagad Fort*, spectacularly sited at the top of the escarpment above the caves. Established by Shivaji, it preserves well finished ramparts and an arched gate. The only feature of interest inside is a circular well, partly rock-cut. From here there are fine views over the valley, also to nearby Vishapur fort.

E. BEDSA

The small group of Buddhist rock-cut monuments at this site, 9 km. southeast of Karla, is assigned to the 1st century CE, Satavahana era. Two excavations are of interest.

Cave 7, a well preserved chaitya hall, is reached through a narrow passageway cut into the cliff. The exterior is richly embellished. Four large columns in the verandah have octagonal shafts, pot-shaped bases, and inverted bell-shaped capitals. The main doorway is flanked by pierced stone windows; the large arched opening above displays timber-like ribs. Side walls are enlivened with architectural facades, complete with arched windows and railings. The hall interior has octagonal columns, inclining inwards slightly, creating triple aisles. An unadorned hemispherical stupa is located at the rear. The timber ribs of the vault above have vanished.

Cave 11 consists of a verandah with subsidiary cells giving access to an apsidal-ended vaulted hall. Nine small cells cut into the side walls have arched motifs over the doorways, linked by railings in shallow relief.

F. KHED

This small town on the Bhima River, known also as Rajgurunagar, 44 km. north of Pune on NH50, was the headquarters of Dilawar Khan, commander of the Ahmadnagar forces in the struggles against the Mughals. The *Mosque and Tomb of Dhilawar Khan*, dating from 1613, are important examples of Nizam Shahi architecture. The mosque has triple arches of lobed design, with lotus medallions in the spandrels, sheltered by an overhang carried on curved brackets. The petalled base of the dome above is partly concealed by the parapet with domical finials. The interior is divided into six bays, the central ones unusually roofed with a single dome. The adjacent tomb has its outer walls divided into double tiers of recesses consisting of pointed arches alternating with lobed arches. Corner finials resemble miniature pavilions.

G. BHIMSHANKAR

This site, reached from Khed by following a road that runs for about 48 km. along the bank of the Bhima River, is celebrated for the *Mahadeva Temple* enshrining one of the 12 jyotirlingas, or luminous emblems of Shiva. The village of Bhimshankar is situated at more than 1,100 m. altitude, just beneath the wooded heights of the Sahyadri Ranges. The Bhima, which rises nearby, trickles into a small cistern known as *Moksha Kund*. While the temple dates back to Yadava times, only the Nandi pavilion of the original 12th-13th century monument survives. The main structure is assigned to the Peshwa period, being completed in 1800 by funds supplied by the widow of Nana Phadnavis. Shivaratri, the popular festival held here in February-March, attracts crowds of devotees.

The temple is built in a revivalist style that recalls earlier Yadava projects, with a curving tower surrounded by a cluster of half-towered elements. Like the main shaft, these lesser elements are crowned with circular ribbed elements and pot-like finials. The adjacent mandapa has triple set of lobed arches. A squat tapering column outside the entrance displays 12 diminishing tiers of curved brackets for lamps.

H. JUNNAR AND SHIVNERI

Junnar lies a short distance west of NH50, on the way to Nasik [4], a total of about 90 km. north of Pune. This town was a flourishing Buddhist centre during the Satavahana and Kshatrapa periods, between the 2nd century BCE and 3rd century CE. Junnar's significance derived from its location on a trade route leading through a pass in the Sahyadris down to the Arabian Sea port of Bharuch (Broach), in Gujarat.

Little is known about Junnar until it became an outpost of the Bahmanis of Gulbarga [24A]. In 1486 the town was taken by Ahmad, the first ruler of the Nizam Shahi kingdom. In later times it was disputed by the Mughals and the Adil Shahis of Bijapur [23A], both of whom came into conflict with local Maratha commanders. Jijibai, wife of the Maratha general Shahji, took refuge here, and in 1627 gave birth to Shivaji, future founder of the Maratha state, an event for which Junnar is best known today. Shivaji actually never lived here as an adult, and the town never passed into his hands. Junnar was taken in 1705 by Aurangzeb, who halted here for more than seven months before marching on to Bijapur. In 1716 Shahu obtained Junnar for the Marathas, in whose possession it remained until 1818, when it was ceded to the British.

The town is enclosed by irregular arcs of basalt outcrops with steep escarpments and flattish tops. Shivneri is the name given to the triangular hill that rises 300 m. above Junnar, immediately to the west. A line of about 50 *Buddhist caves*, mostly simple excavations, are cut into the cliffs on its eastern flank. The fortifications protecting the hill on the south mostly date from the 15th-16th century. They are joined by cross walls to a sequence of gateways that line the approach road. The arched entrances are relieved by lion blocks and the occasional double-headed eagle motif.

A flight of rock-cut steps climbs to a domed tomb and a prayer wall on the flat crest of Shivneri. Buildings of greater interest are seen to the north. They include the small *Kamani Mosque*, which dates from Nizam Shahi times. A cut-out arch connects the corner minarets. Persian inscriptions are set into the rear wall. The mosque, which looks down on the houses of Junnar, can also be reached directly from the town by a steep flight of steps. The two-storeyed pavilion that stands nearby is pointed out as *Shivaji's Birthplace*. A balcony with arched windows projects from the east wall. The pavilion forms part of a palace complex, now ruined. The adjacent modern Bhavani temple commemorates the spot where Jijibai is supposed to have worshipped.

Buddhist caves spanning the Satavahana aand Kshatrapa periods are situated on the outskirts of Junnar. The *Tulja Lena Group*, 2 km. west of the town, consists of 11 excavations. *Cave 3*, the most important, has an unusual circular chaitya hall with 12 tall octagonal pillars surrounding a plain hemispherical stupa. The ceiling is fashioned as a rock-cut dome.

The *Ganesha Lena Group* of caves, 4 km north of Junnar, has 26 excavations, two of which are chapels, the others being viharas. *Cave 7* has a verandah with doorways and windows. The octagonal columns have bell-shaped capitals and seated animals. 19 small cells open off the hall within; a later Ganesha image has been placed in one of these. The adjacent chaitya hall, *Cave 6*, has columns similar to cave 7. Its facade is marked by a blind horseshoe-shaped arch. The vaulted interior of the hall has rock-cut ribs, the devotional focus being a hemispherical stupa raised on a plain drum.

Three groups of caves are excavated into the north and west side of Manmodi Hill, 2 km. south of Junnar. Of the 50 or so excavations, four are chaitya halls. *Cave 40*, the largest, has a well preserved facade. The horseshoe-shaped arch over the entrance contains petal-shaped compartments filled with reliefs of Lakshmi, elephants and devotees. The finial of the arch is flaked by relief stupas, as well as a winged animal-headed figure (left) and a naga deity (right). The whole composition is framed by arched facades in shallow relief. The hall interior is incomplete.

Several Nizam Shahi monuments are scattered around Junnar, the most impressive being a large *Tomb*, 1.5 km. east of the town. The founder of this mausoleum is unknown. Finely carved medallions adorn the south doorway. The large dome is partly concealed by a brick parapet of interlaced battlements; corner finials have miniature domes. A smaller tomb with a pyramidal roof stands to one side. Afiz Bagh, a garden mansion with balconied windows, lies 1 km. further east.

I. SASVAD

This picturesque town, 31 km. south of Pune, was the ancestral home of Balaji Vishvanath, first of the Peshwas. In 1719 Balaji returned to Sasvad for safety, and died here in the following year. In the middle of the town stand several fortified palaces, known as *Wadas*, residences of the Peshwas and those in their service. Each consists of a quadrangle of bare walls with rounded corners, entered through arched portals on one side. Dilapidated wooden structures preserve finely carved columns, brackets and beams. Small shrines are built up to the outer walls.

Hindu monuments of architectural interest are located just outside Sasvad, to the west. The *Sagameshvara Temple* is built on a platform with steps leading diagonally down to a point where the Karha River joins one of its tributaries. The *Changla Vateshvara Temple*, 1.5 km. further west, stands near the south bank of the Karha. Both monuments date from the 18th century Maratha period and are virtually identical. The linga sanctuaries have multiple wall projections between axial niches. Brick towers above, rising in diminishing tiers with lobed arched recesses, are crowned with bulbous domes with petalled fringes, framed by quartets of inward-curving brackets. The adjacent mandapas have brick parapets with corner domical finials framing petalled domes. Tortoises are carved in shallow relief on the floors within. The open verandahs in front have columns with elaborate brackets; seated Nandis are placed inside. Pairs of lamp columns, with projecting brackets, occupy the corners of the terraces on which the temples stand.

J. PURANDHAR

This celebrated citadel, 15 km. west of Sasvad, or about 40 km. from Pune via NH4, occupies one of the highest points in the Sahyadri Ranges, the summit rising 1,475 m. above sea level. A road climbs about 500 m. from the plain to a lower terrace, but the remaining 350 m. ascent to the main entrance of the stronghold must be made on foot.

Purandhar was fortified by the first Bahmani rulers, remaining in their hands until 1486, when it was taken by Ahmad Nizam Shah. Shivaji captured the fort in 1670, but it succumbed to Aurangzeb in 1705. Soon after, Purandhar was granted to Pant Sachiv, an influential officer under the first Peshwa, Balaji Vishvanath. The treaty signed here in 1776 between Nana Phadnavis and the East India Company granted Saslette Island in Mumbai to the British. After the capture of Sinhagad in 1818, Purandhar was occupied by the British, who used it as a sanatorium and detention camp.

Purandhar's *Citadel* spreads across an L-shaped ridge with precipitous sides, approached from the north by means of a steep road. After passing through an austere arched gate, the road arrives at a grassy terrace with an abandoned church surrounded by dilapidated barracks. The hill above is lined with walls. These fine examples of Bahmani fortifications have prominent round bastions and square crenellations.

An overgrown path climbs upwards from the terrace, partly by way of rock-cut steps, to the *Delhi Gate* at the eastern extremity of the citadel. This is the first of a sequence of three arched entrances at successively higher levels, arranged along a narrow ridge. From here there are fine views of Wazirgad, the fortified lower hill immediately to the east, and the plains beneath. The path continues to an *Overgrown Complex*, with ruined residences, barracks and stores, possibly dating back to Bahmani times. Further on, beyond several rock-cut cisterns, is a long rectangular chamber that may have served as a *Prison*, with a single doorway and a curving brick vault. The small Mahadeva shrine crowns the summit of the rise in the middle of the citadel. Another well defended entrance to the fort is seen immediately below.

K. JEJURI

This popular place of pilgrimage, at the eastern end of the Purandhar Ridge, 16 km. east of Sasvad, is famous for its fairs held in April and December. These honour the god Khandoba, a warrior form of Shiva who killed a demon called Mala.

The Khandoba cult rose to prominence in the 17th-18th centuries, under the support of pastoral and mercantile communities in Maharashtra and northern Karnataka. In 1622 the Khandoba temple at Jejuri was the setting for the reconciliation between Shahji and his son Shivaji, the father bringing offers of peace from Bijapur. Aurangzeb was driven away from Jejuri by the miraculous appearance of a swarm of hornets, after which the emperor bestowed on Khandoba a diamond worth 125,000 rupees. The temple was substantially enlarged by the celebrated Holkar queen Ahilyabai and her general Tukoji.

The *Khandoba Temple* is reached only after passing through the streets of the town, and climbing a long flight of steps punctuated by arched portals and subsidiary shrines containing effigies of donors. Throughout the ascent, vendors offer brass masks of Khandoba, recognised by staring eyes and curling moustaches, as well as bright yellow turmeric powder used in rituals of worship; musicians entertain pilgrims with devotional songs. The temple stands in the middle of a polygonal fortified compound, defined by arcades, some overlooking the town beneath and the plains beyond.

Four massive lamp columns stand in front of the main temple. Carved out of the pavement nearby is a tortoise, almost 7 m. in diameter, sheathed in brass. The temple, much renovated in recent years, has a Tamil styled tower capped with a hemispherical roof and flanked by minaret-like towers. The sanctuary doorway within is adorned by an embossed silver frame. The effigies that receive worship in the sanctuary consist of two stones clad with brass masks of Khandoba and his consort Mahlasa, embedded in turmeric powder and sheltered by a gilded domed canopy. The *Panchalinga Shrine* at the rear is distinguished by an octagonal tower with triple tiers of niches topped with a decorated dome. The adjacent hall stores the ceremonial palanquins used at festival times.

West of Jejuri town is the *Mahadeva Temple*, erected by Malhar Rao Holkar II in 1800. The hall interior is roofed with a large dome embellished with painted figures; a tortoise is carved in the middle of the floor. The chief object of worship in the sanctuary is a linga accompanied by statues of the donor and his three wives. The square tank nearby is associated with Tukoji.

L. SINHAGAD

The hill fort closest to Pune, Sinhagad lies about 30 km. southwest of the city; it is most easily reached via NH4. Like Purandhar, Sinhagad occupies a high point in the Sahyadri Ranges, 1,315 m. above sea level, or more than 700 m. above the plain. A metalled road almost reaches the summit, which is marked by a communications tower.

The history of Sinhagad, known originally as Kondhana, goes back to 1340, when the forces of the Delhi emperor Muhammad Tughluq marched against it. In 1486 it was one of several forts in the Pune region that fell to Ahmad Nizam Shah. Shahji, father of Shivaji, was regent of Kondhana under the kings of Ahmadnagar. In 1647 Shivaji held the stronghold for a time, renaming it Sinhagad, Lion Fort. The citadel subsequently changed hands on several occasions between the Marathas and the Mughals. It was the scene of a daring exploit in 1670 when it was captured by Shivaji's army under the command of Tanaji, who used ropes to raise troops and animals up the sheer sides of the hill. Aurangzeb laid siege to Sinhagad in 1701-03, but could not hold it for long. It was thereafter disputed by different Maratha factions until 1818, when it surrendered to the British. The fort was later used as a warm weather retreat for European residents of Pune.

The triple-pronged *Fort* of Sinhagad is ringed with steep cliffs, from which rise sheer walls of basalt more than 40 m. high. These are reinforced by ramparts with regularly spaced towers. On the west flank the ramparts seal the mouth of a steep gorge. The hilltop is reached by a tortuous path from the northeast, passing through a line of three gates. The first gate, flanked by a conical tower on the outer face, has a pointed arched recess topped by battlements. The second gate is similar, but ruined; the third gate is complete with towers and a barbican wall. The undulating and irregular interior of the fort retains few buildings of interest. Tanaji's monument, near the gorge, commemorates the 1670 exploit. Several British period bungalows are dotted about.

M. RAJGAD

One of the most spectacular hill forts in Maharashtra, Rajgad is built on top of a triple-pronged hill with sheer drops on all sides. The incomparable views over the surrounding crests of the Sahyadri Ranges include distant prospects of hill forts at Torna, 10 km. west, Sinhagad, about the same distance north, and

Purandhar, 30 km east. Rajgad citadel lies no more than 50 km. in a direct line from Pune, but is difficult to reach. A climb of about two hours is required from Vajeghar, a small hamlet near Naraspur on NH4, 40 km. south of Pune.

Little is known about the history of this remote and rugged region until 1646, when Shivaji captured Torna from the Adil Shahis. With the treasure that he obtained, Shivaji brought arms, cannon and ammunition to strengthen another hill nearby, naming this Rajgad, King's Fort. In the following year he established Rajgad, making it the seat of his government. The task of fortifying the site was undertaken by Moro Pingle, one of his most loyal commanders. Shivaji returned to Rajgad in 1668 after a successful series of campaigns, and from here mounted his expedition to the Konkan Coast. In 1672 he was persuaded by his father, Shahji, to shift his capital to Raigad [7C]. Like the other forts in the Pune region, Rajgad was taken on several occasions by the Mughals, and then recaptured by the Marathas. However, it declined in importance in the 18th century, and was already abandoned by the time the British stormed Purandhar.

Rajgad is approached by a steep path from the north, passing through an arched gate tucked into the walls at the extreme end of the northern spur of the hill, known as *Padmapathi Machi*. Ruined stores, granaries, residences and reception halls are scattered around the level terrace of this spur.

An additional climb is required to scale *Bala Kila*, the inner fort that occupies the triangular rise that forms the summit in the middle of the hill, rising 1,317 m. above sea level. A pointed arched gate on the east is surrounded by sculpted panels and flanked by polygonal bastions. On the top are a few cisterns, some partly rock-cut, and the overgrown remains of *Shivaji's palace*. This consists of a series of rectangular structures, each with a verandah and a long chamber raised on a platform, standing within a walled compound.

Two very long and narrow spurs fan out from *Bala Kila* to the southeast and southwest. These natural features are protected by fortifications that follow the curving edges of the cliffs to create sinuous lines of walls. The walls are doubled with a trench in between at the extreme ends of the spurs. Round bastions occur irregularly, some with internal steps to give access to outworks at the lower level.

An arched gate in the middle of the east side of the fort, immediately beneath *Bala Kila*, leads to a staircase that descends to the plain beneath.

4. Nasik

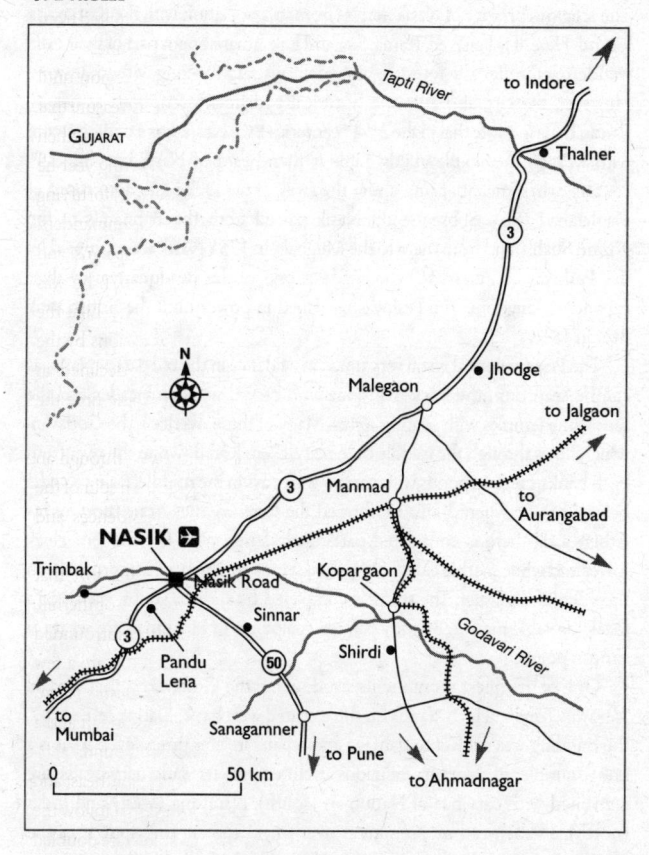

Nasik forms part of the rapidly developing Mumbai-Pune-Nasik industrial triangle. Yet it is one of the holiest cities of Maharashtra, being located on the Godavari River, considered as blessed as the Ganga. Overlooked by temples, the Godavari gives Nasik a picturesque quality. A few hours should be set aside to explore the ghats and nearby temples [A].

Excursions may be made conveniently from Nasik to historical sites in the area, including the Buddhist cave-temples at Pandu Lena [B], the pilgrimage temple at Trimbak [C], near the source of the Godavari, and the ruined monument at Sinnar [D]. A trip to the abandoned temple at Jhogde [E] and Faruqi tombs at Thalner [F] will require a full day and more.

A. NASIK

The religious prestige of Nasik derives from its association with the Ramayana legend. Here, it is believed, Rama, Sita and Lakshmana spent part of their exile wandering through the forest, fighting demons, and meeting with local sages. However, the city also enjoys a historical pedigree. Inscriptions at nearby Pandu Lena indicate that in the 2nd-1st centuries BCE Nasik was a trading centre with wealthy mercantile guilds. Little is then heard of Nasik until the 14th century, when the city came under the sway of the Delhi kingdom based in Daulatabad [5C]. Subsequently, Nasik passed from the Bahmanis to the Nizam Shahis, and from them to the Mughals. In 1751 Nasik was occupied by the Peshwas of Pune [3], who made it one of the headquarters of their expanding kingdom. The Peshwas remained in power until the British took over in 1818.

The Peshwa period is still very much in evidence in the old part of Nasik, as can be seen from the brick mansions with carved wooden facades and the sandstone temples with soaring spires. Many of these overlook the Godavari, which flows through the middle of the city. *Ghats* lead down to the river from both banks, creating ponds with narrow walkways in the middle. *Rama Kund* is believed to be where Rama performed the funerary rites in memory of his father; a dip here is considered particularly auspicious. The modern clock tower and white marble *Gandhi Memorial* stands somewhat incongruously on the edge of the water. The scene is completed by shrines, shops, stalls and a local vegetable market. Brightly painted sculptures of Hanuman are set up at various points.

One of the finest monuments overlooking the Godavari is the *Sundara Narayan Temple*, which stands on the elevated west bank. Dating from 1747, the building was subject to damage and repairs in later times; even so, it is a fine example of Maratha religious architecture. Its sanctuary walls are enlivened with carvings of Hanuman (south), Narayana (west) and Indra (north), all sheltered by prominent overhangs. The curving spire is of the clustered type, capped with a circular ribbed element. The adjoining mandapa is entered through three porches, each with balcony seating, lobed arches and slightly bulbous domes. The mandapa is also roofed with a dome, but this has a flattish profile and is composed of multiple ribbed elements. Doorways inside the porches are headed by overhangs and serpentine shaped pediments.

The *Narashankar Temple*, on the east bank of the Godavari, near Rama Setu Bridge, a short distance downstream, stands in an arcaded compound with corner circular bastions. The entrance gate, roofed with a curving vault, is approached by steps from the river. The temple resembles the Sundara Narayan in most respects. Among the few differences are the carved animals on the upper tiers of the roof. A large bell of Portuguese workmanship is set in the middle of the west compound wall.

Narrow streets running east of Narashankar temple lead to the Kala Rama temple, also known as *Ramaji's Temple*. This popular place of worship dates from 1782, though it has been remodelled recently. The building stands in the middle of a walled enclosure, entered on the east through an arched portal. In front of the main temple is a long pavilion with lobed arches, used for sermons and devotional chanting. A small shrine inside houses a standing image of Hanuman. The smooth surfaces of the curving spire that rises above the temple sanctuary attains a height of 27 m. The dome over the adjoining mandapa is crowned with a triple set of ribbed motifs and a pot finial, while smaller domes cap the porches on three sides. Modern murals within the mandapa illustrate Ramayana scenes. Black stone images of Rama, Sita and Lakshmana are displayed on an embossed silver throne inside the sanctuary.

B. Pandu Lena

Buddhist monuments at this site are among the oldest in Maharashtra. Pandu Lena refers to a group of rock-cut viharas located high up on the north face of a hill, 8 km. south of Nasik, just off NH3. The 24 excavations here are accompanied by inscriptions spanning the 2nd century BCE to the 3rd century CE, from the Satavahana and Kshatrapa periods. Buddha images were added to many caves in the 5th-6th centuries.

The path ascends partly by way of steps to the middle of the line of excavations. *Cave 3*, towards the end at the right, is the largest and most elaborate of the monasteries. Octagonal columns in the verandah have bell-shaped capitals carrying pairs of seated elephants, bulls and fantastic animals with riders. The balcony walls are carved with dwarfs that appear to support railing reliefs, now worn. Imitation rafters and railings adorn the ceiling inside. The hall doorway is framed by representations of a wooden gateway, the lintel of which has rolled ends; guardian figures are positioned at either side. Small cells, each with a rock-cut bed, open off the large hall. The rear wall has a stupa in shallow relief, flanked by female worshippers.

Cave 10 is similar to Cave 3, but there is no balcony, the verandah columns being fully exposed, revealing their pot-shaped bases. An inscription with large letters is incised on the porch wall. A Buddha figure is cut into the stupa panel in the rear wall of the hall.

The only chaitya hall at Pandu Lena is *Cave 18*, towards the left end of the group. Its facade has finely carved details. The entrance is framed by a horseshoe-shaped arch containing ribs interspersed with auspicious emblems and animals; a single guardian figure stands on the left. A similarly shaped, but larger arch above has timber-like ribs. This forms part of an elaborate facade with railings, columns, stupas, cornices and windows, all in shallow relief. The hall interior is plain, except for octagonal columns with pot-shaped bases. Actual wooden ribs were once inserted into the vaulted ceiling, but only the impressions remain. The votive stupa has a high drum crowned with a railing; the finial is an inverted stepped pyramid.

The chaitya hall is flanked by two viharas, *Caves 17* and *20*, linked to it by access staircases, preserved only on the left. Cave 20 was enlarged in later times, when images of teaching Buddha and of Bodhisattvas were added in the rear shrine. The pot-like bases and capitals of the porch columns, however, are original features. *Cave 19*, immediately beneath Cave 20, is a small monastic excavation with perforated windows in the porch, and decorated railings and arches over the cell doorways.

C. TRIMBAK

This small town, 31 km. west of Nasik, is famous for its temple enshrining one of the jyotirlingas of Shiva. The town is dramatically framed by an amphitheatre of cliffs; the wooded slopes conceal a small spring identified as the source of the Godavari River. Fairs held here in October-November and February-March are attended by large crowds.

The imposing *Trimbakeshvar Temple*, begun by the third Peshwa, Bajirao, was completed in about 1785. It is built in a revivalist manner, harking back to earlier temple traditions in neighbouring Gujarat. The deep-red sandstone building stands in a spacious courtyard entered through an arched gate on the north. The Nandi pavilion in front has lobed arches containing stone screens and a pyramidal roof with miniature ribbed elements.

The temple itself is entered through a mandapa with triple porches and balcony seating decorated with lotus medallions. The mandapa walls have small niches filled with sculptures. Above rises a pyramid of ribbed motifs, with triangular vertical faces on three sides. The adjoining sanctuary is laid out on a complicated plan that almost approaches a circle. Numerous wall projections are carried up into the tower, where they are transformed into model elements clustering around the central shaft. Each towered element is crowned with a part-circular ribbed motif. Internally, both mandapa and sanctuary have domed ceilings decorated with ribs and lotuses. The chamber in between has a corbelled vault; wall niches here are capped with fighting elephants. The floor of the sanctuary, reached by descending a few steps, has a circular pedestal filled with Godavari water. Three diminutive lingas here are worshipped as Brahma, Vishnu and Shiva.

Trimbakeshvar Temple, Trimbak.

A curving market street lined with shops leads to *Ganga Sagar*. This 17 m. square tank, which traps water from the Godavari spring, is surrounded on three sides by arcades. A small shrine at the southeast corner has carvings on its outer walls. A stepped path leads from this reservoir to the small shrine that marks the source of the Godavari.

Distant views my be had of the fort that occupies a sheer scarp above the town. Though associated with events in Maratha history, it is of little architectural interest.

D. Sinnar

This walled town, with arched gateways on four sides, lies 27 km. southeast of Nasik on NH50. An abandoned 11th century monument, the best preserved from the Yadava period, stands 1 km. to the northeast.

The *Gondeshvara Temple* stands isolated against a backdrop of distant hills. The main shrine, its associated Nandi pavilion and four smaller corner shrines are all elevated on a high plinth. The complex stands in the middle of a walled compound with entrances on the east and south. The main temple consists of a towered sanctuary and a mandapa with triple porches, both with well articulated wall projections. The basement has friezes of elephants, interrupted by a makara spout on the north. Sculptures adorn the walls, but the axial niches are empty. The sanctuary spire has tiers of model towers arranged either side of central bands filled with meshes of arch-like motifs. The mandapa is roofed with a pyramid of masonry. The mandapa interior has four central columns, with figural brackets supporting a corbelled dome with a lotus carved in the middle. The dome is set within a square vault with curving corbels. The corner shrines repeat many of these features, but on a smaller scale. They preserve the circular ribbed capping elements that are missing on the tower of the main temple.

From Sinnar it is possible to proceed to Shirdi [6C], about 90 km. east via Sanganmer.

E. JHODGE

This small town is situated just off NH3, 115 km. northeast of Nasik. Like the monument at Sinnar, the *Mahadeva Temple* here belongs to the Yadava period. The abandoned 12th century monument stands in a spacious landscape west of the town. It has triple sanctuaries, two of which were originally porches opening off a common mandapa; that on the west preserves its balcony slabs and carved columns. Though damaged, the exterior presents a dignified composition dominated by the soaring curved spire over the main sanctuary. The walls beneath have multiple projections enlivened with carvings of celestials and attendants; the figures are framed by basement and cornice mouldings. The tower above has central tapering bands filled with mesh-like motifs; they are flanked by eight superimposed tiers of model towers. The whole is capped with a massive circular ribbed element. The pyramidal tower over the mandapa is incomplete, but the corbelled dome within has a full set of brackets fashioned as maidens and musicians.

F. THALNER

Located on the north bank of the Tapti River, just off NH3, about 70 km. north of Jhodge, this insignificant village was once the capital of the Khandesh kingdom on the frontier between Maharashtra and Madhya Pradesh.

The history of Khandesh begins in 1370 when Firuz Shah Tughluq, ruler of Delhi, granted Malik Raja Faruqi an estate on the southern border of Gujarat, including the fort at Thalner. By the time of Malik's death in 1399

Khandesh was virtually independent of Delhi, with Thalner as its capital. Malik's successors came into repeated conflict with Gujarat, whose kings invaded Khandesh, laying waste the countryside and sacking Thalner. In 1498 Mamud Shah Begra, the Ahmedabad sultan, occupied Khandesh, granting some of its territories to one of his nobles. A further battle between Thalner and Ahmedabad took place in 1566. Akbar absorbed Khandesh into the Mughal empire in about 1600, later shifting his headquarters upstream to Burhanpur, in Madhya Pradesh. The French traveller François Tavernier, who passed through Thalner in 1660, described the town as a thriving commercial centre on the route linking Burhanpur with the Arabian Sea port of Surat in Gujarat, both with European factories. Due to its strategic location, Thalner attracted the Marathas, who occupied the town until it was made over to the British in 1818.

The *Fort* of Thalner, built on a rise overlooking the Tapti, has mostly collapsed, with only a single wall still standing. The 15th century *Tombs of the Faruqis*, clustered in a group west of the village, are of greater interest. They show affiliations with the architecture of the Malwa region to the north, best seen in the combination of cubic forms and flattish domes on high drums. Smaller domes of the same type are placed at the corers of one tomb. The decoration is fairly restrained, with shallow arched recesses and angled overhangs carried on corbelled brackets.

The octagonal, but domeless *Tomb of Miran Mubarak*, who died in 1457, is the most elaborate of the Thalner monuments. Each side is marked by a pointed arched opening lined with a fringe of lotus buds. The opening on the south frames a doorway with jambs and lintel. The walls on all sides are entirely covered with relief designs of arabesque and foliate motifs, as well as lotus medallions.

5. Aurangabad

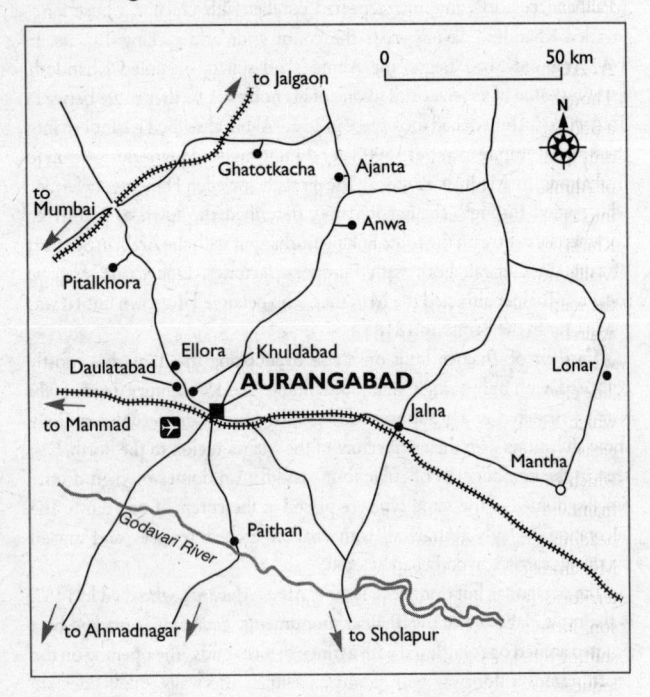

Aurangabad is familiar to tourists as a convenient base from which to visit the cave-temples at Ellora and Ajanta, Maharashtra's most famous antiquities. Yet Aurangabad itself [A] and the surrounding area [B] deserve attention for their Mughal monuments, the finest in Southern India, as well as for a series of Buddhist caves. A full day should be set aside to tour these sights.

The nearby citadel at Daulatabad [C], the tombs at Khuldabad [D] and the caves at Ellora [E] can be covered in a single long day, though more time is recommended. The excursion to Ajanta [F] will occupy another full day; an overnight stay permits an early morning tour of the caves before the crowds arrive. Visitors should be alerted that Ajanta is closed on Mondays, and the great Kailasa temple at Ellora on Tuesdays.

Travellers with additional time and interest should be encouraged to explore the outlying sites of Pitalkhora [G] and Ghatotkacha [H], both with early Buddhist caves, as well as the ruined temple at Anwa [I]. A journey to see the mosques and tombs at Jalna [J] and the unique crater lake at Lonar [K], with ruined temples on its shore, can be combined. The historical city of Paithan [L] may be visited en route to Ahmadnagar [6].

A. AURANGABAD

Though the rock-cut monuments on the outskirts of Aurangabad testify to a Buddhist settlement going back to the 1st century CE, the city itself dates only from 1610. It was founded by Malik Ambar, Prime Minister of Murtaza of Ahmadnagar, close to the village of Khirki. This settlement soon grew into a populous city, attracting the attention of the Mughal invaders. In 1621 Khirki was pillaged and burnt by the Mughal troops under Shah Jahan. Malik Ambar was succeeded as Prime Minister by Fateh Khan, who changed the name of the city of Fatehnagar in 1626. The city was captured once again by the Mughals in 1633. Some 20 years later, when Prince Aurangzeb was Viceroy of the Deccan provinces, Fatehnagar was renamed Aurangabad. The city was threatened by Maratha bands in 1668 and again in 1681, after which Khan Jahan Bahadur, the Mughal Viceroy, ordered new walls and gates to be built. In 1683 Aurangzeb shifted the Mughal court to Aurangabad, which then assumed the dimensions of an imperial capital, a position it maintained until the emperor's death in 1707. In 1723 the city became the headquarters of Nizamul Mulk, Prime Minister of the Mughal emperor Muhammad Shah. Nizamul Mulk managed to gain control of the Deccan territories from Delhi, thereby establishing the breakaway Asaf Jahi state. His son, Nizam Ali Khan, who succeeded him in 1762, was responsible for shifting the Asaf Jahi capital to Hyderabad [26], after which Aurangabad was reduced to a provincial city.

The crowded streets and markets of Aurangabad are contained within a circle of *Walls* laid out on the east bank of the Khan River. Dating from the Mughal era, the walls are about 4.5 m. high, with crenellated parapets and slit holes for guns, punctuated by regularly spaced round bastions. The four principal gates have imposing arched openings surmounted by lines of prominent battlements. *Bhadkal Gate*, on the west side of the city, is an earlier monument, dating from Nizam Shahi times. It displays tiers of shallow arched recesses, with lotus medallions in the spandrels. The dome over the interior passageway is carried on eight intersecting arches.

Aurangabad benefits from an ingenious *Hydraulic System*, first established by Malik Ambar. This conveys water from distant springs and wells into the city by means of an extensive network of aqueducts, channels and pipes, some more than 4 km. long. Many features are cut into the bedrock and roofed with masonry. Pressure is regulated by ventilation towers built of lime masonry, in which water is forced up into an elevated tank and then down again; such towers are still to be seen. *Panchakki*, the water mill overlooking the Khan River just outside the west walls of the city, has a tower of this type. Water falling from the tower drives a large Persian wheel, once used for grinding grain. The cistern in the middle of the courtyard in front forms the roof of a large subterranean chamber. (The adjacent Dargah of Baba Musafir is described below.)

Important examples of religious architecture are found throughout the walled city of Aurangabad. *Kali Mosque*, erected by Malik Ambar in about 1600, is the oldest. Its triple-bayed prayer hall has arches with lotus medallions on curving brackets in the spandrels. The octagonal corner buttresses are decorated with ornamental niches and topped by domical finials. A fluted dome rises over the middle of the hall. Interior bays are roofed with smaller domes on faceted pendentives. *Chauk Mosque* of 1662 was built by Shaista Khan, the maternal uncle of Aurangzeb. Steps ascending to its raised terrace are framed by an arched gate. The prayer chamber here is five bays wide, with a single central dome and a pair of corner octagonal buttresses. *Lal Mosque* of 1665 is the work of Zain al-Abidi, a government official. This is similar in layout but has lobed arches carried on fluted columns.

The *Shah Ganj Mosque* of 1720 occupies the great market square laid out by Aurangzeb, now marked by a modern clock tower. The mosque is raised high above street level, with shops built into its sides. Flights of steps on the north and south climb to a spacious terrace with a large cistern in the middle. The prayer hall on the west presents a line of lobed arches with finely polished plasterwork. A polygonal mihrab is set into the rear wall of the hall interior.

Several Mughal period tombs in Aurangabad enshrine the remains of saintly figures. The *Tomb of Hazrat Qadar Auliya*, near Jaffa Gate, has a central chamber roofed with a bulbous dome carried on a high drum. This is surrounded by an arcaded portico roofed with a curving vault. The *Tomb of Nizamuddin Auliya* is a simple cubic chamber with a prominent dome on a leafy acanthus base. Its corner finials are conceived as miniature pavilions. The *Tomb of Pir Ismail* stands in the well maintained garden adjoining the Maulana Azad College, beyond Delhi Gate on the north side of the city. The mausoleum is a flat-roofed arcaded building with domed corner pavilions. The central octagonal chamber within accommodates the grave of Aurangzeb's tutor. The complex is entered on the south through a gate with triple arches and rooftop pavilions.

Aurangzeb's citadel, *Kila Arg*, laid out in 1693 immediately north of the city, is provided with its own walls. Here stands the *Shah Mosque*, erected by the emperor for his private use. It has unusual trilobed arches and triple vaults with curved cornices. The open pavilion, with a curved roof and corner pyramidal vaults, that served as Aurangzeb's audience hall is located at the highest part of Kila Arg, in the dilapidated compound of the Government School of Art. The hall is aligned with Naubat Gate, the main entrance to the citadel beneath.

The *Jami Mosque*, a short distance south of Kila Arg, was founded in 1615 by Malik Ambar; its prayer hall was enlarged in Mughal times. Eleven undecorated arches are overhung by eaves carried on sculpted brackets. The court in front, with a large cistern in the middle, is partly surrounded by domed chambers. Nearby *Kaudiya Luti Mosque*, standing just inside the city walls, is of greater architectural interest. The Mughal period monument has perforated stone windows set into the walls of the prayer hall. Doorways to the side chambers are framed by curved cornices in relief plasterwork. The lobed arches carry domes; that in the middle is elevated on a high drum.

The *Dargah of Baba Musafir*, enshrining the remains of Aurangzeb's spiritual guide, stands in a walled complex next to Panchakki water mill (described above). The tomb is a cubical, pink stone structure with fluted columns and lobed arches built up to the rear of a mosque. The latter has finely polished plaster piers, lobed arches and corner rooftop pavilions, in the typical Mughal manner. Triple domes rise on bands of acanthus leaves. Tomb and mosque, together with a madrasa and sarai, face a delightful garden crowded with flower shrubs, water channels and fountains.

B. Around Aurangabad

Additional monuments of historical importance are located on the sweeping plain to the north of Aurangabad. The road leading north from Panchakki passes by the campus of Marathdwara University, close to which stands *Soneri Mahal*. This two-storeyed pavilion was erected by a Rajput warrior from central India who accompanied Aurangzeb into the Deccan. Little is left of the golden tinted murals, after which the building is named. It faces an extensive, but neglected garden with a long water channel.

The road continues for another 1.5 km. until it arrives at the mausoleum known as *Bibi-ka Maqbara*, set against a sweeping vista of rugged basalt escarpments. This was erected in 1650-57 by Azam Shah, son of Aurangzeb, for his mother, Begum Rabia Darani. The tomb stands in the middle of a large walled garden, 457 by 274 m., entered on the south through an imposing gateway. Arabesques in the spandrels over the main arch and the faceted decoration inside the corner niches are executed in finely worked plaster. The brass-clad doors are inscribed with the name of the architect, Ataullah, and the date 1661. The garden is contained by high crenellated walls, with bastions topped by open pavilions. It is divided into 32 plots by 12 waterways, with sandstone platforms containing pools and fountains at the crossings; carved stone screens line the axial walkways.

Bibi-ka Maqbara, Aurangabad.

Though Bibi-ka Maqbara is obviously modelled on the Taj Mahal, comparisons with the Agra monument usually fail to acknowledge its inventive design and high quality surface ornamentation. Brass-clad doors with elegant embossed flower designs lead to the steps that ascend the broad terrace on which the tomb stands. Like the Taj, this is a grandiose and strictly symmetrical building. Each facade is dominated by a lofty portal with a pointed arch flanked by a double tiers of small arched niches of similar design. A great dome with a bulbous profile and a brass pot finial crowns the composition; it is framed by a quartet of domed pavilions and a similar number of slender finials with domical tops. Doorways lead to an inner octagonal gallery bounded by stone screens, from where it is possible to view the grave at a lower level, a feature unique to this monument. The tombstone is surrounded by an octagon of perforated marble screens carved with considerable delicacy. Corner squinches carry the lofty dome above. White marble cladding alternating with delicate moulded plasterwork is used throughout.

Like the Taj, the mausoleum is framed by four tapering minarets that stand freely at the corners of the terrace. These examples, however, are octagonal rather than circular, as at Agra. They are topped by diminutive domed pavilions. The small mosque on the terrace to the west of the tomb displays finely finished lobed arches and corner minarets. Small recesses with lotus flowers and arabesque motifs embellish the facade. The mosque interior is roofed with shallow fluted domes.

A distant prospect of Bibi-ka Maqbara may be had from the *Buddhist Caves*, 2 km. to the north. The basalt hill here presents precipitous scarps, the sides of which have rock-cut monuments divided into two groups, those to the west (Caves 1 to 5) being separated from those to the east (Caves 6 to 9) by almost 1,000 m. The earliest of the series, *Cave 4*, is assigned to the 1st century CE, Satavahana era. It is a rectangular chaitya hall containing an apsidal ended colonnade that runs around a monolithic stupa at the rear. Much of the facade and many of the columns have deteriorated, but the wood-like ribs on the vaulted roof are relatively complete. All the other excavations are assigned to the 5th-6th century, Vakataka era.

Cave 1 was never completed, except for its entrance verandah and porch. *Cave 2* has a small sanctuary surrounded by an ambulatory passageway, preceded by a columned verandah. Bodhisattvas flank the shrine doorway, inside which is seated Buddha in teaching posture, with devotees at his feet. *Cave 3* is the largest and most important of the western group. It consists of a columned hall approached through a pillared verandah. An antechamber and sanctuary are cut into the rear wall of the hall, with small cells lining the side walls. The 12 columns inside the hall have multi-faceted shafts with medallions containing seated couples, and pot-and-foliage capitals. All these elements are embellished with scrollwork, foliation and jewelled garlands. Friezes on the beams above illustrate Jataka scenes. The sanctuary interior preserves a remarkably lifelike, sculpted tableau of fervent devotees, some with folded hands, kneeling before preaching Buddha. Little remains of *Cave 5*, in which Jains appear to have repainted the image of Buddha as a Tirthankara.

Cave 6, the first of the eastern group to be visited, consists of a sanctuary entered directly from the verandah and interior porch. Some of the subshrines in the surrounding passageway have Buddha images; finely carved Bodhisattva figures with attendants and flying celestials appear on either side of the sanctuary doorway. The teaching Buddha within is accompanied by a congregation of devotees, a later version of the arrangement seen in *Cave 3*. Traces of paintings can be made out on the verandah ceiling.

Cave 7, the finest of the eastern group, resembles Cave 6 in many respects. Columned shrines at either end of the verandah house images of Panchika and Hariti (right), and a panel of six goddesses with Padmapani and Shakyamuni (left). The passageway doorway is flanked by bold figures, including Avalokiteshvara surrounded by scenes of rescue (left). Goddesses with attendant dwarfs adorn the sanctuary doorway, with the usual preaching Buddha within. Side walls have seated Buddhas accompanied by Avalokitesvara and Tara (right), and female dancer and musicians (left). *Cave 9* consists of three unfinished sanctuaries, with porches opening off a common verandah. Among the numerous Buddhist carvings is a Parinirvana scene, now damaged, as in Cave 26 at Ajanta.

The *British Cantonment* lies 2 km. west of Aurangabad, on the road to Daulatabad and Ellora. Several old bungalows can still be seen. *Holy Trinity Church* of 1879 is a modest Neo-Gothic building with steep gables and pointed arched openings. The British cemetery, 1.5 km. beyond, is dominated by a finely carved stone obelisk. This commemorates Richard Seyer of the Bengal army, who died in 1853.

C. DAULATABAD

The most spectacular hill fort in Maharashtra, associated with almost all of its rulers from the 12th to 18th centuries, lies 14 km. north of Aurangabad. The site is overshadowed by a mighty rock that rises dramatically 183 m. above the plain. Its artificially excavated sides create a partly vertical profile that is easily distinguished from the natural hills around.

Originally known as Devagiri, Hill of the Gods, the citadel was capital of the Yadavas, the most powerful rulers of Maharashtra in the centuries prior to the conquest of the Deccan by the Delhi forces in 1296. Renamed Daulatabad, Abode of Prosperity, the fort served as the principal stronghold of the Khaljis and Tughluqs in Southern India. In 1327 Muhammad Shah moved his court from Delhi to Daulatabad, which for several years afterwords served as the principal centre of Tughluq power. It was here in 1347 that the Bahmanis declared their independence from Delhi, shifting their capital soon after to Gulbarga [24]. The stronghold remained under Bahmani control until the end of the 15th century, when it was taken over by the Nizam Shahis. Daulatabad became the seat of the remnant of the Nizam Shah kingdom after Ahmadnagar was lost to the Mughals. It succumbed in 1633, and over the next 20 years was used by the Mughals as their principal headquarters in the Deccan. When Nizamul Mulk asserted his autonomy from Delhi, Daulatabad became a part of his dominions; it was eventually absorbed into the breakaway Asaf Jahi state of Hyderabad.

The first feature to be noticed beside the road when travelling from Aurangabad is a *Pavilion* with raised vaulted chambers and overhanging balconies. This dates from Bahmani times. The nearby *Dargah of Hazrat Shah Bahauddin Ashri* is a small garden tomb, also of the same period. The road continues for about 1.5 km. before passing through a gap in the outer fort and running beside fortifications until it arrives at the outer gate. A short distance from the outer gate, on the other side of the main road, stands the *Shahi Hammam* of 1582. This well preserved bath house dating from Nizam Shahi times comprises two domed chambers surrounded by small cells.

The Daulatabad site is divided into three distinct zones: *Balakot*, the conical hill itself; *Kataka*, the inner fort, an approximately circular walled area that adjoins the base of the hill on its north and east sides; and *Ambarkot*, the outer fort, defined by walls that create a vast area fanning out from Kataka for almost

2 km. on the north and south. The *Fortifications* of both Kataka and Ambarkot employ double circuits of massive walls set at a marked angle, and lined with slit holes and battlements. The lower outer walls of Kataka have polygonal and round bastions; the higher inner walls are provided with projecting, box-like guardrooms and both square and round bastions. The frequent re-use of 12th-13th century temple materials indicates that these works post-date the Yadava period; they constitute most substantial example of Tughluq military architecture in Southern India.

The *Outer Gate* on the east is the one used by most visitors. It presents a sequence of arched entrances shielded by curving outworks that project almost 80 m. beyond the line of fortifications. The entrances preserve wooden doors with great iron spikes; the chambers within have shallow domes with traces of plaster decoration. Here are displayed cannons with "VOC" markings taken from Dutch ships, and musketry with finely worked animal heads.

On passing through the outer gate visitors arrive at the beginning of a street that traverses Kataka, running west towards Balakot. Royal and religious structures on either side are now reduced to overgrown piles of rubble. Excavations here have revealed vestiges of courtly residence, service structures and waterworks.

The road passes beside a large tank, to the left of the main street. Immediately to the west is the *Jami Mosque*, founded in 1318 during the occupation by Qutbuddin Mubarak, the Khalji ruler of Delhi. The vast square court of the mosque, some 80 by 60 m., is the largest in Southern India. It is entered on three sides through gateways, that on the east roofed with a dome and approached by a flight of steps. The spacious prayer hall on the west has a columned facade interrupted by a trio of arched portals. The interior consists of 25 aisles, five bays deep, roofed with shallow domes. An enlarged dome rises over the bay immediately in front of the deep, chamber-like mihrab in the rear wall. Some columns have figures and floral motifs and obviously come from dismantled temples; others were purpose made. Abandoned for many years, the mosque has recently been converted into a temple by installing an image of Bharata Mata in the mihrab.

Although the Jami mosque has no minaret, *Chand Minar* standing freely a short distance away, on the north side of the main street, probably assumed the function of a prayer tower. It seems also to have served as a victory monument. Its 30 m. high shaft is divided into four stages by circular balconies on projecting brackets. Chand Minar dates from the Tughluq occupation of Daulatabad, but the third fluted section was added by Alauddin Hasan, founder of the Bahmani kingdom, to celebrate his break with Delhi. A brass crescent moon protrudes form the bulbous dome-like summit of the tower. The small structure at the base includes a tiny mosque of 1445. Traces of glazed tiles are seen on the walls.

An overgrown path behind Chand Minar proceeds north to a restored Mughal styled pavilion, and from there to the collapsing remains of the *Mughal Palace*, immediately north of Balakot. Arcaded pavilions are grouped formally around two large courts, each with a four-square garden. Two brick built hammams form part of the complex.

A small mosque stands beyond Chand Minar, also on the north side of the main street. Its unadorned prayer hall is raised on a high plinth. The imposing inner gate nearby functions as the only access to Balakot. Its arched entrance is flanked by tapering round buttresses. Walls with prominent battlements create a discrete fortified zone that forms the lower part of Balakot. Dilapidated and overgrown buildings here are the remains of the residences of the Bahmanis and Nizam Shahis. The best preserved feature is *Chini Mahal*, so-called because of the blue-and-white tiles set into its plastered facade. The double-storeyed hall within, roofed with transverse arches, is flanked by raised chambers, that on the right is now ruined. The *Bahmani Palace* opposite, standing in a walled court, consists of three halls, the side ones with triple arcaded facades. Plaster medallions in the spandrels over the arches have finely worked geometric and arabesque motifs; wooden beams and brackets project from the walls. Pyramidal vaults roof the corner chambers at the rear. Steps nearby ascend to a circular bastion, on top of which is a cannon decorated with geometric patterns and lions in full relief; the opening is cast as a ram's head.

From here visitors cross over a deep trench artificially cut into the base of the hill. This was originally provided with a heavily guarded drawbridge, replaced in modern times with a footbridge. The ascent passes through rock-cut chambers and tunnels, some of which are reworked excavations contemporary with those at Ellora. The path climbs up the wooded slope of the hill, passing by a *Mughal Pavilion* with a frontal arcade, from which there are magnificent vistas of the surrounding countryside. A magazine and remnants of artillery are seen at the summit. From here visitors must descend by retracing their steps until they reach the outer gate of the fort.

The road running north from Daulatabad passes through the *Delhi Gate* in the outer walls of Ambarkot. Its austere arched opening is relieved by sculpted lions in the spandrels. The road then ascends an escarpment, from where there are fine views of the whole site.

Various monuments are scattered over the hills to the east of Daulatabad. The whitewashed *Dargah of Sayyid Mohmin Arif Ballal* is popular with devotees. The adjacent ruin has stone screens in the doorway and windows; the corner finials are conceived as miniature domed pavilions. About 750 m. to the south is a Mughal Period *Garden Tomb*. The walled enclosure has a dilapidated gateway on the west, and octagonal pavilions with fluted domes at the corners. Square flower plots surround the graves raised on a dais in the middle of the garden.

D. KHULDABAD

This small settlement lies 8 km. north of Daulatabad, merely 4 km. from Ellora, just beneath the crest of the hill into which the famous caves have been excavated.

Several Sufi teachers of the Chishti order chose to reside in Khuldabad, Abode of Eternity, during the first occupation of Daulatabad by the Tughluqs, a practice that continued into later times. As a result, numerous legends grew up about the site, including the miracle of the staff which sprouted leaves, carried by a pious disciple. Khuldabad's reputation reached its height under the Mughals. Aurangzeb gave orders to be buried here next to the tomb of his favourite saint. Other royal figures also chose Khuldabad as their last resting place: they include Ahmad Shah, first of the Ahmadnagar rulers; Malik Ambar, founder of Aurangabad; Azam Shah, builder of Bibi-ka Maqbara; and Nizamul Mulk, first of the Asaf Jahi line, the future Nizams of Hyderabad.

Khuldabad Village is contained with a square of high brick walls topped with a line of battlements, dating from Aurangzeb's reign. This emperor was also responsible for the gateways on the north and south, which have arched entrance surmounted by pavilions with curving cornices set between polygonal bastions. Major monuments face onto the street that runs between these gateways.

The *Dargah of Shaykh Zaynuddin Shirazi*, on the east side of the street, is entered through an austere domed gateway dating from Bahmani times. This gives access to a court surrounded by Mughal styled arcades, with a mosque on the west. The tomb of the saint, who died in 1370, stands in a small enclosure to the north. This unadorned structure has sloping walls, a battlemented parapet, and a flattish dome. The grave of the Mughal emperor is the southwest corner is surrounded by a superbly worked marble screen, a gift by the Nizam of Hyderabad in 1912. The southeast corner is occupied by the graves of Azam Shah and his family members. Relics of the Prophet are displayed in a small chamber nearby.

Opposite, on the west side of the street, stands the *Dargah of Shaykh Burhanuddin Gharib*. This, too, is entered through a domed gateway, next to which is a two-storeyed Mughal styled pavilion. The spacious court within is surrounded by arcades. A doorway in the rear wall leads to the tomb of the saint, who died in 1344. This is a modest structure with corner pilasters; a perforated window with an inscribed panels is seen on the east. The tomb is aligned with a small mosque to the west. This has lobed arches and a central cut-out arch in front of the dome, a characteristic Nizam Shahi feature. The graves of Nizamul Mulk and his descendants are surrounded by red sandstone screens.

Immediately south is *Lal Bagh*, a funerary garden complex laid out by Khan Jahan, Aurangzeb's foster-brother. The dilapidated octagonal tomb that stands in the middle of the four-square garden has traces of yellow tilework. Similar tilework is seen on the stone gateway facing the main street.

Leaving the town by the north gateway, the road climbs for about 500 m. before passing through another gate and winding around a dargah. Here is located the *Tomb of Zar Zari Zar Bakhsh*, another Sufi saint who ended his days in Khuldabad. The dargah is recognised by its brightly painted green gateway. The road continues another 500 m. until it arrives at the *Tomb of Malik Ambar*, who died in 1626. This isolated monument displays crisply worked stonework, best seen in the geometric screens of great variety and beauty set into the wall recesses. The walls are overhung by a bold cornice on ornate brackets; corner turrets above are conceived as miniature pavilions. A flattish dome above rises on a fringe of petals. Perched on the crest of a hill a short distance to the northwest is an unidentified tomb. This unadorned monument has double tiers of arched recesses. No graves are seen inside. The garden of the adjacent Guest House offers a grand panorama of the plain below. A path from here descends steeply to the Ellora caves, passing by the excavated court of Cave 16.

E. ELLORA

The celebrated cave temples at this site, 26 km. northwest of Aurangabad, are scooped out of the vertical face of a linear basalt escarpment to face west across the Deccan plain. The caves are described in numerical order that more or less accords with their chronology. Buddhist monuments (Caves 1 to 12) occupy the southern part of Ellora, while Hindu monuments (Caves 13 to 29), are located in the middle; Jain excavations (Caves 30 to 33) are confined to the northern extremity of the site. Most visitors begin their tour of the site at the stupendous, monolithic Kailasa temple (Cave 16).

Ellora's caves span a period of almost 400 years. The earliest are the minor excavations assigned to the 6th century Kalachuri era above Cave 28, at an original holy spot next to the Girija stream that traverses the site, forming a waterfall in the rainy season. Dhumar Lena (Cave 29), the grandest of the early monuments, is stylistically related to the cave temple at Elephanta [2A]. Another Kalachuri monument at Ellora is Rameshvara (Cave 21). The Vishvakarma (Cave 10) and twin Do Tal and Tin Tal (Caves 11 and 12) date from the 7th-8th century Early Chalukya period. The next phase of activity coincides with the era of the Rashtrakuta rulers from the middle of the 8th to the 10th centuries. Two records link these figures with Ellora: the inscribed grant of Dantidurga on Dashavatara (Cave 15), and a set of copper plates discovered in Gujarat, mentioning the involvement of Krishna I in the excavations of Kailasa (Cave 16). The Jain group is also assigned to the later Rashtrakuta period.

The first nine caves at Ellora are all variations on the standard vihara layout, with a columned verandah leading to a hall, with cells opening off the sides, and a Buddha shrine at the rear. *Cave 2* has a verandah with images of Panchika with Hariti at the end (right). Guardians flank the entrance, next to which is a profusion of Buddha figures and divinities. The square hall is defined by fluted columns with cushion-shaped capitals. Side walls have sculptures of seated Buddhas flank by Bodhisattvas and celestials. A similar but larger Buddha occupies the end shrine. Porches lead from the sanctuary to small side cells. The right porch displays a relief of the miracle at Sravasti.

Cave 4 is a two-storeyed excavation, now mostly ruined. *Cave 5*, a larger excavation entered at a higher level, consists of a long hall divided into three aisles. Benches carved out of the floor may have been used by monks for reading and eating. The porches in the middle of the side walls are flanked by small cells. The columns are delicately carved with medallions surrounded by exuberant foliage.

Cave 6 has a rectangular columned hall with smaller side halls, each with two cells. Columns here have large pot-and-foliage capitals. A columned antechamber leading to a small shrine has its walls covered with Bodhisattva figures and goddesses. The shrine doorway is guarded by large Bodhisattvas, with river goddesses on pilasters. The seated Buddha within is flanked by multiple smaller Buddhas, attendants and devotees.

As at Aurangabad, *Cave 8* has a shrine surrounded by a processional passageway on three sides. This has three cells on the left, an incomplete gallery at the rear, and two columns in front. Its sculptures include Panchika and Hariti. *Cave 9* is reached by proceeding through the hall, which consists of an open terrace with a balcony. The facade is enlivened with Buddhist deities, and an unusual scene of Tara rescuing devotees from the perils of snake, sword and elephant (left), and fire and shipwreck (right).

The only chaitya hall at Ellora, *Vishvakarma (Cave 10)*, takes its name from the mythical architects of the gods. A gateway raised on a basement enlivened with animals leads to an excavated court. The hall at the end has a colonnaded portico with a gallery above. Columns at the lower level have partly fluted shafts and pot-and-foliage capitals; a long hunting frieze appears above. The upper gallery has a verandah with a parapet wall embellished with amorous couples and scrollwork. The antechamber walls of the shrine to the right are covered with reliefs of Buddhas and goddesses; a figure of Lokeshvara is seen within. The chaitya hall is entered through three doorways. Access to the upper gallery is by steps to the left of the verandah. The facade behind this gallery has a central doorway flanked by Buddhist figures. The pediment above contains a three-quarter circular window between arched motifs adorned with celestials, naga deities with coiled bodies, and scrollwork. The side niches, containing Bodhisattvas with female attendants, are capped with pyramidal pediments composed of horseshoe-shaped motifs. Timber-like beams are cut out of the monolithic ceiling above.

Vishvakarma (Cave 10), Ellora.

The upper verandah of Vishvakarma leads to an internal gallery (above the front bays of the hall), with a balustrade adorned with embracing couples and maidens. The spacious apsidal-ended interior is divided into three aisles by slender octagonal columns. Central columns on either side have pot-and-foliage capitals. A frieze of dwarfs and panels showing preaching Buddhas is seen above the column brackets. Curved ribs sprouting from seated dwarfs accentuate the soaring vault of the interior. Teaching Buddha carved on the front of the votive stupa sits within a frame adorned with flying attendants; Bodhisattvas stand at either side. The stupa is raised on a tall drum and topped with a multi-tiered finial.

Both *Do Tal* and *Tin Tal (Caves 11* and *12)* have three storeys. (Cave 11 is erroneously named Do Tal, or Two Storeys, because its ground floor was once buried.) Each monument is entered through a spacious excavated court, reached by a passageway cut through the cliff. A flight of steps at the north end of the verandah of Cave 11 ascends to the intermediate level. This consists of five excavations, of which the first is incomplete, and the last is a cell with a rock-cut bed; the remaining excavations have sanctuaries housing Buddha images attended by Bodhisattavas. The uppermost level has a shrine, while to the left is a second sanctuary. Intrusive carvings of Durga and Ganesha indicate that the monument was later converted to Hindu usage.

The lower floor of Cave 12 consists of a long hall with three rows of columns. An antechamber leading to the Buddha shrine is recessed into the rear wall. Steps from the southwest corner of the hall ascend to the topmost level, which consists of a verandah, a hall with four rows of columns, and an antechamber and shrine. Five large Bodhisattvas flanked by attendants are carved on each of the side walls; seven Buddhas, meditating or touching the earth with one hand, with flying figures above, appear either side of the antechamber entrance. Twelve goddesses seated on lotuses held by nagas appear inside.

Ravana-ki Khai (Cave 14), first of the original Hindu excavations to be described, consists of a verandah, square hall and small sanctuary surrounded by a passageway. Large guardians and river goddesses flank the sanctuary doorway; a broken image of Durga is seen inside. Deities carved on the side walls include (left wall, front to back) Durga, Lakshmi bathed by elephants, Vishnu as Varaha, seated Vishnu with Shri and Bhudevi, and Vishnu with single consort: (right wall, front to back) Durga, Shiva and Parvati playing dice, dancing Shiva, Ravana shaking Mount Kailasa, and Shiva spearing Andhaka.

Begun as a Buddhist vihara, *Dashavatara (Cave 15)* has an open court with a free-standing monolithic pavilion in the middle. This has pilastered walls with shallow niches and pierced windows overhung by eaves. The entrance is flanked by river goddesses; other female figures are carved on the walls. Reclining lions and seated dwarfs populate the roof. A flight of steps to the left of the entrance ascends to a spacious hall on the upper floor of the two-storeyed temple at the rear of the court. Shrines are recessed into the middle of three sides of the hall. The shrine at the rear, housing a linga, is approached through a porch flanked by guardian figures.

Large, deeply sculpted compositions occupy the space between the wall columns. In spite of their worn condition and the plaster that partly obscure their details, they are unsurpassed for the range of mythological topics and vitality of figural compositions. In clockwise sequence they portray: (left wall, front to back) Shiva spearing Andhaka, Nataraja, Shiva and Parvati playing dice, the marriage of Shiva and Parvati, and Ravana shaking Kailasa; (rear wall, left side) Shiva emerging from the linga to rescue Markandeya, and Shiva receiving Ganga in his hair; (antechamber walls) Ganesha, Parvati and musicians, Lakshmi bathed by elephants, and standing Karttikeya; (rear wall, right side) Shiva emerging from the linga, and Shiva in the chariot shooting arrows at the demons of the triple cities; (right wall, back to front) Krishna holding up Govardhana, Vishnu sleeping on Shesha, Vishnu on flying Garuda, Vishnu as Varaha, Trivikrama with one leg kicked up, and Narasimha disembowelling Hiranyakashipu.

A stepped path between Caves 15 and 16, ascending to the Guest House at the top of the cliff, offers elevated views of the Kailasa temple.

Cave 16, with its colossal monolithic Kailasa temple, represents the artistic and technical climax of the rock-cut phase of Southern Indian architecture. The monument was initiated by Krishna I (756-63), and subsequently patronised by later Rashtrakuta rulers. The temple is obscured from the outside by a screen wall, in the middle of which is a two-storeyed gateway with an upper gallery overhung by eaves. Flanking walls have shallow pilasters framing dikpalas and river goddesses. Carved panels of Durga (right) and Ganesha (left) are seen within the passageway. The inner faces of the enclosure walls have figures of Durga on the lion, and Shiva in the chariot. A free-standing Nandi pavilion stands at the entrance to the temple. Lakshmi seated in a lotus-filled pool, being bathed by elephants, faces towards the entrance. Monolithic columns, 17 m. high, at either side have their shafts adorned with lotus friezes, garlands and sculpture niches. Huge, three-dimensional monolithic elephants, their trunks broken, stand nearby.

The west facing *Kailasa Temple* stands in the middle of a spacious artificially excavated court. It is raised on a lofty basement sculpted with fully modelled torsos of elephants gathering lotuses in their trunks. Staircases climb to the mandapa with triple porches at the upper level, an arrangement that recalls the larger Hindu monuments at Pattadakal [22D]. An antechamber at the rear (east) leads to the linga sanctuary. This is surrounded on three sides by an open terrace with five small shrines. Bridges link the frontal (west) porch of the mandapa with the Nandi pavilion, and in turn with the upper storey of the entrance gateway. The basements of the mandapa and sanctuary appear to be supported on the elephants beneath. The walls above, with pilastered projections, have sculpted panels and perforated stone windows. A parapet of miniature roof forms is seen above.

The tower over the sanctuary is divided into three receding stages, and is capped with an octagonal-domed roof rising more than 32 m. above the pavement. The arched projection on the front face shows seated Shiva surrounded by dwarfs and jewelled garlands. Subsidiary corner shrines have similar but smaller towers. The middle of the flat roof over the mandapa is marked by a large lotus surrounded by a quartet of majestic striding lions carved in three dimensions. Porches have intricately decorated columns overhung by generously curved eaves. Balcony seating is adorned with a frieze of auspicious pot and foliate motifs.

The sculptural scheme of the Kailasa is elaborate and well throughout. Staircases at the lower level are flanked by walls enlivened with narrative friezes depicting episodes from the Mahabharata (above), and Krishna's birth and youthful exploits (below) on the north staircase; battle scenes with monkey armies on the south staircase are from the Ramayana. Large-scale figures on the lower storey of the temple walls show Shiva in various aspects: dancing with the skin of the elephant demon, and as Dakshinamurti (both beneath the bridge linking the mandapa with the Nandi pavilion); with Parvati being disturbed by Ravana (middle of the south wall); and spearing Andhaka (north). Flying Jatayu attacking Ravana, an episode taken from the Ramayana, appears on the upper storey. The sanctuary walls have additional icons of Shiva framed by pairs of pilasters supporting foliated makaras, or arched motifs containing miniature temple towers, attendant maidens and amorous couples.

Kailasa's mandapa is entered through a doorway on the west flanked by pairs of guardians with attendants. On the walls to the left is a panel showing Shiva with Ganga; on the right Shiva emerges out of the linga. The hall interior has 16 decorated columns supporting a ceiling embellished with an icon of dancing Shiva. Further depictions of Shiva and Parvati are seen within the antechamber. The sanctuary doorway is highly ornamented, with river goddesses on either side; the linga within stands on a circular pedestal. Fragmentary paintings can be made out on the porch ceilings: those in the west porch show flying figures with dwarfs amid clouds, a deity riding a mythical beast, and battle scenes with elephants, horses and infantry.

Sanctuaries, halls and porticoes are cut into the artificially excavated cliff face that forms the sides of the temple courtyard of the Kailasa. A shrine dedicated to the river goddesses is seen immediately to the left of the entrance gateway. This has delicately worked reliefs of Sarasvati, Ganga and Yamuna, each framed by an arch issuing from a pair of open-mouthed makaras. The *Lankeshvara Temple* in the middle of the north side of the courtyard is reached by a staircase with an image of Lakshmi carved onto the wall of the intermediate landing. The temple consists of a mandapa with 36 columns, and balcony seating on two sides, and a sanctuary surrounded by a passageway at the rear (east). A seated Nandi image is set into a recess in the west wall. Columns are adorned with jewelled bands and large pot-and-foliage motifs with exaggerated cushion-shaped capitals, typical motifs of the later Rashtrakuta style. Balcony slabs are enlivened with amorous couples between pilasters. Panels on the side (north) wall depict Ganesha, Narasimha, the trio of Brahma, Shiva and Vishnu, and Parvati, Varaha and Surya, while river goddesses and guardians flank the sanctuary doorway. The rear wall of the linga sanctuary has a relief depiction of a triple-headed bust of Shiva.

The *Portico* that wraps around the eastern half of the courtyard shelters multiple images of Shiva and Vishnu. The three-storeyed shrine cut into the middle of the south side of the courtyard has a doorway flanked by female guardians and attendants. A short distance to the right is a smaller shrine, of interest for its remarkable, high relief sculptures. To the right are seated Durga, Chamunda and Kali, the last in front of an emaciated corpse. The Saptamatrikas with Ganesha, and Parvati, are at the rear, and female attendants on the left.

The tour of Ellora described so far is easily conducted on foot, the distances between the different caves being only a few metres. After the Kailasa, however, it is necessary to take the road that leads northwards for about 250 m. in order to reach the next group of monuments. *Cave 17* is entered through a projecting porch, mostly collapsed, set in a small court. This gives access to a columned hall and a linga sanctuary surrounded by a passageway. Among the deities represented in the wall panels are Ganesha (left) and Durga and Vishnu (right). An unusual image of Brahma is seen outside the court (left wall).

Rameshvara (Cave 21) is notable for the sensuous beauty of its carvings. A court with a monolithic Nandi in the middle leads to a verandah with side shrines. Female figures adorn the column brackets, while amorous couples animate the balcony walls. A gracefully posed Ganga is seen left of the verandah, while Yamuna appears in a corresponding position to the right. Panels within the verandah depict, in clockwise sequence: Karttikeya, the marriage of Shiva and Parvati in the presence of the gods, Durga (left end shrine); Shiva and Parvati disturbed by Ravana, Shiva and Parvati playing dice with Nandi beneath (rear wall); and dancing Shiva, the Saptamatrikas with Ganesha and Virabhadra, and skeletal Kali (right end shrine). Guardians flank the doorway of the linga sanctuary that opens directly off the verandah.

Nilakanatha (Cave 22) is distinguished by its free-standing pavilion, now damaged, and separate shrines for the matrikas.

Three entrances guarded by seated lions give access to the columned interior of *Dhumar Lena (Cave 29)*. The columns of the spacious hall have fluted shafts and cushion-shaped capitals. A square linga sanctuary at the rear of the hall is detached from the surrounding walls. Its four doorways are flanked by pairs of tall guardian figures with female attendants. Large-scale wall panels portray Shiva spearing Andhaka, and the divine couple disturbed by Ravana (west); Nataraja, and Lakulisha (north); and the marriage of Shiva and Parvati in the presence of the gods, and playing dice (south). River goddesses are positioned outside the north and south entrances.

Ganesha Lena and *Jogeshvari* groups of caves are situated in a ravine, about 90 m. above Cave 28. The last cave in Ganesha Lena has traces of paintings showing Shiva appearing out of the linga, and the scene of the churning of the ocean.

A further 1 km. north lies the Jain group, the latest in the Ellora series. *Chhota Kailasa (Cave 30)* is a small but incomplete replica of Cave 16, with a monolithic shrine standing freely in the middle of an excavated court. This shrine has a columned hall entered through a porch with balcony seating adorned with pots, pilasters and elephants. Carved ornamentation decorated the hall interior. Mahavira seated on a lion throne is seen within the sanctuary.

Indra Sabha (Cave 32), the largest of the Jain caves at Ellora, also has a monolithic shrine in the middle of an open court. Miniature Jina figures adorn the arched niches of the roof projections. A free-standing elephant and column, the latter with four figures on top, stand nearby. The vertical sides of the court are embellished with lion and elephant friezes, as well as with Tirthankaras. A double-storeyed temple is cut into the rear of the court, but only the upper hall was completed. Its verandah has carved images of Indra (left) and Ambika with a child seated on her lap, a lion beneath, and a spreading tree above (right). Panels inside the hall show Indra seated on the elephant, as well as various Tirthankaras. Exuberant foliation and garlands, partly cut out, adorn the fluted column shafts. Fragmentary ceiling paintings show flying figures and maidens.

With Cave 32, this itinerary of the rock-cut monuments at Ellora comes to an end. It is now necessary to return to Ellora village, about 500 m. west of the car park in front of the Kaliasa temple, in order to tour the other features of the site.

The sustained reputation of Ellora as a religious spot in later centuries is demonstrated by the *Ghrishneshvara Temple*, the most popular place of worship for most visitors today, located just outside the village. Enshrining an auspicious jyortirlinga, the Ghrishneshvara was financed by Ahilyabai, the celebrated Holkar queen, in the late 18th century. The temple stands in a walled compound, entered from the car park to the west.

The Ghrishneshvara temple is built in a revivalist style that recalls Yadava architecture of the 11th-12th century. The sandstone walls of its sanctuary are articulated by deeply cut horizontal mouldings defining the plinth and basement. The brick and plaster tower that rises above is divided into diminishing tiers of miniature towered elements, with vertical bands in the middle of each side, terminating in a fluted dome on a petalled base. The frontal projection of the tower has an encrusted arch framing Shiva and Parvati riding on Nandi. Corner rooftop finials are conceived as miniature pavilions. The adjoining open mandapa has porch projections with balcony seating on three sides. Columns are enlivened with relief carvings of divinities, as well as of horsemen and hunters; cubic brackets are fashioned as crouching dwarfs. A sculpted Nandi is placed in the middle. Male devotees must remove their upper garments before stepping down into the domed sanctuary in order to worship a linga set into a circular yoni.

Three small *Domed Structures* are dotted around the temple compound, one just above the road leading from the caves. They appear to resemble tombs from the Nizam Shahi period, complete with arched recesses, perforated windows, ornate parapets, and domes rising on friezes of petals. In actuality, they are early 17th century Hindu memorials commemorating the ancestors of Shivaji, who hailed from the Ellora area.

The last feature to be visited at Ellora is a square tank known as *Shivalayatirtha*. This is located some 300 m. further west, along the road leading from the village. Also attributed to Ahilyabai, this tank comprises a square pond surrounded by steps and eight diminutive linga shrines with different types of towers.

F. AJANTA

World renowned for their paintings, the caves at Ajanta lie just over 100 km. northeast of Aurangabad, the nearest railhead being Jalgaon, 55 km. to the north. *Ajanta Village*, 6 km. from the ancient site, is a well preserved fortified settlement dating from 1730; it was established by Nizamul Mulk. The village is contained in a square of crenellated walls reinforced by polygonal bastions. The principal gate on the south is approached by a bridge over the Vaghora River. The principal features of interest within the walls are a mosque and octagonal caravanserai.

The Buddhist excavations at Ajanta were accidentally discovered in 1819 by Captain John Smith, who was out on a hunting expedition. The site then attracted the attention of Major Robert Gill, who lived in the caves in 1849-53, painstakingly copying the paintings and photographing the ruins. Since then the monuments have been studied extensively, and much restored. The fragile condition of the paintings means that the caves are closed from time to time for conservation.

Ajanta's natural setting is incomparable, especially during the rainy season. The monuments are cut into the rocky sides of a crescent shaped gorge, at the head of which is a waterfall feeding a natural pond, the source of the Vaghora River. A viewpoint in the middle of the gorge, giving a panorama of the whole site, marks the spot where Smith first glimpsed the caves. 30 Buddhist excavations, some unfinished, are divided into two distinct phases separated by a period more than 500 years. The earlier Hinayana monuments date from the 2nd-1st century BCE, Satavahana period. Among these are Caves 9 and 10, both chaitya halls, and several viharas, or monasteries (Caves 8, 12, 13 and 15A). The later Mahayana monuments, assigned to the 5th century CE, include two more chaitya halls (Caves 19 and 26), and a number of monasteries (Caves 1, 2, 16 and 17). They are the work of the Ashmakas and Rishikas, feudatories of the Vakataka rulers based near Ramtek [10B].

The tour describes the excavations in numerical order, beginning with *Cave 1*, reached after a climbing a stepped path. *Cave 1* is one of the finest viharas of the Ajanta series. A verandah with cells and porches at either end has three doorways leading into the hall. This consists of 20 columns defining a central square space, with small cells set into the walls on three sides. An antechamber in the rear wall gives access to a shrine where seated Buddha is flanked by Bodhisattvas and flying figures bearing garlands. Sculpted devotees are seen seated either side of the wheel and deer beneath the throne.

The sculptural treatment is elaborate throughout. The columns have medallions adorned with scrollwork and flutings with jewelled motifs; the capitals are circular and ribbed. Brackets have flying couples framing scenes from Buddha's life. Figurative friezes running over the verandah columns include the Four Sights – a sick man, old man, corpse and saintly man – encountered by Siddhartha (left porch). Doorways are embellished with naga deities, musicians and amorous couples; maidens beneath trees are seen above at either side.

Cave 1, Ajanta.

The murals of Cave 1 are among the greatest at Ajanta. Jataka scenes cover the walls of the hall. Left of the verandah doorway is the Sibi Jataka, where the Bodhisattva as a king rescues a pigeon from a hawk. The next panel depicts the conversion of Nanda, who abandoned his wife Sundari. The palace scene which forms the end panel belongs to the Samkhapala Jataka. This narrative is continued beyond the corner onto the left wall, where the Bodhisattva as a serpent king listens to an ascetic; to the right, his wounded snake body is dragged by hunters. Beneath is Alara, the householder who delivers the serpent king by offering his oxen as ransom. The remainder of the left wall is devoted to the Mahajanaka Jataka. On the right is the shipwreck of king Mahajanaka, with a queen and her attendants tempting the prince with worldly pleasures on the left. Next, Mahajanaka comes out of the city gate to meet an ascetic in a rocky shelter. He then announces his decision to renounce the world, and finally leaves his capital on horseback.

Paintings of graciously posed and richly attired Bodhisattvas with elaborate headdresses flank the antechamber doorway. Padmpani (left) and Avalokiteshvara (right) are accompanied by attendants, divine musicians and flying figures. Further right, another Bodhisattva is offered a tray of flowers by a king. The antechamber side walls record the assault and temptation of Mara (left), and the miracle of Sravasti, when the Master multiplied himself (right). Incidents from the Champeyya Jataka occupy the right end of the rear wall. The serpent king Champeyya is captured and made to perform by a snake charmer. Champeyya's wife begs the ruler of Varanasi to release her husband. In the final deliverance scene both kings are seated together with ladies and attendants. Right of the front doorway, foreigners with peaked caps and beards offer gifts to a seated royal figure, sometimes identified with the Vakataka ruler, Harishena. The hall ceiling is covered with painted panels filled with floral and leafy motifs, as well as embracing couples, drinking figures, dwarfs, elephants and geese.

Cave 2 repeats the basic scheme of the previous example, though with additional carvings. End shrines of the verandah contain a seated naga king with yakshi attendant (right), and Hariti with a child on her lap (left). Subsidiary shrines in the rear wall of the hall house Panchika and Hariti (right), and corpulent yakshas with attendants (left). The vihara interior is remarkable for the painted ceiling, with numerous compartments filled with a variety of large medallions with delicate bands of lotus ornament, scrollwork and geometric patterns.

Nativity episodes, such as the dream of Maya, the interpretation by priests, and the birth of Gautama, are painted on the left wall of the hall of Cave 2. Jataka stories cover the remainder of the walls. In the Hamsa Jataka, the Bodhisattva as a goose is captured, then released at the order of a royal couple, to whom he delivers a final sermon (left wall). A large portion of the right wall is devoted to the Vidhurapandita Jataka, especially the courtly scene with the princess Indrati in a swing, Punnaka's proposal of marriage, the game of dice in which Punnaka defeats Vidhurapandita, the Bodhisattva in an earlier birth, and the happy final union. The conversion of Purna and the rescue of Purna's brother from shipwreck are seen beneath. Miniature seated Buddhas are painted on the side walls of the shrine and antechamber, also in the hall (left side). Buddha and Bodhisattva figures flank the doorways to the antechamber and sanctuary. Processions of gracefully posed female devotees carrying offerings adorn the walls of the subsidiary shrines. Seated Buddhas cover the walls of the central shrine.

Cave 4, the largest vihara at Ajanta, was never completed. The verandah has eight octagonal columns, with cells at both ends. Three doorways lead into the hall, where part of the ceiling has collapsed. The jambs of the central doorway are embellished with guardians, couples, flying celestials, and maidens clutching trees; Buddhas and garland-bearing dwarfs appear on the lintel. A relief panel to the right of the doorway depicts Avalokiteshvara surrounded by worshippers suffering torments; the miracle of Sravasti is shown on the left. Only a few of the cells are complete. The shrine has the usual arrangement of teaching Buddhas attended by Bodhisattvas. The antechamber is provided with additional standing Buddhas, two of which are unfinished.

Cave 6, is a vihara excavated on two levels. The lower hall has 16 octagonal columns arranged in four rows. The shrine doorway has an ornamental arch springing from open-mouthed makaras. Mural fragments on the antechamber walls include the temptation of Mara (right), and the miracle of Sravasti (left). A flight of steps climbs to the upper hall. Here, Buddha figures are sculpted in the verandah shrines, as well as on the walls of the hall, antechamber and shrine within.

Cave 7, another vihara, has two small porticoes with squat octagonal columns. Fluted cushion-shaped capitals support eaves relieved by ornamental arches. The cells are positioned at a high level at both ends. The focal shrine houses the usual arrangement of teaching Buddha with Bodhisattvas. The miracle of Sravasti is illustrated in relief carvings on the side walls.

Cave 9 is the first of the earlier series of excavations at Ajanta to be visited. The outer elevation of this chaitya hall has a large horseshoe-shaped window, complete with ribs imitating timbers. The doorway and two windows beneath are surmounted by similar but smaller arches in relief. The Buddha figures here are later additions. The interior of the rectangular hall has two rows of octagonal columns creating triple aisles. The central nave is roofed with a curved vault, but the wooden ribs that were once inserted into the vault are lost. The hemispherical stupa at the end is raised on a high drum and crowned with an inverted stepped pyramid. Traces of paintings survive in two layers; the earlier being contemporary with the excavation. Left of the doorway: the heads of two ascetics are superimposed on an earlier composition of a naga deity and attendants seated in a rocky shelter. At the end of the left wall a procession of devotees makes it way towards a stupa and monastery. The remnants of another older mural survives in a thin band above the left colonnade. The Buddha figures higher up are later additions.

Cave 10 in the middle of the site is a chaitya hall. It one of the first to be discovered by Captain Smith, and is possibly the oldest excavation at Ajanta. Its wooden facade has vanished. The nave is roofed with the usual curved vault, while the side aisles have half-vaults displaying rock-cut ribs. The votive stupa at the end of the rectangular hall has a plain, double-storeyed drum. As in Cave 9, there is evidence of two phases of painting. Earlier fragments on the left wall include the worship of the bodhi tree and stupa by a royal figure accompanied by soldiers, musicians and women.

Among the later paintings in *Cave 10* is the Sama Jataka on the right wall. The composition begins with a king shooting an arrow towards Sama, the Bodhisattva, who holds a pitcher on his shoulder. The story continues with the penitent king, the sorrowing parents of Sama, the restoration of Sama to life, and the reconciliation of the king and Sama. The remainder of the wall illlustrates the Chhaddanta Jataka, in which the Bodhisattva assumes the form of a royal elephant. The main events here are Chhaddanta's pleasurable life in the Himalayas, the queen of Varanasi ordering that he be killed, his tusks being cut off to satisfy the queen, who subsequently swoons, and the royal couple approaching a chaitya hall. Traces of later Buddha figures are painted on the columns and aisle ceilings. The cave also preserves a number of inscriptions.

Cave 11 is a clumsily excavated and partly incomplete vihara. The high plinth and parapet of the exterior are decorated with railings. The verandah columns and doorway are covered with painted motifs. Those on the ceiling showing foliation, birds and animals are better preserved. Sculpted Bodhisattvas with attendants appear either side of the doorway. Four columns with pot-shaped capitals stand within the hall. The shrine, without an antechamber, has a Buddha sculpted against an unfinished stupa.

Caves 12 and *13* belong to the earlier phase at Ajanta. Their facades have completely collapsed, exposing the interior square cells with rock-cut beds. The doorways in Cave 12 have arched motifs connected by friezes of railing motifs. Cave 14 was planned on a large sale, but never finished. The hall doorway is adorned with attendants and maidens clutching branches.

The verandah of *Cave 15* has mostly fallen. A stupa sheltering a canopy of serpent hoods is seen above the entrance. Buddha images appear in the shrine and on the rear wall of the hall. *Cave 15 A*, reached by descending a flight of steps, preserves only portions of the front wall. The doorway beyond is flanked by elephants and a delicately modelled seated naga deity. This is considered one of the masterpieces of 5th century Vakataka period sculpture.

Cave 16, one of the largest viharas at Ajanta, is provided with a 5th century inscription of Varaha Deva, a feudatory of Harishena. The ceiling of the front side of the hall is carved in imitation of wooden beams, the ends supported by sculpted dwarfs, musicians and flying couples. The narrow side aisles, with richly adorned columns, are later additions. Only portions of the hall have paintings. The left wall is covered with scenes depicting Nanada's wife fainting, Nanda's efforts to practice self control, and his journey to heaven in the company of Buddha. On either side of the shrine in the rear wall is the miracle of Sravasti, and a fragment of an elephant procession.

Incidents from the life of the Master cover the right wall of the hall: Buddha begging, Bimbisara's visit, Gautama's first meditation, Gautama at school, and (at the extreme right) the sleeping figure of Maya, and a royal couple in a circular pavilion. Jataka narratives cover the front wall of the hall (left side). In the Hasta Jataka the Bodhisattva appears as an elephant which throws itself from a cliff to provide food for hungry travellers. Episodes from the Maha Ummagga Jataka illustrate the legend of Mahosadha, in which the wise Bodhisattva settled disputes over the motherhood of a child and the ownership of a chariot.

Like Cave 16, which it resembles in overall layout, *Cave 17* dates from the period of Harishena. The vihara preserves the greatest number of murals at Ajanta, among which are many outstanding compositions. A row of eight seated Buddhas above amorous couples are seen over the doorway in the verandah. The incomplete panel to the left shows Indra flying through the clouds, accompanied by celestial maidens and musicians. Further left are successive scenes of a princely couple seated in a pavilion drinking wine, then proceeding towards a city gate, and finally distributing alms to a large assembly. An unusual Wheel of Life covers the left wall of the verandah. Celestial women to the right of the verandah doorway include one beauty with her eyes cast to one side, her jewelled necklace askew. Further right is a panel showing Buddha subduing the furious elephant sent by Devadatta to crush him. The verandah ceiling is painted with a lobed medallion surrounded by delicate foliation; similar themes adorn the interior ceiling.

Jataka subjects cover the interior hall walls of Cave 17. The Chhaddanta Jataka, immediately left of the entrance, is recognised by scenes showing the royal elephant. The Mahakapi Jataka, in which the Bodhisattva appears as a monkey, is seen further to the right: the king on horseback, together with his retinue, shoots arrows at the monkeys; the monkeys escape over the stretched body of the Bodhisattva; the monkeys preach to the king. The entire left wall is occupied by the Vessantara Jataka. The episodes include the farewell of Prince Vessantara, the drive with his family in a chariot, their life in the hermitage, the gift of his children to a brahmin in a forest hermitage, the redeeming of the children, and the return of the family to the capital.

The story of the Bodhisattva as the lioness Sutasoma curing a prince of cannibalism is illustrated on the wall to the left of the antechamber doorway in Cave 17. The scenes of this Jataka show the education of the prince, the cutting and cooking of human flesh, the appeal to the prince to give up cannibalism, and the final banishment to the forest. Paintings within the antechamber depict (left wall, top to bottom) Buddha preaching, descending from heaven accompanied by Indra, and addressing an assembly. The shrine doorway beyond is profusely sculpted with Buddhas, female guardians, river goddesses, scrollwork and lotus petals. Four Jataka scenes appear on the wall of the hall to the right of the antechamber doorway. The scenes of the elephant refusing food, and later bathing with other elephants, are from the Matiposaka Jataka. The youth carrying his blind parents in slings from bamboo rods refers to the Sama Jataka.

The paintings on the right wall of the hall of Cave 17 are mostly devoted to the story of Simhala's conquest of Sri Lanka. The sequence begins (bottom right end) with the shipwreck of Simhala and his merchants, and continues with Simhala accepting the aid of the Bodhisattva, born here as a horse, and leading an expedition against the demonic forces of an ogress, after which he is crowned king of the island. The pilaster beyond is covered with the celebrated composition of a princess with maids and a female dwarf. Returning to the front wall (left of the entrance), there are a number of forest scenes in which a king and his retinue appear. They possibly derive from the Ruru Jataka, in which the Bodhisattva assumes the form of a deer. The Nigrodhamriga Jataka occupies the remainder of this wall. The episodes also depict the Bodhisattva as a deer, here offering itself for slaughter to the palace cook in order to save a pregnant doe.

Cave 19 is the first of the two chaitya halls belonging to the later series at Ajanta. Its richly carved facade has an elegant portico with standing and seated Buddhas carved onto the flanking walls framed by pilasters decorated with foliation, scrollwork and jewelled bands. The facade is dominated by a large horseshoe-shaped window, on either side of which are corpulent yakshas with elaborate headdresses. The side chapels have columns with luxuriant pot-and-foliage capitals. A fully modelled naga couple seated on a rock is sculpted on the left wall. Seated Buddhas, riders, flying couples, hermits and musicians adorn the column capitals within the hall. The panels above show Buddhas surrounded by bands of scrollwork. The central aisle of the interior has a vault with fully modelled, cut-out ribs; the ceilings over the side aisles are flat. The Buddha image sculpted on the votive stupa stands beneath an arch springing from open-mouthed makaras. A monolithic tier of umbrellas with supporting figures rises above. Paintings on the ceiling depict figures, animals and lotuses.

Cave 20 is a small vihara with an antechamber protruding into the hall. The verandah columns and brackets are delicately carved, while the roof has rock-cut beams. *Caves 21* and *22* are almost identical in layout, though incomplete. Richly ornamented columns are seen in the verandahs and halls. Hariti and attendants (right), and a court of a naga king (left), are sculpted above the side shrines of both verandahs.

The tour of Ajanta concludes with a visit to *Cave 26*. This chaitya hall is larger than Cave 19, but is otherwise similar in layout and decoration. A columned verandah, partly collapsed, extends across the facade; small chambers are seen at both ends. The court in front has subsidiary shrines, cells and verandahs. The focal stupa of the hall interior has an image of the Master seated within a pavilion. Compositions are carved on the wall of the left aisle. The dignified Parinirvana scene shows a 7 m. long Buddha figure reclining on a couch, his eyes closed, accompanied by mourning disciples. In the temptation of Mara scene, Buddha is assaulted by elephants, demonic forces and alluring dancing maidens. A collapsed chamber to the left leads to *Cave 27*, a modest excavation of little interest.

G. Pitalkhora

This remote site, 40 km. northwest of Ellora, has 13 Buddhist excavations, mostly viharas, cut into the side of a secluded ravine. Dating from the 2nd century BCE to the 1st century CE, they constitute the largest group of Satavahana period monuments in Maharashtra. Two monuments are of particular importance.

Cave 3, a chaitya hall, is conceived and executed on a large scale, though its original facade has now collapsed. The apsidal-ended interior is divided into three aisles by octagonal columns. Half-vaults in the side aisles have rock-cut ribs, but the timber ribs employed in the central nave have been lost. The stupa has a monolithic base and a structural drum, now disintegrated. Painted fragments indicate that the hall was in use until the end of the 5th century.

Cave 3 shares a common court with the adjacent vihara, *Cave 4*. The basement of its monolithic outer wall is sculpted with elephants and attendant figures. The doorway is flanked by guardians, armed with spears and shields. The panel above, with two elephants flanking an image of Lakshmi, has been removed to the museum in Mumbai [1B]. A covered flight of steps ascends to the vihara. The upper part of its facade, now badly weathered, has traces of ornamental horseshoe-shaped arches. The interior columns have mostly crumbled. Cell doorways are topped with arched motifs, railings and pilasters with decorated capitals. Six cells have vaulted ceilings with rock-cut beams and rafters.

H. Ghatotkacha

The two rock-cut features at this isolated site, some 40 km. northwest of Ajanta, can be reached only with some difficulty. The monuments are historically related to Cave 16 at Ajanta since they share the same 5th century donor, Varaha Deva. The caves are scooped out of the rocky sides of a picturesque forested ravine, overlooking a waterfall.

The *Vihara*, which is the more important of the two Ghatotkacha excavations, has a verandah and four columns, now broken. The central doorway is enlivened with amorous couples and river goddesses. Seated Buddhas are positioned above the side windows. The long inscription near the left doorway gives the genealogy of the patron. The shrine extending beyond the rear wall of the hall houses a seated Buddha with devotees, while; deer flanking a wheel are carved on the pedestal beneath. Antechamber columns have medallions adorning the shafts, with pot-and-foliage capitals above. At the right end of the front aisle is a stupa with Buddha images. A pilaster in the left aisle has a Buddha and an inscription of about the 8th century.

I. Anwa

This small village, 10 km. east of Golegaon on the main road to Ajanta, a total of 75 km. northeast of Ajanta, is worth visiting for its 12th century, *Madhava Temple*. This consists of a sanctuary, an inner closed mandapa, and an open outer mandapa with porch projections on three sides. The high basement displays deeply cut mouldings. The walls are divided into projections that rhythmically expand outwards. Niches with images of Vishnu are positioned at the cardinal directions, with ascetic figures in the side recesses. The balconies of the open mandapa and porches are relieved by flat pilasters with stylised lotuses. The interior doorways are embellished with Vaishnava divinities in the company of Ganesha. Celestial dancers adorn the columns, but the bracket figures above are mostly lost. Corbelled domes are created from concentric rings of delicately worked petalled lobes. The Nandi and linga are later insertions.

J. Jalna

This city, 60 km. east of Aurangabad, was a provincial centre under the Nizam Shahis and Mughals, attaining importance in the early 18th century, when it became the seat of Kabil Khan, one of Aurangzeb's generals. The city was fortified in 1723 by Nizamul Mulk. However, its most interesting monuments date from Nizami Shahi times.

In the middle of the city stands the *Kali Mosque* of 1578. It is surrounded by a rectangle of walls, with an arched gate on the south flanked by pierced stone windows. The prayer hall within has octagonal columns carrying six small domes. The corner finials have domical tops. The adjacent Hammam, added in 1583, has chambers roofed with domes on faceted pendentives. *Jamshid Sarai* opposite, now a school, has a large square court surrounded by arcaded chambers, with a pool in the middle.

The *Dargah of Zacha and Bacha*, on the west side of the city, is also assigned to the late 16th century. It consists of a simple cubic tomb, with stone screens set into arched recesses on three sides. Sculpted lotuses adorn the doorway on the south. The dome rises over a parapet with corner octagonal finials.

The *Dargah of Jam Allah Shah*, 1 km. east of Jalna, is a popular pilgrimage monument dating from 1681. Double tiers of recesses display both pointed and lobed arches. The dome above has a petalled base, repeated within the interior. A small mosque, tank and dilapidated wooden colonnade occupy the surrounding enclosure.

K. LONAR

The Crater Lake outside Lonar, a small town 85 km. east of Jalna via Mantha, is one of Maharashtra's most remarkable natural features. Scientists identify the lake here as a meteorite impact crater dating back some 50,000 years. The circumference of the lake is almost 6 km. Its sloping forested sides, crowded with monkeys and deer, rise more than 130 m. above the water. Dilapidated temples from the Yadava period dot the edge of the lake. Decorated columns with sculpted blocks, many overturned, once defined mandapas and porches.

The *Daitya Sudana Temple* in Lonar town is better preserved. Begun in the 13th century but never completed, it presents an imposing pile of intricately carved blocks. The walls of the sanctuary and mandapa are raised on a high basement enlivened with bands of stylised foliation. Multiple projections treated as niches display figures of Vishnu and Krishna. Pavilion-like niches sheltering icons project outwards on three sides of the sanctuary.

Returning to Mantha, the road continues for about another 140 km. before reaching Nanded [9F].

L. PAITHAN

Built on the north bank of the Godavari River, some 50 km. south of Aurangabad, Paithan owes its reputation to Shalivahana, the Satavahana ruler who made this city his capital in 78 CE. The date is fixed in Indian history as the starting point of the Shaka era, a chronological system that is still widely used. Paithan disappears from history after the Satavahanas, but emerges again in the 18th century as an important centre disputed by the Marathas and the Nizams of Hyderabad. The city is renowned for its woven silks and cotton fabrics.

Exacavations carried out in the sandy mounds near *Nag Ghat*, on the river bank, revealed brick structures, wells and drains of a Satavahana settlement. These features are still partly visible. Among the associated finds were copper coins, shell objects, beads of semiprecious stones, terracotta figurines, and pottery utensils with incised marks.

Paithan is best known today as the birthplace of the Hindu saints Eknath, Dhondinath and Mukteshwar. The *Samadhi of Eknath*, near the Godavari, is a popular shrine with a large fair held in March. Contained within a wooden colonnade, the samadhi marks the spot of Eknath's burial after death by ritual drowning in 1598. The memorial stands in the middle of court, surrounded by wooden arcades, and entered through an arched portal on the east. A path to the west leads to the bathing ghats, from where there is a distant prospect of the earthen embankment of *Nath Sagar*, a large hydro-electric project on the Godavari.

The *House of Eknath Maharaj*, in the middle of Paithan, is a traditional mansion with an arcaded court used for devotional readings; a small chamber at the rear accommodates a deified image of the saint. Modern wall paintings illustrate episodes from Eknath's life. Another mansion that also serves as a place of worship is that associated with *Dhondinath Maharaj*. A path from here leads down to the river, where stands the abandoned *Koti Mosque*.

The only monument at Paithan of any antiquity is the *Tirthakambha*, an 11th century victory column assigned to the Yadava era. The *Jami Mosque* of 1630, immediately to the north, is believed to occupy the site of the Satavahana palace. Its fortified enclosure has tapering fluted bastions at the corners. The prayer hall within is of little interest.

Funerary complexes mark the eastern fringe of Paithan. The *Dargah of Maulana Moazuddin* crowns a small rise overlooking the river. An arched gateway with triple arcade over leads to a flight of steps. The walled compound at the top of the hill contains the domed tomb of the Chishti saint after whom the dargah is named. The adjacent hall with wooden columns conceals the stone remnants of a Yadava period shrine.

6. Ahmadnagar

While it is possible to visit Ahmadnagar (also spelt Ahmednagar) as a day trip from Pune [3] 116 km. to the southwest, Nasik [4] 145 km. to the northwest, or Aurangabad [5] 110 km. to the northeast, an overnight stay is recommended. This will permit sufficient time to tour the most important mosques, tombs and palaces in and around the city [A and B]. Another day needs to reserved for a trip to the pilgrimage town of Shirdi [C].

A. AHMADNAGAR

This city is linked with the Nizam Shahis, beginning Ahmad Nizam Shah (1495-1510), founder of the dynasty, originally a commander in the service of the Bahmanis of Bidar [25]. In 1496 Ahmad declared his independence, and with the aid of local Maratha chiefs seized Daulatabad [5C] and Panhala [8B]. One of his outstanding achievements was to establish a new city that he named after himself, and which came to serve as the capital of a newly launched line of rulers.

On the death of Ahmad the throne passed to the infant Burhan (1510-53), whose able ministers resisted attacks from the Imad Shahis of Achalpur [10D] to the east, and rulers of Gujarat to the northwest. The Shia sect was adopted as the state religion, bringing Ahmadnagar into sympathetic relations with Iran. In the wars against Bijapur [23A], Burhan allied himself with Vijayanagara [20B-C] and Golconda [26E]. Burhan's son and successor, Husain (1553-65), secured the frontiers of Ahmadnagar, and for a time enjoyed an accord with the Portuguese in Goa [11B]. Husain's forces joined those of Bijapur, Bidar and Golconda to counter the threat of Vijayanagara, participating in the great victory of 1565. Murtaza (1565-88), the next ruler, annexed the territory of Berar to the northeast in 1574, but his reign was marred by plots and assassinations, as well as by renewed aggression from Bijapur. The appearance of the Mughals in 1586 posed a new threat.

The last years of the 16th century witnessed a sequence of weak rulers and the invasion of the Mughals. The Mughals were checked for a time by Chand Bibi, sister of a short-lived, deceased king. Her able Abyssinian commander, Malik Ambar, managed to expel the Mughals in 1600, and in the process became effective ruler of the kingdom, leading successful expeditions against Bidar and Golconda. After Malik Ambar's death in 1626 the Mughal intensified their efforts, permanently occupying Ahmanagar in 1636. The city passed from the Mughals into the hands of the Nizams of Hyderabad [26A], from whom it was taken by the Marathas in 1760. In 1808 Ahmadnagar surrendered to Arthur Wellesley. Under the British the city served as the headquarters for a military contingent. Jawaharlal Nehru was among the Indian nationalist leaders imprisoned here by the British. His most popular book, *The Discovery of India*, was written within the walls of the great circular *Fort*.

The tour of Ahmadnagar begins at the circular *Fort*, concealed in the scrublands east of the city. This ring of well finished masonry, some 1.8 km. in diameter, dates from 1563. The 20 m. high walls were erected at the orders of Husain to replace the mud ramparts thrown up by Ahmad more than 60 years earlier. Some 22 semicircular bastions are positioned at regular intervals; one example in the northeast quadrant has triple lobes. Rectangular openings for cannon, originally crenellations, were filled in when a new brick parapet was added during the first Mughal siege in 1586. A 10 m. wide moat shielded by an earthen embankment encircles the walls. It is crossed by a bridge on the north, which leads to a powerful bastion-like barbican. This contains two arched gates, with spiked wooden doors giving access to the interior. Scattered, overgrown and dilapidated relics from the Nizam Shahi period are seen within. The temples that now stand here are additions of the Maratha period.

The Damri Mosque, 500 m. north of the fort, is a small but exquisitely decorated building dating from 1568. Its triple arched facade is enlivened with delicately carved interlaced strapwork. Lotus buds carry the angled overhang with a fringe of lotus buds. Square corner buttresses display panels with deeply sculpted niches and medallions. The parapet of cut-out trefoil elements above has finials topped with miniature octagonal domed pavilions; the central pair of finials supports a cut-out arch. The floor of the six-bayed prayer chamber imitates the pattern of the roof slabs above. The rear wall has three prayer niches, polygonal on the sides and square in the middle, surrounded by geometric ornamentation, with additional foliation filling the central niche. Side windows, also ornamented, are missing their balcony slabs.

The *Dargah of Hazrat Shah Sharif* stands in a shady garden about 1 km. to the east of of Damri mosque. Founded in 1596, this simple structure has double tiers of alternating pointed and lobed arched recesses. The corner finials are conceived as miniature domical pavilions. The dome of the tomb chamber rises on faceted pendentives.

The tour of Ahmadnagar continues with a selection of monuments located in the crowded heart of the city. The *Jami Mosque*, one of the earliest Nizam Shahi projects, has 15 bays roofed with shallow domes on alternating octagonal and circular drums. The building was altered in later times. The *Mecca Mosque* of 1525 is the work of Rumi Khan, a Turkish military officer under Ahmad. (Rumi Khan was responsible for casting the celebrated canon known as Malik-i Maidan, Lord of the Plain, mounted on a bastion in Bijapur.) The Mecca Mosque is elevated on top of a vaulted sarai, or rest house, and is reached by a steep flight of steps. The triple arches of its facade are supported on circular columns of polished granite, supposedly shipped from Mecca; hence the name. The finials have clusters of curved brackets carrying miniature eaves and fluted domical tops. The interior is roofed with unusual transverse flat and barrel vaults. The *Tomb of Rumi Khan*, who died in 1568, stands in the grounds of a nearby student hostel. It displays double tiers of triple arched recesses with doorways and windows in the middle of each side. The pavilion-like corner finials, now missing their domical tops, are crowned by a large dome with a petalled base.

Kotla, in the northern part of Ahmadnagar, was erected by Burhan in about 1537 as a Shia educational college. The complex consists of a large square compound surrounded by arcaded rooms for students. It is entered from the east through an arched gate and a domed rest house, now partly fallen. A large platform in the middle of the court marks the site of a covered cistern. The prayer chamber on the west has 15 bays roofed by pyramidal vaults and shallow domes. The arcaded facade is overhung by a deep overhang carried on brackets; additional angled struts imitate carved woodwork.

The nearby *Farhad Khani Mosque* of 1569 has three plain arches shaded by an overhang. A lobed arch with ornamental minarets surmounts the entrance gate to the compound. The *Tomb of Sharza Khan*, known somewhat fancifully as Do Noti Chira, 'Two Fingerhold', is a unique miniature building dating from 1562. Its central domed bay is flanked by curved vaults.

Bagh Rauza, on the west side of Ahmadnagar, is a garden complex containing the imposing *Tomb of Ahmad*, the only funerary monument to be associated with a Nizam Shahi ruler. Dating from 1509, the tomb stands in a walled compound entered through a domed gate on the south. The cubic building has double tiers of arched openings flanked by arched recesses, with temple-like jambs flanking the entrance. The facade is decorated with relief panels of different designs, including calligraphic medallions and lotuses. A brick frieze of arched recesses is shielded by an angled overhang on sculpted brackets, linked by suspended beams. Corner and intermediate finials above are capped with domical tops. The interior of the tomb is lavishly embellished with plaster arches, some with lobed interiors, surmounted by a calligraphic band. Traces of painted cartouches filled with arabesques are seen in the dome above.

Amhad's Prime Minister, Shah Tahir, is buried in the southwest corner of Bagh Rauza. His small tomb is recognised by its unique pyramidal vault. Just outside the enclosure stands the tomb of the king's astrologer, Malik Ahmad.

B. Around Ahmadnagar

Nizam Shahi period monuments of historical and architectural interest are scattered around the city.

The *Dargah of Alamgir*, 8 km. east of Ahmadnagar, on the road to Paithan [5L], for example, is a small arcaded structure marking the spot where Aurangzeb collapsed and died in 1707. 2 km. further east, at the summit of a hill rising more than 1,000 m. above sea level, stands the *Tomb of Salabat Khan*. Known also Chand Bibi's Mahal, this austere tower commemorates Salabat Khan, Prime Minister of Murtaza. The tomb stands on a spacious terrace with commanding views of the plain beneath, as far as Ahmadnagar. The graves of the patron and one of his wives are housed in an octagonal chamber. Above rises a three-storeyed octagonal tower of impressive dimension, each side marked triple tiers of arched openings, the topmost ones provided with balconies. The double-height chamber inside is surrounded by domed bays on eight sides.

4 km. south of Ahmadnagar stands another impressive Nizam Shahi monument. This is the pavilion of *Farah Bagh*, the centrepiece of an extensive palace complex laid out by Salabat Khan in 1583. With its emphasis on ceremonial portals and axial symmetry, Farah Bagh is distinctly Iranian in conception. Sadly, the pavilion is in poor condition; its bare walls and collapsing vaults give little idea of the sumptuous ornamentation with which it was once furnished. Even so, it is an impressive building, especially since it anticipates by almost 50 years the scheme of the Taj Mahal at Agra, though without the crowning dome. Farah Bagh stands in the middle of a vast pool, now dried up, approached from the north by a 72 m. long causeway. It is laid out as an irregular octagon, with four identical facades displaying on each side double-height arched portals flanked by tiers of smaller arches, repeated on the shorted angled corner faces. The portals have interior half-domes with multiple facets and lotus petals. Internal chambers with similarly decorated vaults at two levels, open onto or look down onto an immense double-height chamber in the middle. This is roofed with a lotus dome rising 18 m. above an octagonal fountain set into the plaster floor.

Another Nizam Shahi palace, *Hayat Behisht Bagh*, is located 6 km. north of Ahmadnagar, on a lane running between the Aurangabad and Nasik roads. The focus of this ensemble is a two-storeyed octagonal pavilion standing in a similarly shaped pond. Pointed arched openings on two levels are decorated with plaster roundels in the spandrels; similar but smaller openings mark the sides. The central chamber is surrounded by an arcade, and overlooked by a windowed gallery at the upper level. The dome above is carried on faceted pendentives. A monumental portal on the south bank of the pond incorporates a hammam, with two chambers roofed by perforated brick vaults. Adjoining rooms for bathing, with cisterns for hot and cold water, can still be seen.

About 500 m. south of Hayat Behisht Bagh is an *Underground Water Palace*, with a unique ventilation tower. This distinctly Iranian feature, known as a badgir, consists of a chimney-like tower with angled vents at the top, designed to capture the wind. This creates a draught that cools a series of domed chambers arranged around a subterranean pool. Terracotta pipes set into mortar are evidence of the extensive water system with which the complex was once provided.

C. SHIRDI

The small town, 85 km. north of Ahmadnagar, is celebrated for its association with Sai Baba, the much revered saint.

After settling in Shirdi in 1872, Sai Baba attracted many Hindu and Muslim devotees since his teachings embraced both religious traditions. Though Sai Baba was a Hatha Yoga specialist, this did not prevent him from residing in a mosque. The number of followers has grown steadily sine his death in 1918. A fair held here in March-April is attended by huge crowds. The image of Sai Baba, with one leg resting on the other, his head cloaked in a long white cloth, is a familiar icon throughout India. An indication of his enduring influence is the international fame of Sai Baba of Puttaparthi in Andhra Pradesh, a teacher who claimed spiritual descent from the Shirdi saint.

Sai Baba Temple is the chief feature of interest at Shirdi. Visitors worship a full-height image of the saint, sculpted in white marble and elevated on a silver-plated throne, flanked by gilded lions. A glass chamber to the left exhibits articles once used by Sai Baba, including a gramophone and umbrella. The black marble Samadhi, or memorial, within the temple, contains the mortal remains of Sai Baba, his head lying to the north and his feet to the south. The small mosque within the precinct marks the original residence of the saint.

7. Mahabaleshwar

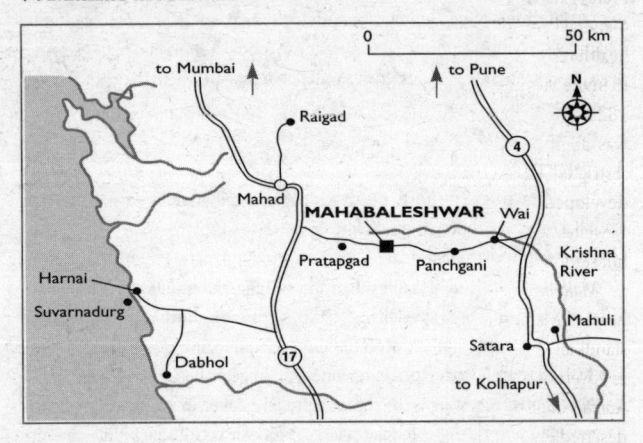

A stay at this verdant hill station [A], the highest and most populous in Maharashtra, may be combined with the itineraries for Pune [3] and Kolhapur [8]. Mahabaleshwar makes an attractive base from which to visit the mountain citadels at Pratapgad [B] and Raigad [C], both linked with Shivaji, founder of the Maratha state. They can be combined in a day trip that winds through the rugged crests of the Sahyadri Ranges west of Mahabaleshwar.

Another day may be taken up with an excursion along the Konkan Coast to reach the island fort of Suvarnadurg [D], reached from the port of Harnai, and to the sleepy port of Dabhol [E], once an international emporium.

Temples at Wai [F] and Mahuli [H], on the Deccan plain east of Mahabaleshwar, can be visited together with Satara [G] in another full-day journey.

A. Mahabaleshwar

This hill station spreads over a wooded undulating plateau that tops one of the spurs of the Sahyadris. With an average height of almost 1,400 m., Mahabaleshwar offers a welcome relief from the humidity of the coast and the heat of the plain; the monsoon rains, however, are severe. The promontories that protrude north and west offer magnificent views of the precipitous edges of the Sahyadris and the valleys below. Streams issuing from springs at the heads of ravines form waterfalls in the wet season. Here rises the Krishna, one of the longest rivers of Southern India.

The history of Mahabaleshwar goes back to the days of Shivaji, who in 1653 visited the sacred spot that marks the source of the Krishna. The hill was one of the first territories that Shivaji acquired while based at nearby

Pratapgad. However, it was not until British times that the hill was settled. General Peter Lodwick explored the area in 1824, with the idea of creating a health resort. Lodwick persuaded the ruler of Satara, whose territory it was, to invite Sir John Malcolm, then governor of Bombay [1], to visit the site in 1828. The next year a treaty delivered the hill into British hands. The station was at first called Malcolm Peth, after Sir John, but this name is now restricted to the main bazaar street. Roads were laid out, and the resort developed quickly with the construction of bungalows, churches and a club, as well as a polo ground and race course. Mahabaleshwar is now the largest hill station in Maharashtra.

Malcolm Peth, crowded with shops and new hotels, marks the commercial heart of Mahabaleshwar. Above the bazaar is the *Civic Hospital*, near to which stands an obelisk in memory of Sir Sidney Beckwith, who succeeded Malcolm as governor of Bombay in 1830, and who died in Mahabaleshwar in 1831. The *Roman Catholic Church* and the more impressive Anglican *Christ Church*, now deserted, but with fine stained glass, stand near the bus station. The *Mahabaleshwar Club* still flourishes.

Yenna Lake lies 1.5 km. northwest of Malcolm Peth, via a winding road that passes by many guest houses. Its pleasant tree lined shore is ringed with popular walks and pony trails. Mahabaleshwar's lookouts provide more dramatic scenery. *Bombay* Point, 2 km. southwest of the bazaar, offers an extensive view of the Konkan. *Sidney Point*, 4 km. west of the bazaar, is marked by a 7.5 m. high pillar crowed by an urn, commemorating Lodwick.

The *Lingamma Falls*, 4 km. east of Malcolm Peth, are the finest in the area. The cascade has a sheer descent of 165 m., unbroken after heavy rain. From here it is only a short walk to *Wilson Point*, at 1,435 m. the highest peak in Mahabaleshwar. It is named after yet another governor of Bombay.

Old Mahabaleshwar, 6 km. north of Malcolm Peth, is the site of the *Mahabaleshvar Temple*, after which the hill station is named. Founded in earlier times, but rebuilt in the 19th century, this simple black basalt structure enshrines a natural rock saturated with spring water, symbolising the source of the Krishna River. The Atibaleshvar temple, in an adjacent walled compound, has pyramidal roofs with tiers of undecorated eave-like mouldings.

The nearby *Temple of Krishnabai* was erected in 1888 by the ruler of Ratnagiri on the Konkan Coast. It consists of an arcaded court, later roofed over, with a high stone wall at the rear. Water flowing out of five holes at the base of the walls is identified with the Panchganga, the five sacred rivers, which include the Krishna. The chutes unite before passing through a stone spout carved as a cow head, and then flowing into a square stepped cistern. Bathing in the water is considered particularly auspicious and the temple is usually crowded.

Other lookouts are located beyond Old Mahabaleshwar. *Elphinstone Point* lies 3.5 km. west, and *Arthur's Seat* is 3 km. north, across a valley of the Gayatri and Savitri Rivers. The cliffs at these two sites rise more than 800 m. above the plain. From Arthur's Seat, named after Sir George Arthur, another governor of Bombay, it is possible to make out the hill forts at Rajgad (1,317 m.) [3M] and Torna (1,535 m.) in the distance.

B. Pratapgad

This citadel occupies Par Ghat, the hill that guards a strategic pass in the Sahyadri Ranges, 13 km. west of Mahabaleshwar. In 1636 Par Ghat was occupied by Moro Pingle, Shivaji's trusted general, who thereby opened up a strategic route that descended to the Konkan Coast. Four years later Pratapgad was the scene of Shivaji's encounter with Afzal Khan, commander of the army of Bijapur [23A], who Shivaji brutally stabbed in a notorious incident. The fort remained an important Maratha outpost throughout the 18th century, being used by Nana Phadnavis, Prime Minister of the Peshwas, as a refuge from the intrigues at Pune. Pratapgad surrendered to the British in 1818.

The *Grave of Afzal Khan*, beside the main road below the hill, is sheltered by a modern roof; it marks the spot where the commander's decapitated head was buried. A path from here climbs to the *Citadel* that crowns the hill, rising 1,080 m. above sea level. To the west and north are sheer precipices, in certain places with a vertical drop of up to 250 m. The south and east flanks of the hill have double lines of fortifications, with 12 m. high circular towers and bastions. The walls follow the curving lines of the escarpment, creating lower and upper forts. On passing through the east gate, the outworks of an impressive tower are seen to the right; to the left is the path to the upper fort. The *Temple of Bhavani*, founded by Shivaji and recently remodelled, overlooks the east flank of the lower fort. The temple enshrines a black stone image of the same goddess as that worshipped at Tuljapur [9C]. Two squat stone lamp towers with curved brackets stand on the terrace in front. A further attraction is the equestrian bronze statue of Shivaji, installed in 1957 and unveiled by Jawaharlal Nehru.

C. Raigad

This fort, 25 km. north of Mahad on NH17, about 60 km. northwest of Mahabaleshwar, spreads over the top of a great wedge shaped rocky bluff that rises 940 m. above sea level. The bluff is separated from the main range of the Sahyadris by a deep valley on the east. The ascent requires a climb of about 400 m. on foot from the spur where vehicles are parked. A ropeway with cabins, however, is now also available.

Under the name of Rairi, this fort was held successively by the Bahmanis and Nizam Shahis. In 1636 it was made over the Adil Shahis of Bijapur, who entrusted it to the Sidis of Janjira [21]. Shivaji captured Rairi in 1656, thereby opening up the coastal routes for the extension of Maratha power. In 1672 he selected Rairi as his new headquarters, renaming it Raigad, Royal Fort. Two years later Shivaji made Raigad his seat of government, striking coins for the first time in his own name. In June 1674 Shivaji was crowned here with much splendour as Chhatrapati, Lord of the [Royal] Umbrella. English embassies visited Raigad to congratulate his son and successor, Sambhaji, when he assumed the throne in 1681. But this ruler did not enjoy Raigad for long, because in 1689 the Mughal forces besieged the citadel. It was thereafter handed over to the Sidis, with orders to defend it against the Marathas. In spite of repeated attempts, the Marathas were unable to retake Raigad until 1734. The fort remained in Maratha hands until 1818, when it was captured by the British. Sir Richard Temple, Governor of Bombay, visited Raidgad in 1885 and ordered the restoration of some its buildings. In 1896 Lokmanya Tilak, a popular leader, initiated an annual ceremony commemorating Shivaji's death.

Shivaji's Throne, Raigad.

The *Fortifications* ringing Raigad plateau, though discontinuous, are built of massive basalt blocks laid without any mortar, but reinforced by round bastions. The walls shielding Takmak Point, the jagged northwestern promontory of the fort, are particularly strong, as are the walls defending the *Great Gate* that serves as the entrance to the fort from the west, used by most visitors. The arched opening, concealed by curving outworks, is adorned with lotus medallions, relief panels showing lions crushing elephants, and a battlemented parapet.

The path ascends from the great gate until it arrives at the comparative level top of the hill. The first feature of interest to be seen is the circular *Ganga Sagar*, Raigad's chief reservoir. To the south rise the walls of the immense *Bala Kila*, Shivaji's citadel. Two ruined, 12-sided towers with multiple tiers of arcaded openings stand freely outside the walls. An arched entrance in the walls leads to a long flight of steps that climbs to a passageway. Doorways on the right give access to six rectangular compounds, believed to have accommodated female members of Shivaji's court. The zone at a lower level to the left has five residential suites, possibly for Shivaji's officers. Each suite has a rectangular chamber standing in the middle of a square compound; a toilet block is provided to one side. The walled zone at a higher level of the left was the setting for ceremonies and official business. All that can now be seen are the stone foundations of formally arranged columned halls and colonnades. The platform in the middle supports *Shivaji's throne*, the remains of which can be viewed through a glass panel. The restored platform is sheltered by a modern, cast-iron domed canopy. A *granary* and *treasury* are located to the north and south of the throne, respectively. A small fountain in front (east) is overlooked by a Hall of Justice. The main gate on the east side of the enclosure has a lofty arched opening with upper panels showing lions clawing elephants. The interior passageway is roofed with a corbelled vault.

A path leads north from the main gate of the Bala Kila to the *Bazaar*. This comprises two lines of 22 shops facing each other across a broad north-south street. The *Temple of Jagadishvar*, erected in 1674, the year of Shivaji's coronation, stands in a high walled compound some 500 m. northeast of the bazaar. Its somewhat austere exterior is relieved by a parapet of trefoil elements framed by corner domical finials. A plastered dome on petals rises over the linga sanctuary within. The adjoining mandapa is roofed with a pyramidal vault.

An arched gate in the east wall of the temple compound leads to the *Samadhi of Shivaji*, an octagonal plinth on which the Chhatrapati's body was cremated in 1680. A bust of Shivaji erected in 1926 commemorates the event. *Waghya's Samadhi* nearby is dedicated to Shivaji's faithful dog that died with its master on the same funerary pyre. It consists of a sculpted animal raised on a 4 m. high pillar. A path running east from here, following one of the spurs of the hill, leads to the remains of extensive barracks.

D. Suvarnadurg

This island fort is located approximately 500 m. offshore from Harnai, a small port located 130 km. from Mahabaleshwar, via Khed on NH17. The sea around Suvarnadurg is shallow, and it is only possible to reach the island by boat at high tide. The fort is more of interest for its striking location than its architectural features.

Survarandurg was the second coastal citadel after Vijayadurg [8C] to be extensively renovated by Shivaji in a bid to counter the power of the Sidis of Janjira. The walls of the island, as well as its name, Golden Fort, date from 1669. In 1696 it was used as a naval base by Khanoji Angre of Alibag [2G]. Under Khanoji's successor, Tulaji, Suvarnadurg became one of the chief posts of the Angre fleet, which threatened European and Indian shipping. After a joint attack on the island by the British and the Marathas in 1756, Suvarnadurg was given over to the Peshwas. In 1801 Bajirao, the last Peshwa, fleeing Yeshwantrao Holkar, sought refuge here. The island was finally taken by the British in 1818.

Suvarnadurg is surrounded by *Fortifications*, now much overgrown, that follow its irregular outline. The walls are partly cut out of solid rock and partly constructed out of square basalt blocks. They are strengthened by round bastions, and broken only by a single, roughly fashioned gate just above the high tide mark. A tortoise is carved on a stone at the gate's threshold; on the walls to the left is an image of Hanuman. Tanks and a small step-well with abundant water are seen inside the fortifications. A plastered stone building is identified as a magazine. Extensive foundations beyond are all that remain of the Angre residences.

E. Dabhol

This historic port, 37 km. south of Harnai, is situated on the north bank of the Vaishishti River, 3 km. from its confluence with the Arabian Sea.

Dabhol was an important centre of shipping when it came under the control of the Bahmanis and Adil Shahis. The Portuguese attempted to capture it in 1514, but were repelled. In the middle of the 16th century Dabhol attracted traders from Gujarat and Malabar, as well as from Aden and Ormuz. Large quantities of textiles, grain and vegetables were exchanged here for imported copper, quicksilver, vermillion and horses. The Portuguese successfully raided Dabhol in 1547, but held it only for a few years, after which its seaborne trade declined. The port was taken twice by Shivaji in 1660 and 1666. In the 18th century it came under the joint governorship of the Marathas and Sidis, except for a period of 11 years when it was occupied by the Angres. By 1818, when Dabhol passed into the hands of the British, virtually all shipping had ceased.

The only building of interest to be seen at Dabhol today is the *Jami Mosque*, which stands in coconut groves close to the water. It was erected in 1649 by Pir

Ahmad Abdullah, an Adil Shahi officer. The building is raised on a terrace with a small pool, in the middle of which is a graceful fountain with eight spouts fashioned as birds. The triple arches of the prayer chamber are sheltered by an angled overhang on sculpted brackets. The parapet above is interrupted by two pavilion-like finials. Corner octagonal buttresses have rows of petals, repeated at each of the five stages. A dome rises over the central bay. Arcades defining a market square are seen immediately north of the mosque.

F. WAI

This charming town lies 40 km. east of Mahabaleshwar, 6 km. from NH4, on the bank of the Krishna River, which here issues from the wooded slopes of the Sahyadri Ranges. At the west end of Wai, the river is traversed by a weir that forms a pool; bathing ghats line the banks for about 500 m. downstream. Nearby temples and shrines were erected by the Rastes, a local family that rose to prominence under the Peshwas in the second half of the 18th century. Only the most interesting of these are described.

The *Ganapati Temple* on the north bank, built by Gangapatrao Raste in 1762, is the most striking of the Wai series. Its 22 m. high plastered brick tower takes the form of a fluted cone, capped with a smaller dome; diminutive conical finials mark the corners. The spacious rectangular sanctuary within, roofed by a pyramidal vault, enshrines a 2 m. high stone sculpture of Ganesha. The rear west face of the temple has angled walls to buttress the building in times of flood.

The adjacent *Kashivishveshvara Temple*, at a slightly higher level, was built in 1757 by Anandrao Bhikaji Raste. It stands in a fortified enclosure, entered on the east through an arched gate. The walls of the temple are featureless, except for small pierced stone windows, one with an attractive design of knotted snakes. The 12-sided spire above the sanctuary rises in three diminishing tiers of plastered niches, each occupied by a seated figure. Similar niches framing Durga, Ganesha and Sarasvati form a parapet above the doorway to the hall. The domed interior has a tortoise engraved on the floor. Steps descend to the linga sanctuary, which is roofed by a curved vault. The detached Nandi pavilion, with lobed arches on four sides is flanked by a pair of tapering, octagonal stone lamp columns.

Another project of Anandrao Bhikaji Raste is the *Mahalakshmi Temple*, dating from 1778. It, too, is contained in a walled compound, but faces west. The entrance to the hall is through a series of lobed arches. The spire over the sanctuary consists of five diminishing tiers, each with 12 plastered niches framing divinities and attendants. The spire is crowned with a fluted dome; similar but smaller domes cap the finials at the lowest stage.

Wai is dotted with many mansions dating from the 18th century, the finest being *Moti Baug*, principal residence of the Raste family (permission required to visit). This is fronted by a double-height verandah leading to wooden panelled rooms. The panels frame brightly coloured paintings of diverse courtly and mythological topics, surrounded by delicately toned floral bands. The large garden to the rear of the mansion has a brick tower with a water wheel, to feed the pools and fountains.

G. SATARA

This historical city is located on NH4, 30 km. south of Wai, between Pune, 110 km. to the north, and Kolhapur, 120 km to the south.

In 1669 Rajaram, Shivaji's grandson, made Satara the headquarters of Maratha power, thereby alerting the Mughals, who besieged it in 1700 and 1706. After retaking the city in 1708, Shahu, Rajaram's successor, was formally crowned here, thereby confirming Satara as centre of the rapidly expanding Maratha empire. Upon Shahu's death in 1749 the city was occupied by the Peshwa, Balaji, who then proceeded to Pune, making this the principal Maratha capital. Satara, however, continued to serve as the residence of a local line of rulers, who gradually emerged as independent, assuming the title of Chhatrapati. Pratapsinh of Satara was recognised by the British after the fall of Pune in 1818, and the princely state of Satara survived until Independence.

The chief focus of Satara is the royal complex in the central square. The west side of the square is occupied by the residences of Pratapsinh and Appa Saheb, now the *Pratapsinh High School* and *District Judge's Court* or New Palace, respectively. They are built in traditional style, with wooden columns, brackets and arches set into brick walls, and sloping roofs of terracotta tiles. The great columned hall inside the court, now crowded with judicial officers and petitioners, was originally used for public ceremonies. A small interior hall in the northeast corner of the palace has fanciful wooden brackets carrying an upper walkway. Wall paintings at the lower level show mythological scenes, such as the churning of the cosmic ocean, as well as Ramayana episodes, including Rama receiving Hanuman. The vividly toned figures are set on a bright yellow background.

On the southern edge of Satara is the *Adalat Wada*, or Old Palace (permission required to visit). Once used by Shivaji and the Peshwas, it is now the residence of the descendants of the local Chhatrapatis. Several of Shivaji's own weapons are reputedly stored here. The fort occupies a triangular flat-topped hill that rises steeply 300 m. above the town. Its walls and circular bastions can be made out from below. There is little of interest on top, except for two gates, a few barren ponds, and a dilapidated residence. The *Shrine of Mangali Devi*, guardian goddess of the fort, is situated in the northeast tower.

The *Shri Chhatrapati Shivaji Maharaj Museum*, near the bus stand in the city, has a small but interesting collection of Maratha memorabilia. This includes weapons, costumes and regalia. Musical instruments, paintings, some on glass, and fresco fragments are also on display.

H. Mahuli

The memorials of the Satara rulers are located at Mahuli, a picturesque site on the Krishna River, 6 km. east of Satara. The nearby riverside shrines are associated with the Pant Pratnidhis, Viceroys of the Peshwas. They are among the most curious examples of Maratha religious architecture.

The largest of the Mahuli monuments is the *Vishveshvara Mahadeva Temple*, erected in 1735 by Shripatrao Pratnidhi. This is raised on a polygonal terrace, with an octagonal lamp column at the top of the steps descending to the water. The east facing temple consists of a sanctuary with angled wall projections carried up into the tower. The lower stage of the tower has axial niches with curved cornices, set between octagonal buttresses capped with domical finials; the upper stage displays an octagon of niches topped with a bulbous fluted dome. A smaller spire over the antechamber repeats several of these elements. The adjoining open mandapa has porch projections with balcony seating on three sides. A European bronze bell, engraved with the date 1744, hangs inside. Turrets treated as miniature pavilions enliven the roof of the mandapa, as well as that of the Nandi pavilion in front.

The nearby *Sangameshvara Temple* marks the confluence of the Venna and Krishna Rivers. Its spire presents a simple curving scheme, with central panels curving up on four sides of the domical roof.

On the opposite bank of the Krishna stands the *Rameshvara Temple*. This occupies a large terrace with corner circular bastions at river level. Only one pair of lamp columns stands complete. The main shrine consists of a towered sanctuary, entered through a small porch with a Nandi pavilion in front. The rear arcade conceals a small sanctuary roofed with a dome.

8. Kolhapur

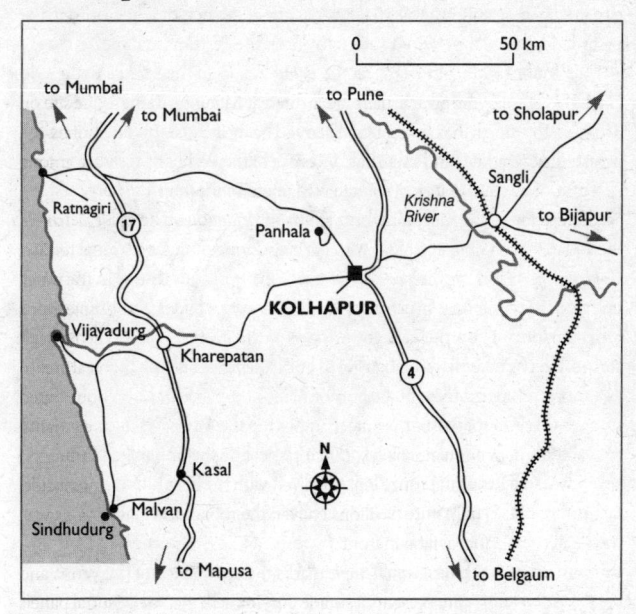

Located in the extreme southwestern corner of Maharashtra, Kolhapur is a commercial and educational city with an interesting historical background. A half day may be devoted to its palaces and temples [A], with another half day for the nearby fort at Panhala [B].

Kolhapur makes a convenient base from which to visit the Arabian Sea strongholds of Vijayadurg [C] and Sindhudurg [D], the latter being an island reached by boat from Malvan.

Kolhapur may be combined with itineraries of Pune [3], Mahabaleshwar [7] and Sholapur [9]. Journeys can also be made from here to Panaji in Goa [11A], and Belgaum [21A] in Karnataka.

A. Kolhapur

Formerly the capital of a princely state, Kolhapur is attractively located in the plains east of the Sahyadri Ranges. Kolhapur traces its history back to the Satavahana period, with remains found here dating from the 2nd century BCE to the 2nd century CE. The discovery of Greek styled figurines and medallions indicates early contacts with the Mediterranean world. Kolhapur attained importance in later times, serving as the headquarters of the Shilaharas, the most powerful rulers of western Maharashtra in the 11th-12th centuries. The city emerged again in the 18th century as the residence of a line of Maratha commanders, which achieved autonomy from the Peshwas of Pune.

The tour of Kolhapur begins at the *Palace Square* in the middle of the Old City. This is entered through elaborate gateways dating from the 19th century. That on the north has an imposing lobed arch flanked by finely detailed balustrades, windows and small balconies carried on elephant-tusk-like motifs. A statue of a wrestler inside the gateway refers to the khushtis, or wrestling academies for young men, for which Kolhapur is famous. The east gateway of the square has an upper pavilion with curving cornices, flanked by towers. The *Government Offices* in the middle of the square occupy the Old Palace, a traditional 18th century structure with wooden colonnades and sloping tiled roofs. A doorway on the east gives access to what was once an open court surrounded by colonnades, later roofed in. A small chamber on the west serves as a shrine for the goddess Bhavani.

A short distance west of the palace square is the *Mahalakshmi Temple*, the largest and most popular in Kolhapur. This relic of the Shilahara period was severely damaged at the time of the Delhi invasion of Southern India at the beginning of the 14th century. It was restored to its present state in 1722 by the local ruler, Sambhaji. The temple stands in a walled compound, entered through arched portals on four sides, that on the west being the highest. A pair of stone lamp columns stands inside. A hall with reused columns and a long inscription is built against the walls immediately to the left. The west-facing temple is entered from the north through a porch with inclined balcony slabs decorated with carved figures. This is partly concealed by a later structure with wooden columns and a tiled roof. The porch leads to a sequence of mandapas with finely carved stone columns and corbelled domed ceilings, partly repaired.

The mandapas lead to the shrine of Mahalakshmi, whose gorgeously attired image is set in a silvered frame. Subsidiary shrines dedicated to Mahakali (north) and Sarasvati (south) open off the innermost hall. The outer walls of all three shrines preserve their complicated faceted outlines, echoed in the high plinth and basement mouldings, as well as in the pilastered niches and angled overhang. Most of the niche carvings have been remodelled in plaster, but a few original stone sculptures of maidens can be made out in the recesses. The five pyramidal towers, each topped by a domical finial, are 19th century additions. The Sheshashayi sanctuary, next to the east entrance, is of interest for the columns, doorway and corbelled dome taken from a dismantled 11th-12th century Jain temple.

The next feature of interest in the city is the *Kolhapur Museum* (closed Mondays), on Bhausingji Road, 1 km. east of the temple. This sombre Neo-

Gothic structure was built as the Town Hall in 1872-76 by Charles Mant, a British architect active at the time in Chennai [36]. The frontal porch of the museum is flanked by towers with steeply pyramidal metal roofs. Two European cannon are on display here; the example dated 1609 is engraved with a relief of the god Mars. The museum houses Satavahana period aretefacts discovered in excavations at nearby Brahmapuri Hill. They include figurines of the Greek god Poseidon, riders on an elephant, and a medallion with Hellenistic figures (replicas only on display). Pottery fragments, coins and beads from Brahmapuri are also shown. Graceful female musicians are among the sculptures rescued from the Mahalakshmi temple. The finest sculpture is a female attendant bearing a fly-whisk from Panhala. A bronze bell displayed here was brought from the Portuguese fort at Vasai [2E] in 1739 to be installed in the Mahalakshmi temple. The raised gallery at one end of the museum is given over to arms.

New Palace, Kolhapur.

The *Chhatrapati Pramila Raja Hospital*, opposite the museum, was built by Mant in 1881-84. Its entrance porch has exuberant Corinthian columns with monkeys and demonic heads incorporated into the arches above. Mant's masterpiece at Kolhapur is, without doubt, the *New Palace*, 1.5 km. further north on Bhausingji Road. Completed in 1884, this complex presents a novel blend of disparate features, in contrasting basalt and sandstone blocks. The principal south facade has a double-storeyed range, with Mughal styled, lobed arches beneath, and temple-like columns and brackets above. This scheme is interrupted by trefoil arches capped with curving cornices and small domes. The same elements cap the octagonal corner towers. The central tower is marked by a pronounced curved cornice. To one side rises a 45 m. high clock tower topped by an octagonal domed pavilion.

The *Shahji Chhatrapati Museum*, which occupies the interior of the palace, is devoted to memorabilia of the Kolhapur rulers. Its furnished apartments and corridors are crammed with arms, howdahs, paintings and photographs. The *Darbar Hall* is a double-height space, with stained glass panels illustrating scenes from the life of Shahji, and a cast-iron balcony supported on carved columns. A throne is placed at one end.

The tour of Kolhapur continues with a visit to *Panchaganga Ghat*, 1.5 km. northwest of the palace square. The south bank of the river is overlooked by Brahmagiri Hill, the site where the Satavahana period objects in the museum were discovered. Nothing can now be seen of the brick structures that were uncovered here during the excavations. The ghat itself is lined with funerary monuments of the Kolhapur rulers. The *Memorial of Shivaji III*, the largest of these, dates from 1815. It stands in a walled compound, entered on the east through an arched gate. The memorial has a sandstone portico with lobed arches. Above the faceted walls rises a brick and plaster tower with tapering bands in the middle of four sides. Adjacent memorials within the same compound are surrounded by a cluster of stone lamp columns.

The last feature to be described is *Shalini Palace* facing onto Rankala Lake, west of the city. This palace was built in 1931-34 as a private guest house for the Kolhapur ruler; it is now a hotel. Its arcades and balconies rise in three stages, dominated by a central clock tower topped with a domed pavilion, recalling that of the New Palace. The interiors are distinguished by the use of Belgian glass etched with Maratha motifs and the Kolhapur crest.

B. PANHALA

This imposing fort, 20 km. northwest of Kolhapur, is built on an outlying spur of the Sahyadri Ranges, rising more than 400 m. above the plain. The strategic importance of Panhala can be judged from its long and varied history guarding one the principal routes through the Western Ghats. After serving as the headquarters of the Shilahara ruler Bhoja II (1178-1209), Panhala passed into the hands of the Yadavas. It was a favourite outpost of the Bahmanis of Bidar [25A]. Mahmud Gawan, the powerful Prime Minster of these rulers, encamped here during the rainy season of 1469. By the beginning of the 16th century Panhala was absorbed into the kingdom of Bijapur [23A]. The Adil Shahis were responsible for strengthening and rebuilding the ramparts and gateways. The fort was raided by Shivaji in 1659, but it was not until 1673 that he was able to occupy it permanently. In 1701 Panhala surrendered to Aurangzeb, and it was here that the Mughal emperor received the English ambassador William Norris. Within a few months the fort was retaken by the Maratha forces under Ramachandra Pant Amatya, who asserted his autonomy by founding in independent dynasty. After a local rebellion in 1844, Panhala was occupied by the British.

More than 7 km. of *Fortifications* define the approximately triangular zone of Panhala fort. The walls are protected for long sections by steep escarpments, reinforced by a parapet of slit holes. The remaining sections have 5 to 9 m. high ramparts, strengthened by round bastions. Unfortunately, the east gate through which the road passes on arrival, was demolished by the British. A Dargah, painted green and white, is seen to the left of the entrance.

The road continues west for about 400 m. until it arrives at *Tin Darawza*, or Triple Gate. This elaborate example of military architecture is assigned to the Adil Shahi era. The first, innermost gate displays an arched recess framing a lobed arch. A nine-domed chamber gives access to an inner court lined with arcades. The second gate is topped with a lintel set within a lobed arch. This frames a plaster composition with lions and an image of Ganesha, additions of the 19th century. Side panels have intricately etched patterns of interlocking merlons and stylised arabesques. Prominent battlements are seen above. The west side of the court is overlooked by an elevated guardroom with triple arches separated by decorated jambs. A passageway beneath leads to the third and outermost gate. A slab set into the arched recess over the lintel has a Persian inscription of 1545 mentioning Ibrahim Adil Shah I. A short distance west of Tin Darwaza is a step-well built into the inner portion of a bastion. Chambers at the upper level are arranged around three sides of the deep well.

The irregularly shaped *Bala Kila*, occupies the middle of the comparatively flat top of Panhala hill, some 1 km. to the north. This fortified zone is defined by high walls with bastions, now much dilapidated and overgrown. Three great rectangular granaries, capable of provisioning an entire army, stand freely within the walls. The largest, some 42 by 10 m., has 16 compartments roofed with flat vaults, rising more than 8 m. above the ground, each with a square hole through which to deposit grain. A domed pavilion is set over the balconied entrance at the east end of the building. Decaying foundations and plinths hidden in the undergrowth are all that remain of the surrounding palace and barracks. *Sajja Koti*, a pleasure pavilion set into the ramparts, is situated another 500 m. to the north. This two-storeyed structure has an upper chamber with flattish domes on vaults, decorated in the typical Bijapur manner. An arcaded balcony on the west looks down into the fort, while the chamber on the east enjoys fine views of the approach to Panhala from the plains beneath.

C. Vijayadurg

This isolated, but magnificently located fort overlooks the mouth of Vaghotan Creek, 140 km. southwest of Kolhapur, via Kharepatan on NH17. The route descends through the rugged bluffs of the Sahyadri Ranges before crossing the Konkan Coast. Vijayadurg's harbour is one of the finest on the Arabian Sea coast of Maharashtra, but is little used. The fort here occupies a rocky promontory rising almost 40 m. above the water, joined to the mainland by a narrow neck on the south. The sleepy settlement here gives little indication that this was once a great port.

Vijayadurg dates back to the 16th century, when it was first occupied by the Adil Shahis. It was much strengthened by Shivaji, to whom it owes its final features as well as its name. Vijayadurg assumed a crucial significance in Shivaji's naval campaign against the Sidis of Janjira [2I]. In 1689 the Maratha admiral Khaoji Angre of Alibag [2G] used Vijayadurg as a base from which to attack European and Indian shipping. These disruptive activities continued until 1756, when a flotilla of British and Maratha vessels managed to take Vijayadurg. The port was subsequently held by the Peshwas of Pune, but piracy flourished as vigorously as before. Vijayadurg passed into British hands with the conquest of the Maratha territories in 1818.

Vijayadurg takes the form of an irregular circle ringed by three concentric *Lines of Fortifications* set at different levels, rising abruptly out of the water. The outermost and innermost rings, both of which are complete, have massive round bastions with slit holes and openings for cannon. The intermediate ring serves as additional reinforcement on the landward side only. Visitors enter Vijayadurg by passing across a moat, now filled in, cut into the narrow neck of land on the south. The path leads through curving outworks, but the gateway inside is lost. A small domed Hanuman shrine stands within. Steps cut into the rock descend to the harbour to the right. Straight ahead lies a gate with an arched opening. This gives access to a passageway that runs between the curving second and third lines of fortification until it arrives at the main gate on the east side of the innermost citadel. Steps ascend between curving outworks to the gate, which preserves its wooden doors and traces of plaster decoration.

Dilapidated Structures within the fort are attractively shaded by mango and banyan trees. To the left of the main gate is a vaulted magazine, entered through a doorway set beneath a lobed arch. Steps climb to a flag tower, from which a path follows the top of the innermost and highest ring of walls, with dramatic panoramas of the ocean below. The path passes by multi-storeyed structures, possibly residences, with balconies but no floors or roofs.

A path running from the right of the main gate leads to the *Barracks*. This is a long rectangular structure, approximately 40 by 10 m., with two doorways below and window openings above. The intermediate floor on posts has disappeared. A large tank is partly excavated into the rock nearby. The path continues to the northern extremity of the fort, where there is another tank. This is overlooked by a *Granary* divided into four vaulted compart-ments, entered on the east through a single doorway. The pavilion on top of the granary is a British period addition. From here there are sweeping views of both the ocean and the harbour.

D. MALVAN AND SINDHUDURG

The charming port of Malvan lies 75 km. south of Vijayadurg, by way of a scenic back road running along the Konkan Coast. Malvan can also be approached from Kasal on NH17, 34 km. east, about 115 km north of Panaji. Malvan is a typical fishing village, with old wooden stores and residences crowding the busy waterfront. This faces a curving palm-fringed bay, sheltered from the ocean by rocks and reefs, including the island fort of Sindhudurg, about 1 km. south of the port (private boats available). The collapsing relics of *Padmagad*, a lesser citadel, can be approached by a causeway at low tide.

In about 1665 Shivaji selected Malvan as his coastal headquarters, fortifying the nearby islands, and installing members of his family as governors. Three years were required before the walls of Sindhudurg were completed; some 6,000 workmen, including Portuguese experts, are supposed to have been employed. With the division of Shivaji's territories between the Maratha chiefs in 1713, Malvan came under the control of the Kolhapur rulers. The port was taken by the Portuguese in 1746, and 20 years later by the British, who then returned it to Kolhapur. Like Vijayadurg, Sindhudurg was notorious for its aggressive attacks on European shipping. The port was finally ceded to the British in 1812.

Sindhudurg is the most remarkable of Shivaji's coastal citadels. Its *Fortifications* extend for more than 3 km., following the irregular indentations of the island. The walls, some 4 m. thick and up to 10 m. high, are partly damaged by the sea on the west. More than 50 round towers, spaced at regular intervals, have slit holes and rectangular openings for cannon. The citadel is entered through a single gate near the north-east corner of the island. This is concealed by curving outworks, on top of which is a guardroom with arched windows. The gate has a single opening bridged by a lintel set in arched recesses. Lime impressions of handprints and footprints, popularly believed to be those of Shivaji himself, are seen on the inner faces of the tower immediately north of the gate.

From the gate a path runs west through coconut groves to the *Shivarajeshvara Temple*, erected in 1695 by Ramaram, Shivaji's second son. The temple is unique since it enshrines a sculpted portrait of Shivaji himself, now much venerated. The great warrior is shown seated, wearing a gilded mask. The sanctuary is preceded by a hall with triple vaulted aisles, later extended; a stepped pyramidal tower capped by domical finial rises over the sanctuary. The path continues to the *Mahadeva Temple*, originally a well, with a small linga placed in a side niche. Beyond lies the Bhavani temple.

Except for overgrown rubble walls, and small step-wells, the interior of Sindhudurg is devoid of features, The fortifications skirt a small beach at the southwest corner of the island, an ideal picnic spot.

9. Sholapur

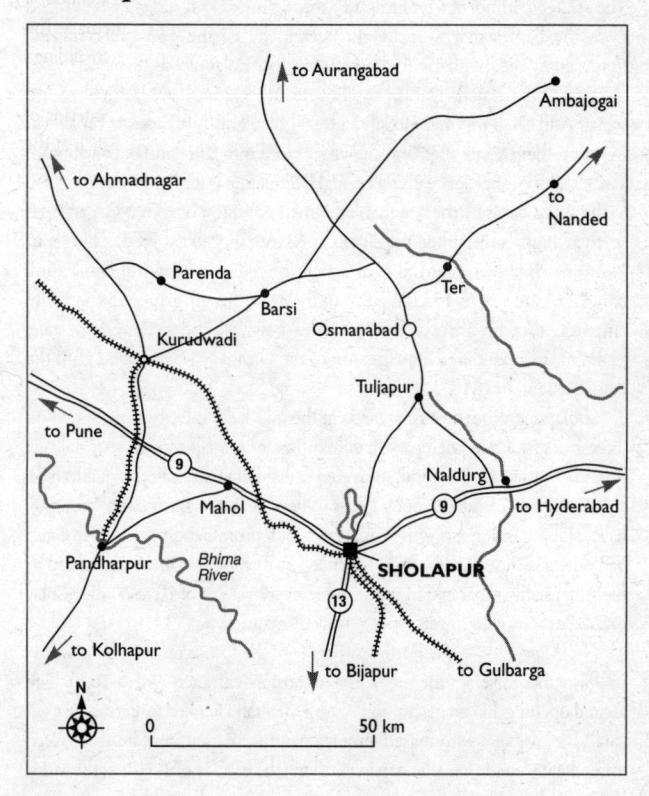

The city of Sholapur is located in the extreme south of Maharashtra, at the junction of NH 9, linking Pune [3] and Hyderabad [26], with NH 13, running south to Bijapur [23] and Hampi [20] in Karnataka. Sholapur is a lively manufacturing centre, best known for its machine woven blankets, sheets and shawls. But it is also a place of historical importance, with a prominent fort and several temples [A], making a stay here worthwhile.

From Sholapur it is possible to make day excursions to the imposing citadels at Naldurg [B] and Parenda [G], the popular Hindu pilgrimage temples at Tuljapur [C] and Pandharpur [H], and the ancient site of Ter [D]. A visit to the monuments at Ambajogai [E] and, beyond, the Sikh shrine at Nanded [F], however, will require one or more overnight halts.

A. SHOLAPUR

The strategic importance of this city through the centuries may be judged from the battles that were fought over it during the 16th-18th centuries. Founded by the Bahmanis in the 14th century, Sholapur was disputed by the rulers of both Ahmadnagar [6] and Bijapur. In 1532 Burhan Nizam Shah and Ismail Adil Shah met here to sign a treaty of friendship, but war broke out between them soon after, and the city passed into the hands of Bijapur. In 1623 Malik Ambar successfully besieged Sholapur, but the fort was returned to the Adil Shahis by the Mughals after their conquest of Ahmadnagar. Even so, the Mughals reclaimed the city in 1668. Aurangzeb camped at Sholapur in 1686 while planning the final assault on Bijapur. Nizamul Mulk took control of the city in 1723 in a bid to throw off his allegiance to the Delhi emperor, thereby absorbing it into the newly founded Asaf Jahi state. Sholapur remained in the possession of the Nizams of Hyderabad until the British assault in 1818.

Sholapur's impressive *Fort* stands in the middle of the city, surrounded on three sides by a tree-lined park that incorporates a small zoo; an artificial lake extends to the east. The double-layered walls define an irregular quadrangle, some 320 by 175 m. The outer lower walls, which date from Bahmani times, have sloping sides, polygonal bastions and prominent guard-rooms and battlements. The moat is now mostly filled in. The inner higher walls added by the Adil Shahis, separated from the outer layer by a gap of 10 to 20 m., display round bastions with towers, occasionally dismantled.

The *Main Gate*, at the northeast corner of the fort, is reached by a timber walkway that traverses the moat. The innermost entrance, with a 10 m. high arched opening, has an inscription of Ali Adil Shah I flanked by carved lions. A small *Jami Mosque*, with reused temple columns, brackets and beams, is seen immediately on the left after passing through the gate. The interior of the fort is now a public garden with fountains, much enjoyed by the local population.

The other significant feature of Sholapur is the *Siddheshvara Temple*, which stands in the middle of the lake to the east of the fort, from where there are fine views of the ramparts. This religious monument commemorates a Hindu saint who died here in 1167, and who came to be worshipped in deified form as Siddheshvara. It is believed that the city achieved prosperity under his auspicious blessings. The saint is particularly revered by members of the Lingayat sect.

Reached by a causeway from the south, the temple stands in a fortified enclosure, with an arched gateway on the west. The garden within the enclosure contains the samadhi, in which the saint is entombed, as well as altars for fire offerings. A wooden colonnade within surrounds the square sanctuary of the temple, in which small lingas covered with gilded brass face-masks, all representing Siddheshvara, receive worship. A painted plaster spire rises above. A large clock is set into the Neo-Classical gable on the front.

Sholapur is furnished with fine civic buildings. The Neo-Gothic *City Corporation* stands in a small park on the main road near the central stadium. Its polished basalt columns, interlaced pointed arches, projecting balconies and octagonal pavilions are painted in striking painted colours. The similarly styled N.G. Mills has a tall octagonal tower.

B. Naldurg

Overshadowed by a magnificent fortress, this small town is located on NH9, 45 km. east of Sholapur. Naldurg served as the headquarters of the Bijapur rulers on their various military campaigns. It was later occupied by the Mughals and the forces of the Nizams.

The *Fort*, at the east end of the town, is dramatically sited on basalt bluffs that rise up sheerly to 60 m. above the Bori River. The ramparts define an approximately quadrangular plateau to the west, from which a long promontory extends north into a great bend in the river. Walls cut off the constricted neck by which these two zones are joined. A third enclosure on the other side of the river, roughly circular in shape, is connected with the northern promontory by a wall thrown across the river. This creates a dam that ensured the fort with adequate water supply.

Sloping walls with slit holes are buttressed by massive circular bastions with guardrooms on top. Two bastions on the west take variant square and lobed shapes. The battlemented parapet has mostly fallen. The principal gate to the fort, on the west, is set between bastions in double lines of walls. Domed structures, possible stables, now much dilapidated, stand immediately inside. From here a street runs through the quadrangular fort. The *Mosque* in the middle dates from 1560, in the early years of the Adil Shahi occupation. Its arches display both pointed and lobed profiles, with ornate arabesque ornamentation in the roundels above.

To the north of the mosque are the ruins of a *European Villa*, built for the representative of the Nizam, but occupied for several years by Colonel Meadows Taylor, the British Resident, formerly of Shorapur [24H], after he took command of Naldurg in 1853. Delicately worked friezes with Neo-Classical patterns contrast with the massive stonework of the ramparts against which the villa is built. One room leads to a balcony jutting out over the river. A *Palace* set into the east walls of the fort, a short distance away, consists of a domed chamber with balconies projecting over the tops of the walls, and a small hammam, both of which open off a court with a fountain.

A walk of almost 500 m. is required to reach the promontory extension to the north. Almost at the end is a remarkable *Lookout Tower*, built as an isolated circular bastion, more than 30 m. in diameter. A long fight of steps ascends to the top, from where a fine panorama may be had of the entire fort. Here is mounted a canon with an animal head. The large *Granary* immediately to the east has pointed vaults roofing two long chambers, with domes at the ends. A small viewing pavilion is set into the west walls of the promontory extension. The *Dam* on the Bori River serves as a causeway to the smaller circular fort on the opposite bank. A balcony beneath the causeway belongs to an unusual water palace built into the dam wall.

C. TULJAPUR

This popular pilgrimage centre is located 40 km. northeast of Sholapur, and almost the same distance directly from Naldurg. The Bhavani temple here attained fame in the 17th century as the shrine of the goddess who rewarded Shivaji with the legendary sword, thereby inspiring him to victory. (A sign in the temple indicates that this weapon is now on display in the British Museum; there is, however, no record of it in London.) Shivaji sought the blessings of Bhavani before embarking upon all important expedition; her name is even supposed to have been shouted as a battle cry by the Maratha troops. Two fairs held at Tuljapur each year, one in September-October, the other in April, attract huge crowds from all over Maharashtra.

The *Bhavani Temple* dates mainly from the Maratha period, but has been substantially remodelled in recent years. It occupies the west slope of a hill, beside a small stream. Steps descend from the crowded bazaar at the top of the hill, past an attractive fountain, the *Gomukh Kund*, named after the sculpted cow head out of which water gushes. The *Kallol Kund*, nearby is surrounded by steps. *Gateways* with plain arched openings, arranged in a descending sequence, leads to the main enclosure of the temple.

The main shrine is surrounded by arcades that follow the polygonal outline of the enclosure. The east facing sanctuary is of little interest, except for its tapering 12-sided spire. This is divided into three stages, and capped with double petalled domes, all brightly painted; the plaster niches are filled with relief sculptures of deities and sages. The sanctuary is approached through an inner mandapa with doorways set into arched recesses, and an outer mandapa with 16 columns and balcony seating on three sides. The pavilion has arched openings standing freely in front, topped with a shorter but similar spire; it is used for fire sacrifices. An arched gate in the west wall of the compound leads to a flight of steps that descends to the village in the plain beneath.

D. TER

This small town (sometimes spelt Thair), 80 km. northeast of Sholapur via Osmanabad, rose to prominence under the Satavahanas in the 1st-2nd centuries CE. Ter's ancient commerce with the Mediterranean is confirmed by the many Roman coins unearthed here. The town is even mentioned in the famous Roman travel work, the *Periplus of the Erythrean Sea*, as one of the two premier centres in this part of India, the other being Paithan [5L]. Ter rose again to prominence in the 11th-12th centuries, when it served as the headquarters of a branch of the Shilahara rulers of Kolhapur [8A].

Excavations in and around the town have yielded old bricks, pottery fragments, beads, garlands, combs, conch shells, and artistically worked ivories. A selection of these artefacts are displayed in the *Ramalingappa Lamture Museum* (closed Mondays) at the entrance to the town. Among the Satavahana items shown here are terracottas, pots, beads, jewellery, coins and lamps; portions of a limestone railing from a Buddhist stupa; and fine worked stucco heads and stone figurines of goddesses. (The celebrated ivory statuette of a yakshi from Ter is generally stored in a bank.) A superbly modelled, though damaged standing image of Narayana dating from the 7th-8th century Early Chalukya era comes from the Trivikrama temple. A remarkable item is a Shilahara period wooden temple doorway adorned with stylised foliation and a row of divinities.

The most important of Ter's ancient monuments is the *Trivikrama Temple*, near the river at the north end of the town. This dates back to Satavahana times, making it the oldest standing structure in Maharashtra. Though substantially renovated over the centuries, it preserves its original apsidal-ended plan and curving vault, features familiar from rock-cut chaitya halls. The shrine was originally a Buddhist foundation, but was later converted to Hindu usage. It is built of plastered brickwork without internal columns, the roof consisting of a smoothly curved vault. The large horseshoe-shaped arch on the front frames a later image of Hanuman. The damaged, but still impressive 1.5 m. high stone image of Trivikrama under worship in the sanctuary probably dates from the Early Chalukya period; it shows the god with one leg kicked up high. A comparable statue of Karttikeya riding the peacock is worshipped in a side shrine.

E. Ambajogai

This small town, some 160 km. north of Sholapur via Osmanabad, is known for its many temples, attractively situated on both banks of the Jayanati River. Ambajogai was an important centre in Yadava times, judging from the numerous monuments found here dating from the 12th-13th centuries. The dilapidated *Sakaleshvara Temple* to the west of the town is situated amidst collapsed blocks overgrown with bushes. Only the 12 central columns of the mandapa, complete with figural carvings, still stand. To the north of the town is the *Kholeshvara Temple*, also assigned to the Yadava era, though much rebuilt. It preserves its original doorway, decorated with river goddesses and guardians.

The town takes its name from the *Jogai Temple*, located in the centre of the town. Of greater artistic interest is the *Yogeshvari Temple* in a fortified compound on the west bank of the Jayanti River. This is entered through a gateway on the south, surmounted by a musicians' gallery. The 12-sided brick and plaster spire over the sanctuary is typical of the Maratha period. Its lowest stage has corner pavilion-shaped finials.

About 500 m. to the northeast, on the river bank, are the *Hattikhama Caves*, assigned to about the 11th century. The complex consists of a line of rock-cut chambers approached through a long columned hall with a court. Two huge stone elephants face the entrance. In the middle of the court stands a pavilion sheltering a Nandi image.

F. NANDED

Site of the most celebrated Sikh shrine in Maharashtra, Nanded is located on the Godavari River, 150 km. northeast of Ambajogai, a total of more than 300 km. from Sholapur, or about 270 km southeast of Aurangabad [5]. Nanded can also be reached from Bidar [25] in northern Karnataka, 185 km. to the south.

According to Sikh tradition, the tenth and final Guru, Gobind Singh, travelled to Nanded in August 1708 to meet with Bahadur Shah, the Mughal emperor who was stationed there on his Deccan campaign. However, the friendship that grew up between the Gobind Singh and Bahadur Shah was opposed by the Mughal nobles, and the Guru was assassinated in October that same year. Before dying he bestowed his succession on the holy book of the Sikhs, the Guru Granth, thereby bringing the line of Gurus to an end.

The great *Shrine* that stands on the bank of the Godavari on the edge of the town is largely the work of the Sikh ruler of Lahore, Ranjit Singh, in the early 19th century. Built in imitation of Sikh gurudwaras in the Panjab, the Nanded shrine is a two storeyed building, embellished in the late Mughal manner with lobed arched recesses and domical balconies. It is topped by a square rooftop chamber with a fluted dome, a characteristic motif of Sikh religious architecture. The chamber is framed by a rooftop parapet with prominent corner pavilions. The flat-roofed, double-height interior houses the Guru Granth Sahib, as well as personal relics of Gobind Singh, such as swords, shields and daggers. The chamber is overlooked by a gallery at the upper level. The shrine stands in a marble paved courtyard surrounded by subsidiary structures.

G. Parenda

This small town, 96 km. northwest of Sholapur via Barsi, is famous for its fort, one of the most perfect specimens of military architecture in Maharashtra.

Parenda was founded during the late 15th century by Mahmud Gawan, Prime Minister of Muhammad Shah of Bidar. It was taken from the Bahmanis by the Nizam Shahis, and subsequently passed several times between them and the Adil Shahis, until it was seized by the Mughals in 1657. It was eventually occupied by the Nizams of Hyderabad.

The *Fort* comprises a quadrangle of double walls, the outer faces of which incline inwards slightly. They are topped with battlemented parapets with regularly spaced box-shaped guardrooms. The outer lower line of walls has polygonal bastions, doubled at the corners; the inner higher line displays circular bastions on the west, where a polygonal bastion accommodates a small mosque. Many bastions are still mounted by cannon. A moat runs around the outside of the walls.

The *Main Gate*, at the northeast corner of the fort, consists of a line of three arched openings with intermediate courts. The first entrance projects into the moat, where it was originally approached by a drawbridge. The robust teak doors are protected by iron plates and spikes. The cannon placed on the corner bastion rising above the gate is embellished with Persian calligraphy in cartouches, friezes of palmettes and reliefs of lions.

Situated to the right immediately on entering the fort is the *Armoury*. Some 300 stone cannonballs are stored in one of its vaulted chambers. To the south is the rectangular compound of the *Jami Mosque*, entered through an arched opening on the north wall, as well as through a domed gateway on the east. The prayer hall, which is assigned to the 16th century Nizam Shahi period, employs temple-like columns with blocks, capitals and brackets, decorated with stylised ornamentation; the outer row is sheltered by an angled overhang. The 27-bayed interior is roofed with flat slabs decorated with lotus medallions. The two bays at the north end of the hall are screened off. Triple stone windows are placed in each of the end walls. The mihrab is of delicately worked polished basalt. It is distinguished on the exterior rear wall by a pair of minaret-like finials.

West of the mosque stands the *Hammam*, now a depository of loose stone carvings. It opens off a small court with a raised area on the south, possibly once used for formal assemblies. A short distance west is a deep octagonal step-well surrounded by arcades. The *Ruined Palace* nearby is entered through an arched gate. Only the raised floor area facing towards an open court can now be made out.

The ground to the south and east of the fort permits access to the top of the walls. Overgrown piles of rubble indicate numerous collapsed and buried structures.

H. PANDHARPUR

This pilgrimage town, the most frequented in Maharashtra, lies on the bank of the Bhima River, 75 km. west of Sholapur via Mohol on NH9. Paharpur is crowded with shrines, monasteries, rest houses and shops, all of which cluster around the Vithoba temple. This monument faces a busy street that leads to the bathing ghats, about 400 m. to the east.

In spite of the antiquity of the cult of Vithoba, known as Vithala in the 13th century (this name has recently been revived), little that predates the Maratha period can now be seen. The shrines of Pandharpur were much developed in the middle of the 17th century during the time of Shahji, the father of Shivaji, and also under the Holkars and Shindes in the second half of the 18th century. The number of visitors to the temple reaches vast numbers during festival time in June-July. On this occasion, saintly persons from all over Maharashtra are carried in palanquins to Pandharpur by singing devotees belonging to the Akari sect.

The *Vithoba Temple* is dedicated to Vishnu in the form of a standing figure, with two hands resting on the hips. Though barely 1 m. high and probably no earlier than the 17th century, this unique image is held in great veneration. According to legend, the original icon was removed at the beginning of the 14th century to save it from the sacrilege of the Delhi invaders, after which it was taken to Hampi, where it was installed in a specially built temple there [20B].

The Pandhapur Vithoba temple occupies a rectangular walled compound, 106 by 52 m. The main entrance, on the east, is through a columned porch and arched gate, beside which are traces of a 13th century structure. The court within is surrounded by arcades, partly occupied by a lofty wooden structure of recent construction. Two stone lamp columns, more than 10 m. high, stand near a pipal tree. The main shrine is approached through two mandapas, both with columns embellished with carved blocks on the shafts, circular capitals and ornate brackets. Other halls open off to the side, that on the south with elaborate columns. The doorways are covered with embossed silver sheets. The exterior plinth and walls of the sanctuary are enlivened with sharply cut mouldings; projecting niches framed by pilasters contain images of Venugopala (north), Krishna on Kaliya (west), and Anantashayana (south). The spire that rises above has multiple projections rising in stages, marked by pilastered niches that contain seated deities. Subsidiary shrines for Rukmini and Mahalakshmi occupy the west corners to the rear of the main sanctuary. Both have vividly coloured spires.

Steps descend to the sandy bed of the Bhima, where many of Pandharpur's holiest shrines are located. *Pundalika's Temple* is an octagonal funerary monument commemorating the spot where a disciple of Vithoba spend the last years of his life. After his death he was buried here, and a linga was set with a brass finial. Nearby *Tukuram's Temple*, built in memory of another holy figure has an arcaded sanctuary topped with a 12-sided tower rising in three stages. *Vishnupad's Temple*, reached by a small causeway, is notable for the funerary ceremonies performed by pilgrims, known as shraddas. Its mandapa shelters natural rocks carved with footprints, believed to be those of Krishna and a cow.

Other important shrines stand in walled compounds next to the Holkar and Shinde mansions that crowd the high bank of the river. The *Dvarkadishvara Temple* has massive circular bastions at the corners of its fortified enclosure. The sanctuary within is topped with a slender octagonal spire. The *Ramachandra Temple*, to the north, enshrines white marble images of Rama, Lakshmana and Sita. A figure to the left represents Ahilyabai, royal patroness of the monument in the late 18th century.

10. Nagpur

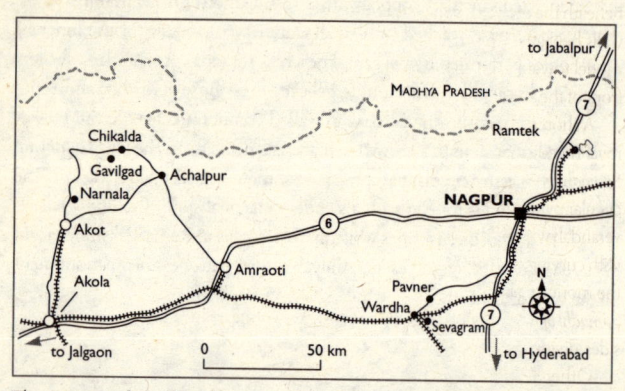

The major industrial and commercial centre of northeastern Maharashtra, Nagpur is located in Vidarbha, the hilly wooded region that is the habitat of the Gond peoples. Famous for its and cotton and silk weaving and for its orange groves, the city also preserves a number of monuments associated with the local Bhonsale rulers [A]. Half-day trips may be made to the sacred hill at Ramtek [B], north of Nagpur, and to the Gandhi Memorial near Wardha [C] to the south.

Longer journeys with overnight stays will be required to the reach the historic town of Achalpur [D], and the nearby hill resort and forts at Chikalda and Gavilgad [E], and Narnala [F].

A. Nagpur

Spreading along the north bank of the Nag River, Nagpur was founded in the 18th century by the Gond chief Bakht Buland. In 1740 it became headquarters of the Bhonsale Marathas who rose to prominence under the Peshwas of Pune [3]. Nagpur was sacked by resurgent Gonds in 1756, after which it came under the protection of the East India Company. The Bhonsale troops rebelled in 1817, but the English forces prevailed and Nagpur thereafter became capital of the Central Provinces.

Old Nagpur in the southern part of the city, known as Mahal, still preserves its arched entrance gates. The Police Station, originally the queen's palace, is a vestige of the Bhonsale period. It is built in a sombre late Mughal manner, with double-storeyed arcades framed by domical corner towers. The nearby Post Office occupies another royal structure. A walled compound in the vicinity accommodates the east facing *Raghurajeshvari* and *Rukmini Temples*, typical examples of the 18th century Maratha architectural style promoted by the Bhonsales. Both temples are approached through wooden mandapas with lobed arcades. The yellow sandstone sanctuaries have complicated star-shaped plans, with multiple angled corners. Basements are decorated with sharply cut friezes of animals, attendants, monster heads and petalled designs. Figures of divinities occupy the wall niches; cut-out sculptures of Krishna with gopis serve as brackets beneath the overhang. The curving towers that rise above repeat the angles of the walls beneath. The central bands have flat geometric patterns flanked by tiers of model towers, each capped with a circular ribbed element. A marble pavilion in front of the Rukmini temple houses a kneeling image of Garuda.

A short distance southeast of Old Nagpur is *Navi Shukrawari*, where a group of royal memorials associated with the Bhonsales stands in a leafy compound. The *Samadhi of Raghuji I*, who died in 1755, has a central linga shrine topped with a circular pyramidal tower divided into shallow facets. The shrine is surrounded by a verandah with pointed arches, projecting as porches on four sides; domed pavilions with curving cornices crown the porches and corners bays. Carvings at the base of the monument show mythological figures and courtly processions. The adjacent *Samadhi of Raghuji III*, a later ruler, is crowned by a square tower with gently curving sides, divided into horizontal facets. The verandah is lined with lobed arches.

Other features associated with the Bhonsales are scattered throughout Nagpur. The *Sukrawari Talao* is a large rectangular tank in the central part of the city. The Shiva temple that stands at its southeastern corner has a red sandstone sanctuary with a star-shaped plan, topped by an intricately worked tower. Delicately carved ornamentation frames the upper chamber on the east face. The buff-coloured sandstone pavilion in front has lobed arcades.

Sitabaldi, the fort established by the British when they occupied Nagpur, extends over a low scrubby hill (permission required to visit). It has two rings of defences, with occasional bastions for gun emplacements. The inner enclosure is occupied by barracks and administrative buildings. The *Bhonda Mahadeva Temple* on the south flank of Sitabaldi is a small but intricately decorated building. Ramayana and Krishna scenes are carved in flat relief on the curving bands of the tower. Wall panels in the porch show yogic forms of Shiva (right) and Vishnu (left).

Spacious tree-lined streets of the former British Cantonment extend to the northwest of the fort. This part of Nagpur is dominated by the *Cathedral of All Saints*, a bland Neo-Gothic project of 1851. Its stone tower with corner pinnacles were added in 1879.

Immediately west of Sitabaldi is the *Central Museum*, established in 1863 (closed Mondays). The archaeology and sculpture galleries display antiquities brought from nearby 11th-13th century temple sites. One of the finest exhibits, Vishnu and Lakshmi riding on Garuda, however, comes from Mandhal; a sanctuary doorway, surrounded by miniature figures, is from Narasingpur, in Madhya Pradesh. Items from distant Southern Indian sites include Buddhist bronzes from Nagapattinam [40M]. The art gallery has various metal and ivory objects, as well as a series of miniature paintings from the Bhonsale period. Wooden memorial posts with unusual carved designs, erected by Gond and Korku people, are shown in the anthropology section.

A short distance west of the Central Museum is the *High Court*. This imposing Neo-Classical styled edifice dates from the last years of British domination. The yellow sandstone complex was built in 1937-42 to designs by Henry Medd, who had worked with Sir Edwin Lutyens in New Delhi. The court is dominated by a central entrance portico, with four Ashokan-type columns, approached by a broad staircase. Above rises a high circular drum, with corner domed pavilions, carrying a smooth hemispherical dome. This is relieved by bands of stupa-like railings. Colonnaded galleries extend to either side.

B. RAMTEK

Located 48 km. north of Nagpur, a short distance east of NH17, Ramtek is famous for its red sandstone hill, known as Ramagiri, believed to be the residence of the god Rama. The hill rises 150 m. above the town, on its eastern flank. The shrines that cluster within the fortified citadel at its summit are a popular destination for pilgrims, especially during the fair in October-November.

Ramtek is associated with the 4th-5th century Vakatakas, who had their capital at Nandivardhana, 5 km. southwest of the hill. Portions of temples, sculptures and inscriptions at Ramtek are assigned to these early rulers. In the 12th-13th centuries Ramtek was incorporated into the kingdom of the Yadavas. The temples erected at this time suffered at the hands of the Delhi invaders, and were virtually abandoned until the 18th century, when the Bhonsales of Nagpur undertook major restoration work. Raghuji I had the images of Rama and Sita installed here in about 1750, thereby reviving religious rituals at the site.

The tour of Ramtek begins at *Ambala Lake*, at the base of the southern extremity of the hill, 2 km. southeast of the town. The road passes through an arched gate, framed by round bastions and topped with a crenellated bastion. The lake beyond is ringed with shrines and memorials from the Bhonsale period crowned with curved and pointed spires.

The route ascending gradually from the lake to the fortified citadel at the top of Ramagiri is now little used; a new, more steeply climbing road is preferred. This winds upwards until it arrives at the *Kalidasa Memorial*, a modern 12-sided structure with a curved roof. The interior provides a setting for painted scenes from the Sanskrit poetry and plays of Kalidasa, the famous 5th century author who resided for a time at Nandivardhana. From here there is a fine panorama of the walls that ring the summit of the hill. Nearby stands the *Kevala Narasimha Temple*, a modest red sandstone structure, much restored. This accommodates a worn 5th century image of seated Narasimha, with the right hand of the god resting on a disc. An inscribed slab of the Vakataka era is set into the walls. A path through the undergrowth leads to the nearby *Rudra Narasimha Temple*, which houses an almost identical image.

From here it is a short distance to *Varaha Gate*. Just outside stands a small mosque with triple domes, erected in memory of one of Aurangzeb's courtiers. Immediately on the right after passing through the arched entrance is an open pavilion. This shelters a large sculpture of Varaha, dating from the 5th century. Steps to the left of the gate lead to the *Bhogarama Temple*, a small Vakataka period structure, much altered. Its twin sanctuaries house 19th century images of Rama and Vishnu; a marble image of Krishna is placed in the central niche of the porch.

The path winds around *Simha Gate*, entrance to the first and lowest walled enclosure of the citadel at the summit of Ramagiri. This quadrangular compound is contained by massive walls with prominent bastions, all dating from the Bhonsale period. In the middle of the west side of the enclosure is *Bhairava Gate*, which gives access to the second, intermediate enclosure of the citadel. This is built at a slightly higher level and is also contained by ramparts. The gate has a lobed arch with Mughal styled niches at either side. In the southeast corner of the enclosure stands the small *Radha Krishna Temple*. A deep rectangular tank and the small *Dasharatha Temple* occupy the southwest enclosure; the latter is fronted by a porch with sculptures, now worn and whitewashed.

To the right of Dasharatha temple is *Gokul Gate*, entrance to the third and highest enclosure of the citadel, extending across the level top of Ramagiri. The triple-storeyed gate has interior columns supporting upper galleries, partly blocked up. The structure dates from the Yadava period, as do the temples beyond. All these structures were substantially renovated by the Bhonsales.

The *Lakshmana* and *Rama Chandra Temples* stand one behind the other at the western end of the third and topmost enclosure. They are the largest and most important religious monuments at Ramtek, invariably crowded with devotees. Each temple is approached through a mandapa with triple porch extensions. The adjoining sanctuary has a complicated faceted plan, carried up into the curving tower above which displays clustered miniature elements. The original carved decoration, damaged through the centuries, is obscured by thick whitewash. Subsidiary shines lining the sides of the enclosure are similarly whitewashed.

The tour continues by retracting the route back to Varaha Gate. The *Trivikrama Temple* that crowns a small rise 200 m. to the east of the gate consists of a damaged 5th century image of Vishnu with his leg kicked up high. From here there are fine vistas of the Jain complex and Khindisi Kund beneath the north flank of the hill.

2 km. north of Ramtek town is a *Jain Complex* dating from the Bhonsale era. The central monument, the west-facing *Shantinatha Temple*, has recently been clad in marble. It enshrines an almost 4 m. high, polished stone image. Side shrines, dedicated to other Jinas, preserve their original 19th century stonework. A short distance west of the complex is the *Kalanka Devi Temple*, a rare example from the 8th-9th century Rashtrakuta period. Its barrel-vaulted roof is raised on a sequence of eave-like mouldings.

The site of *Nandivardhana* is located 5 km. southwest of Ramtek. However, virtually nothing can now be seen of the 5th century Vakataka capital. The 18th century fort that stands here, however, is a fine example of Bhonsale military architecture. High walls with corner octagonal bastions define a quadrangular enclosure, entered on the north through a finely finished, Mughal styled gateway. Rich polychrome effects are achieved through the use of different coloured stones; a carving of Ganesha is seen over the arched opening,

C. WARDHA

The railway junction at Wardha, 62 km. southwest of Nagpur, is of national significance because of Mahatma Gandhi. In 1934 Gandhi selected Wardha as the headquarters of his mission, taking up residence in a nearby village from where he organised political gatherings over the next 13 years. Many decisions of importance, including deliberations such as the Quit India Proposal, were prepared and adopted here.

A small settlement 8 km. east of Wardhan, renamed *Sevagram*, Village of Service, was chosen by Gandhi for his home. *Bapu Kuti*, Gandhi's abode, is a simple cottage with mud walls and a tiled roof. Hand-spinning, initiated by the Mahatma, is still practiced in the village; meetings are held at the open air, multi-faith prayer ground.

At *Pavnar* on the Dharm River, 10 km. north of Wardha, is the *Gandhi Memorial*. This commemorates the spot where some of Gandhi's ashes were immersed after having been brought from Delhi, where the Mahatma was cremated.

D. ACHALPUR

This city, about 185 km. west of Nagpur via Amraoti, attained historical importance as Ellichpur, capital of Berar. Originally a province of the Bahmani kingdom of Bidar [25], Berar emerged as an independent state at the end of the 15th century, under the leadership of Fathullah Imad Shah. In 1491 this figure was encouraged by the governors of Ahmadnagar [6] and Bijapur [23] to proclaim his independence, thereby initiating the Imad Shahi dynasty. Alauddin, who succeeded Fathullah in 1510, participated in the struggles of the era, for a time aligning himself with the Nizam Shahis in an effort to combat the armies of Bijapur and Golconda [26E], and to withstand attacks from Gujarat and Malwa to the north. Burhan assumed the Ellichpur throne in 1562, and three years later participated in the famous battle against Vijayanagara [20B-C]. Berar's independence came to an end in 1572, when it was annexed by Ahmadagar, but the Nizam Shahis were in control only until 1590, when they were ousted by the Mughals. Claims on the region continued to be made by Ahmadnagar, and Ellichpur was occupied by Malik Ambar in 1620. After the city succumbed to Shah Jahan in 1636, Berar was finally absorbed into the Mughal empire. From there it came under the control of the Sultan Khans, subordinates of the Nizam of Hyderabad [26].

Achalpur's short lived role as the Imad Shahi capital is borne out by the dearth of features dating from this era in the city, though there are several earlier monuments. The *Idgah* of 1347 dates from the time of the Delhi conquest. It has a raised domed pavilion over the middle of the wall; only one of the corner minarets survives. The *Jami Mosque*, which is a 15th century Bahmani structure, has a facade of 11 arches.

Of greater architectural interest is *Hauz* Kaora, a ruined Imad Shahi palace 3 km. west of the city. The centrepiece of this complex is a triple-storeyed octagonal tower with arched openings on each side. The interior comprises two superimposed domed chambers. The tower stands in the middle of a circular pond.

E. CHIKALDA AND GAVILGAD

The resort of Chikalda occupies a 1,100 m. high plateau in the Satpura Ranges, 28 km. northwest of Achalpur. Attractively ringed by wooded slopes, the resort was established by the British in the 19th century as a sanatorium and coffee plantation. With its array of colourful birds and animals, Chikalda is a popular destination for nature lovers.

Some 3 km. to the southwest of Chikalda, at a slightly lower elevation, is the impressive fort of *Gavilgad*. Established in 1425 by Ahmad Shah of Bidar, Gavilgad later became the principal stronghold of the Imad Shahis. Double walls with round bastions define a stronghold, approached from the south, where the hill is steepest. Access to the interior is through a line of three gates flanked by guardrooms. The *Delhi Gate* is of particular interest for its sculpted symbols: lions clutching elephants with their paws, and, at either side of a spreading palm tree, a two-headed eagle holding elephants in each beak. The *Jami Mosque* of large dimensions, now dilapidated, occupies the highest point within the fort. The prayer hall is three bays deep behind a seven arched facade. Traces of blue tile decoration and fine stonework can still be made out. Other nearby structures were dismantled in 1858 when Gavilgad was occupied by British troops. The fort is shielded on the north and northeast by an outer ring of walls.

F. NARNALA

This remotely located citadel lies about 40 km. southwest of Chikalda, at the summit of a 1,000 m. high wooded hill, cut off from the main Satpura Range. Like Gavilgad, Narnala dates back to Bahmani times, having also been founded in 1425 by Ahmad Shah of Bidar. The citadel was occupied successively by the Imad Shahis, Nizam Shahis, Mughals and Marathas, before being taken finally by the British in 1818.

Narnala consists of three contiguous *Forts*. The inner fort encloses the upper plateau of the hill, with two smaller outer forts protruding at opposite angles. The battlemented walls, which vary from 8 to 13 m. high, are punctuated by 67 round towers. The fort is entered from the south through a sequence of three arched gates, built in pale cream sandstone. The innermost, *Third Gate* was erected by Fathullal Imad Shah in 1487, four years before he asserted his independence from the Bahmanis. It is profusely decorated with calligraphic designs and lotus medallions; an elaborate parapet runs along the top. Guardrooms projecting from the sides have arcaded balconies filled with delicately worked stone screens.

The area within the fort is dotted with *Decaying Buildings*, including fragments of an aqueduct and stone drains, ruins of a palace and a mosque, and overgrown piles identified as mint, arsenal, powder magazine and stables. Four curious cisterns are covered by a masonry platform with small apertures, with the remains of arches on top. A large cannon with a Persian inscription dated 1670 lies on the west side of the hill.

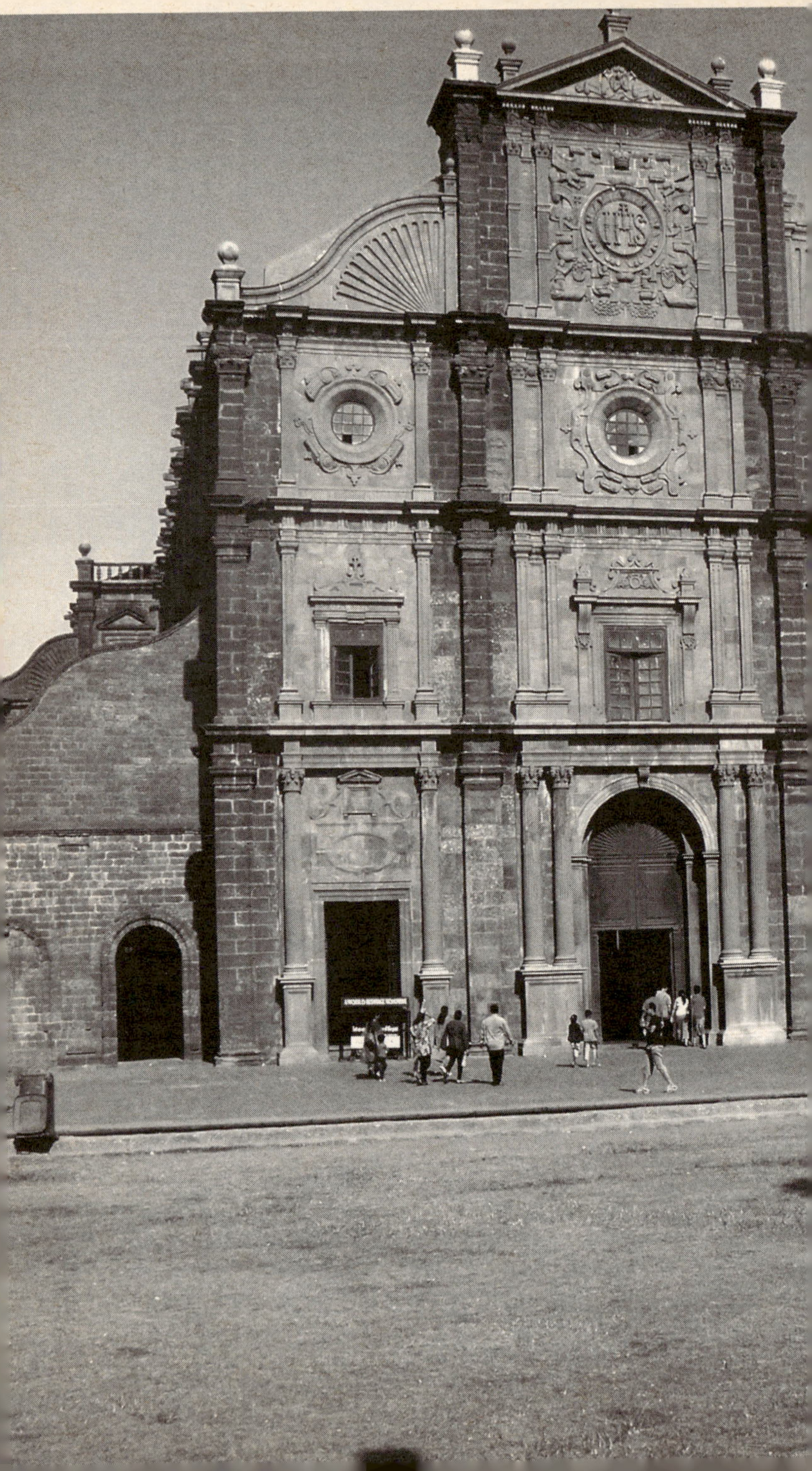

Basilica of Bom Jesus, Old Goa

GOA

Goa

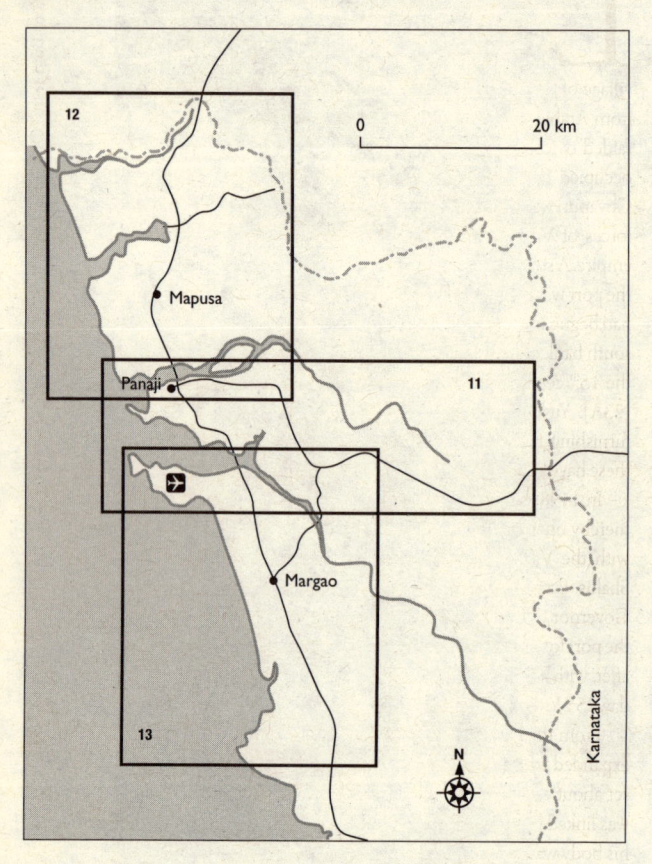

Little is known for certain about Goa until the 11th-13th centuries, when this part of the Konkan Coast came under the sway of the Kadambas. These rulers established themselves at Govapuri, on the north bank of the Zuari, a site marked today be the insignificant village of Goa Velha, on NH17. Govapuri became a major port where horses from Arabia were exchanged for pepper, cardamom and other spices. It was raided twice by the Delhi troops in the early 14th century, and subsequently occupied by the Bahmanis of Gulbarga [24A]. But the Bahmani hold on Govapuri was to last only a few decades. In 1378 the city was conquered by the forces of Vijayanagara [20B-C] and rapidly absorbed into their expanding empire. A struggle for control of the lucrative trade of Govapuri continued, and the port was retaken by the Bahmanis in 1470. By this time, however, the Zuari had begun to silt up and the Bahmanis shifted their headquarters to Ela, on the south bank of the Mandovi, at the spot now known as Old Goa. At the end of the 15th century the Bahmanis were displaced by the Adil Shahis of Bijapur [23A]. Yusuf Adil Khan, founder of the new dynasty, was responsible for furnishing Ela with great mosques, mansions and gardens, though none of these have survived.

In 1498 Vasco da Gama completed the first voyage from Europe to Asia, thereby opening up the direct link with India. The Portuguese made contacts with the Vijayanagara emperors, who encouraged them to expel the Adil Shahis from Goa. Led by Alfonso de Albuquerque, grandiosely entitled Governor of India, the Portuguese attached Goa in February 1510, but held the port for only a few months. Not to be deterred, Albuquerque returned soon after, with additional ships, and the city was finally captured on St Catherine's day, 25 November 1510.

From then on known as Cidade de Goa, City of Goa, the port was much expanded by Albuquerque, who provided it with defensive ramparts. He also set about establishing outposts at Aden, Ormuz and Malacca, to which Goa was linked by regular shipping routes. Albuquerque died in Goa in 1513, and his body was returned to Portugal shortly after. Under later governors, known as Viceroys, Goa was developed as the premier trading post in Asia, unsurpassed in wealth and grandeur. It was for a time the largest European settlement in Asia, with a population of more than 200,000. Goa also served as a base from where Catholic teachings were disseminated. Goa's most famous missionary was the Spanish Jesuit Francis Xavier, who landed here in 1542. In the same year a programme of religious persecution and enforced conversion was initiated. The Inquisition was imported to Goa in 1560, and remained in force until its abolition in 1774.

The Portuguese were challenged on several occasions by both Vijayanagara and Bijapur, but the European grasp on Goa remained firm. By 1543 the

Portuguese had expanded their territories to the districts around their capital, thus completing what came to be known as the 'Old Conquests'. The Adil Shahi threat continued after the fall of Vijayanagara in 1565, and Goa was besieged for almost 12 months by the Bijapur forces in 1570-71. In 1580 Portugal was absorbed into Spain, the enemy of England and Holland, both of whom attempted to expand their own interests in the Arabian Sea trade. Though the Dutch and English seized other Indian possessions of the Portuguese they did not succeed in conquering Goa. After gaining independence from Spain in 1640, Portugal signed a treaty of friendship with England, and there was no further claim on Portuguese territories.

The rise of Maratha power in the later decades of the 17th century signalled a new threat to the Portuguese. In 1680 Goa was occupied by a contingent of Maratha forces under Sambhaji, Shivaji's son. Fortunately for the Portuguese the Marathas retreated soon after, in order to deal with the Mughal advance into Maharashtra. A further incursion on 1739 resulted in a ruinous settlement for Goa. Additional lands were bequeathed to Goa towards the end of the 18th century by the British, in return for Portuguese assistance in subduing Haidar Ali of Srirangapattana [15C]. These gains, known as the 'New Conquests', included territories with predominantly Hindu populations. By this time, however, Goa had lost most of its commercial impetus and there was little attempt to convert these new peoples. The silting up of the Mandovi forced ships to dock further downstream at Panaji, to which the Viceroys eventually shifted. This port remained the capital of Portuguese possessions in India until 1961, when Goa was absorbed into the Indian Union.

11. Central Goa

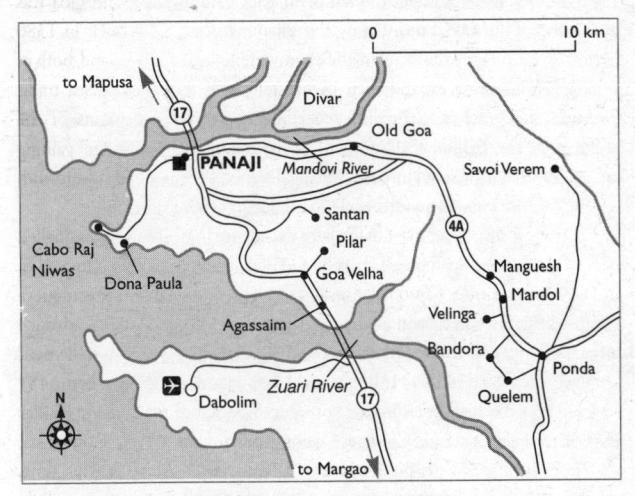

Historical sites are scattered all over the densely populated central districts of Goa that lie between the Mandovi and Zuari Rivers.

Panaji [A] and Old Goa [B], the present and past capitals of Goa, preserve religious and civic monuments spanning some 400 years of Portuguese rule. One full day should be reserved to follow the itineraries described here.

Another journey is to follow NH17 south of Panaji, taking in the recently restored cathedral of Santan [D], the seminary at Pilar [E], and the chapel at Agassaim [F]. Running east from Panaji, NH4 leads to Ponda, a predominantly Hindu district, dotted with temples built in a unique local style. The most interesting examples are those at Manguesh [G], Mardol [H], Velinga [I], Bandora [J] and Quelem [K]. A small mosque, the oldest in Goa, stands just outside Ponda itself [L]. An attractive side trip from here may be made to the rural temple at Savoi Verem [M]. Another half day will be required to reach the remote pre-Portuguese temple at Tambdi Surla [N].

A. Panaji

Formerly called Panjim, following the Portuguese pronunciation, this attractive city is built on the south bank of the Mandovi River, a short distance inland from its confluence with the Zuari. Panaji still preserves a distinctive Portuguese atmosphere. Its streets are lined with brightly painted houses and shops, many with cast-iron balconies and sloping tiled roofs. Before the Viceroys moved their residence here in 1759, Panaji was little more than a ceremonial landing place, with a riverside palace and a large church. In 1844 it became the official capital of Goa.

The tour of Panaji described here begins at the *State Secretariat*, overlooking the Mandovi. This marks the location of the palace erected by Yusuf Adil Khan at the end of the 15th century, known to the Portuguese as the Idalcao (Adil Shahi) palace. The palace was used by the Viceroys for a time before they established themselves at Old Goa. In time it came to be entirely remodelled, and was even provided with a private chapel. After 1918 when the Viceroys shifted their residence to Cabo Raj Niwas, the chapel was demolished and the palace converted into governmental offices. As it stands today, the Secretariat is an 18th century structure with a whitewashed Neo-Classical facade.

The small square on the west side of the Secretariat has a statue of Abbé Faria, a Goan priest who became celebrated in Paris as a hypnotist, dying there in 1819. Further west is the *High Court* of 1878, recognised by its Neo-Gothic windows. To the south is the *Municipal Garden*. This shaded open space is attractively planted with tropical trees and colourful flowers. A monumental column was set up here in 1898 to commemorate the 400th anniversary of Vasco da Gama's landing in India. Da Gama's bust has now been replaced by the lion capital that serves as India's national emblem.

The brilliantly whitewashed *Church of Our Lady of the Immaculate Conception* is built on the side of a hill near the northeast corner of the Municipal Garden. The church stands on an elevated terrace approached by double flights of balustraded steps, the only example of this feature in Goa. Founded in 1540, but entirely rebuilt in 1619, the church presents a somewhat severe facade with pilastered bays, flanked by single-storeyed square towers. The belfry that rises over the middle of the facade was added in 1871 to accommodate a bell brought from the ruined Augustinian church in Old Goa. The plain roofed interior is enhanced by the richly gilded main altar with a central tabernacle. A small statue of the Virgin occupies a blue painted niche above. The pulpit in the north wall has delicately carved details; so, too, the undersides of the canopy. A feast takes place here on 8 December.

Returning to the river visitors should take the second turn to the left beyond the Hotel Mandovi in order to reach the *Menzes Braganza Institute*, incorporating the Central Library. The institute was founded in 1817 by a wealthy philanthropist to promote the arts and sciences. The entrance is lined with blue and white azulejos tiles, manufactured in Portugal in 1935. They illustrate scenes from a literary work of Luis de Camões, the famous Portuguese author who visited Goa in the 16th century. The institute flanks the Police Headquarters, constructed in 1832 as barracks and administrative offices. These buildings form the west side of the *Azad Maidan*. The domed Neo-Classical pavilion in the middle of this square was erected in 1847, with slender Corinthian columns removed from a ruined church in Old Goa. The statue of Albuquerque that once stood here has been replaced by the tomb of Dr Tritao de Braganaza Cunha, hero of the Goan struggle for freedom. A modern memorial to him is seen nearby.

The tour of Panaji continues by returning to the Secretariat and proceeding east towards Ourem Creek. A small square here is overlooked by the Church of St Thomas. The *Post Office*, originally the Tobacco Exchange, and its neighbour, the former Mint, also face onto the square. Narrow streets running south lead to *Fontainhas*, a picturesque quarter with Portuguese styled houses, some converted into hotels, shops and restaurants. Here stands the *Chapel of St Sebastian*, built in 1888 in a Neo-Classical style, with superimposed pediments. Gilded altarpieces are on display within the church, as well as a painted wooden crucifixion taken from the dismantled chapel of the Idalcao palace. The *State Archaeological Museum* is located in an historical building near Fontainhas, on the other side of Ourem Creek. The small collection contains interesting portraits of Goa dignitaries.

A winding road ascends from Fontainhas to *Altinho*, the highest part of Panaji, from where fine views may be had over the Mandovi. The area is dotted with spacious villas, some with beautiful gardens. The grandiose Patriarchal Palace occupies the summit of Altinho.

B. OLD GOA

10 km. east of Panaji, further upstream on the Mandovi, formerly on NH4A, lies Old Goa. Its numerous cathedrals, churches and monasteries constitute the largest and most elaborate examples of European Baroque architecture and art in Southern India. They stand in a landscaped garden setting, that gives little impression that Old Goa was once a great trading city, crowded with civic buildings and grand mansions. With a few exceptions the religious monuments are in excellent condition, since they are jointly maintained by the local Christian community and the archaeological authorities.

The *Basilica of Bom Jesus*, housing the tomb of St Francis Xavier, is located on the south side of the square in the middle of Old Goa. Unlike the other nearby churches the basilica is missing its original plaster coating. The colonnaded west facade presents superimposed Corinthian, Doric and Ionic pilasters fashioned out of basalt set into laterite blocks. These frame doorways at the lowest level, windows at the intermediate level, and circular openings flanked by scrolls and palmettes at the top. The pedimented gable bears the letters 'IHS', the characteristic Jesuit motif, ringed by angels, some clutching ropes, and surmounted by a royal crown and a cross. The free-standing bell tower is placed at the rear of the building, south of the chancel. Flying buttresses on the sides are modern reinforcements. The Professed House attached to the west facade of the basilica was used as monastic quarters until its destruction by fire in 1633. A small teaching establishment is still run here by the Jesuits. The carved panel over the doorway repeats the 'IHS' motif.

Basilica of Bom Jesus, Old Goa.

Bom Jesus is laid out on an unusual cruciform plan, with prominent transepts. Two piers at the west end of the nave, supporting the choir gallery, have Portuguese and Latin inscriptions recording the foundation of the building in 1594, and its consecration in 1605. The heavily gilded altarpieces, among the finest of the period, contrast with the otherwise plain interior. The altar on the left immediately on entering has a polychrome sculpture of St Francis swaying in ecstasy. The high altar in the vaulted chancel is dominated by the statue of St Ignatius Loyola, founder of the Jesuit order. He contemplates the sunburst above, complete with the 'IHS' monogram held by flying cherubim. The Holy Trinity appears in the uppermost tableau. The composition is framed by gorgeously decorated twisted columns headed by a broken pediment. Similarly ornate altars beside the chancel show the Virgin (left) and St Michael (right). The pulpit set into the south wall of the nave is supported by seven angels with foliate bodies. Similar figures cover the back wall and canopy of the pulpit; the sides are carved with the four Evangelists and the four Doctors of the church in the presence of Christ.

The south transept of the basilica accommodates the *Chapel of St Francis Xavier*. The body of the saint, who died on a journey back from Japan in 1552, eventually made its way from to Goa. It was interred here in 1624, only two years after Xavier's canonisation. The tomb itself is the gift of Cosimo III, Grand Duke of Tuscany and a member of the famous Medici family. It was designed and manufactured by Giovanni Battista Foggini in Florence, from where it was shipped to Goa in 1698. The polychrome marble base is inset with bronze plaques depicting the missionary activities of St Francis. The scene visible from the nave shows the saint preaching in the Molucca Islands; one of the side panels shows the saint swimming to safety from the natives of the island of Morro. The silver casket above, in which the saint's body rests, is the work of local craftsmen and dates from 1636. The remains of St Francis are celebrated for their remarkable state of preservation. They are exposed once every ten years, for several weeks from 3 December, the anniversary of the saint's death. On these occasions the body is displayed in the cathedral on the other side of the square. However, not all of the saint's body is intact: one toe found its way to Lisbon, while a section of one arm was dispatched to the Church of Il Gesù in Rome!

A passageway, with tombstones of Goan grandees set into the floor, leads past the Chapel of St Francis, the tomb being viewed through openings on four sides. The *Sacristy*, which opens off the passageway, is entered through magnificently carved wooden doors, surrounded by sculpted stone bands. The 'IHS' motto appears in the pediment above. The sacristy, roofed with a coffered vault, is lined with superb inlaid wooden chests with brass plaques, containing clerical vestments. The apse accommodates a Crucifix set in bright blue azulejos; similar polychrome tiles decorate the altar in front. Steps to one side of the sacristy ascend to the *Art Gallery* (closed Fridays), where paintings illustrating the life of St Francis by a modern Goan artist are on display. From here it is possible to look down upon the tomb of the saint within the chapel. Double-storeyed arcades on noble proportions surround the adjoining garden cloister.

The tour of Old Goa continues by crossing the square in order to reach the group of religious buildings on its northern side. The *Sé*, or *Cathedral*, to the right, reputedly the largest church is Asia, was begun in 1562 by the Dominican order, under the patronage of Dom Sebastião, king of Portugal, apparently on the site of Yusuf Adil Khan's demolished mosque; some 90 years passed before it was completed. The cathedral's principal east facade presents three austere bays on two levels, with an additional pedimented stage in the middle framed by low volutes. The central door is flanked by pairs of fully modelled Corinthian columns. Only one of the two square corner towers still stands; that on the right collapsed after being struck by lightning in 1776. The triple-vaulted nave within, more than 37 m. high, is lined with deep side chapels separated by plain buttresses. The baptismal font in the side chapel to the right, immediately on entering, bears the date 1532; it is believed to have been used by St Francis himself. An interesting oil painting of St Christopher carrying the Christ child shows both figures in Indian dress.

The third chapel on the right, dedicated to the Miraculous Cross, has a carved wooden screen of exceptional workmanship. The high altar at the west end of the vaulted chancel is an assemblage of sculpted and gilded wooden panels portraying the life and martyrdom of St Catherine, to whom the cathedral is dedicated. The panels are framed by richly embellished Corinthian columns. Christ on the cross flanked by saints appears above, and Christ with the Evangelists and church leaders below. Gravestones bearing 17th and 18th century dates are set into the floor in front of the chancel.

Flanking the Sé on its north side is the *Archiepiscopal Palace*, how a Museum and Art Gallery (closed Mondays). This late 16th century complex, occupied until 1695, is now meticulously renovated. The interior halls, apartments and chapel are disposed at the upper level on three sides of a garden court. They are of interest for the elegant plaster wall panels, executed in the graffiato technique, by which a coloured plaster overlay is cut out to reveal patterns in the white underlay. Here wooden furniture, carvings and other ecclesiastical artefacts are on display.

The *Church of St Francis of Assisi* stands a short distance to the west. The present structure of 1682 replaces an earlier one, consecrated to the Holy Spirit in 1521. The west facade is flanked by unusual octagonal towers. The doorway in the middle is reused from the original building. It is the only example in Old Goa of the ornate Manueline style, named after Dom Manuel I of Portugal (1495-1521), recognised by the nautical motifs, including a pair of an astrolabes. The entrance is headed by lobed ribs, with pendant pomegranates and rosettes in panels. Although the church is no longer used for worship, it retains its elaborate altarpiece and coffered masonry ceiling. The pulpit has intricate carved foliation, the density of which reflects the skills of indigenous craftsmen. Oil paintings from the life of St Francis lie the chancel walls. A splendid, though faded altar occupies the rear wall. The panel in its pedimented top shows St Francis standing on a pedestal, being embraced by Christ on the cross. The central portion of the altar is opened up to create a miniature vaulted chamber accommodating the Tabernacle. Figures of the Evangelists in niches are set between Corinthian columns at either side. Equally fine carvings are seen in the altars flanking the nave. The floor of the church is almost entirely paved with tombstones.

The Franciscan convent to the north, with which the church was once linked, now houses the galleries of the *Archaeological Museum* (closed Fridays), the most important in Goa. The bronze statue of Albuquerque in the entrance hall was cast during the lifetime of the commander; it was for a time displayed in Panaji. The equally impressive metal portrait of Luis de Camões was recently removed from the square outside the museum. Carved stone figures in the first galleries are assigned to the 11th-12th century Kadamba period. They include an elaborate icon of Vishnu surrounded by miniature incarnations; Durga decapitating the buffalo demon; and the benign goddess Lakshmi. Hero stones depict martial exploits and naval battles. One example shows a royal personage sitting inside a palace, with warriors beneath. Coins and other items from the excavations at Chandrapura, near Chandor [13F], dating from the 3rd-4th centuries, are also on display. Additional sculptures are to be seen in the adjacent cloister. They include temple images, hero stones, some with battleships, and inscribed panels. A bronze statue of St Catherine, removed from the Arch of the Viceroys (see below), stands in the middle of the court, sheltered by a small pavilion.

The upper gallery of the Archaeological Museum is dedicated to the Portuguese period. Here are show wooden carvings removed from various churches and monasteries. There is also a complete series of Viceregal portraits, the earliest dating from 1547. Even Vasco da Gama makes an appearance, having served briefly as Viceroy in 1524. The oils are of interest for the static poses and ornate costumes.

The nearby *Chapel of St Catherine* marks the site of the first church, erected by Albuquerque in 1510. This was dedicated to the saint on whose special day the Portuguese scored their decisive victory, supposedly at this very spot. A plaque from the original building is set into the side wall of the present chapel, which dates from 1550, but was much restored subsequently. The unusually north-facing building has small flanking towers linked by volutes to a central pediment. A crumbling portion of the original laterite walls of the city is seen nearby.

The tour of Old Goa continues by returning to the front of the Sé, and passing by it on the way down to the river landing. The road passes through the *Arch of the Viceroys*, which once served as the principal ceremonial entrance to the city from the landing on the Mandovi. This is a modern replacement of the arch erected in 1599 by the Viceroy Francisco da Gama, incorporating a portrait of Vasco da Gama, his great-grandfather. Inscribed panels inside the arch record the various reconstructions. The plaque on the west is a memorial to Dom Joao IV, the first Portuguese king after the liberation from Spanish rule.

A dilapidated stretch of the city wall can be made out in the undergrowth east of the arch, but nothing remains of the Customs House that once stood nearby.

The road passing through the Arch of the Viceroys runs down to the ferry crossing to Divar Island in Mandovi. On top of the wooded rise in the middle of the island can be seen the whitewashed bulk of the Church of Our Lady of Piety. The path leading east from the arch leads to the Pastoral Institute and the *Church of St Cajetan*. Immediately inside the compound is a free-standing stone doorway with finely worked jambs and lintel, flanked by perforated screens. This is believed to have come from the Idalcao palace; if so, it must have been reused from a dismantled 12th-13th century temple. The church itself dates from 1656. It was erected by friars of the Italian Theatine order, who were based in Goa for several years. The west facade is modelled on St Peter's in Rome, though at a smaller scale, and with domical towers instead of side wings. The whitewashed facade presented a lofty pedimented portico with Corinthian columns; wall niches accommodate statues of the Apostles.

The interior of St Cajetan is dominated by the dome that rises on a circular drum over the crossing, the only example in Old Goa; it is supported on four great piers. Directly beneath is a covered well. The richly carved high altar at the east end of the nave is consecrated to Our Lady of Divine Providence. Angels here are larger than human size. A small crypt at the base of the altar has lead caskets, in which the embalmed bodies of the Viceroys were stored before being shipped back to Portugal for burial. Subsidiary altars at the ends of the transepts and in the corner bays are in the monumental Baroque manner; so, too, the pulpit with its supporting beasts and birds. The exuberant woodwork of the altar and pulpit contrasts with the starkly plains walls, coffered vaults and dome.

A short distance east of St Cajetan is the whitewashed *Gate of the Conception*, all that survives of the College of St Paul, erected in 1543 to train new converts. St Francis Xavier lodged at the college during his visits to Goa. It was in the nearby Chapel of St Francis Xavier that his remains were kept before being interred in Bom Jesus. The chapel was entirely rebuilt in 1884.

About 100 m. to the north, on the top of a wooded hill, stands the newly restored *Church of Our Lady of the Mount*. A plaque on the side wall at the west end of the building records that Yusuf Adil Khan's troops gathered on this hill in preparation for the battle with Albuquerque. The building has a whitewashed facade topped by a pediment. This gives access to a nave roofed with a coffered barrel vault. The panorama of Old Goa from the terrace in front makes the sleep ascent worthwhile.

The tour of Old Goa concludes with the monuments to the west of Bom Jesus. The first feature to be seen here is the Church of *St John of God*, begun in 1685 and now abandoned. Opposite is the *Convent of St Monica*, founded in the 17th century, but substantially remodelled and buttressed in later times. A formal garden in the middle of the convent is surrounded by a vaulted cloister with ceiling paintings (permission is required to visit). The associated Chapel of the Weeping (Miraculous) Cross is entered on the south through a pair of doors headed by pediments showing a ship (left) and a double-headed eagle (right); the inscribed plaque in the middle gives the date 1636. The altar in the nave is divided into nine round-headed niches filled with figures, with St Monica in the middle. Blue and white azulejos tiles line the lower portions of the chancel walls.

The apartment next to the Chapel has now been converted into the *Christian Art Museum* (no closed days), the finest in Southern India, thanks to a grant from the Calouste Gulbenkian Foundation in Lisbon. The objects were all made in Old Goa for various churches and monasteries, and date mainly from the 17th-18th centuries. Among the silver reliquaries, chalices, crowns, incense holders and other ritual items is a unique 140 cm. high monstrance fashioned as a pelican with a casket set into its chest. Embroidered vestments, capes and ceremonial flags are also on display. Ivory statuettes are of outstanding quality, especially an exquisitely carved 15 cm. high figure of Christ as the Good Shepherd, with a forest scene beneath. Larger ivories show the Infant Christ and Christ on the cross. Wooden carvings include multiple images of St Sebastian. Painted wooden panels are also exhibited, some set in enamelled frames. An inlaid chest with figural legs is the most elegant of several articles of furniture.

The road passing by the convent leads up the hill to the *Church of Our Lady of the Rosary*, at the western extremity of the site. The terrace here offers splendid views over the Mandovi River, from Divar Island to Panaji. The site is believed to mark the spot where Albuquerque witnessed the progress of the successful battle against the Bijapur troops. The church dates from 1549, making it the oldest intact structure standing in Old Goa. The west facade has full-height round towers at the corners, with a part-circular bell tower to one side. The towers are enlivened with sculpted bands fashioned as twisted ropes, a vestige of the nautically inspired Manueline style. The chief object of interest inside the church is a finely chiselled marble monument set into the left wall of the chancel. This commemorates Caterina de Sá, reputedly the first Portuguese woman to arrive in Goa. This incorporates a frieze of pilasters alternating with pots hanging from chains, exactly like a Muslim gravestone in Gujarat, from where no doubt it was brought. The geometric designs in sepia and white plasterwork on the chancery walls, however, are 19th century additions.

Descending to the Convent of St Monica visitors may take the other road running west in order to visit the impressive ruins of the *Church St Augustine*. A good idea of its layout may be had from the surviving walls and vaults. The church is dominated by a portion of a tower, one of a pair that flanked the west facade. Its five stages rise dramatically to a height of 46 m. The church dates from 1602, but the adjoining monastery was founded by the Augustinians in 1572. The complex fell into ruin after being abandoned in 1835, and the bell from the tower was transferred to the Church of Our Lady of the Immaculate Conception in Panaji. The Chapel of St Anthony on the other side of the road dates from 1534, but was entirely rebuilt in 1961.

The only feature of Old Goa that still needs to be noticed are two pillories formed from reused temple columns. One is set up in the garden close to the Archaeological Museum; the other is located a short distance at a road junction to the east of the main square.

C. Cabo Raj Niwas

The headland overlooking the confluence of the Mandovi and Zuari Rivers, with a distant prospect of the Arabian Sea, is one of the most spectacular sites in Goa. Here stands *Cabo Raj Niwas*, once the residence of Goa's Archbishops and Viceroys, now home of the Governor of Goa (permission required to visit).

This comfortable villa, with verandahs on all sides, houses a splendid collection of rosewood furniture, china and glass, mirrors and chandeliers. The building incorporates portions of a Franciscan monastery and chapel, the latter dated from 1594. Its interior is graced with an intricately carved pulpit.

D. Santan

The imposing Baroque monument at Santan is reached by following NH17 south of Panaji for 10 km., and then proceeding east for about 5 km. The grand scale of the *Church of St Anne* that stands here forms a striking contrast to the diminutive settlement that bears its name. A legend that St Anne, mother of the Virgin Mary, appeared here to the local population led to the dedication of the present structure in 1659.

The east facing church has corner square towers divided into five stages and topped by battlemented parapets with pinnacles. The facade has three broad cornices, with the central bays flanked by pairs of Corinthian columns. The pedimented top stage is framed by fan-shaped volutes; a recess here accommodates a figure of St Anne. The central pair of doors bears the date of the building's completion.

The interior, without aisles, is of majestic proportions. The nave is lined with deep semicircular niches with shell-shaped tops that support an upper gallery. Lighting is achieved by three tiers of windows in the niches and gallery above. Raised foliate medallions decorate the plastered barrel vault and the underside of the arch supporting the choir. The high altar is an impressive composition of carved and gilded woodwork, flanked by trios of twisted columns. The central portion is cut away to create a chamber for the tabernacle, lit dramatically by a rear window. The topmost panel of the altar, headed by a broken curved pediment, contains a sculpted tableau of St Anne, the Virgin and the Christ child. The side altars are equally ornate. The pulpit on the south wall is supported by six figures with fish-like bodies. Its sides, rear panel and canopy are all richly embellished.

E. GOA VELHA AND PILAR

The village of *Goa Velha* lies 11 km. south of Panaji on NH17. A signboard beside the highway identifies this as the site of Govapuri, headquarters of the Kadambas in the 12th-13th centuries, of which nothing can now be seen. A side road winds for a short distance through the fields before ascending a small hill to *Pilar Seminary*. In Kadamba times this was the site of a temple dedicated to Shiva, in the form of Govadeshara, from which the name Govapuri is derived. Evidence for this vanished Hindu monument comes from stray sculptures discovered nearby.

The seminary at Pilar was founded by the local Missionary Society of St Francis Xavier in 1890. A revered member of this Society was Father Agnelo de Souza, who achieved fame as a spiritual teacher until his death in 1927. The seminary is a large modern structure. The new chapel has fine stained-glass windows imported from Germany according to designs by a Goan artist. The central panel depicts Our Lady.

Just beneath the seminary stands the *Church and Monastery of Pilar*, founded in 1613. The plain unpretentious building has a frontal porch sheltering a finely carved doorway, with a statue of St Francis of Assisi set into a small niche above. This gives access to the tomb of Father Agnelo de Souza, a major attraction for local pilgrims since this figure is in the process of beatification. A passageway connects the tomb to a charming planted court, surrounded by a two-storeyed arcade. Frescoes here depict the lives and deaths of various saints, including St Francis of Assisi. The unusual fountain in the middle has an octagonal dais with bird-like figures and monster heads.

The church interior is dominated by an ornately carved and painted wooden altar. The central panel shows Our Lady of Pilar standing on a short pillar, flanked by angels. Another depiction of Our Lady is found in a glassed-in niche set in the side wall of the nave. This contains a delicately carved wooden statuette said to have been brought from Spain. The pulpit above is covered with gilded scrollwork, with a painting of Our Lady on the rear panel.

F. AGASSAIM

This village is located 15 km south of Panaji on NH17, just before the highway crosses the Zuari, en route to Margao [13A]. Agassaim is of interest for the *Church of St Lawrence*, consecrated in 1564. The interior is furnished with a remarkable 18th century altar, one of the finest examples of Rococo art in Goa. Set within a barrel-vaulted chancel painted bright blue, the altar is an exuberant composition with leafy pilasters and capping volutes, all in bright gold on a while background. The figure of St Lawrence holding a grid-iron appears in the central niche, with a domed tabernacle beneath, and a risen Christ in a sunburst above. Candles are incorporated into the overall composition. Similar but smaller altars are placed in the side walls of the chancel.

G. MANGUESH

The temple in this small village, 8 km east of Old Goa on NH4A, 12 km. north of Ponda, is one of the largest and most popular Hindu monuments in Goa. Dedicated to a form of Shiva under the name Manguesh, the temple was founded in the middle of the 18th century with income from land donated by a local Hindu ruler during the Maratha period. When the administration of Ponda District was transferred to Goa as part of the 'New Conquests', the Portuguese agreed not to interfere with the temple and its endowment; the estate is still intact.

Manguesh Temple is approached from the main road, a balustraded path, passing by a large square tank. The water is surrounded by arcades; the west side is marked by a tower with a pointed tiled roof. Steps ascend to a spacious court at a higher level, looking down onto the tank. The first feature to be noticed within the court is a the octagonal lamp tower. This whitewashed, seven-storeyed structure is furnished with Neo-Classical pilasters, cornices and round-headed openings, and crowned with a small dome. A wooden chariot is parked nearby, its octagonal frame covered with carvings of deities and leaping yali brackets. The court is lined with service structures.

The temple, which was substantially rebuilt in the 1890s, is entered from the east through an octagonal domed pavilion; similar domes roof the side entrance porches. The hall is painted in ochre and white, with details picked out in bright blue, including the window frames. The sanctuary walls form the lower part of an octagonal tower, complete with Neo-Classical details, and capped with a circular lantern.

Marble floor and tiled walls adorn the temple interior. Arcades on squat columns divide the mandapa into three aisles, with ornate glass chandeliers hanging from the flat wooden roof over the central aisle. Both the antechamber and sanctuary doorway are embellished with embossed silver sheets. They create gleaming frames through which can be glimpsed a small stone linga covered with a brass face-mask. Gilded guardian figures armed with clubs are set in the open recesses at either side, together with stone images of Durga (right) and Ganesha (left).

H. Mardol

The village of Mardol, 1.5 km. south of Manguesh on NH4A, is celebrated for the *Mahlasa Temple*, consecrated to a female aspect of Vishnu. The court in which the temple stands is entered from the east through an arched gateway with an upper chamber for musicians, capped by a tiled roof. Immediately on the right after passing through the gateway stands a seven-storeyed, octagonal lamp tower, virtually identical to that at Manguesh. Close to the town and directly on axis with the temple itself is a modern brass lamp column, with a tortoise base and 21 circular trays. The temple is preceded by a pair of newly completed halls with elaborate stone columns and an ungainly concrete roof. This obscures the original mandapa, which is a timber structure with a sloping copper-tiled roof. Carvings in a curious style beside the side porch entrances show warriors and musicians in vigorous postures; the brackets in between are fashioned as monkeys and yalis. The octagonal tower that rises over the sanctuary has arched niches containing plaster figures. The bulbous dome above is roofed with metal shingles.

The mandapa interior is distinguished by intricately carved woodwork. Columns have 16-sided shafts adorned with stylised foliation and miniature figures in niches; cut-out petals adorn the circular capitals. The brackets are of the lotus type, or show crouching lions. The central part of the ceiling is raised up on panels, with brightly painted gods arranged in niches. The periphery of the mandapa has high timber seating, with wooden balustraded screens admitting light on three sides. Embossed silver doorways give access to the sanctuary, which accommodates a stone image of Mahlasa.

Immediately south of the temple stands the Lakshmi shrine, a similar but smaller structure, also with a sanctuary topped by a domed octagonal tower. Twin images of Vishnu and Lakshmi are worshipped within. An arched gateway in the rear (west) wall of the temple court leads to a delightful tank, with rice fields and palm groves beyond.

I. Velinga

A further example of Goan temple architecture is found in the secluded village of Velinga, 2 km. south of Mardol, or 4.5 km north of Ponda. Though little visited, the *Lakshmi Narasimha Temple* is of interest for the high quality of its woodwork. The court in which the temple stands is entered on the north through a double-storeyed gateway. The mandapa in front of the sanctuary has 28 circular wooden columns carrying a sloping tiled roof; there are no outer walls, only timber balustraded screens. The mandapa abuts the original entrance porch of the sanctuary, marked by a steeply pyramidal roof; porches on the north and south are similarly roofed. The masonry walls of the sanctuary are topped with a square-to-octagonal tower with Neo-Classical pilasters, niches and balustraded parapets. The somewhat squat dome above has unusual vertical sides. The interior has carved columns and silver embossed doorways comparable to those in the Mardol temple (only Hindus admitted).

Much of the charm of the Lakshmi Narasimha temple derives from its peaceful wooded setting, with groves of palm trees on the hill above. Immediately east of the temple is a large square tank surrounded by steps and arcades. The east side is overlooked by a tower with a projecting balcony and a pyramidal tiled roof.

J. BANDORA

This small sprawling settlement, 1.5 km. west of NH17, about 2 km. north of Ponda, is of interest for its pair of Hindu monuments. The first to be reached when arriving from Ponda is the *Nagesha Temple*, almost hidden by groves at the bottom of a small valley. The complex is entered from the east through a Neo-Classical portal. Columns from a dismantled Kadamba period temple are set up nearby. Another Kadamba relic is a sculpted pedestal, now missing its image, placed at the western end of the compound. A five-stage, octagonal lamp column stands just inside the portal. Brightly painted images of deities fill the arches and niches on each side; nagas rear up at the corners.

The temple itself presents the usual arrangement of front and side porches, with pyramidal roofs adjoining a long hall with a gabled roof. Neo-Classical details typical of the 18th century, such as pilasters and round-headed windows, are picked out in pink and ochre. These colours blend pleasingly with the terracotta tiles of the roof and the ceramic lions arranged on the ridge. Finials mark the corners of the balustraded parapet that crowns the octagonal tower that rises over the sanctuary. The flattish dome above is enlivened with a band of interlocking nagas at the base, and a brass pot finial at the summit. The marble clad interior is divided into aisles by arcades on circular columns. The wooden ceiling over the central aisle is raised on panels painted with deities in niches. The sanctuary houses a linga set into the floor, behind which is a sculpted image of Shiva. Nandi appears in the entrance porch. A rectangular tank in front of the temple is surrounded by coconut palms. It is overlooked by an entrance tower with a tiled roof.

The *Mahalakshmi Temple*, 1.5 km to the west, is the second place of worship in Bandora. The temple is of the standard Goan type, except for the fluted dome that crowns the double-stage tower over the sanctuary. Similar fluted domes combined with smoother domes roof the side porches.

K. QUELEM

The road south of Bandora runs through the hamlet of Qelem, about 2 km. distant. On the way the road passes by the *Ramnatha Temple*, a characteristic

Goan styled, Hindu monument, with a predominance of Neo-Classical features mostly dating from the renovation of 1905. Small domes top the sanctuary and side porches. The sanctuary doorway has silver sheets embossed with monkeys, deer and birds intermingling with stalks and leaves. Figures of Shiva and Parvati looking down on Rama with Sita, Lakshmana and Hanuman fill the arch above. Guardians with elephants beneath are set at either side. The Shiva linga that receives worship within the sanctuary is believed to have come from a dismantled 16th century temple. It is accompanied by a gorgeously decked image of Vishnu.

Shantadurga Temple, Quelem.

Shantadurga Temple is situated 1 km. to the east, in a delightful setting on the edge of lush rice fields. One of the most popular Hindu shrines in Goa, it was founded in 1738 by Shahu, ruler of Satara [7G] in Maharashtra. In spite of its attested date, the temple has been totally remodelled in recent times, as is obvious from the bold Neo-Classical detailing of its outer features. The temple is comparatively vertical in elevation. Both the hall and porches have steeply pyramidal tiled roofs. The tower over the sanctuary, one of the highest of any Goan temple, has a triple-stage octagonal drum with a balustraded parapet topped with a flattish dome and a small lantern. The marble clad interior is enriched by glass chandeliers, and embossed silver screens containing small niches accommodating guardian figures. The sanctuary displays the white marble, seated image of the goddess Shantadurga, flanked by icons of Shiva and Vishnu, all sheltered by a richly gilded canopy.

The court in which the Shantadurga temple stands has a huge wooden chariot covered with carvings. Stone blocks beneath a spreading fig tree nearby are fashioned as sculpture niches.

L. Ponda

This town is situated on NH4A, a total of 30 km. distant from Panaji, at the junction of the road from Margao, 17 km. to the south. The only historical feature of interest in Ponda is the *Safa Mosque*, beside NH4A, 1 km. north of the town centre. Built in 1560 under the patronage of the Adil Shahi rulers, it is the oldest surviving example of Islamic architecture in Goa. It is picturesquely sited to one side of a rectangular tank. Six flights of steps separated by arched chambers descend to the water. The prayer hall has pilastered walls divided into shallow arched recesses, with the entrance on the east. The gabled roof is covered with tiles, in the typical Goan manner, with pot finials above. Arched recesses serving as mihrabs line the rear wall of the prayer chamber. Free-standing columns placed around the hall suggest an exterior colonnade, now lost.

M. Savoi Verem

A forested road, with distant views of the Mandovi River, runs 16 km. north of Ponda to this small village, of interest for the *Ananta Temple*. This is built on a hillside, next to a fish pond and a small tree shrine. The temple has a double-tiered roof, the entrance on the east being marked by a tower capped with a pyramidal roof. This is evidently a replacement for the sanctuary tower, which is here absent. The attached open hall is modern. Ornately carved wooden columns and brackets, all brightly painted, are seen within the original interior. A similarly decorated wooden door is placed between two columns. The sanctuary houses a finely carved slab showing Vishnu reclining on Ananta.

N. Tambdi Surla

A side road running 16 km. north of Molem, on NH4A, 28 km. east of Ponda, leads to the *Mahadeva Temple*. This Hindu monument stands in thick forest close to a stream, framed by the ranges of the Western Ghats. Assigned to the 12th-13th century Kadamba period, the temple is the best preserved building in Goa from the pre-Portuguese period. The temple consists of a towered sanctuary and columned mandapa, partly open on the east as a porch, where it is roofed with steeply sloping slabs. The walls are raised on a sharply modelled basement, and are featureless except for shallow pilasters. The triple-stage tower has parapet elements with carvings of Brahma (south), Shiva (west) and Vishnu (north), set in frames headed by monster masks and fanciful scrollwork. The capping roof resembles a dome. Stylised lotuses decorate the inclined balcony slabs of the porch. Four columns within the mandapa carry a ceiling with a star-shaped design incorporating lotuses. Naga stones are set up beside the antechamber doorway, which is flanked by lattice screens. A linga is under worship in the sanctuary.

Returning to Molem, visitors may continue on NH4A to Hubli [21] and Hampi [20].

12. North Goa

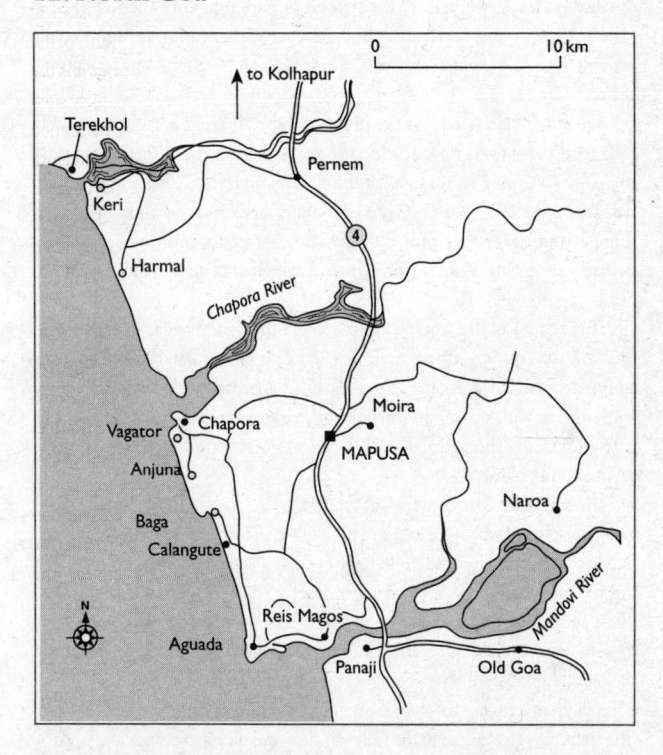

In spite of the recent, intensive tourist development there are many sites of historical interest to be discovered in this part of Goa.

Coastal forts at Aguada [A], Reis Magos [B], Chapora [D] and Terekhol [H] testify to the efforts of the Portuguese to secure the Arabian Sea coast here. Fine churches at Calangute [C] and Moira [E] are witness to the spread of Christianity. Temples at Naroa [F] and around Pernem [G] signal the presence of a vibrant Hindu community.

Because of the short distances involved it is possible to reach many of the sights described in Panaji [11] and South Goa [13] as day trips.

A. Aguada

The fort at Aguada, 10 km. from Panaji [11A], reached by turning off NH17 immediately as it crosses the Mandovi River is one of the most spectacular in Goa. It occupies a headland commanding the Arabian Sea to the north and west, and the estuary of the Mandovi and Zuari Rivers to the south. Part of the site is now occupied by the luxurious Fort Aguada Beach Resort. A restored stone jetty extending into the ocean beneath the resort once provided landing facilities, as well as a base for cannon. Remnants of walls are seen nearby.

Aguada Citadel occupies the highest point of the headland, accessible by a road that winds upwards for about 1 km. from the resort. From here there are sweeping panoramas of the ocean and rivers. The citadel, which dates back to 1617, was besieged on many occasions by the Dutch and English, but never succumbed. It was, however, temporarily occupied by British troops in 1798 during their struggles against Tipu Sultan of Srirangapattana [15C].

The citadel is the finest example of Portuguese military architecture in Goa. It consists of an irregular quadrangle of laterite walls, with attenuated angled corners. The walls have a broad walkway shielded by battlements, with openings for cannon. The surrounding moat is deep and partly rock-cut. The path beyond the moat is protected by a large sloping earthen embankment.

The southeast corner of the citadel is extended to accommodate the main gate, the doors of which are lost, and the vaulted magazine. Here, too, stands the massive circular bulk of the triple-stage *Lighthouse*, added in 1864. (Since 1976 this has been superseded by a modern structure that stands outside the walls.) The central part of the citadel is empty, except for a large cistern with steps descending to arched vaults. This once supplied the fort with fresh water, hence the name Aguada, which is Portuguese for 'watering place'.

A flight of steps climbs from the main gate to the entrance to the lighthouse. The steps also give access to the walkway that runs along the top of the walls. A line of ramparts following the steep side of the hill descends to the water, to protect the river landing below.

The *Church of St Lawrence* crowns a small rise, 1.5 km. east of the Aguada citadel. Completed in 1634, it displays a pedimented gable flanked by square towers. The altar inside shows St Lawrence clasping a boat, a reminder that this saint is the protector of sailors.

B. REIS MAGOS

The recently restored *Fort* at Reis Magos occupies an elevated location overlooking the Mandovi, 4.5 km. upstream from Aguada. Though this fort is earlier than that at Aguada, having been founded in 1551, it was totally rebuilt in 1707. As at Aguada, its walls are laid out in a quadrangular formation, though at a smaller scale. Angled bastions at the corners are topped with circular domed turrets for firing guns (permission required to enter the fort).

The *Church of the Magi Kings* (Reis Magos), beneath the entrance to the fort, dates from 1555, but was remodelled in 1771. A feast is held here each year on 6 January. The church is approached by a broad flight of steps. Carved yali balustrades, removed from an earlier dismantled Hindu temple, flank the bottom steps. The imposing east facade is articulated by slender Corinthian columns. The Portuguese coat-of-arms, surmounted by a three-dimensional half-crown, is placed beneath the central pediment, which is framed by volutes. Faded paintings adorn the nave interior. At the west end is the elaborate high altar, recently modified to create a recessed chamber for the tabernacle, surrounded by figures and flying angels. The richly worked blue-and-gilt woodwork of the altar is headed by a painted panel depicting the three Magi presenting gifts to the Christ child. The gravestone of the Viceroy Dom Luis de Ataide, who died in 1581, is set into the floor of the corridor to the north of the nave. It is marked by the royal coat-of-arms carved in bold relief.

C. CALANGUTE

The 18th century *Church of St Alex* on the edge of this beachside town, 6 km. north of Aguada, presents a fine example of the Goan Rococo style. Its double-storeyed facade has a curious false dome, complete with arcaded drum and capping lantern, rising over the central bays. The dome is flanked by square towers topped with pyramidal arrangements of pinnacles. The white and gold painted interior preserves its original elegance. The nave is lined with window recesses headed by shell-shaped half-domes. The side altar is delicately painted, the canopy being enlivened with tassels and flowers. In contrast, the high altar is an exuberant composition of flattened pilasters, swirling brackets and extended sunbursts.

D. CHAPORA

The fort here overlooks the mouth of the Chapora River to the north and Vagator Beach on the west, a spectacular situation that once marked the northern limit of the Portuguese possessions. Chapora can be reached from Mapusa, on NH17, 10 km. east, or directly from Calangute, 10 km. to the south.

Chapora Fort dates back to the Adil Shahi occupation of Goa in the years prior to the arrival of the Portuguese, but was rebuilt in 1717. The fort fell to the Marathas in 1739, being held for two years by the ruler of Pernem to the north of the Chapora River. It was returned to the Portuguese at the end of the 18th century, but lost its military significance with the acquisition of the New Conquests.

The fort is built on a level topped hill with steep sides. Roughly hewn laterite walls surrounded by dry ditches follow the irregularities of the contours.

Crudely built lookout posts with domical tops punctuate round bastions with large openings for cannon. The main gate, at the top of a steep approach, is small and unpretentious. It leads to a vast emptiness, with no indication of the church, barracks and houses that once stood here.

E. MOIRA

This village, 4 km. east of Mapusa on NH17, is worth visiting for the small *Church of Our Lady of the Immaculate Conception*, one of the finest examples of the Rococo style in Goa. Founded in 1636, the church faces northeast onto a spacious terrace looking out over rice fields and forests. An unusual outdoor pulpit is built to one side. The double-storeyed facade of the church, which was added at the end of the 18th century, is divided into niches with shell-shaped half-domes, those in the middle being higher and lobed. The central tower presents a part-octagonal drum, dome and lantern on the frontal face only. The square side towers have flattish domes framed by small pinnacles.

The nave interior is lined with window niches headed by the same half domes as those on the facade, with which it is contemporary. The chancel, painted entirely in blue, is roofed with a decorated vault. The gilded altar has a central arched recess flanked by pilasters, with angel heads on the capitals and leafy volutes at the sides. The recess is filled with a tiered pedestal accommodating a glass receptacle enshrining an image of the Virgin. Altars on either side of the chancel are consecrated to St Sebastian and Christ on the Cross. A pleasant cloister with a small garden opens off to one side of the nave.

F. NAROA

This small settlement is located 25 km. east of Mapusa, via Bicholim, not far from the northern river crossing to Divar Island. The road passes by Maem Lake, a favourite boating spot. The *Saptakoteshvara Temple* at Naroa is of historical significance, having been founded by Shivaji of Raigad [7C], when the Marathas first took possession of this part of Goa. Begun in 1668, the building was later renovated. An inscribed slab giving the temple's history is placed over the doorway within the entrance porch on the east.

The pilastered walls, large square windows, and the prominent triangular frontal gable of the temple exterior are topped by a sloping tiled roof. The octagonal tower that rises over the sanctuary has arched windows between pilasters, a balustraded parapet, and a flattish dome. A small linga is accommodated within the sanctuary.

The tapering, multi-tiered stone lamp column that stands freely in front of the temple is typical of Maratha architecture.

G. Pernem

This town on NH17, 18 km. north of Mapusa, is attractively situated in the wooded hills that mark the northern extremity of Goa. Pernem is worth visiting for its small Hindu temples, with unusual paintings and decoration, and a grandiose mansion of the former local rulers. Travellers may continue from here along NH17 into Maharashtra.

The *Bhagavati Temple* in the middle of Pernem is a brightly painted monument of little merit, except for its well-proportioned octagonal tower. A greater attraction is the *Desprabhu Mansion*, 200 m. north of the town centre (permission required to visit). This sprawling complex is still inhabited by the descendants of the Maratha family that governed this part of Goa in the 18th century. The mansion is entered through an arched gate between polygonal towers. The reception rooms in the central Neo-Classical block are notable for the collection of local rosewood furniture, Chinese ceramics, silvered palanquins and diverse memorabilia.

The modest *Mulvir Temple* stands in a delightful grove of palm trees next to a spring-fed tank, 2 km east of Pernem. Though this consists merely of a simple arcaded structure with a tiled roof, paintings cover the arches of the hall and sanctuary walls. The faded compositions, with sketchy black linework, are typical of a pictorial tradition that developed in this part of Goa in the 18th-19th centuries. The best preserved scenes show Vishnu on Ananta (over the shrine doorway), Ramayana episodes (arches of side aisles), the churning of the cosmic ocean, Krishna holding up Mount Govardhan, and Vishnu's incarnations (side walls).

Mauli Temple, 1 km. west of Pernem, is similar to the Mulvir temple, except that it has a polygonal porch extension on the front (west). Masonry vaults in the arcaded hall are covered with stylised lotuses and scrollwork executed in the graffiato technique, by which reddish plaster is chipped away to reveal a white background. The black stone image under worship in the sanctuary represents the goddess Devi, armed with sword and shield. Immediately west of the temple is a small stream, overlooked by a fierce stone sculpture of Durga.

H. Terekhol

This coastal fort in the extreme north of Goa overlooks the point at which the Terekhol River flows into the Arabian Sea. It is situated on the north bank of the river, accessible only by ferry from Keri on the south bank, 15 km. west of Pernem.

Terekhol was founded in the early 18th century by the Marathas of Sawantwadi, a nearby town in Maharashtra, and was only captured by the Portuguese in 1788. The *Fort* was contested by the English, to whom it was temporarily surrendered in 1835. Terekhol attained fame during the freedom struggle against the Portuguese; several demonstrators were killed here in 1955.

The road from the ferry leads through the tiny village of Terekhol up the hill to the main gate of the fort. Laterite walls define a small irregular zone on top. Triangular bastions, with lookout posts headed by domical turrets, offer magnificent panoramas of the river and ocean. In the middle of the inner court of the fort stands the *Church of St Anthony*, patron saint of the army and Portugal's national saint. Its facade has an ornate pediment, with voluted sides flanked by open square towers. A luxury hotel now occupies the former garrison quarters of the fort to one side.

13. South Goa

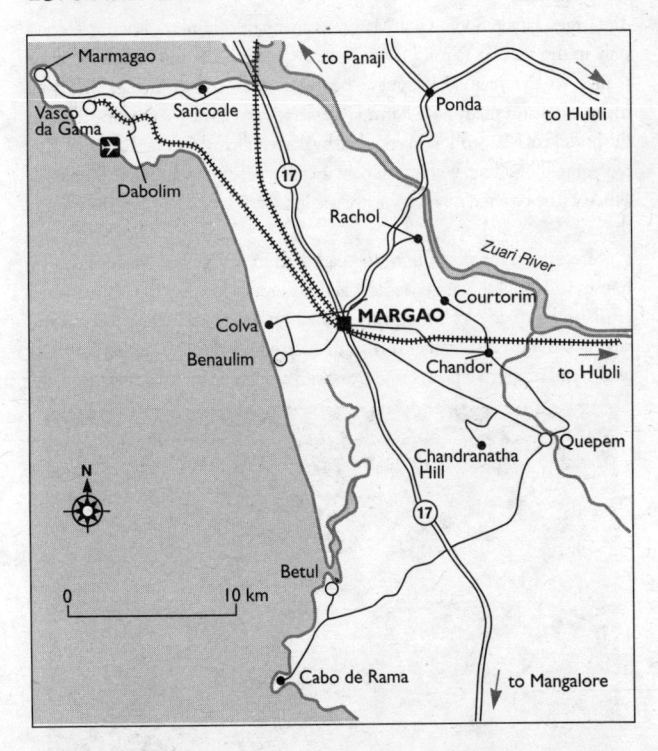

Though less developed than North Goa, South Goa is also a favourite destination for travellers because of its fine beaches and luxury hotels. The Portuguese heritage is still evident in the churches and religious colleges in Margao [A], Colva [B], Sancoale [C], Rachol [D] and Courtorim [E]. An excursion to Chandor [F] provides an opportunity to visit a typical aristocratic mansion of the period.

Hindu temples are a comparative rarity in South Goa, the most interesting being those at the summit of Chandranatha Hill [G]. A journey to the overgrown citadel on Cabo da Rama [H] skirts the beautiful beaches in the southern part of the state.

Visitors based in South Goa may easily reach the sights described in the itineraries for Panaji [11] and North Goa [12].

A. Margao

The largest city in South Goa, Margao is a vibrant commercial centre, second only in the state to Panaji [11A]. The city preserves its traditional character thanks to the many Portuguese period houses and churches. The well maintained and shady *Jorge Barreto Park* serves as a favourite meeting place in the middle of Margao. It is overlooked by the Municipal Council of 1905. This red painted building, with prominent arcades, accommodates the Municipal Library. The covered market, the liveliest in Goa, is located a short distance to the east.

Streets running north from the park lead to the *Church Square*, lined by houses with brightly painted facades and cast-iron balconies. The whitewashed cross in the middle of the square, shaded by spreading mango trees, is the largest and most ornate in Goa. This Rococo edifice displays curling acanthus leaves, and supports a plain stone cross with crudely engraved emblems.

Cross in the Church Square, Margao.

The *Church of the Holy Spirit* overlooks the square from its southeast corner. Founded in 1565 on the site of a demolished temple, the church was substantially rebuilt in 1675. The west facade, the only one to be plastered, presents pedimented windows in three stages. A canopied niche in the middle of the topmost stage frames a relief composition of the Virgin in the company of the Apostles. Balustraded towers at the corners, slightly stepped back, are topped with flattish domes with lanterns. A half-arch on the north side of the church leads to a courtyard formed by residences intended for the clergy, now a school.

The interior of the nave is lined with deep window niches topped by shell-shaped half-domes typical of the 18th century. The barrel vault is coffered throughout. The elaborate altar at the east end is richly carved and gilded. The Crucifix in the topmost recess is framed by angels on ornate columns. Free-standing Corinthian columns placed against the side walls of the chancel carry a cut-out foliated arch. The side altars are equally ornate, especially those consecrated to the Archangel and the Virgin. The pulpit is carried on unusual animal brackets. The sacristy, which opens off the nave on the north, has a finely finished vault. A feast takes place here each year on 9 December.

The road running east from the church leads to *Sat Burnzam Gor*, one of Margao's largest private mansions (permission required to visit). The name refers to seven roofs, of which only three are now preserved, each with a steep pyramid of tiles rising over the long line of doors and windows that marks the street facade. The house was built in about 1790 by the Viceroy's secretary, Inacio Silva. His descendants continue to live here to this day. The grand reception room at the upper level preserves magnificent furniture; there is also a private chapel. The house next door is also of interest for the Neo-Gothic tracery of its windows. A porch shelters a grand staircase ascending to the front door.

In one of the streets leading south of the church square stands the *Damodar Temple*, occupying an old house. A brass face-mask of Shiva covers a small linga set into the floor of the sanctuary.

B. COLVA

This village near the ocean, 5 km. from Margao, is of interest for the *Church of Our Lady of Mercy*, a fine example of the 18th century, Goan Rococo style. The triple-bayed west facade, with pedimented doors and windows, is surmounted by a panel containing the 'IHS' monogram of the Jesuits. Animals are seen in the volutes, while pinnacles crown the capping pediment. A single bell tower rises to one side. Painted blue and white, the chancel frames a four-tiered altar with the Virgin on top. Corinthian columns set against the side walls carry an arch with leafy tracery. The church is famous for the images of Menino (Boy) Jesus, which are credited with miraculous powers. Though the original statue was removed in 1834 to the college at Rachol, its replacements are believed to retain the supernatural attributes of the original. Menino Jesus appears in two side altars, as well as in a painted panel over the pulpit. The crowned youth holds an orb and a flag. The church is attached to a school with an attractive arcaded courtyard.

C. SANCOALE

The *Church of Our Lady* at Sancoale stands in a forested grove on the south bank of the Zuari River, 19 km. north of Margao via NH17. Built by Jesuits in 1606, but almost totally destroyed by fire in 1834, the church is of interest for its surviving, ornate east facade. Pilasters with enlarged Corinthian capitals frame a trio of round-headed doorways below, and rectangular pedimented windows above. The topmost stage has a circular opening headed by a small niche enlivened with pinnacles. Plaster compositions over the side doorways show bearded figures, one holding a sword, the other a book, standing in ornate frames; angels adorn the central doorway. Volutes are disposed symmetrically around the circular opening above.

D. RACHOL

The *College of All Saints* at Rachol, a small village 8 km. northeast of Margao, dates back to 1574. Originally named after Ignatius Loyola, founder of the Jesuit order, it was renamed after the expulsion of the Jesuits in 1759. The college is renowned throughout Goa for its expert training of priests. A press was set up here to print a biblical digest in Konkani, the local language. The translation was by Father Thomas Stephen, the first recorded Englishman to have visited Southern India, who arrived in Goa in 1579. Apart from an extension in the 19th century, most of the present college buildings date from the rebuilding in 1606-10.

The college is sited on top of a small rise, once encircled by laterite walls and a moat, of which only a segment remains. This contains the semicircular headed gate, flanked by Doric columns, through which the road passes. The gate is painted in contrasting bands of colour. The college beyond is entered from the east through a roofed by a vault supported most unusually on a single central column. Murals, now faded, include a scene of fiery hell.

The main rooms of the college are arranged on two levels around a large court (permission required to visit). A raised platform in the middle of the court conceals a subterranean cistern divided into eight cross-vaulted chambers. Remnants of Hindu sculptures discovered here suggest that this may originally have been a temple tank. Paintings of different saints are seen above the doorways to the rooms at the rear (west) of the court. The Last Judgement and Biblical scenes cover the walls of the hall leading to the sacristy on the south side of the court.

The *Church* beyond presents a spacious interior decorated with polychrome carved panels. Those on the chancel walls show various saints, surrounded by angels in foliation. The naive style of these panels contrasts with the gilded magnificence of the high altar and pulpit. The famous statue of Menino (Boy) Jesus, taken from Colva, is exhibited in the altar to the left. Bone relics, believed to be those of Constantine the Great, brought from Rome in 1782, are kept in an altar to the left of the main entrance. The gallery over the east end of the nave houses a pipe organ, the oldest in Southern India, shipped from Lisbon towards the end of the 17th century. The upper corridor outside the entrance to the gallery, running the full length of the church, is lined with mural portraits of the founders of the various religious orders, including St Francis of Assisi. The oil paintings in the main hall beyond depict Goan Archbishops and the youthful Dom Sebastian, the royal founder of the college, on horseback. The adjacent library is amply stocked with rare books.

1 km. east of the college, on the edge of rice fields extending to the Zuari River, stands the isolated *Church of Our Lady of the Snows*. Its modest facade displays Rococo volutes on the uppermost stage; only one of two towers is preserved. The interior has the usual array of ornate wooden altars. Among the gravestones set into the floor of the chancel is a memorial commemorating the burial site of five missionaries who were killed here in 1583. A carved and painted panel of the Last Supper adorns the front altar.

E. Courtorim

This hamlet, 5 km. east of Rachol, provides an idyllic setting for the *Church of St Alex*. This faces west towards a large tank covered with water lilies. The church opens onto a terrace with a small cross, complete with twisted colonettes and exuberant plasterwork. The facade dates from the rebuilding of 1647. The side towers have unusual octagonal uppermost stages with small domes and lanterns; wavy volutes flank the central stage. The interior demonstrates the Goan Rococo style at its most exuberant. The chancel is framed by free-standing Corinthian columns supporting a foliated arch. The triple-arched altar at the end contains images of St Alex and other saints, flanked by foliated and gilded bulbous columns. The tabernacle in front is conceived as a miniature building. The ornate side altars are consecrated to St Sebastian and St Michael. An addition of the 19th century is the cast-iron gallery.

F. Chandor

The road from Courtorim winds its way through pleasant countryside for about 4 km. before arriving at Chandor, a sprawling settlement, also accessible from Margao, 13 km. to the west. At the heart of Chandor is a long narrow square, at the east end of which is the *Church of Our Lady of Bethlehem*. The original facade collapsed in 1949 and was subsequently rebuilt in an unsympathetic, Neo-Gothic style. Of greater interest are the free-standing memorials that dot the square. They include an elaborate Neo-Gothic edifice erected in 1855 by Francisco Xavier Braganza, a member of the family whose grandiose house occupies the south side of the square.

The *Braganza House* is one of the few privately owned mansions in Goa open to the public (no closed days). Though founded in the 16th century, the present building is mostly assigned to the 18th century. The exceptionally long facade consists of 25 bays with window openings, mostly trilobed in shape and partly filled with stained glass. These open onto a balustraded verandah that runs the full length of the building. The lower level of the mansion has simple openings for kitchen, stores and servants' quarters. A central gable marks the staircase ascending to the residential zone at the upper level, now divided into two separate apartments that may both be visited. These give the best possible idea of the gracious living style enjoyed by Goan aristocratic families in the 19th century.

Both apartments have grandiose reception rooms with tiled floors, painted walls and timbered ceilings, off which open smaller galleries for leisure and dining, as well as bedrooms and private balconies. The rooms are furnished with locally produced wooden furniture, among the finest to be seen in Goa, as well as imported glass chandeliers and porcelain; photographs and other personal items crowd tables and chests inlaid with brass or mother-of-pearl. The left hand (east) apartment has its own private chapel. This is adorned with a carved and gilded altar in the Rococo manner. A library of more than 5,000 books is to be seen in the right hand (west) apartment. This was formed by Luis de Menzes Braganza, a journalist and newspaper proprietor at the turn of the 20th century.

1.5 km. east of Chandor square lies the village of Cotta, a short distance beyond which is the archaeological site of *Chandrapura*. Excavations here in 1929 recovered pottery fragments dating back to the 2nd-1st centuries BCE; these constitute the earliest such finds in Goa. An inscribed copper plate dating from the 3rd-4th centuries CE is the oldest historical document in the state. (Some of these items are displayed in the Archaeological Museum, Old Goa [11B.) The decayed brick walls and overturned stone footing blocks form part of an east-facing shrine. That this was dedicated to Shiva is indicated by the large but headless Nandi placed nearby. The shrine is assigned to the 12th-13th century Kadamba era.

G. Chandranatha Hill

The Chandreshwar and Bhutanatha temples on the summit of Chandranatha Hill are reached by following a winding road for about 5 km. from Paroda, a small village 12 km. southeast of Margao. The road climbs for almost 400 m. through increasingly dense forest inhabited by monkeys; the last part of the ascent is by a broad and long flight of steps. The temples occupy the level top of the hill, with fine views of the plain beneath and the ocean beyond. Though no earlier than the 18th century, they mark the site of an earlier Kadamba period foundation.

The *Chandreshwar Temple* presents a rectangle of plain walls with porches sheltering balcony seating; the south porch is topped with a small dome, while that on the east has a pyramidal roof. A high octagonal tower with a domed roof rises over the sanctuary. A natural rock forms the ritual focus of the interior. Small lingas placed here represent Shiva under the name Chandreshwar. The original sanctuary consists of a small domed chamber built up to the south face of the rock. This was later encased within the present structure. The tower above is supported on a vault built on top of the rock. Kadamba period sculptural fragments are assembled in the sanctuary and surrounding corridor. The temple has recently been renovated; vividly painted panels adorn the ceiling of the hall that precedes the sanctuary.

The adjacent *Bhutanatha Temple* is a simple vaulted chamber than enshrines an unshaped stone set at an angle into the ground. The linga is carved out of a large boulder and covered with a brass face-mask. Parked in a shelter to the south of the temples is a chariot made in 1983. This is covered with painted wooden panels, interspersed with three-dimensional yalis and monkeys.

H. Cabo da Rama

This promontory lies 30 km. south of Margao, partly via NH17. Named after the god Rama, the *Fort* here is of little architectural interest, but fine ocean views may be had of the beaches running north towards Colva, and south towards Goa's last headland before Karnataka.

The Portuguese occupied Cabo da Rama in 1761, but abandoned it in 1835. The dilapidated entrance to the fort is reached by crossing a dry moat. The small chapel inside is occasionally still used. Remains of barracks are seen nearby.

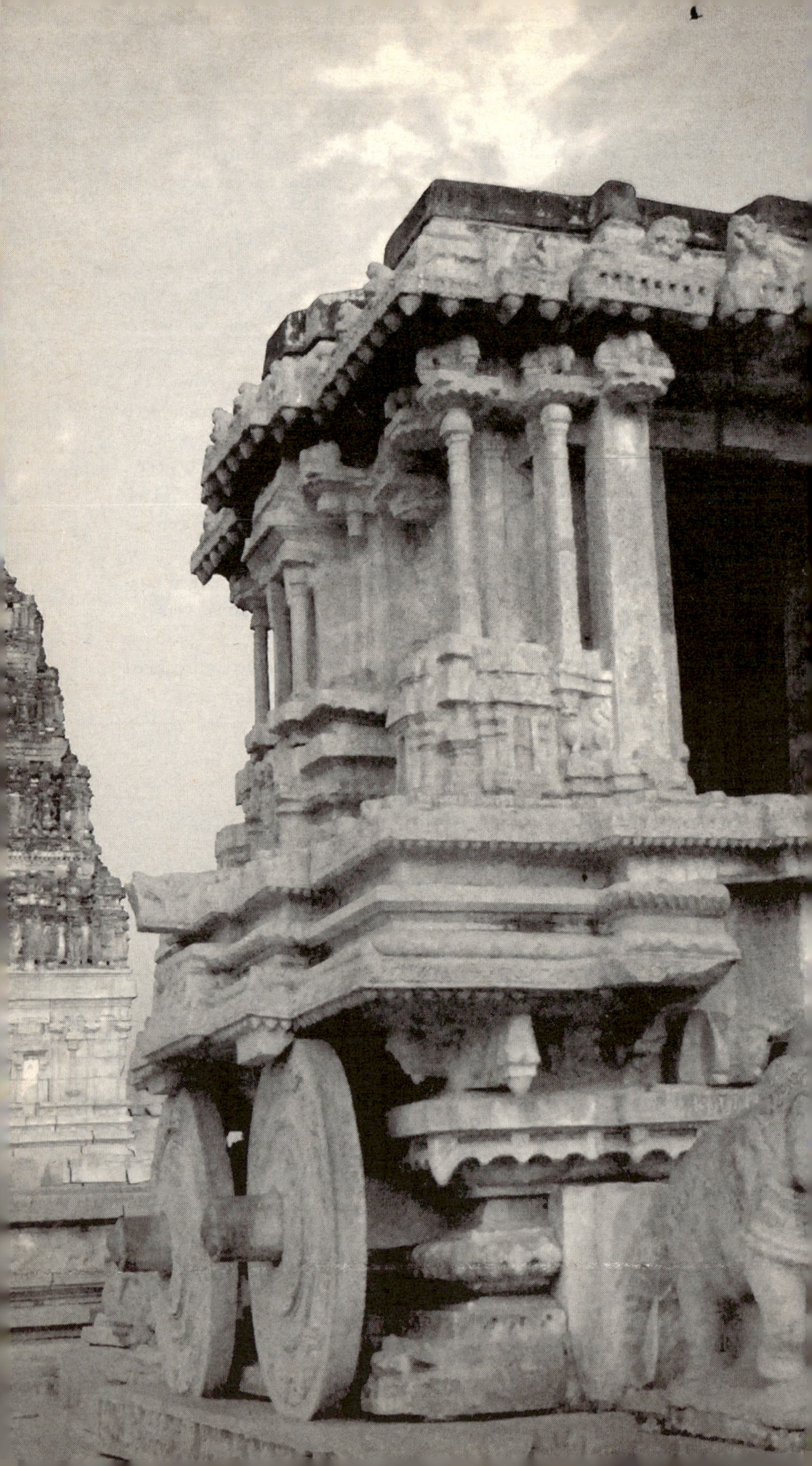

Chariot shrine in the Virthala Temple, Hampi

KARNATAKA

Karnataka

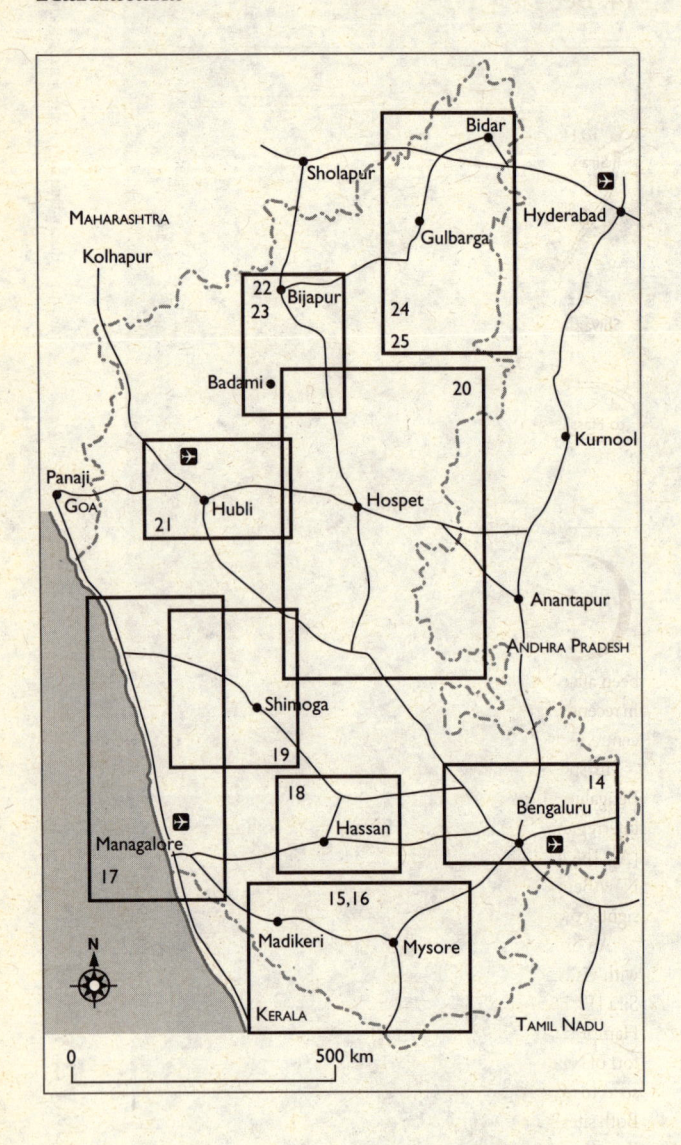

14. Bengaluru

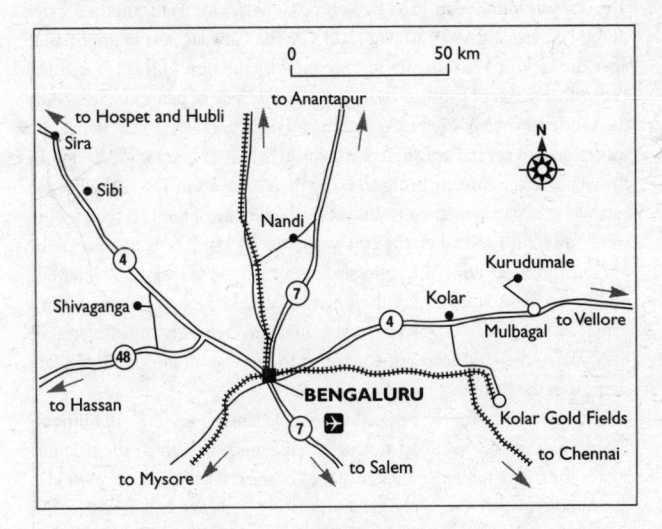

Capital of Karnataka, Bengaluru, the former Bangalore, is situated at the extreme southeast corner of the state, on the southern edge of the Deccan plateau. Its elevation of just over 1,000 m. above sea level guarantees an agreeable mildness of climate, but this has now been affected adversely by traffic pollution caused by unbridled development. In recent years the city has emerged as a leading manufacturing and commercial centre, renowned for its flourishing IT and communication industries.

In spite of rapid growth, vestiges of the past are still to be found in Bengaluru. Isolated monuments associated with Gauda rulers and the interregnum of Haidar Ali and Tipu Sultan dot the streets of Old Bengaluru [A]. The British presence is still in evidence in the monuments and villas of New Bengaluru [B]. A full day should be sufficient to cover the principal sights covered here.

An excursion to the rock citadel at Shivaganga [C] can be combined with visits to the little known temple at Sibi [D], and the unusual tomb at Sira [E], both on NH4. The highway continues to Chitradurga [20K] and Hampi [20B]. NH7 runs north from Bengaluru, passing beneath the hill fort of Nandi [F], from where it is possible to continue into Andhra Pradesh so as to reach the temple at Lepakshi [33G], famous for its ceiling paintings. Both sites can be combined in a single day outing. Temples at Kolar [G] and Kurudumale [H] are located on or near NH4, running east towards Chennai [36].

A. Old Bengaluru

The city was founded in 1537 by Kempe Gowda, a local chief in the service of the emperors of Vijayanagara [20B-C]. The Gowdas rose in importance after the sack of Vijayanagara in 1565, and by the turn of the 17th century controlled much of southeastern Karnataka, in spite of being challenged by the Wodeyars of Mysore [15A] and the Nayakas of Ikkeri [19C]. Bengaluru was raided on several occasions by the Adil Shahis of Bijapur [23A] and by the Marathas, eventually being taken by the Wodeyars in 1687. The English established a garrison in Bangalore at the beginning of the 18th century, but were ousted in 1758 when the city was seized by Haidar Ali, usurper of the Mysore throne. Haidar Ali's aggressive campaigns in the area were continued by his son Tipu Sultan. After the English defeated Tipu at Srirangapattana [15C] in 1799, Bengaluru was incorporated into the newly constituted state of Mysore. The city, however, continued to serve as an important military outpost of the British.

The tour of historical Bengaluru described here begins at *Tipu Sultan's Palace* on Albert Victor Road, just west of the junction with Krishnarajendra Road. The palace is built on the site of the Gowda residence that once stood in the middle of the fort. Only the north-facing audience hall remains. This consists of a double-height hall with wooden columns, overlooked on three sides by balconies. Though now somewhat shabby, the palace would have been sumptuously furnished, somewhat like Daria Daulat Bagh at Srirangapattana.

Immediately east of the palace, on Krishnarajendra Road, stands the *Venkataramana Temple*, dating from the 17th century Gowda era. Its outer walls are carved with rows of divinities in procession; a pyramidal tower rises over the sanctuary. The mandapa in front has yalis sculpted onto the outer columns; quartets of identical animals adorn the central four columns.

A fragment of the stone fort constructed by Haidar Ali in 1761 is seen a short distance to the north. The *Delhi Gate* has prominent arched entrances with fine plasterwork; these give access to a barbican shielding an isolated round bastion. Steps from here ascend to the crenellated walkway that once ran along the top of the walls.

The city market, immediately to the north of the fort, marks the heart of Old Bengaluru. The regularly planned narrow streets, crowded with traffic, are original features, as are the small brick houses with interior courts. Among the religious monuments in this zone is the *Ranganatha Temple*, built in 1628 during the reign of Kempe Gowda II. Its entrance porch has sculpted yalis.

1.5 km. east of Tipu Sultan's Palace is *Lal Bagh*, a garden of about 250 ha. This was originally established as a pleasure resort by Haidar Ali, but later converted into horticultural gardens in 1856, staffed with a professional superintendent from Kew Gardens in London. Lal Bagh contains rare and valuable tropical and subtropical plants, together with indigenous and foreign fruit trees. The spacious glass house, with its delicate cast-iron frame, dates from 1889. Lotus ponds, lakes and shaded avenues are interspersed with natural boulders. The entrance to the park is marked by a handsome equestrian statue of Chamarajendra Wodeyar of Mysore (1868-94).

Gavipur, 2 km. west of Lal Bagh, was once a village but is now absorbed into suburban Bengaluru. Here stands the *Gangadhareshvara Temple*, with a shrine set into a natural rocky crevice. Four unusual granite pillars stand freely in the courtyard. Two carry great stone discs, some 1.5 m. in diameter, representing the sun and moon; the other two pillars support a Nandi and a trident.

Basvanagudi, less than 1 km. to the south, takes its name from the nearby picturesque hill strewn with boulders, one of which is fashioned as a seated *Nandi*. Dating back to Gowda times, the 4.5 m. seated bull is ceremonially decked with garlands and bells. The animal is sheltered by a pavilion of later date. A small Ganesha temple is built at the base of the hill.

Other vestiges of Old Bengaluru survive at the eastern extremity of the modern city, beyond the end of Mahatma Gandhi Road, the principal commercial thoroughfare. *Ulsoor* is a traditional settlement, with old houses facing onto regular lanes. The great tank established by the Gowdas in the 17th century lies to the north. The same rulers were responsible for the *Someshvara Temple*, in the middle of Ulsoor. The largest Hindu monument in Bengaluru, the temple is approached from the east along a street marked by a lofty lamp column. A gopura with sculpted walls and a pyramidal brick tower signals the entrance to the temple. The temple within has an entrance porch embellished with yalis. Carvings of deities relieve the otherwise plain walls. The altar and flag column in front have finely finished stone basements.

B. NEW BENGALURU

The tour of the city continues with a description of the main sights of New Bengaluru. By far the largest and most important building is the *Vidhana Soudha*, completed in 1956, housing both the Secretariat and State Legislature of Karnataka. The imposing granite complex is designed in a revivalist style, the columns, balconies, curving eaves and dome-like tower all being derived from earlier temple architecture. Opposite the Vidhana Soudha, on the other side of a broad ceremonial avenue, stands *Attara Kacheri*, originally the Public Offices. This Neo-Classical stone building of stone and brick, completed in 1868, is painted deep red. Its central Ionic portico is headed by a double pediment. In front is an equestrian statue of Sir Mark Cubbon, Commissioner of Bengaluru in 1834-61.

Attar Kacheri backs onto *Cubbon Park*, named after the same Commissioner. This expanse of more than 120 ha. of pleasant greenery in the middle of the city was laid out in 1864. It is dotted with statues, including an imposing marble sculpture of Queen Victoria near the entrance to the park from Mahatma Gandhi Road. A matching sculpture of Edward VII stands nearby. In the middle of the park stands *Seshadri Iyer Memorial Hall*. Built to accommodate the City Central Library, the building commemorates the Prime Minster of Mysore State in 1883-1901. Its red painted, Neo-Classical front is marked by a pedimented portico.

Kasturba Gandhi Road runs along the eastern flank of Cubbon Park. Here stands the *State Archaeological Museum* (closed Mondays), which is another Neo-Classical building with fully modelled Corinthian columns, painted bright red, dating from 1876. The sculpture gallery displays 2nd century CE, limestone fragments from the Buddhist site at Sannathi [24G], as well as images from the 12th century temple at Halebid [18B], including images of standing Surya, dancing Shiva, and Krishna playing the flute. An impressive icon is the 9th century granite icon of Durga from Avani. The main hall has double-height Corinthian columns supporting a gallery above. Archaeological materials displayed here include items from megalithic burial sites, and 1st century CE pottery from Arikamedu [39B]. The remainder of the space is devoted to memorabilia of Tipu Sultan, with arms, prints, and a relief model of Srirangapattana. Hero stones depicting mounted warriors and foot soldiers engaged in battle are shown beneath the circular cast-iron staircases. Among the paintings that line the walls of the upper gallery are fine examples of the 19th century Mysore school illustrating various Hindu topics. Next door is the Venkatappa Art Gallery, devoted mainly to exhibitions of contemporary art.

The oldest building to back onto Cubbon Park is *Raj Bhavan*, the former British Residency, dating from 1831 (permission required to visit). This whitewashed Neo-Classical villa, with a prominent colonnaded porch, is set in beautifully landscaped grounds. The *General Post Office*, a short distance away, has an imposing corner entrance portico that imitates the Vidhana Soudha.

Mahatma Gandhi Road was originally laid out as part of the *British Cantonment*, with parade grounds and barracks to the north, and churches and bungalows with well-tended gardens to the south. Many of these buildings still stand, giving an idea of Bengaluru in former times; they are, however, increasingly overshadowed by high-rise office buildings, apartment blocks and hotels. Proceeding east from Cubbon Park along Mahatma Gandhi Road, the first historical building to be seen is *St Mark's Cathedral*. This 1812 structure presents a simple Neo-Classical scheme, with a portico on the front, and a curving apse at the rear. A shallow dome marks the internal crossing. *St Andrew's Church* on Cubbon Road, which runs parallel to Mahatma Gandhi Road, is a simple Neo-Gothic building of 1867. Its lofty square tower is relieved by octagonal turrets.

Mayo Hall, at the angle of Mahatma Gandhi Road and Brigade Road, was opened in 1883 as a tribute to Lord Mayo, the Viceroy assassinated in Port Blair. The hall, which now houses a variety of public offices and courts, presents a handsome Italianate facade with pedimented upper windows and vase-like pinnacles. *East Parade Church* in 1863, a short distance east, has a prominent Ionic portico, now painted bright grey, but without any tower. *Holy Trinity Church*, of 1851, marks the eastern terminus of Mahatma Gandhi Road. This, too, is fronted by an Ionic portico, but here the entrance is topped by a triple-stage tower with Neo-Greek palmettes at the corners. Ulsoor, the traditional quarter already noticed, lies further east. *St Patrick's Church*, on Residency Road near the corer of St Mark's Road, dates from 1887, rebuilt in 1894-99. Its impressive Neo-Classical facade displays superimposed colonnettes in the middle. The twin towers have pedimented windows. The interior is roofed with a wooden panelled barrel vault.

This description of New Bengaluru concludes with a notice of *Bangalore Palace* (permission required to visit), 3 km. north of Mahatma Gandhi Road. Constructed in 1880 for a British merchant, the building was taken over and extended by the Wodeyars. The palace faces extensive grounds, partly converted into a formal garden with axial paths and planted plots. The main building, which is built entirely in granite, presents an agreeable clutter of battlemented towers and turrets. Formal apartments are located in the south block. An internal curved flight of stairs ascends to the grand reception rooms at the upper level, adorned with stained glass windows and panelled ceilings.

C. SHIVAGANGA

The most spectacular citadel in southern Karnataka, Shivaganga is located 30 km. northwest of Bengaluru, via Dobbspet on NH4. In the 16th century Shivaganga was the principal headquarters of the Gowdas, who retained this outpost after Bengaluru was occupied by the Wodeyars. The site is dominated by the dramatic, sugarloaf-shaped granite crag, rising more than 100 m. above the plain.

Arcs of walls define a *Fortified Zone* at the base of the hill. Within the walls is a large tank with carvings on its stepped sides. A lofty lamp column beside an entrance gopura leads to a flight of rock-cut steps. The steps path through two more gopuras, one with six steep storeys, before arriving at the *Gangadhareshvara Temple*. This, together with the adjacent Honnadevi shrine, is partly built into a natural cavern. Metal portraits of the Gowdas are placed here. The shrine is entered through an ornately carved doorway, in front of which is a mandapa with lathe-turned columns framing a seated Nandi.

A gateway with a porch and an incomplete gopura give access to Kempe Gowda's hall. This is a detached structure commanding an extensive panorama of the surrounding landscape. The hall has animal columns, doubled at the corners. A tall column headed with a quartet of brackets stands nearby. Steps from here climb to the summit of the hill.

D. SIBI

The small *Narasimha Temple*, beside NH4, 95 km. northwest of Bengaluru, was built towards the end of the 18th century by a local official under Tipu Sultan. The temple is worth visiting for its extensive ceiling paintings, among the finest of the Wodeyar period. Hindu mythological topics on bright red backgrounds contrast with courtly portraits and processions depicted in a provincial Mughal manner.

The panel in the entrance gate shows a rocky landscape populated with beasts, hunters and ascetics in caves; Krishna appears at the summit of a hill. Lines of soldiers in red coats, bearing muskets, are painted onto the beams beneath; courtly scenes, some with sexual couples, adorn the ceilings of the side chambers.

Paintings inside the entrance porch of the temple are divided into nine panels. Over the central aisle of the mandapa appear Shiva and Devi with Ganesha and sages; Vishnu with a diagram of the universe displayed on his body; and Narasimha with Lakshmi flanked by Bhairava and Brahma. Krishna scenes occupy the panels to the left; Krishna scenes are arranged to the right.

Multiple images of Narasimha occupy the ornate plaster niches that serve as a parapet of the colonnade that encloses the temple courtyard. A short distance beyond the temple is a pleasant pipal tree sheltering a cluster of naga stones, overlooking a stepped tank.

E. SIRA

This town lies further along NH4, a total of 123 km. from Bengaluru. Sira gained importance under the rulers of Bijapur [23A], from whom it was captured by Aurangzeb in 1687. It subsequently served as an outpost of the Mughals and the Nizams of Hyderabad [26]. Haidar Ali began his career here before serving under the Wodeyars. The town declined after Tipu Sultan forced many families to move to Srirangapattana.

The most noteworthy monument in Sira is the *Tomb of Malik Rihan*, built in 1651, clearly visible from the highway. An arcade sheltered by an angled overhang on sculpted brackets surrounds the central chamber. The three-quarters hemispherical dome that rises above is framed by corner domical finials, in the typical Adil Shahi manner.

Concealed within the town is the *Jami Mosque* of 1696. Its prayer chamber is entered through five lobed arches, topped by an ornate parapet. The interior is roofed with three domes. Remnants of the town walls and of a fort nearby can still be made out.

F. NANDI

This rock fort lies 50 km. north of Bengaluru, in full view of NH7. Nandi was a favourite retreat of Tipu Sultan, from whom it was captured by the British in 1791. Its cool climate and magnificent scenery make Nandi a favourite picnic spot for visitors.

Nandi village at the foot of the hill is of interest for the twin *Bhoganandishvara* and *Arunachaleshvara Shrines*. These are built in the simple massive style associated with the 9th-10th century Nolamba rulers of Hemavati [33G]. The outer walls have regularly spaced pilasters and superbly worked, perforated stone windows. These contain figures of Shiva (south wall of Arunachaleshvara shrine), Durga standing on the buffalo head (north wall of Bhoganandishvara shrine), and dancers in scrollwork. Pyramidal multi-storeyed towers rise over both shrines. Black stone sculptures of Shiva and Nandi are placed in the upper level of the Bhoganandishvara tower, the roof of which is square. The mandapa that precedes the Bhoganandishvara shrine has a ceiling panel showing Shiva and Parvati surrounded by the dikpalas. Columns here have carved panels on circular shafts. Large polished black stone lingas are housed in the sanctuaries of both shrines. Nandis are seated in small pavilions in front.

The shrines were substantially enlarged in later times. A small pavilion between the two shrines was added in the 16th century. This displays ornate columns with attendant maidens fashioned out of grey-green granite. The ceiling is a dome-like composition with dancing figures surrounding a central lotus. The next addition took place under the Gowdas in the 17th century, at which time the small *Maheshvara Shrine* was added behind the open pavilion. A procession of deities and sages is carved onto its outer walls. A wall linking the two Nolamba period shrines was skilfully worked to resemble the 9th century originals; at the same time a spacious mandapa was built in front of both shrines. The whole ensemble is contained within a large compound surrounded by colonnades, entered on the east through an unfinished gopura. A second compound to the north has a mandapa in the middle, with yali columns and a central dais for displaying images. A large square tank with stepped sides lies beyond.

A road ascends from Nandi village to the top of *Nandi Hill*. After a drive of about 20 minutes the road passes through an arched gate set into the fortifications that ring the upper fort. Just inside the gate is *Tipu Sultan's Summer Palace*. This modest structure with a small verandah overlooks a delightful garden with a large tank. A path ascends to a wooded park at the summit. The nearby *Yoganandishvara Temple* is of interest for the delicately worked brass door frame in front of the sanctuary.

G. KOLAR

Located 40 km. east of Bengaluru on NH4, this city preserves a variety of Hindu and Muslim monuments. On the western fringe of the city is a *Dargah* associated with Haidar Ali, who had a long established connection with Kolar, being born in a small village 16 km. away. The dargah contains graves of his family members, but Haidar himself is buried in Srirangapattana. The building consists of a simple domed tomb with an ornate parapet and corner finials. Similar features are displayed in the adjacent mosque.

Hindu monuments of interest stand within the city itself. The *Kolaramma Temple*, after which Kolar takes its name, dates from the 11th century, when the Cholas of the Tamil zone occupied this part of Karnataka. The temple is contained within a rectangular compound, entered from the east through an imposing gate. The main shrine has wall niches headed with part-circular frames filled with foliation. Columns inside the mandapa have fluted shafts and cushion-shaped capitals.

The ornate 17th century *Someshvara Temple*, immediately to the south, is assigned to the Gowda period. The granite walls of the gopura on the east are crowded with sculptures of various deities. The tower above rises in five diminishing storeys. An ornate lotus is carved onto the ceiling of the passageway beneath. The temple within is preceded by a spacious mandapa, with colonettes and yalis on the outer supports. This gives access to a shrine, the outer walls of which have pilastered niches interspersed with single pilasters standing in ornamental pots. Friezes of animals decorate the lowest mouldings of the basement. The pyramidal tower, restored in later times, is capped with a hemispherical roof. A free-standing mandapa in the southwest corner of the walled compound of the temple has its outer columns embellished with carvings of yalis and maidens. The raised dais within is treated as an independent pavilion, with an ornately worked basement, columns and eaves.

H. KURUDUMALE

This small village, 18 km. northwest of Mulbagal, a town 30 km. east of Kolar on NH4, is worth visiting for the artistic *Someshvara Temple*. This monument dates from the period of Chola occupation of this part of Karnataka in the 11th-12th century. The temple compound is approached from the south by mounting a flight of steps. Tamil influence is seen in the restrained treatment of the basement and pilastered walls of the temple itself, as well as in the sombre design of the wall niches. A pyramidal tower with a hemispherical roof crowns the sanctuary. The entry porch, reached by transverse flight of steps flanked by yali balustrades, has columns with delicately modelled icons of Shiva carved onto the blocks; they include a striking image of the god dancing (right column). A large sculpture of Ganapati is placed on the ground in front of the porch. Carvings on the interior columns portray diverse deities and saints. A rectangular goddess shrine with a barrel-vaulted roof stands freely to the north.

Another Hindu monument in Kurudumale, the *Vinayaka Temple*, is located some 350 m. to the south. This too is a 12th century foundation, though extended in later times. Columns inside the mandapa illustrate diverse aspects of Shiva; other icons are arranged along the wall shelf. An unfinished gopura stands to the east.

15. Mysore

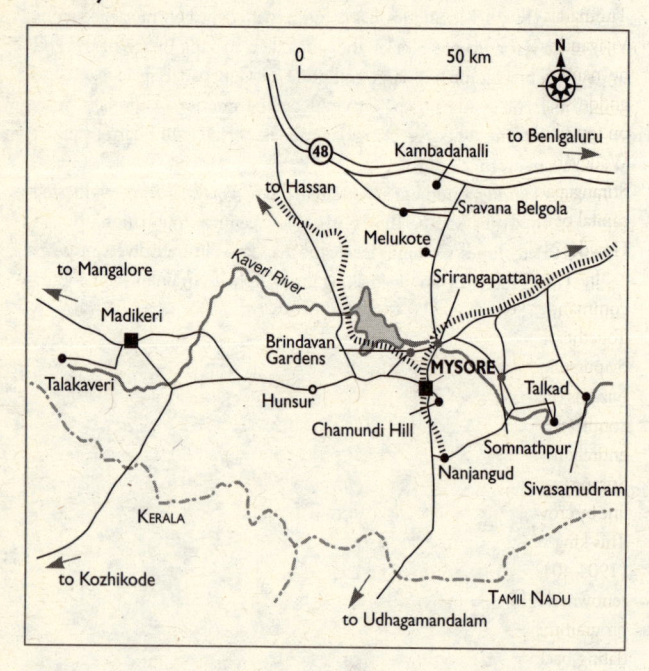

Former capital of the Wodeyar rulers, Mysore is a charming city pleasantly situated at an elevation of about 750 m., surrounded by well watered fields and wooded hills. In recent years it has been developed into an educational centre, with the largest university in Karnataka. The city is renowned for its ivory work, sandalwood carving and silk weaving. A full day may be spent here, visiting the palaces and civic monuments of the city, as well as its vibrant central market.

Excursions may easily be made from Mysore to the shrine on Chamundi Hill [B], the fort at Srirangapattana [C], and the intricately decorated temple at Somnathpur [D]. Religious sites in the vicinity, such as Talkad [E], Nanjangud [F] and Melkote [G], will require additional journeys. The celebrated Jain sites of Sravana Belgola [H] and Kambadahalli [I] may easily be reached as a day trip from Mysore; alternatively, visitors may continue on to Chikmagalur [18].

Mysore serves as a convenient stopover on any trip from Bengaluru [14] to the hill stations of Madikere [16] or Udhagamandalam [43C], the latter in Tamil Nadu, or to the coastal town of Mangalore [27], and the celebrated Hoysala temples near Chikmagalur [18].

A. Mysore

Timmaraja Wodeyar, a governor of southern Karnataka under the emperors of Vijayanagara [20B-C], was responsible for laying out a fort here in 1524. This he named Mahishuru (Mysore), after the demon Mahisha killed by the goddess Chamundeshvari, a form of Durga who was worshipped in a shrine on top of a nearby hill. After the sack of the Vijayanagara capital in 1565, the Wodeyars asserted their autonomy. In 1610 Raja Wodeyar occupied Srirangapattana, a fort on an island in the Kaveri River, making this the second capital of the Mysore kingdom. From here the Wodeyars waged wars on the Gowdas of Bengaluru and the Nayakas of Ikkeri [19C].

In 1761 the Mysore throne was usurped by Haidar Ali, a Muslim commander who rose to power in the service of Krishnaraja Wodeyar II. Together with his son, Tipu Sultan, Haidar Ali expanded the Mysore domains by pursuing aggressive campaigns against the Peshwas of Pune [3A], and the Nizams of Hyderabad [26A]. This policy brought Haidar and Tipu into direct conflict with the British. In 1791 Tipu had Mysore levelled in order to build an entirely new capital, but these plans never materialised since he was killed at Srirangapattana in 1799. Two years later the British re-established the Wodeyar line by crowning the infant Krishnaraja III under the watchful eye of a Resident. This king who ruled until 1868, and his successors, especially Krishnaraja IV (1904-40), were exemplary monarchs who presided over a model state renowned for its enlightened policies of social reform and vigorous building programmes. The Mysore rulers revived Dasara, the spectacular royal festival dating back to Vijayanagara times, which until recently was celebrated each September-October.

The tour of the city described here begins at *Mysore Palace*. This stands in the middle of a quadrangular fort, roughly 450 m. square, built by the Wodeyars in the 18th century, of which only portions of the walls still stand. The main block, a replacement of an earlier palace, was begun in 1897 according to imaginative designs of Henry Irwin, and then later expanded. It survives today as one of the most exotic royal residences in Southern India. The facade presents a grey granite exterior, with corner towers crowned by quartets of painted metal clad domes. The central wing, conceived as a great seating gallery for viewing processions of the Dasara, is emphasised by a higher tower with a central dome surrounded by turrets. On special occasions the facade is spectacularly illuminated by thousands of light bulbs. The palace faces onto a vast parade ground, entered on the east through the Elephant Gate. This has a trio of lofty arches, the central one being more than 20 m. high.

Having removed their shoes, visitors enter the palace through a doorway on the south side and proceed beneath the great grandstand. Passing around an arcaded courtyard roofed with flattish domes, enlivened with a golden howdah and other exhibits, they reach the impressive *Kalyana Mandapa*, first used for marriage ceremonies in 1910. Slender, cast-iron columns and arches support a glass octagonal dome painted with brightly coloured peacocks. All of the iron and glass were imported from Glasgow. Tiled patterns are inlaid into the floor. The side walls are covered with murals portraying the public ceremonial life of the Wodeyars, as represented by various processions that took place in the streets of Mysore in the first half of the 20th century. Side galleries display royal portraits as well as silver thrones.

Stairs lead from the Kalyana Mandapa to the upper level of the palace. Here the principal feature of interest is the *Darbar Hall*, lined with squattish lobed arches carrying shallow domes painted with blue skies and silver stars. Murals on the rear wall against which the royal throne was once positioned depict an array of goddesses, with Chamundeshvari in the middle. The adjacent *Ambar Vilas*, which is smaller, private darbar hall, is roofed with stained glass, with an octagonal, glass domed chamber at one end. From here embossed, solid silver doors give access to a staircase that descends to ground level.

Mysore Palace also incorporates the *Maharaja's Residential Museum*. This houses a collection of furniture and arms, including fearsome 'tiger-claw' daggers. There is also a fine collection of paintings of the Mysore school depicting Hindu deities, as well as royal portraits.

Handsome public buildings and monuments erected by the Wodeyars grace the tree-lined streets of Mysore. Immediately west of Mysore Palace are the *City Corporation Offices* and *Public Offices* of 1920 and 1921, built in a style that recalls that of the palace itself. Several blocks to the west is *Jaganmohan Palace*, erected in 1900 for the marriage celebrations of Krishnaraja Wodeyar IV. An earlier building to the rear serves as the *Jayachamarajendra Art Gallery*. This houses an agreeable mix of royal memorabilia and local crafts. A small shrine at the upper level is adorned with murals of mythological subjects, temple sites and royal pastimes, including various board games and puzzles (permission required to visit).

Mysore's principal commercial thoroughfare, Sayyaji Rao Road, begins at Krishnaraja Circle, near the northwest corner of the palace. A statue of Krishnaraja Wodeyar IV, sheltered by a hexagonal pavilion, stands in the middle, with curving wings of offices and shops on four sides. *Chamarajendra Circle*, a short distance east on Albert Victor Road, has a marble portrait of Chamarajendra Wodeyar (1881-94) beneath a finely worked domed kiosk. Nearby *Government House*, the home of the British Residents from 1805, has a curving arcaded verandah facing a well tended garden (permission required to visit). The *Cathedral of St Philomena*, a short distance north, begun in 1933, is a large French styled, Neo-Gothic monument with twin concrete spires rising almost 60 m. high.

Imposing public monuments in the western part of Mysore include the *Law Courts* and *Krishnarajendra Hospital*, as well as the departments of Manasa Gangotri, the campus of Mysore University. The *Oriental Research Institute* houses an important library of Sanskrit manuscripts. All these buildings display an individual Neo-Classical manner, with whitewashed colonnades and arcades, curving metal-clad vaults and mansard roofs, and domes rising over pedimented porches. The *Folklore Museum* at Manasa Gangotri is home to one of the largest ethnographic collections in Southern India. Its holdings include toys, puppets, household objects, and a series wooden bhuta figures from the village of Mekkekattu in coastal Karnataka [17I].

Some 16 km. north of Mysore are the ornamental *Brindavan Gardens*, laid out below the Krishnarajasagar Dam on the Kaveri River. Formal lawns and plantings line a central channel with spectacular fountains, illuminated three nights a week.

B. Chamundi Hill

The road leading to Chamundi Hill, 3 km. southeast of Mysore, passes near to *Lalitha Mahal*, built in 1921 as a private royal guesthouse, and now a luxury hotel. This spacious Neo-Classical building has a facade with whitewashed colonnades on two levels, dominated by a great dome rising on an extended colonnaded drum. Lesser domes of the same type mark the ends of the facade. Twin banqueting halls, one still used for dining, are roofed with stained-glass vaults.

Before arriving at the summit of the hill the road runs beside a colossal *Nandi Monolith*, some 7.5 m. long and 5 m. high. Sculpted in 1659 out of a single boulder, this monolith depicts a seated bull ceremonially decked with bells and garlands.

Fine views of the city, almost 100 m. below, may be had from the summit of Chamundi Hill. Here stands the *Chamundeshvari Temple*, founded by the Wodeyars in the 17th century, but remodelled in later times. It is entered through a gopura with a steeply pyramidal tower of brightly painted plasterwork. The doors inside the gate, as within the temple itself, have embossed silver panels portraying different goddesses. The sanctuary accommodates a gorgeously attired image of Chamundeshvari, the focal point of the annual Dasara celebrations. Nearby *Rajendra Vilas* was completed in 1938 as a summer retreat for the Wodeyars, but is now a hotel. It is built in a revived Rajput style with rooftop domical pavilions.

C. Srirangapattana

Known to the British as Seringapatan, this island citadel is located on the Kaveri River, 15 km. northeast of Mysore, beside the highway to **Bengaluru**.

The name of the island is derived from the temple of Sri Ranganatha that stands within the fort.

Srirangapattana served as the principal headquarters of the Wodeyars, as well as their usurpers, Haidar Ali and Tipu Sultan. It became celebrated for the battles fought here by the British forces under Lord Cornwallis and General Harris in their attempt to subdue Tipu. In 1799 Harris successfully stormed the citadel and killed Tipu, thereby establishing British supremacy in Southern India. In their zeal to wipe out all vestiges of Tipu Sultan's power, the British demolished the palace and military structures within the fort. However, they spared the bridges, with stone pylons, that cross the two arms of the Kaveri.

The *Ramparts* of Srirangapattana define an irregular zone at the western tip of the island. The polygonal bastions and turreted parapets surrounded by broad moats are the work of French engineers in the service of Tipu. Mysore and Elephant Gates on the south have circular-headed entries and flanking guardrooms. The vaulted dungeons of *Sultan Battery* on the north are where Tipu had British prisoners confined in appalling conditions. Near to Water Gate is a simple enclosure that marks the spot where Tipu was killed.

Religious monuments within the fort are still intact. The *Sri Ranganatha Temple* was substantially remodelled in the 19th century. The walled compound is entered from the east through an imposing gopura with a five-storeyed pyramidal tower. The sanctuary within, accommodating a reclining image of Vishnu, is approached through a succession of mandapas and an intermediate court with a gilded lamp column. A large chariot with carved wooden panels is parked outside the temple walls. The twin minarets of the *Jami Mosque* at the other end of the fort are visible from the Bangalore road. Erected by Tipu in 1787, the mosque has a raised prayer chamber flanked by octagonal minarets that rise in two stages, topped with bulbous domes.

A road from the fort runs east across the island to *Daria Daulat Bagh*. Built in 1784 as a pleasure resort by Tipu, this palace stands in the middle of a spacious garden bounded on one side by the Kaveri (closed Fridays). The palace has wooden verandah with lofty columns on four sides. Mughal influence is apparent in the lobed arches and the ornamental designs of the ceiling. The side walls on three sides of the verandah are covered with murals, partly restored in 1855. Those in the west verandah portray Haidar Ali's victory over the British at Polillur in Tamil Nadu in 1780. One panel shows the British troops surrounded by the Mysore forces, with Colonel Baillie seated in a palanquin in the middle. The interior of the palace, including a pair of double-height audience halls overlooked by balconies, serves as a museum. Among the exhibits are sensitive portraits of Tipu Sultan and his various courtiers by

British artists, including one by Johann Zofanny, as well as a model of Srirangapattana's citadel.

The road from Daria Daulat Bagh continues for 1.5 km. before passing by a small *Church* associated with the French missionary Abbé Dubois, who was active here in 1799-1823. Dubois was an eccentric who dressed and lived like an Indian. His book, *Hindu Manners, Customs and Ceremonies*, is a considered a classic. Memorials to British soldiers are seen in the cemetery nearby. The *Tomb of Haidar Ali and Tipu Sultan*, simply known as the Gumbaz, is located 1 km. further east. Erected by Tipu in 1784, for his father who had died two years earlier, the monument stands in a formal garden with avenues of cypresses, entered from the north through an arched gate. The tomb presents is an imposing domed chamber surrounded by a verandah topped with black marble columns further topped by an ornate parapet. The dome, with a petalled base, is raised high on a circular drum. Father and son are buried side by side, their bodies marked by twin cenotaphs. The ebony and ivory doors were donated in 1855 by Lord Dalhousie, Viceroy of India. A small mosque stands to one side.

The road continues until it meets the tip of the island, overlooking the confluence of the two branches of the Kaveri.

D. Somnathpur

The small village of Somnathpur, next to the Kaveri River, 35 km. east of Mysore, is worth visiting for its exquisite *Keshava Temple*, one of the best preserved monuments from the Hoysala period. Consecrated to *Keshava*, a form of Vishnu, it was built in 1268 by Somanatha, a general of Narasimha III the Hoysala king. The temple stands in the middle of a rectangular court, approached from the east through a gateway with an open portico. An inscribed slab set up here records Somanatha's benefaction.

The east facing temple consists of three shrines, each laid out on a star-shaped plan, opening off a common mandapa that extends outwards as a porch. The shrines are elevated on a plinth that repeats the complicated outlines of the plan. Carved elephants project from the deeply modelled plinth, while the basements of the shrines are animated with intricately sculpted processions of elephants, horses and riders, scrollwork, scenes from Hindu legends, and makaras and geese. The walls above consist entirely of carved panels, set at angles to each other. They depict Vishnu in his various forms and incarnations, as well as other deities. The gods and their consorts are richly encrusted with tassels, jewels and crowns; they stand beneath flowering trees, or frames headed by ornate scrollwork. Labels beneath identify the various artists who worked on the sculptures. The walls are sheltered by an angled overhang with a petalled fringe. Pyramidal towers over the sanctuaries have vaulted frontal projections. The diminishing storeys display pot-like motifs and flattened roof forms; dome-like roofs crown the summits.

The mandapa and porch through which the temple is entered are raised on a high basement enlivened with friezes of temple facades and towers, interspersed with amorous couples. Perforated stone screens above are set between columns and sheltered by an angled overhang. The mandapa interior has columns with gleaming, lathe-turned shafts. Corbelled, dome-like ceilings above have intricate cut-out designs with lobed motifs, pendant buds and looped bands. An imposing icon of Krishna playing the flute, surrounded by attendants, gopis and herds, is installed in the south shrine; an equally impressive image of Janardhana, a form of Vishnu, occupies the north shrine.

A short distance away, partly hidden by trees, stands the *Panchalingeshvara Temple*, also built by Somanatha in 1268. This strikingly unadorned monument was intended as a memorial to Somanatha's ancestors, as represented by the line of five linga sanctuaries, each roofed with a small pyramidal tower.

E. TALKAD

This somewhat remotely situated small village on the north bank of the Kaveri, 45 km. southeast of Mysore via Tirmakudal Narsipur, was once capital of the Gangas, the dominant rulers of southern Karnataka in the 9th-10th centuries. The village is worth visiting for a number of temples partly buried under the sand dunes from the river bed. However, most of these belong to the later Hoysala period. Talkad is best known today for the Panchalinga Darshana, a bathing festival that takes place at intervals ranging from 4 to 14 years.

The *Vaidyeshvara Temple*, the principal place of worship at Talkad, has a shrine with numerous projections, in the typical Hoysala manner. The exterior, partly reconstructed, displays angled wall slabs enlivened with slender pilasters. Niches filled with sculpted deities are sheltered by an angled overhang, with stone chains hanging from the corners. The doorway in the south porch is flanked by guardian figures. Interior columns, with sharply defined capitals, carry a ceiling with a pendant lotus surrounded by figures.

The nearby *Kirti Narayana Temple*, reached by a short walk over the dunes, is less ornate. Its walls are elevated on a basement with precisely cut mouldings. Pilastered projections and niches with pediments are totally devoid of figural sculptures. The pyramidal tower, partly restored, is topped with a domed roof. The adjoining mandapa was originally open, with balcony seating on three sides. Interior columns have slender fluted and multi-faceted shafts.

F. Nanjangud

This town, 23 km. south of Mysore, is situated on the Kabini River, a tributary of the Kaveri. This is home to a three-day chariot festival every March, associated with the *Nanjundeshvara Temple*, a foundation of the early Wodeyars in the 17th century. Donations to the temple were also made by Haidar Ali and Tipu Sultan, but it was Krishnaraja Wodeyar III who substantially extended the monument in the early 19th century. From his time date the outer enclosure walls as well as the principal gopura on the east.

G. Melkote

This religious site occupies a rocky ridge rising abruptly 150 m. above the plain, 55 km. north of Mysore. Melkote is associated with Ramanuja, the celebrated Vaishnava philosopher and teacher, who is believed to have founded the temple and associated mathas here in the 11th-12th century. These institutions were supported through the centuries by successive Hoysala, Vijayanagara and Wodeyar rulers; they continue to be active today.

The road ascending to Melkote passes by *Kalyana Kund*, a large tank surrounded by colonnades, and overlooked by small shrines and rest-houses. A short distance to the east is a small hillock with two incomplete sanctuaries excavated into its sides, in front of which is a 2.5 m. high monolithic Ganesha. Nearby steps ascend to a gopura with a lofty pyramidal tower, from which there are sweeping views of the surrounding landscape. A small Narasimha temple lies beyond.

The road from the tank runs south until it reaches the *Narayana Temple*, Melkote's principal religious monument. This stands in a rectangular enclosure, surrounded by colonnades surmounted by a fanciful plaster parapet. The main shrine is approached through a gopura and a sequence of two mandapas. Fine bronzes of Vishnu and of Ramanuja himself are installed in the main sanctuary, as well as in the surrounding lesser shrines. The most artistic feature of the complex is the hall in front of the goddess shrine on the north side of the enclosure. This was built in 1458 by a Vijayanagara general. Its columns are embellished with intricately worked cut-out pilasters, jewelled garlands and miniature animals and figures. Mythological scenes include Ramayana episodes and the story of Narasimha.

A short distance south of the Narayana temple, at the summit of a rocky rise, is a massive but unfinished *Gateway*, dating from the 15th century. Doorway jambs in the passageway have carvings of maidens standing on makaras, and guardians leaning on clubs. Columns in the chambers at either side are sculpted with diverse divinities.

H. SRAVANA BELGOLA

Celebrated for its colossal Gommateshvara monolith, this town sacred to the Jains is located 50 km. north of Melukte, a total of about 110 km. north of Mysore.

Sravana Belgola was established in the 9th-10th centuries, at a time when southern Karnataka came under the sway of the Ganga kings. The site benefitted from the patronage of Chamundaraya, the minister of Rajamalla IV (974-85), both of whom were converts to Jainism. Temples from the 12th century are associated with Gangaraja, commander of the Hoysala army. Sravana Belgola was further developed under the Vijayanagara and Wodeyar rulers. It continues to flourish today: a great commemorative festival, the Mahamastakbhishekha, takes place here every 12 years, on which occasion the Gommateshvara statue is bathed with coconut milk, rice water, sandalwood paste, turmeric, vermillion powder and flower petals.

Most of Sravana Belgola's monuments are clustered on two granite hills overlooking the town which is situated in the intermediate valley. The visit described here begins with an ascent of *Vindhyagiri*, the granite hill that rises more than 140 m. above the town, on its southern flank. A long line of rock-cut steps climb the shoulder of the hill. The first building to be seen near the top, after passing through a gateway in the walls that encircle the hill, is the 14th century, triple-shrined *Odegal Basti*. This houses images of Adinatha (south), Neminatha (east) and Shantinatha (west). The plain exterior is buttressed by angled props. The nearby *Brahmadeva Mandapa* shelters a column erected by Chamundaraya. This has its circular shaft embellished with unusual, deeply cut leafy scrollwork; a small cubical shrine accommodating a seated image of Brahma is positioned on top. A boulder carved with rows of miniature Jina figures is located next to Akhanda Gate at the top of the last flight of steps. The *Siddhara Basti*, inside the gateway to the right, has inscribed memorial pillars set up beside the doorway. A little further on is Channanna Basti, an unadorned 17th century structure preceded by a tall lamp column.

The *Gommateshvara Monolith*, representing Bahbuli, son of the first Tirthankara, marks the summit of Vindhyagiri. At 17.7 m. high, this is the largest, free-standing figural sculpture in Southern India. The naked saint stands immobile, his glance fixed steadfastly ahead, creepers winding around his legs and arms. The figure has broad shoulders, and elongated arms; the modelling of the body is uniformly smooth. The facial features are delicately carved, as are the coils of hair. Snakes and ant-hills are sculpted out of the rock beneath. Here, too, are inscriptions recording the benefactions of Chamundaraya and the date of 981. The monolith stands in a colonnaded compound of later construction, sheltering subsidiary Tirthanakara images.

The entrance on the north has a ceiling panel that depicts Indra holding a water pot.

The tour continues by descending the same steps until the town is reached at the bottom. The chief place of interest here is the *Jain Matha*, a short distance east of the staircase. Former residence of the Jain pontiff of Sravana Belgola, this mansion has an internal court surrounded by a verandah. The verandah walls are embellished with brightly coloured murals dating from the 18th-19th centuries. They illustrate the various birth stories of Parshvanatha, including the story of Marbhuta and his wicked brother Kamatha, and incidents from the legend of Nagakumara. One composition portrays the annual fair at Sravana Belgola, complete with stalls and crowds of pilgrims. Chambers opening off the verandah house an important collection of fine Jain bronzes, several dating back to the Ganga era.

The adjacent *Bhandari Basti*, substantially rebuilt in recent times, enshrines a full set of 24 Tirthanakaras arranged in a row on a long pedestal. A stone column topped by a small pavilion stands in front.

For the next part of the tour of Sravana Belgola visitors must cross the town, passing by a large tank on the north, opposite which begins the path that climbs *Chandragiri*. The monuments and inscriptions on this hill are contained within a single compound. All the temples have plain exteriors, relieved only by sharply cut pilasters, and topped by multi-storeyed towers. The 10th century *Chamundaraya Basti*, named after the patron of the Gommateshvara monolith, houses an image of Neminatha. Its hollow tower, capped by an octagonal domed roof, serves as an upper shrine for Parshvanatha. Miniature sculptures adorn the parapet elements. The interior ceiling shows a seated Jina in the company of the dikpalas.

Chandragupta Basti, a temple assigned to the 12th century, is notable for its perforated stone screens. Miniature panels depict incidents from the legendary lives of Bahubali and of Chandragupta, his royal disciple. A huge, 5 m. high image of Parshvanatha is housed in the sanctuary of the adjacent *Parshvanatha Basti*. In front stands a lamp column capped with a small pavilion, dating from the 17th century.

About 300 km. north of the Chandragiri complex is *Santishvara Basti*, the only temple at Sravana Belgola to have been built in the ornate Hoysala style. Though dilapidated, the walls panels preserve Jinas standing in niches headed by tower-like pediments. These figures are flanked by attendant maidens, musicians and dancers, beneath panels of decorative scrollwork. An enthroned Jina is worshipped within the sanctuary.

From Sravana Belgola it is possible to return to Bengaluru [14], 165 km. to the southeast, via NH 48 and NH4, or to continue northwards to Chikmagalur [18], some 115 km. to the northwest.

I. Kamabadahalli

This village lies 15 km. east of Sravana Belgola, just off NH48. The Jain monuments here form an ensemble of two coordinated groups of temples within the same compound. The 10th century shrines are typical of the Ganga style, with clearly articulated basement mouldings and wall pilasters; their pyramidal towers are crowned with square or dome-like roofs.

The triple-shrined *Panchakuta Basti* houses images of Adinatha (south), Shantinatha (east) and Neminatha (west). The adjacent double-shrined *Shantinatha Basti* has a later porch with several fine carvings, including a superbly modelled seated Jina attended by guardians. The ceiling inside shows the dikpalas arranged around a seated Jina. A lofty stone column to the north of compound is capped by a pot-bellied yaksha.

16. Kodugu

Formerly called Mercara, Madikeri is the headquarters of Kodugu District, known to the British as Coorg. This area of Karnataka is unsurpassed for its natural beauty. The highlands occupy both sides of the Western Ghats, offering delightful panoramas of verdant valleys with fast flowing streams, and rocky peaks rising some 1,700 m. above sea level.

A drive through Kodagu, with a stop in Madikeri, forms an attractive part of any journey between Mysore [15], 96 km. to the east, and Mangalore [17], 132 km. to the west, or even Kannur [48G] in Kerala. Other than the sights of Madikeri itself [A], for which a few hours should be sufficient, a half-day trip may also be made to Talakaveri [B], a sacred spot that marks the source of the Kaveri River, which flows from here for about 785 km. through southern Karnataka and central Tamil Nadu into the Bay of Bengal.

Kodagu is home to a community with a distinctive way of life, as is evident from local customs, festivals, dress and language. Coffee is the most important regional product, with about one third of all plantations in Southern India being located here. Kodugu is also celebrated for its oranges, as well as for its crops of cardamom and pepper.

A. Madikeri

In 1681 Madikeri became the capital of a local line of chiefs, which successfully resisted domination by the Nayakas of Ikkeri [19C] and the Wodeyars of Mysore. The region was overrun by Haidar Ali in 1773, and subsequently occupied by Tipu Sultan. In 1790, the local ruler Virajendra allied himself with the English against Tipu who, according to a treaty of 1792, was excluded from Kodagu. Later rulers, such as Lingarajendra, remained loyal to the English. Even so, Kodagu was annexed by the British in 1834, but remained independent until its absorption into Karnataka State.

The town dominated by a *Fort* which crowns a small hill. This is shielded by an irregular hexagon of walls, with bastions at each angle, surrounded by a ditch. The circuitous entrance on the east is guarded by a sequence of three gates. These lead to the *Palace*, begun in 1812, which for a time was the residence of the Kodagu rulers. It now houses government offices. Its sombre whitewashed facade has double arcades capped with a sloping tiled roof. The clock tower at one corner is an addition of 1933. A temple of Virabhadra nearby was removed to make way for *St Mark's church*, built in a plain Neo-Gothic style, with a prominent spire.

The *Omkareshvara Temple*, situated in a hollow to the east of the fort, was founded by Lingarajendra in 1820. Standing is the middle of a large tank, the shrine is capped with a three-quarters dome rather like a Muslim tomb.

Of greater architectural interest are the *Memorials of Virarajendra and Lingarajendra*, standing in a compound on top of a hill to the north of Madikeri. Like the temple, just notice that these funerary monuments have bulbous domes framed by slender corner finials. The chambers beneath have plain walls.

Raja's Seat at the western edge of Madikeri is a small pavilion commanding a breathtaking view of the valley beneath, through which the road descends to Mangalore.

B. TALAKAVERI

This pilgrimage spot, about 35 km. southwest of Madikeri via Bhagamandale, is situated on the wooded slopes of Brahmagiri, a peak rising 1,355 m. above sea level. Modest shrines dedicated to Ishvara and Ganapati stand here, with two square tanks in between. The smaller tank is particularly sacred since its water is identified with the *Source of the Kaveri*. An upsurge in water level, signifying the annual rebirth of the river, is observed during the Tula Shanaramana festival in October, an event that attracts crowds of worshippers.

17. Mangalore

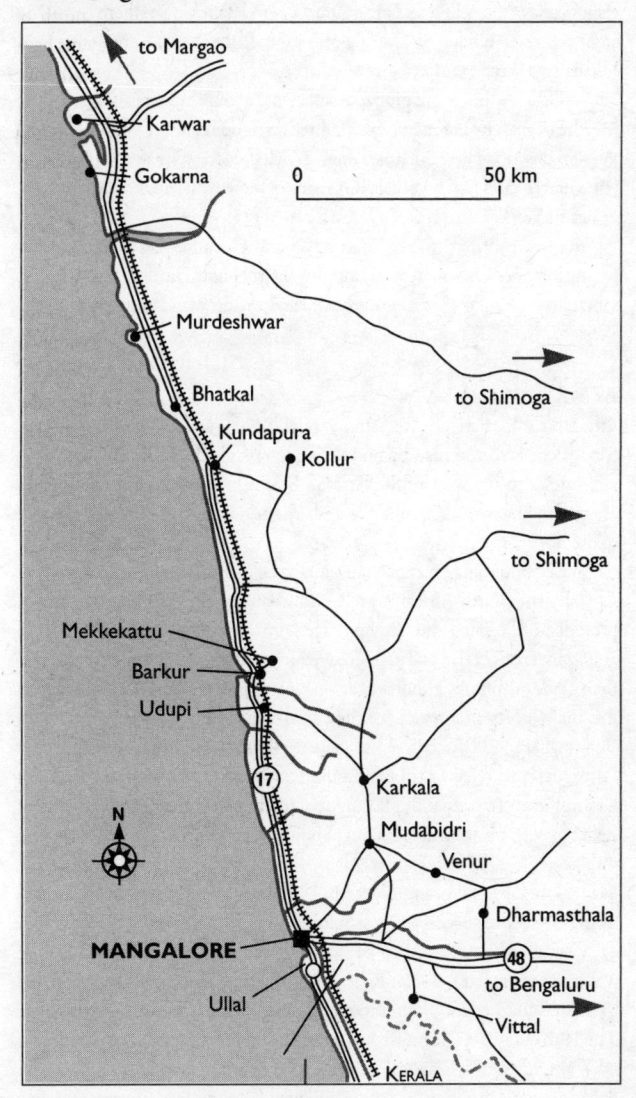

A tour of Kanara, as the narrow coastal strip of Karnataka is known, offers visitors one of the richest and most attractive landscapes in Southern India. The architecture is unique to the region; so, too, the bhuta ceremonies and Yakshagana theatre performances.

While a few hours are probably sufficient to tour the sights of Mangalore [A], the largest city in Kanara, two or three days should be set aside to reach all the sites described here, such as Udupi [B], Mudabidri [C], Karkala [D], Venur [E], Vittal [F] and Dharmasthala [G], many of these with Jain monuments. The village of Mekkekattu [I] is of interest for its bhuta shrine.

The towns of Bakur [H], Bhatkal [K] and Gokarna [L], to the north of Mangalore, are also worth visiting for their Hindu shrines. The goddess sanctuary at Kollur [J] is remotely situated in the wooded foothills of the Western Ghats.

A. MANGALORE

Attractively located on the estuary of the Netravati and Gurpur Rivers, Mangalore is surrounded by undulating terrain cloaked in groves of palms, with views to the west of the Arabian Sea. It is today a busy commercial centre, trading in timber, roof tiles and groundnuts, with a new port situated to the north.

The cosmopolitan mix of Mangalore's population was noticed as early as 1342 by the North African traveller, Ibn Battuta, who commented on the presence of Persians and Yemenis. These merchants were attracted by the abundant crops of rice and pepper for which Kanara was famous, conducting their trade with both Hindus and Jains. At this time Mangalore was one of the main ports of Kanara, coming under the sway of the emperors of Vijayanagara [20B-C]. In 1526 and 1547 the port was raided by the Portuguese, who levied tribute on the Vijayanagara governors. However, it was not until 1670 that the Portuguese made a treaty with the Nayakas of Ikkeri [19C], who permitted them to build a factory here. The Nayakas were displaced in 1763 by Haidar Ali of Srirangapattana [15C], who made Mangalore his naval headquarters. In 1784 the city was taken by the British from his son and successor, Tipu Sultan.

Virtually the only vestige of the fortifications with which Mangalore was once provided is *Sultan Battery*, an isolated circular bastion attributed to Tipu Sultan overlooking the picturesque estuary of the Gurpur River. The 19th century Lighthouse on top of the hill in the central part of the city takes the form of a Classical column. The nearby *Idgah*, with a qibla wall flanked by squat minarets, is now engulfed by a modern extension. A few metres away is the *Jesuit College of St Aloysius*. Its chapel, built in 1882, has an extensive series of wall frescoes and ceiling oil paintings executed in a typical European manner by the Italian artist Antonio Moscheni. The *Rosario Cathedral*, recently renovated, is the only church in the city with a dome. Tucked away in the narrow streets near the old port is the *Jami Mosque of Zinad Baksh*, entirely rebuilt during Tipu's occupation in a typical indigenous style with ornate wooden columns, brackets and beams. The prayer hall is topped with a double gabled roof clad in copper sheets and terracotta tiles. The mimbar within is also of intricately worked wood. British remains are mostly confined to the graves and obelisks in the cemetery adjoining the *Church of St Paul*. Erected in 1843, this simple structure is dominated by a triple-stage tower.

The *Seemanthi Bai Government Museum* in the northern part of Mangalore has a small collection of antiquities, including a remarkable bronze bell, complete with a miniature Lakshmi shrine. There are also wooden carvings of divinities, such as Bhairava and Hanuman, as well as bhuta figures from Mekkekattu. Stone sculptures discovered at Barkur date back to the 13th century; later sculptures portray local warriors.

Kadri Hill, a wooded rise with caverns reputedly inhabited by local yogis, is located 3 km. from the centre of Mangalore. The *Manjunatha Temple* at the base of the hill dates from the Nayaka period, though its history must be much earlier, since it is associated with the Hindu saints Matsyendranath and Gokarnath. While devotees worship the Shiva linga in the sanctuary, they also pay respect to Buddhist images installed in the verandah according to a local syncretistic rite. The temple is contained within a rectangular compound, entered on the east through a gateway in front of which is a tall lamp column. Steps from here ascend to sacred spots on the hill. The Manjunatha shrine, a modest square chamber, is roofed with a pyramidal tower.

The concrete screens of the temple verandah, replacing timber originals, are overhung by angled eaves and projecting lotus brackets. The three Buddhist images kept here are among the largest bronzes in Southern India. They are assigned to the 10th-11th century, and were probably cast in Tamil Nadu and then shipped to Mangalore. The 1.6 m. high Lokeshvara is dated 968. The three-faced figure with six arms is seated within an elaborate frame with diminutive guardians at either side. The bronze statue of Manjushri is of exceptional quality, with delicately cast face and headdress.

B. UDUPI

The religious significance of this town, 50 km. north of Mangalore, is enhanced by the fact that this was the birthplace of Madhava, the famous 12th century Vaishnava teacher. The focus of Udupi is a square surrounded by temples and mathas with ornate wooden verandahs. The latter serve as headquarters for a number different monastic orders.

The *Krishna Temple*, on the north side of the square, supposedly founded by Madhava himself, is a celebrated place of pilgrimage, especially during the Pargaya festival in January. The core sanctuary has a gilded metal screen through which Krishna holding the spear can be viewed. This image is said to have been miraculously rescued from a ship wrecked on the coast nearby. The temple is built in traditional style, with a wooden hall and sloping roofs clad in copper tiles; it faces east towards a large tank. Wooden chariots with three-quarter spherical towers created from brightly coloured ribbons tied to bamboo frameworks are parked outside the entrance to the temple.

The *Chandramauleshvara Temple*, dedicated to Shiva, stands in the middle of the square, surrounded by shops that cluster around its compound walls. The small sanctuary within the compound has a pyramidal roof divided into two tiers clad with metal and terracotta tiles, and topped with a brass pot finial. Similar materials roof the mandapa in front. The west side of the square is occupied by the *Ananteshvara Temple*, consecrated to Vishnu. Its apsidal-ended sanctuary and adjoining columned hall are surrounded by a continuous walled passageway roofed with sloping stone slabs. In contrast, the roofs over the sanctuary and hall are sheathed in copper. The frontal gable has wooden struts with hanging hands and a monster mask at the apex. The rear panel, also of wood, shows a linga flanked by elephants, guardians, peacocks and lotuses. A stone altar with a finely carved base is located immediately outside the east entrance to the temple.

Manipal, 3 km. east of Mangalore, is a progressive industrial and educational centre, famous for its medical college. *Hasta Shilpa Heritage Village* established by Vijayanath Shenoy is an unusual private museum (appointment essential). Here visitors can walk through streets with reconstructed vernacular houses brought from all over the region. The interiors are meticulously restored and crammed with characteristic domestic objects, including bronze vessels. Other highlights include a tile-roofed shrine with wooden bhutta figures, and two modern structures housing collections of Maratha devotional paintings from Thanjavur [40 A], and coloured prints by Ravi Varma, Kerala's most famous artist.

C. MUDABIDRI

This town, 35 km. northeast of Mangalore, is attractively situated in the midst of wooded hills with distant views of the Western Ghats. That this was a Jain centre of importance is indicated by the many temples, known as bastis, and mathas. Many of these shrines and monasteries were sponsored by the local Chauta chiefs and their families in the 15th and 16th centuries.

Chandranatha Basti, Mudabidri.

The largest and most elaborate monument at Mudabidri is the *Chandranatha Basti* of 1429. This stands in a compound at the western end of the main street of the town and is entered through an imposing entrance portico. The main temple consists of a rectangle of walls containing the sanctuary and two interconnecting mandapas. The hall interiors are massive, with elaborately decorated columns and doorways flanked by carvings of guardian figures and pot-and-foliage motifs. Several fine bronzes of Jinas in ornate frames are displayed in the inner hall. The surrounding verandah has full-height columns carrying a stone tiled overhang. Two additional sloping roofs above the sanctuary are coated with copper tiles on angled wooden brackets. The roof over the outer hall has been altered, but its original frontal gable is intact. The wooden panel here shows a Jina flanked by elephants, with guardian figures and female attendants holding flowers beneath. The struts are fashioned as hanging hands, and there is a brass monster at the apex.

In front of the temple stands a detached mandapa, an addition of 1452. This hall is notable for its magnificently carved columns, which display a variety of designs incorporating miniature figures, knotted patterns and lotus motifs. The central bay is roofed with an ornate lotus medallion ceiling. A 16.5 m. high lamp column, with animals and figures on the double capital, stands freely in front.

The *Jain matha* close to the entrance to the Chandranatha Basti is home to an important collection of manuscripts (permission required to visit). Other temples scattered throughout the town present smaller but comparable schemes to the Chandranatha. The *Settara* and *Shantinatha Bastis* are laid out according to the standard rectangular plan, with surrounding verandahs. Each temple has an additional subshrine to accommodate images of the 24

Tirthankaras arranged on a long stone pedestal. Exactly this type of Tirthankara shrine forms the main unit of the *Derama Setti Basti*, which has a long sanctuary approached through a broad columned hall. The temple is roofed with double tiers of sloping stone slabs with a flat area in the middle, with log-like strips covering the joints.

The *Guru Basti*, almost as large as the Chandranatha Basti, conforms to the standard rectangular scheme, with a line of three mandapas leading to the sanctuary, where an imposing, 2 m. high image of Parshvanatha is venerated. The columns in the outer hall are finely worked, as are those in the entrance structure. The latter has sloping stone tiers on four sides of a raised flat roof marked by a battlemented parapet. A stone altar is seen outside the temple compound on the other side of the street. The *Kote* and *Vikrama Setti Bastis*, dedicated to Neminatha and Adinatha respectively, are simpler and smaller structures.

The remains of the *Chauta Palace* are located on the western fringe of Mudabidri. The dilapidated apartments are of interest for the carved wooden doorways and columns showing mythological scenes, attendant figures, animals, birds and foliation.

Jain Memorials stand at the eastern end of the town. These curious laterite monuments are pyramidal in shape, with diminishing tiers of mouldings. *Badagu Basti* is situated just north of the town, on the road to Karkala, overlooking an idyllic landscape. The temple consists of a simple rectangular building with a sloping roof. The frontal wooden gable has a panel showing a seated Jina.

D. KARKALA

Located 18 km. north of Mudabidri, 35 km. southeast of Udupi, this town may also be reached from the other side of the Ghats via Sringeri [19H].

Karkala is an importance centre of Jainism in Karnataka, most of the older temples being bastis associated with the local Bhairavasa rulers. The most interesting monuments are situated outside the town. About 1 km. to the east is a granite outcrop, on top of which is the *Gommateshvara Monolith*, approached by a flight of rock-cut steps. The 13 m. high image was completed in 1432, in obvious imitation of the earlier and larger example at Sravana Belgola [15H]. The Karkala monolith depicts a naked figure, the face staring straight ahead with a serene expression, the arms hanging limp to the sides. The free-standing image is surrounded by a low railing. A column set up outside the enclosure is topped with a seated figure of Brahma.

At the base of the steps leading to the Gommateshvara monolith is the *Chaturmukha Basti*, dating from 1587. The temple is strictly symmetrical in layout: the sanctuary in the middle of a columned hall has doorways on four sides, each of which fames three stone images. In this way a set of 12 Tirthankaras receive worship. The surrounding colonnaded verandah, roofed with sloping stone slabs, has projecting porches in the middle of four sides.

About 1 km. west of the Gommateshvara monolith, at the foot of a densely wooded hill, stands the *Neminatha Basti*. The sanctuary and double halls of this temple are surrounded by a rectangle of walls sheltered by a colonnaded verandah. The subshrines are aligned with an open hall in front. The column that stands to the east of the complex is the finest at Karkala. A triple set of basement mouldings supports a fluted column adorned with bands. The ornate double capital carries a diminutive pavilion.

In the middle of Karkala, at the eastern end of the town's main street, is the *Anantapadmanabha Temple*, founded in 1567. Dedicated to Vishnu, the sanctuary enshrines a reclining image of the god. The doorway is surrounded by delicately worked friezes of lotus ornament and warrior figures. The open hall in front is raised on a basement enlivened with a frieze of elephants, extended as seating on three sides. The columns here have fluted shafts and pronounced double capitals. The roof above has two sloping tiers of stone slabs, with a frontal fable imitating timberwork. In contrast the pyramidal roof over the shrine is sheathed in copper tiles and has a pot finial. The popular *Venkataramana Temple*, located in the same street, has been much renovated in recent years.

E. VENUR

Another side trip from Mudabidri is to the small settlement of Venur, 15 km. to the east, a total of 80 km. from Mangalore. This Jain centre was headquarters of the local Ajila chiefs, who were responsible for commissioning the *Gommateshvara Monolith* in 1604. Similar, but not quite as high as the one at Karkala, this example also stands in a compound, outside which is a column with a seated figure of Brahma on top. Nearby *Parshvanatha Basti*, a contemporary structure, follows the standard rectangular layout already noted for temples at Mudabidri.

Kallu Basti, the largest at Venur, is dedicated to Shantinatha. This 17th century temple presents an imposing colonnade carrying the overhang of the stone roof. Steps ascend to an upper chamber that is provided with its own sloping roof and capping pavilion. The long structure to one side of the temple enshrines a line of 24 Tirthankara images. Beyond the entrance gateway is a lofty column standing on a triple basement. Its fluted shaft with decorated bands carries an ornate double capital with cut-out animals at the corners. The miniature pavilion on top is complete with a stone finial.

F. Vittal

This town, 50 km. east of Mangalore, is worth visiting for the *Panchalingeshvara Temple*, in a style typical of northern Kerala, though now entirely rebuilt. Dedicated to Shiva, the temple is partly apsidal in plan, with a linga sanctuary surrounded by a double passageway approached through twin halls preceded by a porch. The copper clad roof is arranged in three sloping tiers carried on wooden struts. The tiers wrap around the semicircular end of the sanctuary, giving the building a heavy, almost ship-like appearance. An elaborate gable rises over the porch. The temple stands in the middle of a spacious rectangular enclosure surrounded by colonnades. An open pavilion sheltering a large Nandi image, an altar and a flag column stand in front (west). Minor shrines for Ganapati and Dura are located to the north.

G. Dharmasthala

This attractive site, surrounded by forested hills, rice fields and areca (palm) plantations, is located 75 km. east of Mangalore, a short distance from the Netravati River, a bathing centre for pilgrims. Dharmasthala is associated with the influential Heggede family, followers of Jainism and patrons of the *Manjunatha Temple*, in which a linga was installed in 1780. Curiously, the priests of this sanctuary are Madhava Vaishnavas. The sponsorship of the Heggede family continues to this day, as can be seen in the finely executed Gommateshvara monolith, completed in 1973.

The small but interesting *Manjusha Museum* is located opposite the entrance to the temple. Among the religious objects displayed here are carved and painted panels, and bronze sculptures and bells. There is even a selection of ethnographical household objects. Two temple chariots covered in wooden figures stand in front.

H. Barkur

Located just off NH17, 74 km. north of Mangalore, Barkur was one of the richest ports of Kanara in the 15th-16th centuries. However, the river on which the town is situated silted up, and the modern port is now located 4 km. to the west. Barkur's past prosperity is reflected in the many religious monuments that dot the town. The largest is the *Panchalingeshvara Temple* situated beside a tank at the southern end of Barkur. It is approached through an entrance gateway with projecting porticos on two levels; hero stones are set up beside the steps. The inner compound has two east-facing linga shrines, one apsidal ended (south), the other rectangular (north), both with Nandi pavilions in front. Though extensively renovated, the sloping roofs are original features, including that which wraps around the part-circular shrine. Plastered niches with different pediments and false doors can be made out on the outer walls of the north shrine.

The *Ganapati Temple* in the northern part of Barkur also consists of twin east-facing shrines standing in a compound. These rectangular structures are consecrated to Shiva and Ganapati. The Shiva shrine has two storeys with shallow niches and false doors. Both levels are overhung by sloping tiled roofs. A large entrance structure running the full width of the compound has a continuous sloping stone roof. Interior columns are elaborately carved with deities, dancers, musicians, creepers and buds. The rear walls are enlivened with murals of recent date. A short distance further north, on the outskirts of the town, is an earthen fort dating from the 17th century Nayaka era. It is laid out as a square, with an entrance on the east.

Other monuments in Barkur include the *Someshvara* and *Somanatheshvara Temples*, both with focal sanctuaries in the middle of small compounds. The Someshvara has deities carved on the wooden brackets that carry the angled roof. The frontal gable is ornate, with an embossed metal mask at the apex. The Somanatheshvara is the only temple at Barkur to preserve stone carvings of guardians beside the sanctuary doorway.

I. Mekkakattu

This small settlement, 8 km. north of Barkur, is celebrated for its *Nandikeshvara Temple*, dedicated to the bhuta, or spirit, cult. This shrine was totally renovated in the 1960s, with the result that the original wooden sculptures were dispersed, some to the Folklore Museum in Mysore [15A]. The new set of some 170 bhuta images is the largest and most complete series of any such shrine in Kanara. They are carved out of the wood of the jack-fruit tree and are painted in bright red, with boldly modelled faces outlined in white and black. The temple has two shrines arranged one above the other: the lower shrine accommodates the winged bull Nandikeshvara, surrounded by warrior figures; the upper shrine displays Nandikeshvara's consort sitting on the bull, surrounded by female attendants. A shed to one side is crowded with large and fierce guardian figures holding swords, mounted warriors, female attendants, bulls and even a tiger. Donor figures, also in brightly painted wood, occupy a subsidiary shrine.

J. Kollur

The pilgrimage temple at this site, 106 km. north of Mangalore via the port of Kundapura on NH17, is picturesquely situated at the foot of the Western Ghats, on a road that climbs through the Ghats to Shimoga [19A]. Though the *Mukambika Temple* at Kollur has a long history, the present building was erected in 1616 by Venkatappa, one of the Ikkeri Nayakas. The shrine is dedicated to the goddess Mukambika, who is worshipped in the form of a jyotirlinga incorporating aspects of Shiva and Shakti. The small sanctuary is topped by a pyramidal tower with an arch-shaped frontal projection; this is surmounted by a square roof sheathed in gilded copper. The building stands in a small compound surrounded by subsidiary structures with arched openings, angled overhangs and battlemented parapets. Yalis are carved onto the columns either side of the entrance portico on the east.

K. BHATKAL

This town on NH17, 155 km. north of Mangalore, is an important port with a large Muslim population; even so, it is well provided with Jain and Hindu monuments dating from the 16th-17th centuries. The two most important Jain temples face onto the main street. The *Chandranatheshvara Basti* consists of three east-facing shrines (with intermediate walls missing) adjoining a sequence of two long halls. The surrounding verandah has peripheral supports carrying a double-tiered sloping stone roof. An additional square hall in front has stone screens with circular and leaf-shaped perforations, overhung by angled eaves. The double-storeyed entrance structure has chambers on either side of a central passageway. Sloping roofs shelter both storeys. *Parshvanatha Basti* is situated a short distance to the south, set back slightly from the street. The temple's location is marked by a tall lamp column that stands outside the walled compound. It resembles those at Mudabidri.

Bhatkal also has several interesting Hindu shrines. The 17th century *Choleshvara Temple* within the town is a small but ornate building with intricately worked wall pilasters and niches filled with flattish carvings of divinities. The pyramidal tower is crowned with a square roof. The *Raghunatha Temple* resembles the Choleshvara, except that its interior is more decorated, with guardian figures either side of the shrine doorway.

The next group of monuments at Barkur to be described are situated on the other side of NH17, 2 km. east of the town. The most important of these is the *Khetapai Narayana Temple*, consecrated to Vishnu and named after a local chief who erected it in 1540. This small, but finely finished building consists of a sanctuary and hall enclosed in a rectangle of stone screens with slats imitating those of wood. The screens are raised on a basement covered with reliefs illustrating Ramayana episodes and other mythological subjects. The supports and intermediate pilasters are carved with figures and decorative motifs. Cut-out yali balustrades with rolled ends mark the main entrance to the temple on the west. The doorway is flanked by guardian figures sculpted in full relief; the lintel is partly concealed by a beam with cut-out lobes and carved decoration. Similar beams surmount the slatted screens. The sloping stone roof rises steeply on four sides, the upper part being flat with log-like strips.

The interior of the Khetapai Narayana temple has squat columns with lathe-turned slats. The ceiling over the central bay has a finely carved central lotus panel with the dikpalas in the corners. The temple stands in the middle of a small compound, outside which stands a lofty column. Carvings of a donor figure, Agni, Varuna and Kubera adorn the base. An adjacent small structure has a sanctuary and open hall, both with peripheral supports carrying pyramidal roofs composed of angled stone slabs.

A short distance to the south stands the *Shantappa Nayaka Tirumala Temple*. This resembles the Khetapai Narayana in all respects, except that the outer screens are supported on blocks rather than a sculpted basement. The beam in front of the outer doorway has triple lobes, with a foliated mask in the middle, and riders on makaras at either side. The interior shrine doorway is flanked by images of Hanuman and Balakrishna (left), and Garuda and Krishna holding up the Govardhana Mountain (right). Ramayana friezes cover the beams supporting the central ceiling bay.

L. GOKARNA

This pilgrimage town on the Arabian Sea lies 62 km. north of Bhatkal, some 10 km. west of NH17. (From here it is only 115 km. north via Karwar to Margao in South Goa [13A].) Gokarna owes much of its charm to the traditional brick houses with tiled roofs facing narrow streets than lead down to the magnificent beach.

The principal monument here is the *Mahabaleshvara Temple* (only Hindus admitted). Destroyed by the Portuguese in 1714, the temple was subsequently rebuilt under Maratha patronage. It stands in a high walled compound, entered on the west, from the direction of the ocean. The pilastered walls with battlemented parapets and the octagonal domed tower over the sanctuary reflect the influence of contemporary architecture in Maharashtra. Triple porches give access to a spacious hall, the floor of which is engraved with a giant tortoise. A doorway decorated with embossed brass sheets frames the small stone linga that serves as the principal object of devotion. This is partly concealed by a brass face-mask and sheltered by naga hoods.

18. Chikmagalur

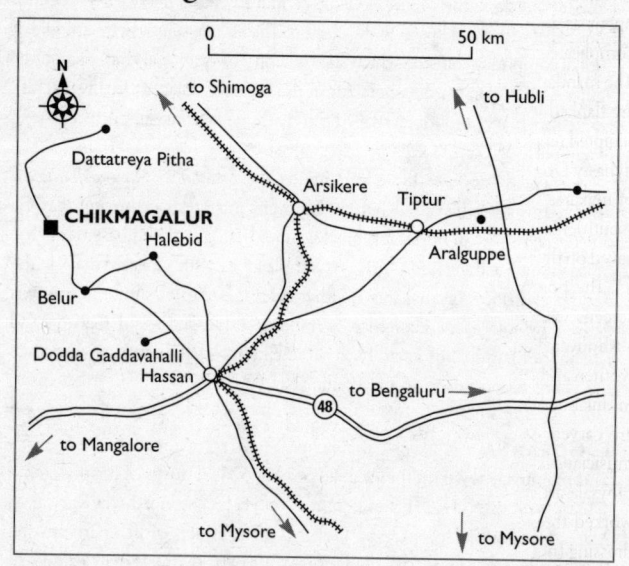

This market town, surrounded by coffee plantations and dense forests, is attractively situated beneath Mulainagiri, which, at 1,923 m., is one of the highest peaks in Karnataka. Chikmagalur makes a convenient base from which to visit the celebrated Hoysala temples at Belur [A] and Halebid [B], for which a full day is recommended. Those with extra time and interest may also take in the unusual shrine at Dodda Gadavahalli [C].

Visitors interested to see more of the elevated landscape of the Western Ghats should make a half-day excursion to the shrine of Dattatreya Pitha [D]. Those journeying on to Hampi [20] or Hubli [21] can pass by the temples at Arsikere [E] and Aralaguppe [F], both of artistic merit. Travellers to Shimoga [19] can select a scenic route through the wooded landscape, via the celebrated matha at Sringeri [19H].

A. Belur

Located 22 km. south of Chikmagalur, the lively town of Belur is famous for the *Chennakeshava Temple*. This outstanding example of Hoysala architecture and art was erected in 1117 as a victory monument by the Hoysala king Vishnuvardhana.

The temple stands in a walled compound at the end of the main street of the town, entered through a Vijayanagara styled gopura of the 16th century. Built entirely of grey-green schist, the temple itself consists of a sanctuary with subsidiary shrines facing outwards in three directions, and a mandapa that opens as a porch on the east. Both sanctuary and mandapa are laid out on complicated stepped plans, repeated in the plinth on which they are elevated. The mandapa is approached by double flights of steps on three sides. The steps are flanked by double tiers of model shrines with pyramidal towers, also by sculpted representations of a youth stabbing a lion, an emblem of the Hoysala dynasty. Doorways at the tops of the steps are headed by arches framed by pairs of makaras with profusely foliated tails sitting on pilasters. Icons of Vishnu (south), Narasimha (east) and Varaha (north), each mounted on Garuda, are caved on the middle of the lintels.

The porch extension of the mandapa is enclosed by perforated stone screens with geometric designs. They incorporate courtly scenes showing Vishnuvardhana, the royal patron of the monument, seated with his ministers, women and attendants (either side of the east doorway). Friezes of elephants, undulating lotus stalks, maidens, dancers and musicians on the walls beneath are carved with remarkable precision. Angled brackets sculpted as female musicians are sheltered by an angled overhang. These masterpieces of Hoysala art depict sensually modelled dancing maidens beneath intricately worked trees and foliage. The figures appear in diverse poses: hunting or dressing (north); and dancing, plaiting hair, gazing into a mirror, or holding a parrot (east). Label inscriptions identify the different artists. The walls of the sanctuary are raised on a basement that is comparatively plain. Deities beneath temple-like towers, carved in relief, cover the wall projections. No tower is preserved above. Subsidiary shrines on three sides, complete with stunted towers, have basements with rows of elephants, yalis and horses. Wall panels here depict multiple incarnations of Vishnu with consorts beneath elaborate pediments.

The interior of the Chennakeshvara temple is dominated by majestic, polished polygonal and lathe-turned columns, with prominent double capitals. The four central supports have angled brackets fashioned as gracefully posed maidens standing beneath ornate foliation. The ceiling here and elsewhere in the mandapa consists of dome-like compositions with corbelled rings of masonry decorated with scrollwork and lotus buds. Large guardian figures dressed in richly jewelled costumes flank the sanctuary doorway. The lintel shows Vishnu and Lakshmi seated within an arch, framed by outsized makaras with fanciful tails. An almost 2 m. high image of Krishna, partly coated with silver and brass, receives worship in the sanctuary.

The 12th century *Ammanavara Temple* occupies the northwest corner of the Chennakeshava enclosure. Sculpted panels set into the walls show maidens and divinities beneath trees. Additional carvings are seen in the *Kappe*

Chennigaraya Temple, to the south. A stepped tank with a pair of model shrines is situated in the northeast corner of the complex.

B. HALEBID

This small village, 14 km. east of Belur, is identified with Dorasamudra, the Hoysala capital. The first great ruler of Dorasamudra, Vishnuvardhana (1108-41), was responsible for expanding the Hoysala domains. He subdued the Late Chalukyas of Basvakalyan [25D] to the north, and secured the south against the Pandyas of Madurai [44A]. The reigns of the later kings Ballala II and Narasimha, which spanned 1173-1235, were marked by military triumphs that established the Hoysalas as the most powerful dynasty in Southern India at the time. The territories under their control encompassed most of Karnataka, as well as substantial parts of the Tamil lands. The last great Dorasamudra kings, Narasimha III and Ballala III, spent much of their reigns battling against the Yadavas of Devagiri [5C]. Both the Hoysalas and Yadavas succumbed to the Delhi invaders at the beginning of the 14th century.

The overgrown and crumbling Ramparts of the Hoysala capital at Halebid enclose an approximate half circle, almost 4 km. across. The granite walls have gateways with bent entryways interspersed with square bastions. The ramparts on the east overlook Dorasamudra, a vast tank after which the capital was named. Religious monuments of the period stand within the walls, but nothing can now be seen of the Hoysala palace.

The double-shrined *Hoysaleshvara Temple*, begun in 1121, but not completed until after the middle of the 12th century, represents the climax of the Hoysala artistic achievement. Like its counterpart in Belur, the temple is built entirely of grey-green schist. Each shrine consists of a sanctuary with three subsidiary shrines opening outwards, the walls of which are laid out on star-shaped plans. The sanctuaries open off mandapas with multiple projections. These halls are linked so as to form a spacious interior, partly open with porches and balcony seating on the east. In front (east) of each mandapa is a free-standing pavilion sheltering a large seated Nandi image. Richly decked with bells and jewels, the animals face towards the lingas that receive worship within the sanctuaries.

All of these architectural components are elevated on a high plinth that repeats the complicated outlines of the building. The basement that runs around the mandapas and sanctuaries are enlivened with friezes of elephants, lions, horses, scrollwork, epic scenes, makaras and geese with foliated tails. Scenes from the Ramayana and Mahabharata (west side) include Rama killing the golden deer, Rama and Sits with monkeys, and Bhishma dying on a bed of arrows. Krishna with gopis, or the same god fighting demons, are seen on the east. These legendary subjects are interspersed with courtly subjects: royal receptions, hunting expeditions and military exploits. The precision of the carvings and the variety of the compositions are unsurpassed in Southern Indian stone sculpture.

Divinities in animated poses cover the outer walls of the Hoysaleshvara temple. The figures all wear richly decorated costumes and headdresses. They stand beneath luxuriant scrollwork or foliation. Among the finest panels are those on the west side: Shiva dancing with the flayed skin of the elephant demon, Krishna holding up Govardhana to protect the herds, and the same deity playing the flute, Vishnu on flying Garuda, and dancing Devi. Panels on the north side show Shiva dancing on the dwarf, and Ravana shaking the mountain.

Doorways to the mandapas are approached by flights of steps flanked by model shrines with pyramidal towers. They give an idea of the forms of the superstructures over the sanctuaries, which were never completed. Swaying guardians encrusted with jewels and tassels are positioned either side of the doorways. The lintels are adorned with dancing icons of Shiva in foliated frames terminating in makaras. Perforated stone windows with geometric designs are set between the peripheral columns of the mandapas. Brackets angling outwards are fashioned as three-dimensional dancing maidens and musicians.

Corbelled ceilings carried on lathe-turned columns inside the temple incorporate friezes of miniature figures, such as Shiva dancing surrounded by the dikpalas and musicians. Guardians with ornate costumes and headdresses flank the sanctuary doorways.

The attractively landscaped grounds in which the temple stands partly serve as an open-air *Archaeological Museum*. Among the many 12th-13th century sculptures displayed here are a large seated image of Ganesha, and a fine Nandi.

A road running further south from the Hoysaleshvara temple for about 500 m. leads to a group of *Jain Bastis*. Three 12th century temples, built along side each other, have severely plain exteriors. The only sculptures to be seen here are striding elephants beside the steps, and an enlarged figure of Parshvanatha in the sanctuary of the central temple. Mandapa ceilings have rotating octagons filled with carved scrollwork, with central panels of Krishna. The road continues southwards for about another 300 m. until it reaches the *Kedareshvara Temple*. This star-shaped shrine has a moulded basement and a series of carved wall panels. Perforated screens illuminate the mandapa interior.

C. Dodda Gaddavahalli

This small village is reached from a small turnoff, about 28 km. south of Belur, on the road to Hassan. The *Lakshmidevi Temple* of 1113 here is an early example of the Hoysala style. Standing in the middle of walled compound, the temple consists of a central mandapa with sanctuaries on four sides. These are dedicated to Kali (north), Mahalakshmi (east) and Bhairava (south); the western sanctuary accommodates a Shiva linga. The shrine walls have shallow niches headed by tower-like pediments of different designs. The two-storeyed tower over the Bhairava sanctuary presents a sequence of intricately worked elements arranged in pyramidal fashion, capped by a multi-faceted square roof. Plainer towers with horizontal cornices are seen above the other three sanctuaries. Prancing yalis are positioned on the frontal projections.

The doorway to the Kali sanctuary within the temple is flanked by remarkable skeletal figures displaying daggers and skulls. The goddess enshrined within is an imposing seated figure brandishing various weapons.

D. DATTATREYA PITHA

A road running north of Chikamagalur skirts the peak of Mulainagiri, and continues along the ridge of Baba Budan Hill. This takes its name from a saintly Sufi figure who is supposed to have introduced coffee from Yemen to Southern India in about 1670. While this attribution is partly legendary, a shrine associated with Baba Budan is located 37 km. north of Chikmagalur, at an altitude of 830 m. above sea level. The *Shrine of Baba*, which consists of a natural cavern, accommodates four graves, believed to be those of the Saint's disciples, with an additional grave of his adopted daughter. (Baba Budan himself apparently returned to Yemen where he died.) The cavern, however, has also been claimed by Hindu devotees, who worship an empty niche cut into the rock, which they identify as Dattatreya, a Hindu saint, sometimes considered an aspect of Vishnu. The shrine is a popular place of pilgrimage for both Hindus and Muslims.

E. ARSIKERE

This small town, 75 km. east of Chikmagalur via Kadur, is worth visiting for its 13th century, Hoysala period *Chandramauleshvara Temple*. Both the sanctuary and open mandapa that stands freely in front are laid out on star-shaped plans. The sanctuary is topped by a tower that continues the angles of the plan all the way to the summit. Sculptures on the walls beneath are mostly defaced. The sanctuary is approached through an antechamber, the outer walls of which have niches topped by model temple towers. The open mandapa in front has balcony seating on all sides. Eight columns in the middle carry a great corbelled dome, almost 5 metres in diameter. Its interior is enlivened with cut-out ribs and pendant buds.

Hero stones showing scenes of battle are set up in the courtyard. Immediately to the north is an unadorned temple with twin-linga sanctuaries, fronted by a long mandapa.

F. ARALAGUPPE

This insignificant village, about 35 km. east of Arsikere via Tiptur, is of interest for its monuments dating from the Nolamba and Hoysala eras.

The 9th century *Kalleshvara Temple* is a modest structure, unadorned on its exterior except for pilastered walls and perforated stone windows. The inner mandapa is roofed with a small, but exquisitely crafted ceiling that may be considered the masterpiece of Nolamba art. The ceiling is divided into nine panels, with dancing Shiva in the middle surrounded by the dikpalas, all smoothly modelled in high relief. Flying attendants carrying garlands are seen at the corners.

A short distance away stands the Chennakeshava temple, assigned to the 13th century. Columns here are elegantly treated in the typical Hoysala manner. Richly carved friezes on the basement, though worn, show episodes from the Krishna story. Sculptures on the walls above are topped by sharply cut pilasters.

19. Shimoga

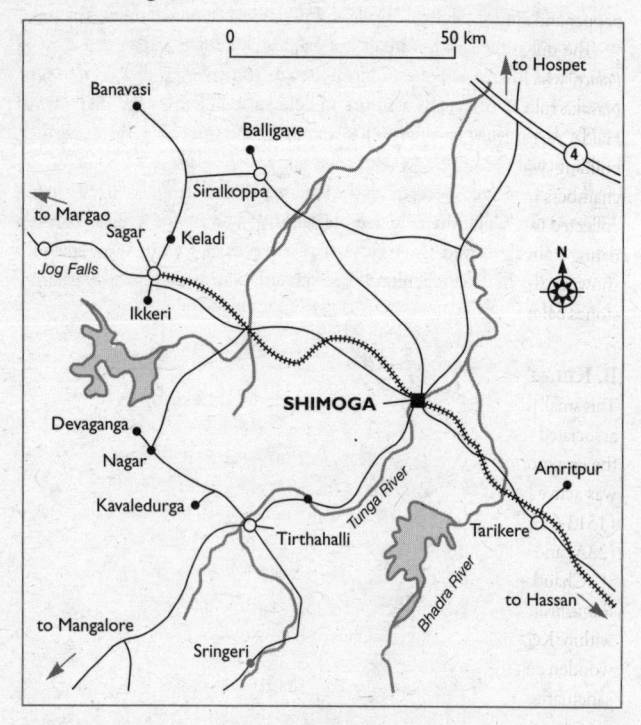

Shimoga is the principal centre of Malnad, the forested region of western Karnataka, renowned for its wooded peaks and spectacular waterfalls, especially that at Jog. Shimoga [A] makes a convenient base from which to visit monuments and sites associated with the local 16th-17th century Nayaka rulers. The temples at Keladi [B] and Ikkeri [C] may be combined in a single day excursion, with another day set aside for the more remotely situated forts at Nagar [F] and Kavaledurga [G].

The pilgrimage shrine at Sringeri [H] can be visited en route to Karkala [17D] in Kanara. Additional time will be required to reach the Late Chalukya and Hoysala period temples at Balligave [D], Banavasi [E] and Amritpur [I].

A. Shimoga

Located on the bank of the upper Tunga River, Shimoga was an important centre under the Nayakas. In 1763 it was taken by Haidar Ali of Srirangapattana [15C], but by the beginning of the 19th century it had been absorbed into the kingdom of the restored Wodeyars of Mysore [15A]. Shimoga is today a lively market town noted for its trade in areca nuts and groundnuts, paddy rice, pepper and sandalwood.

The only historical feature of note within Shimoga is *Shivappa Nayaka's Palace*, which overlooks the Tunga. Though named after a prominent 17th Nayaka ruler, this recently restored structure actually belongs to the time of Haidar Ali in the latter half of the 18th century. The darbar hall is a two-storeyed building with massive wooden columns and lobed arched panels. Side chambers with balconies at an upper level look down into the hall. Sculptures collected from nearby temple sites are displayed in the palace grounds. Those dating from the 13th century Hoysala period include a panel from Balligave showing Shiva and Parvati seated beneath an ornate frame. Most of the hero stones belong to later times.

B. KELADI

This small town is located 6 km. north of Sagar, 72 km. northeast of Shimoga, is associated with the Nayaka rulers who began their careers as governors under the emperors of Vijayanagara [20B-C]. The first known Nayaka, Chaudappa, was active here at the beginning of the 16th century. His successor, Sadashiva (1513-63), gained renown in the campaigns against the Adil Shahis of Bijapur [23A] and was granted parts of Kanara in reward.

Chaudappa and Sadashiva were responsible, respectively, for the twin *Rameshvara* and *Virabhadra Temples* that stand within a walled compound within Keladi town. This is entered through a traditional structure with wooden columns and a sloping tiled roof. Both shrines have small east-facing sanctuaries roofed with pyramidal towers capped with square roofs. The walls are plain, except for shallow pilasters. A unique motif is the architect's measuring rod carved in shallow relief on the rear (west) wall of the Virabhadra shrine. Its height (78.5 cm.) is scaled into halves, quarters and eighths. Both shrines are approached though open mandapas with peripheral columns carved with riders on horses; intermediate slabs serving as balcony seating are decorated with friezes of temple facades. The angled overhangs are surmounted by battlemented parapets. The ceiling inside the hall of the Virabhadra temple is adorned with elaborate geometric patterns, some derived from textiles, as well as looped and knotted designs, Surya with the dikpalas, and the double-headed eagle, the gandabherunda, which served as an emblem of the Keladi rulers.

The smaller *Parvati Temple* stands within the same compound. Its hall has finely worked wooden columns and ceiling panels dating from the 17th century.

The *Keladi Museum*, immediately outside the compound, is home to a modest collection of artefacts and documents connected with Nayaka history.

C. Ikkeri

This site, 3 km. south of Sagar, served as the second Nayaka capital under Doddashankanna, who moved his headquarters here in 1563. The two next rulers, Ramaraja and Venkatappa, whose combined reigns spanned the period 1570-1629, were monarchs of an increasingly autonomous kingdom. In 1614 Venkatappa declared his independence from Vijayanagara. Many victories are attributed to Venkatappa, who extended the Nayaka domains into central Karnataka and even northern Kerala. Ikkeri lost importance in about 1639 when the Nayaka capital was shifted to Nagar.

Nothing remains of the palace at Ikkeri described by Pietro della Valle, the Italian traveller who passed through this part of Karnataka during Venkatappa's reign. The only surviving monument of the era, the imposing *Aghoreshvara Temple*, is assigned to the reign of Doddashankanna in the second half of the 16th century.

Aghoreshvara Temple, Ikkeri.

The outer walls of the passageway that surrounds the north-facing sanctuary of the Aghoreshvara temple are raised on a high plinth with sharply defined mouldings. The stone tower that rises in a succession of storeys is capped by a three-quarters spherical roof. The large square mandapa in front is entered by doorways on three sides, with access steps flanked by yali balustrades. Wall slabs here imitate balcony seating with friezes of temple towers; arched windows with pierced stone screens above are sheltered by angled eaves. The spacious interior of the hall has 16 impressive columns, the shafts and double capitals of which are divided into multiple facets. Rings of concave lotus petals alternating with deeply carved scrollwork decorate the central ceiling panel. The sanctuary houses a huge pedestal that supports a polished basalt linga.

In front of the Aghoreshvara temple stands a *Nandi Pavilion*. The large sculpture of Nandi inside is glimpsed through arched windows separated by slender pilasters and overhung by angled eaves. A battlemented parapet with finials conceals the roof. A subsidiary shrine, possibly intended for an image of Devi, stands next to the temple. Prancing yalis are carved on the porch columns, with decorated balcony slabs between them. Perforated stone windows light the hall within.

D. BALLIGAVE

This small village, 2 km. north of Siralkoppa, 70 km. northwest of Shimoga, was once an important centre of learning, with mathas belonging to devotees of different Hindu theological schools. Balligave is also known for its 12th-13th century monuments dating from the Hoysala period.

The *Kedareshvara Temple* consists of three shrines opening off a common mandapa. The west and south sanctuaries have lingas, one of which is worshipped as Brahma; the north sanctuary houses a statue of Vishnu. The ornate pyramidal towers of these shrines have dome-like roofs and frontal projections with ornate arches topped by monster masks. The hall projects outwards as a porch, with peripheral seating slabs enlivened with rows of miniature temple towers. A carving on the central ceiling shows dancing Shiva surrounded by the dikpalas. The stone screens beside the doorways are fashioned as interlaced nagas.

To the northeast of the village stands the *Tripurantaka Temple*, now somewhat dilapidated. The mandapa in front is elevated on a plinth adorned with figures and animals, some illustrating Panchatantra fables, others in animated sexual postures. Hero stones are set up beside the entrance steps. The magnificently sculpted lintel over the doorway to the main sanctuary shows Shiva dancing within the skin of the elephant demon, with gods and miniature figures on either side.

A short distance from the Tiruparantaka temple, beside Jiddikera tank, is a 10 m. high *Commemorative Column* erected in the 12th century by a Late Chalukya ruler as a victory monument. The sculpture of a double-headed eagle, or gandabherunda, that tops the column is a 20th century replacement. The damaged original is now kept in a small shrine near the column base.

E. BANAVASI

This site, which overlooks the Varada River, 105 km. north of Shimoga via Siralkoppa, was a capital of the Kadamba rulers of western Karnataka in the 10th-11th centuries, and then an outpost of the Late Chaluykas. That Banavasi was also of importance in earlier times is indicated by Buddhist antiquities dating back to the 3rd century that were excavated here. They include several stupas, which are no longer visible.

The chief monument of interest today is the 12th century *Madhukeshvara Temple*, which stands in a compound extending to the river. Two shrines stand next to each other, set at a slight angle. They are approached through open mandapas with balcony seating sheltered by steeply sloping roofs, added in the 17th century. The interiors are notable for the fine, lathe-turned and multi-faceted columns typical of Late Chalukya architecture. An ornate sculpted panel of Shiva with Parvati is placed beside the doorway of the larger shrine.

F. NAGAR

This somewhat remote town is located in the forested hills of the Western Ghats, 86 km. west of Shimoga, via Hosanagara.

In 1639, during the reign of Virabhadra, the capital of the Nayaka kingdom was shifted from Ikkeri to the fort at Bidnur, later renamed Nagar. This move was prompted by an invasion of troops from Bijapur, followed by incursions from Mysore and Goa [11B]. Shivappa (1645-60) developed Bidnur into an impregnable citadel, and from here recovered most of the territories lost to the Wodeyars and Portuguese. But the Nayaka kingdom declined in later times; in the second half of the 18th century it was absorbed into the dominions of Haidar Ali.

Shivappa Nayaka's Fort, at the end of the town, is named after the ruler who did the most to improve and enlarge it. The citadel presents a formidable exterior of overgrown laterite ramparts, enhanced by European styled battlements with musket holes and cannon openings. The entrance, flanked by circular buttresses, is reached by a causeway over the moat. Little is preserved inside the walls, other than crumbling chambers and column blocks of the audience hall. An octagonal well and several small tanks testify to the need for providing the inhabitants with water.

A few modest shrines in the town beneath the fort date from Nayaka times. The most interesting is the Nilakanteshvara temple.

Devaganga, a pleasure restort of the Nayakas, is located in a delightful forested setting, 3.5 km. north of Nagar. This complex consists of tanks and fountains connected by a water channel fed by a natural spring. The largest tank, 25 by 18 m., has a small pavilion in the middle reached by a bridge; other smaller ponds have circular and lotus shapes. At the south end is a bathing place paved with slabs. A small Shiva shrine is elevated on the earthen bank overlooking the complex. There are no surviving royal structures, presumably originally built of wood.

The road from Devaganga continues through the Western Ghats before descending to Kollur [17J].

G. KAVALEDURGA

This isolated citadel, also known as Bhuvanagiri, was one of the chief headquarters of the Nayakas in the 16th-17th centuries. It is located 25 km.

southwest of Nagar, some 90 km. west of Shimoga via Tirthahalli. Kavaledurga occupies one of the most elevated points in the Malnad. A stone pathway climbs through a set of gates, each marking a circuit of walls at successively higher levels protecting the innermost fort.

The crumbling *Ramparts*, overgrown by trees, present a picturesquely ruined spectacle. The remains of walls and column blocks indicate decaying courtly structures; wells and tanks are located nearby. From the summit, 969 m. about sea level, there are spectacular views across the peaks of the Western Ghats towards the Arabian Sea.

The *Kashivishvanatha Temple*, the most complete monument Kavaledurga, occupies the innermost fort of the citadel. This Nayaka period building stands in a small compound, with an unusual pair of lamp columns outside. The temple itself has plain walls overhung by angled eaves, surmounted by trefoil battlements with corner finials. The pyramidal tower over the sanctuary is topped with a square roof. The arched entrance to the hall is flanked by rearing yalis carved onto columns.

Similar, but smaller shrines are seen in the town below the fort. They include the Anjaneya and Virupaksha temples, the former with animals and figures carved in relief on the sanctuary walls.

H. SRINGERI

This small settlement is located 103 km. southwest of Shimoga via Tirthahalli, the access road winding beside the upper Tunga River. Beyond Sringeri, the road follows the river to its source and then passes over the ridge of the Western Ghats before descending to Karkala.

The *Matha* at Sringeri was founded in the 9th century by Shankara, the celebrated teacher who is credited with founding the Advaita Vedanta school of Hindu philosophy. The pontiffs of Sringeri attained considerable renown as advisors to the first Vijayanagara emperors. The matha has maintained its religious importance through the centuries, and is today a popular pilgrimage centre.

The main complex at Sringeri is attractively situated on a terrace overlooking the forested bank of the Tunga. The 16th century *Vidyashankara Temple*, the principal monument here, enshrines a Shiva linga worshipped as a memorial of Shankara himself. The unusual appearance of the building is partly explained by the influence of earlier Hoysala architecture. The temple has a double apsidal-ended plan created by multiple setbacks, echoed in the high plinth on which the building is raised. The outer walls contain an east-facing sanctuary surrounded by antechambers and a passageway, and approached through a spacious mandapa. The high basement displays superimposed friezes of animals and figures, including the story of Arjuna fighting Shiva disguised as kirata, the hunter. Yali balustrades flank flights of steps ascending to each of the six doorways. The walls of the Vidyashankara temple are composed of angled panels carved with various deities, the most important being accommodated in niches headed by shallow relief temple towers. Among the many aspects of Shiva depicted here are Nataraja, and the god slaying the elephant demon, shooting the arrow at the demons of the triple cities, and appearing out of the linga to rescue Markandeya. All of Vishnu's avataras are represented, including Krishna playing the flute, and Rama seated with Lakshmana. The tower rising above the sanctuary has two multi-faceted storeys that are crowned by a hemispherical roof and pot finial. The massive piers inside the hall are treated as rearing yalis with riders, doubled at the corners, in the typical Vijayanagara manner. The piers carry heavy brackets and ceiling slabs with a central dome-like lotus. Fine bronzes are displayed in the sanctuary.

The *Sharada Temple*, a short distance north of the Vidyashankara temple, is a modern structure built in the Tamil style. The focal shrine is surrounded on four sides by a spacious corridor flanked by piers with animal brackets.

I. AMRITPUR

This small village, some 50 km. southeast of Shimoga via Tarikere, is of interest for the *Amriteshvara Temple* erected in 1196 by a general of the Hoysala ruler Ballala II. This outstanding example of Hoysala architecture is remarkable for its clearly articulated ornamentation. The outer walls of the linga sanctuary are carved with rare refinement, as is evident in the single pilasters headed by relief temple towers of different designs. Delicately incised creeper ornament occupies the intervening wall surfaces. The pyramidal tower that rises over the sanctuary presents superimposed sequences of elegantly carved parapet elements, each headed with a monster mask. Multiple images of Shiva occupy the arches in the middle of three sides, ascending to the dome-like roof. The frontal projection of the tower is capped with a fully modelled sculpture of a warrior battling a yali, a typical Hoysala motif. The spacious mandapa extending outwards, with projections in the middle of each side, is partly open as a porch. The peripheral seating is decorated with panels showing hunters, dancers, musicians and diverse Krishna scenes and Ramayana episodes. Shallow reliefs of model temples with complicated towers are positioned beneath. Lathe-turned columns are overhung by generous curving eaves.

20. Hampi

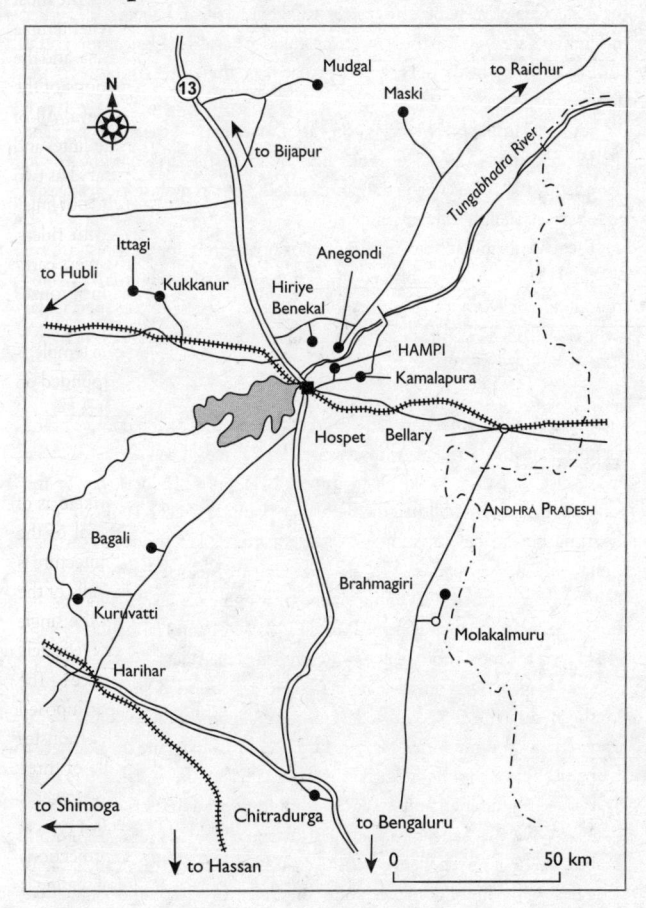

The remains of Vijayanagara, capital of the greatest of all Hindu empires in Southern India, constitute a spectacular ensemble of ruins set in a remarkable rugged landscape traversed by the Tungabhadra River. Known today as Hampi, Vijayanagara is one of the most celebrated tourist destinations in Karnataka.

Two full days are recommended to adequately visit the Hampi ruins, the most extensive of any in Southern India. The site encompasses the towns of Hospet [A] and Kamalapura [C], as well as the village of the Hampi [B]. Another day will have to be set aside for an excursion north of river, to explore the historical town of Anegondi [D] and the remarkable megaliths at nearby Hire Benekal [E].

The journey west towards Hubli [21], in the direction of Goa, passes near the Late Chalukya temple towns of Kukkanur [F] and Ittagi [F]. Other monuments attributed to these rulers are found at Bagali [H], Kuruvatti [I] and Harihara [J], southwest of Hospet. The road from these sites continues in the direction of Shimoga [19].

South of Hospet NH13 meets NH4 at Chitradurga [K], the most imposing citadel in central Karnataka. From here it is possible to continue on to Bengaluru [14]. An excursion to Brahmagiri [L], with its prehistoric vestiges, is possible via a slightly different route.

The road northeast from Hospet, passing not far from the early historic site of Maski [M], leads to the fortified city of Raichur [N]; from here it is possible to continue to Kurnool [32] in Andhra Pradesh. A visit to the spectacular fortress at Mudgal [O] is best made as an excursion from NH13, between Hospet and Bijapur [23].

Vijayanagara was founded in 1336, when the Sangamas seized control of the territories of the Hoysalas, whose power had already been eroded by the invasion of Karnataka by the Delhi army in 1311. Sons of a local warrior, the Sangama brothers established themselves at Hampi, a small religious spot on the Tungabhadra, before shifting their headquarters 2 km. south to a fortified capital, which they named Vijayanagara, City of Victory. From here they planned the campaigns that brought almost the entire peninsular south of the Tungabhadra under their control. Bukka I (1354-77) and Harihara II (1377-1404) were the most prominent of the early Sangamas rulers.

Vijayanagara was not the only state to be founded in this part of Southern India the 14th century. Several commanders of the invading Delhi army remained at Madurai [44A] in Tamil Nadu, from where they declared their autonomy. Simultaneously, the Bahmanis to the north of Hampi established an independent kingdom from their headquarters at Gulbarga [24A]. While the Sangamas managed to annex the Madurai dominion, thereby ending all challenge to their authority from the south, their struggles with the Bahmanis were ongoing. Even so, the Sangamas maintained their position as mighty rulers. Abdul Razzaq, Persian envoy to the court of Devaraya II (1424-46), describes the city of Vijayanagara, and the great Mahanavami festival to which all of the governors and lesser chiefs of the empire were summoned.

The influence of the Sangamas declined in the second half of the 15th century, and in 1485 the Vijayanagara throne was usurped by Narasimha Saluva, governor of Chandragiri [35C]. At about the same time the Bahmani kingdom also began to disintegrate, eventually splitting into five smaller states, including those of Bijapur, Bidar [25A] and Golconda [26E]. The

Saluvas did not remain in power for long, being displaced in 1503 by the Tuluva rulers. Under Krishnadevaraya (1510-29) and his successor and half-brother Achyutaraya (1529-42), Vijayanagara attained the height of its wealth and influence. Both emperors toured extensively throughout the empire, subduing rebellious chiefs and making donations to prominent temples in Andhra Pradesh and Tamil Nadu. They conducted battles against the sultans of Bijapur and Golconda, and also against the rajas of distant Orissa. The arrival of Europeans on the Arabian Sea coast brought Vijayanagara into contact with the Portuguese, who profited from shipments of horses from Arabia to the Hindu capital. Accounts of Vijayanagara by Portuguese traders confirm the magnificence of the city and the ostentation of the Tuluva court.

Achyutaraya was succeeded by Sadashiva, but this ruler was prevented from taking power by Ramaraya, commander of the imperial forces. Ramaraya kept Sadashiva virtually prisoner, while effectively controlling all state business. But Ramaraya's policies antagonised the Deccan sultans to such an extent that they formed an alliance intent on destroying Vijayanagara. This led inexorably to the great battle of January 1565 on the bank of the Krishna River, not far from Aihole [22E], where Ramaraya faced the combined armies of Bijapur, Bidar, Golconda and Ahmadnagar [6A]. The Vijayanagara forces were defeated and Ramaraya's head was paraded before the troops, who fled in panic. Ramaraya's brother, Tirumala, rushed back to the capital, where he collected Sadashiva and the imperial treasury before fleeing southwards to Penukonda [33D] in Andhra Pradesh. Left undefended, Vijayanagara was sacked and burnt. So complete was the devastation that the site was never again reoccupied. Except for the Virupaksha temple at Hampi, which is still a living religious centre, the Vijayanagara monuments were totally abandoned. They remain dilapidated and deserted to this day.

A. Hospet

Iron ore mines in the nearby hills means that Hospet is now a rapidly growing, dusty industrial city. However, it was originally a royal suburb of Vijayanagara, called Hosapattana. The largest monument here is the *Anatanashayana Temple*, 1.5 km. northeast of the centre, on the road to Hampi and Kamalapura. Dating from 1524, during the reign of Krishnadevaraya, this impressive building stands in a walled compound, entered from the road through a large but unfinished gopura. The temple has a partly open hall, with rearing yalis carved onto the outer columns. The rectangular sanctuary at the rear of the hall was intended for a reclining image of Vishnu, but only the pedestal remains. The brick and plaster tower above, which attains a height of 24 m., has a unique double-apsidal-ended roof.

An unfinished 15th century *Muslim Tomb* in the southern part of Hospet is another vestige of the Vijayanagara era. A massive *Earthen Dam Wall* about 1 km. further south, over which runs NH13, dates from the time of Krishnadevaraya. A Portuguese visitor observed that human sacrifices were performed here when the dam wall broke.

The *Tungabhadra Dam*, 3 km. southwest of Hospet, completed in the 1950s, is the largest in Karnataka, and a popular attraction. Regular supplies of water and electricity generated by this project have brought prosperity to the region.

B. Hampi

This small village on the south bank of the Tungabhadra River, 13 km. northeast of Hospet, has a longer history than that of Vijayanagara itself, having already been a sacred spot as early as in the 8th-9th centuries. Hampi was until recently an active village, with shops and stalls crowding the main bazaar street leading to the Virupaksha temple. Together with other large religious complexes, lesser shrines and monolithic sculpted images, the temple occupies a rocky gorge through which flows the Tungabhadra in a northeasterly direction. This group of monuments constitutes the *Sacred Centre* of Vijayanagara.

Natural features in the landscape here are identified with episodes in the Ramayana, especially those in which Rama enlists the aid of the monkey king Sugriva and his monkey general Hanuman. In spite of these Ramayana associations the *Virupaksha Temple* is dedicated to an aspect of Shiva. The deity here is commonly referred to as Pampapati, Lord of Pampa, the goddess after whom Hampi village takes its name. The legend of Pampa being betrothed and married to Virupaksha is celebrated in the chariot ceremonies that still take place along the bazaar street each March-April and October-November.

The Virupaksha temple is entered from the east through a lofty whitewashed gopura, a later renovation of an earlier structure. Its pyramidal brick and plaster tower, rising almost 50 m. high, is one of the loftiest in Karnataka. The gopura gives access to the outer enclosure of the temple, on the opposite side of which is a smaller gopura, dating from the reign of Krishnadevaraya, in the early 16th century. This emperor was also responsible for extending the main shrine that stands at the west end of the inner enclosure. The open mandapa was added in 1510, on the occasion of his coronation. Its outer columns are transformed into complex piers carved with yalis with riders. The animals are sheltered by deeply curved eaves; the brick and plaster parapet above is no older than the 19th century.

The mandapa interior is defined by 16 columns with rearing animals and riders. Ceiling paintings from the early 19th century have been restored to reveal deities on bright red backgrounds. In the middle of the ceiling are pairs of matching panels showing marriage scenes of Rama and Sita (front), and of Virupaksha and Pampa (rear). Both couples are shown standing with trees in the background, in the company of deities. Side panels depict Shiva shooting an arrow at the demon of the triple cities (right), and Kama aiming a similar arrow at Shiva (left). At the east end of the ceiling is a long panel depicting a procession with a pontiff being carried in a palanquin, accompanied by soldiers and musicians. The enclosed hall beyond, usually entered from the sides, leads to the main linga sanctuary. Minor shrines to the north house Bhuvaneshvari and Pampa, two aspects of Shiva's consort. The intricately worked grey-green schist columns, doorway and ceiling are taken from dismantled 11th-12th century temples.

The gopura in the north side of the inner enclosure of the temple gives access to *Manmatha Tank*. This is overlooked on the west by a group of small shrines dating back to the 9th century. The shrine dedicated to Durga has squat columns and sloping roof slabs. In the porch is a sculpted panel showing a warrior battling with a yali, a motif typical of the 13th century Hoysala period. The Tungabhadra River lies a short distance further north.

The crowded colonnaded street, which stretches some 750 m. east from the Virupaksha temple, serves as the *Hampi's Bazaar*. Persian and Portuguese visitors in the past commented on the jewels and sumptuous cloths that were sold here, as well as the beauty of the courtesans. Today, less glamorous squatters occupy the double-storeyed mansions that were once homes of the Vijayanagara courtly elite. Restored structures at the extreme end of the bazaar street include a mandapa with reused schist columns, and a monolithic Nandi, its head defaced, sheltered in an open pavilion. A stepped path from here leads over a rocky ridge to Achyutaraya's temple (see below).

The temples on *Hemakuta Hill* overlook Hampi from the south. They are built in the massive, unadorned style typical of the 14th century. Several have multiple sanctuaries topped with pyramidal stone towers divided into horizontal layers. One triple-sanctuaried example was built by a local chief as a family memorial at the turn of the 14th century, just prior to the foundation of Vijayanagara. Multi-storeyed gateways define a path climbing to the summit of Hemakuta Hill. The *Ganesha Temple* beyond occupies an elevated ridge with a fine view of the Tungabhadra. Its elegant portico has slender columns. An impressive 4.5 m. high image of Ganesha, carved out of a single boulder, is enshrined in the adjoining sanctuary. A similar, but smaller Ganesha is housed in an open pavilion at the southern base of Hemakuta Hill.

The *Krishna Temple*, built by Krishnadevaraya in 1516 to commemorate his victorious Orissa campaign and the conquest of the hill fort at Udayagiri [34D], is located a short distance further south. The colonnaded street of this complex extends east into groves of sugar cane. A tank to one side, with a pavilion in the middle, is surrounded by colonnades. The temple itself is entered through an imposing gopura with a frontal porch. The brick tower has partly collapsed but vestiges of the plaster reliefs illustrating Krishnadevaraya's troops can still be made out.

The main shrine is approached through a pair of mandapas. An unlit passageway surrounds the sanctuary; its outer walls divided into pilastered bays and niches. The brick tower over the sanctuary is capped with a hemispherical roof, but the image of Balakrishna looted from Udayagiri is now in the Government Museum in Chennai [36D]. Minor shrines cluster around the main temple; some have their walls covered with inscriptions. A granary with six flattish domes stands in the outer enclosure of the temple, the south.

The road in front of the Krishna temple passes through a triple-bayed gateway before continuing south to the Royal Centre of Vijayanagara, and Kamalapura. A few metres off this road, just south of the gateway, is the *Narasmiha Monolith*, a remarkable representation of the man-lion form of Vishnu, seated in yogic posture. This 6.7 m. high sculpture, the largest at Hampi, was commissioned by Krishnadevaraya in 1528. A shrine nearby shelters a rock-cut linga, now flooded by water from recent irrigation work.

The tour of the Sacred Centre described here continues by returning to Hampi and proceeding east along the bazaar street. A path turning off the north to follow the Tungabhadra provides majestic vistas of the surrounding rocks and hills. *Chakra Tirtha*, an auspicious bathing spot at a bend in the river, marks the place where Lakshmana, Rama's brother, crowned Sugriva. The tirtha is overlooked by Kodandarama temple, of interest for the Ramayana scene carved onto a boulder contained within the sanctuary. Multiple lingas in geometric formation are carved onto the boulders nearby. Here, too, there is a fine image of Anantashayana.

The path continues past *Achyutaraya's Temple*. In spite of its name this large-scale complex was actually built by the emperor's brother-in-law, and dedicated to the god Tiruvengalanatha in 1534. The temple is approached from the north along a colonnaded street, with a tank to one side. A pair of gopuras of almost equal size give access to two concentric walled enclosures. The shrines of the inner enclosure are much dilapidated. The free-standing mandapa in the outer enclosure has carvings of ascetics and seductive maidens on the column blocks. A path leads form the rear (south) of the temple to the irrigated valley that separates the Royal Centre of Vijayanagara from the Sacred Centre. Steps from this path that runs along the side of the valley ascend to the summit of *Matanga Hill*. Visitors who make the effort to climb the hill will be rewarded with a magnificent panorama of the Tungabhadra Valley and an aerial view of Achyutaraya's temple.

The next monument to be encountered on the riverside path is the *Narasimha Temple*. This 14th century temple stands within a small courtyard that is entered through open gateways on two sides. The main shrine has a pyramidal stone tower resembling those on Hemakuta Hill. *Sugriva's Cave*, immediately in front (north), is a natural cleft marked by painted white and ochre strips. This feature is believer to be the spot where Sugriva hid the jewels that were dropped by Sita when she was abducted by Ravana in his aerial chariot. A shallow pond nearby is known as Sita Sarovar. The river at this point is crossed by a *Bridge*, of which only the stone pylons survive. The *Purandaradasa Mandapa* on the bank nearby is named after a famous musician at the Vijayanagara court.

The path passes beside an exposed rocky shelf strewn with small mounds of stone assembled by pilgrims to ensure fertility and good fortune. Further along, the path passes through a double-storeyed gateway and beside a portal known as the *King's Balance*. This consists of two posts and a lintel, from which a balance or swing was once suspended. Here the Vijayanagara kings are supposed to have been weighed against gold and jewels, which were then distributed to brahmins.

The path continues to the *Vitthala Temple*, the finest at Vijayanagara, a total of 1.5 km. northeast of Hampi. The temple is sometimes thought to have been erected to house the celebrated image of Vithoba from Pandhapur [9H] in Maharashtra, which was removed for safety during the period of the Nizam Shahis. The foundation date of the Vitthala is not known for certain; it was possibly founded by Narasimha, first of the Tuluva emperors, at the beginning of the 16th century.

The main shrine stands in a rectangular walled compound entered through gopuras on three sides. Free-standing halls with internal podiums for displaying images of divinities are arranged around the east-facing main unit. This presents a somewhat severe exterior, concealing an inner passageway around the main sanctuary and an adjoining enclosed hall with porches.

The glory of the Vitthala temple is the open mandapa in front, an addition of 1554. This is elevated on a basement decorated with friezes of lions, elephants and horses, the last with Portuguese attendants; miniature shrines in relief house a complete set of Vishnu's incarnations. The mandapa columns present different combinations of cut-out colonettes and carved divinities and rearing yalis. (Contrary to popular belief, the tones emitted from the colonettes when slightly struck do not form part of a musical scale.) The outer piers are deeply overhung by curving eaves with ribs and rafters on the undersides. Ceiling slabs of no less than 10 m. span, carried on massive beams, once roofed the central hall: those still in place are carved with elaborate lotus medallions. The Garuda shrine that stands immediately in front (east) of the mandapa is conceived as a model chariot, complete with four decorated granite wheels. Its walls have cut-out colonettes; sadly, the brick tower is lost.

Colonnades line the streets outside the principal gopura of the Vitthala temple. That running northwards leads to the dilapidated *Ramanuja Temple*, which is contained within its own rectangle of walls, entered through a gopura with Ramayana carvings. The shrine within is approached through a mandapa with rearing yalis defining a central space. The colour aded street running eastwards from the Vitthala temple proceeds past a large tank, with an open pavilion in the middle. The street terminates some 900 m. away at a small pavilion with a podium, standing in the middle of the fields. The road from here proceeds south to Kamalapura, and north to Talarighat, the river crossing to Anegondi.

C. KAMALAPURA

This village situated at the edge of the Royal Centre of Vijayanagara lies about 12 km. northeast of Hospet. Kamalapura itself is of little interest, except for a dilapidated 18th century fort, and a large tank dating from Vijayanagara times, beside the main road running south of the village.

The *Archaeological Museum* (closed Fridays) is worth visiting for the instructive large-scale model of the Vijayanagara site that occupies the central court. Sculptures in the surrounding galleries include slabs carved with Virabhadra, Bhairava and Hanuman, as well as naga deities. Two headless figures appear to represent a royal couple. Jewellery, weapons and manuscripts are also shown. Commemorative stones collected from all over the site illustrate scenes of battle, and of heroes being received in heaven.

The road leading northwest from Kamalapura in the direction of Hampi arrives after a short distance at the fortifications of the *Royal Centre*. This part of the site is identified with the residence of the Vijayanagara emperors, and comprises the earliest and most complete example of a Hindu palace zone in Southern India. Some buildings stand relatively complete, having been constructed entirely of masonry, including their roofs and towers. The arched openings and stylized plaster decoration of these buildings, as well as their internal domes and vaults, have an Islamic appearance. This is not surprising since they are modelled on the architecture of the contemporary Bamani sultans at Gulbarga and Bidar, with whom the Vijayanagara rulers were in constant contact. Other structures in the Royal Centre were fashioned out of wood, terracotta and plaster, and were dismantled and burned in the sack of the city. Only their masonry foundations and column footings, revealed by recent excavations, can now be seen.

Soon after leaving Kamalapura, the road passes through the massive fortifications of the city, now repaired. The first monument to be seen inside the walls is the *Queens' Bath*. This is a pleasure pavilion with balconies projecting over a central square pool, now devoid of water. Little of the original plasterwork survives, except in the vaults of the arcaded passageway. The pavilion is surrounded by a water channel, once fed by a nearby aqueduct. The *Chandrashekhara Temple*, a short distance away, stands in the middle of a walled compound, with a gopura on the east. The two sanctuaries that open off a common mandapa present an unadorned appearance.

Returning to the Queens' Bath, the road proceeds around the outer walls of the enclosures of the Royal Centre. These walls have thin tapering profiles composed of irregularly shaped, but tightly fitting granite blocks. Though certain enclosures are known as the Zenana and the Mint, these identifications are not authentic.

The first enclosure to be visited is the largest. In one corner is the elevated floor of the *Hundred-Columned Hall*, probably the audience hall where the Vijayanagara emperors dispensed justice. Immediately to the south are the remains of other columned halls, some facing onto paved courts with wells and ponds. The functions of these structures are uncertain. An *Underground Chamber* with re-used schist blocks from a dismantled temple probably served as a treasury.

The highest point of the enclosure is the *Mahanavami Platform* at its northeastern corner. This monument is unique in the architecture of Southern India. It is built on ascending levels, its slightly tapering sides covered with animated reliefs of royal activities, including performances of music and dance, wrestling matches, the reception of visitors and hunting expeditions. Turkish figures with pointed caps, possibly slaves, also appear, in addition to parades of elephants, horses and even occasional camels. Staircases give access to the top of the platform, that on the west are flanked by intricately worked schist slabs. The Portuguese describe the Vijayanagara emperors ascending a platform to make sacrifices to a goddess, and to witness the processions of animals, soldiers and courtly women on the occasion of the Mahanavami festival. Hence the name of the monument.

Bathing tanks to the south of the platform include a remarkable *Stepped Pond* surrounded by steps and landings, all fashioned out of grey-green schist. Numbers and letters incised on the blocks indicate directions and levels. The pond was fed by a nearby aqueduct, which formed part of a complex hydraulic system that transported water to the Royal Centre from the tank at Kamalapura.

Returning to the entrance of the enclosure, visitors proceed along a road that passes through two massive gateways, of which only the bases still stand, before they reach the *Ramachandra (Hazara Rama) Temple*. Serving as a private chapel for the Vijayanagara emperors, this is the finest example of 15th century religious architecture at the site. The temple faces onto a plaza where many of the roads of the city once converged. Directly opposite are a reconstructed lamp-column and a small Hanuman shrine. A road leading in a northeasterly direction, lined with small shrines, now dilapidated, passes by the Yellamma temple. This shrine is still used by local villagers for worshipping a powerful goddess to whom goats are sacrificed.

The Ramachandra temple is contained within a rectangle of walls, the outer faces of which are covered with friezes of elephants, horses with Arab attendants wearing long cloaks, soldiers in military formations and female dancers. These parades correspond to the Persian and Portuguese descriptions of the Mahanavami festival. A modest gateway with a pillared porch leads into to the compound. Friezes on the inner face of the enclosure walls portray episodes from the Ramayana. They begin with the Shravanakumara prologue (right side of north gateway), recognised by the youth carrying his parents in baskets.

The outer walls of the main Ramachandra shrine are raised on a moulded basement and are divided into projections and recessed by pairs of pilasters. This scheme is relieved by single pilasters standing in ornate pots. A brick tower with a square roof (restored) rises above. The attached mandapa has elegant porches, that on the east are contained within a later extension. The outer mandapa walls are covered with reliefs arranged in three tiers. These depict the main events of the Ramayana. The story begins with the fire sacrifice of Dasharatha (north end of west wall), and ends with the enthronement of Rama with Sita (south end of west wall). Scenes on the east wall show Rama shooting the golden deer, and the climactic battle with Ravana.

The mandapa interior of the Ramachandra temple is of interest for the quartet of polished dolorite columns carved with different aspects of Vishnu. No icons are preserved inside the sanctuary, but the pedestal has slots for a trio of images, presumably for Rama, Lakshmana and Sita. A smaller twin-shrined temple stands immediately to the north. Sculpture panels here illustrate additional Ramayana episodes, as well as the story of Narasimha.

A path running west from the Ramachandra temple leads to the 'Mint Enclosure'. Here can be seen the cleared remains of a *Palace Structure*, with an inner court defined by verandahs on three sides. Circular brick-lined depressions in the court to the north indicate a garden for plants or trees. A recently discovered stepped pond to the rear has an unusual cow-headed water spout. The *Nine-Domed Pavilion* in the adjacent enclosure is a reception hall divided into vaulted bays. It is overlooked by a *Two-Storeyed Octagonal Pavilion* with a fanciful roof.

Returning to the Ramachandra temple visitors should then continue along the road leading to the Lotus Mahal (Zenana) Enclosure. The best preserved courtly structure in the Royal Centre, the *Lotus Mahal* is laid out on a symmetrical plan, with projections on each side. The double-storeyed facade has openings framed by lobed arches overhung by curved eaves at each level. A staircase tower provides access to the upper storey. The pavilion is roofed with nine towers, the central one being higher than the others, so as to achieve an overall pyramidal composition. In spite of its fanciful name, the pavilion probably served as a reception hall for the Vijayanagara emperors or their principal military commanders.

Standing in the northwest corner of the enclosure, immediately the left of the entrance, is a *Rectangular Building* with a long gabled roof, partly concealed by a perforated parapet. It is entered through a small doorway, while light and air are admitted only through small openings. These features suggest that the building may have served as a treasury. A collection of artefacts discovered in the excavations at Vijayanagara are displayed inside. They include (reused) limestone Buddhist panels dating back to the 2nd century, as well as Late Chalukya period columns and panels, and Vijayanagara era Jain icons. *Watchtowers* incorporated into the enclosure walls once surveyed the approaches to the Lotus Mahal. The example in the north walls has a square staircase tower topped by balconies on four sides; that in the southeast corner of the enclosure is octagonal in plan, with double arcades at the top surmounted by a pyramidal tower.

A doorway in the east wall of the Lotus Mahal Enclosure leads to an open space, probably used as a parade ground overlooked from the east by the *Elephant Stables*. This imposing structure consists of a line of 11 chambers, each accommodating one or two of animals used by the Vijayanagara emperors on state occasions. The stables are roofed with alternating domes and 12-sided vaults, arranged symmetrically either side of a central upper chamber, probably for drummers and musicians. The arched doorways and remnants of plaster decoration are Bahmani in style. The north side of the parade ground has an *Arcaded Structure* with a raised verandah, possibly used as a grandstand from which to review parades of troops and animals. The interior court would have been suitable for martial sports and animal fights. It is now used to display stray stone sculptures of Hindu diversities and Sati and hero stones.

A path behind the stables leads to a number of ruined temples. These face onto the road that begins in front of the Ramachandra temple. Here can be seen a dilapidated *Jain Temple* dating from the 15th century.

The tour of the Royal Centre concludes by returning to the Ramachandra temple and continuing west to reach the *Underground Temple*. Dedicated to Virupaksha, the same deity worshipped at Hampi, this monument derives its name from the fact that it was discovered buried under washed out soil. Irrigation in nearby fields is responsible for the water that constantly floods its interior. At the core of the temple is a shrine with a pyramidal tower that resembles those on Hemakuta Hill. The complex is entered through a simple gopura, missing its brick tower.

On the opposite side of the road is another palace structure with its characteristic inner court surrounded by verandahs and small chambers. About 50 m. to the north is a complex of similar structures, recently uncovered by the archaeologists. Labelled by them as the *Noblemen's Quarter*, this zone is crowded with palaces of the type just noticed. The density of the planning, with narrow lanes between the different palaces, together with the many water channels and wells, gives the best possible idea of a suburb of the Royal Centre.

The road from here proceeds west until it joins the main route linking Kamalapura and Hampi. The visit of Kamalapura, however, continues with the *Pattabhirama Temple*, 1 km. east of the village. This religious monument is notable for its grand scale. The towered gopura on the east is the best preserved at the site. A short distance to the northwest stands the *Domed Gateway*, with its circular drum elevated on four soaring arches. Unfortunately, almost nothing can be made out of its plaster decoration.

Further features of interest are seen outside the Royal Centre of Vijayanagara, beside the road running north from Kamalapura to Talarighat. The *Ganagitti Jain Temple*, about 500 m. north of Kamalapura, has two sanctuaries, as well as two mandapas with squat columns. A lofty lamp-column stands freely in front; on its shaft is an inscription recording that the temple was erected in 1385 by a Jain minister of Harihara II. A lane to one side leads to *Bhima's Gate*, named after the epic hero brandishing a sword carved on a loose slab placed inside. Massive walls define a passageway roofed with lintels on decorated brackets.

A short distance further north is a fork in the road, overlooked by Malyavanta Hill, 150 m. to the east. This is believed to be the spot where Rama waited while Hanuman went in search of Sita. The Ramayana association is confirmed by images of Rama and his retinue carved on a boulder inside the sanctuary of the *Raghunatha Temple* at the summit of the hill. The rock itself protrudes above the roof of the sanctuary where it is topped with a small tower. A well preserved mandapa on the south side of the walled compound in which the temple stands has an interior stage for performances of sacred dance and theatre. The adjacent gopura has a delicately carved basement, and a pair of rearing yalis with riders on the frontal portico. The pyramidal tower that rises above preserves much of its original plaster details. A doorway in the west wall of the temple compound gives access to a natural cistern, with multiple Nandis and lingas carved onto its sides. From here there is a fine panorama of the Royal Centre.

The *Muslim Quarter* of Vijayanagara is located further to the north. The principal remains here consists of a mosque and a domed tomb, both erected in 1439 by a military commander of Devaraya II. The road continues northwards, passing through *Talarighat Gate* in the outer fortifications of the city. The gateway has an upper chamber with arched openings and a crenellated parapet. From here visitors may continue to Talarighat, or take the road running westwards to the Vitthala temple.

D. Anegondi

Situated on the opposite bank of the Tungabhadra River, 4 km. downstream from Hampi, Anegondi is reached by roundabout road from Hospet, more than 30 km. distant. It is, however, quicker and more enjoyable to take the short coracle ride from Talaright. (The new bridge here collapsed in 2010.) Anegondi was an important town prior to the foundation of Vijayanagara. After the sack and abandonment of the capital it continued to thrive under a line of local rulers that survives to this day.

The visit to Anegondi starts at a monumental gate on the Tungabhadra, from which a path runs to the town, 1 km. north. The path passes by a dilapidated *Matha*, a religious structure with re-used schist columns. A short distance further on are the stone walls with circular bastions that encircle the town.

The main town square of Anegondi is dominated by the *Gagan Mahal*, a courtly structure that resembles the Lotus Mahal. The Gagan Mahal faces towards the *Ranganatha Temple*, of little interest except for its re-used schist columns, painted vivid green. The gate nearby, now in danger of collapse, is a 14th century structure with finely finished granite columns. Lanes on the east side of the town lead to bathing ghats. At the south end of the steps is a group of shrines with fine views of the river, which here makes a turn to the north.

Anegondi Citadel is located 1 km. west of the town. The rocky hill is ringed with massive walls, partly dating back to Vijayanagara times. Fortified gateways between round bastions give access to enclosure with barracks, wells and other military structures.

E. Hire Benekal

This prehistoric site is located just off the Hospet-Gangavati road, 42 km. northeast of Hopset, partly via NH13, or about 15 km. west of Anegondi. A local guide is essential in order to find the route through the boulder-strewn territory to a cluster of remarkable *Megaliths*, the largest group of such features in Southern India. More than some 50 standing megaliths, dating back more than 2,000 years, are to be seen here. They consist of quadrangular burial chambers defined by upright slabs laid on edge, up to 3 m. high, capped with large circular slabs. The most interesting megaliths are distinguished by unusual circular holes cut into the side slabs.

A short distance from the main group of megaliths are two natural shelters with paintings on rocky overhangs. Faint ochre compositions depict horsemen with spears, figures brandishing clubs, and antelopes, horses and bulls.

F. Kukkanur

This small town, 48 km northwest of Hospet via Koppal, is celebrated for its temples assigned to the Rashtrakuta and Late Chalukya periods.

The 9th century *Navalinga Complex* consists of three shrines built in sandstone, each with a multi-storeyed square tower, opening off three interconnecting mandapas. In spite of the presence of votive lingas, the shrines were originally dedicated to female divinities. Niches in the unadorned temple walls are headed by makaras with foliated tails, as well as parapets of roof forms in relief. The lintels over the interior shrine doorways are elaborately carved, that in front of the west shrine has cut-out makaras, looped garlands and flying figures. The shrines stand in the middle of a large compound, together with smaller structures and a tank. The two entrance gateways are 16th century additions.

A short distance away is the 10th century *Kalleshvara Temple*. Its square sanctuary has a triple-storeyed tower with a frontal projection. The walls are adorned with temple-like reliefs of different designs. The capitals of the lathe-turned columns inside the adjacent mandapa are intricately worked. Rectangular Ganesha and Durga shrines face each other across the middle of the hall.

G. Ittagi

That this village, 5 km. west of Kukkanur, dates back to Early Chalukya times is evident from an 8th century *Portal* with a sculpted lintel, which stands in between mud-clad houses on the main street.

The chief monument at Ittagi, the *Mahadeva Temple* erected in 1112, is one of the outstanding examples of Late Chalukya architecture. The temple, which faces east towards a large square tank, comprises an open mandapa with triple porches, an enclosed mandapa, and a towered sanctuary. The carving of the schist blocks is exceptional throughout. The sanctuary and mandapa walls display pilastered projections expanding outwards in the middle of each side. The niches, now empty, are headed by tower-like pediments. The parapet has deeply cut arch-motifs surrounded by foliation and monster masks, repeated in diminishing tiers on the pyramidal tower. Both lathe-turned and multi-faceted columns are seen within the porches and mandapas. The lintel over the sanctuary doorway shows dancing Shiva flanked by makaras set in elaborate scrollwork. The ceiling panels are conceived as corbelled domes with ornamental ribs and intricate lotus designs.

H. Bagali

This small village is located 35 km. southwest of Hospet, on the Harihar road. The *Kalleshvara Temple*, northeast of the settlement, dates back to Rashtrakuta and Late Chalukya times. The original 10th century monument consists of a sanctuary and adjoining mandapa, articulated by boldly modelled basement mouldings and wall pilasters. Imaginative sexual acts are carved on the cornice blocks above the sanctuary walls: coitus between two and sometimes three figures; women displaying their vulva; male figures with enlarged phalluses, some engaging in self fellatio. A triple-storeyed tower rises above.

The 11th century extensions to the temple include the south doorway to the mandapa. This is surrounded by bands of finely carved miniature figures, including couples; Lakshmi flanked by elephants appears on the lintel. The spacious open mandapa, laid out on a stepped plan with balcony seating all around, is another addition. This gives access to a Narasimha shrine on the north. The sharply moulded basement and varied shapes of the interior columns are typical of Late Chalukya architecture, as are the sharply angled eaves and ornate parapet. Loose sculptures brought from dilapidated temples in the vicinity are assembled here. A small detached shrine to the east accommodates a finely worked image of Surya.

I. KURUVATTI

Overlooking the Tungabhadra River, 90 km. southwest of Hospet via Harpanahalli, this village is of interest for the 11th century *Mallikarjuna Temple*. Slender pilasters on the outer walls of the sanctuary and mandapa frame niches capped with miniature towered pediments. The multi-storeyed tower has a dome-like roof and a frontal projection with an arched face. The inclined bracket figures on the pilasters framing the east doorway of the mandapa are masterpieces of Late Chalukya art; they show fully modelled female dancers against intricately cut-out foliate backgrounds. A large Nandi faces towards the mandapa doorway. The columns within have finely worked shafts, both lathe-turned and multi-faceted. A lintel suspended in front of the sanctuary doorway is sculpted with Brahma, Shiva and Vishnu. The divinities stand inside an ornate arch with flowing foliated tails.

J. HARIHAR

This small town on the Tungabhadra lies on NH4, 107 km. southwest of Hospet. Harihar takes its name from the *Harihareshvara Temple*, erected here in 1224 by a minister of the Hoysala king Narasimha II. The extensive building has its outer walls articulated by slender niches headed by miniature temple towers in relief. The tower rising above is a later restoration. The open mandapa in front, with multiple projections three sides, has inclined balcony seating decorated with friezes of temple-like towers in relief. The interior aisles are flanked by lathe-turned columns with sharply cut details. The main shrine houses a 1.3 m. high image combining Shiva (left) with Vishnu (right).

The large number of inscribed slabs set up in the temple compound shows the enduring significance of the temple in Hoysala and Vijayanagara times.

K. Chitradurga

Located 180 km. south of Hospet on NH13, or 200 km. from Bengaluru on NH4, this city lies at the foot of a massive fort built on the flank of a rugged chain of granite hills that rises to 1,175 m. above sea level.

The strategic importance of Chitradurga fort is revealed by the Late Chalukya and Hoysala occupation in the 11th-13th centuries, after which the site came under the sway of Vijayanagara. A line of local Nayakas declared their independence from Vijayanagara in 1602, making Chitradurga their capital. The fort was taken from the Nayakas by Haidar Ali of Srirangapattana [15C] in 1779, but was captured by the British merely 20 years later. The fort preserves monuments associated with all of these occupants; other vestiges are found in the city itself.

The visit to Chitradurga described here begins at the *Fort*, at the western end of the city. Four successive lines of walls gird the rocky hill, constructed of great blocks of granite fitted between the boulders, rising from 5 to 12 m. high. The ramparts are protected by a moat, and strengthened by bastions of different shapes and sizes. They enclose an irregular elevated zone that is comparatively flat, but strewn with rugged boulders to create an impressive rocky wilderness.

A sequence of massive *Gates* provides access to the fort from the east. The first gate, which dates from the Vijayanagara period, is approached through a barbican that creates three bends. Sculptures of a double-headed eagle, naga and Ganesha are carved onto the walls. At the south end of the elevated ground within is a cave temple enshrining a headless seated goddess. A powder magazine nearby has a pit with four large grinding stones, 1.5 m. in diameter. Passing by a stone trough, the path leads through the second and third gates, both with guardrooms, set into the 15 m. thick walls. A small Ganesha shrine and an oil pit are located within the third gate.

The monuments of greatest interest within the fort comprise a line of two *Free-Standing Gateways* and a number of lamp columns and swing portals lining the path between the Hidimbeshvara and Sampige Siddheshvara temples. Both shrines were founded in the second half of the 13th century by generals of the Hoysala kings. The *Hidimbeshvara Temple*, to the north, is built at the summit of a rocky hill, facing onto a boulder. Its mandapa and projecting porch are typical of Hoysala architecture, but the brick parapet is a later addition. The two gateways already noticed are independent structures erected by the Nayakas in the 17th century. They have double colonnaded storeys and upper pavilions with pyramidal towers and dome-like roofs.

A third, double-storeyed gateway with a rooftop pavilion serves as the entrance to the *Sampige Siddheshvara Temple*, to the south. A square platform inside the temple compound is where the Nayakas performed their coronation ceremonies. The sanctuary in the southwest corner consists merely of a porch leading to a natural cavern, where a Shiva linga is worshipped. Another monument nearby, the Ekanatheshvara temple, founded by the Nayakas, is of lesser interest.

Tanks and *Wells* are scattered about. They include a circular well, 7 m. in diameter, with two flights of steps leading down to the water, and a large tank in a natural crevice. Rubble and mud remains of *Residential Quarters* and *Storage Granaries* associated with the Nayakas occupy the southern part of the fort,

City Walls enclose the houses of Chitradurga in a rectangle on the eastern flank of the fort. Several gates still stand, including one with guardrooms that now houses a small museum. The 17th century *Ucchalingamma Temple*, enshrining the protective goddess of the Nayakas, faces onto the principal street of the city. It is entered through an entrance structure flanked by a high basement supporting a double-storeyed portico. A lofty lamp column stands in the middle of the street in front. The shrine within is a modest unadorned structure approached through a double hall. It is crowned with a pyramidal tower capped with a dome-like roof; this resembles the towers of the gateways within the fort.

That Chitradurga was of importance in earlier times is demonstrated by artefacts discovered at *Chadravalli*, 1.5 km. northwest of the city, at the foot of the fort. Excavations here conducted some years ago uncovered lead coins, Roman silver coins, ornaments of gold, silver and copper, and painted and polished pottery shards, all associated with the 2nd-3rd century Satavahana period. (Some of these items are now displayed in the Government Museum, Chennai [36D].) Faint traces of brick walls were also discovered, but no overall structures can be made out. An inscription on a boulder giving information about the site is located near the Bhadreshvara temple. This Hoysala period monument has been much renovated in recent years. Prehistoric remains were also discovered in the caverns in the nearby hills.

L. BRAHMAGIRI

This remote site, 8 km. north of Molakalmuru, a small town located about 120 km. southeast of Hospet via Bellary, is of importance for its prehistoric and early historic remains. Under the name Isila, Brahmagiri seems have had contact with Northern India in the 3rd century BCE. *Ashokan Inscriptions* are found on two boulders on the western perimeter of Brahmagiri; a third is located 5 km. to the northwest. These records of the Maurya empire are the earliest historical documents to be discovered in Southern India.

The central part of the Brahmagiri site is bounded on the east by the Chandreshvara tank, on the north by the Chinna Hagar River, and on the south by a hill with caves and rocky shelves bearing evidence of habitation. Here can be seen the remains of *Megalithic Burial Chambers*. They consist of stone circles and slabs defining stone cists, some as large as 2 by 1.6 m, capped with circular slabs up to 2.6 m. in diameter. Archaeologists believe that these chambers were constructed over many centuries, including the Maurya era. Rubble structures all around indicate a settlement of considerable size. Pottery fragments, stray bricks, stone tools, copper coins and iron slag are among the stray finds.

Modest temples belonging to the Rashtrakuta and Late Chalukya periods are located on the hill above the prehistoric site.

M. Maski

This small town, 113 km. northeast of Hospet, is flanked by a long chain of granite hills with caverns in the sides and extensive flat surfaces on top.

A number of *Prehistoric Sites* in the vicinity have yielded an abundance of artefacts, including Neolithic implements, such as stone axes and hammers, as well as funerary urns of burnt clay. Beads of crystal, amethyst, carnelian, lapis lazuli and agate testify to trade with distant places; so too the proliferation of items made from conch shells. Metal finger-rings, earrings, bangles and necklaces were also among the remains. These finds have been dated to the 5th-3rd centuries BCE.

Maski is also known for its *Ashokan Inscription*, which was discovered on a boulder inside a cave on the west slop of the hills. Unlike the records at Brahmagiri, this example mentions the 3rd century BCE Maurya emperor by name. Iron slag, furnaces and grinding stones found at the foot of the hills indicate early smelting activity. A large field of menhirs, arranged in regular avenues, is located to the southwest. Various inscriptions from the 10th-16th century are also found at Maski.

N. Raichur

The provincial city lies 185 km. northeast of Hospet by road, and about the same distance south of Gulbarga. It is also possible to reach Raichur from Hyderabad [26], about 200 km. northeast.

Raichur was a city of considerable importance under the Kakatiyas of Warangal [28A], before being seized by the Delhi forces in 1312. Soon after, it was absorbed into the Bahmani kingdom, giving its name to the richly irrigated triangle of land between the Krishna and Tungabhadra Rivers, over which many wars were fought between Gulbarga and Vijayanagara. After passing into the hands of the Adil Shahis, Raichur was captured by Krishnadevaraya in 1520, only to be retaken by Bijapur 22 years later. It remained under the control of Bijapur until the Mughal conquest in 1686. The city then became part of the Mughal Deccan province, and was in time assimilated into the territories of the Nizam.

Raichur is dominated by two irregularly shaped, concentric citadels. The *Outer Fort*, assigned to the 14th-15th century Bahmani period, has tapering granite walls reinforced by a mix of quadrangular and round bastions protected by a broad moat. The *Inner Fort*, encompassing a smaller area, belongs to the 12th-13th century Kakatiya era. It is built with extremely long granite blocks, finely joined without any mortar, but strengthened by square bastions. Both forts incorporate a rocky hill on the south side of the city, which overlooks a large tank beyond the walls.

The most important monuments of Raichur belong to the Bahmani and Adil Shahi periods. They are located on the crowded commercial street that runs just over 1 km. from east west through the middle of the city. The tour begins at *Mecca Gate* in the outer fort. This is a Bahmani structure with a plain arched opening surmounted by a Persian inscription dated 1470. The gate is topped with a small pavilion roofed with a pyramidal vault. *Shailini Gate*, a short distance east, is set between two massive bastions of the inner fort. Its arched opening is framed by a parapet of rectangular battlements with curved backs. A small mosque and dargah dating from Adil Shahi times are built into the gate. *Shallow Engravings* are seen on the fort walls on the opposite (south) side of the road. They include a 1294 record of the Kakatiya commander of Raichur, and an unusual scene depicting a long stone slab being transported by bullock carts.

A path leading off the main street, just opposite the Post Office, runs south towards the *Kali Masjid*. This modest mosque of six bays incorporates re-used temple columns of polished black basalt. The overhanging angled eaves are partly obscured by a concrete extension in front. The path continues toward the Dargah of Mian Babu and its accompanying mosque before arriving at a dilapidated staircase. This ascends to the *Bala Hisar* at the summit of the rocky hill. This citadel consists of a simple triple-bayed hall and a detached prayer chamber. A circular platform with a cannon is placed nearby.

Returning to the main street of the city, the *Fort Jami Mosque* stands a short distance east of the Post Office. Its simple prayer hall, roofed with domes and vaults, has artistically worked inscribed panels set into the rear wall. The compound in front is entered through a small domed chamber on the east. The District Prison diagonally opposite is believed to mark the site of the Kakatiya palace. The Daftar-ki Masjid nearby is of little interest.

The street runs east, making a bend around *Sikandar Gate* in the inner fort. This has a well preserved arcaded passageway framed by a handsome arched portal capped with a battlemented parapet. A small Adil Shahi mosque is built into the walls nearby. To reach *Naurang Gate* it is necessary to turn off the main street here, and proceed north, following the walls of the inner fort. This served as the principal north entrance to the outer fort, but is now in disuse. It has a large central court surrounded by arcades, into which are built blocks carved with female stick-dancers, Hindu gods and goddesses, yalis and squatting lions, all typical of Vijayanagara art. Arched portals are positioned on two sides.

This tour of Raichur continues by returning to the main street and continuing to the *Ek Minar Masjid*, so-called because of the single cylindrical minaret that stands detached from the small prayer chamber. This feature dates back to the first years of Bahmani occupation of the city. The *Kati Gate*, a short distance away, marks the eastern extremity of the outer fort. It is set between massive round bastions, and is headed by a lintel and an inscribed panel dated 1623 set into an arched recess. The *Jami Mosque*, about 350 m. east on the same street, is a Bahmani foundation. Its prayer chamber consists of 33 arcaded bays employing re-used Kakatiya temple columns. The interior is of interest for the geometric patterning of the calligraphy that adorns one of the prayer niches, added during the Adil Shahi period. The octagonal buttresses with ornate bases at the corners also belong to the same era.

7 km. south of Raichur is the small village of *Maliyabad*, with its remarkable 12th-13th century Kakatiya periodfort. The inner walls of finely fitted granite blocks define a partly rectangular enclosure. Two life-size stone statues of elephants stand inside the walls.

O. MUDGAL

Located 110 km. north of Hospet via NH13, this town is worth visiting for its exceptionally well preserved fort. Mudgal was a strategic outpost contested by the Vijayanagara and Gulbarga rulers, whose commanders occupied it successively in the 14th and 15th centuries; it eventually came under control of Bijapur in the middle of the 16th century.

Mudgal's citadel adjoins the western side of the modern town. The *Ramparts* define an approximately elliptical zone, some 800 m. along the greater north-south axis, with major entrances on the north and east. The massive walls are doubled throughout. The outer circuit, built in the early 17th century at the orders of Ibrahim Adil Shah II, has noticeably angled walls with prominent round bastions; it is shielded by a broad moat. The inner circuit of walls, assigned to the 15th-16th century Vijayanagara occupation, is more vertical and employ square bastions. Battlements with rounded merlons on top of both circuits are inscribed with records of various governors.

Fateh Darwaza, or Victory Gate, the eastern entrance to the citadel, is reached after passing through a bent entryway flanked by bastions and ramparts. A hall beside the inner passageway, dated 1560, has a column with a defaced relief of a courtly figure. The same date is inscribed on the outer face of the wooden doors, which are studded with iron spikes.

The southern portion of the Mudgal citadel occupies elevated rocky terrain. Within this zone stands an inner fort, or *Kila*, with walls reinforced with square bastions. A dilapidated pavilion and a round platform intended for cannon are the only features of interest. A large rectangular tank is located nearby.

21. Hubli

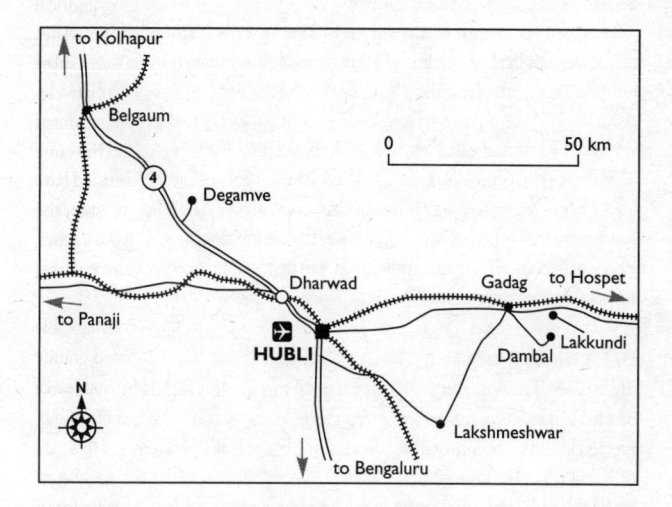

The largest city in northwestern Karnataka, Hubli is a leading manufacturing centre. Dharwad, 21 km. to the north, is smaller and quieter, being the home of Karnatak University. While there is little of historical interest in either city, visitors tend to pass through Hubli and Dharwad on their way from Bengaluru [14] to Kolhapur [8] and other destinations in Mahahrastra, or when travelling from Goa to Hampi [20], Bijapur [23] or Badami [22]. Such journeys provide ample opportunities to visit the fort at Belgaum [A] and the rare Kadamba period shrine at nearby Degamve [B].

The Late Chalukya temples at Gadag [C], Dambal [D] and Lakkundi [E] may be combined as a full day excursion from Hubli, or visited en route to Hampi. The monuments in the Hubli area also include the exquisite Adil Shahi period mosque at Lakshmeshwar [F].

A. Belgaum

This city, northwest of Hubli on NH4, near the border of Maharashtra, rose to prominence under Asad Khan, the Adil Shahi governor of Belgaum in the first half of the 16th century. The city fell to the Marathas in 1673, and was absorbed into the Mughal empire soon after, serving for a time as a provincial centre. It was taken by Haidar Ali of Srirangapattana [15C], and then again in 1818 by the British, who used Belgaum as a military outpost. The *Cantonment*, with many of its buildings still standing, is located in the western part of the city. *St*

Mary's Church, begun in 1864 in a Neo-Gothic style, preserves its flying buttresses and stained glass windows.

Belgaum Fort stands east of the city. Its stone walls, surrounded by a ditch, define an elliptical zone almost 1 km. across. Blocks taken from dismantled temples are set into the walls. The main gate on the north was added in 1631 by Asad Khan. A dilapidated hall in the middle of the fort reuses temple columns.

The Safa Masjid outside the fort dates from 1590. Three dilapidated Jain Temples in the vicinity are Late Chalukya monuments of the 12th century. The larger, north facing temple preserves its pyramidal roof. The adjacent mandapa has an ornate corbelled dome-like roof; the shrine doorway is richly carved. The smaller, south facing temple, now missing its sanctuary, has a verandah with angled seating slabs carved with panels of figures.

B. Degamve

This village lies 5 km. north of Kittur, a small town on NH4, 30 km. northwest of Hubli. The chief feature of interest here is the Kamala Narayana Temple, erected in the 12th century by a queen of one of the Kadamba rulers of this part of Karnataka. The monument has twin shrines, now consecrated to Vishnu and Mahakali, and an intermediate chamber housing an image of Lakshmi Narayana. These divinities all face into a long mandapa, open on the east as a porch. The outer row of columns carries the angled overhang of the eaves. Balcony seating below is adorned with a frieze of temple towers. Carvings enliven the interior columns and doorways.

C. Gadag

This city, 54 km. east of Hubli, is of interest for its extensive Late Chalukya monuments. The 11th-12th century Trikuteshvara and Sarasvati Temples stand next to each other in the same compound in the southern part of the city. The sanctuary of the Trikuteshvara temple, with a pedestal with three lingas, faces east into a large open mandapa with side projections and balcony seating all around; a second sanctuary is situated directly opposite. The Sarasvati temple is also incorporated into this scheme. Both temples have their outer walls adorned with pairs of pilasters carrying temple towers in relief. The porches have balcony seating enlivened with figural panels overhung by steeply angled eaves. Sculpted figures, many arranged in shallow niches, decorate the columns. The towers over the sanctuaries are incomplete.

In the middle of Gadag stands the intricately decorated, but abandoned and neglected Someshvara Temple. Figural panels headed by foliation on the outer walls partly conceal slender pairs of pilasters capped with pediments conceived as model temple towers. The parapet above is encrusted with sculpted elements. The doorways to the mandapa are surrounded by densely carved figures and foliation; that on the south is approached through a small porch. The adjacent Rameshvara temple is similar, but more ruined.

D. DAMBAL

Located 21 km. southeast of Hubli, this village is renowned for the *Dodda Basappa Temple*, one of the finest examples of Late Chalukya architecture. The outer walls of the linga sanctuary have multiple angled facets that almost approach a circle in plan. The facets are decorated with elongated pilasters, singly or in pairs, terminated by tower-like motifs. The pyramidal tower, which continues the wall projections beneath, culminates in an unusual star-shaped roof. The interior columns of the adjoining mandapa have gleaming lathe-turned shafts and capitals. The doorways are surrounded by bands of stylised foliation, with miniature figures beneath. A hall attached to the east of the temple shelters an unusually large polished stone image of Nandi, know locally as Dodda Basappa; hence the temple name.

E. LAKKUNDI

This village, 11 km. east of Gadag, lies on the main road from Hubli to Hospet, from which some of its temples may be glimpsed. Lakkundi preserves a number of Jain and Hindu monuments dating from the 11th-12th centuries. These Late Chalukya structures are built entirely of finely worked grey-green schist. The basements have deeply cut mouldings; slender wall pilasters frame niches headed with tower-like pediments of different designs. The mandapas and porches have columns with both lathe-turned and multi-faceted shafts. They support decorated beams and corbelled ceilings. The richly encrusted doorways are flanked by perforated screens incorporating miniature figures and foliate motifs. Porches have balcony seating overhung by steeply angled eaves.

The *Jain Basti*, the largest and most prominent temple in Lakkundi, is situated on the west side of the village. Its sanctuary walls rhythmically expand outwards in shallow projections that are repeated in the parapet of miniature roof forms above. The five-storeyed pyramidal tower is capped with a square roof. Enclosed and open mandapas, the latter with projections on three sides, adjoin the sanctuary.

The other major monument at Lakkundi is the *Kashivishvanatha Temple*, a short distance away. This comprises twin sanctuaries facing each other across a porch, now partly collapsed. The sanctuary walls have pairs of pilasters capped by makaras with flowing tails or with temple-like reliefs of different designs. Niches topped with curved tower-like profiles mark the most prominent projections; they contrast with the pyramidal shape of the tower itself, preserved incompletely over the west sanctuary. Doorways are surrounded by bands of stylised foliation with guardian figures beneath. The temple also serves as a museum, its compound being a depository of sculptures, hero stones and inscribed slabs found in an around the village.

Another historical feature of interest in Lakkundi is the *Stepped Tank* on the other side of the main road. This comprises a square pond surrounded by landings and miniature shrines, with triple flights of steps descending to the water. A two-storeyed colonnade serves as a bridge across the staircase on the south.

F. LAKSHMESHWAR

This town, 48 km. southeast of Hubli, or 38 km. directly south of Gadag, is worth visiting for its small but highly decorated *Adil Shahi Mosque* of the early 17th century, which resembles the finest monuments in Bijapur. The mosque is entered from the main street of Lakshmeshwar through an imposing gateway, with an arched recess framing a doorway with temple-like jambs and lintel. The doorway is topped by a parapet with finials in shallow relief. Sculpted brackets carry the angled eaves, above which is a cut-out parapet of luxuriant design with intermediate domical pinnacles. The facade is flanked by slender octagonal domical minarets.

The gateway leads to a compound in which stands the mosque. The prayer hall presents a triple-arched facade, the central opening with lobes cut into the outer plane. Crisply carved stone roundels fill the spandrels. The arches are sheltered by sloping eaves on sculpted brackets, with hanging stone chains in between. The intricately worked parapet employs cut-out battlement motifs, and intermediate pinnacles fashioned as model pavilion, complete with miniature eaves and domes. The facade is framed by octagonal minarets that rise high above the roof line.

The interior of the prayer hall consists of six bays, five of which are roofed by 12-sided domes, with faceted pendentives beneath, and cut-out chains suspended from the apexes. The dome in front of the ornate mihrab is raised up high on a double-stage drum, with perforated windows.

Several 11th century monuments stand on the eastern fringe of Lakshmeshwar. Though much damaged, they preserve traces of the precise detailing that characterise Late Chalukya architecture. The *Someshvara Temple*, the largest example, stands in an open court entered through gateways on three sides. The sanctuary has wall niches topped with model temple tower. This adjoins a free-standing mandapa with multiple side projections. A small stepped tank is situated immediately to the west.

The other Late Chalukya monument of interest is the nearby *Lakshmi Lingeshvara Temple*, which gives its name to the town. Here, triple linga sanctuaries open off a common mandapa that in turn adjoins a larger mandapa with doorways on three sides. Unfortunately, the outer walls have been substantially rebuilt

22. Badami

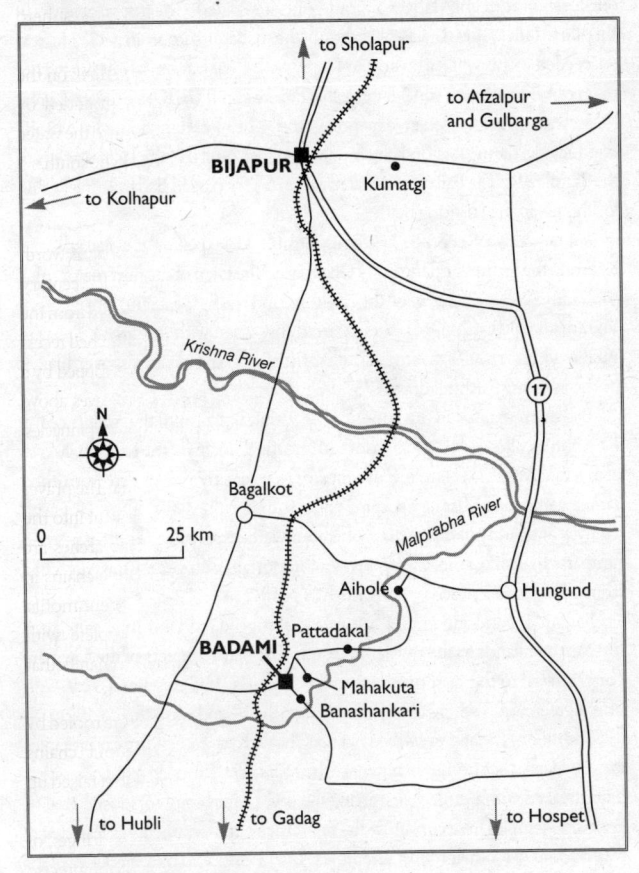

The Early Chalukya temples in and around Badami, the oldest Hindu monuments in Karnataka, are celebrated for their varied architectural forms and splendid carvings. An added attraction is the natural beauty of the Malprabha Valley in which the temples are set. Two full days are recommended to visit the monuments in Badami [A], the nearby holy spots of Banashankari [B] and Mahakuta [C], and the temples in the villages of Pattadakal [D] and Aihole [E].

A. Badami

Badami is associated with the Early Chalukyas, the dominant rulers of Karnataka in the 6th-8th centuries. Under the name of Vatapi, this town served as their capital. From here they conquered substantial parts of Karnataka and territories in adjacent Maharashtra and Andhra Pradesh. The first great figure of this line, Pulakeshin I, was already on the Badami throne in 543. He was succeeded by his son Kirttivarman I (556-97). Civil war broke out during the reign of Kirttivarman's son Mangalesha. Pulakeshin II (610-42), the next great ruler, was instrumental in expanding the Chalukya kingdom. In 612 he conducted a daring raid on Kanchipuram, [37E], capital of the Pallava rulers of the Tamil zone. The Pallavas retaliated and in 642 occupied Badami. Pulakeshin lost his life in the ensuring battle.

Vikramaditya I (655-81) was responsible for expelling the Pallavas and restoring the fortunes on the Early Chalukyas. The reign of the next major ruler, Vijayaditya (696-733), was the longest and most peaceful, but that of Vikramaditya II (733-44) was marred by wars with the rival Pallavas. Vikramaditya's son, Kirttivarman II, last of the Early Chalukyas, was overthrown by the invading Rashtrakutas in 757.

Badami remained in the hands of the Rashtrakutas until the middle of the 10th century, after which it was absorbed into the domains of the Late Chalukyas of Basvakalyan (25D), a line of kings only indirectly descended from their earlier namesakes. The town came in turn under the sway of the Hoysalas, Tuluvas and Adil Shahis, the last of whom were responsible for the gates and ramparts that still stand. Badami was an important outpost for the Marathas, from whom it was seized by the British in 1818.

Badami is surrounded by a horseshoe of rugged red sandstone cliffs, with fortified headlands to the north and south. The narrow streets of the town are concentrated to the west of a dam wall with ghats. This contains a *Tank* with bright green water, where townsfolk regularly bathe and wash their clothes.

The tour of Badami described here begins with the 6th century cave temples excavated into the sheer escarpment of the *South Fort*. The deep red sandstone is here streaked with purple veins, giving the caves a gorgeous colouristic quality. Four cave temples here constitute the finest rock-cut monuments in Karnataka, much admired for their robust sculptures. They are reached by a strenuous flight of steps, interrupted by terraces offering spectacular views over the town and tank.

Cave 1 is entered through a porch that gives access to a spacious square mandapa with a small square sanctuary set into the rear wall. The column shafts are decorated with jewel-and-garland motifs and small medallions containing figures and fantasy foliation; the capitals are fluted. Sculpted panels at either end of the porch depict Harihara (left) and Ardhanarishvara (right). The ceiling panels show a deeply modelled coiled naga divinity, with Shiva and Parvati in the company of flying celestials at either side. Outside the porch to the right is a small shrine housing images of Durga, Karttikeya and Ganesha. A magnificent 18-armed icon of dancing Shiva is carved onto the nearby cliff face.

Cave 2 repeats the scheme of the previous example, except that the deities are all Vaishnava. Panels at either end of the porch portray Varaha (left) and Trivikrama (right), both with friezes of dwarfs beneath. The brackets are fashioned as lions emerging from open-mouthed makaras. The ceiling panels include a wheel of radiating fish, and a design incorporating swastika motifs and flying couples. Gracefully posed warriors guard the porch entrance.

Cave 3 is laid out in accordance with the others, but at a larger scale and with greater emphasis on ornamentation. The historical importance of the monument is confirmed by an inscription dated 578, during the reign of Kirttivarman I. Panels crowded with animated dwarfs adorn the basement, while the columns present a variety of multi-faceted and fluted designs. The brackets of the outermost row of columns are fashioned as embracing couples and maidens beneath flowering trees. Winged Garuda is carved on the inner face of the curving eaves. Faint traces of paintings showing courtly scenes are preserved at either side.

Major figural compositions are carved on the porch walls: to the left, Vishnu seated on the coils of the serpent Ananta (end panel), Varaha and standing Vishnu (side panels); to the right, Narasimha (end panel), Harihara and Trivikrama (side panels). The last deity forms the central figure of an enlarged scene, with Vamana (smashed), deities and attendants. 'Scenes' at the top of the walls illustrate mythological scenes, such as the churning of the ocean, and Krishna vanquishing demons. The porch ceiling is decorated with medallions showing Vishnu flanked by Lakshmi and Garuda surrounded by the dikpalas (middle), Shiva, Indra and Kubera (left), and Brahma and Varuna (right). Ceiling panels in the hall include Brahma with the dikpalas.

The topmost *Cave 4*, the last of the series, is a Jain monument. It is smaller and less elaborate than its predecessors. Both standing and seated Tirthankaras adorn the walls; the full modelling of these figures distinguishes them from later, more shallow carvings of Jinas.

Since it is not possible to proceed further along the stepped path visitors must descend to the base of the cliffs. Near the car park here stands a red sandstone *Muslim Tomb*. This finely finished building commemorates Sidi Abdul Malik Aziz, governor of Badami under the Adil Shahis. The prominent cornice, ornate trefoil parapet and three-quarter spherical dome are typical features of the architecture of Bijapur [23A]. The tomb, which is entered from the east through a small porch, stands in a walled cemetery. From here visitors should follow the path that runs beside the dam wall.

The *Yellamma Temple* overlooking the tank is a Late Chalukya monument, dated 1137. Its walls and multi-storeyed tower are divided into narrow projections framed by slender pilasters; secondary pilasters are capped with miniature roof forms. Turning left soon after brings visitors to a central crossing in the middle of the town. From here a passageway between houses leads to the

Jambulinga Temple. This Early Chalukya building, dating from 699, is of interest for its trio of sanctuaries opening off a common mandapa. Ceiling panels in front of the sanctuaries show Shiva, Vishnu and Brahma. Other ceiling compositions depict a coiled naga, and swastikas with flying celestials. The adjacent Virupaksha temple is assigned to the Late Chalukya era.

The tour of Badami proceeds along a path that passes through several of the town gates before it arrives at the *Archaeological Museum* (closed Fridays), on the north bank of the tank. On entering the museum visitors will see a large, double-sided pediment from a free-standing portal showing Shiva flanked by makaras carved on both sides. Among the other sculptures exhibited here are two panels from Pattadakal portraying Shiva spearing a demon, and the same god riding in a chariot, shooting arrows. Here, too, is displayed a remarkable sculpture of Lajja Gauri, a squatting goddess with a lotus head, displaying her sexual parts. The path continues around the tank, running past the Mallikarjuna group of temples. Their squat pyramidal tower and open porches are typical of Late Chalukya architecture.

The path terminates at the *Bhutanatha Temple*, picturesquely located on the eastern edge of the water. The sanctuary and enclosed mandapa are Early Chalukya in date, but the open mandapa is later. Sculptures are seen in caverns in the nearby boulders. The most impressive is an enthroned, richly jewelled seated figure, probably of Buddha. Another relief carving shows Vishnu sleeping on Ananta, attended by Lakshmi.

Visitors must now return to the Archaeological Museum, from where they may pass through an arched gate so as to reach the stepped path that ascends the *North Fort*. This somewhat strenuous route climbs through a deep gorge with dramatic overhanging cliffs. The first monument to be seen, the *Lower Shivalaya*, stands on a rocky promontory overlooking the town. Only the tower, with a dome-like roof, survives. Small pavilions opposite may have been ceremonial structures used by the Early Chalukya kings. The next features to be noticed are the crenellated fortifications and conical stone granaries, dating from the 18th century Maratha period.

At the summit of the headland is the *Upper Shivalaya*, probably the first free-standing temple to be erected by the Early Chalukyas. Though not all of its 7th century fabric is preserved, the building is impressive for its tower capped by a massive, square domical roof. Angled slabs roof the surrounding passageway. The basement has friezes of animated dwarfs, as well as scenes from the Krishna legend (south). Additional Krishna figures are carved on to the pilastered walls.

The final monument of Badami to be described here is the 7th century *Malegitti Shivalaya*. This can only be reached by taking a side path next to the Police Station on the main road. Sited on top of a huge boulder, out of which it seems to grow naturally, the temple consists of a towered sanctuary, mandapa and entrance porch. The outer walls have clearly articulated basement mouldings, pilastered projections, and cornice and parapet. Perforated stone windows, headed by makaras and garlands, flank sculpted icons of Vishnu (north) and Shiva (south). The tower has an octagonal domed roof.

B. Banashankari

This pilgrimage spot, 5 km. east of Badami, is celebrated for the *Banashankari Temple*, which enshrines a fierce Kali-like form of Durga. A chariot festival takes place here at the end of January each year, together with a busy market. The temple dates back to Rashtrakuta times, but was substantially remodelled in the 18th century. The three octagonal tapering stone lamp columns that stand in the courtyard are typical Maratha features. A vast square *Tank* in front of the temple is fed by water from a nearby spring. The tank is surrounded by arcades, with a triple-stage arcaded lamb tower near its southwest corner.

C. Mahakuta

This attractive wooded site lies 8 km. beyond Banashankari, along a road that passes beneath a rocky outcrop, or about the same distance along another road that turns off the route leading from Badami to Pattadakal.

The Mahakuta shrines stand within a walled compound, grouped around a rectangular *Tank* fed by a natural spring. A small pavilion in the middle of the water shelters a four-faced Shiva linga. The principal shrine here, the *Mahakuteshvara Temple*, belongs to the late 7th century, slightly later than the Badami monuments, but earlier than those at Pattadakal. It consists of a sanctuary surrounded by a passageway, approached through a mandapa with a small porch on the east. The outer walls are raised on basement mouldings with intricately carved friezes of mythological and courtly subjects interspersed with foliate panels. Pierced stone windows with ornate pediments of different designs are positioned at either side of niches with Ardhanarishvara (north) and Shiva (south and west); guardian figures appear beside the east doorway. A storeyed tower capped with an octagonal domical roof rises over the sanctuary. A small Nandi pavilion stands freely in front.

Almost exactly the same architectural scheme is repeated in the *Mallikarjuna Temple* on the south side of the tank. The interior has ceiling compositions with different deities.

The west side of the tank at Mahakuta is lined with smaller shrines, including the almost identical *Sagameshvara* and *Mahalinga Temples*, both capped with curving shikhara towers typical of northern Indian architecture. Delicately carved deities are seen in the wall niches: Harihara (north), Ardhanarishvara or Narasimha (west) and Lakulisha (south).

A *Gateway* stands outside the complex, at it southeast corner. This has a pair of remarkable skeletal guardian figures, identified as Kala and Kali. An inscribed column found nearby many years ago has been removed to the Archaeological Museum in Bijapur.

About 2 km. southwest of Mahakuta, at the head of a ravine, stands the *Naganatha Temple*, which may be compared with similar monuments at Mahakuta. Perforated stone windows admit light to the mandapa and the passageway surrounding the sanctuary. Couples embracing beneath trees are carved onto the porch columns.

D. Pattadakal

This village, 22 km. northeast of Badami, overlooks the Malprabha River, which here flows in a northerly direction. Before reaching the village the road from Badami passes by a newly restored *Jain Temple*, assigned to the 9th century Rashtrakuta period. Its outer walls have slender pilasters, but are devoid of sculptures. The stepped tower has a square roof. Unusual elephant torsos are sculpted in full relief either side of the mandapa doorway, where they are framed by makaras with ornate tails.

The main group of monuments at Pattadakal is located another 500 m. east, at the edge of the village. The temples and smaller subshrines, all dedicated to Shiva, face east towards the river. They are remarkable for their architectural variety, demonstrating the meeting of Northern and Southern Indian styles. Their grand scale and sculptural elaboration represent the climax of the Early Chalukya art in the first half of the 8th century. The temples are described in a sequence from north to south, as visited from the entrance to the landscaped compound at its northwest corner.

The almost identical, small *Kadasiddheshvara* and *Jambulinga Temples* have northern Indian curved spires adorned with horseshoe-shaped motifs and ribbed elements. The frontal faces have circular panels containing mages of Nataraja. Other sculptures of Shiva appear in wall niches below. The *Galaganatha Temple* presents a more evolved version of the same Northern Indian scheme, comparable to monuments at Alampur [32B] dating from the late 7th-early 8th centuries. The most striking feature of the Galaganatha is its well preserved tower, divided into horizontal tiers of horseshoe-shaped motifs and ribbed elements; it is crowned with an enlarged circular ribbed finial. Porches once projected outwards on three sides of the passageway that surrounds the sanctuary, but only that on the south is preserved. It shelters a carved panel depicting Shiva energetically spearing the demon Andhaka. Damaged river goddesses and an icon of dancing Shiva adorn the sanctuary doorway.

Though founded by the long reigning king Vijayaditya in the early 8th century, the *Sangameshvara Temple* was never completed. Its finely proportioned elevation is typical of Southern Indian style, with walls divided into projections and recesses by pairs of pilasters, topped by a parapet of model roof forms, and a multi-storeyed tower with a square domical roof. Perforated stone windows in the wall recesses have bold geometric patterns.

The *Kashivishvanatha Temple* was built at about the same time as the Sangameshvara, but in a highly evoled version of the Northern Indian style. Wall projections have pediments composed from horseshoe-arch motifs. Meshes of similar motifs cover the curving facets of the spire that rises above. A dancing Shiva is positioned on the front face of the tower.

The neighbouring, almost identical *Virupaksha* and *Mallikarjuna Temples* were erected by two queens of Vikramaditya II to commemorate their husband's victory over the Pallavas in 745. The temples each have a linga sanctuary surrounded by a passageway that opens into a spacious square mandapa entered through porches on three sides. Free-standing Nandi pavilions are positioned on axis to the east. Walls contain the temples in rectangular paved courts, with subshrines and entrance gates on the east. The diagonal arrangement of the two enclosures is unusual.

A marked stylistic evolution is seen in the Virupaksha and Mallikarjuna temples, the largest and most elaborate of the Early Chalukya series. The slight differences between the two monuments are worthy of note: wall projections in the Virupaksha are flanked by two sets of pilasters, while three sets are employed in the Mallikarjuna; a square domical roof caps the tower of the Virupaksha, while that of the Mallikarjuna is hemispherical. Both towers have horseshoe shaped projections on the front, but only that on the Mallikarjuna contains a dancing Shiva icon.

The vitality of Early Chalukya art is amply illustrated by carvings on the outer walls of both temples. Panels on the wall projections either side of the east porch of the Virupaksha depict Shiva appearing out of the linga (left), and Vishnu as Trivikrama (right). Other notable icons on this temple are dancing Shiva (east end of south wall), Bhairava (south wall sanctuary), and Vishnu with Durga beneath (north wall of sanctuary). Perforated stone windows with delicately carved foliate and geometric motifs are inserted into the intervening wall recesses. Both the sculptures and windows are surmounted by arch-like pediments filled with figures or with makaras with foliated tails. Porch columns have carvings of embracing couples, as well as divinities: Shiva subduing Ravana (south porch), and Vishnu riding on Garuda (north porch). Panels either side of the doorway within the east porch show auspicious pot-bellied attendants. The ceiling panel here portrays Surya riding in a horse-drawn chariot. Fully modelled figures with clubs guard the doorways within the porches.

Interior columns of the Virupaksha temple are covered with reliefs, including bands of narrative friezes depicting mythological stories, as well as decorative designs with lyrical scrollwork and lotus ornament. Wall columns are enlivened with gracefully posed courtly couples. Ceiling panels over the central aisle are carved with a coiled naga, and Lakshmi between elephants surrounded by lotus petals. The sanctuary doorway has river goddesses and attendants beneath at either side, and makaras with foliated tails raised above. A polished granite linga on a high pedestal is installed within. A remarkable, cut-out icon of Durga spearing the buffalo demon is housed in the minor shrine to the right of the linga sanctuary.

Steps ascend to the large Nandi image housed in the pavilion in front of the Virupaksha temple. The animal, decked with garlands and bells, is carved with convincing naturalism, but is sometimes draped with a cloth. Massive circular columns with similarly shaped capitals carry the ceiling above. A gate on the east side of the enclosure leads down to the river, and the path that leads to the Papanatha temple.

The art of the Mallikarjuna temple parallels that of the Virupaksha, but in general the carvings are less refined and somewhat unfinished, as in the vigorous Nataraja (west wall of sanctuary).

The tour of the Pattadakal monuments concludes with a visit to the *Papanatha Temple*, some 200 m. south of the main group, on the other side of the village. This temple consists of a pair of interconnecting mandapas, which give the building an unusually long low elevation. Elements derived from both the Northern and Southern Indian styles are here combined: the curving tower over the sanctuary resembles the superstructures of the Kadasiddheshvara and Jambulinga temples, while the parapet of model roof forms and the makaras with foliated tails on the pilasters flanking the doorways relate closely to similar features of the Virupaksha and Mallikarjuna temples.

The basement of the front (east) porch of the Papanatha is carved with a dynamic frieze of fighting elephants and lions. Carvings on the outer walls illustrate episodes from the Mahabharata and Ramayana. The latter series is recognised by the processions of monkeys (eastern end of south wall). The porch columns are adorned with courtly couples, maidens and guardians; similar figures appear on the peripheral columns inside both halls. Side niches within the first mandapa are occupied by images of Durga and Ganesha. Columns here have cushion-shaped capitals and ornate brackets decorated with monster masks and foliation. Brackets carrying transverse beams are fashioned as open-mouthed makaras disgorging lions. Ceiling panels in the two mandapas have finely executed Nataraja figures and coiled naga deities.

E. Aihole

This village can be reached directly from Pattadakal, the road running for about 15 km. through the picturesque Malprabha Valley, as well as from Hungund, on NH13, 22 km. to the east. Aihole is worth visiting for its large number of Hindu and Jain monuments belonging to both the Early and Late Chalukya periods, as well as to the intervening Rashtrakuta era, a period spanning more than 500 years. Built of local sandstone, the temples are dotted in and around the village, the houses of which are partly contained in a circuit of stone walls.

Only the most interesting monuments of Aihole are described here. However, it is worth noting that the names by which many of these are now known derive from the villagers who inhabited these structures in recent years, rather than from the deities that once received worship here.

The visit of Aihole begins with the *'Durga' Temple*, the largest and most elaborate at this site. A foundation of the early 8th century, the temple takes its name not from the goddess Durga, but from the fact that it once served as a durg, or fortified lookout. The apsidal ended plan of the temple recalls earlier Buddhist chaitya halls, but it was never a Buddhist establishment, being originally dedicated to Surya. The semi-circular sanctuary and adjoining rectangular mandapa and entrance porch are surrounded by a continuous open colonnade, all raised on a high basement. An incomplete Northern Indian styled tower rises over the sanctuary.

The sculptures of the 'Durga' temple are among the masterpieces of Early Chalukya art. Columns at the entrance are carved with amorous couples and guardian figures; those inside the porch have medallions, garlands and jewels; the ceiling panel here shows a coiled naga and a wheel with fish spokes. The mandapa doorway is flanked by river goddesses and guardians. Perforated stone windows alternating with niches headed by pediments of different designs line the colonnade. Surviving sculptures in the niches represent (in clockwise sequence): Shiva with Nandi, Narasimha, Vishnu with Garuda, Varaha, Durga and Harihara. Traces of flying couples are seen carved onto the sloping roof slabs. (Two more complete couples from the temple ceiling are now displayed in the National Museum, New Delhi.) In contrast to the rich treatment of the exterior, the mandapa interior is plain. A circular pedestal devoid of any image is placed in the sanctuary.

Stray sculptures are displayed in the adjacent *Archaeological Museum* (closed Fridays). The finest exhibit is a damaged image of the Jain goddess Ambika seated on a lion beneath a tree, removed from the Meguti temple.

A short distance south of the 'Durga' temple stand a number of other Early Chalukya monuments grouped around a tank, with sculptures set into the stepped sides. The *Surya Narayana Temple* presents a simple combination of towered shrine, mandapa and porch. A Late Chalukya image of Surya is placed inside the sanctuary. The 8th century *Ladkhan Temple* is of interest for its obvious reliance on timber architecture. A spacious square columned hall is roofed with sloping tiers of stone slabs in two levels, with log-like stone strips protecting the joints. River goddesses and embracing couples embellish the outer porch columns. Inclined balcony seating in between is decorated with auspicious pot-and-knot motifs. The hall interior is monumental in scale but undecorated; a large Nandi is placed in the middle. A small sanctuary is placed against the rear wall; perforated screens on three sides illuminate the interior. A second sanctuary is positioned at the summit of the roof originally (reached by stone steps in the porch below). Icons of Vishnu, Surya and Ardhanarishvara are carved onto its outer walls.

The nearby *Gauda Gudi* is set at a lower level, suggesting an earlier date in the 7th century. This temple consists of an open quadrangular mandapa containing a small sanctuary. Inclined balcony slabs between the peripheral columns are decorated with pot motifs. The roof slabs above slope on four sides. Niches with triangular pediments on the sanctuary walls are empty, but the doorway is elaborately carved. The adjacent *Chakra Gudi* is ruined, except for the well preserved Northern Indian styled tower over the sanctuary. This is capped with a circular ribbed finial.

A short walk through the streets of Aihole is required to reach the *Kunti Group*. Four temples built close together consist of partly open halls with sloping roofs. Each temple has a small sanctuary positioned against the rear wall. The southeast example, probably the first to be built, is entered from the north, where the columns are carved with amorous couples. The northwest temple also has sculpted figures. Its interior is of interest for the trio of finely carved ceiling panels portraying Shiva with Parvati, Vishnu on Ananta, and Brahma on the lotus. Guardians flank the sanctuary doorway. The two remaining temples are assigned to the 9th century Rastrakuta era, as is evident from the squat proportions of the columns and their circular capitals. A free-standing portal with animal brackets links the two northern temples.

The *Hucchappayya Matha* lies further south, beyond the houses of the village. Its severe exterior is relieved by carvings of embracing couples on the columns flanking the east porch. One of these figures shows a woman with a horse's head. The mandapa is roofed with ceiling panels depicting the same trio of divinities noted in the Kunti group.

Visitors with additional time and interest should follow the path to the south of the village that runs beside the river. This leaves Aihole near the *Hallibasapa Gudi*, a Rashtrakuta period temple recognised by the unusually large figures of river goddesses beside the entrance. The path then traverses a small stream and continues for about 1 km. before arriving at the *Hucchappayya*

Gudi (not to be confused with the Hucchappayya Matha, already described). This Early Chalukya temple has a well preserved, curving, Northern Indian styled tower. Couples and guardians are carved onto the porch columns, but the trio of fine ceiling panels representing Shiva, Vishnu and Brahma that once graced the interior has been removed to the museum in Mumbai [1B]. The nearby *Galaganatha Group* belongs to the Rashtrakuta era. The main temple is entered through a doorway with a lintel decorated with large makaras and looped garlands.

The tour continues by returning to Aihole in order to ascend the hill that overlooks the village from the southeast. The most convenient route is to follow the main road that runs around the walls of the village, passing by the *Mallikarjuna Group*. The main temple here is an Early Chalukya foundation, but the tower is later. Its entrance doorway is adorned with makaras.

A short distance further south begins the stepped path that is best climbed in the cool of the morning. Just beneath the flat top of the hill is a 6th century *Buddhist Temple* fronted by a two-storeyed colonnade. A ceiling panel here shows a seated Buddha. At the summit of the hill is the *Meguti Temple*, from where fine views may be had of Aihole and the Malprabha Valley as far as Pattadakal. The temple is a Jain foundation with an inscription of 634, making it the earliest dated structure in Southern India. It presents a rudimentary version of the Southern India style, with its elevation divided into basement, pilastered walls, and cornice and parapet. The upper chamber is a slightly later addition, as are the porch and mandapa in front (north). A impressive seated Jina figure is placed within the sanctuary. Beyond the stone walls defining the temple compound is an interesting group of *Megaliths* dating back some 3,000 years. These qudrangular chamber tombs have stone slabs supporting capping pieces.

Visitors must now descend Meguti Hill in order to rejoin the road that runs around the village walls. A side road from here passes by the *Jyotirlinga Group*, incorporating several modest Early Chalukya shrines, and leads to *Rawana Phadi* to the northeast of the village. This 6th century cave temple is excavated into a sandstone outcrop, in front of which stands a broken fluted column and several rudimentary small shrines. Ravana Phadi has a triple bayed-entrance flanked by worn guardian figures in foreign dress. This gives access to a hall, with a linga sanctuary to the rear and chambers to either side. Subtly modelled sculptures of Ardhanarishvara, Harihara, Shiva with Ganga, and guardians enliven the walls of the hall. The ceiling is decorated with delicate lotus ornament. An elaborate sculptural composition in the left side chamber shows ten-armed Shiva dancing in the company of Parvati, Ganesha and the Saptamatrikas; the figures all wear unusual pleated costumes. The side walls of the antechamber preceding the linga sanctuary has carvings of Varaha and Durga.

After leaving Ravana Phadi, the road passes by the *Huchimalli Gudi*. This temple has a sanctuary surrounded by a passageway and a mandapa surrounded by rectangle of walls. The interior is partly roofed with sloping slabs. A curved, Northern Indian styled tower rises over the sanctuary. The porch has a unique ceiling panel of Karttikeya riding on the peacock.

About 125 m. south of the point where the side road leading from Ravana Phadi rejoins the main road north of Aihole stands the *Chikki Gudi*. This temple is laid out in the same manner as the previous example, but lacks a tower. Finely executed lotus ornament decorates the interior columns and beams. Two elaborate ceiling compositions show Shiva dancing and spearing Andhaka, and Vishnu sleeping on Ananta, and the same god kicking his leg up as Trivikrama. The adjacent ruined structure has an apsidal-ended plan with a Shiva linga raised on a circular pedestal. The car park outside the Durga temple compound lies a short distance to the south.

The itinerary described here does not include the *Tarabasappa Gudi*, beside the main road almost 1 km. north of Aihole. This temple follows the standard tripartite layout, with sanctuary, mandapa and porch. The sanctuary has pilastered walls and a fully preserved, Northern Indian styled tower.

23. Bijapur *(see map on p 267)*

Bijapur is situated in the middle of a desolate plain that presents a striking contrast to the imposing fortifications and gateways and richly decorated monuments within the city itself. Celebrated for its splendid mosques, tombs and palaces erected by the Adil Shahi rulers in the 16th-17th centuries, Bijapur is a rewarding stopover on any tour of northern Karnataka. It is today a thriving market city, with new buildings crowding ancient ones.

A visit to Bijapur may conveniently be combined with the itineraries for Hampi [20], Badami [22] and Gulbarga [24], also with that for Sholapur [9] in Maharashtra. At least one full day should be devoted to the monuments of Bijapur [A] and its immediate environs [B]. An excursion to the royal resort of Kumatgi [C] and funerary complex at Afzalpur [D] will require a full day.

Bijapur was already well established in 1294, when it was annexed by the invading Delhi army. The city subsequently became a provincial centre of the Bahmanis. At the end of the 15th century Bijapur was under the governorship of Yusuf Adil Khan. An immigrant from Central Asia, this able officer, served under Mahmud Gawan, the influential Prime Minister of Bidar [25]. Yusuf was posted to Bijapur, from where he proclaimed his independence in 1490, thereby transforming the city into the capital of a new kingdom. He did not, however, assume the title of Shah, but continued to profess allegiance to the Bahmanis.

Almost all the Adil Shahis succeeded each other in direct father-to-son line. The most prominent figures were Ali I (1558-80), Ibrahim II (1580-1627). and Muhammad I (1627-56). The careers of these rulers were taken up with the struggles with the rival states of Bidar and Golconda [26E]. The Adil Shahis also waged wars with neighbouring Vijayanagara [20B-C], contributing to the army that defeated this great Hindu empire in 1565. The Adil Shahis benefitted enormously from the victory, seizing much of Vijayanagara's wealth and territories.

The greatest fortunes of the Adil Shahis and the period of their largest monuments coincide with the reigns of Ibrahim II and Muhammad. Though the Mughals besieged Bijapur in 1636, during the reign of Muhammad I, it was not until 1686 that the Mughal forces under Aurangzeb finally succeeded in permanently invading the kingdom, occupying the capital and bringing to an end the Adil Shahi line. The city declined thereafter.

Constant warfare did not prevent the Adil Shahis from enthusiastically patronising art and literature, and many painters and poets flocked to the Bijapur court, where a distinct school of miniature painting flourished. Their sponsorship extended also to religious learning, especially to the Sufi dargahs, where the intellectual climate of Bijapur was further developed. The Bijapur kings were also well acquainted with Hindu mythology and astronomy.

Ibrahim II, for instance, even adopted the traditional Indian title of Jagatguru, Preceptor of the World.

A. BIJAPUR

The city of Bijapur is strongly fortified, being contained within a circuit of *Outer Walls* that define an elliptical zone, some 2.5 km. along the greater east-west axis. The walls were erected in 1565 under Ali I, and are fairly complete, reaching an average height of 10 m. The outer faces are reinforced by no less than 96 round bastions with intermediate projecting guardrooms and a prominent battlemented parapet. A broad pathway runs continuously along the top of the walls. The bastions were modified in later times with the introduction of artillery, and many fine guns are still in place. The most famous is the Malik-i-Maidan, Lord of the Plain, which sits on Sharza bastion, named after the lions carved onto its sides, surveying the approaches to Bijapur from the west. The walls are broken by six gates that define the principal roads of the city. The gates follow a standard pattern, with lintels on corbelled brackets surmounted by lofty arches and battlemented parapets.

Only the most important of Bijapur's many monuments are described here. The tour begins at the east end of the city with the Gol Gumbaz, the tomb of Muhammad I. This faces onto M.G. Road, the principal east-west artery of the city, a short distance from the Railway Station. Completed at the time of Muhammad's death in 1656, this is the major achievement of the Adil Shahs and one of the greatest structural triumphs of Indian architecture.

The design of the *Gol Gumbaz* is strikingly simple, with a hemispherical dome, nearly 44 m. in external diameter, resting on a cubical mass 47.5 m. square. The exterior is majestic, with triple sets of arched recesses on three sides. Medallions on brackets are etched into the plasterwork in the spandrels. The central recesses are filled with stone screens pierced by doorways and windows. An overhang cornice, cantilevering outwards for more than 3 m., is supported on tiers of sculpted brackets and surmounted by an arcade and parapet of trefoil elements. Corner octagonal towers have open stages, each marked by arcades concealing staircases. They are topped by bulbous domes on petalled bases, imitating at a smaller scale the great dome that serves as the climax of the whole composition.

The tomb interior is dominated by eight arches in overlapping squares that form interlocking pendentives. The arches curved inwards to create a circular gallery, from which the dome rises. The austere quality of the chamber emphasises the overall structural system. A cenotaph slab in the floor is positioned over the true grave, which lies concealed in a ground level chamber. A part-octagonal domed chamber projects outwards in the middle of the north side.

The Gol Gumbaz stands in the middle of a formal garden. To the west is a small but handsome mosque, with a restrained facade of five arches flanked by slender minarets with domed turrets. The finely finished gateway on the south has an upper vaulted chamber intended for musicians. The building now accommodates the *Archaeological Museum* (closed Fridays). Early Chalukya temple sculptures and an inscribed pillar from Mahakuta [22C] are displayed here, as well as elegantly worked calligraphic slabs from the Adil Shahi period. The upper rooms house a collection of worn carpets and Chinese porcelains. An interesting 17th century watercolour map of Bijapur shows the concentric rings of the city walls and all the major buildings and waterworks.

Gol Gumbaz, Bijapur.

The *Jami Mosque* is reached by proceeding west and south from the Gol Gumbaz. Begun by Ali I in 1576, this great project was never completed. Corner buttresses indicate where tall minarets would have risen on either side of the prayer hall. This presents a row of nine pointed arches, only that in the middle is lobed, with medallions in the spandrels. The overhang is carried on sculpted brackets, but the parapet above was never begun. The great hemispherical dome at the rear rises on a cubic clerestory, relieved by arched recesses and a pierced parapet with prominent finials.

The mosque interior is impressive for its monumental simplicity, with the nine central bays being roofed by a single lofty dome. Two intersecting squares of arches with intermediated faceted pendentives create an octagonal space, over which the dome appears to float, the first appearance of this structural device in Bijapur. Traces of colour tile mosaic are seen in the medallions and string courses of the supporting arches. The treatment of the stone mihrab, added in 1636, is sumptuous, with receding sculpted planes of stylised foliation framing the central arch, and traces of painted decoration. The prayer chamber faces onto a court, only partly surrounded by arcades. The free-standing gateway on the east was added by Aurangzeb at the turn of the 18th century.

Continuing west along the same street as the Jami Mosque, visitors will reach *Yusuf's Old Jami Mosque*. Dating from 1513, this is one of the earliest Adil Shahi monuments in the city; Its hemispherical drum on a ring of lotus buds rising on tall circular drum anticipates the mature Adil Shahi style. The prayer chamber has three bays, the central one wider than those on the sides. A short distance south, down a side street, stands the *Complex of Ali Shahid Pir*, assigned to the reign of Ali I. This consists of a small mosque, little more than 10 m. square, superbly decorated with sharply cut plasterwork. The wagon-vaulted roof running parallel to the facade is a rarity in Adil Shahi architecture.

The *Mihtar Mahal* stands on the same street as the Jami Mosque. This complex, which belongs to the period of Ibrahim II, is entered through a multi-storeyed gate opening directly onto the street. The projecting balconies with arched openings are overhung by prominent eaves. The supporting angled struts are decorated with relief and cut-out stylised lions, geese and foliation, in obvious imitation of timberwork. Slender finials with bulbous domes rise above the parapet. The passageway interior is roofed with eight half-arches that support a square ceiling on curving brackets. The gate gives access to a mosque, notable for the elaborate brackets carrying the overhang and the ornate trefoil battlements of the parapet. Slender minarets flank the facade. The six-bayed interior is roofed by alternating domes and vaults.

The *Asar Mahal*, reached by taking a turn north, is situated just outside the citadel (see below), to which it was once linked by a great bridge, portions of which still survive. The building was originally intended as a hall of justice, but in 1646 was converted into a sacred reliquary to house two strands of the Prophet's hair, thereby ensuring its preservation over the centuries.

The Asar Mahal gives the most complete idea of a typical Adil Shahi palace. Its east front consists of double-height portico with massive timber columns carrying a ceiling with inlaid wooden panels. (Portions of the original wooden columns are seen lying about.). The portico surveys a formal garden with a central pond. To the rear of the portico are chambers on two levels, connected by staircases at either end (only men admitted). The upper chambers are ornamented with murals depicting courtly scenes, but these have mostly faded. Better preserved are the compositions of vases and blue flowers in the south chamber. The chambers have inlaid wooden doors with geometric screens above. The ruins of the Jahaz Mahal, another palace, are seen nearby to the north.

The tour described here continues with a visit to the *Citadel* in the middle of Bijapur. This is contained within a circle of inner walls, no longer continuous but occasionally doubled, repeating many of the features of the outer walls already noticed. The citadel walls, which date mainly from the period of Ali I, are surrounded by a moat with water on the west; elsewhere the moat has been filled in. The southern gate to the citadel, the only one to be completely preserved, is reached only after crossing a causeway that passes beneath a broad arch. The gate is shielded by a curved wall that creates a bent entryway.

The first building to be noticed after passing through the south gate is *Karimuddin's Mosque* of 1310, erected during the occupation of Bijapur by the Delhi army when it invaded the Deccan. Entirely built out of pillaged temple materials, the mosque has a long columned hall with a raised clerestory in front of the mihrab. The courtyard is entered through a temple-like chamber.

Remains of the palace area of the Adil Shahis are located immediately to the west. The core of this zone is a spacious quadrangle surrounded by arcades, today occupied by municipal offices, including the judicial court. The only portion of the quadrangle that preserves any of its original Adi Shahi architecture is the *Sat Manzil*, at the northwestern corner, overlooking the walls and moat. Only four of the original seven storeys still stand. Water basins and ornately decorated vaults within suggest that this building was intended as a pleasure pavilion. The *Jal Mandir*, immediately north, is a finely finished, miniature pavilion originally standing in a small pool. Too small for ordinary use, it may have been intended as a reliquary chamber.

The *Gagan Mahal*, a short distance further north, served as the audience hall of Ali I. Its great central arch is flanked by two narrower ones that face north towards an open assembly area, now a landscaped garden. The spandrels of the arches are filled with stucco medallions of stylised ornament supported on fish-like brackets, a characteristic motif of the Adil Shahis. Little is left of the chambers decorated with ornate woodwork that once opened off the main hall. Immediately east of the Gagan Mahal is another similar hall, the *Anand Mahal*. Completed in 1589 by Ibrahim II, its triple-arched facade has been retained in the conversion of the building into municipal offices. Its entrance chamber, however, preserves its original domes and vaults.

The *Mecca Mosque* of 1669, in the east part of the citadel, is concealed within high walls, indicating that it may have been reserved for courtly women; it is still used by women today. The small, but finely finished prayer chamber, with a dome carried on intersecting arches, has a sombre arcade topped with a hemispherical dome. A pair of minarets is incorporated into the complex. Ruined structures nearby served as stables and granaries.

The tour of Bijapur continues by leaving the citadel and visiting a number of monuments located on its periphery. The *Tomb of Ali II* (1656-72) stands a few metres north of the citadel, just off M.G. Road. This monument presents imposing line of open arcades surrounding the central square chamber, of which only the lower walls were completed. The tomb is elevated on a lofty plinth, approached by steps on the south. The *Mosque* and *Tomb of Yaqut Dabuli*, a short distance east, also off the same road, are named after one of Muhammad I's African slaves. These two modest structures have prominent cornices, but the mosque lacks a dome.

Malika Jahan Begum's Mosque, on the west side of the citadel, is an exquisite building erected in 1586 by Ibrahim II in honour of his wife. Three unadorned arched openings lead to the six-bayed prayer chamber. The treatment of the brackets carrying the overhand is elaborate, with cut-out curving struts, suspended beams and walls panels carved in luxuriant detail with lotus motifs and leafy arabesques. The cornice and parapet above have perforated interlocking designs. The intermediate finials are conceived as miniature pavilions with domical tops. The six bays of the interior are roofed with domes; the dome in front of the mihrab is raised on a high drum adorned with intersecting arches. The mihrab is a part-octagonal domed chamber.

The *Anda Mosque* of 1608 stands on the south side of the citadel, a short distance from the south gate previously noticed. It is the only mosque in Bijapur to be raised on an upper level. The apartment below is closed by a single door, from which a staircase concealed in the walls climbs to the prayer chamber above. These features suggest that the building may have been reserved for women. The triple-arched facade of the mosque has delicately worked medallions in the spandrels and brackets above; the parapet is notable for its lace-like treatment. Four elegant finials with their own projecting cornices cluster around a central dome with fluted sides.

The *Jod Gumbaz*, to the west of the citadel, comprises a pair of almost matching tombs, one octagonal the other square. The octagonal tomb accommodates the remains of Khawas Khan, Prime Minister of the last Adil Shahi ruler, Sikander (1672-86). The square tomb shelters the grave of Abdul Razzaq Qadiri, the religious advisor of Khawas Khan. It is now a popular dargah. Both buildings have elongated facades, capped with overhangs on brackets, and corner finials with domical tops. The slightly bulbous domes rise on friezes of well articulated petalled flutings.

Further west is the *Taj Bauri*, one of the Bijapur's principal water monuments, dating from 1620. This consists of a large square tank with a broad flight of steps on the north descending to the water. The steps are framed by a monumental arched portal with octagonal towers capped by characteristic domes on petals. The dilapidated *Mecca Gate* in the outer walls is located nearby. Another reservoir, the *Chand Bauri*, is located a short distance north, just inside the Shahi Gate.

The tour of Bijapur concludes with a visit to the *Ibrahim Rauza*, the most splendid of all Adil Shahi monuments. This complex, situated 350 m. beyond the outer walls on the west side of the city, was begun by Ibrahim II, but completed by his queen, Taj Sultan, in 1633. The complex consists of a paired tomb and mosque standing in the middle of a formal garden, about 140 m.

square. It is entered through a gateway on the north, from which a raised pathway leads to the podium on which the tomb and mosque are raised.

The exterior of the tomb is a majestically conceived pyramid of turrets and finials, crowned with a three-quarter spherical dome raised high on a frieze of petals. The overhang that runs around the building is carried on a line of ornate brackets that wraps around corner part-octagonal buttresses, capped with octagonal minarets crowned with domical finials on petals. The parapet above has model pavilions, complete with miniature cornices and bulbous domes. The outer walls, doorways and windows of the cenotaph chamber, within the interior verandah, are decorated with superbly executed panels of calligraphic, floral and geometric designs, both in shallow relief and as cut-out screens. There are even traces of painted decoration. The chamber itself, devoid of decoration, is roofed with a flat vault divided into nine squares, with curving sides. The grave of Ibrahim is positioned in the middle and that of Taj Sultan at the eastern end.

Directly opposite the tomb, on the other side of a deep pool with fountains, stands the mosque. The mosque repeats the overall scheme of the mausoleum, but at a slightly smaller scale, and with cut plasterwork adorning the five arches of the facade. Corner buttresses are carried up above the roof line as slender minarets. Arcaded balconies project outwards from the side walls of the prayer chamber. The central bay of the prayer hall is raised up into the interior of the capping dome

B. Around Bijapur

The immediate environs of Bijapur are dotted with Adil Shahi remains. Ibrahim II was actively involved in the expansion of Bijapur, and in 1599 began work on a twin circular city called *Nauraspur*. This idea never came to fruition, but portions of the unfinished fortifications can still be seen 6 km. west of Bijapur. Among the few completed, though now ruined structures in Nauraspur is the Sangith Mahal. This is a slightly smaller copy of the Gagan Mahal in the Bijapur citadel, though with its internal lofty vault still mostly intact. The hall faces towards a rectangular pool, located in the middle of a vast enclosure with broad low arches on each of nine sides.

Monuments at *Ainapur*, 3 km. east of Bijapur, include the tomb of Ain-ul Mulk, which is built in a style reminiscent of Bahmani architecture. The cubic mausoleum has double tiers of arched recesses. The crenellated parapet is enlivened with pavilion-like turrets at the corners; the dome has flattish proportions. The adjacent mosque is a small structure with remarkable ornamentation. The plaster tracery in the medallions of the spandrels is particularly noteworthy. These plaster details complement the delicately carved stone brackets, cornice and parapet.

A short distance further east is the unfinished tomb of Jahan Begum who died in 1651. Judging from its surviving corner turrets and connecting arcades, this was intended as a replica of the Gol Gumbaz, but at a lesser scale. This is an appropriate reference since Jahan Begum was once of Muhammad's principal queens. Five graves on a double platform include that of the queen and her family members. A palace built for Jahan Begum, with a dilapidated triple-arched facade, stands nearby.

C. KUMATGI

The small village of Kumatgi, 18 km. east of Bijapur on the road to Gulbarga, is of interest for the remains of a pleasure resort dating from Adil Shahi times. The complex is dominated by a double-storeyed pavilion, square below and octagonal above, topped by a small dome. This stands in the middle of a pond, surrounded by water channels, reached by a bridge on the east. Vaults with fanciful designs are seen within, while pipes projecting outwards from the walls were for cooling sprays. Water also descended through a perforated rose sprinkler set into the ceiling of the upper chamber. The required pressure was achieved by means of a tower standing outside the complex. This had a system of superimposed Persian wheels, now vanished, that raised water to a cistern, from where it was then conducted into pipes.

Beside the double-storeyed pavilion is a rectangular building. Its interior is divided into ten bays roofed with vaults carried on fan-like, fluted pendentives. Traces of the murals with which the interior was once ornamented can barely be made out. They portray scenes of courtiers hunting, drinking, listening to music, playing polo and enjoying wrestling matches. Some figures seem to be European.

A few metres west of the complex is a large tank which fed the channels and fountains. The pavilion in the middle of the water can only be only be reached by boat.

D. AFZALPUR

This town on the bank of the Bhima River, about 95 km. northeast of Bijapur via Sindgi on the road to Gulbarga, is worth visiting for its finely finished mosque and tomb. The complex was built in 1654-59 by Afzal Khan, a commander of Ali II, before he was treacherously murdered in 1660 by Shivaji at Pratapgad [7B] in Maharashtra. Elevated on a terrace in a walled garden overlooking fields to the south of the town, the mosque and tomb face each other across a small pool, with an unusual column in the middle. The triple arches of the prayer hall of the mosque are decorated with plasterwork, while the perforated parapet with pavilion-like finials above are of stone. The nine interior bays of the hall interior are roofed with alternating domes and flattish vaults; the mihrab is a polygonal chamber. The adjacent tomb is roofed with a dome raised on faceted pendentives. Leaf-like motifs on floral stands, in relief plasterwork, enliven the corners.

24. Gulbarga

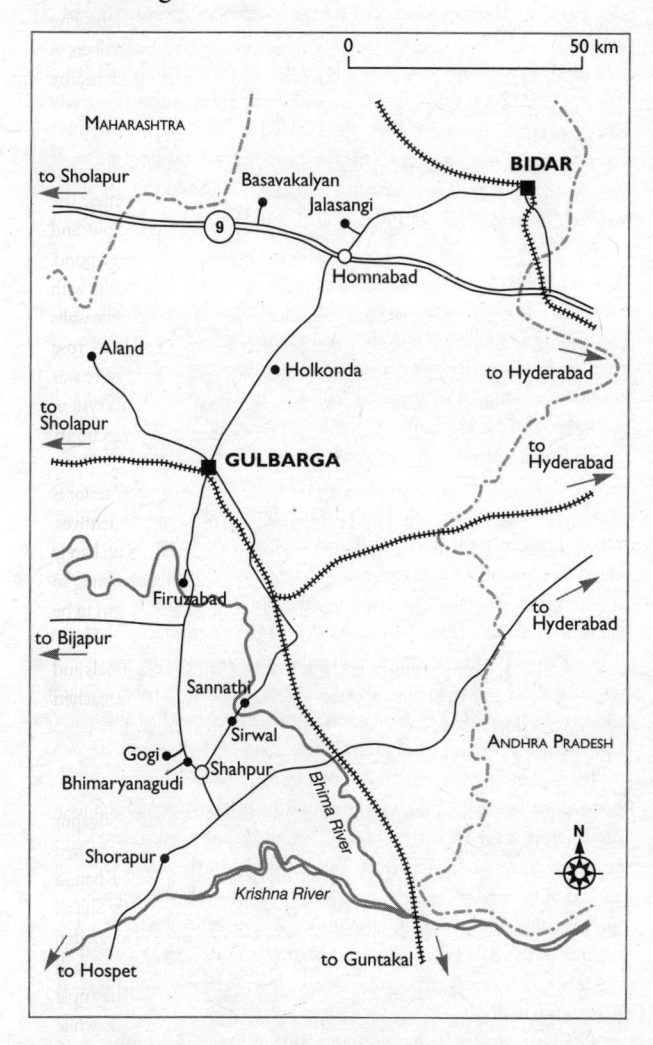

The largest city in northern Karnataka, Gulbarga is both a historical site and an important religious centre due to the popularity of the dargah of Hazrat Gesu Daraz. This is the largest Muslim shrine in Karnataka, attracting thousands of pilgrims during the Urs festival held in honour of the saint. Gulbarga is dotted with a profusion of structures dating from the Bahmani and Adil Shahi periods. One day should be set aside to visit the most important mosques, tombs and shrines [A].

Half-day excursions may be made to the dargahs at Holkonda [B] and Aland [C], to the north of Gulbarga, and to the ruins of the palace city of Firuzabad [D] to the south. More than a full day will be required to journey further south of the city in order to visit the mosque and shrines at Gogi [E], the prehistoric remains at Bhimarayanagudi [F], the Hindu temples at Sirwal and Buddhist remains of nearby Sannathi [G], and the palaces at Shorapur [H].

A. GULBARGA

Soon after Alauddin Hasan Bahman Shah proclaimed his independence from Delhi in 1347 Gulbarga was chosen as the capital of the newly founded Bahmani kingdom. Though Alauddin and his successors waged wars with the neighbouring kings of Vijayanagara [20B-C] in the second half of the 14th and during most of the 15th centuries, these rulers built up an extensive kingdom that encompassed much of northern Karnataka, western Andhra Pradesh and almost all of Maharashtra. Tajuddin Firuz (1397-1422), an outstanding figure, established a close relationship with the Chishti saint, Hazrat Gesu Daraz, but this relationship turned sour after the saint predicted that Firuz's brother, Ahmad, would inherit the throne; this indeed is what happened. In order to avoid conflict with the Firuz's immediate descendants, Ahmad promptly shifted the Bahmani capital to Bidar [25A] in 1424, upon which Gulbarga was reduced to a provincial centre. After the fragmentation of the Bahmani kingdom at the end of the 15th century, the city came under the sway of the sultans of Bijapur [23A]. In 1658 it was absorbed into the Mughal dominions, from where it passed into the hands of the Nizams of Hyderabad [26A].

The tour of Gulbarga described here begins at the *Fort* that once served as the headquarters of the Bahmanis and governors of the later Adil Shahi rulers. The tapering stone walls with massive round bastions define an irregularly shaped circle, about 250 m. across. The east gate, now the principal entrance, reached at the end of a causeway crossing the moat, has a pointed arched opening flanked by bastions. Opposite the gate, immediately after entering the fort, stands the Bala Hisar. This solid keep is built on top of a north-facing audience hall. Masonry arches traversing the hall can be seen from the staircase that ascends to the top.

The *Jami Mosque*, a short distance further on, was probably built by Tajuddin Firuz. Unlike any other mosque in Southern India it is entirely roofed over, without any internal court; this unusual scheme is explained by the fact that it may have served originally as a ceremonial reception hall. The building has been much altered: external arched openings of the mosque were once been filled with screens, while the battlements and finials of the parapet are restorations. The outer aisles within the mosque present impressive perspectives of broad arches with angled profiles; the central zone has multiple domed bays. An enlarged chamber in front of the mihrab is roofed with a lofty dome on pendentives, raised high above the roof.

Dargah of Hazrat Gesu Daraz, Gulbarga.

A few metres northwest of the Jami mosque is a *Bazaar Street* flanked by vaulted chambers, dating from Bahmani times. This runs east from a massive gate set into the northwest corner of the fort, the original entrance to the citadel. The gate is shielded by curving outworks fitted into the ramparts.

Funerary Monuments associated with the first Bahmani rulers in the second half of the 14th century lie to the west of the fort, now partly concealed by recent housing. The tombs of Alauddin Hasan, Muhammad I and Muhammad II are unadorned cubic chambers with slightly sloping walls, corner finials and flattish domes. The *Chor Gunbad*, on top of a rising slope about 1.5 km. further west, was erected in 1420 for Gesu Daraz, but the saint was never buried here. The domed mausoleum has double tiers of arched recesses in its outer walls; miniature domical pavilion-like finials mark the corners.

About 500 m. north of the royal tombs is the *Dargah of Shaykh Sirajuddin Junaydi*, spiritual preceptor of the first Bahmanis. The compound houses a simple domed mausoleum and small unadorned mosque. In the early 16th century Yusuf Adil Khan, founder of the Adil Shahi kingdom of Bijapur, added a monumental gateway to the complex. This monumental structure stands freely to the east, serving as a focal point for a long street. The gateway has double tiers of arcades on either side of a central arched portal. The facade is flanked by lofty cylindrical minarets with intermediate balconies, capped by flattish domes.

Proceeding down the street from the gateway just described visitors reach the *Shah Bazaar Mosque*. Dating from the period of Muhammad I (1358-75), it has a courtyard entered through a domed chamber on the east. The simple arched opening and battlemented parapet are typical of early Bahmani architecture. The prayer hall on the west side of the court has 15 aisles, each with six domed bays.

The commercial heart of Gulbarga ciy, to the east of the fort, is marked by a crossing of two principal streets. They are lined with shops and stores accommodated in arcaded chambers, now partly hidden by modern shop fronts.

Several groups of monuments are situated on the eastern edge of the city, originally facing onto a large tank, now partly dried up. The first to be described is the royal funerary complex known as the *Haft Gunbad*. The tomb of Alauddin Muhajhid (died 1378), has unadorned sloping walls with corner fluted finials and a flattish dome. That of Dawud (died 1378) is a double mausoleum, with two domed chambers linked by a narrow corridor. The largest and most elaborate funerary monument of the Haft Gunbad complex is the tomb of Tajuddin Firuz (died 1422). Like that of Dawud, this comprises a pair of twin domed chambers. Here, however, the walls are divided into double tiers of recesses with arched tops in multiple planes. The upper recesses are decorated with geometric patterns in pierced plasterwork; similar panels appear above the doorways in the middle of each side, sheltered by angled eaves on brackets, above which are half-pyramidal vaults. The facades are further embellished with bands of foliate and arabesque patterns, as well as roundels containing geometric designs, all in precisely cut plasterwork. Similar themes adorn the arched recesses, supporting arches and domes of the interior.

About 750 m. east of the Haft Gunbad is the *Dargah of Hazrat Gesu Daraz*. In addition to the tombs of the saint and his son, the complex is crowded with prayer halls, schools, rest houses, stores and gateways. The whitewashed mausoleum of Gesu Daraz, dating from the death of the saint in 1422, has a double storeyed facade divided into arched recesses. Exterior decoration is confined to roundels in the spandrels over the arches, and the parapet with domical finials. A lofty dome rises above. The original designs painted onto the corner arches and dome within are now concealed by modern mirrorwork. A cloth canopy covers the grave of the saint. The tomb of Sayyid Akbar Husayni, the son of Gesu Daraz, who died during the lifetime of the saint, stands in front. It is of the same type, with a sumptuously decorated polygonal mihrab.

The small mosque in the south court of the dargah is of architectural interest, having been built in the middle of the 17th century by Afzal Khan, general of Muhammad Adil Shah. This finely finished building is furnished with sculpted brackets carrying an ornate overhang topped by clusters of domical finials, and crowned by a dome raised on a petalled frieze. An immense ceremonial arch springs from high towers positioned at the two southern corners of the court. This structure has unusual carved roundels containing heraldic animals on fish-like brackets. The arch originally crowned a gateway that led down to the lake, on the edge of which the dargah was built.

About 250 m. southeast of Gesu Daraz's dargah complex is the *Dargah of Shah Kamal Muharrad*, another saint who resided in Gulbarga during early Bahmani times. The complex consists of a domed tomb, mosque, rest house and long building with a line of domed chambers, possibly for student accommodation. The original exuberant plaster decoration of the mosque facade is partly concealed behind a modern extension.

The last monument at Gulbarga to be described here is the *Kanchan Mahal*, 1.5 km. north of the city, close to the main road to Bidar. The mosque here, known as Langar ki Masjid, is of interest for its prayer chamber roofed with a pointed vault with imitation timber ribs. Fine plaster ornamentation enlivens the wall niches and mihrab. Another feature of interest in the city is the *Government Museum* (closed Fridays). This occupies two small domed tombs opposite the Government Hospital in the southern part of the city. Among the sculptures housed here are several brought from Sannathi.

B. Holkonda

The funerary complex at this site is reached by turning right off the main road leading to Bidar, about 30 km. north of Gulbarga. Seven Bahmani period tombs are preserved here, five standing within a walled complex entered from the east through an arched gateway. The most prominent monument is the *Tomb of Shaykh Muhammad Mayshakha*, the saint to whom the Holkonda complex is dedicated. This 14th century tomb presents a plain whitewashed exterior, interrupted only by the arched entrance on the south. Finer plasterwork is seen on other smaller tombs.

C. Aland

Located 42 km. northwest of Gulbarga, this town is of interest for the *Dargah of Ladle Sahbi*. This is dedicated to the Chishti Sufi saint who was the spiritual guide of Gesu Daraz. The most impressive aspects of this complex are the two 16th century gateways that define a processional pathway leading to the main tomb. The first gateway has a central arch flanked by lofty minarets on octagonal bases. The cylindrical shafts of the minarets are interrupted by arcaded galleries and topped by bulbous domes. The second gateway has similar styled minarets at the two outer corners. The tomb itself is of little architectural interest.

The nearby *Kali Mosque* of 1642 is a modest structure with three rectangular bays each roofed with a dome on extended pendentives.

D. Firuzabad

Beside the road running south of Gulbarga, 30 km. from the city, stands the *Dargah of Khalifat al-Rahman*, a saint about whom little is known. The building dates from the early Bahmani era, as is evident from the plain walls that taper slightly, with raised portals in the middle of each side, the battlemented parapet with domical finials, and the smooth hemispherical dome. The interior of the tomb is unusual, with vaulted corridors on four sides leading to a central domed chamber. A gateway outside the tomb leads to a small mosque, with six shallow domes.

The dargah appears to be a contemporary with the nearby palace city of Firuzabad. This takes its name from Tajuddin Firuz Shah, who founded it in 1400 to commemorate a victory over the Vijayanagara forces. Intended as a base for future campaigns, Firuzabad also functioned as a royal pleasure resort. It was, however, abandoned after the move of the capital to Bidar.

Firuzabad is laid out as an irregular square, almost 1 km. across, defined by the Bhima River on the west, and massive ramparts on other three sides. Two lines of vaulted chambers defining a bazaar street are visible behind the houses of the modern village, immediately to the north, leading to the riverside (west) gate of the city. This has an arched entrance flanked by polygonal bastions. A path through the overgrown ruins inside the walls runs towards the *Jami Mosque*, the largest monument of the city. Only its domed entrance chamber and perimeter walls defining a vast rectangle still stand. The prayer chamber within has mostly collapsed. Immediately to the west of the mosque is the *Palace Zone*, entered through a dilapidated arched portal, with traces of royal animals in stucco in the spandrels. The palace itself now presents a confused mass of overgrown chambers, halls and courts. Better preserved is the hammam immediately south of the palace zone. This is of interest for its combination of pyramidal vaults and domes. A second, more decayed hammam is located north of the mosque.

Another prominent feature of Firuzabad is the north-facing *Audience Hall* located some 100 m. east of the mosque. This has transverse masonry arches defining a double-height interior. The roof, presumably of wood, is lost. A path from the mosque leads towards the east gate of the city. A pointed vault with ribs roofs the passageway leading to the outer arched entryway, protected by an extensive barbican enclosure.

E. GOGI

This small town, 45 km. south of Gulbarga, is worth visiting for its mosque and tombs associated with the Adil Shahis of Bijapur.

The *Kali Mosque* commissioned by the sister of Ali I (1558-80) is a small, but superbly finished monument. It is entered through a gateway decorated with interlaced bands surrounding the arched opening. The interior is roofed with a flat vault enlivened with timber-like ribs. The prayer hall that stands within the courtyard has a triple arcaded facade. Ornate plasterwork is seen in the bands around the openings and in the roundels of the spandrels. Elegantly curved brackets carry the overhanging eaves. Octagonal corner buttresses are topped with domical finials. The hall interior consists of a single chamber with a small dome carried on eight intersecting arches, with faceted pendentives in between. The polygonal mihrab in the rear wall serves as the base of a hollow tower crowned with a small dome that rises above the roof.

The *Dargah of Hazrat Chandra Husayni*, a short distance west, is a popular place of worship. The complex is entered on the north through an arched gate. The focal building is the open tomb of the saint, surrounded by modern stone screens. To the rear (west) stands the domed mausoleum of the royal patroness of the nearby mosque. It is built in a simple style, with double tiers of arched recesses on four sides.

That Gogi was important for the Adil Shahis is indicated by an unadorned arcaded structure nearby, which shelters the graves of the first four Bijapur rulers. A gateway in the west of the complex leads to a large lake.

A small and much rebuilt *Jain Temple* tucked away in a side street of Gogi is worth visiting in order to view a small but beautiful image of Parshvanatha. This polished, green schist image is assigned to the 10th-11th century, Late Chalukya era.

F. Bhimarayanagudi

This small settlement, near the main road running south from Gulbarga, 5 km. from Gogi, preserves one of the largest prehistoric sites in Karnataka. *Stone Alignments* are here combined with Neolithic ash mounds. Overgrown granite boulders and collapsed menhirs in both basalt and reddish granite are arranged in long parallel lines, stretching more than 150 m. The remains are believed to be about 2,000 years old.

G. Sirwal and Sannathi

A visit to these two villages, located opposite each other on a bend in the Bhima River, about 60 km. south of Gulbarga, is in the nature of an expedition. The easiest approach is from Shahpur to Sirwal, and then fording the river to visit Sannathi.

Sirwal has a large number of temples dating from the 10th-11th centuries, during the Rashtrakuta and Late Chalukya eras. Though now mostly abandoned and dilapidated, these buildings preserve outer walls with crisply carved pilasters, and internal columns with relief carvings of garlands. The largest monument is the whitewashed *Siddheshvara Temple* on the western flank of the village, now in worship. This has a central sanctuary with four doorways, each leading to a separate mandapa. Linga sanctuaries were later appended to these mandapas, thereby creating an unusual five-sanctuaried scheme. To the northwest of the village is a step-well with carvings of Hindu divinities on its side walls.

Sannathi, on the other side of the Bhima, is of interest for its extensive *Buddhist Remains* dating from the 1st century BCE-3rd century CE, Satavahana period. The outlines of brick fortifications delimit a roughly quadrilateral zone some 600 m. across. Surface remains from the elevated walled citadel include coins and pottery. Mounds outside the walls indicate the locations of Buddhist stupas. One example, 2 km. north of the village, has a mound measuring 70 m. in diameter, and is more than 8 m. high. Limestone slabs found at these stupa sites have animated carvings of Jataka stories and scenes from the life of Buddha. Some slabs have been removed to the State Archaeological Museums in Gulbarga and Bengaluru [14B].

Sannathi is best known today for the *Chandralamba Temple* dedicated to a form of Devi. This 11th century shrine is visited by large numbers of plilgrims, especially in March-April. The sanctuary, which faces east, is unusually circular in plan. A slab with an inscription of Ashoka, the 3rd century BCE emperor, is displayed in the temple compound.

Further Buddhist vestiges are found near the village of *Kanganhalli*, 5 km. upstream from Sannathi. Limestone slabs from a destroyed stupa dating from the 2nd-3rd century CE are of interest for their fine carvings of courtly figures, lotus flowers, and representations of stupas with parasol finials. One slab depicting a king and queen is inscribed with the name Ashoka.

H. SHORAPUR

This historic town, 100 km. south of Gulbarga, was capital of the Bedars, a line of local chiefs whose domains comprised much of the territory between the Bhima and Krishna Rivers. The Bedars resisted the incursion of the Mughals at the end of the 17th century, and in the following century rose to prominence under the Nizams of Hyderabad. Colonel Meadows Taylor, author of the celebrated *Confessions of a Thug*, was posted here as a British Political Agent in 1841. The town was the scene of an uprising against the British in 1857.

The walls surrounding Shorapur are almost intact, with arched gateways positioned on four sides. In the middle of the town stands the 19th century *Bedar Palace*. Its unadorned exterior contrasts with the decorated, though dilapidated interior. Three levels of reception rooms employ intricately worked wooden columns, brackets and beams. Fanlights over the windows are Neo-Classical. The older 18th century palace nearby, now a primary school, has a small court with a fountain overlooked by a Mughal styled loggia.

The *Venugopala Temple* of 1709 stands on a elevated terrace above the middle of the town. It has a large open mandapa with balcony seating on three sides. The outer row of columns, which stand clear of the balcony, have sculpted elephants at their bases. A pyramidal tower with a hemispherical roof crowns the plain sanctuary to the rear.

A path ascends to the *Residence of Meadows Taylor*, now the PWD Guest House, perched on a rocky eminence. Dating from 1844, this simple villa has a gracious colonnaded verandah giving access to two circular reception rooms.

25. Bidar *(see map on p. 287)*

Elevated more than 700 m. above sea level in the northern extremity of Karnataka this historic city is celebrated for its magnificent fort, mosques, tombs and madrasa. These monuments are associated with the Bahmanis and their successors, the Baridis, and date mainly from 15th-16th centuries. The city is also known for its fine arts, especially the intricately worked inlaid metalwork known as bidri, named after the city itself, that continues to be manufactured here.

Most of the important monuments of Bidar [A] and its environs [B] may be covered in a full day of sightseeing, either as an excursion from Gulbarga [24A] or Hyderabad [26]. But an overnight stay is necessary in order to visit the temple at Jalasingi, with its charming sculptures [C], and the impressive citadel at Basavakalyan [D]. From Bidar it is also possible to travel to Sholapur [9A] or the Sikh pilgrimage shrine at Nanded [9F], both in Maharashtra.

A. BIDAR

Bidar served as the capital of the later Bahmanis, after Ahmad I (1422-36) shifted his headquarters here from Gulbarga in 1424. During the reigns of Alauddin Ahmad II (1436-58) and Shamsuddin Muhammad III (1463-82) the Bahmani kingdom reached its greatest extent, stretching from the Arabian Sea to the Bay of Bengal. The outstanding personality of the era was Mahmud Gawan, Muhammad's Prime Minister, the effective ruler of the kingdom. He strove to maintain a balance between Indian Muslims and recent emigrés from Iran and Central Asia, but in the end was unable to prevent internal conflict.

Several powerful figures emerged as the Bidar court disintegrated towards the end of the 15th century. They include Yusuf Adil Khan and Nizamul Mulk, founders of the future kingdoms of Bijapur [23A] and Golconda [26E] respectively, and also Qasim Barid I, first ruler of the Baridi dynasty. Qasim's son, Amir Barid (1504-43), gained control of the Bidar territories, but it was his successor Ali Barid (1543-80) who was an active patron of architecture, and a participant in the confederacy that defeated the army of Vijayanagara [20B-C] in 1565. In 1619 Bidar was conquered by Ibrahim Adil Shah and the Baridi territories were annexed by Bijapur. The city was conquered by the Mughals in 1656, from whom it then passed into the hands of the Nizams of Hyderabad.

Visitors generally approach Bidar from the south. About 1 km. before reaching the city they will catch a glimpse of the whitewashed dome of the *Dargah of Hazrat Shah Abul Faid* [in B]. From here they road leads to the southern gate of the city. This is one of several well defended entryways, set into the *Fortifications* that contain the city in an approximate quadrangle. The walls are reinforced by polygonal bastions, and topped by a massive trefoil parapet. Two main streets divide the city into four quarters. The crossing is marked by a squat circular tower known as the *Chaubara*. A short distance to the south, partly hidden behind houses, is the *Jami Mosque* of Bidar. This consists of a modest prayer hall with seven arched openings decorated with fine plasterwork. The openings are sheltered by an angled overhang carried on brackets and surmounted by a parapet of trefoil battlements.

Proceeding northwards along the main north-south street of Bidar visitors soon arrive at the *Madrasa of Mahmud Gawan*, named after the famous Prime Minister, who completed it in 1472. Built to house the teachings of the Shia doctrines that were propagated in Bidar at this time by Iranian emigrants, the madrasa is a unique imitation on Indian soil of a Central Asian theological college. Though severely damaged, its original scheme is still apparent. The facade was flanked by a pair of tall cylindrical minarets, only one of which still stands. It has two intermediate stages cantilevering outwards as balconies; the summit is domed. Both the minaret and the adjacent arcaded facade are cloaked with tile mosaic in brilliant blue and white colours, with touches of yellow and green. The calligraphic tile panel quoting a passage from the Koran that runs across the facade is the finest in Southern India. The interior of the madrasa is dominated by a great square court, originally approached through lofty arched portals on four sides, each of which is surmounted by a dome. Triple tiers of arched chambers in between were intended as accommodations for teachers and students.

A short distance further north, on the east side of the same street, stands the *Takht-i Mahal*. This early 15th century gateway is of interest for its finely worked plasterwork decorating the bands around the arched openings, the roundels in the spandrels, and the trefoil battlements of the parapet. Nothing remains of the tomb that once stood beyond the gateway.

From here visitors soon arrive at the *Fort* at the northern end of the city. Though originally laid out by the Bahmanis, Bidar Fort and its various monuments were extensively remodelled under the Baridis. The double walls that contain the fort are protected on the south by a triple moat, partly hewn out of the basalt out of which it is built. The walls are reinforced by round and polygonal bastions, many with gun emplacements, interspersed with guardrooms cantilevering outwards on brackets. The walls are topped with a parapet of arched battlements.

Entry to the fort is through a line of three gateways in the southeast quadrant of the fort. The intermediate *Sharza Darwaza*, so called because of the sculpted animals set into the facade, has an arched gateway flanked by polygonal balconies, above which is a decorative frieze of polychrome tiles. The innermost gateway, the *Gumbad Darwaza*, is reached only after passing through a causeway. Its double arches with pronounced angled contours are surmounted by a flattish dome.

An ensemble of royal buildings occupies the southern part of the fort. Though partly ruined, these give the best possible idea of formal courtly architecture in the 15th-16th centuries. The first features to be noticed on entering this zone are the multi-domed bath on the right, and the *Rangin Mahal* on the left (key is kept at the nearby Archaeological Museum). The latter, dating from the period of Ali Barid, is one of the best preserved palaces in Bidar. An arched entrance on the north gives access to a small court at the far end of which is a hall with intricately worked timber columns, brackets and beams, a rare survival of a presumably widespread wooden tradition. The lower parts of the walls are embellished with elegant arabesque patterns in blue, turquoise and yellow tile mosaic. A suite of vaulted chambers opens to the rear. Doorways here are surrounded by polished basalt panels inset with delicate mother-of-pearl patterns and inscriptions.

The next important building to be visited within the fort is the *Solah Khamba Mosque*, which served both as a place of assembly and prayer. Founded in 1327, during the occupation of Bidar by the forces of the Delhi army, it was later extended. Its long line of 15 arched openings is relieved by a parapet of interlocking perforated battlements. The flattish dome is raised on a circular drum ornamented with trefoil merlons in relief. The interior of the mosque is five bays deep. Squattish circular columns carry small domes on faceted pendentives. The mihrab in the middle of the rear wall is framed by a lobed arch.

The Solah Khamba Mosque faces eastwards onto a rectangular garden known as *Lal Bagh*, with a podium in the middle containing an elegant, oval-shaped fringed pool. Water was conveyed by means of a channel from an angled chute set into the apartments on the southern periphery of the garden. To the north is an arcaded building, now the *Archaeological Museum*. Here are displayed various sculptures, ceramics, stone inscriptions and other artefacts gathered from all over the fort.

Solah Khamba Mosque, Bidar Fort.

A path leads west from Lal Bagh to the *Diwan-i Am*, the public and ceremonial focus of the Bahmani and Baridi courts. This comprises a large rectangular court flanked by high walls with arched recesses. On the south side is a spacious hall with finely worked stone blocks indicating the locations of wooden columns, now vanished. Chambers opening off the hall on three sides were embellished with polychrome tiled panels, but these are lost. The floors in some chambers have geometric designs in different coloured stones.

The *Takht Mahal*, located further west, is where the Bidar rulers held private audience. It, too, has a columned hall facing north into a walled court. The court is entered from the northeast corner through a gate with a bent entryway. A Portal on the western side of the court has a lofty arched opening with a markedly pointed profile. Traces of hexagonal coloured tiles depicting royal tiger and sun emblems can be made out in the spandrels. A chamber to the rear (south) of the columned hall has an ornamental pool with lobed sides.

A dilapidated pavilion located a short distance to the southwest offers views of a well irrigated lower zone where the palace gardens were once located. An extensive plain extends beyond the walls of the fort.

B. Around Bidar

Royal and saintly funerary monuments are dotted around Bidar. Those linked with the Bahmanis are located at *Ashtur*, 3 km. northeast of the city. The first building to be glimpsed from the road running from Bidar is *Chaukhandi*, the tomb of Khalilullah, a Persian saintly figure who died here in 1460. His father was Shah Nimatullah, the famous Sufi teacher of Kirman in Iran, who was invited by Ahmad I to settle in Bidar, but who sent his son instead. The Chaukhandi is entered from the south through an arched gateway with plaster decoration. The mausoleum itself consists of a double-height octagonal screen surrounding a small domed chamber. This wall has arched recesses flanked by panels with diagonal squares, outlined with finely worked basalt bands. The south doorway is headed by a majestic basalt Koranic inscription, the finest in Southern India. Its overlapping cursive script is set against a delicately carved foliate scroll.

A short distance east along the road lies the royal necropolis, with the mausoleums arranged in a single line. The *Tomb of Ahmad I* (died 1436), at the furthest (eastern) end is the earliest and most impressive of the group. The walls of its square domed chamber are relieved with triple tiers of pointed arched recesses, four on the lower two registers, seven above. Ornamentation is restricted to superb calligraphic bands and foliate roundels, all in crisply carved plasterwork. The battlemented parapet has corner finials, repeated on the 16-sided drum of the impressive hemispherical dome that rises above. Remarkable paintings adorn the interior of the tomb. These show foliate, geometric and arabesque patterns in brilliant gold, vermillion and turquoise tones. The painting in the mihrab recess seems to portray a textile drape. The dome is embellished with concentric bands of calligraphy and arabesque motifs. Unlike the other royal tombs at Ashtur, that of Ahmad I is under worship, the sultan being venerated as a saint.

The adjacent *Tomb of Alauddin Ahmad II* (died 1458) presents a quite different exterior. Each facade employs a set of five pointed arches of unequal height, symmetrically disposed about the central largest niches. Here the arched profiles are gently curved. Panels above are adorned with polychrome tiles. The later adjacent *Tomb of Shamsuddin Muhammad* (died 1482) recalls earlier schemes in its use of arched recesses and bold parapet. There is, however, a total absence of decoration.

Another funerary complex is situated beside the main road running west of Bidar, 2 km. from the city walls. This is associated with the later Baridi rulers. The tombs are distributed on either side of the road. To the north is the *Tomb of Qasim Barid* (died 1504), which is a small unremarkable building with a plain dome. The nearby *Tomb of Amir Barid*, his successor, was left incomplete, with two tiers of arched recesses but no dome. Here, too, are the tombs of Ibrahim and Qasim Barid II, who died in 1587 and 1591 respectively.

Considerably larger and of greater architectural interest is the *Tomb of Ali Barid* (died 1580) on the south side of the road. Dating from 1577, three years before the death of this ruler, the tomb is elevated on a podium in the middle of a vast four-square garden, of which only the axial walkways are still preserved. The tomb itself comprises a dome raised on four lofty pointed arches. Horizontal recesses above the arches were probably intended for tile panes. The walls are topped by an elaborate parapet with trefoil elements, while the base of the dome has a frieze of petals. The tomb interior is enhanced by coloured tile panels and roundels. Pendentives with net-like patterns are decorated with arabesque plasterwork. The sarcophagus of Ali Barid is of polished black basalt. The gate to the garden stands to the south of the tomb. A small mosque next to the gate has three broad arched openings. Ornate plasterwork decorates the roundels in the spandrels and the interior arched recesses.

The *Dargah of Hazrat Shah Abul Faid*, already noticed above, commemorates the saint who died in Bidar in 1474. This figure exercised considerable influence on the later Bahmani rulers and is still held in great reverence. The tomb has its facades divided into tiers of arched recesses; the imposing dome that rises above is the largest of any in Bidar. The arched doorway is outlined by a basalt set in magnificent polychrome tiles painted with fanciful arabesque designs (now concealed by modern paint). The central grave inside the tomb is that of the saint himself.

C. JALASANGI

This small village, 44 km. southeast of Bidar, 2 km. west of the road to Homnabad, is worth visiting for its small 11th century *Shiva Temple*. Though damaged and partly rebuilt, the temple preserves fine examples of Late Chaluyka carvings. Only the sanctuary and antechamber walls stand complete; the tower is missing. Sculptures include deities in the axial niches, notably Shiva (south), Narasimha (west) and *Devi* (north). Beautiful maidens occupy the intervening recesses. Those on the south wall are particularly alluring, especially one figure who holds up a slate on which she inscribes the name of Vikramaditya, royal patron of the monument. A frieze of mythological beasts is positioned beneath the cornice. Several columns and an ornate doorway are preserved in the adjacent mandapa.

D. BASVAKALYAN

The city is located 6 km. north of NH9, about 55 km. west of Bidar, via Homnabad. Originally known simply as Kalyan, the city has recently been renamed in honour of Basava, a Hindu teacher who died here in 1196. This figure launched a series of radical social and religious reforms that later came to constitute the Virashaiva movement. Suppressed by the Late Chalukya rulers, the movement was revived in the 18th-19th centuries, and has today a sizeable number of followers known as Lingayats distributed throughout northern Karnataka and neighbouring Maharashtra and Andhra Pradesh. Basava and other Virashaiva teachers who lived in Kalyan are commemorated in shrines, known as gadigges, scattered in and around the city. They mostly consist of arcaded courts overlooked by meeting halls with vaults and domes.

Basvakalyan also has a small *Archaeological Museum*. The collection includes sculptures from the 11th-13th centuries, among them a fine a kneeling Garuda, and standing Vishnu. Excavated artefacts from Maski [20M] and Sannathi [24G] are also on display, as well as several small cannons and other arms.

Basvakalyan is also a historical city, having served as the headquarters of the Kalachuri and Late Chalukya rulers during the 10th-13th centuries. Its impressive citadel, the largest in northern Karnataka, was substantially rebuilt by the Bahmanis after they gained control of the region in 1347. It subsequently served as an outpost for the Bijapur kingdom in the 16th-17th centuries. After being occupied by the Marathas in the 18th century, the fortress came under the control of the Nizams of Hyderabad.

Basavakalyan's *Citadel* is reached by proceeding northwards along the full length of the main bazaar of the city. This street leads to an imposing gate that gives access to a spacious arcaded court, with a ceremonial platform in the middle dating from the period of the Nizams. A canon with a fine Persian inscription lies on the ground nearby. An arched gate at the northwestern corner of the court gives access to the citadel itself (closed Mondays).

The outer walls define an elliptical zone, measuring about 650 by 550 m. The walls date from both the Bahmani and Adil Shahi periods, and also incorporate earlier carved blocks. They are strengthened with massive round and polygonal bastions, with guardrooms projecting outwards on corbelled brackets. A stone lined moat, now empty, surrounds the walls on all sides. A sequence of three gates with arched entrances and vaulted passageways is located to the south. Wooden doors here have metal spikes for repelling elephant attacks. A 30 m. long causeway shielded by a rectangular barbican leads to the first gate. Discarded sculptures assembled between this and the second gate include Hindu and Jain deities, as well as a charming naga couple with entwined serpent bodies.

The second and third gates are linked by a stepped path that ascends steadily to the open and raised area of the lower fort. Among the overgrown and collapsed structures here are a power magazine (right) and rectangular barracks (left). The path continues until it meets the base of the upper fort, distinguished by massive circular bastions. Rectangular openings at the top are for cannon, many of which are still in place.

A flight of steps wrapping around the bastions ascends to the *Upper Fort*. This contains residential, ceremonial and religious structures, mostly dating from the period of the Nizams. On the left after passing through the arched gate in the inner walls stands the *Raj Mahal*. This is a palace with a small court and a pond in the middle, overlooked by arcades on the north decorated with ornate plasterwork. Steps to the left of the Raj Mahal climb to a bastion on top of which is a superb cannon with engraved and coloured designs and an animal head inlaid with brass. Other steps lead to a court lined with arcades at the topmost level of the citadel. A restored pavilion on the east looks out over the walls onto a large square tank below.

Returning to the arched gate in the inner walls, a path to the right passes by a whitewashed pavilion fronted by a Corinthian colonnade. Immediately to the north stands the *Rangin Mahal*, with an arcaded pavilion of delicate workmanship facing onto a small garden with a central fountain. A passageway here gives access to a small triple-bayed mosque, with a bulbous dome raised high on a petalled drum. Further apartments beyond lead via a domed granary to the darbar hall facing onto a rectangular court. The court is overlooked by balconies on three sides topped by curving cornices. Steps climb to a bastion at the east end of the court, where is placed a huge, roughly cast cannon, some 7.5 m. long.

From Basvakalyan it is possible to continue westward on NH9 to Sholapur [9A].

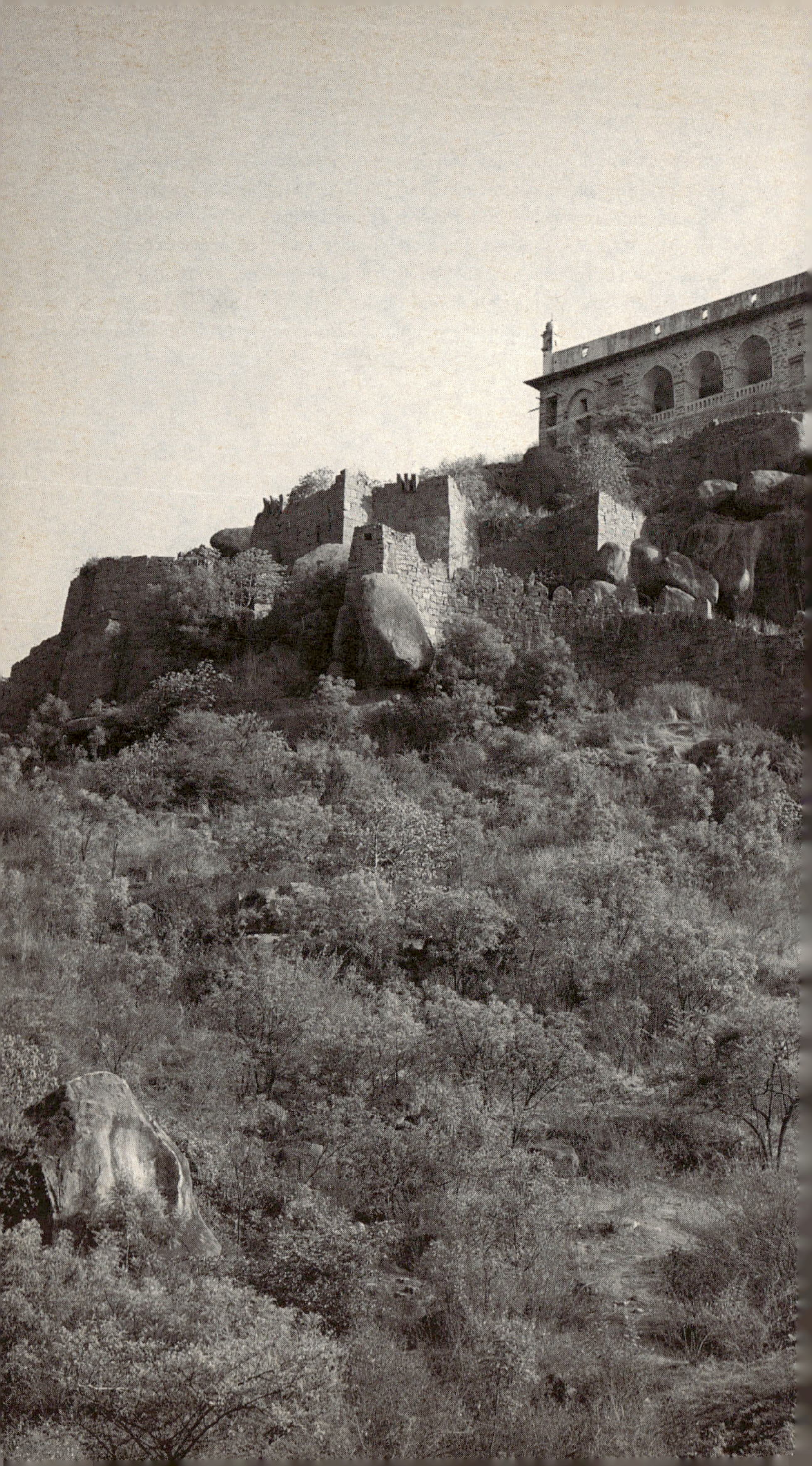

Darbar Hall, Golconda Fort

ANDHRA PRADESH

Andhra Pradesh

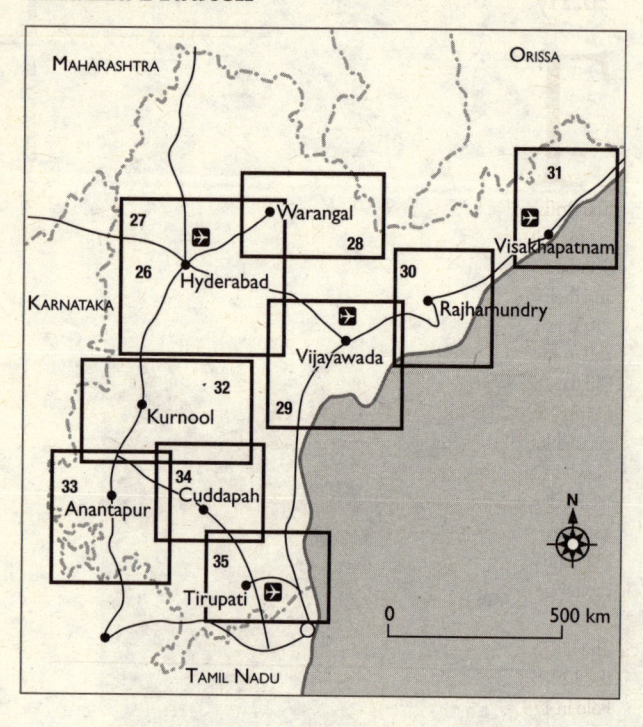

26. Hyderabad

The capital of Andhra Pradesh has a long and illustrious history. Together with nearby Golconda, Hyderabad served as the capital of the Qutb Shahis and their successors, the Asaf Jahis, better known by their title of Nizam. A splendid courtly culture and building tradition flourished here for more than 400 years. The British developed the twin city of Secunderabad as a military base.

In spite of the rapid growth that has transformed Hyderabad and Secunderabad into a huge metropolis, vestiges of the Qutb Shahis, the Nizams and their nobles are visible, everywhere.

At least one full day needs to be reserved for visiting the mosques, palaces and museums in both Old Hyderabad [A] and New Hyderabad [B]. Another half day should be set aside for a tour of Golconda City and Fort [E] and tombs nearby [F] on the western fringe of the city. For those interested in the British occupation, a few hours may also be spent at Secunderabad [D], northeast of New Hyderabad.

Hyderabad is also an obvious starting point for any tour of Andhra Pradesh, a suitable base from which to reach Warangal [28], Vijayawada [29], Kurnool [32] and other historical centres in the state. Full-day excursions beyond the capital are described in the following itinerary [27].

The hill fort at Golconda was a major outpost of the Kakatiyas of Warangal in the 12th-13th centuries. It was famous for its wealth and was noted by Marco Polo in 1291. In 1364 Golconda was ceded by the Kakatiyas to the Bahmanis of Gulbarga [24A], who had previously declared their independence from Delhi. Golconda was retained as an important citadel commanding the eastern tract of the Bahmani kingdom. However, it was not until the emergence of the Qutb Shahis that Golconda became a dynastic capital. Sultan Quli Qutb al-Mulk (1494-1543), the founder of this line, rose to power under the Bahmanis of Bidar [25A]. Though never formally declaring his autonomy, this outstanding military leader and strategist steadily consolidated his gains over rival rulers, including the emperors of Vijayanagara [20B-C] and the kings of Orissa. The territories under his control equalled those of the Adil Shahis of Bijapur [23A]. Golconda was strongly fortified, and the city was furnished with imposing civic, military and religious structures.

Golconda reached the height of its power under Ibrahim Qutb Shah (1550-80), who reorganised the Qutb Shahi state, appointing Hindu officials to high military, administrative and diplomatic posts. But these were unstable times, and Ibrahim frequently came into conflict with the competing kingdoms of Bijapur and Ahmadnagar [6A]. These difficulties were temporarily overcome in order to create the alliance that resulted in the defeat of the Vijayanagara forces in 1565. This confederation soon disintegrated, and by 1569 Golconda was already quarrelling with Bijapur over lands previously held by Vijayanagara. In 1579 Golconda and Ahmadnagar joined forces to raid the Bijapur kingdom.

The threat of Mughal expansion into Southern India began to be felt during the reign of Muhammad Quli Qutb Shah (1580-1612). Ahmadnagar fell to the Mughals in 1600, leaving the Qutb Shahis and the Adil Shahis to bear the impact of attacks from the north. Meanwhile, Venkatapatideva, one of the later Vijayanagara kings of Chandragiri [35C], proved a potential enemy on the southern borders of the kingdom. It was during Muhammad Quli's reign that it was decided to expand the congested Golconda capital. A bridge was thrown across the Musi River in 1578, permitting the move of the city to the east. The plans for Hyderabad were made in 1591, and over the next few decades the principal monuments, parks and gardens were laid out. Though affairs of state were conducted thereafter in the new capital, Golconda continued to be used as a fortified citadel, with an international reputation as an emporium of the diamond trade.

Under Muhammad Qutb Shah (1612-26), Golconda-Hyderabad enjoyed a period of comparative peace, though the Mughals continued to threaten the frontiers. Contacts were maintained with Persia and Europe, and factories of the Dutch, French and English merchants were established on the Bay of Bengal Coast. In 1636, during the reign of Abdullah Qutb Shah (1626-72), Aurangzeb was appointed Viceroy of the Mughal province of the Deccan. From this time on, Golconda-Hyderabad was under the surveillance of the Mughals, who were attracted by its prodigious wealth and famous hoards of diamonds. Maratha military power emerged as an additional threat in the period of Abul Hasan Qutb Shah (1672-87). Golconda-Hyderabad finally succumbed to the Mughals in 1687, thereby losing its status as a capital. However, the Mughal hold on the former Qutb Shahi territories was repeatedly challenged by the Marathas.

In 1723 Nizamul Mulk, Prime Minister of the Mughal emperor Muhammad Shah, was sent to Aurangabad [5A] to crush rebel forces. He stayed on in the Deccan, and soon after proclaimed himself independent of Delhi, thereby initiating the Asaf Jahi dynasty. Within a few years Nizamul Mulk shifted his headquarters to Hyderabad, which became home to a new line of rulers. The Nizams recovered the fortunes of the earlier Qutb Shahi capital, resisting the encroachment of the British and French, and even occasionally joining forces with the Europeans, as in 1790 and 1792, during the wars against Tipu Sultan of Srirangapattana [15C]. In the course of the 19th century the Nizams became allies of the British, concluding treaties by which they retained virtual autonomy, although a Resident was appointed to oversee the Hyderabad court. The Nizams continued in power for some years after Independence, but in 1956 Hyderabad was absorbed into the newly constituted state of Andhra Pradesh.

A. OLD HYDERABAD

Situated on the south bank of the Musi River, Old Hyderabad was laid out with two principal streets intersecting at right angles: these survive today as crowded commercial thoroughfares. The crossing is dominated by the *Char Minar*, built in 1592 as the chief landmark of the newly established capital and a monumental entrance to the Qutb Shahi palace. The Char Minar presents imposing portals on four sides, each spanning more than 11 m. Arcaded storeys and geometric screens are seen above. The four corner minarets, after which the monument takes its name, rise to a height of 56 m. above the ground, and are capped with domical finials. They contain spiral staircases, which ascend to triple tiers of balconies, from which there are fine views across the city in all directions. The upper levels were used both as a madrasa and mosque (access restricted); from here royal proclamations were read out to the assembled public.

The *Jami Mosque* of 1598 stands immediately northeast of the Char Minar. It is entered through a narrow lane lined by shops, above which rise its whitewashed minarets. The east facade of the prayer hall has three lobed arches on either side of a central pointed arch. The interior is roofed with shallow domes, except in front of the mihrab, where there is a rectangular vault. Inscriptions cut into basalt blocks flank the polygonal prayer niche. The rear walls of the mosque almost touch one of the four arches of the *Char Kaman*, erected in 1594 to define a great open square a short distance north of the Char Minar. The west arch served as a ceremonial gateway to the parade grounds where Muhammad Quli reviewed his troops; drummers were housed in a chamber elevated on the east arch. The square is now mostly occupied by buildings, through which run two main streets. A portion of the octagonal cistern, the Gulzar Hauz, is still seen in the middle.

The *Lad Bazaar*, one of the original market streets of the city, runs west from the Char Minar, marking the main route connecting Hyderabad with Golconda. The street terminates in a square where a large 19th century clock tower looms over a delicate whitewashed mosque of the same period.

Immediately south of the Char Minar is the *Mecca Mosque*, begun in 1614 by Muhammad Qutb Shah. The mosque takes its name from the belief that the bricks inserted over the central arch were baked out of clay brought from Mecca. Its grandiose, but undecorated prayer chamber, the largest in Hyderabad, is 74 m. long and 59 m. deep. It is entered through five lofty arches carried on solid stone piers. The facade is topped with boldly overhanging eaves. The polygonal minarets at either end have octagonal galleries and Mughal styled domes, added by Aurangzeb in 1687. On the south side of the large paced court onto which the mosque faces is a long arcaded pavilion. This accommodates the tombs of the later Nizams and their family members. (The first Asaf Jahis are buried at Khuldabad [5D]).

The *Chowmahalla Palace*, the principal residence of the Nizams, to the rear of the Mecca Mosque has recently been restored and is now open to the public as a museum (closed Fridays). Formal audiences and grand entertainments and banquets were held here during the period of Mir Osman Ali Khan Bahadur, the 7th Nizam (1911-48). The main entrance to the complex is on the west through an arched gateway topped by a slender clock tower, but visitors now enter the complex from a gate on the north. The palace comprises a linear sequence of garden courts with pools and fountains surrounded by whitewashed wings, some of which house collections of old photograph, costumes and other memorabilia of the Nizams. The first garden court is overlooked from the south by the *Khilawat Mubarak*. This imposing reception hall, with an arcaded facade and ornate corner towers surrounded by turrets and finials, is decorated in finely cut plasterwork. The double-height interior is enhanced by marble floors and crystal chandeliers; the marble throne at the rear is where the 8th Nizam was crowned in 1967. An armoury is accommodated in the side chambers. The second garden court has identical Neo-Classical pavilions with lofty porticos in the middle of four sides. That on the west, the Mahtab Mahal, was for receptions, while that on the east, the Aftab Mahal, was used for dining and sleeping. The Afzal Mahal on the south side is furnished in an ornate European style.

The next group of monuments to be described is situated near the Musi River. This is crossed by the Afzal Ganj Bridge, reconstructed after a disastrous flood in 1908 to serve as the major link between Old and New Hyderabad. The *High Court*, on the south bank of the Musi, west of the bridge, was erected in 1916 as the first major project of Vincent Esch, a British architect in the service of the 7th Nizam. The outer walls of the court are enriched with panels of relief decoration in red sandstone, used also for the columns, arches, balustrades and eaves. The building has a central portal, 18 m. high. The dome above is surrounded by smaller domes, all cloaked in blue tiles and topped with gilded finials. The court faces across the river to the Osmania General Hospital [described in C].

The nearby *Badshahi Ashurkhana* was intended as a congregational hall for Shia Muslims to gather during the Muharram festival, held each year in April-May. Dating from 1594, this is the oldest such building in Southern India. The inner hall, with double-height timber columns, is decorated with superb tile wall mosaics, added in 1611. Though partly damaged by floods, the original brilliant yellow, orange, blue and turquoise colours are intact. The arched panels are filled with hexagonal tiles with floral designs and calligraphic alams representing ceremonial standards. Metal alams are displayed only during Muharram.

A short distance east of the Badshahi Ashurkhana, on the other side of the main road leading to Afzal Ganj Bridge, is the *Diwan Deorhi*. This was once home to Hyderabad's Prime Ministers. Nothing remains of this palatial complex except the outer gates, one with a Neo-Classical parapet, the other with Mughal styled arcades. It was here that Salar Jung assembled his superb collection of art objects. In 1968 these were shifted to a newly built museum overlooking the Musi River. (The collection is described in [B].)

Purani Haveli, 1 km. east of Afzal Ganj Bridge, was another favoured ministerial residence. The central part of the palace consists of two long wings embellished with Neo-Classical colonnades, facing each other across a garden, with octagonal towers at the ends. The eastern wing now houses the Nizam's Museum (closed Fridays). This of interest for the long wardrobe still stocked with personal garments of the 7th Nizam, as well as assorted souvenirs, mementos and models, most of which were presented to the Nizam on the occasion of his Silver Jubilee in 1937. The European styled villa at the south end of the garden served as one of the homes of Mahboob Ali Khan Bahadur, the 6th Nizam (1869-1911).

About 250 m. south of Purani Haveli is the *Darush Shifa*, or House of Cure. Founded by Muhammad Quli Qutb Shah in about 1595 as a hospital and sarai, the somewhat dilapidated complex now accommodates mechanics and small businesses. Its central court is overlooked by double-height arcades. A small ashurkhana in the middle of the court, a later addition, is home to a fine collection of alams. The mosque that stands outside the north entrance, dating from the same period, has a triple-arched facade framed by gracefully proportioned minarets, partly hidden by an ugly concrete extension. Coloured tiles decorate the medallions in the spandrels.

Other historical features on the peripheries of Old Hyderabad are now contained by sprawling suburbs. A curiosity is the *Tomb of Michel Raymond*, set on a terrace at the summit of a rocky eminence 3 km. east of the Char Minar. An obelisk marks the grave of this French adventurer who died in Hyderabad in 1787. A small reconstructed Neo-Classical pavilion stands in front. The nearby Asman Garh palace houses the *Birla Archaeological Museum*. This unusual Gothic Revival building with a castelated round tower dates from the turn of the 20th century.

The *Paigah Tombs*, 3 km. southeast of the Char Minar, comprise a virtual city of the dead, with streets lined with funerary structures. These served as graves for the family of commanders and nobles who rose to prominence under the Nizams. The earliest tomb dates back to 1786, the most recent from

1968. The central group is attractively set in a well maintained garden. A line of flat roofed arcaded pavilions is decorated with intricate plasterwork. Geometric and foliate patterns cover the arches and jali screens, while clusters of vase-like finials enliven the parapets.

An *Idgah* dating from the 18th century stands a short distance from the Paigah tombs. This consists of a prayer hall of five bays, the arches being surmounted by an open gallery and a battlemented parapet. The facade is framed by massive minarets of unusual stunted proportions, topped with bulbous finials.

Undoubtedly one of the most remarkable sights of Old Hyderabad is the palace of *Falaknuma*, the Mirror of the Heavens, now the luxurious Taj Falaknuma Palace Hotel. The property crowns the summit of Koh-i-Tur 3 km. south of the Char Minar. The main block was begun in 1884 by Sir Viqar al Umra, a Paigah noble who served as Prime Minister of the 6th Nizam. But in 1897 the property was acquired by the 7th Nizam for his personal use, and it was here that he died in 1911. The road ascending to the palace passes through an ornate clock gate, with back-to-back Italianate facades framing a broad arch. The road terminates at a broad terrace overlooked by an imposing two-storeyed Neo-Classical facade, Ionic below and Corinthian above, capped by a pediment with the Nizam's coat-of-arms, looking out over the city below. Curving colonnades terminating in pedimented wings fan out at either side. A double flight of steps, flanked by imported cast-iron lamps, gives access to a colonnaded verandah lined with doors set with stained glass panels. From here visitors enter a fountain lobby with Roman styled marble fountain and benches, and a ceiling entirely covered with a painted blue sky, across which flies an eagle trailing a garland and cloth. Beyond is the library with a magnificent wooden panelled ceiling displaying the 'VO' monograph of the original owner of the palace. A broad staircase lined with oil paintings of the Nizam and the Paigah nobles gives access to the reception rooms at the upper level, mostly decorated in the ornate Rococo Revival style that was popular in Hyderabad at the end of the 19th century. They include a men's games room, with billiards table and card tables, a banquet hall that could seat more than 100 guests, a ballroom and a sitting room. Residential wings, kitchen and service quarters surround a spacious courtyard to the rear. A small museum crammed with wooden items purchased at one of the Delhi exhibitions is situated to one side.

B. SALAR JUNG MUSEUM

The vast numbers of objects accumulated by the Prime Minister Yousuf Ali Khan Bahadur Salar Jung (1889-1949) are of considerable interest not only for their intrinsic artistic worth, but also because they reveal the eclectic taste of the wealthiest Indian collector in the first half of the 20th century. The Museum (closed Fridays) is still growing with the purchase of new objects. The courts and verandahs between the galleries, though unsympathetic in style, are filled with European statuary, most of it belonging to the academic schools of the 19th-20th centuries. Only the most interesting rooms are noticed here.

The Founder's Gallery *(Room 2)*, shows paintings, furniture, porcelain, documents and other objects personally associated with Salar Jung and his forebears. *Room 3* is dedicated to Indian bronzes and painted textiles. Among the Hindu and Jain bronzes from the Tamil zone are several imposing Nataraja and Somaskanda figures dating from the 15th-16th centuries, and a dancing Ganesha of the same period. A variety kalamkari cloths, produced by a mixture of printing and dyeing techniques, includes a long composition illustrating the Shiva Purana, dated 1840. Painted cloth scrolls known as patas, a speciality of Andhra Pradesh, are also on display. *Room 5* is devoted to stone sculptures. Among the highlights is an elegant limestone Buddha wearing a fluted costume, assigned to the 2nd-3rd century Satavahana period, from Nelakondapalli in eastern Andhra Pradesh, and a 5th century sandstone linga showing a face of Shiva, from the Gupta site of Kausambi in Northern India. Other fine pieces are the 12th century polished black basalt figures of Mahavira and Parshvanatha from various sites in Karnataka.

Furniture and minor arts in wood, many from Karnataka, are on display in *Room 6*. They include ostentatious cabinets and tables, intricately fashioned from sandalwood and rosewood. Religious carvings include panels of different divinities, taken from temple chariots. *Room 7* presents a sumptuous collection of printed and embroidered fabrics, such as 18th century appliqué costumes from Rajasthan. Their vivid compositions contrast with the subtle motifs incorporated into contemporary muslins from Dhaka in Bangladesh. *Rooms 9-10*, the children's section, has a marvellous collection from all over the world, including a unique 1939 model of a flying boat. Room 11 contains European styled ivory chairs and tables manufactured in Visakhapatnam [31A], as well as figurines and inlaid boxes, many of them from Mysore [15A].

European statuary, including the 'Veiled Rebecca', made in Italy in 1876, a particular favourite of Salar Jung, is seen in *Room 12*. The 19th century gilded clock immediately outside is a great attraction because of the mechanical figures that move on the hour.

The armaments in *Room 14* include guns, daggers, swords and shields. They give a good idea of the refinement of metal casting in the 17th-18th centuries. Some items are identified as belonging personally to the Mughal emperors and to Tipu Sultan. *Room 15* is dedicated to ornately decorated metalwares, including splendid ewers, basins, trays, spice boxes and huqqa bases, all executed in the inlaid bidri technique. Originating in Bidar, bidri was practiced widely in Deccan workshops.

Room 16 is dedicated to 20th century Indian paintings, and includes significant oils by Ravi Varma and Rabindranath Tagore. *Room 17* is reserved for miniature paintings, with of representative examples from all the Mughal, Rajasthani, Pahari and Deccani schools, as well as 16th century Jain manuscripts from Gujarat and 18th century miniatures from Shorapur [24G].

The jades on view in *Room 27* are the finest in any Southern Indian collection. They include a hunting knife of Jehangir, and an archery ring of Shah Jahan, both in green jade inscribed in gold. Illuminated Islamic manuscripts constitute an important section of the collection. *Room 23* has several magnificent early Korans in bold Kufic script from North Africa. Another Koran, dated 1288, displays the autographs of three successive Mughal emperors. There is also an Urdu poetic composition by Muhammad Quli Qutb Shah, and a manuscript combining Arabic and Indian scripts commissioned by Ibrahim Adil Shah II of Bijapur. The largest work is a Koran dated 1730, from Arcot [38B]. Later treatises on history, astronomy and mathematics, as well as historical romances, come from Persia There is even an example of a female calligraphic hand: that of a famous courtesan in 18th century Hyderabad.

Chinese and Japanese porcelain, statuary and other items are on display in the eastern block of the museum, while European paintings, bronze and marble sculptures and decorative arts are seen in the western block. Among the latter are oils by Calanetto and Guardi, and the English Victorian artists Frederick Leighton, George Frederick Watts and Lawrence Alma-Tadema.

C. NEW HYDERABAD

The commercial heart of New Hyderabad, marked by the Abids area named after an Armenian merchant, lies north of the Musi. The tour of this part of the city begins with the monuments overlooking the river. The *Osmania General Hospital*, another project of Vincent Esch, dating from 1925, faces the High Court, from which its domed silhouette is best viewed. Like the court it too is designed in a Neo-Mughal manner, its long wings being roofed with high domes surrounded by pavilions. The *State Central Library*, begun in 1891, some 750 m. downstream, stands opposite the Salar Jung Museum. It was designed by Indian architects and anticipates the style developed by Esch (The collection has been noticed in [B].)

The University College for Women, backing onto the river 1 km. further east, occupies the former *British Residency* (permission required to visit the interior). The mansion was constructed in 1803 for James Achilles Kirkpatrick, the first Resident to consolidate the British presence in Hyderabad. Designed by Samuel Russell, the Residency is conceived in the grand Palladian manner. The main building is entered from the north through a double-height portico, approached by a grand flight of steps flanked by stone lions, replacing orginal sphinxes. Eight massive Corinthian columns are surmounted by a pediment framing the seated lion and unicorn, the coat-of-arms of the East India Company. The portico gives access to a stately darbar hall with 22 columns carrying an upper gallery all around. Splendid chandeliers and gilded mirrors, apparently removed from the Royal Pavilion at Brighton, add to the splendour. To the rear is a circular staircase with elegant ironwork balustrades in the finest Georgian manner, lit by a skylight in the dome.

The original entrance to the Residency, from the river to the rear of the main building, is marked by a triumphal arch leading to colonnaded loggias. The extensive gardens include a small cemetery where several Residents are buried. Close to the outer walls are the remains of the Rang Mahal, where Kirkpatrick's Muslim wife, Khair-un-Nissa, lived. However, virtually nothing remains of the plaster model of the Residency that Kirkpatrick built for her in the garden.

Many British officers and their Eurasian subordinates lived in the area around the Residency. Their former presence is indicated by the imposing bulk of *St George's Church* of 1844. This presents an unimaginative Neo-Gothic design, with buttressed side aisles and a frontal tower. Nearby Christ Church is a later structure of 1867.

King Kothi Palace, about 1 km. north, was the principal home of the 7th Nizam (permission required to visit). Its original owner was Kamal Khan, a wealthy businessman, who had his initials incised onto the walls and doors of his new mansion, that he had built in a Neo-Classical style. After being taken over by Mir Osman in 1899, before he assumed the Hyderabad throne, it was decided to retain the initials but change the name of the palace to King Kothi. The east block of the complex, now serving as a hospital, includes a great reception room intended for official and ceremonial purposes. The west block contains the main residential apartments, known as Nazri Bagh. The street entrance always has a curtain draped across it; consequently it is known as the Purdah Darwaza. The tallest structure is a clock tower, meticulously maintained over the years. Mir Osman continued to live in Nazri Bagh until his death in 1967. He is buried in a corner of the palace grounds.

The *Public Gardens*, on Mahatma Gandhi Road in the middle of New Hyderabad, are approached through an arched gate flanked by castellated octagonal towers. The small mosque standing immediately inside was occasionally used by the last Nizam. Its horseshoe-shaped arches and tripled domes with moulded designs reflect Egyptian Islamic influence.

The *State Archaeology Museum* nearby (closed Fridays) houses an important collection of early Buddhist antiquities in a separate gallery. These represent art traditions in Andhra Pradesh during the 1st-4th century Satavahana and Ikshvaku periods. Prominent among the sites represented is Amaravati [29K], from where several slabs carved with lotus medallions and pot-and-foliage motifs have been brought. The reliefs of stupas sheltered by tree-like parasols come from Chandavaram. Fully sculpted Buddha figures in white limestone from other sites have elegantly modelled fluted robes. The finest is the Buddha from Nelakondapalli, on view in the entrance hall of the gallery.

Other sculptures are displayed in the main wing and annexe of the museum. They include numerous 12th-13th century Kakatiya panels from Patancheru, especially a 3 m. high standing figure of Parshvanatha. The same era is also represented by two columns with Ramayana scenes, from a temple at Katangur, and a composition with courtly maidens from Warangal. displayed on the lobby, near the ticket counter. Panels from Nalgonda depict unusual scenes of ritual suicide. A columned hall with an ornate ceiling composition from Ghanapur [28D] has been reconstructed in the garden, as has a wooden temple chariot covered with carvings.

The rear wing of the museum accommodates a valuable group of bronzes. Hindu divinities and saints from Motupalli span the Chola and Vijayanagara periods. The Jain figurines from the 9th-10th century site of Bapatla are the finest, especially the icon of Ambika showing the goddess standing in within an ornate frame. Bronze bells and copper-plate grants are also on display, as well as sets of Roman coins discovered at coastal site in Andhra Pradesh. Various inscribed stone slabs from temples and mosques are displayed in the outside verandah. Copies of murals from the Buddhist caves at Ajanta [5F], a site once within the Nizam's domains, are exhibited in the upstairs gallery; here too are Chinese dishes and bowls.

The *State Legislative Assembly*, on the north side of the Public Gardens, dating from 1913, is built in a revived Rajput style. The double-storeyed arcades, overhung by angled cornices, are topped by rows of domed pavilions with lobed arches. The scheme is dominated by a dome raised high on an octagonal pavilion.

The *Birla Planetarium*, reputedly the finest in India, stands opposite the Assembly, on the other side of Mahatma Gandhi Road, at the summit of Naubat Pahad. *Birla Mandir*, consecrated to Venkateshvara, is perched on top of another hill a short distance north. Completed in 1976 and constructed out of white marble from Rajasthan, the temple combines a Southern Indian styled entrance gopura with an Orissan styled sanctuary. The interior walls of the hall are adorned with Ramayana friezes.

Khairati Begum's Mosque, the finest Qutb Shahi monument in New Hyderabad, is situated about 750 m. northwest of Birla Mandir, not far from Hussain Sagar. The mosque, which dates from about 1633, was built by the daughter of Muhammad Qutb Shah for her tutor, Akhund Mullah Abdul Malik. The triple arches of the prayer hall have ribbed fruits at the apexes; the spandrels above are filled with tasselled motifs. A galleried cornice and a battlemented parapet are seen above. The elaborate minarets at either side have double tiers of 12-sided galleries carried on petals. Deeply incised geometric patterns cover the upper stages of the minarets. The adjacent domed structure marks the empty tomb of Akhund Mullah, who died while on a visit to Mecca.

The Secretariat, of no concern architecturally, overlooks *Hussain Sagar*, the immense reservoir with a 3 km. long dam wall, over which runs the road from New Hyderabad to Secunderabad. Completed in 1562, the tank is named after its builder, Hazrat Hussain Shah Wali. Aurangzeb's forces are said to have camped on its bank during the siege of Golconda. Recreational facilities such as the Boating and Sailing Clubs line the shores. Portals imitating those at Warangal were erected in 1978 to mark the ends of the road that runs along the dam wall; bronze busts of cultural and political figures in Andhra's history are placed along the route. The most recent addition is a colossal monolithic statue of Buddha, which stands in the middle of the water.

Another Qutb Shahi monument in New Hyderabad worth seeking out is located 1.5 km. east of Hussain Sagar. The *Mushirabad Mosque*, erected at the same time as the reservoir, is built in an ornate style, best seen in the parapet of pierced interlocking battlement motifs interspersed with petalled finials. Triple-tiered minarets flanked the facade. The bottom 12-sided stages are enlivened with bold curvilinear designs; the top circular stages have geometric patterns. The intermediate balconies are carried on tiers of petals.

Osmania University is located 3 km. east of the Mushirabad Mosque. Founded in 1919 as the only institution with Urdu as the principal medium of instruction, this has one of the largest campuses in Southern India, with many impressive buildings distributed in a spacious parkland. The first structure to built on campus, the Arts College, was completed in 1939 to designs by a Belgian architect. Its faintly Moroccan Islamic style is striking. The central wing of the college, reached by double flights of steps, is emphasised by a trefoil-arched portico and an overhanging cornice with a line of supporting arches. The entrance hall within has a decorated domed ceiling. The college forms the focus for a long pond lined with palm trees. Other buildings of the university are built in a similar manner, but are less distinguished. A botanical garden is located at the south end of the campus.

D. SECUNDERABAD

Hyderabad's twin city, named after the 3rd Nizam, Mir Akbar Ali Khan Sikandar Jah, was founded as a station for British troops following the alliance between Hyderabad and Britain in 1853. Laid out 5 km. north of Old Hyderabad, from which it was originally separated, it is now linked by almost continual development with New Hyderabad.

The British presence may still be felt in the parade grounds in the middle of Secunderabad, which are overlooked on the east by the unpretentious *St Andrew's Church*. The brick clock tower a short distance south, standing in a small municipal garden near the station, is capped by a pavilion with triple arcades. Wesleyan, Baptist, Methodist and Catholic places of worship dot the surrounding streets. Another British relic is the *Secunderabad Club*, 1 km. north of the parade grounds. Founded in 1878 it is still active.

The *Paigah Palace* on Sadar Patel Road, 2 km. west of the parade grounds, is of greater architectural interest. The entrance to the complex is announced by the so-called Spanish Mosque of 1906. This is built in a curious Neo-Gothic style with exaggeratedly horseshoe-shaped arches, suggesting Moorish architecture. The palace to the rear (south), now occupied by the Hyderabad Urban Development Authority, is an elegant Neo-Classical villa dominated by a porch with lofty Corinthian columns.

The Cantonment at *Trimulgherry*, 3 km. north of Secunderabad's parade grounds, preserves British period barracks, hospital, military prison and bungalows, all built in an austere style. *Holy Trinity Church*, 3 km. further north at *Bolarum*, was erected in 1848 with a donation from Queen Victoria, on land given by the Nizam. Its Neo-Gothic exterior is animated by steeples rising above the battlemented parapet. Four additional steeples crown the square tower. The interior has fine stained glass windows. Metal plaques and stone slabs set into the walls record the British soldiers and civilians who died in Hyderabad, as do the tombs in the well maintained cemetery.

E. GOLCONDA

The remains of Golconda, the first capital of the Qutb Shahis and one of the greatest citadels of Southern India, lies 5 km. west of New Hyderabad on an elevated plateau strewn with granite boulders. The highest of these rocky eminences, rising 130 m. above the plain, forms the core of Golconda fort.

Golconda City is delimited by curtain walls that create an irregular circle, some 5 m. in circumference. Round bastions reinforce the massive tapering walls capped with lines of crenellations, rising to an average height of 18 m. The broad ditch on the outside is now mostly dry. *Naya Qila*, or New Fort, dating from 1629 is a roughly quadrangular extension to the northeast. It has an unusual nine-lobed bastion jutting out of the defensive wall. The remains of a formal garden laid out around a central water channel can still be made out within the ramparts.

The *Fateh Darwaza*, or Victory Gate, on the east, through which the conquering Mughal army under Aurangzeb entered Golconda city, is the one most often used by visitors arriving from Hyderabad. It is shielded by massive curving outworks commanded by projecting guard chambers on sculpted brackets. Similar chambers surmount the two arched entrances of the gate. The inner entrance preserves its wooden doors with iron cladding in geometric designs. A 300 m. long *Bazaar Street* connects this gate with the second ring of fortifications that contains the Bala Hisar, or inner fort. The arcaded chambers lining the bazaar street, still used as shops and residences, served as the principal market of Golconda. On the south side of the street is the khazana, or royal treasury, now the *Golkonda Archaeological Museum* (closed Fridays), of interest for its collection of stone sculptures. A 3 m. high figure of Parshvanatha is set up in the middle of the planted central court; slabs showing mounted heroes crushing their enemies and scenes of ritual suicide are strewn about. Inscribed slabs dating from the 11th century are also on display.

The western terminus of the bazaar street is marked by a pair of *Ceremonial Portals*, each with a dome carried on two walls and two open arches. The spandrels are filled with plaster reliefs of fantastic animals, birds and winged figures in pleated costumes; tigers are seen in the medallions. The *Jami Mosque* of Golconda is situated immediately to the rear of the north portal. Erected by Sultan Quli Qutb al-Mulk in 1518, it was the site of his assassination 25 years later. The courtyard of the mosque is entered on the east through a domed chamber incorporating a reused temple doorway. The prayer chamber has 15 bays roofed with flattish domes, the central dome distinguished internally by ribs. A fine calligraphic panel is set into the semi-circular mihrab. Among the cluster of dilapidated and ruined structures immediately to the north is a *Granary* with 16 domed bays, now used as a carpet weaving centre.

The *Bala Hisar Gate*, the principal entrance to the fort at the end of the bazaar street, is concealed by a detached barbican wall. The entrance has a pointed arch enlivened with triple rows of foliate motifs; yalis and ornate medallions fill the spandrels. The composition is topped with three guard chambers carried on curved brackets. The large domed chamber inside the gate serves as a setting for a small collection of Chinese ceramics, coloured tiles and other artefacts discovered within the fort. The gate leads directly to a portico roofed with a flattish dome that exhibits remarkable acoustics.

The royal *Hammam*, immediately north of the gate, comprises a complex of interconnected chambers roofed with perforated domes. Gardens with axial waterways are situated nearby. A road flanked by barracks, stores and granaries proceeds west towards the stepped path that ascends to the summit of Bala Hisar. The tour described here, however, turns south in order to visit the *Palace of the Qutb Shahis*. This complex is laid out in a sequence of vaulted chambers interspersed with high walled enclosures, providing a transition from public to private zones. The buildings are now ruined, with collapsing walls and vaults.

The triple arcades of the shilakhana, or armoury, dominate the first, outermost enclosure. The second enclosure is overlooked from the west by *Taramati Mosque*, a small place of worship used by the Qutb Shahi rulers and their nobles. Traces of fine plasterwork are seen on its triple-arched facade. The *Dad Mahal*, or Hall of Justice, faces onto the eastern half of the enclosure. This comprises a nine-domed hall flanked by residential quarters with small chambers at either side.

An arcade leads by way of a lofty audience hall, with transverse arches supporting heavy vaults and domes, to the third enclosure, marking the beginning of the private zone of the palace. The paved court here has a 12-sided pool in the middle and a part-octagonal chamber with arched openings at the northwest corner. The *Rani Mahal*, on the south, comprises a raised terrace, now missing its high wooden columns, opening onto a triple vaulted hall. The side walls have multiple arched niches for lamps. Delicately worked plaster arabesques fill the roundels above the side arches.

Continuing south, steps descend to a large hall, possibly for courtly assemblies, now ruined except for the supporting piers that once carried masonry vaults. Beyond, at the lowest level, is the *Shahi Mahal*, a small pavilion standing in the middle of a private garden. This dilapidated structure has portals on four sides raised on a vaulted substructure. Additional residential apartments, now almost totally deteriorated, are situated to the east. A short distance on the west is a small *Mosque*, hidden from view by high walls, probably reserved for the female members of the court.

From here more than 200 fairly steep steps climb to the summit of *Bala Hisar*. An alternative and less strenuous route leads from the Bala Hisar Gate, along the street lined with barracks. Both routes pass beside walls built of massive granite blocks that climb up and over the boulders. The ascent from Bala Hasar Gate is lined with stores and granaries, as well as a treasury with six flattish domes, dated 1624. The ruined tanks and water channels beside the steps form part of an elaborate *Hydraulic System*, by which water was raised to the uppermost level of the fort. Immediately below the summit is the Mahakali temple, built up to a large boulder. *Ibrahim's Mosque*, named after the third Qutb Shahi ruler, stands nearby. Its modest triple-arched prayer hall is flanked by slender octagonal buttresses. The terrace in front extends onto the ramparts.

The *Darbar Hall* of the Qutb Shahis occupies the highest point of Bala Hisar. The lowest level of the hall is divided into vaulted bays. A chamber with triple openings set into the rear wall was reserved for the king. The rooftop pavilion offers uninterrupted views of the palace below, as well of the entire city and its surroundings.

The tour of Golconda continues by taking the road north from the Balar Hisar Gate. This runs close to a large stepped tank before passing through *Banjara Gate*, the principal entry to the city from the north. The pointed arched entrance is set between polygonal bastions. Carved blocks set into the side walls depict fantastic animals and birds. The road continues northwest for about 750 m. before arriving at the Qutb Shahi cemetery.

F. AROUND GOLCONDA

Almost all the Qutb Shahi rulers are buried in the *Royal Necropolis* outside Golconda. The ensemble consists of seven royal tombs surrounded by subsidiary funerary structures, a mosque and a hammam, set in a formal garden with water channels, fed by a deep step-well. As the suburbs of New Hyderabad extend steadily west, these monuments no longer enjoy their once splendid isolation.

The first mausoleum to be seen is the *Tomb of Abdullah* (died 1672), which stands just outside the east gate of the complex. This nobly proportioned monument presents a pyramidal arrangement of arcaded storeys, seven arches beneath and five above. Pierced plaster screens are set between the overhang and the battlemented parapet. Finials with dome-like summits mark the corners and intermediate points. The composition is crowned with an imposing, slightly bulbous dome rising on a petalled base. The richly ornamented details include fine plasterwork and coloured tilework. The diminutive tomb of Abu Hasan (died 1687), the last of the Qutb Shahis, is seen to the left of the gate.

The *Tomb of Hayat Baksh Begum* (died 1667), wife of Muhammad Qutb Shah, stands to the right of the gate, after entering the complex. This monument repeats the scheme already noted for the tomb of Abdullah, with additional emphasis on the trefoil battlements on the parapet. Sombre arcades roofed with octagonal domes are seen at the lower level. The contemporary mosque to the rear (northwest) has exquisite plasterwork: the five arches of the east facade have sharply modelled fluted buds at the apexes, from which incised ribbon-like motifs curl outwards; calligraphic medallions fill the spandrels. Pierced masonry screens with different geometric designs are set between domical finials. The corner minarets have double tiers of 12-sided arcaded galleries on petalled bases; the minarets are crowned with three-quarter spherical finials. Nearby are the tombs of Pemamati and Taramati, two noblewomen of the Qutb Shahi court.

The *Tomb of Muhammad Qutb Shah* (died 1626) conforms to the scheme already described, but with an overall increase in scale. The dome, which attains a height of more than 50 m., dominates the entire complex. The petals at its base are enlarged and fully modelled. The mausoleum contains the graves of Chand Bibi, daughter of Ibrahim Adil Shah of Bijapur, as well as other offspring of the Qutb Shahi family.

The *Hammam* built into one corner of the complex nearby was for the use of visitors to the necropolis, not for the preparation of dead bodies before entombment, as is popularly believed. Its internal domed chambers were once provided with hot and cold water according to a sophisticated steam bath system. A 12-sided platform with swirling marble strips in the central chamber was for bathers to relax.

Immediately to the south of the bath, on the other side of a four-squatre garden, is the *Tomb of Muhammad Quli Qutb Shah* (died 1612). This introduces a further variation of the standard scheme. The central bays on each side are recessed for porticos with slender, timber-like granite columns. Decorated corner finials rise on part-octagonal buttresses. The basalt cenotaph within the tomb chamber is decorated with fine calligraphy; the actual tomb, however, is placed in the vaulted substructure beneath.

Mausoleum of the first Qutb Shahi rulers are situated nearby. The *Tomb of Sultan Quli Qutb al-Mulk* (died 1543), the founder of the line, is a modest structure elevated on a low terrace. The black basalt grave within, has beautiful calligraphy. Other graves are laid out on the terrace. The arcaded drum of the dome within is recessed behind a narrow gallery with cut-out baluotrades. A short distance to the west stands the *Tomb of Yar Quli Jamshid* (died 1550). This is the only octagonal example at Golconda. It consists of a double-height chamber, with two tiers of arched recesses and a projecting balcony with ornate balustrades. Eight finials cluster around the petalled base of the dome.

In the southern extremity of the complex is the *Tomb of Ibrahim* (died 1580). This presents an alternative design influenced by earlier Bahmani architecture. The domed chamber comprises a simple cube, with each facade being divided into double tiers of five arches. Traces of coloured tilework are visible in the bands over the upper arches and beneath the parapet. A square open pavilion nearby contains the remains of Ibrahim's chamberlain.

After completing the tour of the Golconda necropolis visitors may wish to explore other monuments in the vicinity. The road running southwest from the Bala Hisar Gate leads to the *Mecca Darvaza*, of interest for the magnificent inscription that runs around three sides of the outer entrance. The arched opening is set between polygonal bastions. The walls create a double barbican.

About 1 km. further west are two hills crowned by buildings associated with noblewomen of the Qutb Shahi court. The *Mosque of Pemamati*, the first to be reached, north of the road, is of little architectural interest, but the terrace in front affords a magnificent panorama of the Bala Hisar. The *Baradari of Taramati*, south of the road, recently restored, is a simple vaulted pavilion raised on a high terrace.

The road running east from the Fateh Darwaza towards Old Hyderabad passes by the suburb of *Karvan*, 2 km. away from Golconda. Next to the road stands the *Toli Mosque*, a highly ornate Qutb Shahi monument dating from 1672. The central arch of its facade is distinguished by shallow lobes and ornate medallions in the spandrels. The angled overhang is surmounted by geometric screens of different designs. Curving brackets carry a cornice, over which runs the parapet of trefoil battlements with domical finials. The part-octagonal buttresses at either end support minarets with triple tiers of arcaded galleries. The fully modelled treatment of the petalled ornamentation is the most elaborate of the period. The minarets are crowned with three-quarter spherical finials. The prayer hall of the mosque is unusually divided into two transverse halls. The outer hall, roofed with a flat vault, has elevated balconies with arcades, parapets and corner finials on its side walls; the inner hall is roofed with triple domes.

27. Around Hyderabad

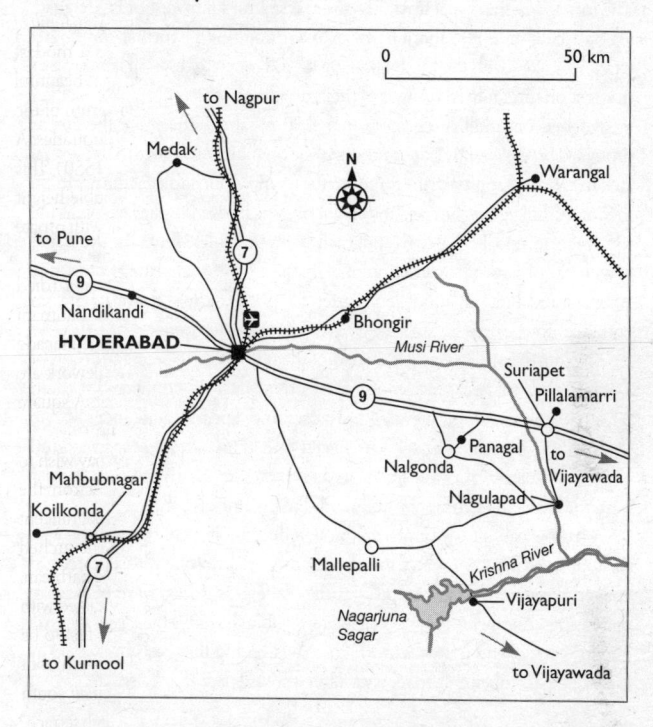

The Hyderabad region is dotted with historic sites that can be reached as full-day trips from the capital. Koilkonda [A], Medak [C], and Bhongir [D] each have impressive citadels associated variously with the Late Chalukya, Kakatiya, Bahmani and Qutb Shahi rulers. Examples of the ornate temple styles that once flourished in the area can be seen at Nandikandi [B], Panagal [E], Pillalamarri [F] and Nagulapad [G].

A journey is recommended to the Buddhist site of Nagarjunakonda, represented by a series of reconstructed monuments and a museum of antiquities on an island in Nagarjuna Sagar, the largest reservoir in Andhra Pradesh. The island can be reached by launch from Vijayapuri (check timings) [H].

Warangal, the ancient Kakatiya capital, may also be visited as a day trip from Hyderabad, but is treated here as a separate itinerary [28].

A. Koilkonda

The fort above this small town lies about 125 km. southwest of Hyderabad, via Badepalli on NH7, about halfway to Kurnool [32A], further south. The citadel is linked with the Qutb Shahis, who did much to develop it as a major outpost on the southern fringes of their kingdom.

Perched on a hill rising more than 250 m. above the plain, the *Fort* is protected on the west by a deep ravine, while on the east it is guarded by several streams. Visitors approach the fort from the town, which nestles at the northern foot of the hill. A long and arduous flight of steps leads in zigzag fashion to the top, where formidable bastions abut each angle. Ponds line the path. The first in a sequence of gates has an inscription of Ibrahim Qutb Shah dating from 1550. Animals and birds in modelled plaster fill the spandrels above its arched entrance. The passage beyond the gate is narrow and tortuous.

The fourth gate leads to a level part of the hill, where there are the ruins of a palace with vaulted apartments. Traces of a water-lift connected with an adjacent tank at the south end of the palace and a nearby aqueduct indicate the method by which water was raised and transported. *Magazines* and *Granaries* nearby survive in dilapidated condition. These rectangular buildings have thick masonry walls and shallow brick vaults.

A narrow passageway climbs up through three more gates before arriving at the top of the hill, from where there is a fine view. A mosque with a prayer hall entered through five arched openings stands here, as does a store of massive dimensions. Another monument of interest within the fort is the *Idgah*. This has curious circular end buttresses with chambers on top that probably served as lookout posts. Lobed arched recesses adorn the wall.

B. Nandikandi

This village, about 50 km. west of Hyderabad on NH9, is of interest for the 11th century *Ramalingeshvara Temple* dating from the Late Chalukya era. The monument is preceded by an unusual portal with a lintel supported on two posts adorned with icons of Nataraja and Lakshmi. The sanctuary has a star-shaped plan with 16 angles, marked by basement mouldings and multi-faceted walls. Single pilasters headed by miniature spires and arched frames fill the recesses. Sequences of deeply recessed cornices, headed by relief representations of curved towers, rise above. They combine to form a complicated superstructure that retains the original star shape of the building as it rises, even to the capping roof piece. A projection on the front face of the tower ends in an arched frame for a sculpted icon, now missing.

The temple's shrine is approached through a hall with triple porch projections, surrounded by balcony seating. The central columns have multi-faceted shafts and capitals covered with minute carvings of divinities.

The shrine doorway is framed by creeper motifs, with attendant maidens beneath. Large guardians are carved on separate slabs at either side. The niches in the rear walls of the hall house icons of Ganesha and Sarasvati.

C. Medak

This town, 86 km. north of Hyderabad, 18 km. west of NH17, is overshadowed by a substantial fort, now much decayed. Founded by the Kakatiyas in the 12th century, the site was taken from them by the Bahmanis of Gulbarga [24A], eventually passing into the hands of the Qutb Shahis.

Medak Fort consists of two lines of walls girdling a hill northwest of the town. It is entered along a road that passes through a sequence of gates, the first of which is of little consequence. The Mubarak Mahal, inside the second gate, is of massive construction. From here the stepped path ascends to the third and largest gate, distinguished by round bastions. The fourth gate is less imposing. The Elephant Gate, the final one, takes its name from the animal carved in relief on one side, beyond which is a ruined court. A flight of steps leads from here to the highest part of the hill, more than 100 m. above the surrounding plain. Here can be seen a 3 m. long brass gun, manufactured in Rotterdam in 1620. There are several granaries and stores stand nearby. There is also a small mosque dating from the Qutb Shahi period. A tomb beneath the fort, however, is an earlier monument dating from the Bahmani era.

By far the most imposing building in Medak town is the Neo-Gothic *Catholic Church*. Completed in 1924 this is one of the largest Christian monuments in Southern India. More than 5,000 worshippers can be accommodated in its prayer hall, which is more than 90 m. long and 60 m. high. The facade is dominated by a single soaring tower framed by buttresses. The tall arched windows have wooden slats, and delicate tracery filled with stained glass.

D. Bhongir

This city, 47 km. northeast of Hyderabad, is celebrated for its great citadel dating mainly from the 12th century Kakatiya period. This occupies a dramatically isolated hill rising 120 m. above the countryside.

The granite rock on which the *Citadel* is built naturally divides the defences into two parts: the upper fort crowns the summit, while the lower fort extends along a spur that descends towards the town on the west. A deep cleft between the two forts is dammed by cross walls to form a descending chain of ponds fed by rock-cut channels. A ruined palace in the upper fort has a splendid outlook. Nearby is a detached bastion that supports two guns, one of bronze, the other of iron. Close to the fortifications on the north lies a mutilated Nandi; together with stray columns in the lower fort this indicates one or more dismantled temples.

Portions of walls and gates have massive dry stone masonry and quadrangular bastions. They form a striking contrast to the Bahmani and Qutb Shahi additions, in which walls of rubble set in mortar are strengthened by polygonal and round bastions.

The idgah and tombs dotted around Bhongir town at the base of the fort date mainly from the Qutb Shahi period.

The road and railway continue to Warangal, 94 km. to the northeast.

E. Panagal

Located 3 km. north of Nalgonda, a town 112 km. east of Hyderabad, reached partly via NH9, the village of Panagal has a large tank with a long dam wall. A basalt tablet here bears an inscription of 1551, during the reign of Ibrahim Qutb Shah. Two Late Chalukya monuments dating from the 11th century stand next to each other on the edge of the tank. The *Pachhala Someshvara Temple* consists of four linga shrines, a fifth having fallen, arranged on two sides of an open mandapa. Only two shrines survive with their walls and multi-storeyed towers fully intact. Carvings of miniature figures set in creeper motifs cover the wall projections and intervening recesses. Among the divinities that appear here are Shiva and Parvati on Nandi, Vishnu riding on Garuda, Vishnu and Brahma adoring the linga, multi-armed Ravana shaking Kailasa, and a remarkable panel showing Shiva dancing, the tresses of the god's hair flying outwards. The other shrines have plain walls devoid of any carvings, occasionally relieved by chambers in the middle of each side, complete with balcony seating, columns, eaves and square towers. Columns inside the mandapa display figures carved onto the cubic blocks.

The other monument at Panagal occupies the middle of a compound with six subshrines, and an entrance gate on the south. It consists of a trio of shrines, dedicated separately to Shiva, Vishnu and Brahma, each roofed with a fully preserved pyramidal tower. The shrines open off a common mandapa, the columns of which have multi-faceted shafts and cubic blocks covered with carvings of mythological scenes.

F. Pillalamarri

The *Ekakeshvara Temple*, established in 1208 by the wife of a provincial governor, stands northwest of Pillalamarri, a small village located 5 km. north of Suriapet, 133 km. east of Hyderabad on NH9. Though only incompletely preserved, the monument is a fine example of the Kakatiya style. The building is elevated on a plinth with deeply recessed mouldings. Steps on three sides ascend to the porch extensions of the mandapa, originally open on the front, with balcony seating all around. The sanctuary has pilastered walls overhung by deeply angled eaves. The tower above, missing its upper portion, displays ascending tiers of miniature model roof forms on either side of a central band. An arched frame adorns the frontal projection.

Inside the village stands another Kakatiya monument, the *Nameshvara Temple*. Partly restored, it has finely worked columns with sharply cut mouldings. The temple is of interest for the traces of frescos that survive on the beams inside the mandapa. The best preserved composition shows the churning of the cosmic ocean, with gods and demons pulling the serpent Sesha coiled around the axial mountain. The sculptural ornamentation of the doorways and columns is of high quality.

G. NAGULPAD

Two fine specimens of Kakatiya religious architecture are found in this remotely situated village on the east bank of the Musi River, reached partly by dirt road, 25 km. south of Suriapet. The temples are situated close to each other, partly concealed by houses, with a small mosque in between.

The linga sanctuaries of the *Triple-Shrined Temple*, south of the mosque, were consecrated in 1234. The outer surfaces of the sanctuaries are poorly preserved, in striking contrast to the excellent condition of the interior ornamentation. Column shafts have octagonal sections between cubic blocks, while the capitals have sharply moulded discs and square upper portions with circular petalled undersides. They carry beams carved with friezes of figures illustrating Ramayana and Mahabharata episodes. Battle scenes, with armed warriors riding in chariots and royal figures accompanied by retinues, are among the most remarkable of these compositions. The undersides of the beams have finely modelled lotus medallions. The ceilings display lotus flowers surrounded by rings of petals raised on rotated squares; triangular corner portions are packed with sharply cut divinities flanked by attendants. The doorways to the shrine are equally embellished.

The *Kameshvara Temple*, north of the mosque, dates from 1358. Its hall has porch projections on three sides, each approached by a flight of steps. Parts of the walls and roof of the mandapa have now collapsed. The shrine exterior has alternating projections and recesses, with deeply set horizontal grooves, overhung by a deep cornice with fringes of buds and cut-out ribs and rafters on the undersides. No tower is preserved above. Those columns still standing in the mandapa have precisely defined ridges and bands, with exaggerated double capitals.

H. NAGARJUNA SAGAR

The waters of Nagarjuna Sagar, dammed by a massive stone wall bridging a deep gorge through which flows the Krishna River, have submerged the Buddhist site of Nagarjunakonda. However, several rescued remains from this site have been rebuilt on an island in the middle of the lake. The island may be reached as a day trip from Hyderabad, 166 km. distant, via Mallepalli.

The ancient site of *Nagarjunakonda* was first occupied by the Satavahanas between the 2nd century BCE and 2nd century CE. They were succeeded by the Ikshvakus, the most powerful rulers in Andhra in the 3rd-4th centuries, who made Nagarjunakonda their capital. That the Ikshvakus were great supporters of Buddhism is evident from the large number of monasteries and shrines that they erected here to meet the needs of the different sects. Inscriptions on limestone blocks name some of these religious communities, as well as individual donors. The Ikshvakus were ousted by the Pallavas of Kanchipuram [37E] in the 7th century, after which the site fell into disuse.

Excavations conducted in 1954-61 brought to light more than 30 Buddhist establishments at Nagarjunakonda. These mostly consisted of different combinations of hemispherical stupas, chaitya halls with circular, apsidal-ended or rectangular plans, and monastic complexes with cells arranged in wings around a central court. The stupas have concentric or radial infill walls of brick or rubble, the exteriors being coated with plaster or limestone slabs. The halls and monasteries are constructed with finely finished limestone columns set into brick or rubble walls: of these, only the lower portions have survived, including pavement slabs and access steps.

Not a single Buddhist monument at Nagarjunakonda survives intact in its original location. The flat-topped hill that once overlooked the Krishna from the south is now an island with reconstructed monuments and an Archaeological Museum (closed Fridays). The rescued limestone sculptures and relief carvings displayed here, together with those from the contemporary site of Amaravati [29K], constitute the most important collection of Buddhist sculptures in Andhra Pradesh. Nagarjunakonda art is distinguished by animated compositions with vigorously posed figures. Unlike the Amaravati reliefs, which are badly eroded, those from Nagarjunakonda are amazingly well preserved.

The first group of carvings to be seen in the *Archaeological Museum* are capping panels from stupas. Some slabs show representations of stupas in the company of flying celestials and seated Buddhas. Other panels depict incidents from the life of the Master: leaving the palace, the God's carrying Siddhartha's crown, and the report of the departure, combined on one slab; and, on another, the protection of Buddha by Mucchalinda, Buddha receiving alms, and the first sermon. One double-sided panel shows courtly couples, elephants and ganas. Long friezes, originally capping pieces of railings that surrounded the stupas, are also on display. The panels on one frieze illustrate episodes from the Mandhatu Jataka. Another example shows the conversion of Nanda, interspersed with amorous couples. Yet a third frieze depicts typical episodes from the life of the Master, such as the renunciation, the departure from the palace, the assault of Mara, the enlightenment, and the first sermon, all separated by figural medallions.

Columns collected from different monuments are adorned with lively courtly scenes an dancing dwarfs. There are also free-standing sculptured images of Buddha attired in elegantly modelled robes, the most impressive of which is more than 3 m. high. A few 16th century carvings, such as seated Narasimha, executed in granite, show that the site was inhabited in later times.

A short distance from the museum, on the edge of the water, is a *Bathing Ghat*, originally located on the bank of the Krishna River, at the edge of the Nagarjunakonda site. Its steps are entirely constructed of finely finished limestone slabs. About 150 m. to the rear of the museum is a line of rubble fortifications, dating from the 16th century. Simple gateways give access to a garden in which a number of monuments have been reconstructed. The first to be seen is a *Megalith* dating back more than 2,000 years. It consists of a stone circle enclosing a heap of stones. These once concealed a simple burial chamber containing four skulls.

Simha Vihara 4, on the opposite side of the path to the megalith, dates from the Ikshvaku period. It comprises a stupa built on a high platform, accompanied by twin chaitya halls, one enshrining a stupa, the other an imposing standing Buddha. The *Bodhishri Chaitya* nearby presents a simple hemispherical stupa raised on a cylindrical drum encased in limestone slabs. The stupa is contained within an apsidal-ended brick structure.

The path continues to the *Maha Chaitya*. With a diameter of 27.5 m., this was one of the largest stupas at Nagarjunakonda. The radial, spoke-like pattern made by its internal rubble walls is a distinctive feature of stupa architecture under the Ikshvakus. Projections with columns are positioned at the cardinal points. The stupa once contained a reliquary with a tooth relic. An apsidal-ended shrine stands to one side. The *Svastika Chaitya*, towards the end of the path, is named after the pattern made by the rubble walls inside the stupa.

Other reassembled features from Nagarjunakonda may be visited on the mainland at *Anupu*, 8 km. south of Vijayapuri. A stadium, possibly intended for musical and dramatic performances or sporting contests, presents tiered galleries with seating on four sides of a rectangular court. A short distance further along the road is a pair of *Monastic Complexes* next to each other. One of these consists of a square hall with 36 columns, with two chaitya halls in front, surrounded by cells on three sides; the other has a 16-columned hall with cells on four sides. Stupas with six radial spokes are situated outside each complex. A refectory, store and bath are seen nearby. The principal residence here has three wings of cells disposed around a court, within which is a 36-columned hall. A temple, comprising a rectangular sanctuary and mandapa, stands close to the present bank of the Krishna.

28. Warangal

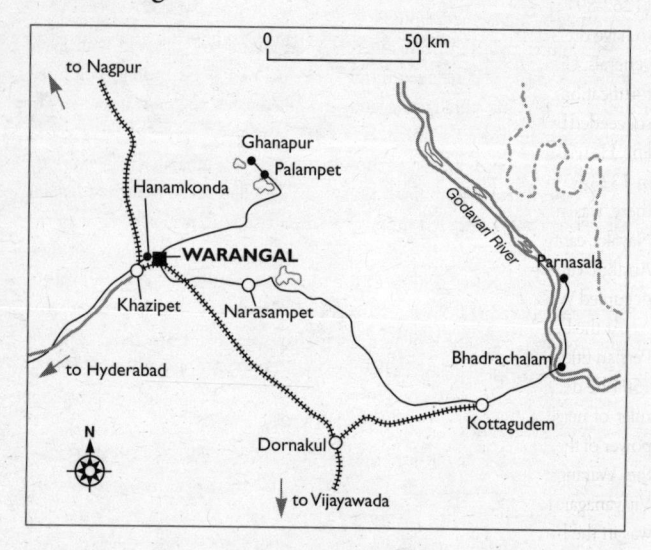

Located 140 km. northwest of Hyderabad, Warangal is of historical importance, having served as the capital of the Kakatiyas in the 13th-14th centuries. It is today particularly known for its wool trade and its production of wooden toys. A half day should be sufficient to visit the remarkable circular fort and ruined temple on the outskirts of the city [A], as well as the better preserved Hindu monument at Hanamkonda [B].

The finest examples of Kakatiya temple architecture and sculpture are to be found at Palampet [C] and Ghanapur [D], both of which may be reached as a half-day excursion from Warangal. However, a trip to the pilgrimage site of Bhadrachalam [E] on the Godavari River will require one full day and more.

The Kakatiyas emerged as the most powerful rulers of the Andhra country at the beginning of the 12th century. Rudradeva (1158-95), the first great Kakatiya monarch, had his headquarters at Hanamkonda, from where he waged war against the Late Chalukyas and Cholas. The next important figure, Ganapatideva (1199-1262), the outstanding personality of the era, extended the Kakatiya domination as far as the Bay of Bengal Coast, thereby coming into conflict with the kings of Orissa. His other campaigns were aimed against the Cholas and their successors, the Pandyas. Ganapatideva's generals even managed to raid Kanchipuram [37E], within the Tamil country. It was during Ganapatideva's reign that the Kakatiya capital was shifted to the newly laid out city of Warangal.

Ganapatideva, having no male issue, nominated his daughter Rudramadevi (1262-89) as his heir. She took an active part in government, and is supposed to have dressed in male garments when holding meetings with ministers and generals. Under her direction the new city of Warangal was ringed with triple fortifications, and many new monuments were constructed. Rudramadevi was succeeded by her grandson, Prataparudra (1289-1323), the last of the Kakatiya line. He resisted the conquest of Southern India by the Delhi army in 1303, but in 1323 was compelled to pay tribute in cash and elephants. After his death there was rebellion among local chiefs, and in 1336 their leader, Kapaya Nayaka, captured Warangal from the Delhi commander. Soon after, this part of Andhra came under the sway of the Bahmanis of Gulbarga [24A], who occupied Warangal in 1366.

At the beginning of the 16th century a local chief, Sitapati, who adopted the Persian title of Shitab Khan, was governor of Warangal under the Bahmanis. In 1504 he declared his independence and allied himself with Ramachandra, the ruler of neighbouring Orissa. Shitab Khan was soon threatened by the rising power of the Tuluva kings of the Vijayanagara empire [20B-C], which bordered the Warangal territories to the southwest. Shitab was vanquished by the Vijayanagara forces in 1510, when they took control of the city. By 1532 Warangal was in the hands of Quli Qutb al-Mulk, who incorporated it into the growing kingdom of Golconda [26E]. With the later transformation of Golconda into the state of Hyderabad, Warangal passed into the dominions of the Nizams.

A. Warangal

Modern Warangal is situated a short distance north of the Kakatiya capital. The original city was laid out according to a unique *Circular Plan*, with three concentric rings of walls. The first ring, about 1.2 km. in diameter, constitutes the innermost part of the capital, usually referred to as the fort. The *First Ring of Walls*, more than 6 m. high, are of massive granite blocks laid with out any mortar. The rectangular bastions overlook a broad moat, still filled with water. The inner faces of the walls have steps ascending to a path that runs continuously along the top. The watchtowers and lines of battlements here date from the Bahmani period. Four **Gateways** at the cardinal points are preceded by sturdily built barbican enclosures, each requiring a double turn to the left on entering the fort. The identical arrangements of the four gateways create a pattern of rotational symmetry, somewhat like a swastika. These entrances were renovated in Bahmani times as is clear from the sculpted balustrades and other blocks taken from dismantled temples, and the curved protective walls on front of the east and west gateways.

The area contained within Warangal fort is now partly inhabited, with houses lining the axial east-west road. The archaeological zone in the middle coincides with the enclosure of a great Shiva Temple, of which only the free-standing *Entrance Portals* in the middle of four sides still stand. Each portal consists of a pair of posts with angled brackets carrying a massive lintel, achieving an overall height of more than 10 m. The treatment of the portals is elaborate throughout, with boldly carved lotus buds, looped garlands, mythical beasts, and birds with foliated tails. The absence of religious themes partly explains why the portals were spared by the invaders.

Entrance portal to demolished Shiva Temple, Warangal.

Of the *Shiva Temple* itself that stood within the enclosure nothing remains intact, but there is an abundance of fallen wall slabs, brackets and ceiling panels, now formally displayed in an outdoor museum. Several columns still stand, but these are actually redeployed as part of a mosque that was begun out of temple spoilia by the Bahmanis, but never completed. A broken mihrab lies fallen to the rear. The four-faced Shiva linga that was originally worshipped in the temple is now venerated in a shrine to the south of the complex. Excavations at the southeast corner of the complex have uncovered remains of a row of subshrines, each with a votive linga.

More complete is the *Kush Mahal*, a 14th century audience hall erected by the Delhi invaders, about 150 m. west of the archaeological zone. This consists of a rectangular hall flanked by massive sloping walls, broken by six arched openings on each side. Five transverse stone arches once carried a timber roof, but this is lost. Steps at the northwest outer corner of the building ascend to the roof, from where excellent views may had of the whole site.

A short distance south of the archaeological zone is a large tank. It is overlooked from the east by a prominent rock, which rises abruptly from the water. This natural feature is known as *Orugallu* (Single Rock) in Telugu, after which Warangal derives its name. A small shine occupies its summit. Further shrines and pools are scattered throughout the fort. Three long granaries stand near the south gate.

Warangal's *Second Ring of Walls*, defining a circle 2.4 km. in diameter, completely contains the inner ring. The fortifications are of earth rather than stone, but also have a broad moat, now partly filled in. The area within this circuit is mostly given over to agriculture. Gateways at the cardinal directions are aligned with those of the fort. Those on the east and west have arched stone structures dating from the Bahmani period. Their passageways are guarded by massive earthen embankments that protrude beyond the walls.

The *Third Ring of Walls*, again of earth, delimits a vast irregular circle, approximately 12.5 km. in diameter, containing the modern city of Warangal. The fortifications are interrupted on the northwest by rocky hills and the earthen walls of Hanamkonda Fort.

B. HANAMKONDA

The site of the first Kakatiya capital is located 3 km. northwest of Warangal, the two cities now being connected by almost continuous development. The principal monument of interest in Hanamkonda is the so-called *Thousand-Pillared Temple*, located beside the main road. The impressive example of Kakatiya architecture dates from 1163, during the reign of Rudradeva. An inscribed slab set up beside the entrance gate on the east gives the details of its foundation.

The south facing temple is built of grey-green basalt and is finely worked throughout, though no longer complete. Three shrines separately dedicated to Shiva, Vishnu and Surya open off a large mandapa that extends outwards as a porch lined with balcony seating. The outer walls of the shrines and mandapa rise upon a deeply moulded basement. Vestiges of carvings are seen in the wall niches of the sanctuaries, which are headed by tower-like pediments. The towers, presumably of brick, are lost. The mandapa interior has columns displaying sharply cut, multi-faceted shafts; the capitals are adorned with sculpted jewels and petals. The central ceiling panel is an elaborate composition, with an icon of Nataraja surrounded by scrollwork. Cut-out lintels, with dancing Shiva figures flanked by makaras, are set before the shrine doorways. Worship today only takes place in the linga shrine on the west.

The temple plinth extends to the south, so as to accommodate a magnificent polished Nandi, facing into the mandapa. Yet further south is another mandapa, less finely worked and now dilapidated, constructed entirely out of granite.

The earthen ramparts and granite entrance portals of *Hanamkonda Fort* are situated about 1 km. south of the temple, on the far side of a rocky outcrop. The

Siddheshvara temple, inside the south entrance to the fort, consists of a small linga shrine adjoining an open mandapa with seating on three sides. Infill walls and the spire over the sanctuary are later additions. A mound nearby has bricks and other debris and ruined structures. Rock-cut Jain vestiges are found in cavers high up on the nearby rocks.

C. Palampet

This site, 68 km. northeast of Warangal, is of interest for the *Ramappa Temple*, built by Recherla Rudra, a general of Ganapatideva. Dating from 1213, it is by far the best preserved example of temple architecture from the Kakatiya period. The sanctuary and antechamber open off a large mandapa laid out on a stepped plan, with balcony seating all around, raised on a high plinth. The reddish sandstone exterior of the sanctuary has a sharply moulded basement with a frieze of miniature elephants: slender wall pilasters frame tiers of multiple niches, now empty, in the middle of each side. A deep overhang runs continuously around the building. The brick tower over the sanctuary has successive storeys with pilastered walls and parapets, somewhat restored. A vaulted projection is seen on the front face.

The front porch of the mandapa is contained within high balcony walls adorned with pilasters framing maidens and stylised lotus ornament. The polished basalt columns within the mandapa have cubic shafts, occasionally covered with carvings, separated by octagonal sections. The double capitals are sharply cut. The peripheral columns have angled brackets fashioned as yalis or as female dancers and musicians. These masterpieces of Kakatiya figural art are notable for their smooth modelling, sinuous postures, and curiously elongated bodies and heads. The ceiling panel over the central bays within the mandapa incorporates similar figures within rotated and ascending squares.

A detached mandapa accommodating a sculpted Nandi, and a subsidiary shrine stand within the walled compound of the temple. An inscribed slab giving the historical circumstances of the monument is sheltered by a small pavilion.

Ramappa Cheruvu, the great lake created by Recherla Rudra, lies 1.5 km. south of the Ramappa temple. Its waters, which encompass nearly 24 sq. km., are surrounded by picturesque forested hills.

D. Ghanapur

The temples at this site, 13 km. northwest of Palampet, are also associated with a vast lake. *Ghanapur Cheruvu* has an earthen dam wall more than 2 km. long and 16 m. high. It is contemporary with a 13th century group of monuments, now much ruined, constructed during the reign of Ganapatideva, after whom the settlement takes its name.

The *Kotagullu*, as the complex is known, consists of two east-facing Shiva temples, both with mandapas on stepped plans with seating all around. A Nandi pavilion stands in front of the larger example. Both temples are raised on high plinths with deeply cut mouldings. The outer walls, now dilapidated, have ornate pilasters in regularly spaced recesses. Nothing remains of the towers. The balcony slabs of the porches in one temple are adorned with friezes of elephants, ducks and stylised flowers, as well as temple towers in shallow relief. Internal columns have cubic shafts separated by sharply cut octagonal bands. A few bracket figures survive in situ. Additional sculptures are seen on the richly decorated doorway jambs.

The temples stand in the middle of a square compound, with a row of comparatively well preserved linga shrines near the west perimeter wall. Some of these have curved towers enhanced by diminutive replica towers placed at each level. The multiplied elements are separated by vertical strips in the middle of each side. Other shrines have pyramidal multi-storeyed towers capped with square-domed roofs. Elaborate gateways are seen on two sides of the compound. The gateway on the south is laid out as a large hall, with projections on four sides; only several of its columns still stand.

E. BHADRACHALAM

This celebrated pilgrimage site on the east bank of the Godavari River lies about 180 km. east of Warangal, the road winding through forested hills. Bhadrachalam can also be reached from Vijayawada [29A], about 200 km. to the south, or from Rajahmundry [30A], approximately the same distance to the southeast.

Bhadrachalam is related to the Ramayana epic, since it is here that Rama and Sita are believed to have spent part of their forest retreat. The *Shrirama Temple*, which marks the spot where Rama crossed the river, was built by Kancherla Gopanna, a Hindu governor under the last Qutb Shahis in the second half of the 17th century. This figure was accused of appropriating funds from the royal treasury for its construction, and was subsequently imprisoned. After a miraculous rescue he adopted the title of Ramdas.

Despite the beauty of its natural setting the Shrirama temple is of little interest architecturally, having been substantially rebuilt in recent years, though it is entered through an impressive gopura. The main shrine houses an unusual four-armed icon of Rama, in the company of bronze images of Sita and Lakshmana. The *Ushnagunda* in the bed of the Godavari a short distance away is a hot spring that emerges when the sand at the bottom of the river is disturbed.

Parnasala, beside the Godavari, 35 km. upstream from Bhadrachalam, is believed to mark the hermitage where Sita was approached by the demon Ravana in disguise as an ascetic; he then assumed his real form and abducted her in his aerial chariot.

29. Vijayawada

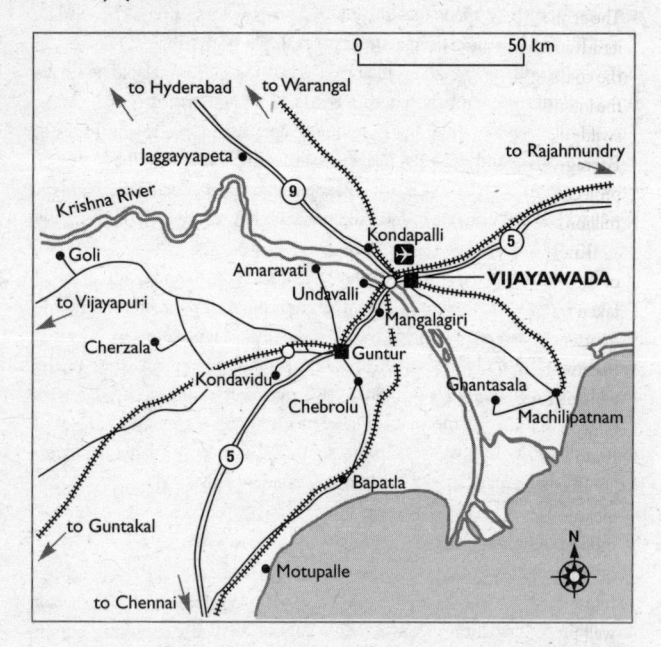

Strategically located at the head of the richly irrigated and densely populated Krishna River Delta, 270 km. southeast of Hyderabad via NH9, Vijayawada is a thriving business centre and a convenient base from which to visit interesting and varied historical sites.

A few hours should suffice for Vijayawada itself [A], with a half-day excursion northwest of the city to the hill fort at Kondapalli [B] and the Buddhist remains at Jaggayyapeta [C].

The Dutch tombs at Machilipatnam [D] and the Buddhist structure at Ghantalsala [E], southeast of Vijayawada, may be combined in another day trip.

A full-day journey southwest of Vijayawada can take in the rock-cut monument at Undavalli [F], the temples at Mangalagiri [G], the museum at Guntur [H], and the shrines at Chebrolu [I] and Bapatla [J].

The Buddhist site of Amaravati [K], the most famous in Andhra Pradesh, deserves a half day in itself, so as to visit the sculptures in the local museum and the active place of worship overlooking the Krishna River nearby.

Additional time will have be set aside to reach the remotely located Buddhist vestiges at Goli [L], the forts at Kondavidu [M], and the unusual early brick shrine at Cherzala [N].

A. Vijayawada

The economic importance of Vijayawada through the centuries is explained by its advantageous location, 70 km. inland from the Bay of Bengal, commanding the coastal trading routes as well as the those following the Krishna upstream to the interior. The city is picturesquely surrounded by hills on three sides, with the swiftly flowing waters of the river on the south. The 1 km. long **Prakasam Barrage**, on the outskirts of Vijayawada, is one of the earliest major irrigation projects in Southern India. First finished in 1855, the scheme irrigates nearly one million ha., converting the delta area into the richest granary in Andhra.

Known in former times as Bezwada, Vijayawada was an important centre of the Vishnukundin rulers in the 5th-6th centuries. In about 605 the city was taken by the Early Chalukya rulers of Badami [22A], who made it the headquarters of their eastern domains. The governors of Vijayawada eventually became separated from the main line of rulers and began their own dynasty, generally referred to as the Eastern Chalukyas. Hiuen Tsang, the Chinese pilgrim, stayed in the monastery at Bezwada in 639 and noted the decline of Buddhism in the area.

Isolated Buddhist vestiges are still to be seen within Vijayawada city. They include *Rock-Cut Steps* on the east hill, believed to indicate the presence of a monastic establishment. It was here that the colossal, but much damaged statue of Buddha was discovered, now on display in the *Victoria Jubilee Museum* (closed Fridays). Among the other Buddhist antiquities in this collection is a well-preserved standing Buddha from Alluru, dating from the 3rd-4th century. This white limestone figure is gracefully dressed in a fluted robe; the head is modelled with particular refinement. Prehistoric materials, such as stone tools, microliths and Neolithic implements are also to be seen in the museum. Coins, arms, metalwork and miniature paintings form the 17th-18th centuries illustrate the arts that flourished here under the Qutb Shahis and Nizams.

The Eastern Chalukya presence in Vijayawada in the 7th century is testified by two groups of excavated monuments in the vicinity. Five rock-cut sanctuaries at *Mogalrajapuram*, 3 km. east of the city centre, are located at the extreme end of a row of hills. They have porches with undecorated squat columns. Cave 2 shows an overhanging cornice with artificial windows. Worn images indicate a variety of Hindu deities. Two additional cave-temples may be seen in the west part of the city, beneath Telegraph Hill. The larger of these two examples has a dilapidated but spacious colonnade that gives access to a trio of small linga shrines.

B. Kondapalli

Located 14 km. west of Vijayawada on NH9, Kondapalli is best known today as a place of manufacture of brightly painted wooden dolls.

The picturesque hill fort at Kondapalli was founded by the Eastern Chalukyas in the 8th century, before being occupied by the Reddi chiefs in the 14th-15th centuries. It was conquered by the Bahmanis in 1471, and from them passed to the Qutb Shahis, who made it into the most important stronghold in the Krishna Delta. Kondapalli was eventually absorbed into the domains of the Nizams, though it also served for a time as an outpost for the British.

The *Lower Fort* at Kondapalli, entered by means of a path through three successive gates at the foot of the hill, is thickly overgrown with jungle and cactus. The English barracks within the walls are much decayed. Winding between two ridges, the path climbs up for more than 1 km., mostly by way of a stone staircase. The ruins of an old palace appear dramatically perched on a crest above the path.

The *Upper Fort*, which may be more conveniently reached by road via NH9, is entered through a trio of large gateways, with 5 m. high stone walls and lintels up to 4 m. across. The whitewashed dargah of Ghulab Shah nearby, which gives its name to the gateways, commemorates a commander who was killed here defending the fort. Immediately above is the Tanisha Mahal, a Qutb Shahi structure. The ground floor consists of colonnades divided into separate chambers. A small stone staircase gives access to the upper level, where there is a reception hall with subsidiary chambers, and bathrooms with stone cisterns and terracotta pipes set into the walls, all lacking their roofs. Traces of intricately worked plaster decoration can still be made out.

A path leads to a deep tank fed by a natural spring. The granary beyond is supported on high arches, with different compartments serving as separate receptacles, each with an opening in the roof. Close to the granary are the magazines. The hill around is defended by fortifications, strengthened with towers and ramparts.

C. Jaggayyapeta

This town, 77 km. northwest of Vijayawada on NH9, was once an important Buddhist centre. Relics were discovered here in the 19th century on a low hill called Dhanu Bodu that runs parallel to the road leading to the town. As at Amaravati, 50 km. southeast, these vestiges suffered from pillaging by local people.

The principal Buddhist remains consists of the *Maha Chaitya*, as the stupa is referred to in the 3rd-4th century inscriptions, a ruined pillared hall immediately southeast, and a few inconspicuous mounds. The drum portion of the stupa, 21 m. in diameter, stands to a height of about 1.3 m. and has four cardinal projections. It is faced with greenish limestone slabs fixed to the masonry ring wall contained within the brick and earthen core. The slabs at the base of the drum are carved with figures showing worship of the stupa by devotees bearing garlands. Other items, including a representation of a royal figure, are now in the Government Museum, Chennai [36D]. Fragments of Buddha images and the carved plinths of subsidiary votive stupas suggest the existence of other Buddhist shrines nearby.

D. Machilipatnam

Known to Europeans as Masulipatnam, this town, 70 km. southeast of Vijayawada, was once the principal port of the Krishna Delta. In the 17th-18th centuries it was renowned for its cotton textiles, especially finely woven muslins and brightly coloured prints. Trade declined after 1864, when an enormous tidal wave penetrated some 30 km. inland, drowning more than 30,000 people. In spite of this and other similar calamities, the town is once again a thriving textile centre. It is currently a focus for the Church Missionary Society.

Machilipatnam's commercial history beings with the arrival of the English. The East India Company established an agency here in 1611 and a factory some 11 years later. Except for a brief period in 1628-32, when they were expelled, the English made this port their major headquarters on the Coromandel Coast. Their advantage over rival Dutch and French companies was confirmed by a decree from the Mughal emperor Aurangzeb in 1698, granting them trading monopolies. The French obtained a similar grant from the Nizam in 1733, but were forcibly ousted by the English six years later.

Little can now be seen of Machiliptanam's mercantile past. The only sights of interest are the *Dutch Tombs* in the burial ground. Their handsomely carved inscriptions and coats-of-arms bear dates ranging from 1649 to 1725.

E. Ghantasala

This somewhat isolated village, 21 km. west of Machilipatnam, was once a renowned mercantile centre dependent on seaborne trade. Roman gold coins and locally produced copper and lead coins with ship motifs testify to the flourishing Indo-Roman trade. Buddhism played an important part in the life of Ghantasala, but unfortunately the monuments were subjected to large-scale pillage. Decorated limestone columns of various sizes have been discovered in the village and surrounding fields. They come from pillared halls associated with 2nd-3rd century monastic establishments. Some columns are still seen lying on the ground near low mounds.

The ruined *Maha Chaitya* was excavated in the early part of the 20th century. Like other stupas in the region, it has radial and ring walls of rubble, once filled with rammed mud to create a solid hemispherical mass. (One casing limestone slab carved with a relief depiction of the assault and temptation of Mara has found its way to the Musée Guimet, Paris.) The recent find of a coping stone carved with dwarfs bearing garlands suggests that the stupa was originally encircled by a high railing.

F. Undavalli

Rock-cut sanctuaries at this site, overlooking the south bank of the Krishna River, lie 2 km. west of NH5, just 4 km. south of Vijayawada. Contemporary with similar caves at Vijayawada, the Undavalli examples are assigned to the 7th-8th century Eastern Chalukya period. The architecture is massive and unrelieved, with undecorated squat columns with angled cuts and curved brackets.

The most impressive sanctuary at Undavalli is the *Triple-Storeyed Cave*. This consists of three halls at different levels, linked by internal staircases with terraces in front. On the outside, these halls present superimposed colonnades, one set back from the other, separated by overhanging cornices with false windows. The fully sculpted lions and seated sages in stucco that serve as parapet elements are later additions, as are many of the carved panels. The hall inside the top level has a large panel of Vishnu reclining on Ananta at one side, now much restored.

Monolithic temple models and other excavated halls are seen nearby.

G. Mangalagiri

This town on NH5, 13 km. south of Vijayawada and 19 km. north of Guntur, is overlooked on the south by a wooded hill with a natural cave, which is accorded great sanctity. There are also indications of rock-cut sanctuaries, now greatly worn, dating back to Eastern Chalukya times. A *Victory Pillar*, set up near the foot of the steps that ascend the hill, is inscribed with the account of the capture of Kondavidu fort in 1515 by a commander of Krishnadevaraya, emperor of Vijayanagara [20B-C].

The principal attraction of Mangalagiri is the *Lakshmi Narasimha Temple*. This monument goes back to the time of the Reddi chiefs in the 14th century, but was substantially remodelled in the 17th-18th centuries. Entrance gopuras in the middle of four sides provide access to the walled compound. The east gopura presents a steep pyramidal tower of eleven storeys, topped by a barrel vaulted roof. There are no sculptures on the tower or on the walls beneath. The north gopura is shorter, but is covered with plaster figures, now somewhat decayed. The unfinished gopura on the west was begun during the Qutb Shahi period, judging from the arches with lobed profiles.

The east facing shrine in the middle of the temple compound is raised on a high terrace enlivened with rows of pilasters. The outer walls of the shrine and adjoining mandapa have regularly spaced niches and single pilasters standing in pots, all in shallow relief. The double-storeyed tower over the shrine is capped with a hemispherical roof. The shrine is approached through an open mandapa, with some columns fashioned as rearing yalis. The outer piers are overhung by deeply curved eaves. A small Garuda shrine in front has wheels carved onto the side walls, suggesting a chariot. Its pyramidal roof is crowned with a lotus finial.

H. Guntur

This city, 32 km. southwest of Vijayawada on NH5, came into prominence after being granted to the French in the early 18th century as a trading depot, developing thereafter as a place of commercial importance. Guntur is dotted with tobacco curing factories and mills for rice, cotton and oil. There are no historical features of note within the city, but the *Baudhasree Archaeological Museum* (closed Fridays) is worth visiting. Sculptures discovered at 2nd-4th century Buddhist sites in the region are displayed here. They include elegantly modelled Buddha figures dressed in flowing robes, and stupa slabs showing devotees and scenes from the former lives of the Buddha. Associated finds, such as black-and-red polished ceramic fragments, are also exhibited. There is, in addition, an unusual limestone stool with cut-out lotus flowers. Carvings associated with the Eastern Chalukyas include 8th century panels of seated Brahma and standing Vishnu. Later art is represented by 15th-16th century bronze figures.

I. Chebrolu

This small town, 10 km. south of Guntur, has an ancient history going back to Ikshvaku times. The high mound on which the houses are built has yielded terracotta figures and coins, two of which, in gold, pertain to the Roman emperor Constantine.

The earliest monuments at Chebrolu belong to the 9th-10th century Eastern Chalukya period. The finest example is the *Bhimeshvara Temple*, raised on a solid lower storey, with entrance porches on three sides sheltered by deeply overhanging eaves. They give access to a corridor running around four sides of the central linga shrine. The tower above, with its capping hemispherical roof, is of a later date.

The nearby *Adikeshvara Temple*, dating from the 12th century, has double shrines roofed with multi-storeyed towers, somewhat altered. The shrines are preceded by an enclosed mandapa, entered through a small porch with columns fashioned as seated yalis on squatting elephants. The adjacent *Nageshvara Temple* presents a different arrangement, the main shrine being approached through an open mandapa with balcony seating all around, now partly obscured by infill blocks. The entrance gopura has a steeply pyramidal tower typical of the 17th-18th century. A Nandi pavilion stands outside the temple compound.

That Chebrolu flourished in later times is revealed by the unusual 18th century *Brahmalingeshvara Temple*. This consists of a small shrine surrounded by a colonnade, standing in the middle of a large square tank. The main object of worship here is a linga with four images of Brahma carved onto its shaft, set into a lotus bowl. The linga is viewed through doorways on four sides, each with cut-out screens and sharply modelled overhanging eaves. The ceiling within presents a corbelled pyramidal vault. A bridge on the east provides access from the bank, where steps lead down to the water. Eight subshrines were originally positioned around the tank facing the water; those at the corners are dedicated to different goddesses.

J. BAPATLA

This town lies 38 km. south of Chebrolu, 7 km. inland from the Bay of Bengal. The *Bhavana Narayana Temple* here was erected by the Cholas when they conquered the Krishna Delta region in the 10th century. Architectural links with the Tamil country are seen in the multi-storeyed pyramidal towers of the triple shrines, capped with prominent hemispherical roofs. A standing Vishnu is under worship in the central shrine, with subsidiary divinities in the corners. The temple, together with minor sanctuaries, stands in a walled compound.

Motupalle, where Marco Polo is supposed to have landed in 1298, is a forgotten port 32 km. further south along the coast.

K. AMARAVATI

This small town on the south bank of the Krishna River, 34 km. north of Guntur, is best known for the Maha Chaitya, or Great Stupa, which once stood on its outskirts. The remains of this monument were first noticed in 1796, but systematic investigation did not take place here until the middle of the 19th century, by which time many limestone portions had been pillaged. Virtually nothing can now be seen of the stupa, other than a low earthen mound, 45 m. in diameter, surrounded by a pathway defined by upright slabs.

The *Maha Chaitya* at Amaravati is probably the largest and most elaborate in Southern India. It was founded in the 3rd-2nd centuries BCE during the Satavahana era, and was enlarged on several occasions during the 3rd-4th centuries CE under the Ikshvakus. The stupa is celebrated for its finely worked limestone capping posts and posts and railings, most of which have been removed from the site. The largest collections are in the Government Museum, Chennai, and the British Museum, London. Together with sculptures from Nagarjunakonda [27H], those from Amaravati are of outstanding artistic importance for the development of the Buddha figure and the narrative tradition illustrating the life of the Master.

The *Archaeological Museum* (closed Fridays), next to the Maha Chaitya, is home to a collection of recently discovered panels, posts, railings and sculptures, dating from both the Satavahana and Ikhvaku era. The first gallery displays large standing Buddhas, some more than 2 m. high, with elegantly fluted robes. Another sculpture depicts a maiden gracefully posed beneath a horseshoe-shaped arch. Several panels show stupas with flying celestials, and the worship of Buddha's seat. There is also a fully modelled embracing couple, probably celestials. The second gallery is dominated by a remarkable life-size bull, ceremonially decked with garlands and tassels. This has been assembled from fragments discovered in 1980 in the vicinity of the Amareshvara temple. Nearby is a wheel with cut-out spokes, symbolic of Buddha's teaching, as well as two elegant standing Buddha figures.

A reconstruction of part of the stupa railing, reaching an impressive height of almost 6 m., stands in the museum courtyard. It is composed mostly of plaster casts taken from pieces in the Chennai collection, but also incorporates several original cross bars. They show a mixture of full lotus flowers and narrative scenes, such as the birth of the Buddha, and various miracles. A useful model presenting the original scheme of the Maha Chaitya is also on view.

Stupa slab, Archeological Museum, Amaravati.

The *Amareshvara Temple*, elevated on a mound overlooking the Krishna, a short distance away, was founded by the Eastern Chalukyas in the 10th-11th centuries, but was substantially renovated in the 17th century by Venkatadri Nayadu, a local chief. That the monument occupies an earlier Buddhist mound is suggested by the curiously shaped linga under worship in the upper shrine. This actually forms part of a yupa, or stone pillar inserted into the body of a stupa as a symbolic axis of the universe. The temple is approached by freestanding gateways on the south and east, the former marking the end of the main street of Amaravati town. The temple itself is surrounded by a double enclosure, the inner compound raised up on retaining walls as a solid structure, with flights of steps on three sides. The shrine exterior is of little interest, but the columns in the adjacent mandapa, which has balcony seating all around, have well shaped cubic blocks and double capitals. Here is placed a brass clad image of Venatadri Nayadu, his hands held together in adoration.

The remains of the fort of *Dharanikota*, part of which goes back to the 18th century, are located 1 km. upstream, beside the river.

L. GOLI

This small village lies about 100 km. west of Guntur, a short distance from the route to Vijayapuri, 43 km. further west, a stopping off point for Nagarjuna Sagar [27H]. Goli is best known for its *Buddhist Antiquities*, dating from the Ikshvaku period, but other remains are also of interest. They include three prehistoric dolmens west of the village, and the dilapidated Malleshvara temple in an old fort to the southwest.

An irregular pit with stray bricks marks the site of a small, but profusely decorated stupa. Most of the limestone slabs discovered here in 1926 and now on display in the Government Museum, Chennai. An exception is the panel showing Nanda's forced ordination, which has made it way to the Metropolitan Museum of Art, New York. One item still to be seen at Goli is a panel with a seven-hooded serpent, presently in worship in a small shed.

M. KONDAVIDU

The Kondavidu Range west of Guntur is dotted with forts of different periods. They are most easily reached by taking a diversion of 5 km. from Phirangipura, 27 km. west of Guntur.

Puttakota, or Lower Fort, dates back to the 11th-12th centuries, when the Eastern Gangas of Orissa controlled this part of coastal Andhra. It occupies a valley in the middle of the hills, the mouth of which is closed by a high embankment of earth and stone. The area inside, now much overgrown, is filled with remains of temples, mandapas, wells and stone mortars.

The *Kila*, or Upper Fort, on top of the hill, is reached by a path from Puttakota. This citadel is associated with the Reddis, for whom it served as the principal stronghold in the 14th-15th centuries. The fortified zone is surrounded by battlemented ramparts with high towers. The area inside is filled with disintegrating dwellings, treasuries, magazines and granaries. One structure with a rock-cut chamber may have served as a store. Overturned mortars are seen everywhere around. There are many springs and three large tanks, one feeding into another. Several shrines have had their sculptures chipped away. One was even transformed into a mosque by Ghulab Ghazi, a local commander, whose tomb stands nearby.

The Reddis were repeatedly challenged by the Vijayanagara emperors for supremacy in this part of coastal Andhra. They were finally vanquished in 1515, after which another citadel at Kondavidu, known simply as *Kota*, was built beneath the northern flank of the hill. The ramparts, broken by two well defended gateways, still stand to a considerable extent. The chief monument of interest inside Kota is the *Gopinatha Temple*, a 16th century structure, later converted into a mosque. It is entered through a spacious open mandapa, the outer columns of which have cut-out colonettes and sculpted yalis overhung by deeply curved eaves. An inner mandapa with side porches leads to the main shrine. The walls, partly concealed by cactus, are relieved by pilastered niches. No tower is preserved over the sanctuary.

N. Cherzala

This remote village, 56 km. west of Guntur via Narasaraopet, is of interest for the *Kapoteshvara Temple*. Though currently in use as a Hindu place of worship, its apsidal-ended plan and barrel vault recall similar, though incompletely preserved, 3rd-4th century Buddhist structures at Nagarjunakonda. Only 7 m. long, the Kapoteshvara is built entirely of brick, including the vaulted roof. The frontal arch created by the vault is ornately treated with plaster decoration framing a temple tower in shallow relief.

Monolithic model shrines, evidently votive in purpose, are scattered around the temple precinct.

30. Rajahmundry

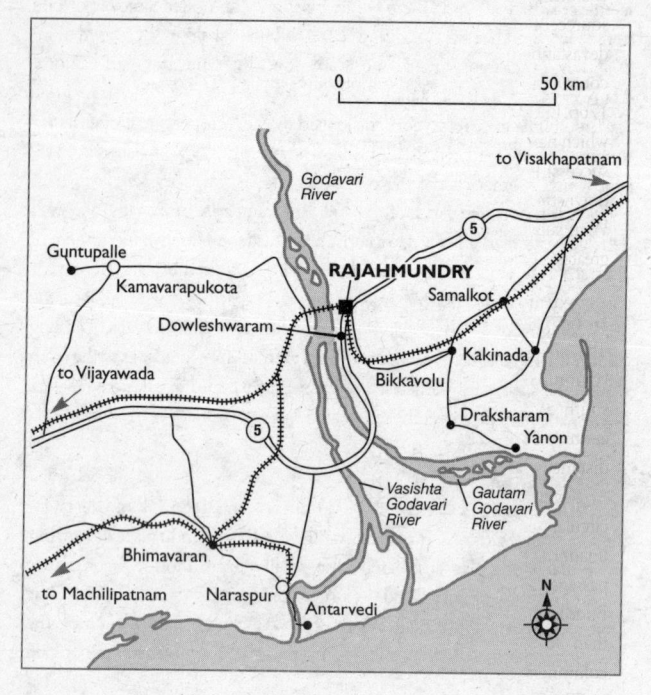

The densely populated Godavari Delta is dotted with historical sites that testify to the sustained economic significance of this richly watered zone through the centuries.

Rajahmundry, the largest city in the delta, is situated only a short distance from the great dam at Dowleshwaram [A]. From here the Buddhist relics at Guntupalle [B] can be conveniently visited as a half day trip. A visit to the Eastern Chalukya temple at Bhimavaran [C] and the pilgrimage shrine at Anatarvedi [D] can be combined in a single day excursion.

Another full day journey to the eastern part of the delta can take in the religious monuments at Bikkavolu [E], Draksharam [F] and Samalkot [H]. This excursion can be extended to include the scanty European vestiges at the coastal trading posts of Yanon [G] and Kakinada [I].

A. DOWLESHWARAM
The Godavari Delta draws its wealth from extensive cultivation of rice, sugar cane, areca nut, turmeric and bananas, as well as local industries as cotton

dyeing and printing. All these depend on an immense system of canals and channels that fans out all over the region. Unfortunately, the Godavari, the source of the water, is prone to flooding: severe storms, sometimes with devastating tidal waves, poses another threat. There were several attempts to control the river after Rajahmundry was ceded by the Nizams to the English in 1766. Enormous physical difficulties were encountered in harnessing the river, which here attains a width in excess of 6 km. Sir Arthur Cotton was eventually successful in constructing the *Great Dam* at Dowleshwaram, 10 km. downstream from the city. More than 4 km. long, the dam was built in 1848-52. With subsequent repairs and alterations it survives to this day as one of the greatest engineering works in Southern India.

B. Guntupalle

This small village lies 87 km. west of Rajahmundry via Kamavarapukota. (Guntupalle is also accessible from Vijayawada [29A], via Eluru, 35 km. south of Kamavarapukota.) *Buddhist Antiquities* dating back to the 2nd-1st century BCE, Satavahana era are to be found in a wooded ravine a short distance east of Guntupalle.

Several features stand on a terrace approached by a long flight of steps. A circular complex, occupying a commanding positioned, includes an unadorned brick stupa, more than 9 m. in diameter, surrounded by a passageway. Part of the limestone cladding is intact. Here are placed standing Buddha images, some up to 2 m. high, dating from the 3rd-4th century CE. More than 30 stupas of varying sizes are located nearby; so, too, the ruins of a columned hall and an apsidal-ended shrine.

Two groups of rock-cut shrines are located a short distance away. The excavated *Chaitya Hall* has an unusual circular plan and a dome-like ceiling with a network of radiating ribs that imitates wooden rafters. The entrance is framed by a horseshoe-shaped arch.

C. Bhimavaran

Situated 126 km. southwest of Rajahmundy, this town has an important East Chaluyka monument, though now somewhat worn and poorly restored. The core shrine of the 11th century *Someshvara Temple* houses a 1.5 m. high linga. The outer walls of the passageway surrounding the shrine are severely plain, except for pilasters set in recesses. The pyramidal tower above has flattened model roofs in ascending tiers, capped by an enlarged square roof with a dome-like top.

D. Anatarvedi

The pilgrimage shrine at this small settlement is most conveniently reached by boat from Naraspur, 112 km. south of Rajahmundry, on the Vaishishta branch of the Godavari River. Naraspur was an important European trading post, but nothing can now be seen of the Dutch, French and English presence. As in the past, small ships are built here; it is also an important centre of lace making.

It is about a 10 km. trip from Naraspur to the confluence of the Vaishita River with the Bay of Bengal. Here, on the opposite bank, lies Anatarvedi, the most sacred bathing spot in the Godavari Delta, sometimes also know as *Dakshina Kashi*, Southern Banaras. Great numbers of pilgrims visit the Lakshmi Narayana temple in February-March to attend the wedding festival of the god.

According to legend, Narasimha manifested himself in an ant hill where the existing stone image of the deity was miraculously discovered. This was originally kept in a shed and then installed in the temple, which was erected for it in 1823. Its brightly painted towered gateway is visible along the sands.

E. BIKKAVOLU

This village is located about 45 km. east of Rajahmundy. The *Chandrashekhara, Gollingeshvara* and *Rajarjeshvara Temples*, which stand in a row, are all assigned to the 9th century Eastern Chalukya period. Characteristic features are the moulded plinths, pilastered walls with regular projections, parapets of miniature roof forms, and multi-storeyed towers crowned with square roofs, some restored. Finely sculpted icons of Ganesha, Karttikeya and Durga are set into the wall niches. Additional images of Vishnu, Surya, Brahma and the dikpalas appear on the Gollingeshvara temple. The central panels are framed by secondary pilasters that support makaras with foliate tails. Each temple adjoins a mandapa, generally with unadorned walls. Fine carvings of Durga and Virabhadra are placed inside the mandapa of the Gollingeshvara temple.

Abandoned and dilapidated strucures stand on the fringe of Bikkavolu village. They include the *Nakkalagudi* and *Virabhadra Temples*, both with squat pyramidal towers. The sculpture panels, though worn, are similar to those seen in the Gollingeshvara. The slightly later, 10th century Kanchanagudi temple, now abandoned and overgrown, presents an elegantly heightened triple-storeyed tower.

F. DRAKASHARAM

A locally celebrated pilgrimage spot, this village lies 40 km. south of Rajahmundry, via Ramachandrapuram. The 10th century *Bhimeshvara Temple* here is of interest for the enormous, 5 m. high linga that received veneration in its sanctuary, which stands in the middle of a mandapa arranged unusually on two levels. The outer walls, single pilasters and capping cornices at both levels. Columns with sharply modelled capitals are employed within. The pyramidal tower over the linga sanctuary is capped with a square roof.

Evidence of European presence at Drakasharam is seen in the *Dutch Tombs* on what is called Ollandu Dibba, or Holland Mound. They date variously from 1675 to 1728, and have finely carved slabs.

G. Yanon

This former French settlement, barely more than 900 ha. in extent, is located 37 km. east of Drakashrama, about 20 km. from the mouth of the Gautam Godavari River.

The French built a factory at Yanon in 1750, shortly after which they were defeated by the British in the battle of Pithapura. Yanon was temporarily occupied by the British in 1802-03, and thereafter remained under French control into the 20th century. It now forms part of the Union Territory of Puducherry [39A].

Few European remains are to be seen in Yanon, partly because in 1839 the town was laid waste by a hurricane, accompanied by an inundation of the sea. The Catholic church postdates this catastrophe. A spacious walled parade ground is laid out on the south side of the town, bordering the river.

H. Samalkot

The 11th century *Bhimeshvara Temple* in this town, 47 km. east of Rajahmundry, is the largest East Chalukya monument in the region. It resembles the slightly earlier monument at Drakasharam, with it shares the same name. The tower over the central shrine at Samalkot has two distinct storeys capped with a square roof. Porches on two levels project outwards on three sides of the mandapa: the lower portions of the columns here are fashioned as seated lions. Supports with finely finished double capitals are seen inside the mandapa, some of the shafts being enlivened with figural carvings. Gateways on the north and south of the temple compound have pilastered walls, but no towers.

It is worth noting that Samalkot attained some measure of notoriety in the 18th century when it became the headquarters of a group of landowners who resisted European traders. The fort here was also the scene of fighting between the English and French, both of whom occupied the town on different occasions in 1759. The fort subsequently served as a sanatorium for British troops, but was eventually demolished in 1838. Since then, Samalkot has emerged as a commercial centre, with numerous sugar cane refineries and distilleries.

I. Kakinada

This busy seaport, 18 km. south of Samalkot, was in the past renowned for its cotton exports attracting various European traders. The Dutch built a factory and mint in 1628 at *Jagannathapuram*, on the south side of the harbour, by a decree from the Mughal emperor. The British attacked the settlement in 1781, occupying it for three years. During the war of the French Revolution in 1789-95, Jagannathapuram was once again captured, only to be returned in 1814. The port reverted finally to the British in 1824. Surviving European remains are confined to a *Small Cemetery*. The earliest identifiable graves are those of a Dutch family dated 1775-78.

In the course of the 18th century the bay silted up, and Kakinada replaced Jagannathapuram as the principal port. A second impulse to seaborne commerce was provided by American Civil War in 1861, during which time Kakinada rose to prominence because of huge shipments of cotton textiles. The town is today an important Christian centre. The *Protestant Church* in the town apparently possesses one of the finest organs in Southern India. A Roman Catholic church and convent stand nearby.

31. Visakhapatnam

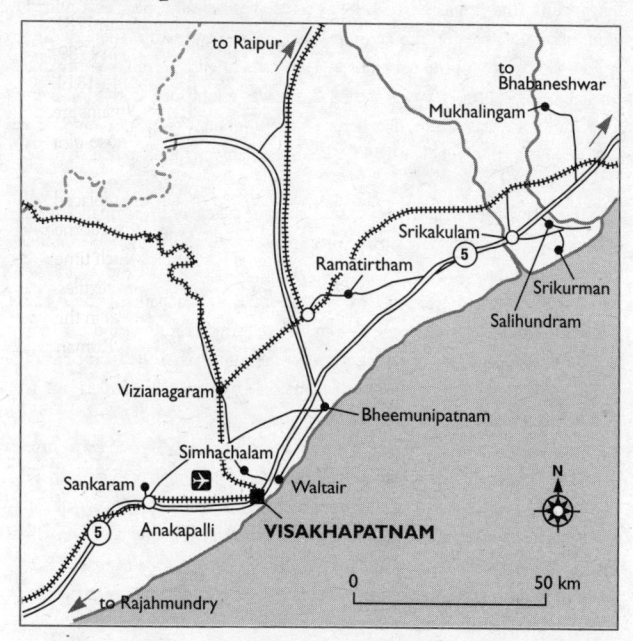

Dotted with historical sites, both Buddhist and Hindu, the Visakhapatnam area benefits from delightful scenery with forested hills descending to rocky headlands on the Bay of Bengal Coast.

A few hours should be reserved for the sights of Visakhapatnam [A], with half-day trips to the hill temple at Simhachalam [B], the Buddhist relics at Sankaram [C], and the curious Dutch tombs at Bheemunipatnam [D].

The Buddhist sites at Ramatirtham [E] and Salihundram [F] will require a longer journey, especially if this is extended to include the pilgrimage shrines at Srikurman [G] and Mukhalingam [H], from where it is possible to continue up the coast to Orissa.

A. Visakhapatnam

Formerly known as Vizagapatnam, or simply as Vizag, this city is a major industrial centre and naval base known for its heavy industries, with an oil refinery, zinc smelting plant and specialist steelworks. Visakhapatnam benefits from what was until recently the only deep water harbour on the Bay of Bengal, and the second biggest shipyard in Southern India, after Mumbai [1]. The port serves as a major export terminal for bulk iron and manganese.

Little is known of Visakhapatnam's history prior to the arrival of the Europeans. The English established themselves here in 1682, and quickly built up a lucrative commerce in textiles, tobacco and ivory. The city came under the control of the Mughals in 1689; the English were taken prisoner and all of their property was seized. Peace was established in the following year, and trade was resumed as before. Except for attacks by local chiefs and an invasion by the French in 1757, Visakhapatnam remained in British hands until Independence.

The city benefits from a splendid setting, facing onto a broad bay. Its southern extremity is bounded by a promontory with a hill rising 175 m. above the sea, known as *Dolphin's Nose*. The lighthouse here has a beam visible for more than 60 km. out to sea. The oldest part of Visakhapatnam, the *Fort*, is separated from Dolphin's Nose by a small river, which forms a sand bar. Here can be seen the remains of 18th century barracks, an arsenal, the Court House, and the Protestant church, the last being marked by a graceful domical lantern. The cemetery nearby contains European graves going back to 1699.

Visakhapatnam is framed by a line of three hills, each topped by a shrine associated with a different religion. The *Venkateshvara Temple*, on the south hill, has a small, steeply pyramidal entrance gopura. The central hill is crowned with the *Church of the Virgin Mary*, approached by a path lined with the Stages of the Cross. Its whitewashed facade is flanked by slender towers. The *Dargah of Isai*, a Muslim saint much venerated by seafarers, is set beneath the north hill. It is roofed with a flattish, bulbous dome.

Waltair, once a separate town, but now part of greater Visakhapatnam, is located near Ramakrishna Beach, at the northern end of the bay. Originally established as a health resort for British offices, it preserves several Christian places of worship. *St Paul's Church* of 1847 is a simple Neo-Classical building with a modest portico displaying a quartet of Ionic columns. A semicircular arch divides the congregation from the altar, enhanced by the stained glass in the apse. The Catholic Pilgrimage Chapel dates from 1867. Waltair is renowned for *Andhra University*, one of the largest campuses, founded in 1931.

B. SIMHACHALAM

The popular *Varaha Narasimha Temple* at Simhachalam is dramatically sited in the secluded forest of the Kailasa Hills, 16 km. north of Visakhapatnam. This shrine is believed to have been dedicated originally to Shiva, but was later transformed into a Vaishnava place of worship after a visit by Ramanuja, the famous teacher, at the end of the 11th century. The story is borne out by the principal votive image of the temple: this is a linga-shaped form, composed of sandalwood paste, concealing a diminutive effigy of Vishnu. Dating back to the 8th-9th century, the temple was entirely rebuilt in 1268 by a military commander of Narasimha, the Eastern Ganga king of neighbouring Orissa. That Simhachalam continued to be a place of importance in later centuries is evident from the visit in 1516 of Krishnadevaraya, emperor of Vijayanagara [20B-C]. The growth of nearby Visakhapatnam ensures that the temple continues to expand.

The Varaha Narasimha temple is approached by a long winding road that ascends the hill, arriving at a car park from which flight a of steps climbs to gateways on the north and west. These take the form of gopuras with steeply pyramidal towers, recently renovated. Most visitors enter through the north gopura, inside which is a large mandapa built into the northwest corner of the enclosure. Peripheral columns of polished granite have seated lions supporting shafts with carved reliefs, and sharply modelled capitals. Internal columns are enlivened with bands of foliation and jewelled garlands. A lofty flagpole stands in front (west) of the porch that gives access to the inner enclosure.

The temple within consists of a pair of mandapas aligned with the square sanctuary and its surrounding passageway. The outer open mandapa has circular columns decorated with figural friezes and garlands. One of these columns is identified as the pillar out of which Narasimha miraculously appeared. The 12 columns of the inner enclosed mandapa support a ceiling of rotated squares. The sanctuary which lies beyond is roofed with a corbelled vault. The outer walls of both shrine and mandapas are raised on a high basement adorned with yalis and makaras. Wall projections have framing pilasters, with yalis in full relief. Images of deities, ascetics and royal figures stand beneath ornate trees carved in shallow relief.

Panels in the middle of the sanctuary walls depict Varaha (north), Narasimha disembowelling Hiranyakashipu (east), and Trivikrama (south), each surmounted by a small icon of Krishna in the pediment. These sculptures are executed in the finest Orissan style, with smoothly rounded bodies contrasting with intricately etched facial features, costumes and jewellery. The panels are interspersed with exuberant scrollwork and creeper motifs. Windows capped by ornate pediments admit light to the mandapa. Orissan type pyramidal towers over the sanctuary and mandapa are crowned by circular ribbed elements.

The inner enclosure of the temple is surrounded by a colonnade incorporating three small shrines. That in the northeast corner is conceived as chariot, with large wheels carved onto the basement; life-size prancing horses are placed either side of the access steps.

C. Sankaram

The village of Sankaram, 3 km. north of Anakapalli, 38 km. west of Visakhapatnam, is known for its 3rd-4th century Buddhist antiquities, the dilapidated remains of which are located on two hills to the north of the settlement.

On the level top of the east hill, known as *Bojjanakonda*, are the basement and lower portions of a large *Stupa*, around which are disposed smaller votive stupas, both rock-cut and brick built. The brick Monastery nearby has a central court surrounded by small square cells, with an apsidal-ended shrine in the middle. *Rock-Cut Sanctuaries* are cut into the sides of the fill, four with Buddha reliefs. The cave with a monolithic stupa has 16 columns. Images of Ganesha and Bhairava in another excavated monastery indicate that the site was used in later times for Hindu worship.

Lingalakonda, the west hill, has numerous rock-cut stupas arranged in ascending tiers. They are dominated by the outlines of a large monolithic stupa.

D. BHEEMUNIPATNAM

This small, quiet fishing port town lies 24 km. northeast of Visakhapatnam; the road runs picturesquely along the coast past a series of splendid sandy beaches.

Bheemunipatnam was once known as Bhimlipatan, one of the major Dutch settlements on the Coromandel Coast. The Dutch used it as a port for exports of rice in the 17th century. In later times it became famous for jute manufacturing, with large mills located in the surrounding villages, many still in operation today. Bhimlipatan was sacked by the Marathas, who invaded the coastal region in 1754, and was destroyed again in 1781, during the Anglo-Dutch wars. It surrendered to the British in 1795, but was not finally given over to them until 1825.

Hints of Bheemunipatnam's Dutch past are evident in the European styled houses, with colonnaded verandahs and sloping tiled roofs, and the crumbling fort. Of greater interest are the *Dutch Tombs* in the cemetery overlooking the sea. These include a series of remarkable obelisk-shaped monuments bearing Dutch inscriptions, the earliest dating from 1750, as well as a French record of 1785. The lighthouse nearby is more recent.

British period vestiges include the 19th century clock tower in the middle of the town. The *Church of St Peter*, some 2.5 km. north, built in 1864, is recognised by its 20 m. high belfry. The interior is notable for its tiled floor and wooden furniture.

The small Krishna shrine on the top of the hill outside the town is approached by a steep flight of steps.

E. RAMATIRTHAM

This village, 27 km. northeast of Visakhapatnam via Vizianagaram, is known for its Buddhist remains dating mainly from the 3rd-4th century Ikshvaku era. The principal group of monuments is located on a hill north of the village, known as *Gurubhaktakonda*. They are dramatically sited on a narrow ledge 165 m. above the plain, hemmed in by the vertical cliff of bare rock on one side and a deep ravine on the other.

The first feature to be seen at Ramatirtham is the *Main Stupa*, 22 m. in diameter, of which only the base survives. At the foot of the cliff nearby is a tank fed by water dripping from the rocky overhang. Further along is a terrace of boulders, with rows of monastic cells and the ruins of an imposing plastered *Apsidal Hall*. The apse of the hall contains a small brick stupa faced with stone slabs. Here was discovered a small relief casket containing lead coins and clay sealings, one with a legend written in characters of the 2nd century. A columned hall is situated nearby.

The next features to be seen are four *Chaitya Halls* laid out in an irregular line, all apsidal in plan. Votive stupas partly survive in two of the halls. Two monasteries nearby, bordering the ledge, have long rows of cells, the doorways of each chamber flanked by stone pilasters,

Remains of similar Buddhist structures may be seen on the adjacent hill, called *Durgakonda*. The 8th-9th century images of Jain saviours found here belong to the period when Buddhism had disappeared from the region.

F. Salihundram

The Buddhist remains at this site form an important landmark, picturesquely situated on top of a hill overlooking the Vamsadhara River, 8 km. from its confluence with the Bay of Bengal. Salihundram lies 15 km. east Srikakulam, a town on NH5, about 100 km. northeast of Visakhapatnam.

A rubble paved path, lined by structural remains, ascends to the crest of the hill. Two *Apsidal-Ended Sanctuaries* stand immediately inside the gate. One enshrines a seated image of Buddha made of plaster covered brickwork; the other has a stone cased votive stupa with a brick core. A number of stupas higher up the path include one with eight radial spokes. The *Circular Sanctuary* at the summit is 7.5 m. in diameter, with walls almost 5 m. thick, standing to a height of barely 1 m. Nothing survives of the roof or the votive stupa inside. The main stupa nearby is made of wedge shaped bricks around a central hollow shaft. Here, excavators recovered three stone caskets, each contaiing a crystal reliquary with gold flower.

Dilapidated walls indicating a group of monasteries are concentrated beneath the hill, near to the bank of the Vamsadhara.

G. Srikurman

The *Shri Kurmanatha Temple* at this coastal village, 13 km. east of Srikakulam, was founded by the Eastern Chalukyas in the 10th century. However, the monument was substantially remodelled in the 12th-13th centuries, when the Cholas temporarily occupied coastal Andhra. The temple is unique in having the tortoise form of Vishnu as its principal object of adoration. The main shrine stands within an enclosure, the walls of which have shallow pilasters. Gateways with columned porches are placed in the middle of the east and south sides. Two lamp columns stand inside. The main shrine is surrounded by a colonnade, adorned with wall paintings depicting Krishna episodes and aspects of Vishnu, no older than the 19th century. Sculpture niches are positioned in the outer projections of the sanctuary and attached mandapas. The walls are capped with a parapet of miniature roof forms. The tower over the sanctuary rises in two diminishing storeys with an octagonal-domed roof.

H. Mukhalingam

This remotely situated small town, on the east bank of the Vamsadhara River, lies 46 km. north of Srikakulam, partly via NH5. Mukhalingam was the first capital of the Gangas, rulers of Orissa in the 12th-13th centuries, and patrons of the great temples at Puri and Konarak.

The 9th century *Madhukeshvara Temple*, in the middle of the town, is the most important and best preserved monument at Mukhalingam. It consists of a sanctuary and an adjoining rectangular mandapa with unusual subshrines built into the four corners. Sculpted panels on the walls between the corner shrines are set into niches with tower-like pediments in shallow relief. Among the numerous icons are finely carved images of Narasimha and dancing Shiva (south). The corner shrines are distinguished by curved towers with horizontal divisions, capped with disc-like ribbed motifs. The curving tower over the sanctuary is larger and higher, but also simpler, with plain horizontal divisions and duplicated disc-like elements. The central projections on each side of the tower have horseshoe-shaped niches containing images of different deities: Shiva appears twice on the front (east face) as Bhikshatanamurti (above) and Nataraja (below). The doorways on the east and south have jambs adorned with guardians, maidens and gracefully posed amorous couples, all set in elegant, luxurious foliation. The lintel over the east doorway shows scenes from the Krishna story, as well as miniature friezes of battle, with soldiers and elephants. The south doorway is surmounted by multiple images of Shiva, showing the god spearing Andhaka, and dancing within the skin of the elephant demon.

The Madhukeshvara temple stands within a rectangular compound with a curious screen wall dividing it into two parts. Shrines at the corners imitate those already noticed on the mandapa. The detailed ornamentation of the doorways and towers of these shrines is finely executed, particularly over the doorways. A sculpted naga set close to the north compound wall holds a pot for water to flow into a small basin. The entrance gateway in the screen wall has intricately carved ascetics in meandering creepers on the jambs. The east entrance to the enclosure has a curving vaulted roof with a trio of ribbed finials on the ridge.

Madhukeshvara Temple, Mukhalingam.

About 200 m. to the southeast is located the 11th century *Bhimeshvara Temple*. This repeats the basic scheme of the Madhukeshvara, but is less well preserved. Most of the original detail has been lost, except for the delicately worked doorways.

At the entrance to the town stands the *Someshvara Temple*, a 9th century monument with a sanctuary topped by a curved tower, about 15 m. high, with narrow horizontal bands. There is no mandapa. The principal doorway on the west has panels of scrollwork, with the navagrahas and seated Lakshmi on the lintel; river goddesses enliven the jambs. Triple niches on each of the side walls of the sanctuary house finely worked figures of Shiva, ten-armed Durga, and a curious one-legged form of Shiva (north); Harihara, Karttikeya and Ardhanarishvara (east); and Lakulisha, Ganesha and Shiva (south).

32. Kurnool

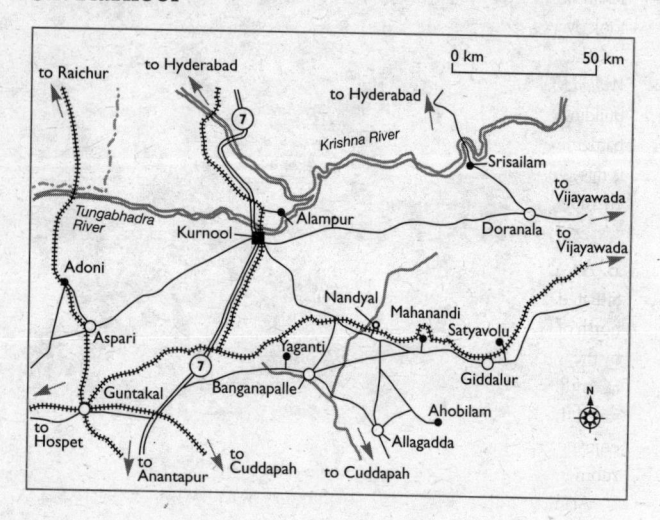

Kurnool lies near the south bank of the Tungabhadra River, about 30 km. upstream from its confluence with the Krishna. Though there only a few sights to draw visitors to Kurnool [A], the city makes a convenient stop on the journey along NH7 from Hyderabad [26], 291 km. to the north, to Anantapur [33], 140 km. to the south, and, beyond, to Bengaluru [14].

Historical monuments accessible from Kurnool include the temples at Alampur [B], rescued from the rising waters of the Krishna, and an easy half day trip. Separate full-day excursions will be required to reach the more distant but picturesquely located pilgrimage temples at Srisailam [C], Mahanandi [D], Satyavolu [E], Ahobilam [F] and Yaganti [G], all situated to the east of Kurnool. At least two days should be set aside to visit these sites, with a recommended overnight stay at Srisailam or Ahobilam. A stopover at the citadel at Adoni [H] is possible en route to Hampi [20] in Karnataka.

A. KURNOOL

The importance of this city as an administrative centre is apparent from the fact that in 1950-56 it served as the capital of Andhra Pradesh.

This history of Kurnool goes back to 1620, when it was conquered by Abdul Wahad Khan, commander of the forces of Bijapur [23A], whose tomb remains the chief monument of the city. Kurnool gained further prominence under the Mughals and their successors, the Asaf Jahis of Hyderabad. A local family of chiefs controlled most of the district, the first member of which, Daud

Khan, was installed by Aurangzeb. This line of Khans lasted until the British took over Kurnool at the beginning of the 19th century.

The only historical monument of interest in Kurnool is the *Tomb of Abdul Wahad Khan*, in the eastern part of the city. Dating from 1639, this finely finished building consists of a domed chamber surrounded by an arcaded passageway. A battlemented parapet with corner pavilion-like finials frames a central dome that is raised on a circular drum and enlivened with a frieze of petals. A lesser tomb chamber adjoins the building on the east.

B. ALAMPUR

Situated on the north bank of the Tungabhadra River, this village lies 30 km. north of Kurnool, about half the distance along NH7. Alampur was threatened by the waters of the Srisailam Project, one of the largest hydro-electric schemes in Andhra Pradesh, some 85 km. downstream. A barrage built here has now saved the temples, but deprived them of the view of the river that they once enjoyed. Other temples at nearby sites were dismantled before being submerged, and then re-erected on the outskirts of the village.

Alampur formed part of the kingdom of the Early Chalukyas of Badami [22A], and was evidently a settlement of some importance judging from the many fine temples erected here in the 7th-8th centuries. These comprise the largest and earliest surviving Hindu monuments in Andhra Pradesh. The group of nine temples at Alampur is known as the *Nava Brahma*, even though they are all dedicated to Shiva. With the exception of the Taraka Brahma, they conform to a standard scheme, each with an east-facing sanctuary surrounded by a passageway and preceded by a mandapa, contained within a rectangle of walls. The Northern Indian styled, curved towers that rise above the sanctuaries are divided into tiers adorned with horseshoe-shaped motifs and capped by circular ribbed elements.

Temples at Alampur.

The first feature to be seen on arriving at Alampur is the *Sangameshvara Temple*, the blocks of which were brought from Kudaveli, at the confluence of the Tungabhadra and Krishna Rivers, now a flooded site some 20 km to the east. The temple is elevated on a high terrace embellished with a frieze of animals, pilastered projections and a prominent parapet. Niches on the outer walls of the temple have pediments of different designs, some with pairs of makaras. Those on either side of entrance frame large pot-bellied ganas. The tower above the sanctuary is of the standard Alampur type, though somewhat worn.

The *Nava Brahma Group* stands in the middle of Alampur village, surrounded by houses and protected by ancient fort walls. The temples are described from north to south. The *Vira Brahma Temple* has its outer walls divided into projecting niches framed by pairs of pilasters, with triangular pediments composed of interlocking horseshoe-arched motifs. The niches are empty, but flying celestials embellish the tops of the walls. The tower above has pronounced central projections. The *Vishva Brahma Temple* is more elaborate. Pediments with complicated designs surmount the niches and widows. The basement blocks are carved with ganas, musicians, dancers, monster masks and geese with foliated tails. Interior columns have seated lions at the base, fluted shafts and ribbed pot-shaped capitals. The beams are embellished with scrollwork. Triple niches appear on the sanctuary walls within the passageway. The adjacent *Arka Brahma Temple* is now partly ruined.

The *Kumara Brahma*, the earliest temple of the Nava Brahma group, has a plain exterior with perforated screens lighting the interior passageway. Columns and beams in the mandapa are decorated with foliation and miniature figures. The *Bala Brahma Temple*, the only one currently in worship, has its outer walls partly concealed by a later colonnade. Various loose sculptures, including a series of matrikas, are placed here. A gateway to the east once led down to the river. The *Garuda Brahma Temple* is similar to the Vishva Brahma, but is almost devoid of carved decoration. The sanctuary doorway has bands of foliation, guardian figures and a flying Garuda.

Dated 698, the *Svarga Brahma* has a frontal porch of six columns with fluted shafts and pot-and-foliage motifs on the bases and capitals. Additional porches with similar supports shelter windows on the three sides of the passageway. The temple is notable for its elaborate sculptures, including a complete set of the dikpalas occupying pairs of niches at the four corners. Other icons show Shiva dancing, appearing out of the linga, shooting arrows at the demon of the triple cities, and seated in a teaching posture beneath a tree; accessory images include amorous couples and, at the top of the walls, flying celestials. An icon of dancing Shiva is contained within the arch-shaped frontal projection on the tower over the sanctuary.

The *Padma Brahma Temple*, the latest of the Nava Brahma group, displays complicated pediment designs above the niches on the outer walls and on the sanctuary walls inside the passageway. The tower is incomplete; there is no entrance porch. The *Taraka Brahma Temple* has an unusual multi-storeyed tower with the usual arch-shaped frontal projection. The gate in the wall nearby served as the original entrance to the complex. Deities are carved onto its ceiling.

Next to the temples stands the *Archaeological Museum* (closed Fridays), home to a fine collection of early Chalukya sculptures. The masterpiece is a refined image of dancing Shiva with multiple arms holding different weapons, trampling a dwarf; the facial expression of the god is serene. Other exhibit items include images of Durga, and ceiling panels showing dancing Shiva and a coiled serpent. A slab for libations is carved with the squatting figure of Lajja Gauri. Numerous decorated columns and beams are also on display. Among the sculptures assigned to the 10th-11th century Late Chalukya period is a polished basalt Nandi ridden by Shiva and Parvati.

That Alampur continued to be an important site in later times is indicated by the fortifications and gateways inside the village, and by the *Papanasam Group of Temples*, 1.5 km. southwest of the village. These small structures are assigned to the 9th-10th centuries, a period of transition between the Rashtrakuta and late Chalukya periods. Most examples of this group display pyramidal multi-tiered towers; one has an unusual apsidal-ended roof. Though there is little external decoration, internal columns are carved with figurative and foliate motifs. A fine Durga image is preserved in one of temples; another temple has a ceiling panel showing Vishnu's incarnations.

C. Srisailam

A visit to Srisailam, 180 km. east of Kurnool, is best accomplished with an overnight stay. The drive to this site, particularly the last 35 km. from Doranala, is through the wooded slopes of the Eastern Ghats. Srisaialm occupies a superb site overlooking the gorge of the Krishna River, some 200 m. below. (Srisailam may also be reached directly from Hyderabad, 190 km. to the north.)

The *Mallikarjuna Temple* at Srisailam is a popular place of pilgrimage, especially during the Shivaratri festival in February-March. The cult of Shiva celebrated here is closely linked with the Chenchus, the hunters who inhabit the surrounding forests. Though the worship of Mallikarjuna dates back to early times, the present monument does not predate the 14th-15th century. It enjoyed the patronage of the emperors of Vijayanagara [20B-C], several of whom personally visited the site.

The temple is surrounded by high walls topped by a crenellated parapet defining a rectangular compound, some 208 by 168 m. The walls are of outstanding artistic interest because of the remarkable reliefs carved onto the exterior blocks. The bottom course is ornamented with a procession of elephants, some uprooting trees, while the second course is devoted to equestrian and hunting scenes. The panels on the third and fourth courses depict processions of soldiers, dancing girls, musicians, sages, pilgrims and mythical beasts. A host of scenes represent Shiva in diverse forms: as the wandering ascetic, disguised as the hunter fighting Arjuna, as the slayer of the elephant demon, and as the rescuer of his devotee Markandeya, who is shown clutching the linga. A large panel of a seated king near the east gateway may represent the emperor Krishnadevaraya; a model shrine nearby frames a standing icon of Shiva. Royal motifs on the south wall include the double-headed eagle known as gandabherundha.

Modest gateways with columned porticos on four sides, some with pyramidal brick towers, give access to a spacious compound. This is filled with shrines and open halls. The temple itself consists of a modest sanctuary capped by a pyramidal tower with diminishing tiers. The jyotirlinga that is worshipped in the sanctuary is approached through a mandapa with triple porches, an addition of 1405. The pilastered walls and pierced stone windows have been entirely replaced, except for the columns on the porch, inscribed with edicts of the Vijayanagara kings. A minor shrine near the north porch of the temple shelters a linga with multiple miniature replica lingas carved onto its curved shaft.

D. MAHANANDI

This pilgrimage spot is attractively situated in the wooded foothills of the Eastern Ghats, about 100 km. east of Kurnool via Nandyal. The temples at Mahanadi belong to the Early Chalukya period. Like those at Alampur, with which it is contemporary, the *Mahanandishvara Temple* has its core shrine contained within a rectangle of walls that accommodate a spacious mandapa and an ambulatory passageway. The spire that rises above the shrine has its curving sides adorned with horseshoe-shaped arched motifs. It is a crowned by a circular ribbed element.

Two subsidiary temples, as well as several model shrines nearby, are of the same age as the main monument.

E. SATYAVOLU

This village, 30 km. east of Mahanandi via Giddalur, is the setting for two other Early Chaluyka monuments. The *Ramalingeshvara* and *Bhimalingeshvara* Temples stands next to each other, the first being the larger. Both have shrines with wall niches in the middle of three sides, roofed with curving spires of the Alampur type. The frontal projections of the towers, with vaulted roofs and arched faces, frame icons of dancing Shiva. The mandapa attached to the Ramalingeshvara has pierced stone screens. It is preceded by an outer open mandapa with triple porches, surrounded by balcony seating, an addition of the 14th-15th century. Panels of divinities, accessory figures, animals and birds are seen on the basement of the original temple. Mythological topics and decorative motifs embellish the blocks of the central four columns of the inner mandapa.

F. AHOBILAM

Located at an elevation of 925 m. in the forested hills of the Eastern Ghats, this somewhat remote pilgrimage site lies 148 km. southeast of Kurnool, via Nandyal and Allagadda; it may also be reached from Cuddapah, 112 km. to the south.

Ahobilam is linked with Narasimha, the man-lion incarnation of Vishnu. According to local legend, Narasimha fell in love with a local Chenchu girl and had to undergo tests to prove his valour before marrying her. While the Narasimha cult at Ahobilam was first promoted by the Reddis of Kondavidu [29M] in the 14th-15th centuries, it was the emperors of Vijayanagara who gave prominence to the site in the 16th century. It has continued since as a significant religious centre, and attracts large numbers of pilgrims. It is presently the headquarters of an importance Vaishnava matha.

Ahobilam is the name given to two sites, 8 km. apart. *Lower Ahobilam* is a small settlement offering simple accommodation and facilities for devotees. The *Narasimha Temple* here is a grand edifice, dating mostly from the 16th century. An ornate pavilion and lamp column mark the main street that proceeds west towards the complex. The temple is entered through a pair of gopuras, the outer one lacking its tower. The inner gopura has pilastered walls raised high on a double basement, and a five-storeyed pyramidal tower above. The walls within the passageway are covered with reliefs of figures, creeper motifs and superimposed temple facades.

The spacious mandapa of the Narasimha temple appears to have been built in imitation of an almost identical mandapa in the Vitthala temple at Hampi [20B]. Its basement has an ornate frieze of elephants and attendants. Clusters of cut-out colonettes surround the outer columns, with secondary shorter colonettes and squatting dwarfs above. The eaves are replacements. As in its counterpart at Hampi, the interior is divided into open halls defined by sculpted columns. The north hall is enlivened by multiple aspects of Narasimha, while the hall to the rear is flanked by riders on yalis, as well as by richly attired courtiers. The shrine beyond is comparatively unadorned and modest in scale. The mandapa that occupies the southwest corner of the compound has slender colonettes and animals on the outer columns; rearing beasts flank the central aisle.

Upper Ahobilam is set in a pleasant wooded ravine with a waterfall and stream. The approach path leads by a large square tank with stepped sides. It is overlooked by a 16-columned pavilion with a central dais; the columns here display yalis and colonettes. The gopura that gives access to the compound of the Narasimha Temple from the west has a whitewashed three-storeyed tower. The interior of the gopura is of interest for the friezes of courtly figures and Ramayana scenes that enliven the side chambers. The temple mandapa is built up to a natural cavern, where the most important image of Narasimha is venerated. The walls of the mandapa are covered with friezes of deities and accessory figures, including Chenchu huntresses with bows and arrows. Squat columns have double blocks covered with carvings, and extended double capitals and lotus brackets. Other 16-columned pavilions, resembling the one already noticed outside the complex, stand to the east. A gateway here leads to the rough trail that ascends the hill, leading to various clefts and shrines sacred to Narasimha.

G. Yaganti

This little visited spot, 90 km. south of Kurnool via Banganapalle, is delightfully located at the head of a rocky valley framed by a crescent of sandstone cliffs. A cascade feeds a large square tank in front of the 16th-17th century *Uma Maheshvara Temple*. This pond is surrounded by friezes of courtly and mythological scenes carved on the blocks just above water level. The surrounding colonnades and central pavilion are later additions. A towered gopura, a short distance west, leads to the main temple. This has an outer mandapa with porch projections on three sides, each with balcony seating. the slightly irregular layout of the interior is explained by the sculpted Nandi which is accommodated here. Interior columns have figures of deities, many standing in arched niches, and diverse decorative patterns carved onto the shafts.

A doorway in the northwest corner of the temple compound leads to a track that crosses a stream and then climbs up to a number of natural caverns that serve as linga shrines.

H. Adoni

This strategically located stronghold, 80 km. southwest of Kurnool via Aspari, was much contested by the emperors of Vijayanagara and the Bahmanis of Gulbarga [2A]. In 1568 Adoni was captured by the Adil Shahis of Bijapur, who installed a garrison here under a series of commanders. Adil Shahi control of Adoni lasted until Aurangzeb's generals arrived in 1690. In 1756 Salabat Jung of Hyderabad presented Adoni to his brother Balasat Jung, who made it his headquarters. In 1778 Adoni was twice besieged by Haidar Ali of Srirangapattana [15C], but it was not until 1786 that it was occupied by his son, Tipu Sultan, who demolished the fortifications and removed the stores and guns to Gooty [33A]. Adoni was ceded to the Britiish in 1800.

Adoni town is situated to the south of a series of rocky hills that forms the nucleus of the citadel. The main street is dominated by the imposing bulk of the *Jami Mosque*, erected in 1660 by Madu Qadiri, the Adil Shahi governor. The mosque is entered through a lofty portal framed by buttresses. The prayer hall overlooking a spacious court has a five-arched facade. This is surmounted by an angled overhang on sculpted brackets, and a parapet of trefoil elements. Corner octagonal buttresses, with stone chains hanging from brackets, rise as minarets. The composition is topped with a dome raised high on a petalled drum. The interior bays of the hall are roofed with alternating shallow domes and vaults. Doorways to the side chambers in the outer aisle of the hall are framed by temple-like colonettes and pediments. The mihrab is conceived as a domed chamber.

A road from the town proceeds for about 500 m. before passing through the walls of the sprawling lower fort. Disintegrating structures are seen beside the road. Better preserved features are found in the *Upper Fort*, including the Rangin Mosque, erected by Masud Khan, governor of Adoni in 1662-87, partly out of material from dismantled temples. Piles of stones nearby are all that remain of what must have been an elaborate Vijayanagara period monument. Venkanna Bhavi is a large well named after a minister of Masud Khan. The *Tomb of Malik Raman Khan*, a local holy figure, stands a short distance beyond, on the southern edge of the fort, overlooking the town. Its domed chamber was later extended with the addition of extra funerary chambers.

33. Anantapur

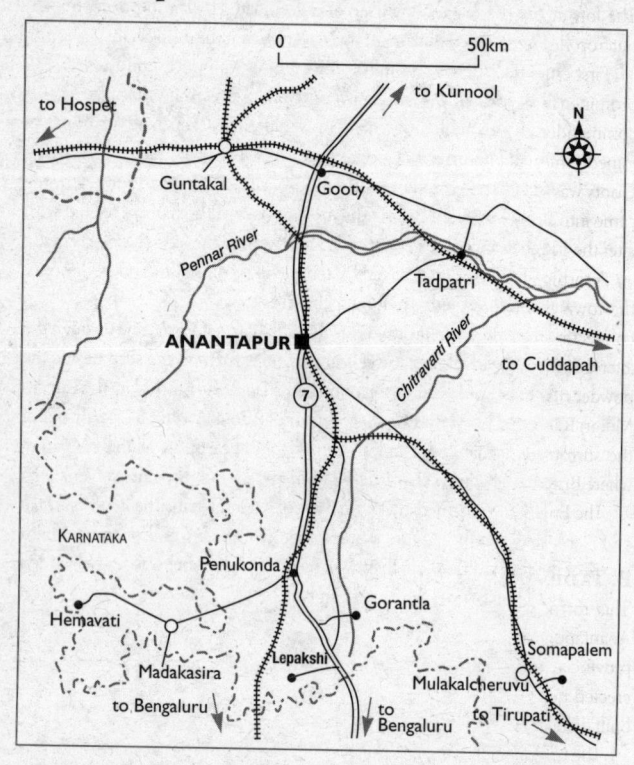

Anantapur makes a convenient stopover on any journey along NH7 from Kurnool [26], 140 km. to the north, and Bengaluru [14], 224 km. to the south. Though there is nothing of historical interest in Anantapur itself, the surrounding area is rich in monuments.

The fort at Gooty [A] and the ornate Vijayanagara period shrines at Tadpatri [B] can be combined in a single-day excursion north of the city, with the possibility of continuing on to Cuddapah [34], via Gandikota [34C], 165 km. to the east.

A trip southeast of Anantapur can take in the elegant shrine at Somapalem [C], with the option of proceeding to Tirupati [35], 305 km. southeast.

The fort at Penukonda [D] and the temples at Gorantla [E] and Lepakshi [F], the latter celebrated for its ceiling paintings, are located on or near NH7. Additional time will have to be set aside in order to reach the isolated village of Hemavati [G], with its unusual Nolamba styled temples.

A. Gooty

The fort at Gooty, 50 km. north of Ananatapur, occupies a striking granite outcrop elevated more than 300 m. above the plain.

First established by the emperors of Vijayanagara [20B-C], Gooty rose to prominence in the 18th century, when it became the stronghold of the Maratha commander, Murari Rao. This figure became well known to the British, and joined forces with Robert Clive against the Nawab of Arcot [38B] in 1751. Gooty was lost to Haidar Ali in 1773 after a siege of nine months, but eventually came into British hands by way of a settlement with the Nizam of Hyderabad after the defeat of Tipu Sultan in 1799.

A tortuous path, shielded from the southwest by a single gate, climbs from the town to the *Fort*. This is contained by walls that run around the rock connecting 14 massive round bastions. The highest part of the site, reached after passing through two more gates, is occupied by a gymnasium and a powder magazine. A small pavilion of polished limestone, known popularly as Murari Rao's Seat, is perched on the edge of a cliff nearby, with fine views across the surrounding landscape. The ruined ancillary buildings include prisons where British soldiers were held. There are also a number of wells in the rocks.

The English cemetery at the base of the fort has several fine graves.

B. Tadpatri

This town, on the south bank of the Pennar River, 53 km. northeast of Anantapur, rose to prominence in the 15th-16th centuries, when it became a provincial outpost of the Vijayanagara empire. The religious monuments erected here at this time are among the most ornate of the period. They are built of local grey-green granite, intricately worked throughout.

The *Chintala Venkataramana Temple*, in the middle of the town, is contained within a rectangle of high walls, entered on the east though a gopura with a steeply pyramidal tower, partly incomplete. Sculptures enliven the granite basement and walls. A ceremonial swing and a tall lamp column stand in the street outside. Most visitors to the temple, however, enter the enclosure through a modest doorway on the north. This gives access to the temple, which is approached through an open mandapa with a central space defined by raised platforms; its eastern end is partly blocked off by a small Garuda shrine. The open mandapa gives access to a smaller closed mandapa with side porches, beyond which is the sanctuary dedicated to Vishnu.

The outer walls of the Vishnu sanctuary and its adjoining mandapa are raised on a finely modelled basement. Sculpted figures between the wall pilasters illustrate episodes from the Krishna and Ramayana legends. Leaping yalis enliven the porch columns. The lintels of the doorways within the porches show Sita's ordeal by fire in the presence of the gods (south), and Rama's final enthronement (north). The multi-storeyed tower over the sanctuary, with later plaster figures, is topped by a hemispherical roof.

The outer columns of the open mandapa are raised on an ornate basement with crouching dwarfs. Maidens bearing offerings, carved almost in the round, grace the central columns on the sides, replaced by yalis on the front (east). The Garuda shrine is treated as a miniature chariot, complete with stone wheels. The interior space of the mandapa is surrounded by piers with leaping yalis ridden by armed warriors. Traces of paintings are seen on the ceilings over the side bays.

A goddess shrine to the northwest of the main temple is connected by way of an open porch with an unusual circular shrine. The eaves overhanging its peripheral columns are animated with carvings of life-like lizards and playful monkeys. The ceiling within is an ornate corbelled dome ringed with tiers of petals, with a central pendant bud. The adjacent circular shrine has multi-faceted basement mouldings and walls.

Overlooking the sandy bed of the Pennar, 1 km. north of the town, stands the *Bugga Ramalingeshvara Temple*. The gopuras on the north and south sides of the temple enclosure, though incomplete, are the most ornate of any in Southern India. The architectural elements are obscured by carved divinities, donors, guardians, sages and dwarfs. The double basement is interrupted by figural niches with lobed and arched profiles; tower-like pediments rise above. Other mouldings are embellished with friezes of jewels and elegant scrollwork. The door jambs in the passageway of the north gopura are carved with maidens clutching luxuriant creepers. Similar maidens bearing lotuses, and riders on horses, decorate the columns in between, with squatting dwarfs beneath.

The west facing temple within the enclosure has a shrine housing a linga set in a pedestal filled with water, perpetually fed by a small spring. The adjoining mandapa is entered through side porches with yali columns. The outer walls of the mandapa and shrine have ornate basement mouldings and pilastered niches. The pyramidal tower over the sanctuary is topped with a hemispherical roof. The temple is aligned with a modest gateway leading down to the river. Immediately to the south is a another smaller temple with two sanctuaries, dedicated to Parvati and Rama. They open off a common mandapa with piers fashioned as cut-out colonettes in double tiers, one above the other, as well as sculptures of rearing yalis and attendant maidens. The outer walls of the two sanctuaries have complex basement series interrupted by miniature niches. The doorways are surrounded by bands of creeper motifs.

C. Somapalam

This isolated village is reached by taking a diversion of about 6 km. from Mulakacheruvu, a small settlement about 130 km. south of Anantapur, on the route to Tirupati. The Chennakeshvara Temple at Somapalem was built by a local governor of the Vijayanagara emperors towards the middle of the 16th century. Just in front (east) of the temple is a remarkable 18 m. high lamp column. This is raised on a double basement enlivened with friezes of dwarfs, mock battles and royal animals. The base of the column shows figures in niches, including a courtly donor, while the tapering shaft is covered with bold undulating stalks and scrollwork. A hall projects out from the temple enclosure, immediately to the right of the ruined entrance gopura. The hall has a central dais, contained by columns carved with richly dressed donor figures and attendant maidens. A lobed wall niche on one side is provided with an unusual stone bolster.

The temple within the walled enclosure is approached through an open mandapa, with colonettes on the outer piers overhung by deeply curved eaves. The brick parapet above shows niches devoid of plaster sculptures. A small Garuda shrine, treated as a chariot, with small stone wheels on the sides, protrudes partly into the mandapa. Traces of faded paintings illustrating Ramayana episode, can be made out on the ceiling within. The central aisle leads to the main sanctuary.

The hall set into the southwest corner of the enclosure contains a small pavilion, exquisitely worked in grey-green granite. Its four columns have slender cut-out colonettes with carvings of maidens holding lotuses. The shrine beyond is entered through a doorway with a lintel embellished with a frieze showing Rama enthroned.

D. PENUKONDA

This town, 74 km. south of Anantapur, was a strategic citadel for the Vijayanagara emperors from the 14th century onwards. However, after the capital was sacked and burnt in 1565, Penukonda served for a time as the chief headquarters of the Aravidu rulers, successors to the Vijayanagara throne. Repeated raids on Penukonda by the forces of Bijapur [23A] and Golconda [26E] persuaded these rulers to shift eventually to Chandragiri [35C]. The Qutb Shahis captured Penukonda in 1610, retaining it as an important outpost of their kingdom; it was subsequently taken by the Mughals and the Marathas.

Penukonda is dominated by a rocky hill, with Fortification climbing up its steep sides to create an approximately triangular fort. Vestiges of past occupation lining the path to the summit include gateways, watchtowers, collapsing halls and small shrines. The walls beneath the hill contain much of the city in a quadrangle. The major gateways, with bent entrances, are located in the middle of the north and east sides, while a large tank provides protection on the south. Religious and royal monuments face onto the north-south road that runs through the middle of the town.

The *Parshvanatha Temple*, facing east onto the road, enshrines a remarkable sculpture from the 12th-13th century Hoysala era. This depicts the Jain saviour sanding in front of an undulating serpent. The nearby *Sher Shah Mosque* belongs to the period of the Qutb Shahi occupation, as is obvious from the plaster decoration on the arcaded facade, and the bulbous profile of the dome that rises on a petalled drum. The vaulted bays of the prayer chamber are defined by lobed arches. The mihrab is particularly ornate.

About 250 m. further south are the twin *Rama* and *Shiva Temples*, which stand side by side, both dating from the Vijayanagara period. The pilastered walls of their long low facades are covered with carvings: Ramayana and Krishna legends on the 15th century Rama temple; scenes from Shaiva mythology on its neighbour. Sanctuaries in both temples have pyramidal towers capped with hemispherical roofs. The sanctuary of the later, 16th century Shiva temple is enclosed within a dark passageway, with carved icons in wall niches. The mandapa that precedes this shrine has piers with colonettes. A later mandapa adjoins the Rama temple, in front of which stands a lamp column and a gateway.

The nearby *Gagan Mahal* is a courtly monument belonging to the period when Penukonda served as an imperial capital. It resembles pavilions in the royal enclosures at Vijayanagara [20C]. An arcaded verandah leads to a vaulted hall with chambers at the rear. A domed pavilion above is roofed with an octagonal pyramidal tower capped by a ribbed finial. An adjoining staircase block is capped with a similar, but smaller tower. (These features anticipate the larger and more symmetrical schemes at Chandragiri.) About 50 m. to the east is a detached *Square Pavilion*, the unadorned sloping walls of which are overhung by curved eaves; an octagonal pyramidal tower rises above. Richly worked plaster decoration is preserved inside. The adjacent well has an ornate entrance fashioned in the semblance of a lion. The free-standing gopura in the vicinity is an 18th century construction, apparently unattached to any temple.

The city of Penukonda now extends beyond the fortification walls. The *Dargah of Babayya*, about 500 m. to the north, was much patronised by Haidar Ali and Tipu Sultan of Srirangapattana [15C]. It remains a popular place of worship, with a great fair in December.

E. GORANTLA

This small town on the east bank of the Chitravati River, 30 km. southeast of Penukonda, is worth visiting for the Madhavarya Temple, a fine example of the early Vijayanagara style, erected in 1354 by a local chief. In spite of its relatively plain exterior the temple preserves interesting reliefs. The compound in which it stands is entered through a massive gopura, never completed and now neglected. The open mandapa of the temple has balcony seating on three sides, the peripheral columns partly transformed into yalis standing on elephants. The beasts have fierce faces with protruding eyes and open jaws. Internal columns have their shafts divided into blocks sculpted with Krishna legends and Ramayana episodes, scenes from the story of Narasimha, and acrobats, fighters and musicians. The shafts terminate in double capitals and elegant lotus brackets with pendant buds. The ceiling over the central bay of the mandapa has a larger flower surrounded by petals. The doorway leading into a second, enclosed mandapa is surmounted by a frieze of Rama enthroned.

F. Lepakshi

The Virabhadra temple in this small town is worth visiting for its outstanding sculptures and ceiling paintings, which represent the climax of Vijayanagara art in the middle of the 16th century. Lepakshi lies 12 km. west of NH7, just near the point where the highway meets the Karnataka border, 35 km. south of Penukonda. (Lepakshi is about 120 km. north of Bengaluru, from where it may easily be reached as a day excursion.)

The first feature to be seen on arriving at Lepakshi is a colossal *Monolithic Nandi*, 1 km. east of the town. This imposing granite sculpture shows Shiva's mount seated comfortably to one side. The animal is ceremonially decked with garlands and bells.

Monolithic Nandi, Lepakshi.

The *Virabhadra Temple* itself is the work of two brothers, Viranna and Virupanna, governors of Penukonda under the Vijayanagara emperor Achyutaraya in about 1540. The monument, which occupies a rising granite outcrop to the south of the town, stands in the middle of two concentric irregular enclosures. The outer enclosure is entered through gateways on three sides, that on the north being most often used by visitors. This is somewhat awkwardly angled in relationship to the inner east gateway, which leads directly to an open mandapa with a large central space. The peripheral columns of the mandapa are elevated on an ornate basement, with blocks carved as horses and warriors. The columns have slender colonettes, and are overhung by deeply curving eaves. The central space within is defined by massive piers fashioned with trios of figures at the corners: Natesha between Brahma and a drummer (northeast); dancing maiden between a male drummer and cymbalist (southeast); Parvati between female attendants (southwest); and a drummer between three-legged Bhringi and Bhikshatana-murti (northwest). Musicians and ascetics adorn the intermediate piers.

The extensive paintings that cover the ceiling of the mandapa constitute the most important examples of Vijayanagara pictorial art. The frescos have recently been cleaned to reveal the fresh black linework and the vibrant ochre, brown and green colours. The compositions are of outstanding interest for the details of costumes and facial types. They are arranged in long strips that correspond with the bays that surround the central space of the mandapa, and illustrate legends from the Puranas and the Mahabharata and Ramayana epics. One of the most interesting composition shows the boar hunt of Shiva. This animated forested scene forms the climax of the story of Arjuna's encounter with Shiva as the hunter (west corridor).

Steps on the south side of the mandapa with the sculpted piers and ceiling paintings ascend to an inner enclosed mandapa. Its outer walls (as visible from the outer mandapa) are covered with friezes of elephants, as well as the legend of Sriyala and of Arjuna fighting Shiva disguised as the hunter. The central space of the inner mandapa is defined by piers fashioned as yalis; the animals are doubled at the corners, angling outwards. Figures carved on the sides of the piers include Shiva dancing, and spearing the demon, as well as an icon of Durga (northwest corner), now worshipped independently. The ceiling above has a large painted composition of standing Virabhadra in the company of one of the sponsors of the monument, Virupana, and his wife. The principal cult deity of the temple, a fierce figure decked with skulls and carrying weapons, receives veneration in the principal shrine on the south side of the mandapa. Side shrines are dedicated to Keshava, Kali, Uma and the linga, the last being partly set into a natural cavern. The shrines are modest structure capped with brick towers, visible only from the outside.

Additional features of interest are seen in the outer compound of the Virabhadra temple. Inscriptions are carved onto the blocks of the inner enclosure wall, especially near the northeast corner where they even extend onto the bedrock. A large, unfinished mandapa occupies the southwest corner of the inner enclosure. Its peripheral columns are sculpted with figures of sages, while those in the middle have divinities. No roof slabs seem ever to have been added. A natural boulder to the east of the mandapa is partly fashioned as a huge coiled *Monolithic Naga*. Its multi-hooded head rears up to shelter a polished granite linga.

G. HEMAVATI

This somewhat remote village, located 80 km. southwest of Penukonda via Madakasira, once served as the capital of the Nolambas. The temples erected here testify to the distinctive architectural idiom developed by these rulers in the 9th-10th centuries. Though some of the finest sculptures from Hemavati have been removed to the Government Museum in Chennai [36D], others survive in situ.

The *Doddeshvara Temple* is a modest, unadorned structure with regularly spaced wall pilasters. The perforated stone windows are adorned with standing divinities, including a gracefully posed figure of Ganga (east), as well as foliate designs. The internal columns are decorated with looped garlands in sharp relief. The adjacent *Siddheshvara Temple* has been much reconstructed. Original columns with sculpted panels are seen in the mandapa in front of the sanctuary, which houses an impressive seated Bhairava image. The Virupaksha temple has a finely carved doorway.

Additional sculptures are displayed in a small museum near to the temples. Also of interest in the vicinity are two tanks, one with a bent flight of steps, the other now overgrown.

34. Cuddapah

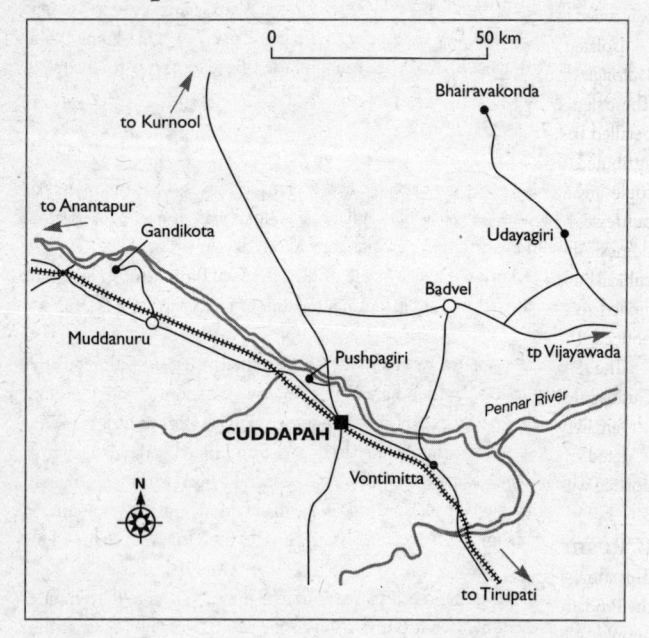

Cuddapah makes a serviceable stopover on any journey from Vijayawada [29], Kurnool [32] or Anantapur [33] to Tirupati [35], 140 km. to the southeast. While there are only a few historical features in Cuddapah itself [A], worthwhile excursions may be made to the temples at Pushpagiri [B] and the fort at Gandikota [C]. Each of these sites may be reached as a day trip from the city, with the possibility of continuing on to Tadpatri [33B] and Anantapur.

A full day will be required to reach the mountain stronghold of Udayagiri [D] and the rock-cut shrines at Bhairavakonda [E]. Visitors travelling from Cuddapah to Tirupati may also wish to inspect the temple at Vontimitta [F].

A. CUDDAPAH

This city is located on a major route along the Pennar Valley, leading from interior Andhra Pradesh through the Eastern Ghats to the Bay of Bengal Coast. The Cuddapah region, though somewhat arid, is famous for its crops of turmeric, onions and melon. Quarrying has become a significant industry, and Cuddapah stone is now widely exported.

Cuddapah as annexed by the Mughals in 1687. The line of commanders that they installed here assumed almost independent status under the title of Nawabs, until they were ousted by Haidar Ali of Srirangapattana [15C] in 1776. The city was ceded to the British after the defeat of Tipu Sultan in 1799.

Isolated vestiges of the Nawabs are scattered throughout Cuddapah. Two *Watchtowers* in the heart of the city are all that survive of the dismantled palace. These slender structures have arched openings and miniature domes sitting on petalled bases. The *Azam Mosque*, dating from the early 18th century, is also attributed to the Cuddapah Nawabs. Its six-bayed prayer hall is entered through triple arcades overhung by sloping eaves on ornate brackets. The circular buttresses have miniature arcaded balconies and slender finials with miniature domes. About 200 m. to the south is the *Dargah of Syed Ahmed Sahib*. This cubical building has triple arched recesses on each side, surmounted by tiers of arched recesses. The corner buttresses resemble those on the mosque just noticed. The dome is low and flattish.

The *English Cemetery*, on the outskirts of the city, is a reminder of Cuddapah's former foreign population. The tomb of Webb Thakeray, a civil servant in the Madras Presidency and uncle of William Makepeace Thakeray, is dated 1807. Nearby Christ Church, erected in 1881, has an arcaded portico with slender columns.

B. PUSHPAGIRI

This somewhat remote village is reached along a road that runs 6 km. west from the Prodattur road near Chennur, 17 km. north of Cuddapah. Two groups of temples at Pushpagiri date back to the 12th-13th centuries, when the region was under the sway of a line of Chola rulers, remotely connected with those of the same name in the Tamil zone. The monuments were substantially renovated during the Vijayanagara period in the 15th-16th centuries. The village is today the seat of a well known Vaishnava matha.

The main group of temples at Pushpagiri is situated north of the village, near the west bank of the Pennar River. The principal monument here is the *Vaidyanatheshvara Temple*, a typical late Chola styled building. It stands in the middle of an enclosure entered through a small side gate. Carved panels are set up in the surrounded colonnades. The *Trikuteshvara Temple*, immediately north, has three shrines with plain pilastered walls, each capped with a square-domical roof, opening off a common mandapa.

The nearby *Bhimalingeshvara Temple* comprises a shrine and mandapa raised on a double basement, with carvings on the lowest band. The walls have sculpted panels set between the niches and pilasters. The pyramidal tower rises in an ascending series of projections and miniature roof forms, and is crowned by a prominent square-domical roof. The mandapa is somewhat unfinished on the front (east), where double steps flanked by balustrades climb to a small platform that supports a Nandi sculpture.

The *Chennakeshvara Temple*, the most artistic at Pushpagiri, is picturesquely situated beneath a bare hill rising from the east bank of the Pennar, directly opposite the village. The temple faces west towards the river, which has to be forded in order to reach the towered entrance to the enclosure. The Chennakeshvara consists of three shrines opening off two mandapas. Not all parts of the complex were finished at one time, as is clear from the makeshift walls on the front (west). The basements of the shrines are remarkable for the dense carvings of animals and figures, interspersed with fully modelled pots sprouting foliation, surmounted by pilasters with ornate circular shafts. Even the spouts for the outflow of libations are highly embellished.

The walls of the two west-facing shrines of the Chennakeshvara temple are almost entirely covered with reliefs showing Ramayana and Krishna episodes, the story of Arjuna fighting Shiva disguised as the hunter, and repeated icons of dancing Shiva in the company of attendant maidens, dancers and musicians. The most important compositions are headed by foliated frames. The pyramidal towers that rise over the shrines have receding storeys, with pilastered projections capped by square or hemispherical roofs. The less decorated south-facing shrine shows sculptures of Brahma and Dakshinamurti on its outer walls.

C. Gandikota

This celebrated citadel, 75 km. northwest of Cuddapah, is reached by turning north at Muddanuru on the Anantapur road, and then west just before the bridge across the Pennar River, and following the road for about 8 km. Gandikota, which means Gorge Fort, is aptly named, as the citadel is perched dramatically about 100 m. above a rugged gap, no more than 200 m. wide, through which the river forces its way.

Gandikota's history goes back to Vijayanagara times, but the fort itself dates mainly from the period of the Qutb Shahis, who captured it in 1589. In spite of claims by the Vijayanagara rulers of Chandragiri [35C], the forces of the Qutb Shahis continued to occupy Gandikota, and were still in control when François Tavernier, the famous French traveller, halted there in 1652. Gandikota was captured by Aurangzeb's general in 1687, and by the beginning of the 18th century had come under the control of the Cuddapah Nawabs. Haidar Ali improved and garrisoned the fort, but it was taken by the British in 1791.

Few citadels in Andhra Pradesh enjoy such a spectacular natural setting, yet this is not immediately apparent on arrival. The first view of the fort is of a line of massive stone Walls with prominent square bastions, topped by a crenellated parapet. The main entrance, on the east, is through a sequence of barbican enclosures that leads to an arched gate. This is surmounted by battlements with six squat finials. A *Triple-Storeyed Tower* rises above the houses of the small settlement inside the fort. This elegant structure, possibly a remnant of a Qutb Shahi palace, has arched opening below and fretted windows for pigeons above. A short distance north is an imposing *Jami Mosque* standing in a large quadrangle, that may have served as a caravanserai. The triple-arched openings of its facade are overhung by sloping eaves; above rises a parapet with arched openings. The massive circular buttresses at the corners are capped with minarets topped by domical finials. A large *Granary* with a vaulted roof stands to the north.

The dilapidated *Ranganayaka Temple*, beyond the granary, is entered through a collapsing gateway devoid of any tower. The mandapa inside has finely finished animal piers, but is otherwise in poor condition. An unusual feature is the architect's measuring rod incised onto the enclosure walls to the south of the main shrine.

The *Madhavaraya Temple*, west of the settlement in Gandikota fort, is more impressive. It is recognised by its gopura, which has a four-storeyed, steeply pyramidal tower. This incomplete and worn gateway has elaborately modelled basement mouldings and crowded wall pilasters. The double chambers flanking the passageway interior of the gopura have columns with figural carvings. The main shrine inside the enclosure is preceded by a spacious mandapa, with elegantly proportioned piers overhung by deeply curved eaves. The interior space is defined by columns fashioned as rearing yalis with riders, some in European dress.

D. UDAYAGIRI

The fort at Udayagiri lies 98 km. northeast of Cuddapah; the last part of the journey from Badvel passes through the forested highlands of the Eastern Ghats. Udayagiri occupies the comparatively level top of two narrow hills that run north-south, rising more than 600 m. above the plain. The sides of these hills are so precipitous as to be virtually inaccessible; the rocky bluffs at the top are nearly 300 m. high in some places. Because of these natural defences Udayagiri was the preferred citadel for all those who controlled this part of Andhra Pradesh.

The site first enters history as a stronghold of the Reddis of Kondavidu [29M], from whom it was captured in 1512 by Krishnadevaraya of Vijayanagara [20B-C]. It then came under the command of the Qutb Shahis, who occupied it until the Mughal invasion of 1687. It had already fallen into disuse by the time the fort passed into the possession of the Cuddapah Nawabs in the course of the 18th century.

At least two hours are required to ascend the *Fort*, the preferred route being from the west. From the path it is possible to view the panorama of ruined bastions, lookout towers and gateways that gird the tops of the hills. In spite of their considerable scope, the ramparts are unremarkable. Of greater interest is the *Mosque* on the highest part of the west hill, though its facade and flanking towers are now virtually hidden by growth. An inscription over the mihrab within the prayer hall indicates that it was erected in 1643 by Ghazi Ali, a general of the Qutb Shahis. Numerous carved blocks indicate that it was partly built of re-used temple materials. The granary nearby is an earlier structure, possibly a renovated temple mandapa.

Almost nothing survives of the walls and gateways that protected Udayagiri at the base of the eastern flank of the hills. The only historical feature to be seen is the dilapidated 16th century *Ranganayaka Temple*, which stands at the end of the main street of the town. Its towerless east gopura leads into an outer enclosure, which has another smaller gopura on the south, with a virtually intact pyramidal tower. The main shrine within has been despoiled.

The *Krishna Temple*, another 16th century monument, is situated 1 km. south of the town, overlooking a stepped square tank. Its main shrine is damaged, but several carvings of Balakrishna can be made out on its outer walls. The nearby gopura serves as an entrance to an attractively shaded compound. A broken mandapa here preserves finely finished yali columns.

E. BHAIRAVAKONDA

Eight *Rock-Cut Shrines* at this remote site, about 45 km. northwest of Udayagiri, are among the earliest Hindu monuments in Andhra Pradesh. They date from the 7th-8th century, during which period the Early Chalukyas and Pallavas struggled for control of this region.

The Bhairavakonda shrines are situated on the bank of a stream at the bottom of a small wooded ravine, near to a 60 m. high waterfall. Though excavated at different levels, the shrines are almost identical. They consist of columned verandahs sheltered by curved eaves with false windows, leading to small sanctuaries with polished black basalt lingas. Seated lions adorn the bases of the outer columns. Icons of Shiva, Vishnu, Brahma and Ganesha are carved onto the verandah walls, and guardian figures appear at either side of the sanctuary doorways. Some shrines have Nandis set into roofless courts.

The shrines all face towards the diminutive *Durga Bhairava Temple*, after which the site is named. This houses an unusual eight-faced goddess.

F. VONTIMITTA

This town, 28 km. east of Cuddapah, is notable for the *Kodandarama Temple*, the largest in the area. This 16th century monument stands within a rectangle of walls, entered through three imposing gopuras. That on the east, crowned with a steep five-storeyed tower, is approached by a long flight of steps. The unadorned treatment of the walls of the temple within contrasts with the elaborate sculptures on the mandapa that precedes it. The columns here have cut-out colonettes, on which attendant maidens are carved, replaced by icons of Krishna and Vishnu on the central supports on the south. Maidens and deities are combined in triple sets at each corner, a unique device. The central space within the mandapa is defined by yali piers, the animals being doubled at the corners, where they frame attendant figures. The ceiling over the central space is raised on brackets with multiple corbels.

35. Tirupati

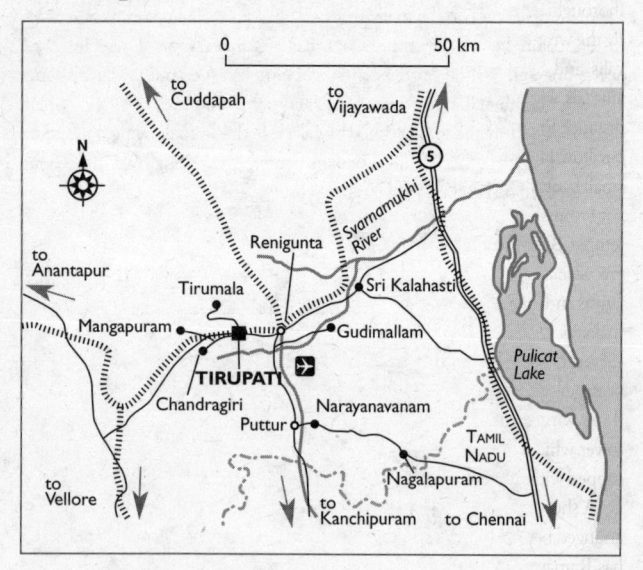

Located in the extreme southeast corner of Andhra Pradesh, this city is the destination of countless pilgrims who make the ascent to Tirumala in the nearby hills to worship at the Venkateshvara shrine, reputedly the wealthiest in Southern India. The substantial revenues earned by the local temple management, known as the Tirumala Tirupati Devasthanams (TTD), have funded renovations at many religious sites in the vicinity, as well as supporting civic projects and numerous charitable and educational institutions.

Other than a visit to the temples at Tirupati [A] and Tirumala [B], which may be covered in a single day, a side trip is easily made to the nearby fortress of Chandragiri [C] and the religious monument at Mangapuram [D].

Excursions to the early shrine at Gudimallam [E] and the popular temple at Sri Kalahasti [F] follow the Suvarnamukhi River on its course east towards the Bay of Bengal. Both places can be reached in a single day.

The lesser known temples at Narayanavanam [G] and Nagalapuram [H] can be visited on the way to Chennai [36], 150 km. to the southeast.

A. Tirupati

Dramatically sited at the foot of a bluff of red sandstone that marks the beginning of the Tirumala Hills, Tirupati is a lively commercial city focused on the Govindaraja temple. Its crowded streets echo the rectangular plan of the monument, which is laid out on an east-west axis, approached along a thoroughfare lined with shops and stalls. The eastern end of this road is marked by the west-facing *Anjaneya Shrine*, of interest for its elaborate carvings. Trios of yalis and horses mark the corner columns of its mandapa. Similar cut-out animals, with riders on the columns, flank the central aisle of the interior. A short distance to the east of the Anjaneya shrine is a large square *Tank* with a central pavilion. Here take place float festivals, in which sacred images are displayed in small boats illuminated by lamps.

From the Anjaneya shrine the road runs west towards the Govindaraja temple. Before it reaches the temple, however, it passes through a magnificent, *Free-Standing Gopura*, erected in 1624. Its passageway is flanked by decorated jambs and lintels carried on ornate brackets. Maidens on either side, standing on makaras, clutch creepers with curling stalks that frame miniature divinities. A carved portrait of the sponsor of the gopura appears on the south wall of the passageway. This shows Matla Ananataraja, a local chief, in the company of his three wives, paying homage to Govindaraja. The seven-storeyed pyramidal tower, which rises almost 50 m. above, is covered with finely finished projections capped with model roof forms, with openings in the middle of each storey.

A short distance west are the twin enclosures of the *Govindaraja Temple*, one arranged behind the other, linked by modestly scaled gopuras. The outer gopura has Ramayana scenes carved onto the passageway walls. A tall swing pavilion outside has columns covered with elegant foliate designs. Twin shrines at the western end of the inner enclosure are dedicated to Ranganatha, the reclining form of Vishnu, and Krishna with consorts. A minor shrine nearby has an icon of Lakshmi identified with the poetess Andal. The sanctuaries open off a common mandapa, the piers of which have crouching lions and extended brackets. The mandapa in the southwest corner has finely finished colonettes on the outer piers; the central space is lined with yalis projecting inwards. An exquisitely finished pavilion in the middle has columns of grey-green granite and a wooden roof.

Immediately north of the Govindaraja temple stands the Kacheri Nammalvar temple, now converted into the *Shri Venkateshvara Museum of Temple Art*, entered on the south through a small gopura. The photographs, architectural models, diagrams and metal ritual items shown here explain the principles of the Vaishnava artistic tradition. The exhibits are displayed in the spacious mandapa that precedes the shrine.

B. Tirumala

The wooded crags of the Tirumala Hills, rising about 700 m. above Tirupati, provide a splendid natural setting for the Venkateshvara temple, 22 km. distance from Tirupati via a winding steep road. Pious devotees make the trip by foot, starting at the modern gopura at the base of the hill, and then following a picturesque path through the forest. Because of the great crowds that regularly exceed 10,000 in a single day, worshippers often have to wait in line for hours before entering the temple. Pilgrims come from all over the country and abroad; their offerings in notes and coins, sometimes even in gold and silver, are sorted in the hundi, or treasury, within the complex.

The worship of Venkateshvara, Lord of the Seven Hills, is traced back to the 9th-10th century Chola era. It was, however, under the patronage of the 15th-16th century emperors of Vijayanagara [20B-C] that the shrine was expanded and Venkateshvara adopted as the protective deity of the royal family. The promotion of this god, known variously as Venkataramana, Tiruvengalanatha and Srinivasa, amounted to no less than an imperial cult, the god appearing together with rulers on their seals and coins. (He is nowadays portrayed with a black face and his eyes covered, to prevent his gaze from scorching his devotees.) The emperor Krishnadevaraya visited Tirumala seven times, making lavish gifts and endowments on each occasion. His portrait and those of his queens are still be seen within the complex. Achyutaraya, his successor, who began his career at nearby Chandragiri, ordered special ceremonies at Tirumala and Sri Kalahasti before hastening to the Vijayanagara capital where he was crowned in 1529. The Tirumala shrine continued to attract benefactions under the later Vijayanagara rulers of the Aravidu line in the first half of the 17th century.

The *Venkateshvara Temple* has been renovated extensively to provide facilities for the ever expanding numbers of worshippers, thereby obscuring many original features. The complex is contained with a rectangle of walls, entered in the middle of the east side through a modest 13th century gopura; the tower is later. The portico immediately inside the gateway is a 17th century structure, with warriors on yalis projecting carved onto the columns. Almost life-size sculptures of the Vijayanagara emperors paying homage to Venkateshvara are displayed here. The brass images of Krishnadevaraya and his two queens (right) and a polished granite sculpture of Achyutaraya (left) are the finest portraits of the Vijayanagara era. Two mandapas with carved columns, those on the front and side aisles fashioned as rearing yalis, stand to the south of the entrance gopura. A small pavilion inside one of these halls has ornate supports, with cut-out colonettes overhung by curving eaves. The north part of the enclosure is occupied by the kitchen where food is prepared for pilgrims; sweets known as laddus are a speciality. A lamp column cloaked in gold sheet stands in front of the gopura that gives access to the inner enclosure. Similar metal covers the threshold and jambs of the doorway itself.

The main shrine in the middle of the inner enclosure is a modest Chola period structure. The tower, with a hemispherical roof covered in gold sheet and topped by a gilded pot finial, has been rebuilt. The preceding mandapa has sculpted columns overhung by curved eaves, also cloaked in gold. A portion of the interior is given over to the hundi, already noted. The standing crowned image of Vishnu within the temple sanctuary is ornamented with diamonds and rubies; metal icons of Shridevi and Bhudevi are placed at either side.

The remainder of the enclosure is occupied by colonnades and minor shrines, one 14th century example housing an image of Varadaraja, and an office where donations to the temple can be made.

A small *Art Museum* is situated in the colonnade outside the temple, opposite the east gopura. This has a collection of stone, metal and wooden sculptures, as well as paintings and copper-plate inscriptions, many from Vijayanagara times. There are also votive figurines, lamps, musical instruments and arms.

A large rectangular *Tank*, with stepped sides and a pavilion in the middle of the water, is located a short distance to the north.

C. CHANDRAGIRI

This citadel, 11 km. west of Tirupati, attained importance during the Vijayanagara period. It was the headquarters of Narasimha Saluva, founder of the second line of Vijayanagara rulers in 1485. It was also the principal capital of the Aravidus in the first half of the 17th century, after they shifted here from Penukonda [33D]. It was from here that Venkatapatideva (1586-1614), the greatest of the Aravidu rulers, presided over the diminishing territories of Vijayanagara. The civil war that broke out at his death hastened the dissolution of the empire.

Royal and religious structures at Chandragiri occupy an impressive site, on the southern flank of a great granite hill. *Massive Walls* with bastions of different shapes, surrounded by a ditch, contain these features in an irregular quadrangular fort. An east-west road, passing through a succession of gateways, defines a sequence of three compounds, with the palaces situated in the middle compound. Further massive walls climb up the side of the hill, with lookout towers surveying the approaches from all directions.

The north-facing *Raja Mahal*, traditionally associated with Venkatapatideva, is the masterpiece of Vijayanagara palace architecture. It is both larger and more formal in layout than earlier courtly buildings at Hampi [20B]. Its facades are arranged in three arcaded storeys, linked by eaves and walkways, with a rooftop pavilion topped by a steeply pyramidal tower in the middle, and smaller versions of this tower capping staircase blocks at the four corners. The interior of the palace is dominated by a central double-height audience chamber. The fresh plaster-work gives little idea of the original decoration. A tank shaded by trees stands immediately to the north.

The nearby *Rana Mahal* is smaller, but similar in appearance to the Raja Mahal; however, a passageway passes through the lower storeys, indicating that the building may have served as a gateway. Its upper level has a domed chamber and an arcaded verandah. The end staircase towers are topped by octagonal pyramidal roofs. The central tower resembles that of the Raja Mahal, but is slightly higher. The east facade preserves traces of the original exuberant plasterwork. Here, foliate motifs embellish arched openings, with medallions filled with geometric designs above. The Rana Mahal faces east onto a court once surrounded by colonnades, now mostly lost. The excavated remains of a royal residence are seen to the north.

Several *Abandoned Temples* stand in the vicinity of the palaces. These modest 15th-16th century structures have small stone sanctuaries topped by pyramidal brick towers with hemispherical roofs. The outer walls have regularly spaced pilasters and small niches, but there are no sculptures.

The *Kodandarama Temple*, at one end of the village of Chandragiri, 1 km. east of the fort, is still under worship. Its sanctuary is approached through an open mandapa and an inner closed mandapa, the latter with triple niches on each side wall. Finely detailed walls are visible in the passageway, which was only added later around the sanctuary.

D. Mangapuram

The *Kalyana Venkateshvara Temple* at this site, 14 km. west of Tirupati, has recently been reinvested for worship by the TTD. The monument is of historical interest, having been founded in 1540 by a governor of Chandragiri. The temple is entered on the east through an imposing gopura with a renovated five-storeyed tower. The shrine in the middle of the rectangular enclosure is preceded by an open mandapa with yali columns; the animals are tripled at the corners, where riders are also seen. The entrance steps on the front skirt a small Garuda shrine. The walls of the mandapa and sanctuary present rows of shallow pilasters, many standing in relief pots. The pyramidal tower has two storeys capped with a hemispherical roof.

E. Gudimallam

This somewhat remote village on the south bank of the Svarnamukhi River lies 30 km. east of Tirupati. It is reached by turning east off the Puttur road, about 5 km. south of Renigunta. Gudimallam is famous for the remarkable *Linga* venerated within the sanctuary of the *Parashurameshvara Temple*. This 1.5 m. high phallic emblem of Shiva dates back to the 1st century BCE, Satavahana period, making it the earliest such cult object in Southern India. It is of interest for the well preserved male figure carved onto its naturalistic shaft. He is shown with matted hair, holding a trident in one of his two hands, and a slaughtered deer in the other. The lower part of the body is clearly visible beneath the folds of the costume. Sometimes identified as Shiva himself, the figure is more likely to represent a worshipper of the god.

Linga in the Parashuraneshvara Temple, Gudimallam.

Excavations indicate that the linga once stood freely, surrounded by a low stone railing. During the Pallava period, in the 9th century, this open-air shrine was contained within an apsidal-ended sanctuary preceded by an antechamber. The temple was further extended under the Cholas in the 12th century, but the apsidal-ended tower was only added in the 16th century. The building was again remodelled only a few years back.

F. Sri Kalahasti

Like Tirupati and Tirumala, Sri Kalahasti is also a celebrated pilgrimage shrine but the deity worshipped here is Shiva rather than Vishnu. The town is attractively situated on the south bank of the Svarnamukhi River, 33 km. east of Tirupati, at the foot of the Kailasa Hills where the valley opens up into the plain. While the bathing ghats and shrines on the hill attract a steady flow of devotees, religious life in the town is mainly concentrated in the Kalahastishvara temple. This complex enshrines the vayu (air) linga, one of the five elemental emblems of Shiva in Southern India. Sri Kalahasti is also associated with Kannappa, the legendary hunter who plucked out his eye in a frenzy of adoration, to offer it to the linga. A small shrine consecrated to this saintly devotee of Shiva is located at the summit of the hill above the town.

The villages around Sri Kalahasti are known for the production of kalamkaris, the brightly coloured cotton fabrics showing traditional mythological subjects, produced by a mixture of printed and dyeing techniques.

Sri Kalahasti was until recently dominated by an imposing *Gopura* that stood freely at the end of the main street of the town. This towered gateway was erected by Krishnadevaraya in 1516 but altogether collapsed in May 2010.

A sequence of two gateways, one with a portico, leads to the outer enclosure of the *Kalahastishvara Temple*. This wraps around the main temple on three sides. On the east is the rocky side of the hill; on the west are the popular bathing ghats, reached through another gopura. Mandapas, pavilions, lamp columns and altars crowd the enclosure. The large mandapa in the southwest corner is raised on a high basement with finely carved friezes; the peripheral piers have animal carvings.

The temple itself is contained within a rectangle of high walls, with a single towered entrance on the south. The four shrines inside all date from the Vijayanagara period. The most important shrine is that opening to the west, which houses a curiously elongated linga protected by a brass cobra hood. A brass-covered lamp column stands in front. Other shrines dedicated to Jnanaprasumbha, Dakshinamurti and Ganesha open off a 19th century colonnade. This is laid out as a vast corridor that surrounds the principal linga sanctuary on four sides. Massive piers have leaping horses and riders lining the approach from the south, while animal brackets cover the side aisles. Among the bronzes on display here are processional icons of Shiva and a complete set of the 63 Nayanmars (north corridor). A stone representation of Kannappa as a hunter is housed in the west corridor.

A short distance south of the Kalahastishvara temple is the dilapidated and overgrown *Manikanteshvara Temple*. Dating from the 12th century Chola era, this monument stands in a square enclosure built up to the base of the hill. Its east facing sanctuary and mandapa have finely detailed basement mouldings, pilastered walls and niches, the last filled with icons of Shiva. A towered gateway is capped with an enlarged vaulted roof, much renovated in later times.

G. Narayanavanam

This small town, 35 km. south of Tirupati, just 2 km. east of Puttur, is famous for its weaving, with looms set up in the main street. The *Kalyana Venkateshvara Temple* was established here in 1541, but was extended in later times. The large gopura on the east is of interest for the relief compositions in the passageway. Ceiling panels here show a kneeling soldier with a gun shooting a prancing deer, between a pair of geese and a sexual scene; the central lotus is surrounded by the dikpalas. Doorway lintels have carvings of a fish and makaras, a camel with a rider, and Kama and Rati on parrots. The second gopura, defining the inner enclosure of the temple, has an entrance portico with cut-out colonettes. The sanctuary, which is approached through a mandapa with side porches, is roofed with a brick tower capped by a hemisphere.

H. Nagalapuram

An important monument of ambitious proportions stands in this small town, 24 km. east of Narayanavanam. The *Veda Narayana Temple* dates back to Chola times, but in the first half of the 16th century it became the nucleus of a vast complex with three concentric enclosures linked by axial gateways.

The complex is entered from the west through a grandiose gopura, begun by Krishnadevaraya. Intended as one of the largest projects of the Vijayanagara era, comparable in size to that at Sri Kalahasti, the gateway was never finished beyond its imposing granite basement and walls. A path leads to a second, smaller gopura, also attributed to Krishnadevaraya. This is raised on a double basement with pilastered walls devoid of niches. The gateway has been much repaired, as can be seen from the crisp whitewashed details of its five-storeyed tower. A lamp column stands on an ornate plinth within. Among the subsidiary structures standing in the second enclosure is an east facing goddess shrine with finely finished walls. A portico with colonettes and yalis on the outer piers gives access to the main temple, where a mandapa lined with animal columns leads to the original shrine surrounded by a colonnade. The shrine has an ornate basement embellished with Krishna scenes and diverse figures. Carved icons of Shiva and Brahma are fitted into the wall niches.

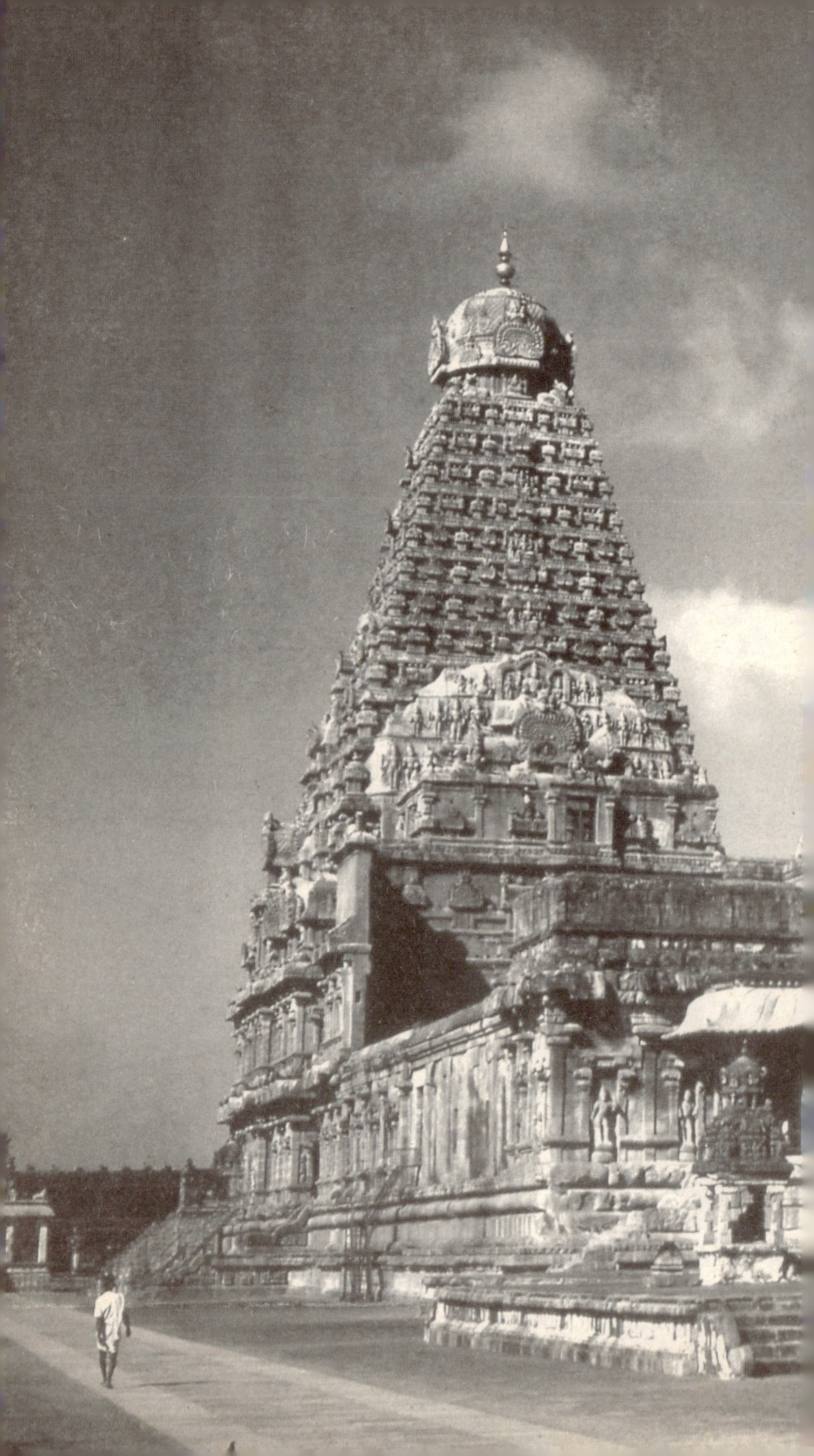

Brihadishvara Temple, Thanjavur

TAMIL NADU

Tamil Nadu

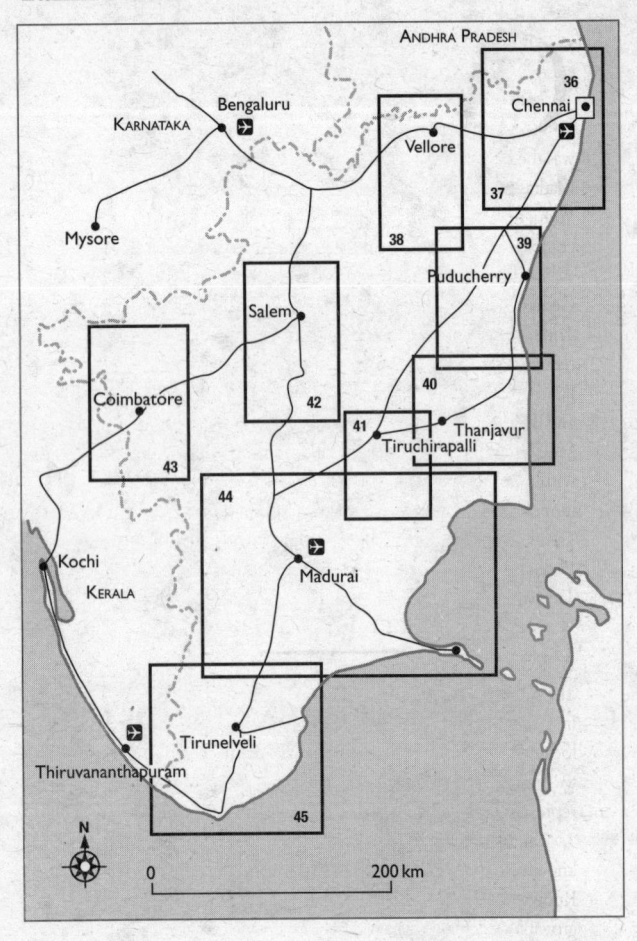

36. Chennai

Chennai, the capital of Tamil Nadu, formerly Madras, is built on the shore of the Bay of Bengal, but lacks any natural harbour. Even so, from its foundation in 1639 until the middle of the 19th century, when it was eclipsed by Mumbai (then known as Bombay) [1], Madras was the busiest and wealthiest seaport in Southern India. Throughout its history Madras is closely identified with European commerce, as testified by its remaining Portuguese and British vestiges. The city also incorporates earlier settlements, complete with temples and markets, that preserve their traditional Tamil character.

Two full days may be occupied with the major sights of Fort St George [A], George Town [B], Poonamallee High Road [C], Anna Salai [E], Chepauk and Triplicane [F], and Mylapore and San Thomé [G]. But additional time will be required to visit the art collections of the Government Museum in the Pantheon Complex [D], as well as the outlying districts of Adyar [H], Guindy and the two Mounts of St Thomas [I].

Chennai makes a convenient base from which to visit historic localities within an approximate 100 km. arc. These are described in the following itinerary [37]. The city also makes a logical starting point from which to tour Tamil Nadu, and may be combined with itineraries for Vellore [38], Puducherry [39] and points further south. The temples in and around Tirupati [35] in Andhra Pradesh are also easily accessible from Chennai.

A. FORT ST GEORGE

The tour of Chennai described here begins at Fort St George, the site of the first settlement of the East India Company in Southern India. This was located on a sandy spit near the estuary of Cooum Creek, on territory ceded to Francis Day in 1639 by Venkatadri Nayaka of Chengalpattu [37C], representative of the Vijayanagara ruler at Chandragiri [35C].

The earliest buildings, surrounded by earthen ramparts at what was then known as Madraspatnam, were consecrated on St George's Day, 23 April 1640. Known thereafter as Fort St George, they formed the nucleus of a rapidly growing settlement that soon established itself as the principal headquarters of British commerce on the Coromandel Coast. The lucrative trade in textiles and spices soon attracted the attention of the French, and the fort was temporarily lost to Labourdonnais in 1746 and Lally in 1758; it was further threatened by Haidar Ali of Srirangapattana [15C] in 1769. The original military, administrative and religious functions of the fort have been retained through the centuries, and the buildings that crowd the 17 ha. of the fort are still mostly in use.

Nothing remains of the original walls of Fort St George; the sloping *Ramparts with Battlements* for gun emplacements are 18th century works constructed after the French attacks. Designed by Bartholomew Robbins, they form an irregular pentagon, with the longest wall running parallel to the ocean on the east, now separated from the sands by Kamarajar Road. Two triangular bastions protrude into the moat at the north and south ends of the seaward side; three more bastions are positioned on the landward side. This scheme is further reinforced by a ring of earthen walls provided with numerous angles. The result is the most complete example of British military architecture still to be preserved in Southern India. There are five main gates, each with a rounded masonry entry, once approached across drawbridges, now replaced with roads. Most visitors arrive through the Sea Gate on the east.

The first building to be seen on entering the fort is the *Legislative Assembly of Tamil Nadu*. Its long Neo-Classical facade, dominating the seaward aspect of the fort, incorporates portions of the original 1694 Government House. The 20 polished black granite Doric columns that grace its front and side porticos come from a colonnade constructed in 1732. This originally ran from the Sea Gate to the parade grounds within the fort, but was demolished in 1910.

Immediately north of the Legislative Assembly stands the *Fort Museum* (closed Fridays), originally the Public Exchange Hall. The Hall of Arms, occupying the original warehouse on the ground floor, contains artillery, regimental flags, weapons and armour associated with various British campaigns. One room displays the silver dishes and ewers presented in 1687 to St Mary's Church by Elihu Yale who, after serving as Governor of Madras in 1684, went on to bequeath his name to Yale University. Finely worked 17th century silver dishes and a cup removed from the church at Pulicat [37H] are also exhibited, as is a large-scale model of the fort. A somewhat severe statue of Lord Cornwallis, sculpted in 1800 by Thomas Banks, stands at the foot of the stairs. It shows the Governor General accepting Tipu Sultan's two young sons as hostages.

The first floor, housing the Portrait Gallery, is where merchants daily met for trade and news. The paintings shown here include portraits of both British worthies and Indian nobility of the Chennai region, such as the Wallajah Nawabs of Arcot [38B]. The gallery is overlooked by a wooden balcony at one end. The adjacent room retains items of correspondence by Clive, Wellesley, Cornwallis and Bentinck. The Prints Section, on the second floor, displays early views of Madras. The elegant Ionic rotunda, standing freely near the south end of the museum, was erected in 1799 as a monument to Cornwallis, whose statue was originally placed here.

A short walk leads to the *Parade Grounds*, formerly Cornwallis Square, laid out in 1715 on the site of the first Fort House, the residence of the Madras Governors. Ministerial offices are seen on the east of the open space, with barracks for regiments on the other three sides. *St Mary's Church*, reputedly the oldest Protestant place of worship in Asia, stands near the southeast corner of the parade grounds. Erected in 1678-90 as the religious focus for the growing British population of the settlement, the church is still in worship. St Mary's was built by Streynsham Master, Governor of Madras, from subscriptions contributed by residents of the fort, including Elihu Yale. Both Yale and Robert Clive were wedded here. Job Charnock's three daughters were baptised in the church before the family moved to Bengal, where Charnock founded Calcutta in 1690. Thoms Pitt, subsequently Governor of Fort St George, Warren Hastings, Lord Cornwallis and Arthur Wellesley, later the Duke of Wellington, were all members of St Mary's congregation.

The church presents a plain whitewashed facade, broken by arched openings with shuttered windows set into 1.2 m. thick brick and line walls. The battlemented parapet is a later addition. The restrained Neo-Classical tower was added in front of the west door in 1701; its octagonal steeple was only completed in 1795. Curving staircases climb to doorways set between the tower and the nave. The arcades creating triple aisles support masonry vaults intended to withstand bombing, siege and cyclone. At the west end is a raised gallery with an ornate wooden balustrade, reserved for the Governor and Council. A rich assortment of tombs and memorials is seen in the nave. The early 19th century monuments on the north wall include a panel by John Flaxman, commemorating Josiah Webbe, and another by John Bacon, dedicated to Frederick Schwartz, the distinguished missionary. The Italian oil painting of the Last Supper, which serves as the altarpiece in the sanctuary, a 19th century extension, is supposed to have been captured in 1761 in a raid on Puducherry [39A]. An interesting item in the possession of the church is a Bible printed in 1660. Gravestones removed in 1763 from an earlier cemetery are set into the pavement that surrounds the church. They include that of Elizabeth Baker, wife of the first President of Madras. The words inscribed on her tombstone and the date of 1652 are the oldest English inscriptions in Southern India.

Immediately west of St Mary's is the *Archaeological Survey of India*, once Admiralty House. This Neo-Classical mansion, with its imposing double-height columned portico, was where Clive, the Steward of the fort, and his newly wedded wife lived in 1753. State receptions were held here prior to the construction of the Banqueting Hall on Anna Salai.

After finishing the tour of Fort St George, visitors have a choice of routes through the city: north along Rajaji Road to George Town; west along Poonamallee High Road to Egmore and the Pantheon Complex; southwest along Anna Salai; or south along Kamarajar Road, skirting the Marina to Chepauk and Triplicaine, with Mylapore and San Thomé beyond.

B. George Town

The indigenous population of Madras at the turn of the 18th century, estimated at some 300,000, was accommodated in a walled quarter known originally as Black Town, later George Town, located immediately north of Fort St George. Much of the wealth and trade of the city is still concentrated here in the crowded streets and tiny shops. Though the walls have now disappeared, the regular layout of the streets is still apparent. George Town is flanked on the east by Rajaji Road, running past the modern harbour, and on the south by N.S.C. Bose Road.

The first feature of interest to be noticed on Rajaji Road is the 38 m. high *Lighthouse* of 1841. This is conceived as a massive Greek Doric column, its beam visible 25 km. out at sea. The adjacent *High Court* of 1888-92, one of Chennai's most distinguished monuments, was designed by J.W. Brassington, but was revised by Henry Irwin and J.H. Stephens. The imposing complex employs Islamic-styled portals with arched recesses surrounded by fringes of buds, topped by battlemented parapets. The flanking octagonal towers, their corners marked by circular ribs, are capped with square pavilions with bulbous domes painted with stylised arabesque patterns. An octagonal central tower, added in 1912, rises almost 50 m. above the east block of the court. Domed pavilions cluster against its base; the summit is marked by a large bulbous dome framed by eight domical finials. Originally intended as a lighthouse with a fine view over the city and ocean beyond, it now serves as a memorial. One of the chambers inside the tower houses a marble statue by George Wade of T. Muthaswami Iyer, the country's first Indian judge. The interior of the court is of interest for the liberal use of carved woodwork and stained glass.

Parry's Corner, immediately north of the High Court, where N.S.C. Bose Road runs into Rajaji Road, takes its name from the oldest British mercantile company still operating in Chennai. The site is occupied by *Dare House*, erected in 1940 in the International Modernist style. Further along Rajaji Road is the *State Bank of India*, built in the 1890s in a manner recalling that of the High Court. The main entrance is marked by a sequence of lobed arches headed by arcaded windows. The square towers at either side, with projecting balconies lined with ornate balustrades, serve a platforms for finely worked octagonal domed pavilions. The *General Post Office* next door, which opened in 1884, is the work of Robert Fellowes Chisholm, one of the city's most celebrated architects. Its arcaded ranges are terminated by square towers with curious multi-gabled roofs. The central arched entryway is flanked by larger and higher square towers devoid of roofs.

Bentinck's Building stands a short distance further north along Rajaji Road. This 1793 structure, now somewhat dilapidated, was used variously as the Supreme Court and the Collectorate of Madras. It is one of the few original

Neo-Classical projects overlooking the ocean to survive. Its superimposed Doric and Ionic colonnades are emphasised by a part-circular projection in the middle.

Diverse religious and educational buildings are located on or near N.S.C. Bose Road, formerly Esplanade Road. The first to be seen is *Anderson's Church*, recognised by its octagonal tower capped with a gabled steeple. Next comes the *Armenian Church*, entered from a side street through a modest gate bearing the date 1712. Gravestones with Armenian script in curious designs are set into the pavement of the planted court inside. A detached belfry tower with rounded openings is roofed with a petalled from framed by vase-like pinnacles. The church itself, which dates from 1722, has an octagonal lantern rising over the curving vaults that roof the sanctuary. The interior consists of a long narrow nave with an unusual stepped altar at the east end. This incorporates small oil paintings of the life of Christ.

St Mary's Co-Cathedral, immediately north, is a reminder that George Town's population once had more Catholics than Protestants. The date 1642 inscribed over the central door commemorates the year of the first Catholic place of worship in the city, as distinct from San Thomé. A stark Neo-Classical tower of four stages, topped with an octagonal lantern, rises from one corner. Oil paintings within show the Crucifixion and Mary Magdalene.

Pachaiyappa's College, further along N.S.C. Bose Road, is named after Pachaiyappa Muthiar, an interpreter who worked for the East India Company. It opened in 1850 to provide education for poor boys. Built in an authentic Neo-Greek style, the college has an imposing portico elevated on a high terrace above the traffic. Six Ionic columns topped with a bold pediment shelter the grand doorway leading to the school.

A short distance west are the twin *Chennakeshava Perumal and Chenna Mallikeshvara Temples* facing onto N.S.C. Bose Road. Known collectively in the past as the Town Temples, these shrines were consecrated in 1766. They are built in a traditional Tamil idiom, with square towers covered with plaster sculptures and topped by square domical roofs. Two modest Jain temples in nearby Mint Street testify to the long-standing presence of Gujarati merchants in George Town.

C. POONAMALLEE HIGH ROAD

The principal route proceeding west from Fort St George is lined with impressive civic structures. At the extreme east end of the High Road stands *Memorial Hall*, erected in 1857 as a thanksgiving for the preservation of Southern India from the Mutiny. Its handsome Ionic portico is now rarely used. The adjacent *Southern Railways Office*, completed in 1922, presents a lively fusion of Neo-Mughal and European motifs executed in local granite. *Madras*

Central Railway Station next door was built in 1868-72, according to designs by George Hardinge. Double-storeyed arcades with corner pavilions flank the 40 m. high central clock tower, topped with a pyramidal roof. The nearby *Victoria Public Hall*, completed in 1889, is the work of Chisholm. This red-brick composition is distinguished by its corner tower, topped by a sloping tiled pyramidal roof relieved by small wooden gables. Next door stands *Ripon Building*, named after one of the Governors of Madras, accommodating the offices of the City Corporation, inaugurated in 1688. Dating from 1913, it presents an imposing three-storeyed Italianate facade dominated by a central clock tower.

Further along Poonamallee High Road, on the south side, is the *College of Arts and Crafts*, founded in 1850. It occupies a later mansion built by Chisholm, that still occupies a tree lined garden. *St Andrew's Kirk*, a short distance west, was erected in 1818-21 by Thomas de Havilland to a design by Lieutenant Grant. This handsomely proportioned Neo-Classical church, arguably the grandest in Southern India, is entered through a monumental pedimented Ionic portico. This is surmounted by a slender triple-stage tower with a tapering octagonal spire. The outer walls of the unusual circular nave have Ionic columns with louvred doors set in between. The circular hall within is ringed by 16 fluted columns with finely modelled Corinthian capitals. They support a 15 m. diameter dome painted with golden stars on a bright blue background.

A footbridge next to St Andrew's Kirk leads to *Egmore Station*, another project of Chisholm. This presents a synthesis of pointed Islamic styled arches with towers topped by Rajput domed pavilions. The left portico is headed by a tympanum filled with leafy scrolls and the monogram of the South Indian Railway. An imaginative curved vault with triple pot finials rises above. The library and museums of the Pantheon Complex are situated a short distance to the west.

D. PANTHEON COMPLEX

Taking its name from the Public Assembly Rooms that once stood on this site, the Pantheon Complex houses the major cultural institutions of Chennai. The collections of the *Government Museum* (closed Fridays) are displayed in four separate blocks.

The *Archaeological Galleries* house an important series of stone sculptures collected from various sites in Tamil Nadu and Andhra Pradesh. The first room displays 8th century Pallava carvings, including a large seated Vishnu. Among the Nolamba period items is a charming 10th century ceiling panel from Hemavati [33G]. This shows Shiva and Parvati on Nandi riding through the clouds. 10th-12th century Chola art is best represented by Ardhanari from Tiruchennampundi, Shiva appearing out of the linga from Mudiyanar, and

Ranaganatha from Villupuram. One of the finest statues is the elegant figure of Surya from Uttani, placed at the top of the stairs. A finely worked 11th century Late Chalukya doorway from Karnataka is also on display. Among the exhibits assigned to the 16th century is a somewhat damaged sculpture of seated Balakrishna from Hampi [20B]. The upper balcony that rings this room accommodates epigraphs from different eras, sandstone fragments from 2nd century BCE monument at Bharhut in Madhya Pradesh, and stray 1st-2nd century CE pieces from Gandhara in northern Pakistan. The connecting corridor at the end of the room is lined with hero stones, some showing lively hunters or horsemen, such as the panel from Ipuru.

The next room of the Archaeological Galleries is crammed with figures and architectural fragments, mostly from Pallava and Chola period sites. They include a complete set of the Saptamatrikas, several Dakshinamurti images, and large icons of seated and standing Vishnu. Of particular interest are the limestone posts, railings and drum slabs recovered from the demolished Maha Chaitya at Amaravati [29K]. A plaster model to one side gives an idea of the original appearance of the stupa. The carvings, which are mostly assigned to the 2nd-4th century Ikshvaku era, testify to the vitality of early Buddhist traditions in Southern India. Amaravati's art is represented by ornate lotus medallions and long friezes of garlands carried by dwarfs. On the reverse side of the medallions are Jataka stories, with crowded scenes of palaces, courtiers and mounted riders. The drum panels are adorned with pots filled with lotuses, and serpents wrapped around stupas. The most impressive panel of the Aramaravati series depicts a stupa in deep relief, complete with railings, side columns supporting dharma chakras, and flying celestials.

Carvings from other Buddhist sites of the same period exhibited here include those from Jaggayyapeta [29C]. One depicts a royal figure holding a dharma chakra. Jain figures, the largest being a seated saviour from Tuticorin [45H], are seen in one side room. Buddhist relics from Goli [29L], presented in an adjacent room, include a frieze of Vessantara Jataka scenes, in which the Bodhisattva appears as an elephant. The large seated Kali figure nearby comes from Hemavati. The Zoological and Geological Galleries are situated beyond.

The next portion of the collection is housed in a structure of Italianate design, incorporating a part-circular theatre surrounded by an arcade. The cannons placed around the building include a magnificent example with a tiger head, taken from Tipu Sultan's army at Srirangapattana in 1799. Another example displays the arms of the Dutch East Indian Company. The *Arms Gallery* within the building displays many items from the armoury at Thanjavur [40A]. The finest are the elephant goads, or ankushas, in exquisitely chiselled steel, daggers with pierced steel guards, and swords with deeply modelled gauntlets. The adjacent *Prehistoric Gallery* is filled with Iron Age pottery, terracotta burials, and stone and metal tools. The most interesting item is a terracotta sarcophagus with six legs and a ram's head, from Markapuram in Andhra Pradesh. Earthenware urns from Adichanallur [45C] are displayed together with their associated iron weapons and other implements. Roman pottery and diverse ornaments come from Arikamedu [39B].

A grand double staircase leading to the upper level of the building is lined with wooden doors from the Chettinad area [44K], and wooden lintels carved with Ramayana episodes, removed from a temple at Kollam [46H]. Further wooden exhibits are seen in the lofty hall at the upper level, distinguished by its stained glass and papered ceiling and vault. The *Ethnographic and Folk Art Galleries* show assorted items from all over Southern India, the most fascinating being ivory boomerangs, brass masks and musical instruments.

The next building is the *Old Connemara Library* of 1896, designed by Irwin. Its former reading room has an intricately worked ceiling, with varied geometric designs carried on curving panels of stained glass (permission required to visit). The plaster spandrels over the side arcades are embellished with richly cut acanthus leaves and arabesque motifs. The extensive collection of books and manuscripts dates back to 1861.

The *Bronze Gallery*, to the rear of the library, houses one of the largest and most important collections of metal images in Southern India. At the ground level the exhibits are displayed in glass cases. The 10th-11th century Chola period is well represented. The Ardhanarishvara from Tiruvengadu is acknowledged as one of the outstanding masterpieces of the era: the blending of male and female physiognomies, dress and hair styles is perfectly achieved. Sets of similarly large-scale figures include a paired Shiva and Parvati from Kilaiyur [40C], and the group of Rama with Sita, Lakshmana and Hanuman from Tiruvengadu. Also of interest are a Vishnu from Kamal, and Maheshvari, with flame-like headdress, from Velanganni [40N]. A cheerful dancing Ganesha is among the later 17th century bronzes.

Steps lead to an upper balcony where a series of magnificent Nataraja icons are on display. They include an unusual early example from the 9th century Pallava period, showing the god with two bent legs. Here, too, can be seen the 11th century Nataraja from Tiruvelangadu, perhaps the greatest of all Southern Indian dance icons. The magnificently balanced posture and the delicate modelling of the flying hair with snakes, all contained within a flaming halo, are unsurpassed. Several fine Somaskandamurti groups, showing Shiva, Parvati together with diminutive Skanda, are also exhibited. Buddhist bronzes are shown on the other side of the upper balcony. Among those brought from Nagapattinam [40M] is a superb composition showing the Master standing in an ornate frame; another example portrays Buddha seated beneath a profuse, but intricately worked tree, flanked by serpent attendants. Several Avalokiteshvara figures are also of merit.

The *National Art Gallery*, formerly the Empress Victoria Memorial Hall, is another project of Irwin, dating from 1909. It is built in pink sandstone in a refined Neo-Mughal style. The main entrance and pierced stone screens above are framed by a recessed pointed arch fringed by buds. The walls are topped with a crenellated parapet, above which rises a cluster of octagonal pavilions crowned with domes, the pavilion in the middle being larger and higher. The side rooms opening off the entrance accommodate ivory and sandalwood caskets, printed cloths, and paintings on glass and mica representing charming secular and mythological scenes. The central hall is hung with imposing oil paintings, of little worth.

The *Gallery of Contemporary Art* next door is dedicated to temporary shows.

E. ANNA SALAI

This thoroughfare, originally known as Mount Road, in reference to St Thomas Mount to which it eventually leads, was once lined with handsome offices and stores. Only a few historical structures survive, among them Agarchand Mansion, Higgenbothom's and The Mail. Many celebrated landmarks, such as the Neo-Gothic arcades of 1897 of Spence & Co., have vanished forever. Anna Salai begins on an island in Cooum Creek just south of Fort St George, a site marked by an equestrian statue of Sir Thomas Munroe, Governor of the Madras Presidency in 1819-26. This work of 1839 is by Francis Chantrey. The *Gymkhana Club* nearby, a relic of the British era, is still popular.

A portrait of George V stands in front of the iron gates leading to the *Rajaji Hall*, just off Anna Salai, south of Cooum Creek (permission required to visit). This impressive Neo-Classical building was erected in 1802 as a ceremonial setting for state entertainments according to a design by John Goldingham, an astronomer and engineer to the East India Company. Known originally as the Banqueting Hall, the building is approached by a broad flight of steps that leads to an arcaded lower storey, added in 1875, which partly conceals the severe Doric columns of the hall within. The pediments above were adorned with trophies commemorating British victories; these have now been replaced with emblems of Tamil Nadu Sate. The portraits of British dignitaries that once graced the interior of the hall have been removed to the Fort Museum and Raj Bhavan. A fine library of historical manuscripts, however, remains.

Old Government House stands in the estate immediately south or Rajaji Hall (permission required to visit). Originally the residence of a Portuguese merchant, Luis de Madeiros, it was acquired in 1753 by the Governor of Madras, but was later damaged during the French wars. The house was entirely remodelled in

1800 by Goldingham, who added the double staircase and reception rooms of the upper floor. The deep verandah with paired Doric columns dated from 1895.

Another vestige of the city's Neo-Classical past is the *Old Madras Club*, known in its heyday as the Ace of Clubs, now a decaying relic within Express Estate, just off a street running east from Anna Salai. The club was founded in 1832, and its central reception hall was erected in 1842; a spacious colonnaded verandah with pedimented ends was later added.

Christ Church, 1 km. further along Anna Salai, is a small, graceful structure dating from 1852. Its handsome Ionic porticos shelter doorways on three sides. It is topped by a slender, multi-stage tower with an octagonal steeple. More impressive is *St George's Cathedral* on the corner of Anna Salai and Dr Radhakrishnan Salai, still known by its former name of Cathedral Road. This imposing monument was planned by James Caldwell and constructed in 1814-16 by de Havilland. The brilliant whitewashed front portico, with triple side rows of paired Ionic columns, is crowned with a plain pediment. The tower, set well back, has a lower square stage and an upper round stage, capped with an octagonal spire that attains an overall height of 42.5 m. The side walls have louvred doors with semicircular stained glass windows, the glass being repeated in similarly shaped lunettes above. The side doors are sheltered by full porticos. Double rows of nine Ionic columns carry a curved vault decorated with raised plasterwork over the central aisle.

The apsidal chancel of Christ Church accommodates a marble altarpiece of St George crowned with a marble pediment. Among the many fine monuments are Chantrey's memorial of 1830 to Bishop Heber (north wall, east end), and the fully sculpted funerary figures of James Lushington and Reverend Daniel Corrie. A small domed gate once served as the entry to the adjacent cemetery. It now leads to a cluster of graves picturesquely shaded by trees. Here can be found the tombstone of Elizabeth de Havilland, the architect's wife, dated 1818. Some graves are enclosed by railings made of discarded spears, allegedly brought from Tipu Sultan's arsenal at Srirangapattana.

Anna Salai continues to Little Mount, Raj Bhavan at Guindy, and St Thomas's Mount.

F. Chepauk and Triplicane

Kamaraj Road, previously South Beach Road, and the adjacent foreshore serve as a broad marina that runs beside the Bay of Bengal on the eastern fringe of Chennai. Planned by Grant Duff, Governor of Madras in 1881-86, the road connects Fort St George with San Thomé Cathedral Basilica, almost 5 km. distant

Chepauk is the name given to the quarter now partly occupied by the campus of *Madras University*, founded in 1857 as the major educational institution of the city, located just south of Cooum Creek. The university is of architectural interest, with many innovative buildings designed by Chisholm, the most unusual being *Senate House* of 1873 on the corner of Wallajah Road. This red brick building is illuminated by windows with coloured glass in geometric patterns. The windows are set behind lofty arcades carried on solid round pillars and topped with domical finials. Square towers in the middle of the long sides have projecting balconies shaded by angled eaves. The pointed arches in coloured tilework at the top frame triple-set of narrow round-headed windows. The arches merge with domes painted with stylised ornament. Smaller octagonal towers at the corners are topped with domed pavilions. Outside the south entrance is an 1887 Golden Jubilee statue of Victoria. The queen is seated beneath an ornate cast-iron canopy manufactured in Glasgow.

Chepauk Palace, immediately south, on the other side of Wallajah Road, was designed by the English engineer Paul Benfield in 1768 as the Madras residence of Muhammad Ali of Arcot (1749-95). The complex consists of two long blocks, both with arcaded ranges. Chisholm added a tower in 1870 to link the two blocks. This curious structure combines disparate features: broad arched entrances at the base; tiers of superimposed balconies in the middle of each side; slender octagonal buttresses at the corners, protruding above the roofline as minaret-like towers with domical tops; and a capping small dome on a petalled base. The horizontal striped paintwork gives the tower an almost Byzantine appearance. The palace was acquired by the Madras Government in 1885, and now serves as the headquarters of various departments; its original name, however, is retained.

The next building of interest on the Marina is *Presidency College*, founded in 1840. As rebuilt by Chisholm in 1864, the complex presents an austere appearance with round-headed windows. The ribbed dome with clocks on four sides is an addition of 1887.

Vivekananda House, about 1 km. further south, is an architectural curiosity, erected in 1842 to store blocks of ice shipped from Boston. Its semicircular frontage has double rows of arched windows. The rooftop pavilion is capped with a peculiar pineapple shaped finial. The building was occupied for a few months by Swami Vivekananda, the famous Bengali religious leader and philosopher; hence its name.

Triplicaine, a short distance south of Chepauk, is also linked with the Nawabs of Arcot. Muhammad Ali was responsible for the *Wallajah Mosque*, erected in 1795 on what is now Trilpicaine High Road, near the junction with Wallajah Road. Graves of the Arcot family, as well as the tomb of the saint Maulana Bahrul Uloom, are seen in the adjacent graveyard. The mosque presents an austere facade with flanking minarets, square at the base, octagonal in the middle, and fluted and circular in the upper stages where they are topped with bulbous finials. The *Dargah of Hazrat Dastagir Sahib*, further south on Triplicaine High Road, is another prominent Muslim monument. It is crowned by a bulbous dome of squat proportions framed by a quartet of pinnacles.

It is, however, for the *Parthasarathi Temple* that Triplicaine is best known. Identified with the village of Tirupallikeni, this quarter has regularly laid out streets that echo the rectangular walled compound of the temple itself. This monument traces its history back to the 9th century, and was the scene of many battles, with Dutch and French occupying it at various times. It has been extensively renovated in recent years. The twin sanctuaries of Krishna and Rukmini are approached through gopuras with vividly painted towers on both the east and west (only Hindus admitted). A stone colonnade with carved columns leads to the east gopura. A decorated wooden chariot is parked nearby. Further south is a tank with a small pavilion in the middle.

G. Mylapore and San Thomé

Mylapore is located immediately south of Triplicaine, only a short distance inland from the Marina. This traditional quarter is dominated by the *Kapaleshvara Temple*, the largest in Chennai, surrounded by narrow bustling lanes. The original foundation was damaged by the Portuguese in 1566, but was substantially rebuilt in later times. The temple is dedicated to Shiva, who is here conceived as a peacock (mayil), since his consort, the goddess Parvati, assumed the form of a peahen in order to worship the linga: hence the name Mylapore (Mayilapura).

The Kapaleshvara complex is entered on the east through a gopura with a lofty pyramidal tower crowded with plaster sculptures; nine pot finials line the ridge of the barrel-vaulted roof. Depictions of Shiva in diverse forms appear in the creepers held by maidens carved onto the doorway jambs of the gopura. Small east-facing linga and Vinayaka shrines are seen on entering the walled enclosure. The principal linga sanctuary is, however, entered through a mandapa on the west. The same mandapa gives access to a rectangular shrine on the north, consecrated to Devi, and roofed with a barrel vault. A sequence of Nandi, altar and lamp columns stands outside. A smaller gate here leads to a vast tank with stepped sides.

San Thomé Cathedral Basilica, on the Bay of Bengal, marks the legendary burial place of St Thomas the Apostle. This venerable shrine traces its history back to the 7th-8th centuries, when Nestorian Christian migrants from Iran erected a chapel over what they believed to be the grave of St Thomas. The Portuguese rebuilt the chapel in 1523, calling it San Thomé, and used it as the nucleus of their headquarters on the Coromandel Coast. San Thomé remained in their hands until 1672, when it was occupied by the French, followed two years later by the Dutch. The British took command of San Thomé in 1749, but

Portuguese priests remained in charge of the basilica. The building was demolished in 1893, and a new structure was raised three years later in a Neo-Gothic style.

The whitewashed gabled facade of the basilica, framed by octagonal towers, is dominated by a separate higher tower with an octagonal steeple that marks the south entrance. The chief attraction of the interior is a small narrow tomb set beneath the floor in the middle of the nave, alleged to contain the corporeal remains of the saint. The newly completed *St Thomas Museum* (closed Tuesdays), at the rear of the basilica, houses items dating from the Portuguese era, including tombstones, a baptismal font, receptacles, granite carvings, and a map dated 1519. Several pre-European vestiges are also on display. A silver reliquary contains a fragment of the iron spear that is believed to have killed the Apostle.

The Christian character of San Thomé is reflected in the numerous places of worship that dot the neighbourhood. A small Anglican church with a Neo-Gothic verandah stands next to the basilica. A short distance south is *Lazarus Church*, dating back to 1582, rebuilt in 1637 by the prominent Madeiros family, and renovated in 1928. Of greater historical interest is *Luz Church*, west of Myalpore. An inscribed plaque set into the outer south wall of the building records that it was erected by a Franciscan monk in 1516, making it the oldest European structure in Chennai. The Baroque style of its architecture is evident in the pilastered facade adorned with curving volutes and conical finials framing a sunburst motif. The altar within the church depicts the Virgin and Christ crowned by angels. The barrel vault of the nave has relief plaster decoration. 17th century Portuguese tombstones are set into the pavement beneath.

H. ADYAR

This part of Chennai is named after the river that marks the southern periphery of the city. *Chettinad Palace* stands in spacious grounds on the north bank of the Adyar River, close to its confluence with the Bay of Bengal. *Brodie Castle* nearby, an imposing white structure with a Neo-Classical portico and a castellated round tower, takes its name from the East India Company servant who built it 1796-98.

The world headquarters of the *Theosophical Society* occupies the south bank of the Adyar, just across from Elphinstone Bridge, built in 1840. Founded in 1875 in New York by Helene Patrovna Blavatsky and Henry S. Olcott, the Theosophical Society shifted to Madras in 1882, taking over the home of John Huddlestone, one of three Madras Government officers sent to negotiate with Tipu Sultan in 1784. During Annie Besant's Presidency from 1907 onwards, the Society's property was expanded to encompass some 110 ha. of beautifully tended gardens. They include a huge banyan, one of the world's largest trees, estimated at more than 400 years old. The paths are marked by granite columns removed from a temple mandapa. Small shrines of different faiths are concealed in the gardens.

The Great Hall in the main building of the Society is enlivened with plaster reliefs depicting world religious figures, as well as statues of Blavatsky and Olcott. The adjacent museum displays portraits of the Society's Presidents and a few antiquarian items (permission required to visit). The Society's library of more than 165,000 books functions as a centre for postgraduate studies in Sanskrit and Indology.

Vestiges of British recreational life are to be seen further upstream. On the north bank of the Adyar stands the *Madras Club*, formerly the Adyar Club. Established in 1891 in an 18th-century villa owned by George Moubray, who arrived in Madras in 1771, the club stands in gardens sweeping down to the water. The river frontage is embellished with a stately octagonal dome rising over a semicircular bay. The octagonal room within is surrounded by arcades.

I. GUINDY AND THE TWO MOUNTS OF ST THOMAS

Further historical features are located in the extreme southwest of Chennai, in the direction of the airport. *Raj Bhavan* at the western edge of Guindy National Park was the country residence of the Madras Governors from 1817, first used by Munroe (permission required to visit). Sprawling colonnaded wings flank the central hall, the interior of which is enlivened with a bust of Wellington and paintings removed from the Banqueting Hall. The nearby Gandhi Memorial Pavilion was erected in 1956.

Little Mount, an outcrop of granite associate with the refuge of St Thomas, stands a short distance north of Guindy National Park, near Marmalong Bridge across the Adyar. The *Church of Our Lady of Good Health* was founded in 1551. A roughly carved plaque set into the wall to the left of the entrance shows a figure of St Thomas and the date 1612. Steps to one side of the altar descend to a small grotto, reputed to be the retreat of the saint. A crevice behind the church is filled with natural water. The cross incised into the rock here is believed to commemorate the spot where St Thomas preached.

The higher Mount of St Thomas, 3 km. to the southwest, marks the spot where the Apostle is supposed to have been martyred in CE 68, after arriving here from Kerala. The mount rises 90 m. above the plain, and can be clearly seen from the airport. The ascent begins in the village at its base, where there is a whitewashed gate with a central arch surmounted by an icon of St Thomas and the date 1726. A flight of brick-paved steps climbs to the modest *Church of Our Lady of Expectations*. Its west facade has an arched doorway with an inscriptions of 1707, naming an Armenian donor and bearing the royal arms of Portugal. The barrel-vaulted interior is of interest for the gilded altar. This frames a carved stone plaque showing the celebrated Bleeding Cross, surrounded by a Pahlavi inscription. This was discovered by the Portuguese in 1521, but its antiquity remains uncertain. The building next door was once a Franciscan orphanage and school

The *Cantonment* beneath the east flank of the Mount preserves several 18th century Neo-Classical villas, one of which served as the residence of Hastings in 1769-72. The Garrison Church of 1830 is an unassuming edifice with a simple Ionic portico. Its slender tower has been truncated, marring its original four-stage design. The interior is furnished with memorials of military officers.

37. Around Chennai

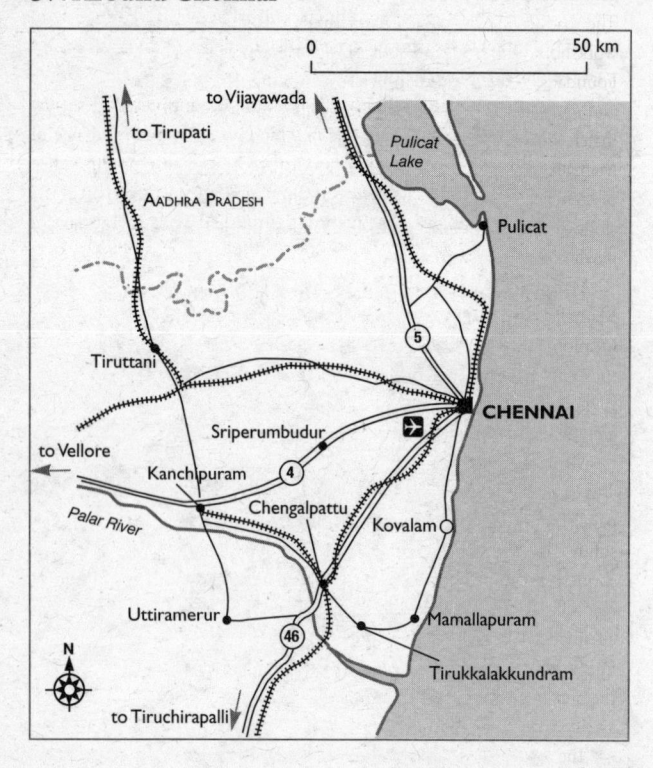

Hindu monuments from the 7th-9th century Pallava period, among the earliest in Tamil Nadu, are scattered throughout the Chennai region, as at Mamallapuram [A], Chengalpattu [C], Kanchipuram [E] and Uttiramerur [F]. Temples from the Vijayanagara and Nayaka periods, dating from the 16th-17th centuries, can be visited at Tirukkalakkundram [B], Sriperumbudur [D] Kanchipuram and Tiruttani [G].

Mamallapuram and Kanchipuram, the two most popular destinations outside Chennai, will require separate trips in order to do justice to their many monuments, even though they can be combined with one full-day visit. Another half day will be needed to reach the Dutch cemetery at Pulicat [H].

Some excursions may conveniently be combined with other itineraries: Kanchipuram is directly on the way to Vellore [39] or Tiruchirapalli [41]; the road from Mamallapuram continues to Puducherry [39]; Tiruttani may be visited en route to Tirupati, 65 km. to the north [35].

A. Mamallapuram

The road from Chennai to Mamallapuram is lined with artists' studios and workshops. About 50 km. south is *Dakshinachitra*, a project of the Madras Craft Foundation, where houses from all over Southern India have been transported and reconstructed. These range from historic mansions to simple mud and thatch huts, some accommodating local pottery and weaving activities. Mamallapuram, 12 km. further away, is celebrated for its Government College of Architecture and Sculpture. This has been responsible for reviving traditional stone carving and bronze casting techniques. The town is full of stalls displaying newly complete artworks.

Mamallapuram, previously Mahabalipuram, takes its name from Mamalla (650-68), one of the Pallava kings of Kanchipuram. Its seaside location suggests that the town served as an active port. Mamallapuram's rock-cut and free-standing monuments and associated sculptures, all fashioned out of local granite, represent the first flowering of Hindu architecture and art in the Tamil region.

Mamallapuram's cave temples and carved panels, dating from the late 7th and early 8th centuries, are cut into the sides of a granite outcrop that runs parallel to the ocean, about 400 m. inland; they are described from north to south. The *Trimurti Mandapa*, at the north end, consists of a row of three shrines, each flanked by pilasters, between which stand guardian figures. The rear walls of the shrines show Brahma (left), Vishnu (centre) and Shiva (right), attended by kneeling devotees. A polished stone linga is placed before the last image. Beyond the Shiva shrine is a niche with Durga standing on the head of the buffalo demon that she has just killed; the goddess is framed by a foliated arch springing from makaras.

The *Kotikal Mandapa*, to the west, has a crudely excavated sanctuary preceded by a small verandah. Female figures flank the doorway. The *Varaha Cave Temple*, further south, conforms to the same scheme, except that the columns have seated lion bases, a favourite Pallava motif. A parapet of roof forms is carved above the eaves. A projecting shrine in the middle of the rear wall is flanked by guardians, as well as Lakshmi (left) and Durga (right). Large-scale carvings on the side walls show Varaha lifting Bhudevi (left) and Trivikrama (right).

The nearby free-standing *Ganesha Ratha* is a rectangular monolith with a columned verandah, with lion columns flanked by guardians between wall pilasters. An image of Ganesha has recently been installed in the small sanctuary. Above the parapet rises a vaulted roof, complete with arched ends and pot and trident finials. East of the Ganesha Ratha is the *Archaeological Museum*, with sculptures and architectural pieces assembled in an outdoor compound.

Arjuna's Penance, a sculpted relief more than 30 m. long and 14 m. high, is located a short distance south of the museum. The composition is remarkable for the vitality and naturalism of the smoothly modelled figures and animals. Two large boulders are covered with flying gods, goddesses and semi-divine beings, as well as elephants and other animals, all converging on the central cleft. The gap is filled with a slab sculpted with male and female naga figures, their hands held together in adoration, over which water once flowed from a tank above into a basin beneath. Arjuna standing on one foot is seen to the left of the cleft. In front of him stands four-armed Shiva holding the magic weapon which Arjuna hopes to win by his penance. Beneath is a hermitage shrine of Vishnu, before which are seated sages, two deer and a lion; disciples beneath engage in various austerities. To the right of the cleft, beneath the elephants, is the story of the cat who performed atonement by standing on one leg, thereby tricking a group of rats.

The relief is sometime also interpreted as an illustration of the penance of Bhagiratha, the sage who persuaded Shiva to receive the Ganga in his matted locks. According to this view the water flowing over the naga figures would represent the descent of the celestial river to earth. Immediately to the right of the composition is a group of life-like monkeys, carved entirely in the round.

A short distance south of the Arjuna's Penance is the *Pancha Pandava Mandapa*, of which only five columns with lion bases were completed. Next comes the *Krishna Mandapa*, with a 16th century colonnade sheltering a long relief composition that follows the curving contours of the rocky face. Here Krishna is shown shielding the herds and gopis from Indra's storm by lifting Govardhana Hill. The naturalistic details, such as the attendant who milks a cow which licks her calf, are remarkably tender. Other figures, shown in affectionate embrace or playing the flute, are modelled with the fluid roundness that is a speciality of Pallava art.

A short distance in front (east) of the Krishna Mandapa stands the *Sthalashayana Perumal Temple*. This 16th-17th century complex is entered through an uncompleted gopura on the east; this leads to a second smaller gopura, recently renovated. The mandapa in between has pillars with donor carvings. The Vishnu shrine within is of little artistic merit.

The path running southward beside the rocky outcrop leads to the *Dharmaraja Cave Temple*. This comprises three empty sanctuaries excavated into the rear wall of an open hall. The architectural elements are unadorned, and the guardian figures flanking the central doorway have been chiselled away. From here the path makes a turn and ascends through a cleft in the middle of the outcrop. The first feature to be noticed is the *Mahishasuramardini Cave Temple* on the left. This consists of three shrines, the central one with a projecting porch, all set within a long verandah with fluted columns. The end panels of the verandah are among the greatest masterpieces of Pallava art. They depict Vishnu sleeping on the coils of Ananta, in the presence of the gods (left), and Durga riding on the lion, approaching the buffalo-headed Mahisha who wields a club (right).

Passing by a lighthouse on a prominence, the path leads to the *Olakkanatha Temple* on the rocky summit, directly above the Krishna Mandapa. The walls of this free-standing sanctuary have pairs of pilasters framing worn images of Shiva; no ceiling or superstructure survives.

Returning to the base of the hill visitors should proceed a short distance westwards in order to reach the *Adivaraha Cave Temple*. Partly obscured by a modern structure, this consists of a verandah with a shrine cut into the rear wall. The shrine doorway, approached through a porch, is flanked by guardian figures: an image of Vishnu receives worship within. Sculpted panels either side of the sanctuary are identified as royal portraits, possibly of Mamalla and other courtly figures. The end panels of the verandah show Lakshmi bathed by elephants (left), and Durga standing on the buffalo head (right).

The next feature of interest at Mamallapuram to be described is the *'Shore' Temple*. This occupies a sandy promontory, now converted into a garden, overlooking the Bay of Bengal, directly east of the Sthalashayana Perumal temple. The 'Shore' temple stands in landscaped grounds, and is approached from the west through ruined courts with altars and decorated plinths; the surrounding walls are topped with lines of Nandi images. A small boulder to the south of the temple is fashioned as Durga's lion; the goddess is shown seated on the hind leg of the animal, with the decapitated buffalo head to one side. Immediately to the north of the temple are several newly revealed features, including a well, a miniature circular shrine, and a boar carved out of a boulder.

Together with the Kailasanatha temple at Kanchipuram, the 'Shore' temple dates from the reign of Rajasimha (697-728). This Pallava king is credited with initiating structural temple architecture in the Tamil zone. In spite of its overall erosion from the sea and wind, the elegant proportions of its twin towers are still apparent. The monument comprises a complex of three shrines. The original sanctuary is a small chamber that shelters an image of sleeping Vishnu, carved onto a low granite boulder. A sanctuary facing east towards the ocean houses a multi-faceted, polished black basalt linga. The worn composition carved onto the rear wall shows Shiva, Parvati and the infant Skanda. A smaller sanctuary, facing west, similarly provided with a linga and Shaiva images on the rear wall, abuts the Vishnu shrine. The rows of pilasters with lion bases on the outer walls are sheltered by eaves and a parapet. Steeply pyramidal towers, with diminishing storeys repeating the features of the walls beneath, rise above the two Shaiva shrines. The towers are capped by octagonal domical roofs with basalt finials. The larger, east-facing shrine is surrounded by an outer wall that encloses a narrow passageway open to the sky.

The group of five monoliths known as the *Pancha Rathas* is one of the chief attractions of Mamallapuram. Hewn out of granite boulders standing in the dunes, some 300 m. south of the main rocky outcrop with cave shrines, they are known somewhat misleadingly as rathas, or chariots. The temple-like monoliths date back to the reign of Mamalla, but were never entirely completed. Their purpose remains enigmatic; so, too, the names by which they are known, which are taken from characters in the Mahabharata epic.

Pancha Rathas, Mamallapuram.

The *Draupadi and Arjuna Rathas*, at the north end of the group, are elevated on a common plinth sculpted with elephants and lions. The square Draupadi Ratha has a hut-like roof with curved ridges. Female guardians between pilasters flank the doorway on the west; a makara arch is incised above. Standing images of Durga are seen on three sides. A similar representation of the goddess is carved onto the rear wall of the shrine. A free-standing lion stands a short distance to the west. The adjacent Arjuna Ratha, is recognised by its square pyramidal tower. Elegant wall pilasters at the lower level frame guardians and couples, with deities in the middle of each side: Shiva leaning on Nandi (south), Indra on the elephant (east), and Vishnu with Garuda (north). The walls are overhung by eaves with a parapet of roof forms. The upper storey of the tower repeats the pilastered walls, eaves and parapet, but at a reduced scale. The capping roof is an octagonal dome. The porch (west) gives access to the verandah and an empty sanctuary. A finely finished Nandi is located to the east.

The rectangular *Bhima Ratha*, the next in line, is incomplete in its lower portions, except for the columns with seated lions at the front (west), and the finely modelled eaves and parapet of roof forms. The ratha is dominated by a vaulted roof with arched ends. Next to this stands the square *Dharmaraja Ratha*, the tallest and most elaborate of the group. This is a triple-storeyed version of the Arjuna Ratha. Columns with lion bases at ground level flank an entrance porch that leads to an unfinished sanctuary. Sculptures framed by pilasters are positioned in the side panels on each face: Ardhanarishvara and Bhima (east); Brahma and Harihara (north); Shiva and the royal patron Mamalla (south); and Shiva (west). The second storey of Dharamaraja Ratha consists of a passageway around a square shrine, the outer walls of which have carvings of deities, guardians and attendants. Devotees with Chandra (north) and Surya (east) can be made out on the walls of the third storey. The chamber at this level has a Somaskanda group accompanied by Brahma and Vishnu carved onto the rear wall.

The *Nakula Sahadeva Ratha*, to the west of the others, is the only example with an apsidal-ended plan. Its crowning vault has an arched face on the south. An imposing, free-standing elephant stands nearby.

Three smaller, less well finished monoliths are located about 500 m. west of the rocky outcrop with cave temples. The twin *Pidari Rathas* and the *Villian Kuttai Ratha* each have two storeys capped with square or domed roofs.

Other features of interest are located to the north of Mamallapuram. The road passing by an unfinished gateway of the 16th century, on the edge of the town, leads to the *Mukundanayanar Temple*, a small 8th century structure that imitates the simpler rathas.

The village of *Saluvankuppam*, 4 km. north of Mamallapuram, is worth visiting for the so-called *Tiger Cave*. This somewhat fantastic monument consists of a large boulder, out of which a small portico has been fashioned in the middle, possibly intended for the display of bronze images during festival time. The portico is surrounded by a ring of fierce yali heads, with two additional elephant heads on the left. About 150 metres north of the Tiger Cave is a simple cave temple with a sanctuary accommodating a polished black basalt linga. Texts in contrasting Southern and Northern Indian scripts engraved on the side walls extol the virtues of Parameshvara, the Pallava king who ruled between Mamalla and Rajasimha. A relief composition of mounted Durga approaching Mahisha is carved on the face of a nearby boulder.

B. Tirukkalukkundram

This town, midway between Mamallapuram and Chengalpattu, is dominated by a quartet of magnificent gopuras that rises above the outer walls of the *Bhaktavatsaleshvara Temple*. This monument is one of the most ambitious architectural schemes of the Nayakas of Gingee [39F]. The 17th century gateways are grandiose structures, with passageways adorned with carved maidens clutching creepers, scenes of linga worship, and various deities. The ceilings show Kama and Rati on parrots (north gopura), and paintings or royal visitors (west gopura). The tower vary from nine storeys on the north and south, to seven on the east and six on the west; they are devoid of plaster sculptures.

The principal entrance to the temple is through the east gopura. This gives access to a spacious enclosure, with a large square tank in the northeast corner, and an elaborate mandapa in the southwest corner. The latter has yalis on the peripheral columns, replaced by horses on the interior central aisle leading the dais at the highest level.

A lofty mandapa with side aisles is reached after passing through the second east gopura. This aisle proceeding north is lined with columns with sculpted horses; a Nataraja shrine is positioned at the end. The aisle to the west leads to the principal linga sanctuary in the innermost enclosure. This small apsidal-ended structure has finely finished basement mouldings and wall pilasters. Deep niches are occupied by carved images of Ganesha and Dakshinamurti (south), Shiva appearing out of the linga (west), and Brahma and Devi (north). The apsidal-ended scheme is repeated in the brick and plaster tower above, which has an ornate frontal arch. The accompanying goddess shrine is located in the northwest corner of the intermediate enclosure.

A steep hill rises to the northeast of Tirukkalukkundram town. About 400 steps climb to the *Vedagirishvara Temple*, perched on the summit 160 m. above the plain. Though of little interest architecturally, its rooftop terrace offers magnificent views of the Bhaktavatsaleshvara temple beneath, and the great tank to the east. Visitors make the strenuous ascent in order to witness priests feed two sacred vultures that appear punctually at midday. The path up the hill passes by the 7th century *Orukal Mandapa*. This rudimentary excavation consists of a linga shrine flanked by sculpted attendants and figures of Vishnu (right) and Brahma (left). Gracefully posed celestials adorn the end walls. The shrine is reached through a mandapa with double rows of pillars. Pallava period inscriptions are seen on the inner columns, while the outer supports preserve graffiti of Dutch visitors, one of which is dated 1664.

C. CHENGALPATTU

Known previously as Chingelput, this town lies 58 km. southwest of Chennai on NH45 28 km. west of Mamallapuram and 35 km. east of Kanchipuram. Chengalpattu is of historical interest for its fort, the most important in this part of Tamil Nadu in the 17th-18th centuries. Founded by the Qutb Shahis of Golconda [26E] and later occupied by the Nawabs of Arcot [38B], it was taken by the French and British. Robert Clive secured the surrender of the French garrison here in 1752, but temporarily lost the fort to Haidar Ali of Srirangapattana [15C] a few years later.

Little remains of Chengalpattu fort, through which the railway now passes, other than the 18th century *Raja Mahal*. This courtly structure, now much altered, originally consisted of five storeys. Its small inner room is surrounded by arcades and roofed with a small dome. The Anjaneya temple nearby dates from the 19th century.

Near the hamlet of *Vallam*, 3 km. southwest of Chengalpattu, three cave temples dating from the Pallava period are cut at different heights into low granite hills. *Cave 1*, the most important, bears an inscription of the reign of Mahendravarman I (580-630), making it one of the earliest Hindu monuments in Tamil Nadu. Later carvings of Ganesha and Jyeshtha occupy niches either end of the walled-up verandah.

D. SRIPERUMBUDUR

This town, 40 km. southwest of Chennai on NH4, was the site of the assassination of Rajiv Gandhi in 1991. A newly completed memorial commemorates the tragedy at a spot beside the highway, just south of the town.

Sriperumbudur is celebrated as the birthplace of the 11th-12th century Vaishnava philosopher Ramanuja, who is worshipped in the *Adi Keshava Temple* in the middle of the town. Though this monument traces its history back to the Chola era, its architecture belongs mostly to the 16th-17th centuries. The complex is entered on the east through an imposing, but austere gopura of standard design. The gateway is of interest for the Ramayana friezes that cover the side walls of the passageway. The gopura gives access to the outer enclosure of the temple, which is surrounded by colonnades and minor structures on four sides. Rama and Lakshmana shrines are located at the northwest and southwest corners respectively, the latter being preceded by a mandapa with ornate columns.

Visitors can only enter the higher inner enclosure of the temple from the entrance porch on the south. Broad steps flanked by yali balustrades climb up to the plinth, which is adorned with sculpted dancers, couples and attendants, as well as aspects of Vishnu and scenes from Vaishnava mythology, such as the story of Narasimha. The columns of the entrance porch are embellished with rearing horses with riders flanking the central aisle, which leads to the main doorway. This aisle continues inside the inner enclosure, the horses being here replaced with yalis. Immediately ahead is Ramanuja's shrine, facing south, while to the left stands Vishnu's shrine, facing east. Both sanctuaries are ornately treated, with pilastered niches set into their outer walls; overhanging eaves have cut-out ribs on their undersides; pendant stone chains mark the corners. Hemispherical towers protrude above the roof line. A lofty swing pavilion and a long mandapa stand outside the east gopura of the complex.

E. KANCHIPURAM

Located 32 km. west of Sriperumbudur, just off NH4, Kanchipuram is one of the most vibrant religious centres in Tamil Nadu, also well known for its flourishing silk industry. No less than 50 temples within the city are dedicated to different Hindu deities; they include major complexes consecrated to Shiva, the Goddess and Vishnu. The profusion of shrines means that religious festivals take place almost continuously through the year.

Archaeological vestiges discovered in Kanchipuram testify to the popularity of Buddhism and Jainism in earlier times, and at least one Jain complex is still in worship. Kanchipuram served as the capital of the Pallavas in the 7th-9th centuries, but continued to maintain its importance during the succeeding Chola, Vijayanagara and Nayaka eras. The religious monuments are distributed in the three distinct zones: the Ekambareshvara and Kamakshi temples and associated sanctuaries in Shiva Kanchi; the Varadaraja temple in Vishnu Kanchi, to the southwest; the Jain shrines at Tiruparuttikunram, on the other side of the Vegavati River, southwest of the city.

The tour of Kanchipuram described here begins at the *Kailasanatha Temple*, which stands on the edge of open fields about 500 km. west of Shiva Kanchi. Begun by the Pallava king Rajasimha in the early 8th century, it is the oldest standing building in the city; however, it lacked priests and worshippers until only a few years ago. It is now the site of the annual Mahashivaratri festival in February. Constructed mostly out of sandstone, the Kailasanatha is a planned complex, with the main temple standing in the middle of a rectangular walled enclosure lined with small shrines. Two doorways are positioned on the east; a single doorway on the west is now blocked up.

Kailasanatha Temple, Kanchipuram.

As in the 'Shore' temple at Mamallapuram, the principal sanctuary of the Kailasanatha complex houses a multi-faceted linga, with a Somaskanda panel carved onto the rear wall. The sanctuary is surrounded by a narrow passageway. Its outer walls are raised on a moulded basement, relieved by friezes of dwarfs and foliate patterns. Projecting shrines at the corners and in the middle of three sides are framed by pilasters with rearing yalis at the base. A full range of Shaiva divinities are accommodated here: for example, Shiva appearing out of the linga, flanked by Vishnu and Brahma (south); and Shiva in the chariot shooting arrows, flanked by Durga and Bhairavi (north). The figures are framed by pilasters supporting makaras with foliated tails. The storeys of the pyramidal tower that rise above repeat the wall scheme below at diminishing scales; the capping roof is an octagonal dome. The flat-roofed mandapa to the east of the sanctuary was originally a detached structure.

The shrines lining the compound wall of the Kailasanatha complex all have dome-like roofs, with seated Nandis and elephants in between. Images of Shiva and other divinities within the shrines are mostly eroded and overlaid with coloured plaster. Paintings from the Pallava period are preserved on the interior shrine walls. They include fragmentary scenes of Shiva with Uma and Skanda (north side), and Shiva accompanied by Vishnu and Brahma (south side).

At the east end of the enclosure stands the Mahendra-varmeshvara shrine, named after Rajasimha's successor. This free-standing structure has a large barrel-vaulted roof with arched ends, obviously a precursor to the barrel-vaults that crown later gopuras. In the middle of its outer walls are carvings of Dakshinamurti (south), a Somaskanda group (west), and dancing Shiva (north). A polished granite linga is enshrined within. The outer face of the enclosure walls are relieved by pilasters. A line of additional minor shrines flank the east entrance. A short distance east is a seated Nandi on a low plinth.

Returning to the crowded streets of the city, the tour of Kanchipuram continues with a visit to the *Ekambareshvara Temple*, the largest in Shiva Kanchi, and the setting for the Panguni Utiram festival in March-April. A lofty pavilion with slender columns stands in the middle of the street leading up to the gopura that serves as the principal entrance to the monument from the south. This impressive 17th century structure has a pyramidal tower of nine diminishing stories rising on a double series of granite walls. The brick and plaster tower is surmounted by a barrel-vaulted roof, rising almost 60 m. above the ground. Its arched ends are enlivened with monster masks; 11 pot finials line the ridge. Smaller gopuras on the south and west give access to the inner enclosure of the temple. The inner south gopura is elaborately treated in the 16th century Vijayanagara manner. Its entrance is concealed by a later mandapa built up to it on the south.

In the middle of the second enclosure stands the temple dedicated to Ekambareshvara, facing east. It is preceded by a long mandapa incorporating an earlier linga shrine, Nandi pavilion, altar and lamp column. A large stepped tank stocked with fish, set at an angle, can be seen to the north. The main temple, contained within yet a third rectangle of walls, is surrounded on four sides by a spacious columned corridor roofed with granite slabs carried on animal brackets. It houses a stone linga, identified as the earth, or prithvi, linga worshipped by Kamakshi, the resident goddess of Kanchipuram. Relief carvings throughout the temple show Kamakshi clutching Shiva's emblem. Numerous multi-faceted lingas are displayed in the colonnades; a sahasra linga occupies the shrine at the northeast corner. A subsidiary shrine accommodating a large brass Nataraja icon opens off to the north. The Somaskanda shrine, in the southwest corner of the enclosure, is approached through a hall with columns showing 16th century carvings of yalis with riders. To the rear (west) of the main temple is an open court with a sacred mango tree, beneath which Kamakshi is believed to have worshipped Shiva. Its spreading branches shelter a raised walkway.

A short distance east of the Ekambareshvara temple is the 8th century *Iravataneshvara Temple*. This Pallava period monument has a square sanctuary with a pyramidal tower crowned by a large square roof. Wall sculptures show Shiva as the yogi (north), dancing Shiva (west), and Dakshinamurti (south). The figures are flanked by attendant deities and guardian figures; makaras with foliated tails are positioned above.

The *Jvarahareshvara Temple*, facing east onto the road running south of the Ekamabareshvara temple, is one of the few monuments in Kanchipuram dating from the 12th century Chola era. Its unusual elliptical sanctuary adjoins a quadrangular antechamber, mandapa and porch. The outer walls, raised on a finely modelled plinth, have pilasters standing in pots, pairs of pilaster framing niches, now empty, and pierced stone windows. The plaster decorated brick tower, crowned with an elliptical domed roof, is a recent renovation. An altar and small Nandi pavilion stand in front.

A short distance southeast of the Ekambareshvara temple is the *Kamakshi Amman Temple*, one of the most popular shrines in Shiva Kanchi. Modestly proportioned gopuras provide access to the almost square outer enclosure from the middle of four sides. The lower parts of the gopuras are 16th century structures. The east gopura, which is the most elaborate, has niches filled with carvings of Ganesha (right) and Subrahmanya (left). An ornate mandapa stands freely within the outer enclosure, north of the main temple. Dating from the 16th century, it is raised on a basement enlivened with a frieze of yalis. The column shafts have blocks covered with carvings. Piers with colonettes line the central aisles in both directions within the hall. In the middle is a dais on a base carved in the semblance of a tortoise. A large tank with a central pavilion occupies the north side of the enclosure.

The inner enclosure, in which the main shrine of Kamakshi is situated, is entered on the east (only Hindus admitted). In times past, however, the enclosure was accessed from the south, judging by the altar, lamp column and Nandi pavilion that are aligned on this side. Kamakshi's rectangular sanctuary within is roofed with a gilded tower that rises above the roof.

A small *Shiva Shrine*, set beneath the present-day street level, is seen near the northeast corner of the Kamakshi complex. This dilapidated 12th century structure has a hemispherical roof with arched motifs. The *Matangeshvara Temple*, a short distance from the southeast corner, is a small square 8th century sanctuary. Its pyramidal tower is capped by a square roof. The sanctuary adjoins a mandapa that opens to the west. Columns with seated lions at the base flank the entrance. This scheme is virtually repeated in the Mukteshvara temple, further south.

The *Vaikuntha Perumal Temple*, built by Nandivarman II (731-96), the most important Pallava king at Kanchipuram after Rajasimha, is located in the eastern part of Shiva Kanchi, a short distance from the railway station. The temple, which is approached through a gateway and entrance hall, both later additions, stands in the middle of the quadrangular walled enclosure. It consists of a trio of sanctuaries arranged one on top of the other. The sanctuary at the lowest level, accommodating a seated icon of Vishnu, is surrounded by a double corridor. The sanctuary at the intermediate level, surrounded by a single corridor, has a reclining image of Vishnu. A standing image of the god was presumably housed in the sanctuary at the top level, but this is now missing. The sanctuaries are linked by internal flights of steps.

The outer walls of the sanctuaries on three levels have pilastered projections framing niches with diverse images of Vishnu and Krishna. Leaping yalis enliven the pilaster shafts. The topmost sanctuary is capped with an octagonal roof. The lowest sanctuary adjoins a mandapa on the west. The enclosure is surrounded by a colonnade with seated lions at the base of the columns. The colonnade shelters wall reliefs, now much worn. They appear to illustrate episodes from Pallava history, including coronation scenes, receptions and battles.

The tour of Kanchipuram continues with a visit to the *Varadaraja Temple*, the largest and most significant religious monument in Vishnu Kanchi. According to local legend this monument commemorates the site where Brahma performed a yagna, or fire sacrifice, to invoke the presence of Vishnu. This rite was carried out on a square altar raised high above the ground. The core of the Varadajara temple, elevated on an artificial square platform, accords with this description of Brahma's altar.

High towered gopuras on the east and west lead into the spacious outermost enclosure of the temple. The east gopura, the grander of the two, was commissioned by Kumara Tatacharya, spiritual preceptor of the Vijayanagara emperor Venkatapatideva of Chandragiri [35C] in the early 17th century. The tower is raised on a double-storeyed granite structure, with duplicated basements, pilastered wall projections and niches, and cornices. The passageway entrance is bridged by a broad lintel carried on lotus brackets. The interior is flanked by jambs adorned with maidens clutching creepers. The brick and plaster tower presents an impressive pyramid of nine diminishing storeys, each with windows in the middle of the long sides. The capping vaulted roof has arched ends.

Most visitors enter the Varadaraja temple from the main street that arrives at the west gopura of the complex. Within the gateway, immediately to the left, is an ornate mandapa that is one of the masterpieces of Vijayanagara art. Its basement is regularly punctuated by small niches; yali balustrades flank the staircase on the south. The sculptural treatment is elaborate throughout. Piers have fully modelled warriors on rearing horses, the animals being doubled at the corners, together with Kama on the swan and Rati on the parrot. The piers are sheltered by curving eaves, with stone chains for lamps at the corners. Animals with riders also appear in multiple forms around the dais at the northern end of the mandapa interior. Column shafts here have blocks covered with reliefs of divinities, saints, amorous couples and jesters. Crouching yalis and elongated lotus buds serve as brackets carrying the roof beams. To the north of the mandapa is a large tank with a small pavilion in the middle.

A comparatively small gopura beyond the mandapa gives access to the intermediate enclosure of the complex (only Hindus admitted). This is mostly occupied by mandapas and subsidiary shrines dating from the 12th century, including the mandapa immediately in front of the west entrance to the innermost enclosure. The shrine here dedicated to Anantalavar is a small Chola period structure with simply moulded basements and pilastered walls; the tower above has a hemispherical roof. The sanctuary of Purundevi Tayar, chief consort of Varadaraja, stands in the southwest corner nearby. This 17th century Nayaka period shrine has sharply cult pilasters standing in ornamental pots, and delicately modelled eaves. Contemporary paintings on the ceiling of the adjacent swing pavilion illustrate the sports of Krishna: the youthful god steals the clothes of the gopis, and dances on the hoods of the serpent Kaliya. In the mandapa opposite the nearby Narasimha shrine, Rati and Manmatha are shown riding in aerial chariots, shooting a profusion of arrow.

The innermost enclosure of the Varadaraja temple is partly occupied by a colonnade lining the perimeter walls. The walls are covered with paintings dating from the 18th century. They show the presiding deities of different Vaishnava centres, as well as diverse saintly and holy men. One scene to the rear (west) of the sanctuary illustrates the Garuda vahana being transported in procession, together with parasols, fly-whisks and other insignia. A royal devotee on an elephant plays cymbals and sings the glory of Varadaraja. A flight of steps on the east side of the colonnade ascends to the raised sanctuary that forms the nucleus of the complex. This enshrines bronze images of Vishnu flanked by consorts: guardian figures protect the doorway. The rectangular tower above has been renovated recently.

The tour of Kanchipuram concludes with an excursion across the Vegavati River to *Tiruparuttikunram* in order to visit the Jain complex. Known as *Trailokyanatha*, this consists of two double shrines, each with a pair of apsidal-ended sanctuaries, built in the 12th century Chola style, with small towers capped by hemispherical roofs. The exteriors have been much renovated, and no sculptures survive. The shrines, one of which is dedicated to Vardhamana, are preceded by a common mandapa with slender columns, an addition of the 17th century. Its ceiling is covered with paintings illustrating the stories of the Jain savious, particularly of Rishabhadeva and Vardhamana in their former lives. The scenes are arranged in long panels with labels filled with processions of elephants, soldiers, standard-beaters, dancers and musicians. One scene depicts the story of Danendra, a naga king, who offered his realm to the relatives of Rishabhadeva so that they would not disturb the meditation of the saint: the relatives are depicted within their walled cities. Another scene relates how Vardhamana overcame Sangama, a jealous god who assumed the form of a serpent: the saviour stands before a tree, around which a snake is coiled. These and other narratives are twice interrupted by circular compositions that represent celestial audience halls. They each show eight concentric rings containing miniature figures, trees and shrines, with a saviour enthroned in the middle.

Immediately north of the Trailokyanatha stands the *Chandraparabha Temple*. Its 9th century Pallava date is indicated by the rearing lions on the wall pilasters, and the squat square tower.

F. UTTIRAMERUR

This town, 25 km. south of Kanchipuram or 27 km. southwest of Chengalpattu, is of interest for two temples of the late Pallava period dating from the reign of Dantivarman (798-817). Their architecture anticipates the Chola style.

The *Sundaravarda Perumal Temple* was inspired by the Vaikuntha Perumal at Kanchipuram, since it consists of three sanctuaries arranged vertically, accommodating seated, reclining and standing forms of Vishnu. Other aspects of this divinity are housed in subsidiary shrines that project from three sides at each level. The upper storeys are reached by steps from the attached mandapa. The moulded basement of the outer walls of the temple have yalis and makaras at the corners. The balustrades flanking the steps to subsidiary shrine are carved with panels, such as Lakshmi (south). The walls have flat pilasters and shallow niches. The brick and plaster parapet that rises over the eaves has pronounced roofs forms over the projecting shrines. The multi-storeyed tower is capped with a hemispherical roof; its ornamentation is recent.

Only the lower portions of the nearby *Kailasanatha Temple* belong to the Pallava era; the tower over the sanctuary and the attached mandapa are 11th century additions. Columns within the mandapa display Chola styled decorated shafts and fluted columns.

G. TIRUTTANI

The *Subrahmanya Temple*, built on top of a hill outside Tiruttani, is today the chief attraction of this small town, 86 km. northwest of Chennai or 45 km. directly north of Kanchipuram. A path leads from the centre of the town past a square tank with a central pavilion and a series of rest-houses, before climbing a long stepped path to the temple. This monument is laid out in a sequence of ascending terraces. Doorways in the middle of the east side, giving access to two concentric roofed enclosures, are cloaked in gilded brass sheets and embossed with peacock motifs, an emblem of the god to whom the temple is consecrated, The flag pole and altar between the two doorways are similarly clad. The main sanctuary at the highest level is a rudimentary structure dating from Pallava times, with icons of Subrahmanya on its outer walls. A gorgeously attired icon of the god serves as the main object of veneration. The same divinity, riding a peacock and accompanied by consorts, is worshipped within two minor shrines. A line of small stone statues of soldiers holding swords, representing Subrahamanya's votive army, is seen in the outer enclosure.

Of greater artistic interest is the modest *Virattaneshvara Temple*, 1.5 km. northeast of Tiruttani, on the other side of a rivulet. This 9th century structure has a small east facing, linga shrine with an apsidal end. The similarly shaped vaulted roof that rises above has a frontal arched projection filled with the figures of a Somaskanda group. The sanctuary is entered through an antechamber and a later mandapa. Niches on the outer walls accommodate splendid examples of late Pallava period sculptures: Vinayaka and Dakshinamurti (south), Vishnu (west), and Durga (north). Loose icons of Shiva, Ganesha, Surya and the matrikas are placed within the mandapa.

H. PULICAT

This somewhat remotely located settlement gives its name to a shallow salt-water lagoon, about 60 km. long and up to 20 km. wide, beside the Bay of Bengal, on the border between Tamil Nadu and Andhra Pradesh. The lagoon is separated from the ocean by a spit of land, on which is situated the town of Pulicat, ancient Palakkadu, 40 km. north of Chennai.

An important port for the Vijayanagara governors of Chandragiri in the 15th-16th centuries, Pulicat was well known to European traders for its finely woven and colourful printed cotton textiles. In 1609 the Dutch built a fort here called Castel Geldria, which rapidly became the principal headquarters of Dutch commerce on the Coromandel Coast. This was occupied by the British in 1781-85 and again in 1705, before finally capitulating in 1824.

Of the original Dutch fort at Pulicat, only the perimeter moat can now be made out. The *Dutch Cemetery*, to the west, is of greater interest. This is entered through an arched gate bearing the date 1656. Posts at either side are carved with unusual, life-sized skeletal figure: one carries an hourglass on his head, the other a skull and a column. The tombstones, which range in date from 1658 to 1776, are elaborately carved with royal coats-of-arms; one example shows a relief view of the original fort. The mausoleum of one Dutch governor is conceived as a small arcaded square structure with a barrel vaulted roof. Its arched ends are filled with plaster renditions of cherubs and coats of arms. A dilapidated church and a sundial adjoin the cemetery.

38. Vellore

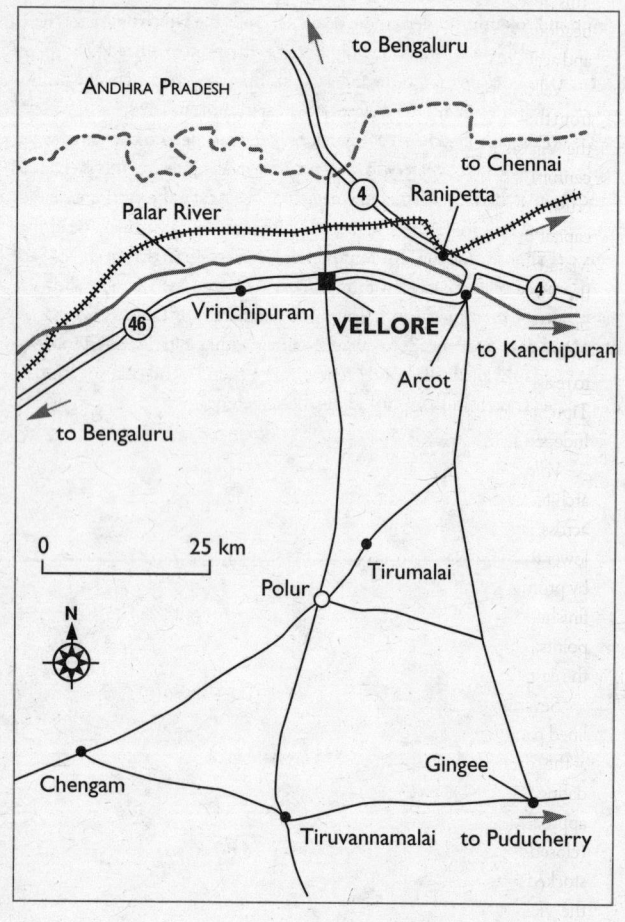

Although Vellore may be reached as a day trip from Chennai, an overnight stay is recommended in order to have sufficient time to visit the fort and temple in the city [A], and the relics of the Nawabs at nearby Arcot [B].

Hindu monuments of religious and artistic significance within easy reach of Vellore include those at Vrinchipuram [C], Tiruvannamalai [E] and Chengam [F]. An excursion to Tiruvannamalai may also include the Jain shrine at Tirumalai [D].

A. Vellore

This historical city, with its celebrated fort, is best known today as the headquarters of the Christian Medical College, founded in 1900; its hospital and academic campus are prominent landmarks in the city.

Vellore Fort, northwest of the commercial heart of the city, a short distance from the Palar River, is traditionally associated with Chinna Bomma, viceroy of the Vijayanagara kings of Chandragiri [35C] in the last decade of the 16th century. This figure attempted to assert his autonomy, but was eventually crushed by Venkatapatideva in 1604, after which Vellore served as the second capital of the Vijayanagara emperors. The fort was captured in 1676 by the Marathas, who held it until they were ousted in 1708 by Daud Khan, general of the Mughal army. Soon after, Vellore became the residence of Murtaza Ali, brother-in-law of the claimant of the Arcot throne. The city remained under the sway of Arcot until 1780, when a British garrison gained control in an attempt to resist the forces of Haidar Ali. After the fall of Srirangapattana [15C] in 1799, Tipu Sultan's family was detained here. The fort remained in British hands until Independence, in spite of a mutiny in 1806.

Vellore Fort is the outstanding example of sultanate influenced military architecture in Tamil Nadu. Its irregular quadrangular interior, almost 500 m. across, is defined by two lines of sloping granite ramparts, the outer skin being lower than the inner one. The walls are reinforced with round bastions topped by prominent curved battlements, with spaces in between for muskets. Finely finished, box-like guardrooms project from the bastions and intermediate points. The ramparts are shielded by a broad moat bridged by a causeway on the east, the only entrance to the fort.

Several 19th century British period buildings are grouped around the tree-lined parade ground in the middle of the fort, the finest being the *Court House* at the southern end. Facing east onto the parade ground is the *Church of St John*, dating from 1846. Its modest but well proportioned Neo-Classical portico is approached by a balustraded staircase. The *Archaeological Museum* next door (closed Fridays) occupies another historical building. The lower galleries are stocked with carvings and architectural pieces gathered from various sites in the vicinity. They include a set of the dilpakas from Malpadi, and a large Lakshmi Narayana assembled from broken pieces. The upper level of the museum has an instructive photographic display of Indian maritime trade, as well as excavated prehistoric stone tools and pottery.

The chief monument of historical importance in Vellore Fort is the *Jalakanteshvara Temple*. Abandoned for many years, the building was never subjected to disfiguring alterations or extensions; as a result it preserves its original late 16th century character. It was re-consecrated as a place for worship only in 1981. The temple is contained within a square enclosure defined by high walls, with some blocks enlivened with shallow carvings of fish. The enclosure is entered on the south through a single imposing gopura. Its lower two granite storeys are adorned with mouldings and ornate pilasters, some standing in pots, others framing niches, now empty. Above rise the seven diminishing storeys of the recently renovated brick and plaster tower. Openings in the middle of the long sides are flanked by guardian figures. Monster masks decorate the arched ends of the vaulted roof.

Immediately inside the gopura, on the left, stands the mandapa for which the temple is famous. The outer piers of the hall are fashioned as rearing yalis, some with elephant trunks, and richly bridled horses, all with riders: accessory themes include warriors, hunters and other beasts. The vitality of these vigorous compositions and the virtuosity of the caving, almost in the round, are unsurpassed in Southern Indian sculpture. Panels of dancers separated by dwarfs adorn the plinth on which the hall is raised. Corner piers and those lining the central aisle of the interior are distinguished by clusters of slender cut-out colonettes. The dais on the elevated floor at the end of the central aisle has a shallow tortoise base. The ceiling above is conceived as a pendant lotus, with parrots hanging upside-down from petals. The flower is surrounded by a ring of dancing figures and rows of miniature deities. Smaller mandapas in the other corners of the enclosure are linked by a colonnade runs along the perimeter wall. Numerous loose carvings are displayed here.

A second gopura, imitating at a smaller scale that in the outer walls, gives access to the inner enclosure of the temple. Here stands the main shrine, a modest structure with undecorated walls, entered through a porch on the south. Opposite the entrance, within the mandapa, is a small Nataraja shrine. A turn to the left is required to approach the linga shrine to the west, which is reached by passing through a doorway flanked by large guardian figures. The plaster towers over the Nataraja and linga shrines have been restored recently. A flag column and Nandi are placed outside the temple, on the east. They are aligned with a pierced stone window set into the east wall of the temple mandapa. Shrines dedicated to Subrahmanya (west) and Devi (northwest) corner are set into the peripheral colonnade of the enclosure. A set of Nayanmars is displayed in the south colonnade.

The only other historical monument in Vellore worth visiting is the *Dargah of Tipu Sultan's Family*, 1.5 km northeast of the fort, next to the road leading to Arcot. Here stand the tombs of Bakshi Begum, wife of Haidar Ali and mother of Tipu, dated 1806, and of Badhsah Begum, Tipu's wife, dated 1835. Both are conceived as octagonal domed chambers surrounded by arcades, and topped by ornamental parapets and domes raised on petalled necks. The nearby graves of other relatives are simpler structures.

B. ARCOT

This town, 27 km. east of Vellore, on the south bank of the Palar River, is associated with a line of rulers known by their title as Nawabs. These figures were descended from Daud Khan, the Mughal governor who occupied Arcot after the fall of Gingee [39F] in 1698. During the course of the 18th century, both the French and the British came into conflict with the Nawabs for supremacy of this part of Tamil Nadu. In 1751 the East India Company sent Robert Clive to Arcot, in order to divert the enemy from the siege of Tiruchirapalli [41A]. The capture and subsequent defence of Arcot are significant events in the military history of the period. Clive was forced to surrender to the French under Lally in 1785, but the town was recaptured by the British in 1760, only to be lost to Tipu Sultan in 1783. It was finally secured by the Government of Madras in 1799.

Because of the fierceness of these various struggles, Arcot preserves few relics of its past. The *Delhi Gate* is the only remaining portion of the brick walls that once surrounded the town. Of greater interest are the monuments near the river. The *Tomb of Sadatullah Khan*, who died in 1732, is surrounded by a colonnade topped with angled eaves and a parapet of domical finials. The same parapet and finials are repeated above the walls supporting the three-quarter hemispherical dome. The *Jami Mosque* in the northeast corner of the compound is surmounted by an ornate parapet running between slender octagonal minarets with domical tops. Other smaller tombs are located within the town.

Ranipetta, 4 km. north of Arcot, on the opposite bank of the Palar, marks the site that functioned as the cavalry station of the European quarter. The old English cemetery has many tombs dating from 17891 onwards. *St Mary's Church* of 1815 is a plain Neo-Classical structure typical of Cantonment religious architecture.

C. VRINCHIPURAM

This small town on the south bank of the Palar River, 14 km. west of Vellore, is worth visiting because of the Marghabandhu Temple. This religious monument is linked with the Nayakas of Gingee, who were responsible for its renovation in the 17th century. The temple is grandly scaled, dominating the surrounding earthen lanes and thatched houses. It is entered on the east through a large gopura of standard design; its seven-storeyed tower being recently refurbished. This gateway gives access to the outer enclosure of the temple. A mandapa with 36 columns, containing a flag column protruding through the roof, partly conceals the three-storeyed gopura that leads to the inner enclosure. A well with a brick and plaster lion built over the steps is seen to the left; to the right is a mandapa with a raised platform at the rear.

Twin mandapas with piers adorned with fine sculptures occupy the northwest and southwest corners of the outer enclosure. They appear to be modelled on the celebrated mandapa at Vellore. The Vrinchipuram examples, however, are smaller and lower, but repeat the same arrangement of yali and horse columns on the periphery, and columns with clustered cut-out colonettes at the corners and along the central aisles. The northwest mandapa has additional figures of the Nayaka patron and his wife carved onto the pair of columns in front of the raised dais at the rear.

The apsidal-ended linga shrine at the core of the inner enclosure of the temple, possibly dating back to the 12th century, is contained within later colonnades. It is approached through a mandapa with lateral steps on the north and south; a window in the middle of the east wall is aligned with the sanctuary. A Natesha shrine is placed against the north wall of the enclosure.

D. TIRUMALAI

This small hamlet lies 18 km. northeast of Polur on the Tiruvannamalai road, 48 km. south of Vellore. The 16th century Jain Complex, built up to a granite outcrop, is of interest for its fragmentary paintings. The lower temple enshrines a large carved image of seated Mahavira, with a tree of life painted onto the wall behind. Steps ascend to the upper temple, inside which brass images are displayed. The rock above has carvings of diverse Jinas, including Bahubali and Parshvanatha. Brick chambers at two levels are built into the rocky overhang. The walls and granite ceilings at the upper level are plastered and painted. In addition to floral patterns there are unusual circular diagrams with Jinas in the middle surrounded by segments filled with miniature figures.

E. TIRUVANNAMALAI

This celebrated pilgrimage town is located 82 km. south of Vellore, but can also be reached from Puducherry [39A], 103 km. to the east. The fort at Gingee, 37 km. east from Tiruvannamalai, can by visited en route to Puducherry.

Tiruvannamalai is celebrated for the Arunachaleshvara temple, one of the largest in Tamil Nadu. The festival that takes place here in November-December is accompanied by a popular cattle fair. On the night of the tenth day of the celebrations, a huge bonfire is lit on the summit of the rocky hill that rises steeply to the west of the town. The fire burns for many days and is visible from a great distance. Devotees prostrate themselves at the sight of the flames, which they consider to be the manifestation of Shiva's fiery linga, worshipped in the temple below.

The town is dotted with small shrines dedicated to different deities, including Durga and Subrahamanya. There are also many tanks associated with the directional guardian deities, such as Indra and Agni, in which float festivals regularly take place.

A popular rite at Tiruvannamalai is the auspicious circumambulation of the mountain. The route is marked by numerous shrines and wells.

Sri Ramanasara, the spiritual retreat founded by the illustrious guru Ramana Mahrishi, who died in 1950, is located in a shady compound 1 km. southwest of the town. Its international reputation is confirmed by the many foreign visitors who flock there.

The innermost streets of Tiruvannamalai echo the rectangular configuration of the *Arunachaleshvara Temple*, the high walls of which define three concentric enclosures that extend eastwards to form a sequence of spacious courts. Gopuras positioned on four sides are aligned with each other in both directions to create a layout of remarkable symmetry. The temple is usually approached from the east, through colonnades with wide central passageways that accommodate a market of lively shops. One colonnade is roofed with corbelled timbers; another has a ceiling with modern painted compositions.

Of the four gopuras in the middle of the outermost circuit of walls, that on the east is the largest, rising no less than 66 m. high. It is assigned to the first half of the 17th century, when the monument was renovated by the Nayakas of Thanjavur [40A]. The ornamentation of the lower granite elements is elaborate, with decorated basements, wall pilasters and eaves. Finely carved figures are inserted into the wall niches, including, on the outer (east) face, Shiva as Bhikshatanamurti (north), and the same god dancing within the skin of the elephant demon (south). The ten diminishing brick and plaster storeys of the gopura create a soaring pyramidal mass, capped with the usual vaulted roof with arched ends. Shallow projections lining the passageway walls are divided into panels framing female dancers, with yalis at either side; dwarfs serve as brackets above. The jambs have maidens clutching creepers. Carved panels on the lintels show the battle of Kama and Rati, as well as Shiva with consorts, and elephants worshipping the linga. A painted ceiling panel over the passageway depicts royal elephants.

The outermost court of the Arunachaleshvara temple is reached after passing through the east gopura. The north side of the enclosure is occupied by an immense mandapa, dating from the 17th century. The inner row of 34 piers has blocks carved with diverse divinities. A linga chamber at one end is set at a lower level. A large stepped tank surrounded by a colonnade is located on the south side of the enclosure. The small east facing Subrahmanya shrine standing next to the edge of the water has intricately worked walls and columns in the late 16th century manner. A large seated Nandi and swing pavilion are placed in the middle of the enclosure. Four smaller gopuras, with less decorated walls, partly dating from the 14th century, give access to the second enclosure. Here there is another stepped tank, as well as a large mandapa with an open colonnade facing south. Traces of ceiling paintings include a scene showing the marriage of Shiva and Paravati.

Access to the third, innermost enclosure of the temple is by means of a single gopura on the east. The lower portions of the gateway are unadorned, suggesting an 11th century, Chola period date. The Shiva shrine standing inside the enclosure, on axis with the gopura, is surrounded on three sides by plain walls, covered with inscriptions. The shrine is entered through a columned porch on the east, partly containing an earlier lamp column, altar and Nandi. Small Subrahmanya and Ganesha shrines, with exquisitely decorated walls and columns, are positioned at either side.

Located within plain walls, the Shiva shrine at the core of the monument is surrounded on four sides by a spacious corridor. This is an addition of the 19th century, as is the aisle that leads to the shrine doorway, enhanced by an embossed brass frame. The shrine itself is a renovated Chola structure, with replacement panels of Dakshinamurti (south), Shiva appearing out of the linga (west), and Brahma (north) on its outer walls. The linga worshipped within is associated with the element of fire. Additional lingas and a complete set of brass Nayanmars are displayed in the surrounding colonnades. The associated Devi shrine is located in the northwest corner of enclosure. It is approached through two mandapas, the central aisle of the inner hall being flanked by an array of sculpted goddesses.

F. CHENGAM

Located 34 km. west of Tiruvannamalai, this small town is of interest for the modest, but artistic *Venugopala Parthasarathi Temple*. The monument consists of a simple east facing shrine preceded by an open mandapa, the inner space of which is defined by piers with yalis and cut-out colonettes. The ceiling over the central space is covered with Ramayana paintings laid out in narrow registers, each incident being identified by captions. Dating from the 17th century, the painted figures are characterised by precise linework and lively postures. Several episodes depict local versions of the Ramayana, such as the scene of Hanuman dragging Ravana's queen by the hair.

39. Puducherry

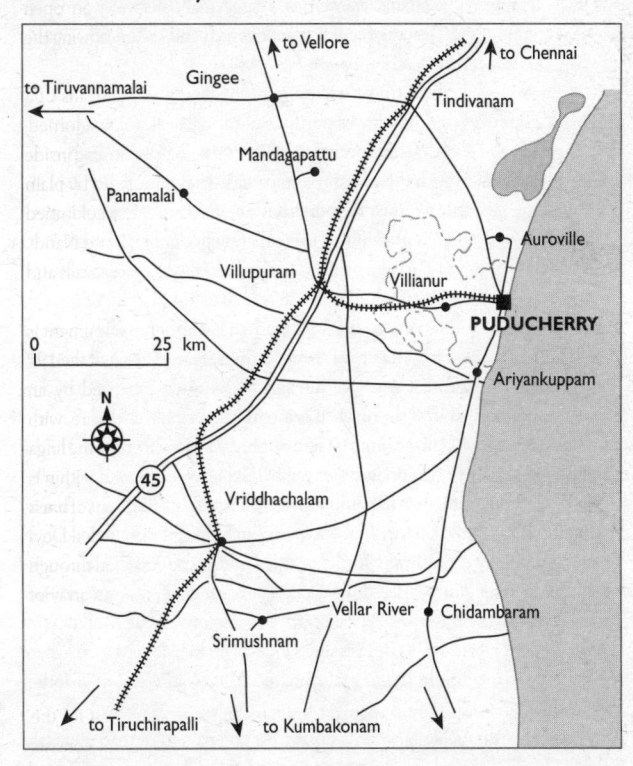

Formerly known as Pondicherry, this city is capital of the Union Territory incorporating the former French settlements of Southern India ceded to the Indian Government in 1954. (They include Yannon [30G], Karaikal [40P] and Mahé [48E].) Though Puducherry, does not form part of Tamil Nadu, it makes a logical point from which to reach a number of historical sites in the state that surrounds it.

At least one day should be reserved for the sights of the city [A] and those of nearby Ariyankuppam [B], Auroville [C] and Villianur [D].

A full day excursion to the fort at Gingee [F], the most spectacular in Tamil Nadu, can be combined with a visit to the cave-temple at Mandagapattu [E], or the hill shrine at Panamalai [G], both dating from the Pallava period. From Gingee it is possible to continue on to Tiruvannamalai [38E] and Vellore [38A].

Another full day from Puducherry will be required to tour the celebrated Nataraja temple at Chidambaram [H], especially if travelling on to Kumbakonam [40G]. The temples at Srimushnam [I] and Vriddhachalam [J] are easily accessible from Chidambaram.

A. Puducherry

The old part of the city facing onto the Bay of Bengal retains much of its traditional French character. The history of the city dates back to 1672, when the French secured land for a trading post from Ali Adil Shah II, ruler of Bijapur [23A], who at the time controlled this part of Southern India. The settlement established by François Martin, laid out over two years, served as the headquarters for the expansion of French influence in the region. Puducherry was occupied by the Dutch in 1693-97, and changed hands between the British and French no less than nine times in the course of the 18th century. Under Joseph François Dupleix, governor in 1741-54, Puducherry regained its former importance. However, in 1761, the British captured the city and demolished many of its finest buildings. Puducherry was finally restored to the French in 1817. In 1940 it declared for Free France.

Puducherry is known internationally as the home of the *Sri Aurobindo Ashram*, founded in 1926 by Sri Aurobindo, one of India's greatest philosopher-poets. Since then the ashram has developed into a popular and affluent organization. After Aurobindo's death in 1950, the running of the ashram was entrusted to Mirza Alfassa, his chief disciple, better known as the Mother, who died at the age of 93 in 1973. The ashram is located on Rue de la Marine, where the samadhi that entombs the mortal remains of Aurobindo and the Mother can be visited.

The plan of Puducherry, with its distinctive grid pattern of roads, was laid out in 1756-77 by Jean Law. The most important streets run perpendicular to the Bay of Bengal. Goubert Salai, the broad *Marina* running beside the ocean, is lined with handsome whitewashed edifices with colonnaded balconies. Among these is the *Municipal Building*, with its grandly scaled, timber floored reception room at the upper level. Similarly styled mansions, many with lush gardens surrounded by high walls, can be glimpsed in the streets behind.

Several villas have been converted into research institutions, such as the Ecole Français d'Extrême Orient and the Institut Français, both with fine libraries. A typical example of Puducherry's domestic architecture is the *House of Ananda Rangapalli*, the diarist and protegé of Dupleix, on Ranga Pillai Street (permission required to visit). Its reception rooms open off a central court with colonnades at two levels. The house is noteworthy for its carved woodwork. Midway along Goubert Salai is the *Gandhi Memorial*, with a statue of the Mahatma. It is surrounded by an arc of eight lofty granite columns, more than 11 m. high, allegedly brought from Gingee. The 27 m. high *Lighthouse* of 1836 stands nearby. The shady *Government Park* lies on axis with the memorial. Its tree lined paths fan out from a central pavilion with pedimented facades, crowned by an urn.

The park is overlooked from the north by the handsome Neo-Classical *Raj Nivas*, built on the site of Dupleix's residence. Next door, on the other side of Rue Louis, is the *Puducherry Museum* (closed Mondays). The lower rooms contain stone and metal sculptures form the Chola and later periods, as well as artefacts recovered from excavations at Arikamedu [B]. They include fragments of 1st-2nd century CE Roman amphorae, gems, lamps and glass moulds. Local pottery from the site is represented by grey and red wares, usually with simple incised designs, and burial urns. Coins and fragments of Chinese celadon porcelains found at Arikamedu date from the 11th-12th century. The upper rooms of the museum are stocked with furniture, paintings and other items assembled from various mansions in Puducherry.

The French presence at Puducherry is still evident in the many Catholic places of worship that dot the city. The *Church of Our Lady of the Angels* on Rue Romain Rolland, south of Government Park, dates from 1855. Its facade, flanked by two unadorned square towers, faces east towards the ocean. The interior is roofed by a barrel vault, with a great dome rising over the crossing. The oil painting of Our Lady in the altar was presented by Napoleon III. The tomb of the Marquis de Bussy, one of Dupleix's most enterprising followers, dated 1785, is located in the cemetery next door. A statue of Jeanne d'Arc stands in the middle of the small square opposite.

The *Church of Our Lady of the Immaculate Conception*, on Cathedral Street, was begun in 1779 by the Jesuits, but not completed until 1791. Its imposing facade presents paired Doric columns below and Ionic above, the latter flanked by curved volutes. A statue of Our Lady occupies a round-headed niche in the central pedimented bay. The interior has plain barrel vaults, with a central dome pierced by eight circular openings, with an octagonal lantern above.

A contrasting Neo-Gothic style, with towers flanking a central gable, and stained glass in the arched side windows, is seen in the *Church of the Sacred Heart of Jesus*, on South Boulevard. The *Church of the Assumption*, of 1851, at *Nellitoppu*, on the western outskirts of the city, has an image of Our Lady placed in a niche over the main entrance; on the left tower is a representation of St George slaying a yali-like monster. The vaulted interior is notable for its elegant gilded wooden altarpieces, the finest in Puducherry. That at the west end accommodates a Crucifix within a canopy enlivened with brightly painted flying angels.

B. Ariyankuppam

This insignificant village, 4 km. south of Puducherry, is of interest for the Church of *Our Lady of Good Heath*, founded in 1690 and subsequently rebuilt several times. The interior has rounded arches carrying a vault over the central aisle. A free-standing Crucifix is displayed on the altar; brightly painted wooden images are set on shelves in the side walls.

The archaeological site of *Arikamedu* is located 1 km east of the village, on the south bank of a lagoon formed by the Ariyankuppam River. Excavations here revealed traces of a port that flourished in the 1st-2nd centuries CE, trading mainly with the Mediterranean region. The architectural remains, which included vestiges of brick structures, possibly warehouses, and a courtyard with two small tanks, are no longer visible. Roman period artefacts discovered here are on view in the Puducherry Museum, and in the Archaeological Galleries of the Pantheon Complex, Chennai [36D].

C. AUROVILLE

The Mother personally conceived the utopian settlement of Auroville, 8 km. north of Puducherry. Founded in 1968, this has grown steadily over the years into a sizeable and cosmopolitan community, with comfortable villas set in spacious grounds on the fringe of the ocean. The names of the residences, Shanti (peace), Grace, Verité, Horizon, Transition, Gratitude, etc., express the spiritual aspirations of Auroville's population. Other than religious pursuits, the community has revived traditional industries; its workshops produce fine woven textiles, marble-dyed silks, handmade papers, perfumes and incense sticks. An active press disseminates the writings of Aurobindo and the Mother.

The visionary plan of Auroville, with lines of buildings spiralling outwards in continuous motion, symbolises the universality of its faith. The nucleus of this scheme is marked by an open-air circular amphitheatre, the *Bharat Nivas*, intended for cultural performances. It is surrounded by meditation rooms and beautifully maintained gardens laid out in petal formation. These features converge on the *Matrimandir* (check timings for visits). This remarkable spherical structure is created from panels hung on a concrete frame. Its staircases ascend to an inner sealed chamber with white marble floor and walls. Daylight entering from a hole in the roof is directed to a large crystal globe that glows mysteriously, providing an appropriate focus for meditation.

D. VILLIANUR

This small town, 11 km. west of Puducherry, is of interest for the *Tirukameshvara Temple*. The monument is entered from the east through a simple portico facing onto the main street. An open colonnade leads to an inner gopura, restored in 1887 with funds provided by a French government official. This gives access to the eastern half of the inner enclosure, mostly occupied by a mandapa, with a central space surrounded by piers with carvings of figures and horses with riders. The central ceiling panel has a lotus surrounded by deities.

The western half of the enclosure contains the principal linga sanctuary, as well as subsidiary Devi and Murugan shrines, dating back to the 12th century Chola era, entirely encased in later colonnades. North of this enclosure is a large square tank with a pavilion in the middle. The large gopura on the south has finely worked niches, filled with carvings. The seven-storeyed tower has been much renovated.

The *Church of Our Lady of Lourdes*, a short distance away, was erected in 1876 in imitation of the Basilica in France. The statue of Our Lady was donated by the French Government a year later. The church boasts its own tank, a unique feature. Large crowds gather here for the ritual bathing during the festival honouring the Madonna, held in June.

E. MANDAGAPATTU

The 7th century *Cave Temple* at this site is located 60 km. northwest of Puducherry, 2 km. east of the road leading to Gingee, about 20 km. north of Villupuram on NH 45. Mandagapattu is one of the earliest Pallava shrines, comparable with examples at Mamallapuram [37A] and Tiruchirapalli [41A]. Although an inscription of Mahendravarman (580-63) mentions the worship of Brahma, Shiva and Vishnu, no icons of these gods are found here. The facade presents a simple line of massive part-octagonal columns leading into a hall. Guardian figures with clubs are seen at either end.

F. GINGEE

This fortified site lies 68 km. northwest of Puducherry, via Tindivanam; alternatively it may be reached from Tiruvannamalai, 37 km. west. A little more than 1 km. west of the town lies Gingee Fort.

Palace Zone, Gingee.

Gingee rose to prominence under the emperors of Vijayanagara [20B-C] in the 15th and 16th centuries as a strategic outpost guarding the northern reaches of the Tamil country. The Gingee governors steadily asserted their autonomy, openly proclaiming their independence during the civil war of 1614, in which they took up arms against Venkatapatideva of Chandragiri [35C]. Gingee was threatened by the Adil Shahi forces of Bijapur, and succumbed to them in 1648. The invaders renamed Gingee as Badshahabad, and occupied it for almost 30 years. In 1677 the Maratha chief Shivaji successfully besieged the fort, followed in 1698 by the Mughal general Zulficar Khan. But the site proved malarial, and in 1716 the Mughal army, now virtually independent of Delhi, shifted their headquarters to Arcot [38B]. In the middle of the 18th century Gingee was taken by a detachment of French soldiers, who held it until the capture of Puducherry by the British. At the time of Haidar Ali's invasion of Tamil Nadu in 1780, Gingee was garrisoned by Arcot troops and a few British soldiers. By the beginning of the 19th century the site was abandoned.

Gingee consists of a trio of formidable *Mountain Citadels*: Krishnagiri (north), Rajagiri (east) and Chandrayanadurg (south), each defended by lines of thick granite walls built into the steep sides of the rocky hills. Substantial ramparts with round bastions and a broad moat connecting the citadels create a vast triangular zone, more than 1.5 km. from north to south. Intermediate walls divide this area into inner and outer enclosures.

The tour of Gingee described here begins at the *East Gate* of the inner enclosure. This is shielded by outworks containing a passageway with no less than four changes of direction before the actual doorway is reached. An arched portal, standing freely inside, provides a ceremonial entrance to the *Palace Zone*. This consists of an ensemble of courtly structures, only partly revealed by the excavators. The complex is dominated by the *Kalyana Mahal*, with a central pool surrounded by an arcade, overlooked on the north by a six-storeyed square tower. This has arched openings surrounding a central staircase block. The pavilion that rises above has a pyramidal roof displaying tiers of eave-like mouldings. The remains of earthenware pipes embedded in the walls of the tower suggest a sophisticated hydraulic system.

Triple lines of arcaded chambers, most likely stables for horses and grooms, stretch north from the Kalyana Mahal, defining a large *Parade Ground*. An excavated structure with a central chamber surrounded by a colonnade at the western side of the parade ground may have been a royal residence. In front (east) is a green stone slab supported on short legs, with a large block imitating a cloth bolster. This could have served as a formal seat for the Nayakas to oversee processions of troops and animals.

A large tank to the south of the parade ground, partly cut into the rock, is surrounded by colonnades. Several large *Granaries* with pointed brick vaults stand in the vicinity. One example has ornate plaster decoration on the sides and arched ends of the vault; another example, further southwest, ingeniously combines three vaulted chambers and a connecting corridor within a rectangle of walls.

The path proceeding southwest from the Kalyana Mahal passes through a gate before ascending *Rajagiri*, rising more than 165 m. above the plain. Though the summit is reached only after a strenuous climb, visitors are rewarded with a splendid panorama of the whole of Gingee Fort. At the top stand two small shrines, several granaries, and a ruined flagstaff tower. The last feature may have once resembled the tower of the Kalayana Mahal. It is necessary to descend by the same route to the east gate of the inner enclosure before continuing the tour.

Immediately in front (east) of the gate stands the *Mosque Sadat Ullah Khan* (1703-10), one of the Arcot rulers. The facade of the prayer hall has seven arches with lobed profiles surmounted by an arcaded parapet, and flanked by octagonal finials with domical tops. A small court with a central pool in front is raised on arcades.

About 500 m. southeast of the mosque stands the abandoned and dilapidated *Venkataramana Temple*. This 16th century monument is entered through a prominent gopura on the east; the seven-storeyed tower is still intact. Ramayana scenes and Vaishnava divinities are carved onto the side walls of the passageway. Mandapas of different designs occupy the outer enclosure of the temple. A second gopura on the east gives access to the inner enclosure. Here stands a trio of east facing, unadorned shrines, the two side ones dedicated to Vishnu's consorts. A fourth shrine projects outwards from middle of the west enclosure wall. Lofty pavilions with unusual slender columns capped by brick towers stand in the fields outside the temple.

Another feature worth seeing in the outer enclosure of Gingee Fort is the *Vellore Gate*, easily reached from the main road that runs through the middle of the site. The gate makes use of extensive curving outworks to shield the entrance. A line of steps worked into the ramparts ascends from the main road to *Krishnagiri*. Among the structures clustered on the summit of this mountain citadel are an audience hall with curious fluted domes and projecting balconies, two vaulted granaries, an oil storage well, and the modest Ranganatha and Krishna shrines.

The last feature to be described at Gingee is the *Pattabhirama Temple*, located 2 km. southwest of the town, hidden from the main road and the fortified site. Even more ruined than the Venkatarakamana temple, with which it is contemporary, the monument is also laid out with a trio of east facing shrines dedicated to the god and his two consorts. A short distance in front (east) of the gopura stands a lofty pavilion raised on a decorated basement. Steps in the middle of each side are flanked by balustrades carved with elephants, yalis, geese, and double-headed birds clutching diminutive elephants in their beaks. The 12 slender columns with 16-sided shafts support stone eaves, and a cluster of five brick towers.

Another historical monument of interest in the Gingee area is located at *Singavaram*, 4 km. north of the town. The 7th century cave temple, cut into the east face of a large boulder perched above the village here, is reached by a long flight of steps. Structural additions from later periods, including a gateway, are built up to its front. Guardian figures are sculpted at either side of the colonnade that frames the hall. The shrine within has its rear wall almost entirely taken up with a 5 m. long image of Ranganatha. A stalk rising from the navel of the reclining form of Vishnu blossoms into a lotus upon which Brahma is seated. Bhudevi appears at the feet of the god, with Garuda and attendants to the sides. Immediately north of the cave temple is a deep niche with an icon of Durga standing on the buffalo head.

G. Panamalai

This small village, 75 km. west of Puducherry on the road from Villupuram to Vettavalam, is of interest for the *Talagirishvara Temple* that crowns the top of a nearby hill. This important 8th century Pallava structure is built entirely out of local reddish granite. The walls of the square sanctuary project outwards on four sides to accommodate an entrance chamber and three subshrines. The regularly spaced pilasters have rearing lions at the bases, a characteristic feature of Pallava architecture. A pyramidal tower with vaulted roofs rising over the projecting shrines and entrance chamber is capped by a hemispherical roof. The central shrine accommodates a multi-faceted linga on a circular pedestal; the rear wall has a Somaskanda panel. Similar, but smaller lingas are placed in the subshrines. Traces of paintings include a mural fragment in the north shrine, depicting dancing Shiva attended by Parvati. The mandapa adjoining the sanctuary on the east is a later addition.

H. Chidambaram

This town, 67 km. south of Puducherry, is celebrated for the great *Nataraja Temple*, in which Shiva is worshipped in his form as Lord of the Dance. The monument is believed to mark the spot of the legendary dance contest won by Shiva in a bid to impress his consort Parvati; legend places it as the source of the original linga. Founded in the Chola era, the temple remains one of the major pilgrimage destinations in Tamil Nadu. The management of the shrines within the complex is under the control of the local Dikshita brahmins.

The monument occupies an area of about 22 ha. in the middle of Chidambaram. It is contained within a double quadrangle of enclosure walls surrounded by broad streets used for chariot festivals at various times throughout the year. When not in use, these chariots are parked in the streets, where they may be inspected for their intricately worked wooden carvings. The outer set of enclosure walls, added in the 17th century, has entrances with simple porticos in the middle of each side. Passageways flanked by low walls lead from each entrance to a towered gopura in the inner set of enclosure walls.

The four *Gopuras* that frame the temple are the finest of the Chola period, demonstrating the monumental architectural style achieved during the 12th century. The gates all conform to a standard scheme. The lower granite walls are divided into two storeys, each with moulded basements, pilastered niches, and overhanging eaves. The upper storeys are heightened, and display additional pilasters standing in pots. All these elements are adorned with deeply incised foliage and scrollwork. Splendid sculpted images inserted into the wall niches at both levels depict the full range of Shaiva images. They include Shiva as the ascetic with a trident, and the same god dancing on the demon (east gopura); Bhikshatanamurti, Durga and Sarasvati (north gopura); Dakshinamurti and the navagrahas (south gopura); and Subrahmanya (west gopura). Sages, guardians and attendants are found on all of the gopuras.

Jambs lining the lofty passageways inside the gopuras are divided into panels with maidens in different dance movements; labels identify each of the 108 postures depicted on the east and west gopuras. Wall niches inside the passageways house sculptures of deities and donors. The delicately modelled portrait of Krishnadevaraya in the north gopura dates from the visit of the Vijayanagara emperor to Chidambaram in 1516. The brick and plaster towers above have been much altered in later times. They are divided into seven diminishing storeys, each covered with plaster sculptures. Shallow projections in the middle of the long sides have openings at each level. The towers are capped by vaulted roofs with arched ends and pot finials.

The gopuras give access to a spacious paved court. The main temple, contained within its own quadrangle of walls, occupies much of the southern half of the enclosure. It is entered on the east of west through lesser gopuras. The space inside is almost entirely filled with colonnades and subshrines, many dating from the 19th century. The *Nritya Sabha*, in the south corridor, is an ornate structure assigned to the late Chola period. The 13th century hall is elevated on a double basement adorned with friezes of dancers, dwarfs and yalis, as well as wheels with prancing horses, partly concealed by later colonnades. The columns of the Nritya Sabha are intricately carved with miniature temple facades; the ceiling is panelled with fully modelled lotuses. A wall niche housing a remarkable Bhikshatana image (restored) is framed by fluted pilasters. Among the other features of interest here is a Devi shrine in the north corridor.

A gate on the south and two on the east, the one with a tower being recent, lead to the innermost enclosure. In the middle stand the the two hut-like chambers that constitute the ritual focus of the Nataraja temple: the south facing *Chit Sabha*, and attached *Kanaka Sabha*. These shrines are unique in the religious architecture of Tamil Nadu, since they reproduce the forms of simple thatched huts. Raised on a common masonry platform, the two chambers are built entirely of wood, with timber columns, wall panels and curving roofs cloaked in sheets of gilded copper. Though founded in Chola times, the two sabhas have been renewed periodically through the centuries. Two forms of Shiva receive worship here: the bronze icon of Nataraja, and the space (akasha) linga, which is invisible. The east facing Govindaraja shrine that stands nearby houses the reclining image of Vishnu.

The *Raja Sabha*, a vast mandapa dating back to the 12th century, occupies the northeast corner of the outer enclosure of the Nataraja temple. This hall may have served a royal ceremonial purpose, and is linked with the Chola kings who are known to have resided at Chidambaram. Large elephants with attendants are sculpted on the east and west sides of the high basement. The broad steps and porch on the south are additions of the 17th century; the curving brick vaults within belong to the 18th century Maratha period. The dais at the north end of the central aisle is for displaying processional images at the Ani Tirumanjanam festival in June-July, and the Markashi Tirvatira festival in December-January. The large rectangular Shivaganga tank nearby dominates the northern part of the enclosure.

Facing east onto the tank is the *Shivakamasundari Shrine*, which houses the goddess associated with Nataraja. The shrine stands in its own rectangle of enclosure walls. Its entrance gate, with curving balustrades flanking the steps, is assigned to the Chola period, as is the colonnade surrounding the enclosure within. The two mandapas preceding the sanctuary are, however, later in date, as is obvious from the paintings that cover the ceiling of the outer hall. The paintings over the side aisles are among the best preserved examples of Nayaka pictorial art, notable for their clear linework and vivid red, ochre, green and white tones. The 17th century compositions are arranged in narrow registers. One set of panels (north aisle) relates the legend of Shiva as Bhikshatanamurti. The god appears as the naked beggar holding a parasol, accompanied by a beautiful, scantily clad woman, identified as Mohini. The next scene shows the sages being seduced by Mohini, while their wives fall under the spell of the god. In a later episode, the sages tend a sacrificial fire, out of which demons are produced, only to be repelled by Shiva.

Scenes from the life of Manikkavachakar, one of the Nayanmars, are mostly devoted to the childhood of the saint, and his exploits as a youth in the service of the Pandya king. A vivid set of panels from this story illustrates Shiva's revenge on the king for punishing Manikkavachakar: disguised as a trader, Shiva delivers a pack of jackals transformed into horses to the king's stables; the jackals pounce on the king's horses; the saint stands on the bank of a river with a stone on his bank; Shiva then makes the river overflow its bank, with people swimming frantically through the water. In the narrative of Cheraman Perumal (south aisle), another of the Nayanmars, the hero is shown riding an elephant accompanied by soldiers, on the way to Chidambaram to worship Nataraja. A further panel illustrates the story of Upamanyu. Modern paintings cover the ceiling over the central space of the hall.

The *Subrahmanya Shrine*, in the compound immediately to the north of the Shivakamasundari shrine, dates from the Chola era, as is clear from the treatment of the outer walls and the hall columns with superimposed building facades on the shafts. The later brick vaults are covered with 19th century paintings, including views of the principal temples in Tamil Nadu associated with Murugan, the god to whom the shrine is dedicated.

I. SRIMUSHNAM

This little visited town, 40 km. west of Chidambaram, has a pair of religious monuments dating from different periods, unusually arranged back to back. The east facing *Nityeshvara Temple* is a Chola foundation of the 10th century, recently restored. It stands in a rectangular enclosure, entered through a gateway overlooking a large tank with a central pavilion. The small square sanctuary of the temple has finely carved figures set in niches headed with makaras: Dakshinamurti flanked by sages (south), Shiva appearing out of the linga (west), and Brahma (north). The adjoining mandapa is a later addition.

The larger, west facing *Bhuvaraha Temple* is an elaborate monument, sponsored by the Gingee Nayakas in the 17th century. The complex is entered through gopuras on the north and west, the latter being more imposing, with a seven-storeyed tower, recently renewed. The outer enclosure has a mandapa, with spacious cross aisles, altars and a Garuda shrine, that gives access to an open pavilion that was originally a free-standing structure. The ornate sculptural treatment of the 16 columns in the pavilion marks it as one of the masterpieces of Nayaka art. The peripheral columns are raised on a basement carved with friezes of musicians and dancers, as well as miniature divinities standing in niches. The shafts here have yalis and horses with riders, projecting outwards, with groups of smaller figures beneath, The four central columns of the pavilion are embellished with portraits of the Nayaka rulers (not identified). The portly figures, sculpted in almost three dimensions, wear finely detailed costumes, jewellery, crowns and daggers. The ceiling above has elaborate lotus medallions surrounded by upside-down parrots and bands of figures, geese and scrollwork.

A nearby doorway leads to the inner enclosure of the temple. At the east end is the main shrine, in which Vishnu is venerated in his boar incarnation. The ornate treatment of the outer walls is typical of the Chola manner, as revived by the Nayakas. The shrine is topped with a brick tower capped by a square-domical roof.

J. VRIDDHACHALAM

Situated 80 km. southwest of Puducherry, this town can also be reached directly from Chidambaram, 55 km. to the east. The *Vriddhagirishvara Temple*, after which the town takes its name, is a Chola foundation, much extended in later times. The outer enclosure is framed by a quartet of imposing gopuras, the finest being that on the north. These 17th century structures have deep niches framed by bold pilasters set into the double wall series. Shallow jambs within the passageways are divided into small panels filled with female dancers. The pyramidal towers that rise above each have six diminishing storeys. Two additional gopuras on the east give access to the inner enclosures. The space between the outermost and intermediate gopuras on this side is partly occupied by a large mandapa built up against the south side of a structure, now used as the temple offices.

The mandapa within the intermediate gopura has slender colonettes on the outer columns; sculpted yalis line the central aisle. Portrait sculptures carved on the corner piers of the central bay of the mandapa resemble those at Srimushnam, suggesting that they may also portray the Gingee rulers. A Nataraja shrine is located at the northern end of this mandapa. The focal linga shrine at the heart of the innermost enclosure is surrounded by later colonnades.

40. Thanjavur

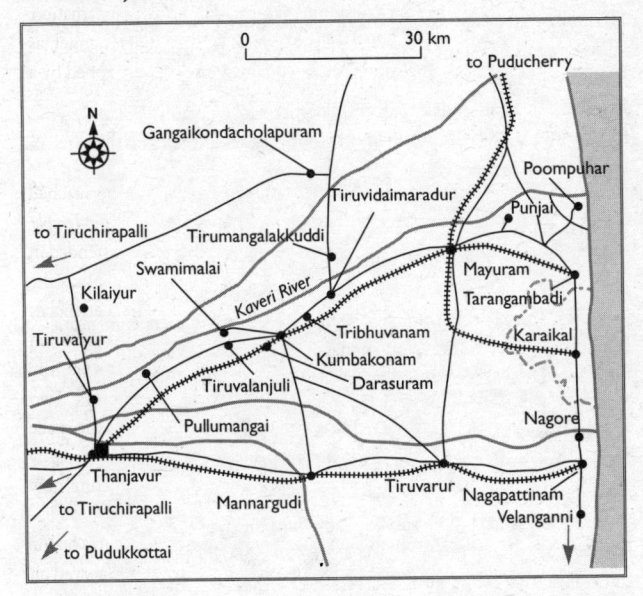

Home to successive Chola, Nayaka and Maratha rulers, Thanjavur served for more than 1,000 years as capital of the densely populated heartland of Tamil Nadu, known traditionally as Cholamandalam. The city stands at the head of the Kaveri River Delta, a richly irrigated zone traversed by innumerable water channels and dotted with towns and villages. Thanjavur lies between Punducherry [39] and Tiruchirapalli [41], the itineraries of which may be combined with that described here. Kumbakonam [G], 37 km. east of Thanjavur, makes an alternative base from where to visit historical localities in the delta area.

One full day is recommended for the temple, palace and museum at Thanjavur [A], with side trips to the shrines at Tiruvaiyur [B] and Kilaiyur [C]. A full-day journey to Kumbakonam may be combined with stops at Pullumangai [D], Tiruvalanjuli and Swamimalai [E], and Darasuram [F], which lie on the way. From Kumbakonam visitors have a choice of alternative routes. The road running northwest passes by the temples at Tribhuvanam and Tiruvidaimaradur [H], Tirumangalakuddi [I] and Gangaikondacholapuram [J], with the possibility of proceeding on to Chidambaram [39H] and Puducherry. The road leading south reaches the temple cities of Mannargudi [K] and Tiruvarur [L].

The Bay of Bengal seaboard east of Kumbakonam, best known to Europeans as the Coromandel (Cholamandalam) Coast, is lined with Hindu, Christian and Muslim places of worship, as well as vestiges of French and Danish settlements. Nagappatinam [M], Velanganni [N], Nagore [O] and Karaikal [P], Tarangambadi [Q] and Poompuhar [R] may all be covered in a full-day outing, with the possibility of visiting the temple at Punjai [S], with its fine carvings, on the way.

A. THANJAVUR

This city, known as Tanjore in British times, first attained prominence under the Cholas, who used it as one of their principal capitals in the 10th-12th centuries. The city seems to have been the preferred residence of Rajaraja I (985-1012), the greatest Chola monarch. Thanjavur continued to dominate the Kaveri Delta in later times. Under Vijayanagara [20B-C], it was the seat of a local line of governors, known as Nayakas, the first of whom was Sevappa Nayaka (1549-72). By the end of the 16th century his successors were ruling as independent kings. Raghunatha (1614-34) and Vijayaraghava (1614-73), the most powerful figures of this line, were challenged by their rivals at Gingee [39F] and Madurai [44A]; subsequently, the Thanjavur domains were raided by the Adil Shahis of Bijapur [23A]. In 1674 the Nayaka throne was captured by Ekoji, brother of Shivaji, the celebrated Maratha chief. Thanjavur thereupon became the headquarters of an independent line of Marathas, whose rulers resisted attacks by the Mughals and their representatives, the Nawabs of Arcot [38B]. By the end of the 18th century the British had taken command of the Thanjavur area, but the Marathas lived on as a declining royal family. Serfoji II (1798-1832) received an English education and achieved renown as a patron of learning and culture.

The circular configuration of Thanjavur as developed under the Nayakas is revealed by the moat that encircles the old city; however, the fortification walls are no longer to be seen, having been demolished by the British at the end of the 18th century. The great *Brihadishvara Temple* stands within its own quadrangular fort, southwest of the old city, where stone ramparts with European styled battlements overlook a broad moat, partly rock cut. The monument is the grandest architectural achievement of the Chola era. Built entirely of granite, it was consecrated in 1010 by Rajaraja I, who personally donated the gilded pot finial at the summit of its tower.

The temple stands in the middle of a vast rectangular enclosure defined by high walls, entered through two *Gateways* on the east. These impressive structures have vaulted roofs with arched ends, adorned with later plaster sculptures. Outsized guardian figures protect the east doorway of the inner gateway. Smaller carvings on the basement illustrate Shaiva legends, such as the marriage of Shiva and Parvati, and Shiva rescuing Markandeya. The *Columned Pavilion* in front (east) of the main temple shelters a huge monolithic Nandi, dating from the late 16th century. The pavilion has slender columns with carvings of donors on the shafts. The adjacent brass-clad flagpole is supported on podium carried by ganas and elephants with upraised trunks.

The *Main Temple* consists of a square linga sanctuary, an antechamber with doorways on the north an south, and a long mandapa entered through a porch on the east. The double-storeyed pilastered walls of the sanctuary are raised on a high basement adorned with yalis and makaras (top mouldings), and inscriptions relating the origins, construction and endowments of the monument (bottom mouldings). A seated dwarf supports the spout emerging from the sanctuary basement on the north. Openings flanked by guardians with clubs mark the middle of the sanctuary walls on three sides. Niche projections at either side are occupied by finely modelled figures, mostly of Shiva, including Bhikshatanamurti (south wall, east end), Natesha (south wall, west end), Harihara (west wall, south end), and Ardhanarishvara (north wall, west end). Other divinities are sculpted in the semi-circular niche tops. Attendant flank the pilasters standing in pots that occupy the intervening wall recesses.

The steeply pyramidal tower over the sanctuary rises to about 66 m. above the pavement. It consists of 13 diminishing storeys with pilastered walls, eaves and parapets that ascend dramatically to the octagonal domical roof crowned by a gilded pot finial. The plaster coated frontal (east) projection, with Shiva seated in a triple-arched niche, is an addition of the Maratha era. Doorways in the antechamber walls are reached by steps flanked by balustrades with curved tops and figural side panels. The long mandapa is only partly complete, and the wall sculptures unfinished. The east doorway is flanked by guardian figures. The entrance porch has columns with cut-out colonettes and rearing animals sheltered by deeply curved eaves. This is a Nayaka extension, as are the columns within the mandapa.

The sanctuary interior of the Brihadishvara is dominated by a colossal linga, almost 4 m. high, elevated on a circular pedestal; worship here has been revived here recently. The surrounding passageway on two levels is divided into chambers (only priests admitted). Sculptures in the lower passageway include a large dancing Shiva (west wall). Paintings from two periods cover the walls. Miniature four-armed dancers in different postures are sculpted onto the basement in the upper passageway.

Subsidiary buildings stand freely in the enclosure. The south facing *Chandeshvara Shrine* imitates features of the main temple, with which it is contemporary. The tower is crowned with an octagonal roof. The *Subrahmanya Shrine* in the northwest corner was erected by Sevappa Nayaka towards the end of the 17th century. Its outer walls have intricately fashioned pilasters, some standing in ornate pots. Icons of Subrahmanya are inserted into niches on three sides; the walls of the attached mandapa have images of Ganapati (south) and Durga (north). Stone windows with geometric designs light the antechamber within. The three-storeyed tower is topped with a hexagonal roof. The shrine is entered on the east through a porch with side steps. The long mandapa to the east was altered during the Maratha eva, as is evident from the 19th century portraits of royal figures of this line painted onto its inner walls.

Another Maratha period addition to the complex is the hall in front of the *Brihadnayaki Temple*. This goddess shrine is approached through a porch on the south, with piers enlivened with colonettes and yalis. The 19th century paintings on the mandapa ceiling inside illustrate Shaiva legends, the scenes being identified by Tamil labels. The nearby south facing *Natesha Shrine* dates from the 17th century, but the metal image of the dancing god installed in the sanctuary is an original Chola period icon.

Colonnades are built up to the temple compound on four sides. The lingas installed in the west and north colonnades, together with the paintings of mythological topics on the rear walls, are additions of the Maratha period. The *Interpretation Centre* in the south colonnade is worth visiting for its explanations of the temple's architecture. Here are displayed almost full size photographic reproduction of the otherwise inaccessible Chola period murals in the passageway around the linga sanctuary in the main temple. These give the best possible idea of the remarkable scenes showing Rajaraja and this queens worshipping Nataraja, and Shiva as Tripurantaka, riding in the chariot. Plaster cast of the sculpted dancing figures in the upper passageway of the main temple are also exhibited.

West of the temple enclosure, but within the ramparts that surround the monument, is the large square *Shivaganga Tank*. The water is overlooked on the east by *Christ Church*, a restrained Neo-Classical building of 1779. The triple vaulted aisles of its interior culminate in an apse roofed with a half-dome. The relief tablet by John Flaxman set into the west wall, depicting the death of the famous missionary, Reverend Christian Schwartz, in 1798, was donated by Serfoji II. The wooden pulpit in the church was used by Schwartz.

The freshly restored *Nayaka Palace*, surrounded by walls in the middle of the old city of Thanjavur, is approached from one of the main streets through two arched gateways. The royal complex was founded by Sevappa Nayaka, but was enlarged and altered in later times. At the heart of the complex is a free-standing, seven-storeyed square tower with arcades on four sides. A domed entrance chamber nearby gives access to a spacious court. Opposite, on the south side, is a two-storeyed building divided internally into halls and corridors, with pointed arches supporting shallow domes and vaults. A square chamber with a steep pyramidal tower rises from the roof. The tiers of diminishing eaves are enhanced with Neo-Classical balustrades and fluted domical finials, evidently 19th century modifications. On the east side of the court is the imposing Nayaka audience hall. Animal brackets carry the eaves that overhang the facade, while domes and vaults crowned with prominent lotus finials protrude above the roof. The interior is dominated by massive circular piers that support broad lobed arches and a pointed vault with ribbed and fluted surfaces. A large plaster composition, depicting the coronation of Rama, enlivens the walls at the rear of the chamber. The tableau looks down on a large green granite throne, above 5 m. square, set into the floor.

The *Thanjavur Art Gallery* occupies part of the Nayaka Palace. Its extensive collection of stone and metal sculptures has been assembled from numerous sites all over the Kaveri Delta. Granite sculptures are displayed in the domed entrance hall and the colonnades that surround the court. Among the 10th century exhibits are a damaged, but delicately modelled Ardhanarishvara, a standing Shiva with an elaborate headdress, and a Dakshinamurti. The existence of Buddhism in the area is confirmed by a seated Buddha from Pattisvaram. A unique set of 12th century figures from Darasuram shows Shiva as Bhikshatanamurti, with begging bowl, fly-whisk and prancing dog, attended by the wives of sages. Another panel from Darasuram depicts Shiva dancing triumphantly in the skin of the elephant demon that he has just slain. The vitality and twisted posture of the god are remarkable.

Of even greater artistic interest in the Art Gallery are the Chola period bronzes, the finest which are displayed in the audience hall of the Nayaka Palace. They include several 11th century figures from Tiruvengadu, such as Shiva as the archer (bow and arrow missing), the body posed with a slight tilt. The god is accompanied by Parvati, taking the hand of the goddess, or seated with her and the child-like figure of Skanda. The masterpiece of the Tiruvengadu series shows Shiva with snakes in his hair, leaning slightly to one side, one arm outstretched, together with Parvati. The refined posture and modelling of the god and his consort are unsurpassed in Chola art.

Among the other Chola period bronzes of artistic interest are an eight-armed Bhairava and a naked Bhikshatanamurti, the latter accompanied by a jumping dog. Standing images of Parvati are represented by examples from Tiruvelikudi and Kilaiyur. Figures of saints include Sundarar from Kilaiyur, and Kannappa from Tiruvengadu. A seated Parvati and a Kali with her hair standing on end are both assigned to the Vijayanagara era. The portrait of Vijayaraghava, almost 1 m. high, shows the Nayaka ruler in the act of devotion.

Additional bronzes, including many splendid Natarajas are housed in galleries at either side of the audience hall. Among these is a majestic dancing Shiva from Tiruvidaimaradur showing the god without the usual flying locks of hair. Other outstanding Nataraja brounzes are those from Tiruvelvikudi, Pattisvaram and Vedranyam.

Next to the Art Gallery, in the adjacent apartments of the Nayaka Palace, is the *Sarasvati Mahal Library*. A statue of Serfoji II, founder of the collection, is displayed in the entrance lobby. A small museum (closed Wednesdays) shows a selection of the library's extensive holdings. The exhibits include palm-leaf and paper manuscripts and albums, many from the Maratha period. Three pages from a Ramayana, with minutely detailed coloured scenes arranged in narrow strips, are of particular interest. There are also European maps, engravings and prints.

The *Maratha Palace* in the wing to the east of the library is now somewhat dilapidated. The audience hall, which faces west onto a large court, has massive circular columns carrying lobed arches. The arches are filled with brightly painted gods, European styled angels and courtly figures, all surrounded by stylised foliation. The attached Royal Museum, occupying part of the private quarters of the descendant of the Maratha ruling family (closed weekends), has a small collection of royal memorabilia. The *Tamil University Museum* (closed weekends), in the south wing of the Maratha Palace, is reached by a separate entrance from the main street. This is home to a diverse assemblage of pottery from prehistoric sites, coins, metalwork, weapons, palanquins, brass lamps and musical instruments.

In addition to the Brihadishvara temple, Thanjavur preserves several other religious monuments. The most interesting is the 17th century Rajagopala temple, located in a narrow lane a short distance north of the Nayaka Palace. A flight of steps from the gopura on the east ascends to the upper temple, preceded by corridors roofed with brick vaults. The sanctuary has pilastered walls and is capped with a five-storeyed tower. 19th century paintings covering the walls of the attached mandapa depict Vaishnava topics.

Among the urban feature of the city that deserve attention is the *Clock Tower* standing near the market. This was built in 1833 in an inventive Indo-Saracenic style with funds provided by a Maratha queen.

B. TIRUVAIYARU

Located 13 km. north of Thanjavur, on the north bank of the Kaveri River, Tiruvaiyaru is famous for its music festival, here each January to commemorate the birth anniversary of Tyagaraja, the celebrated musician and saint (1767-1847) who lived and composed in the *Panchanandishvara Temple* here. This monument dates back to Chola times, but was much extended under the Nayakas and Marathas. It is entered on the east through a sequence of four gopuras. A large mandapa, partly open, faces south into the outermost enclosure. The space between the third and fourth gopuras is filled by an even larger mandapa with broad aisles bounded by yali piers; the animals are tripled at the crossing. The innermost enclosure is occupied by a small east facing linga sanctuary. At the rear (west) is a shrine dedicated to five lingas. A second shrine to Shiva, immediately to the south, is approached through an ornate mandapa with finely worked piers displaying cut-out colonettes. Recent paintings on the peripheral colonnade here depict Shiva's exploits.

C. Kilaiyur

Located 20 km. north of Tiruvaiyur, this small village is worth visiting for the twin *Agastishvara* and *Cholishvara Temples*. These finely finished monuments were erected in the 9th century by local chiefs subordinate to the early Cholas. The two west facing temples have pilastered walls rising on basements with delicately modelled friezes of petals and yalis. The central niches in each temple frame images of Shiva (south), Subrahmanya (east) and Brahma (north). They are shown standing in the Agastishvara temple, but seated in the Cholishvara temple. The niches are headed by semicircular pediments filled with miniature figures. Above rise the two-storeyed towers with sculpted Nandis positioned between the capping square or hemispherical roofs.

D. Pullumangai

Just off the main road, midway between Thanjavur and Kumbakonam, is the insignificant hamlet of Pullumangai, with its splendid 10th century **Brahmapurishvara Temple**. This example of early Chola architecture has finely finished pilastered walls with wider projections at the corners and in the middle of each side of both the sanctuary and attached mandapa. Narrower projections in the intervening recesses have shorter pairs of pilasters carrying arched pediments. The refined carvings in the central projections on the sanctuary walls show Dakshinamurti attended by sages (south); Shiva appearing out of the linga, witnessed by Brahma and Vishnu (west); and Brahma with sages (north). Angled figures are positioned beneath the overhanging eaves. Further carvings are seen on the mandapa walls: seated Ganapati together with a host of lively dwarfs (south), and Durga with devotees (north). The three-storeyed tower over the sanctuary, coated in later plasterwork, is capped with a square roof. The temple is entered through a Maratha styled gopura and arcaded hall.

E. Tiruvalanjuli and Swamimalai

The celebrated Swaminatha temple of Swamimalai stands 3 km. north of the main road, 29 km. east of Thanjavur, 8 km. west of Kumbakonam. At the road junction stands the *Kapardishvara Temple* in the small settlement of Tiruvalanjuli. The focal linga shrine of this monument is approached from the east through a sequence of four gopuras, mostly without towers. In the middle of the second enclosure stands the 17th century Sveta Vinayaka shrine. This small, but exquisitely finished structure consists of a simple chamber with perforated stone screens on the east and a porch on the south, embellished with balustrades, wheels and leaping horses. The shrine is dedicated to a white stone relief icon of Ganesha. A later mandapa, with circular columns covered with tiers of shallow architectural facades, is built up to the shrine on the east. A Nandi stands freely to the west, facing towards the gopura that gives access to the third enclosure.

The northeast corner of the third enclosure is occupied by a Chola period mandapa. The double-bayed opening on the west is framed by unusual bulbous pilasters. The Chola period linga shrine in the fourth and innermost enclosure is topped by a small tower with a hemispherical roof; inscriptions cover its outer walls. The shrine is surrounded by a 17th century colonnade roofed with brick vaults.

A doorway in the south wall of the third enclosure of the Kapardishvara Temple leads to the Devi shrine, which stands in its own walled compound. An extensive painted composition on the ceiling here depicts the course of the Kaveri River, flowing past Srirangam Island [41B] to the Bay of Bengal.

The nearby town of Swamimalai is dominated by the *Swaminathan Temple* built on top of a hill. The complex is entered from the south through a gopura with a vividly painted tower. Double flights of steps ascend to the upper level. The finely detailed sanctuary, housing an image of Murugan, and its preceding mandapa have been entirely remodelled in recent years. Views of the surrounding fields and canals may be had from the surrounding terrace.

Metal casting is a major industry in Swamimalai, and the town has many workshops with brass icons for sale.

F. Darasuram

This small settlement, beside the main road 34 km. east of Thanjavur, just 3 km. from Kumbakonam, is renowned for the *Airavateshvara Temple*. One of the finest monuments of the late Chola era, the temple is assigned to the reign of Rajaraja II (1146-72). The complex is entered on the east through two gopuras. The outer detached gate is conceived on a grand scale, but only the lower granite portion, now dilapidated, was completed. In front of the inner gate are a Nandi pavilion and two small, finely decorated altars. The inner gate is topped by a vaulted roof covered with plaster sculptures. This gives access to a rectangular enclosure surrounded by colonnades, with a small museum displaying sculptures and photographs located in the northeast corner.

The main temple consists of a sanctuary, antechamber and two mandapas, the outer one of which is partly open, with a porch extension on the south. The exterior of the sanctuary and enclosed mandapa are elevated on a basement that runs continuously around the building. The bottom register is enlivened with yalis and dancing dwarfs. The top register has miniature panels framing stories of the Nayanamars. Among these are the legends of Chandesha, the saint who cut off his father's leg when the latter kicked the linga that he was worshipping (south), and of the deliverance of a child from the jaws of a crocodile by the intervention of Sundarar (north). The elongated spout that emerges from the north basement of the sanctuary is supported on a standing dwarf and rearing yali. Full-height pilasters divided the walls into projections; shorter, secondary pilasters frame niches on the projections, or stand in ornate pots in the recesses.

Carved black basalt figures in the sanctuary wall niches depict Shiva as Dakshinamurti (south, partly hidden), Shiva appearing out of the linga (west), and Brahma (north), all with attendant devotees and divinities. Similar panels on the antechamber walls show Ganesha (south) and Durga (north). The wall paintings are assigned to the 18th century, as are the plaster restoration of the figures, and the plaster decoration of the overhanging eaves and extended parapet. The pyramidal tower over the sanctuary presents three diminishing storeys capped with a hemispherical roof.

Steps on the north and south, flanked by curved balustrades, provide access to the temple's antechamber. The walls here, as well as those of the adjoining mandapa, have pilastered niches filled with icons. Among the different aspects of Shiva that appear here is an unusual dancing three-headed Bhairava (south). A small shrine built up to the wall nearby houses a unique form of Shiva as a mythical beast subduing Narasimha.

The porch extension of the outer mandapa is approached from the south by two flights of steps, with balustrades fashioned as large striding elephants with curling trunks. Prancing horses pulling wheels are carved in high relief on the basement, indicating that this part of the temple was conceived as a chariot. Seated Brahma, the driver of the chariot, appears on the central niche of the basement. The peripheral columns of the porch extension have seated yalis at the base; other supports are decorated with medallions of scrollwork containing dancers and musicians, or with superimposed reliefs of temple facades. A detailed account of the story of Subrahmanya is depicted on several panels. Lotus medallions and groups of musicians are carved on the panels of the coffered ceiling of the porch. Pairs of guardian figures flank the doorways leading to the linga sanctuary within the temple.

A few metres north of the Airavateshvara temple stands the contemporary *Daivanayaki Amman Temple*. Contained within its own walled enclosure, this goddess shrine has a sanctuary and antechamber raised on a basement adorned with friezes of dwarfs and yalis; pilasters on the sanctuary walls have rearing yalis at the base. Niches occupied by icons of different goddesses are interspersed with pierced stone windows, one with looped serpents. The tower over the sanctuary is elaborated with later plasterwork. The roof is unusually cruciform in shape; its arched ends are encrusted with flame motifs and monster masks.

About 1 km. north of the temples just described is an unusual *Image of Lajja Gauri*, venerated in a small Amman shrine. The lotus-headed goddess is shown in squatting posture, displaying her sex. The figure is supposed to have been brought from Karnataka as a trophy by the invading Cholas in the 12th century.

G. Kumbakonam

Cultural capital of the Kaveri Delta region, this city on the south bank of the river is second only to Thanjavur in historical significance. An idea of the population and wealth of Kumbakonam over many centuries may be had from the large number of temples and shrines dedicated to different cults, and the elaborate mathas and other religious institutions that still thrive here. Kumbakonam was an importance centre under the Cholas in the 9th-12th centuries; in the 17th century it was the residence of Govinda Dikshita, powerful minister of Raghunatha Nayaka of Thanjavur.

The *Mahamakam Tank* serves as the ritual core of Kumbakonam, the site of a great festival held here every 12 years. The waters of all the sacred rivers of India are believed to unite here. The trapezoidal shaped reservoir is surrounded by steps, at the top of which are 16 small pavilions erected by Govinda Dikshita for Raghunatha to perform religious ceremonies. The pavilion near the northwest corner of the tank has a raised dais in the middle. Carvings on the beams and ceiling inside show the Nayaka ruler seated in a balance, being weighed against treasure, witnessed by warriors and courtiers. As in the other pavilions, the attached shrine has a small brick tower capped with a hemispherical roof. The tank is overlooked on the east by the Abhimukteshvara temple. Of greater interest is the *Kashivishvanatha Temple* near the north bank. This houses a set of river goddesses in a subshrine in the mandapa. The central figure, who personifies the Kaveri itself, gazes through a sequence of doorways towards the tank.

Not far from the northwest corner of the Mahamakam tank stands the *Nageshvara Temple*. Founded in 886, this is the oldest religious monument at Kumbakonam, though it was much extended in later times. The complex is entered from the east through a sequence of three gopuras of diminishing size. A large mandapa occupies the north side of the second enclosure. This is elevated on a carved basement, embellished with wheels and prancing horses in the typical

Chola manner. Outsized stone elephants flank the balustraded steps on the south. Plasterwork from the 18th century covers the perforated windows set into the walls; a modern Nataraja shrine is built over the dais at the end. The pavilion opposite has an unusual wooden roof covered with metal sheets. A small gopura gives access to the third, innermost enclosure, partly filled with colonnades.

The early Chola period temple that stands at the western end of the innermost enclosure is approached through later mandapas. The original shrine is raised on a moulded basement enlivened with lotus petals and miniature scenes. Pilastered wall niches house images of sages and Dakshinamurti (south), Adhanarishvara (west), and Brahma and Durga (north), the last now forming the focus for a modern pavilion. These carvings are unsurpassed for their graceful postures, delicate modelling and sweetly detached expressions. A multi-storeyed tower crowned with a hemispherical roof, much renovated, rises above.

A street running west from the Nageshvara leads to the *Sarangapani Temple*, the largest Vaishnava foundation in Kumbakonam. The vast complex is entered from the east through a lofty gopura topped with a steeply pyramidal tower, more than 45 m. high. Dancing figures in panels brought from an earlier, presumably deteriorated temple, are set into the basement. The ten-storeyed tower is densely packed with plaster sculptures; openings in the middle of each stage are flanked by guardian figures. On the north side of the first enclosure is a detached mandapa, open on three sides, with a dais for processional images at the rear. The second gopura gives access to an extensive mandapa with broad intersecting aisles.

The third gopura, in line with the previous two, gives access to the innermost enclosure. Here stands the original shrine, an ornate structure founded in the 12th century Chola era. The middle of its east wall is marked by three carved stone screens of different designs, through which the doorway to the sanctuary can be glimpsed. A long tray set into the basement is carried on squatting figures and timber-like blocks. Two huge guardians are placed in front. The basement on the north and south sides of the temple displays wheels with leaping horses and striding elephants, typical motifs of the late Chola era. The walls above have deeply set niches interspersed with single pilasters standing in pots, all finely finished. The carved panels in the niches, including several Narasimha icons, are 17th century Nayaka period insertions.

Access to the sanctuary of the Sarangapani temple is through doorways reached by steps on the north and south sides, used alternatively at different seasons. The 12 columns inside the mandapa in front of the sanctuary have shafts covered with superimposed architectural facades. The ceiling above shows a lotus surrounded by rings of geese and interlocking dancers and acrobats. A large reclining image of Vishnu, also an addition of the 17th century, is venerated within the sanctuary. The nearby Lakshmi shrine, in the southwest corner of the enclosure, partly dates from the Chola period, as is evident from the treatment of the basement (as seen from outside the enclosure). The west gopura in the outer walls of the temple leads to a large rectangular tank with a pavilion in the middle.

Other religious monuments of Kumbakonam face onto the main north-south bazaar street that runs through the city. Here stands the *Kumbheshvara Temple*, after which the city is named. The Kumbheshvara myth explains the creation of the world from the waters of the cosmic pot, or kumbha, shattered by Shiva's arrow. The complex is approached from the bazaar street through a long colonnade lined with stalls; wooden chariots parked outside are partly concealed by shops. The colonnade leads to the lofty east gopura, the first of three in a row. Like most other parts of the temple it dates from the 17th-18th centuries.

The outermost enclosure of the Kumbheshvara is partly occupied by a tank with a central octagonal pavilion and a walled garden; an unfinished gopura is seen on the south. The second enclosure has a grandiose mandapa with a flagpole and a large Nandi in the middle. The ceiling over the crossing where two broad aisles meet is carved with signs of the zodiac. The third, innermost enclosure is occupied by three east facing shrines, standing close to each other. The central shrine accommodates the linga that forms the ritual focus of the monument. This emblem of Shiva is allegedly fashioned out of earth, in accordance with the creation myth of the temple; for this reason it is never washed with water. The Devi shrine immediately to the north has an elaborate colonnade in front (east). Columns here are embellished with carvings of attendant women and leaping animals.

The *Ramaswami Temple* marking the southern terminus of the bazaar street of Kumbakonam was founded in 1620 by Govinda Dikshita. A wooden chariot covered with Ramayana panels is parked outside its towered entrance, with bronze workshops located nearby. The brightly painted gopura leads directly to a spacious hall with magnificent sculptures, among the finest of the Nayaka period. The central aisle of the hall is flanked by paired guardian figures (north end), Rama and Sita, donors, attendants maidens, and Rati and Kama (south end). Leaping horses and yalis adorn the peripheral supports.

A second gopura leads to the inner enclosure, in which stands the main Ramaswami temple. The enclosure is surrounded by colonnades, the walls of which are covered with brightly coloured Ramayana scenes, recently repainted. The outer walls of the temple have shallow pilastered niches, but no original sculptures. The five-storeyed tower over the sanctuary is capped with a hemispherical roof. Fully modelled stone images of Rama, Sita, Lakshmana and Hanuman are enshrined within.

The northern terminus of the bazaar street is occupied by the *Chakrapani Temple*. Two gopuras provide access to the monument from the east. The temple itself is raised high on a solid basement, reached by steps from the north and south, used alternatively. In the mandapa in front of the sanctuary are displayed brass portraits of Serfoji II and his consort. The Chola styled sanctuary houses brass images of Vishnu standing in a six-pointed star, or chakra; hence the name Chakrapani. Lakshmi is venerated in a detached shrine a short distance to the north.

While this description of Kumbakonam by no means exhausts the religious monument of the city, a number of secular structures are also worthy of notice, such as the Maratha period pavilions and ghats lining the Kaveri. *Government College* on the opposite bank of the river was formerly the summer resort of Serfoji II; it is recognised by its picturesque clock tower. Founded in 1854 as the first English college in the Madras Presidency, its most famous student was the mathematician Ramanujan.

H. TRIBHUVANAM AND TIRUVIDAIMARADUR

The road that runs northeast from Kumbakonam beside the Kaveri River arrives after 8 km. at Tribhuvanam (also spelt Thirubhuvanam). This village is dominated by the grandly scaled *Kampahareshvara Temple*, built by the late Chola period king Kulottunga III (1178-1218). The monument has a sequence of two enclosures, each with an impressive gopura on the east: the outer enclosure has an additional gopura on the south. Many of the stone sculptures in the walls of these gateways are intact; the upper brick and plaster storeys form squatly proportioned towers.

The core of the main temple in the middle of the inner enclosure comprises a linga sanctuary and attached mandapa. The walls are elevated on a high basement carved with friezes of well formed yalis; miniature panels above depict Ramayana scenes. Single pilasters standing in pots alternate with pilastered niches containing icons. The finest of these are Shiva appearing out of the linga (west), and Durga standing on the buffalo head (north). Paintings on the intervening walls are no earlier than the Maratha era. The steeply pyramidal, five-storeyed tower over the sanctuary repeats at a diminishing scale the features of the walls beneath; the crowning roof is hemispherical. Wall niches on the two mandapas that adjoin the sanctuary to the east are mostly empty, but the semicircular pediments above are filled with reliefs. Stone windows in between have geometric designs. Warrior figures and large yalis enliven the balustrades flanking the steps on the north and south, which give access to the transept between the temple and a sequence of two mandapas. The basement of the porch that projects south from the outer mandapa is adorned with dancing figures and attendant maidens. The columns here have cut-out colonettes or superimposed architectural facades in shallow relief.

A small Chandeshvara shrine with a hemispherical roof stands to the north of the main temple. The Devi shrine nearby has goddess figures on the outer walls; the roof takes the form of a rectangular vault. The Sharabheshvara shrine, at the northeast corner of the enclosure, is dedicated to a composite aspect of Shiva. Vividly painted ceiling panels in the hall in front illustrate the exploits of this deity.

2 km. beyond Tribhuvanam is Tiruvidaimarudur, known for the *Mahalinga Perumal Temple*. This large-scaled complex consists mostly of mandapas and spacious colonnades dating from the 17th-18th centuries. A large rectangular tank with a central pavilion is located just outside the gopura that serves as the main entrance to the monument on the east. This gives access to a columned structure containing a Ganesha shrine, flagpole and large Nandi. Two more gopuras have to be passed through before the innermost linga shrine is reached. Together with its attached hall, this stands in a small compound surrounded on four sides a colonnaded corridor. The shrine itself dates from the Chola era, as is evident from the icons carved onto its outer walls: Dakshinamurti (south), Shiva appearing out of the linga (west), and Brahma (north). Metal images of the Nayanmars are displayed in the outer corridor to the north. The Murugan shrine in the southwest corner of the third, innermost enclosure is also assigned to the Chola period. The Devi shrine on the south side of the second enclosure, provided with its own compound walls and gopura, is also an earlier foundation; it is, however, preceded by later structures.

I. TIRUMANGALAKUDDI

The *Pramanatheshvara Temple* in this village north of the Kaveri River, 15 km. northeast of Kumbakonam, is of interest for its paintings dating from the 18th century Maratha period. These cover the ceiling of the corridor that leads to the Nataraja shrine within the inner enclosure of the monument. One bay is dedicated to local legends: the bottom register has scenes of a hunter arriving at a linga sanctuary; a woman crossing the Kaveri; and a hunter in a grove with two deer, and the hunter killing a tiger. In the middle register three demons meet a guardian inside a pavilion; and a family with two children worship a linga. The top registers shows deities with female devotees, and a family worshipping Shiva and Parvati. The adjacent panel depicts shrines along the Kaveri. Further paintings are seen on the ceiling inside the mandapa attached to the corner linga shrine. They include the story of the life of one of the Nayanmars.

The *Surya Narayana Temple*, about 500 m. northeast, is unique. It comprises a Chola period sanctuary dedicated to Surya, surrounded by eight small shrines, recently renovated, dedicated to the planetary deities.

J. GANGAIKONDACHOLAPURAM

The Brihadishvara temple at this site, 20 km. north of Tirumangalakuddi, lies a total of 35 km. from Kumbakonam. Together with the monument of the same name at Thanjavur, 72 km. distant, this is the greatest structure erected by the Cholas.

Gangaikondacholapuram was established as a capital by Rajendra I (1012-44) after his successful military expedition to Northern India, where he claimed to have reached the Ganga River. Other than the Brihadishvara temple, the only remains of Rajendra's time at this site are the foundations of brick buildings with stone column blocks, believed to be the remains of a palace, excavated in the fields on the outskirts of the village of *Maligaimedu*, 2 km. southwest of the temple.

The *Brihadishvara Temple* stands in the middle of a rectangular enclosure with an imposing gate on the east, now dilapidated. Most visitors enter from a doorway on the north. The temple is obviously modelled on that at Thanjavur, and is today dedicated to Shiva under the same name. The sanctuary has double tiers of pilastered walls elevated on a basement embellished with lions and scrollwork beneath, and yalis and makaras above. The pilastered wall projections house fully moulded sculptures. The lower tier of panels shows (in clockwise sequence): Ganapati, Ardhanarishvara, Dakshinamurti (replacement), Harihara, and Nataraja (south side); Shiva receiving Ganga in his hair; Shiva appearing out of the linga, Vishnu with Lakshmi and Bhudevi, Subrahmanya, and Shiva with Parvati (west side); and Shiva killing the demon, Durga, Brahma with consorts, Bhairava, and Shiva (north side). Miniature figures sculpted on blocks cover the intervening wall surfaces.

The six-storeyed tower, rising almost 60 m. above the ground, has a slightly concave profile. The parapets of roof forms are emphasised, but the dome-like capping roof is smaller than that at Thanjavur. The plaster sculptures on the tower, including the chamber built up to the east face, are 18th century additions. The transept between the sanctuary and the mandapas is entered by doorways flanked by guardian figures on the north and south, approached by flights of steps. Niches on the walls west of the steps house panels of Shiva as Bhikshatanamurti (south), and Shiva bestowing a wreath on the kneeling saint Chandesha, sometimes identified as the royal patron (north), the latter considered one of the finest masterpieces of Chola art. Niches on the walls east of the steps show Lakshmi (south) and Sarasvati (north). A massive linga, raised on a circular pedestal, is enshrined within the sanctuary. The mandapa to the east was never completed, in spite of renovations in the 17th century. Among the bronzes displayed here are Subrahmanya, Devi, and Shiva with Uma. A stone altar carved with a lotus top has the navagrahas carved on the sides. At the east end of the mandapa is a doorway sheltered by a porch reached by double flights of steps.

Subsidiary shrines to the north and south of the main temple, both dedicated to Kailasanatha, were erected by Rajendra's queens. These virtually identical buildings have small towers capped with hemispherical roofs. A small structure at the southwest corner houses a Ganesha image. A large Nandi, fashioned from stone blocks covered with plaster, is positioned to the east of the main temple. A plaster coated lion is built over the entrance to a flight of steps that descends to a circular well nearby.

The small *State Museum* (closed Fridays) just outside the temple enclosure houses items found in the excavations at Maligaimedu. They include coins, coloured glass bangles, terracotta tiles, pots, fragments of Chinese celadon, and sculpted stone fragments.

K. MANNARGUDI

This town, 34 km. southwest of Thanjavur, and about the same distance south of Kumbakonam, is renowned for the *Rajagopala Temple*, housing the protective divinity of the Thanjavur Nayakas. An open mandapa with donor portraits carved onto column bases and a free-standing column topped with a diminutive pavilion stand in the middle of the square to the east of the main gate of the temple. A chariot covered with carved wooden panels is parked nearby. The innermost shrine of the temple is approached though a sequence of four gopuras. The outermost gate, the largest of the series, has double pilastered walls with empty niches. The 11-storeyed tower above has been remodelled. Grandiosely scaled mandapas, with spacious aisles flanked by horses and yalis, some with elephant trunks, occupy much of the second and third enclosures of the monument.

L. TIRUVARUR

The Tyagaraja temple at Tiruvarur, one of the most important in the Kaveri Delta, lies 27 km. south of Mannargudi, a total of 53 km. east of Thanjavur. The monument enshrines the Somaskanda form of Shiva which, together with Nataraja at Chidambaram, was especially venerated by the Cholas. Tyagaraja was also glorified in the hymns of Tamil saints such as Appar and Sambandar. The temple overlooks the immense Kamalaya tank to the west of the town. Outside the main entrance to the complex on the east is a small chariot-like shrine with wheels carved in high relief on the basement of the porch. The figure shown prostrate beneath one of the wheels refers to a legend in which a prince was crushed to death, but then miraculously restored to life by Shiva.

The outer enclosure of the *Tyagaraja Temple* is entered through four gopuras, those on the east and west being massive 12th century structures. They display high basements with rearing yalis in panels, and double pilastered walls with sculptures of different deities set into niches. The squat pyramidal towers are topped with barrel vaulted roofs, much restored. The north and south gopuras date mostly from the 17th century. The rows of detached plain columns immediately inside the east gopura are roofed with thatch during the festival held here in April-May. To the north of these columns is a mandapa with a ceiling almost entirely covered with paintings, also assigned to the 17th century period Nayaka. The animated compositions, on brilliant red backgrounds, illustrate legends from Shaiva mythology. One set of panels (east aisle) is devoted to the story of the saint Muchukunda. The hero is portrayed riding majestically in a procession on an elephant; he is received with great pomp by Indra at the entrance to his heavenly city, where celestial nymphs wave lamps and offer garlands. Other scenes show the seven identical images of Tyagaraja created by Indra to confuse Muchukunda, which are then conveyed to earth in palanquins. Monkeys swing through the coconut trees behind the palace, while fireworks with blazing sparks scatter over the spectators, who carry parasols and standards. Another feature of interest within the enclosure is the Kalamal shrine in the northwest corner.

A second gopura on the west leads to the second enclosure of the temple. The mandapa immediately in front (east) has columns with lion bases. Many Chola period sanctuaries stand nearby. The Achaleshvara shrine, in the southeast corner, has a west-facing sanctuary with pilastered walls framing sculptures of Dakshinamurti (south), Shiva appearing out of the linga (east), and Brahma (north). The pyramidal tower is crowned with a decorated hemispherical roof. The attached mandapa is a later addition. Several nearby structures display brick vaults typical of Maratha architecture, such as the two-storeyed octagonal pavilion roofed with a dome.

A gopura on the west, the third in line, gives access to the third, innermost enclosure. Here stand the twin, east-facing Tyagaraja and Vanmikanatha shrines, both with pyramidal towers capped with hemispherical roofs that date back to the 11th century. The Tyagaraja shrine displays yalis on the basement and wall niches with the usual arrangement of icons of Dakshinamurti (south), Vishnu (west), and Brahma (north). A later colonnade links the two shrines.

M. NAGAPATTINAM

This city overlooking the Bay of Bengal is located 24 km. east of Tiruvarur, a total of 80 km. east of Thanjavur. Nagapattinam was once a famous emporium of textiles and spices, with seaborne links with Southeast Asia and China. It was also an important centre of Buddhism in Chola times as may be gauged from the many fine Buddhist bronzes that have been discovered there, including those now in the Government Museum, Chennai [36D]. In the early 16th century Nagapattinam became one of the first Portuguese settlements on the Coromandel Coast, but was not until the Dutch took it over in 1657 that the port was extensively developed. The city remained in Dutch hands until 1781, when it was occupied by the British. Thereafter the city declined.

Among the few vestiges of European occupation in Nagapattinam is the *Church of St Peter*, with its Dutch-styled facade, near the Railway Station. *Dutch Tombs* dating from 1664 still stand in Karkhopf Cemetery. The most elaborate example has plaster reliefs of angels framing saintly figures on the sides, topped by semicircular volutes and a fanciful octagonal finial.

Among the Hindu monuments of Nagapattinam are the Kayarohana and Tyagaraja temples, both Chola foundations that have been much altered in later times.

N. Velanganni

This small village on the Bay of Bengal, 12 km. south of Nagapattinam, became known in the 16th century as the place where the Virgin miraculously appeared to two local boys, and later to Portuguese sailors in distress. The first Catholic shrine was established at Velanganni under the sponsorship of the Portuguese community of Nagapattinam. With the decline of this port towards the end of the 18th century, Velanganni emerged as an independent parish under the Franciscan order. The basilica that stands here is the most famous Christian shrine in Tamil Nadu, attracting huge crowds of pilgrims throughout the year.

The *Basilica of Our Lady of Health* is a modern Neo-Gothic structure, renovated and extended on several occasion, most recently in 1974. Facing east towards the ocean, its brightly whitewashed facade is flanked by octagonal towers with tapering spires; the crossing within is marked by a lofty octagonal drum with circular windows capped by a small spire. The interior is decorated with an inlaid stone floor and stained-glass windows. The celebrated image of the crowned Virgin holding the Christ Child is displayed on the main altar. The Virgin, dressed in a blue robe, stands on the crescent moon. The altar is surrounded by blue-and-white Dutch tiles. A second church at the rear (west), also with twin towers, is divided into two levels.

The *Museum of Offerings*, in front (east) of the basilica, is stocked with gold and silver items, models of houses and trains, ex voto objects, testimonials and other curiosities donated by grateful devotees. A path lined with the Stations of the Cross leads west from the basilica to Our Lady's Tank. This commemorates the spot where the Virgin first appeared.

O. Nagore

This small town, 8 km. north of Nagapattinam, is known for its tomb of Hazrat Sayyid Shahul Hamid Qadir Wali. Born in Northern India in 1491, this Muslim saintly figure attained fame in Tamil Nadu by curing the son of Sevappa Nayaka, The Thanjavur ruler responded by granting land at Nagore to the saint, who lived here until his death in 1579. The dargah that grew up around his tomb was endowed by the Maratha rulers of Thanjavur, as well as by prominent members of the Muslim communities of Nagapattinam and other towns in the Kaveri Delta. The shrine currently attracts crows of devotees, both Muslim and Hindu, from all over Southern India, and even from Southeast Asia, especially during the Kandiri festival celebrated on the anniversary of the saint's death.

The Dargah is a low arcaded building, with a domed chamber in the middle accommodating the saint's grave. The doors to the chamber are embellished with sheets of embossed silver. Lofty minaret-like towers mark the four corners of the dargah. These tapering square structures are each divided into seven stages, with round headed openings in the middle of each side. They are crowned by low domes. In front (west) stands an isolated fifth tower, erected in 1753 with funds provided by the Maratha ruler of Thanjavur. Its nine stages are topped with a small dome framed by corner finials, attaining an overall height of 43 m.

P. KARAIKAL

Part of the Union Territory of Puducherry, this town is situated a short distance inland from the Bay of Bengal, 12 km. north of Nagore. Karaikal was one of the lesser holdings of the French on the Coromandel Coast. Even so, it still preserves something of its European character, with regularly laid out streets and 19th century residences. *Government House*, a mansion with colonnades and wooden shutters, stands at the north end of the main street. The *Church of Our Lady of the Angels* nearby was erected in 1821 in a distinctive Neo-Gothic manner. The tower that soars over the east porch is crowned with an octagonal lantern, added in 1891.

The main street of Karaikal, proceeding north through the town, passes by the gate of the Ammaiyar Temple. A plaster sculpture over the entrance shows the emaciated female saint to whom the shrine is consecrated. This figure is celebrated in Tamil devotional poetry and is one of the most popular Nayanmars.

Q. TARANGAMBADI

This quiet town, 15 km. north of Karaikal, or 63 km. east of Kumbakonam via Mayuram, was once the headquarters of the Danish East India Company. In 1620, the Company purchased a small piece of land on the Coromandel Coast from Raghunatha Nayaka; four years later Tranquebar, as this territory came to be known, was transferred to King Christian IV. Until 1807, when it was taken by the British, this settlement was the principal headquarters for Danish commercial activities in Southern India. By the time it was restored to Denmark in 1814-45, Tranquebar had dwindled into insignificance.

Tarangambadi, as Tranquebar is now known, preserves its European character due to the many 17th-18th century houses and churches that still stand here. The settlement is entered from the west through the brick archway of the *Town Gate*. The Danish coat-of-arms and the date 1792 are displayed on the pediment. The road which leads from the gate to the sea is lined with houses, many with porticos and round-headed windows. Here stands the *New Jerusalem Church* of the Evangelical Lutherans. Its main entrance is framed by a decorated triangular gable framing a crown, as well as the royal emblem and the date 1718. The interior has four equal transepts roofed by pointed tiled roofs. The church is associated with Bartolomeus Ziegenbalg, the first Lutheran missionary in Southern India, and the translator of the New Testament into Tamil, which he had printed on a newly introduced press. Dying in 1719, he is buried in a grave set into the floor in front of the altar. The cemetery outside contains other interesting tombs. *The Church of Zion* nearby, founded in 1701 but subsequently remodelled, was the main place of worship for Europeans. A bell tower, topped by a shallow dome and a miniature obelisk, rises over the entrance. The long nave is roofed with a pointed brick vault.

A large open square is laid out beside the Bay of Bengal. The north side is occupied by the Governor's bungalow, with an imposing colonnaded verandah, recently restored. Opposite, on the south side of the square and directly overlooking the ocean, is *Dansborg*. This fort was begun in 1620 by Ovo Gedde, the first Danish governor, and was subsequently strengthened on several occasions. It consists of a quadrilateral compound bounded by broad ramparts, entered on the north through a pedimented arched gate. The east side of the fort is occupied by a long low building with sloping walls and small windows. A central upper chamber has a small tower. The vaulted rooms of the lower storey serve as a small museum (closed Fridays), housing a collection of maps, documents, weapons and other artefacts pertaining to Danish history.

R. POOMPUHAR

This popular spot, 12 km. north of Tarangambadi, is situated at the mouth of the Kaveri River, the waters of which are little more than a trickle as they enter the Bay of Bengal. Poompuhar is identified with Kaveripattinam, an ancient emporium with trade links with Rome, that later flourished under the Cholas. Excavations in the vicinity have revealed brick remains dating back to the 2nd-3rd centuries. They include a wharf site and a massive inteh service flightly laber are the traces of a Bhuddhist vihara and shrine.

Recently developed as a recreational centre, Poompuhar benefits from a good beach and tourist facilities. The seven-storeyed *Art Gallery*, built in a bizarre temple-like style, houses a set of modern stone reliefs illustrating the Silappadikaramm, or Story of the Anklet, a Tamil classic. Set in Poompuhar, it tells the tale of Kannagi, the exemplary Tamil wife, and Kovalan, her princely husband.

S. PUNJAI

This small village, also know as Tirunanipalli, 15 km. northeast of Mayuram (Mayiladuthurai), is the setting for the 10th century *Naltunai Ishvara Temple*. The east-facing monument originally consisted only of a towered linga sanctuary adjoining a small mandapa, both with outer walls divided into bays by flat pilasters. Carvings of deities are inserted into wall niches headed by shallow relief pediments: Agastya, Ganesha and Dakshinamurti with sages (south); Shiva appearing out of the linga (west); and Brahma and Durga (north). Carved in deep relief and glistening with applied oil, these figures are among the most majestic sculptures from the early Chola period, comparable to bronzes of the same date. Miniature narrative reliefs are seen in the uppermost moulding of the basement. Guardians flank the east doorway, now partly concealed by a pair of later mandapas.

41. Tiruchirapalli

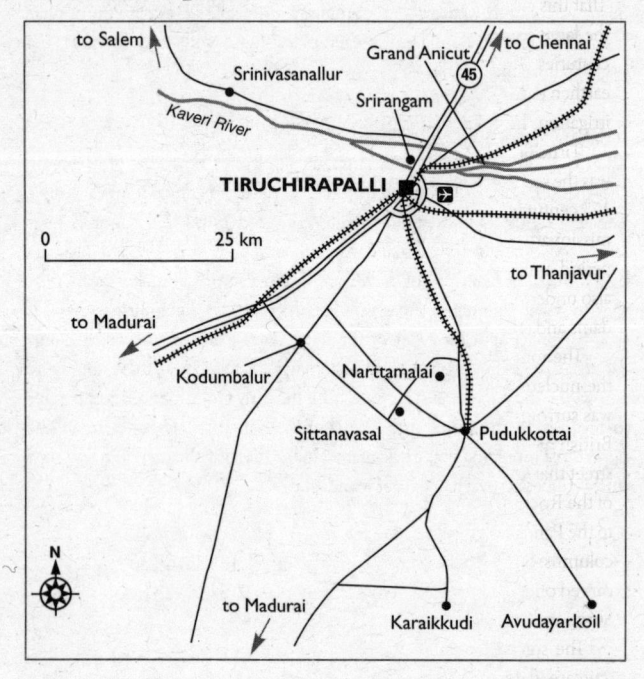

Still known as Trichy, an abbreviation of its British period name, Trichinopoly, this historical city in the heartland of Tamil Nadu stands on the south bank of the Kaveri, overlooking the great Rock rising 83 m. above the river. Tiruchirapalli is now an important industrial centre, second only in Tamil Nadu to Chennai [36]; yet historical features are still to be seen. Visitors should allow a half day for the shrine and churches on and around the Rock [A].

A tour of the two large-scale religious monuments on Srirangam Island, immediately north of Tiruchirapalli, will occupy a full day [B], especially if the Chola temple at Srinivasanallur [C] is included. From here it is possible to continue on to Salem [42].

A day trip south of Tiruchirapalli can take in the temples at Kodumbulur [D], Sittanavasal [E] and Narttamalai [F], all from the Chola era. Additional time will be required to visit the Tondaiman capital of Pudukkottai [G] and the temple sponsored by these rulers at Avudaiyarkoil [H]. Instead of returning to Tiruchirapalli, visitors may travel from Pudukkottai on to Madurai [42].

A. Tiruchirapalli

That this city was an important centre under the Cholas may be judged from the large-scale hydraulic projects undertaken in the area during the 11th-12th centuries. The Grand Anicut, 14 km. downstream (east) of the city, is a long earthen dam traversing the Kaveri River, with side channels to divert water for irrigation. The dam was built by Sir Arthur Cotton in 1839.

Tiruchirapalli served as a second capital for the Nayakas of Madurai, and was the scene of bitter fighting between these rulers and the Mughals in the late 17th century. The city was later occupied by the Nawabs of Arcot [38B]. Much missionary activity took pace here in the 18th-19th centuries, during which period a major military Cantonment was laid out by the British. The British also undertook repairs to the Grand Anicut, as well as the construction of new dams and channels.

The tour of Tiruchirapalli described here begins at the *Rock* that forms the nucleus of the old city. In Nayaka times, this dramatic granite outcrop was surrounded by a ring of fortifications, but these were demolished by the British at the end of the 18th century. Their circuit can still be traced by a street that encircles its base. Two early sanctuaries are excavated into the side of the Rock. The *Lower Cave Temple*, at the base of the south face, is assigned to the Pandyas in the 8th century. It consists of a hall with massive, unadorned columns. Side shrines house images of Shiva and Vishnu. Other deities are carved onto the rear wall: from left to right, Ganesha, Subrahmanya, Brahma, Surya and Durga.

The somewhat steep ascent of the Rock begins nearby, with a covered staircase flanked by mandapas, one with carvings of donor figures and divinities. The first feature of interest to be seen is the *Upper Cave Temple*, associated with the Pallava ruler Mahendravarman I (580-630). Its hall, which is entered from the side, has squatly proportioned columns with lotus medallions on the shafts. The doorway to the shrine (right) is flanked by guardian figures. The panel on the wall opposite (left) in an impressive composition that portrays Shiva receiving the goddess Ganga in his hair. The steps continue upwards until they pass by the *'Rock Temple'*, occupying a bluff on the west flank of the Rock. This religious complex is entered on the east through a towered gate that leads to a mandapa (only Hindus admitted). Here can be seen the tower of a Devi shrine located at the lower level. The west-facing linga shrine, reached only after passing through the hall, is a Chola period structure, but the colonnade that surrounds it is later. The ascent of the Rock ends at a small Ganesha temple at the summit. The columns in the open mandapa that precedes the sanctuary have donor figures, deities and horses carved onto the shafts. Panoramic views may be had from here across the river to Srirangam.

The Rock is surrounded by crowded streets and shops, with a large tank on the west. A short distance north of the tank is *Christ Church*, associated with Reverend Christian Schwartz, who founded in it 1766 on land donated by the Nawab of Arcot. The modest Neo-Classical building has a small square tower at one corner. Plain Doric columns line the central aisle within. The polygonal sanctuary at the end has its walls covered with inscribed slabs. The grave of Schwartz, who died here in 1798, can be seen in the cemetery nearby.

A portion of the 18th century city walls, including an arched gate and a quadrangular bastion, is seen near the southwest corner of the tank, on West Boulevard Road that runs in a north-south direction through the old city. The imposing *Cathedral of Our Lady of Lourdes*, a Neo-Gothic edifice consecrated in 1841, stands on the opposite side of the road. Its east facade has a rose window surmounted by a lofty tower with octagonal and square turrets and a tapering spire, completed in 1895. The nave is roofed with pointed cross vaults. St Joseph's College, a large Jesuit institution founded in 1840, stands next door.

The *Dargah of Nata Shah*, containing the tomb of a popular saint who lived in Tiruchirapalli during the 17th century, is located 500 m. south of the Rock. The building is recognised by its large dome framed by corner pinnacles. The dargah was endowed by the last Nayaka queen, Minakshi (1731-36). It is also the burial place of Wallajah Muhamad Ali (1749-95) of Arcot.

Further features of historical interest are located in the *Cantonment*, 3 km. south of the old city. This area still preserves its broad curving streets lined with bungalows set in spacious gardens. The *Church of St John*, of 1816, has a handsome pedimented portico, partly hidden by a modern porch. Its outer walls are lined with original shuttered doors that are opened for ventilation during worship. Doric columns inside carry a flat wooden roof. The altar and furniture are all finely worked. A small brass table set into the floor marks the grave of Bishop Heber. The adjacent cemetery is crowded with tombs, some with obelisks. The *Government Museum* (closed Fridays) in the vicinity has a small collection of stone sculptures and bronzes, including a fine 12th century image of Manikkavachakar, as well as painted album pages. There are also models of the Rock and of the Ranaganatha complex at Srirangam.

B. SRIRANGAM

This 30 km. long island is formed by two branches of the Kaveri River. Here stand two great religious monuments: the Ranaganatha temple, dedicated to Vishnu reclining on Ananta the cosmic serpent; and the Jambukeshvara temple, consecrated to the water (ap) linga of Shiva. Lesser shrines and numerous tanks dot the island.

Ranganatha Temple, Srirangam.

The *Ranganatha Temple*, 4 km. north of the Rock at Tiruchirapalli, is one of the largest sacred complexes in Tamil Nadu, its outermost walls defining a rectangle of 950 by 816 m. The monument was founded in the Chola period, but benefitted from the sponsorship of the Pandyas and Hoysalas in the 12th-13th centuries before being sacked by the Delhi troops in 1323. After the expulsion of the invaders in 1371, the temple was repaired and expanded under the emperors and commanders of the Vijayanagara [20B-C]. The most vigorous period of growth was during the 16th-17th century Nayaka period. Building works continue into recent times: the great tower over the outermost south gopura was completed only in 1987.

The temple is remarkable for the geometric precision of its plan. It is laid out in a series of seven concentric rectangular enclosures defined by high walls.

They contain an overall area of more than 60 ha. *Gopuras* in the middle of four sides are aligned along roads that proceed axially towards the central shrine. The outer three enclosures are occupied by houses accommodating the town's population. The broad thoroughfares separating these outer enclosures are used for chariot festivals in December-January. Most devotees approach the monument from the south, along Big Bazaar Street; this leads directly to the south-facing shrine of Ranganatha.

The gopura of the seventh (outermost) enclosure dates from the 17th century, being an unfinished project of Tirumala Nayaka of Madurai (1623-60). Its lower granite storeys present a vast mass divided into a high basement, and two pilastered storeys with sequences of niches set into the wall projections. The new brick and cement pyramidal tower, with 13 diminishing storeys, rises to an impressive height of 77.5 m, making it one of the tallest in Tamil Nadu. The road proceeding north passes through a sequence of gopuras of diminishing size, The gate in the next enclosure has paintings of religious processions on the on the passageway ceiling; the gopura in the fifth enclosure displays Vijayanagara emblems, with boar, sun and moon incised on the doorway jambs.

The gopura in the next (fourth) enclosure marks the entrance to the sacred precinct of the Ranganatha complex. The court that is reached immediately on entering is lined with shops at either side, with the *Rangavilasa Mandapa* at its northern end. This 17th century hall has three spacious aisles defined by piers with cut-out colonettes, alternating with yali piers on the south. The small pavilion in the middle has ceiling paintings illustrating the Vasanta festival, with a mock battle between Kama and Rati, as well as episodes from the Ramayana epic.

To the west stands the small east facing *Venugopala Shrine*. This exquisitely finished 16th century structure is entered on the east through a small porch with double flights of steps, now contained within the Rangavilasa Mandapa. The shrine itself is elevated on a boldly modelled basement. The walls above have deeply recessed niches filled with figures that are among the finest examples of Nayaka sculpture. Gracefully posed maidens holding musical instruments, mirrors and a parrot flank icons of Krishna playing the flute in the middle of the sanctuary walls; Tumburu and Narada, the two celestial musicians, appear on the antechamber walls. The pyramidal tower above the sanctuary is crowned with a hemispherical roof. (A rooftop terrace nearby provides a panorama of the whole complex, including the gilded tower of the focal sanctuary.)

The *Art Museum*, immediately east of the Rangavilasa Mandapa, has a small but remarkable collection of Nayaka ivory figurines and caskets, as well as copper-plate grants, bronze statuettes, arms and textiles. The *Sheshagiri Mandapa*, a short distance beyond, is reached by passing around to the east side of the fourth enclosure. This hall is famous for the carvings on its eight northernmost piers. These show riders on richly bridled horses leaping upwards on their hind legs. Smaller warriors beneath the horses slay panthers and yalis. The animation and virtuosity of the almost three-dimensional animals and figures are unsurpassed. Together with the sculptures at Vellore [38A], these are the most notable examples of 16th century Vijayanagara art in Tamil Nadu.

Immediately east of the Sheshagiri Mandapa stands the *Vellai Gopura*, one of the finest of the Ranganatha series. Its well proportioned, nine-storeyed tower has prominent projections in the middle of the long sides; the lowest storey has stone columns set into the window openings. The Vijayanagara emblem, with boar and sword, is seen on one of the lintels within the passageway. The *Thousand-Columned Mandapa* north of the Sheshagiri Mandapa occupies the northeast corner of the fourth enclosure. Ten rows of columns on rising floors lead to a small sanctuary at the northern end. Wheels and prancing horses are sculpted onto the basement of a porch contained within the hall.

The tour of the Ranaganatha temple continues by returning to the gopura on the south side of the third enclosure. This gives access to the 17th century *Garuda Mandapa*. This spacious hall has a shrine at the south containing a huge image of the kneeling, eagle-headed mount of Vishnu. Pillars with cut-out colonettes and clusters of corbelled brackets define seven aisles running north-south. The central aisle to the north of the Garuda shrine has additional carvings of portraits of the later Nayakas of Madurai. The figures stand in attitudes of worship, dressed in finely detailed costumes and crowns, bearing daggers and knives. Among the other features of interest in the third enclosure are the three circular brick granaries on the west, and the elliptical pond on the north.

A small gopura on the south leads into the innermost two enclosures that constitute the core of the complex (only Hindus admitted). Here stands the part-circular *Ranganatha Shrine* housing the reclining image of Vishnu. Its tower is capped by a gilded hemispherical roof, with a frontal (south) arched frame containing a standing figure of the same god. The walls of the corridor that surrounds the shrine are covered with paintings dating from the early 18th century. These illustrate legends pertaining to Ranganatha, as well as scenes from the life of Krishna. At the end of one composition is a portrait of Vijayaranga Chokkanatha of Madurai (1706-32) and his queens, adoring the temple divinity.

Other places of interest associated with the Ranganatha temple stand outside the complex. A large square tank to the west is used for float ceremonies at festival time in February. The *Amman Mandapa* on the bank of the Kaveri, 1 km. to the south, leads to a popular bathing ghat on the river bank. The hall was built by one of the Madurai queens.

2 km. east of the Ranganatha complex is the village of *Tiruvannakoil* and the *Jambukeshvara Temple*, the second great religious monument on Srirangam Island. This impressive temple is entered from the west through a sequence of five gopuras. The gateways follow a standard pattern, diminishing in height from outside to inside. The largest gopura is a vast unfinished project in the middle of the outermost east enclosure wall. The first gopura on the west leads to a large mandapa, facing south towards a square tank with a central pavilion. The sacred precinct is reached after passing through the second and third gopuras. Beyond stands an impressive hall with wide corridors dating from the 19th century. Its spacious central crossing is defined by complex pierce with clusters of heavy brackets carrying the lofty ceiling.

Two more gopuras give access to the two sanctuaries in the middle of the monument (only Hindus admitted). The modest scale and simple features of these gateways contrast with the grandiose architecture of the corridor that surrounds the central two shrines. One shrine consists of a small unadorned chamber housing a linga at a lower level, over which water pours perpetually from a hidden spring. The adjacent shrine, which is open to the sky, contains a jambu tree with spreading branches. Subsidiary Natesha shrines are positioned at the northwest corners of the two innermost enclosures.

The east facing Akhilandeshvari shrine, dedicated to the consort of Jambukeshvara, is situated in the northern part of the complex, within its own walled compound surrounded by a colonnaded corridor. A flagpole, altar, seated Nandi and Ganesha shrine are arranged in a row outside the two gopuras that lead to the shrine.

C. SRINIVASANALLUR

The temple at this small village, 45 km. northwest of Tiruchirapalli, stands beside the road running beside the north bank of the Kaveri River from Srirangam Island. (The road continues to Namakkal [42D], 37 km. northwest on NH7.)

Erected in 927, the *Koranganatha Temple* is a typical example of early Chola architecture. The basement that runs around the building has friezes of fully modelled yalis and makaras. Pilasters on the south wall frame a niche carving of Bhikshatanamurti conversing with sages. No original carvings survive in the west and north niches, but attendant figures are seen on the flanking walls. They are remarkable for the delicate modeling and elegant poses, many turned at a slight angle to the wall plane. Niche pediments are carved with foliated makaras and miniature figures. The brick and plaster, pyramidal tower that rises above is capped with a square roof. Foliate decoration is incised on the jambs of the east doorway.

D. Kodumbalur

This small settlement, 36 km. southwest of Tiruchirapalli, is notable for the *Muvarkoil*, a small complex dating from the 9th century, early Chola era, of which two out of three shrines still stand. These small west-facing structures have moulded basements adorned with boldly sculpted yalis. Pilastered wall niches house icons of Shiva in the middle of three sides, with Bhikshatanamurti appearing on the south. Sculptures are inserted into the upper storeys of the tower. The icon of Shiva dancing (south shrine, east face) is exceptional for the angular posture of the figure, and the delicately incised detail of the staring eyes and curved eyebrows. The two-storeyed towers are capped with heavy, square roof forms topped by pot finials. A platform with moulded stone sides extends in front of the three shrines.

About 500 m. to the east stands the Muchukundeshvara temple, another early Chola period foundation.

E. Sittanavasal

The *Jain Cave Temple*, cut into the west flank of a long granite outcrop overlooking a spacious landscape, lies about 24 km. southeast of Kodumbulur, 17 km. directly northwest of Pudukkottai. This 9th century monument, approached by a flight of steps, presents an austere portico, with three columns with rolled brackets. This leads to a small hall with carvings of Parshvanatha (right) and Mahavira (left) on the side walls; three more Jinas are cut into the rear wall of the small shrine chamber. The interior of the cave is of interest for the delicately toned paintings. Dancing maidens and a royal figure with female attendants are painted onto the columns, while the hall ceiling is covered with a large composition showing a lotus pond with elegantly drawn stalks, leaves and flowers, in deep green and red. The pond is populated by elephants, fish, ducks and youths bearing flowers. The ceiling inside the sanctuary has paintings of textile-like designs with interlaced knotted patterns.

A natural cavern beneath a rocky overhang on top of a hill, a short distance away, has polished beds used by Jain monks. A 2nd-1st century BCE inscription can also be seen here.

A prehistoric *Megalithic Site* is visible from the road, 500 m. east of the cave temple. This consists of a number of stone circles with cists, some up to 4.5 m. in diameter, as well as several dolmens.

F. Narttamalai

Religious structures at this site, 40 km. south of Tiruchirapalli, are built on a natural rocky terrace with a commanding view across the landscape. (The site can also be reached from Sittanavasal, about 16 km. away, via a back road.) Named after the founder of the Chola dynasty, the 9th century *Vijalaya*

Cholishvara Temple at Narttamalai is actually the work of a subordinate chief. The solidly proportioned building consists of a west facing sanctuary contained within a square of outer walls, attached to a small mandapa. The pilastered walls are surmounted by eaves and a parapet, over which rises the two-storeyed tower. Guardian figures are carved either side of the doorway on the west, while Nandis appear beneath the hemispherical roof. Vestiges of paintings inside the hall include a large Bhairava figure. Six subsidiary shrines face towards the central temple.

Two small shrines, 16 m. apart, are cut into the face of the nearby outcrop. The walls of the *Vishnu Cave Temple* are lined with identical, majestic images of the god sculpted in high relief, five on either side of the sanctuary doorway, and one at either end. The sanctuary is devoid of any icon. The moulded plinth of a structural hall is seen outside. The adjacent Shiva cave temple has a linga sanctuary and a 7th century inscription.

Loose carvings found at the site have mostly been removed to the Government Museum at Pudukkottai, 18 km. south.

G. Pudukkottai

This small city, 58 km. south of Tiruchirapalli, was the capital of the Tondaimans, minor chiefs who emerged at the end of the 17th century under the Nayakas of Madurai. From 1753 these figures assisted British troops in their campaigns against Haidar Ali of Srirangapattana [15C] and the French. Thereafter, Pudukkottai was recognised as a princely state.

Nothing is now left of the old palace of the Tondaimans, but the *New Palace*, now the Collector's Office, stands about 1 km. west of the commercial heart of the city. Built for Rajgopala Bahadur in 1929, this handsome stone edifice is entered through a porch with ornate arches on polished granite columns, with the Tondaiman coat-of-arms displayed in the pediments. A dome rises above the two-storeyed arcades of the main block. An inner rectangular court is surrounded by loggias at two levels. Another Tondaiman civic monument is the *District Headquarters*, on the south side of the city. This large red brick complex has twin towers with domical tops on either of the entrance.

Also worth noticing is the *Ceremonial Arch*, erected in 1897 on the occasion of Queen Victoria's Diamond Jubilee, spanning the main street of the city. Among the places of worship at Pudukkottai is the Catholic church, a Neo-Gothic building with a gabled facade framed by tall steeples.

The old part of Pudukkottai, *Tirugokarna*, is located 3 km. northwest of the city centre. Here stands the *Gokarneshvara Temple*, a 7th century foundation much extended by the Tondai-mans. The temple is approached from the south through a long ceremonial corridor, the ceiling of which is covered with Ramayana paintings dating from the 18th century. The first scene over the east aisle show the gods seeking the help of Vishnu. The sequence ends with Rama and Lakshmana leaving for the forest. The panels over the central aisle are devoted to the marriages of Dasharatha's four sons. The narrative continues over the west aisle, where the episode of Hanuman setting fire to Lanka shows an aerial view of Ravana's city. The enclosure between the two gopuras at the northern end of the corridor is occupied by a mandapa with sculpted yalis and riders on horses, as well as figures of Kama and Rati. The innermost enclosure accommodates the small Bakulavaneshvara and Brithadambal sanctuaries, the latter enshrining the protective goddess of the Tondaimans.

A small doorway at the northwest corner of the enclosure leads to the summit of the granite shelf on which the temple is built. Here can be seen a small rock-cut chamber, assigned to the Pandya era. This is entered through a verandah with four squat columns. The side walls have carvings of Ganesha (south) and Shiva receiving Ganga in his hair (north).

The *Government Museum* is situated near to the entrance to the temple. The archaeology section displays sculptures found at nearby sites, such as Kodumbalur, as well as a set of 9th century images from Narttamalai depicting the matrikas, and Shiva as Dakshinamurti. Bronzes date from the Chola and later periods. Copies of the paintings at Sittanavasal are also on show.

From Pudukkottai it is possible to continue on to Karaikkudi [44K], 43 km. south, or to Madurai, 100 km. southwest.

H. Avudaiyarkoil

This small town, 47 km. southeast of Pudukkottai, is associated with the Shaiva saint Manikkavachakar, who reputedly spent much of his life here. The Atmanatha Temple is an artistically interesting complex, dating mainly from the 17th-18th century period. Its outermost gopura is approached from the east through a large mandapa, with a broad passageway flanked by piers raised on a high platform. The columns have carvings of Tondaiman rulers and their ministers; those at the end show three-dimensional images of Shiva in his fierce aspects, as well as armed guardians. A small shrine on the west is preceded by a square hall lined with donors and yalis.

The first gopura of the Atmanatha temple has a double sequence of basement mouldings and pilaster walls. The mandapa located between this and the second gopura has yalis projecting outwards from the peripheral columns. The central part of the hall is surrounded by columns with yalis, warriors and donors, one of whom is identified as a Tondaiman minister. A later brick shrine, consecrated to Manikkavachakar, is situated to the west. It is surrounded by a passageway with walls entirely covered with murals illustrating the life of the saint. That these paintings can be no earlier than the turn of the 20th century is evident from the episodes set in Pudukkottai's busy streets, one of which shows the 1897 Diamond Jubilee ceremonial arch.

A mandapa with carved pillars occupies the second enclosure of the temple. The pillars here have high relief figures of Manikkavachakar and Patanjali accompanied by royal donors, warriors and maidens. The third enclosure accommodates the focal shrine of the complex. Curiously, this contains no image; devotees instead venerate an empty pedestal, apparently in accordance with Manikkavachakar's monistic philosophy. The walls of the shrine are ornately treated with delicately fashioned pilasters. Perforated stone windows admit light to the attached mandapa, which can only be entered through doorways at the two northern corners. The surrounding columns are enhanced by carvings of donors, sages, Manikkavachakar, and aspects of Shiva and Devi. The Ambal shrine, in the northwest corner of the enclosure, is also empty.

42. Salem

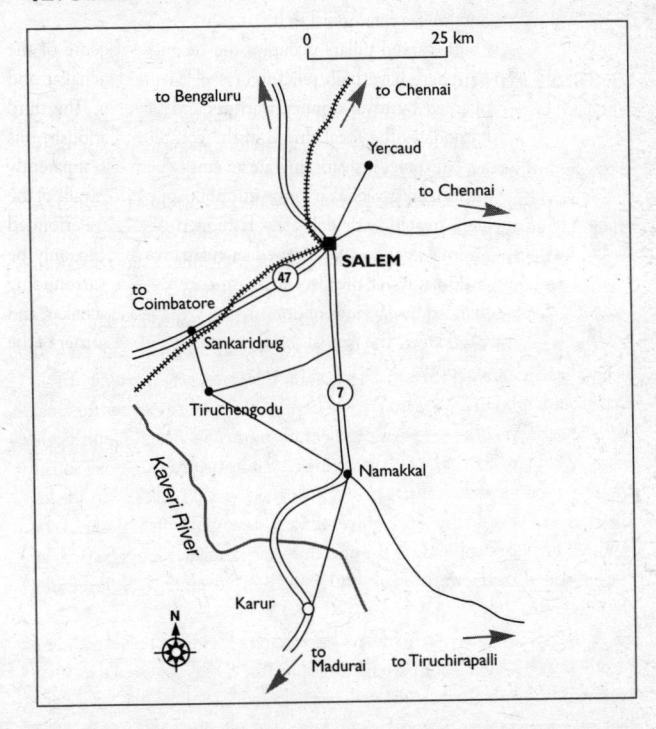

Pleasantly surrounded by the Shevaroy and Nagaramalai Hills, this industrial city in the uplands of Tamil Nadu is an important textile and steel manufacturing centre. Though there is little of historical importance to be discovered in Salem, the city makes a convenient base from which to explore the hill resort of Yercaud [A], the picturesque mountain fort of Sankaridrug [B], and the temples at Tiruchengodu [C] and Namakkal [D].

A. YERCAUD

Nestling in the Shevaroy Hills at an altitude of about 1,500 m. above sea level, this agreeable *Resort* is renowned for its schools and coffee estates. Located 23 km. northeast of Salem, Yercaud was settled by the British in the early 19th century, and coffee was introduced here already in the 1820s. The whitewashed, red-tiled houses of the town stand south of Yerikadu, Forest Lake, which gives its name to the resort. The bazaar square is overlooked by the well maintained *Holy Trinity Church*, a modest gabled building with Neo-Gothic windows. The cemetery at the rear has many of its graves intact. The club below the church is where planters still meet.

B. SANKARIDRUG

Situated 35 km. south of Salem via NH47, Sankaridrug rises about 500 m. above the plain. The hill is crescent shaped in contour, giving the appearance of a conch shell, or shankha; hence its name.

Sankaridrug came under the command of the Nayakas of Madurai [44A] in the 17th century, but was added to the kingdom of the Wodeyars of Mysore [15A] by the conquest of Chikka Deva Raja in 1689. After being taken from Tipu Sultan of Srirangapattana [15C] by the British in 1791, Sankaridrug served as headquarters of a British battalion. It was abandoned in 1828.

The ascent of *Sankaridrug Fort* is most easily made from the east, the path being shielded by a sequence of ten gates. The first gate is set in a circuit of walls that extends around the foot of the hill. Beyond the third gate stands the small Varadaraja Perumal temple. A steep flight of steps climbs to the fourth gate, strongly built in stone. The fifth gate is defended by two bastions, one square the other round. The ramparts here are assigned to Tipu Sultan. On the left they lead to a cave on the south spur of the hill associated with a Muslim saint. Another flight of steps leads to the next three gates, situated about halfway up the hill. These are the work of Lakshmi Kanta Raja, governor of the fort under the Wodeyars.

A magazine with a barrel-vaulted roof stands between the seventh and eighth gates, the latter being partly demolished. The ninth gate, erected in 1799, commands the point where the path reaches the brow of the hill. Steps from here give access to the topmost gate, set in a ring of walls running around the summit. The few structures that survive at this level include a small Vishnu shrine and a modest mosque on the verge of a precipice. The highest point is marked by a platform for a flagstaff, near which stand several rectangular, flat-roofed granaries and a store with three compartments.

C. TIRUCHENGODU

This small town is situated 11 km. south of Sankaridrug, or 50 km. directly southwest of Salem. Two temples, one in the middle of the town and the other at the summit of a bare granite hill that rises to the west, are Chola foundations, much patronised by the Nayaka and Wodeyar governors of Sankaridrug in the 17th-18th centuries.

The lower *Kailasanatha Temple* is entered on the east through a 25 m. high gopura, which faces towards a 16 m. high fluted stone column and a colonnade crowded with shops. Chariots with wooden carvings are parked in the street nearby. The entrance gopura has finely worked basement mouldings and pilastered niches. The brightly painted, multi-storeyed tower is crowded with figures. The leads to the main temple, approached through a spacious mandapa, with outer supports fashioned as leaping yalis with riders. Paintings cover the ceiling over the central space. A small linga shrine is situated beyond. Of interest are the 63 Nayanmars and naga stones housed in a colonnade on the south side of the enclosure. A plaster covered Nandi in the northeast corner conceals steps descending to a small well.

A winding path of about 1,200 steps, passing by mandapas, subsidiary shrines and a large Nandi, ascends to the upper *Ardhanarishvara Temple*, perched near the summit of the hill more than 250 m. above Tiruchengodu. One portion of the steps is treated as a hallowed site for taking oaths. The steps arrive at a terrace with fine views of the town beneath. The gopura here is a large ornate structure, with signs of the zodiac carved onto the passageway ceiling; the doors preserve their original wooden panels. The gopura serves as the main gate on the north side of the temple. Visitors arriving by car, however, will enter through a modern gopura on the west.

Twin shrines of the temple, dedicated to Ardhanarishvara and Subrahmanya, stand in a walled enclosure surrounded by halls with colonnades with elaborate carvings. Leaping yalis with riders adorn the outer columns. The columns lining the central aisles on both the east and west sides of the inner mandapa have fully carved figures of donors and attendant maidens, as well as paired images of Manmatha and Rati, and Virabhadra and Kali. Even an Englishman, hat in hand, is to be seen here. He depicts the British Collector of Salem, who undertook repairs to the temple in 1823. The ceilings are exceptional for their painted depictions of mock battles between Manmatha and Rati, and the ornate central lotuses surrounded by parrots. The west facing Ardhanarishvara sanctuary houses a unique cult object: a tree trunk clad in both a lungi and sari. The adjacent Subrahmanya sanctuary faces in the opposite direction. A subshrine dedicated to Nageshvara, in the west part of the complex, is intricately carved with royal figures and European guardians, as well as with divinities.

D. NAMAKKAL

A massive granite rock, with remnants of a fort on top, marks the centre of this town on NH7, 50 km. south of Salem, or 35 km. southeast of Tiruchengodu. The principal religious monument at Namakkal is the *Narasimha Temple*. This complex is built up to the west flank of the rock, into which is excavated a cave temple with remarkable carvings dating from the 8th century Pandya period. The complex is entered from the west through a gopura, devoid of a tower, beyond which stands an open mandapa sheltering an altar and flagpole. A second gopura, also missing its superstructure, leads to the inner enclosure, where a Garuda shrine is seen. Here stands the main temple, entirely walled in, entered by steps on the north and south. The two mandapas within lead to the original cave temple, which enshrines an impressive image of Narasimha seated with Surya and Chandra. The side walls have additional icons of Varaha and Trivikrama (right), and Narasimha killing Hiranyakashipu, and Vishnu seated on Ananta (left). The large scale compositions and vigorous postures of the figures are typical of Pandya art.

Halfway up the rock at Namakkal is another *Cave Temple* with carvings dating from the Pandya era. Reliefs worth noticing here include Trivikrama (left), Vishnu on Ananta (middle), and Narasimha (right). A further relief of Harihara is seen on a side wall to the right.

At the top of the rock, some 65 m. above the streets of the town, is a *Fort* attributed to Ramachandra Nayaka, governor of the Wodeyars in the 18th century. The fort was taken by the British in 1768, but was lost the following year to Haidar Ali; after 1792 it was garrisoned by the East India Company's troops. The summit is most easily accessible from the southwest, on which side narrow steps have been cut into the rock. Remains of the first line of fortifications are seen on the lower south slope. The stone ramparts are topped by a brick parapet with projecting guardrooms. A masonry platform runs around the walls, giving access to loop holes set into them. A ruined treasury and a magazine stand inside the small walled area at the top.

43. Coimbatore

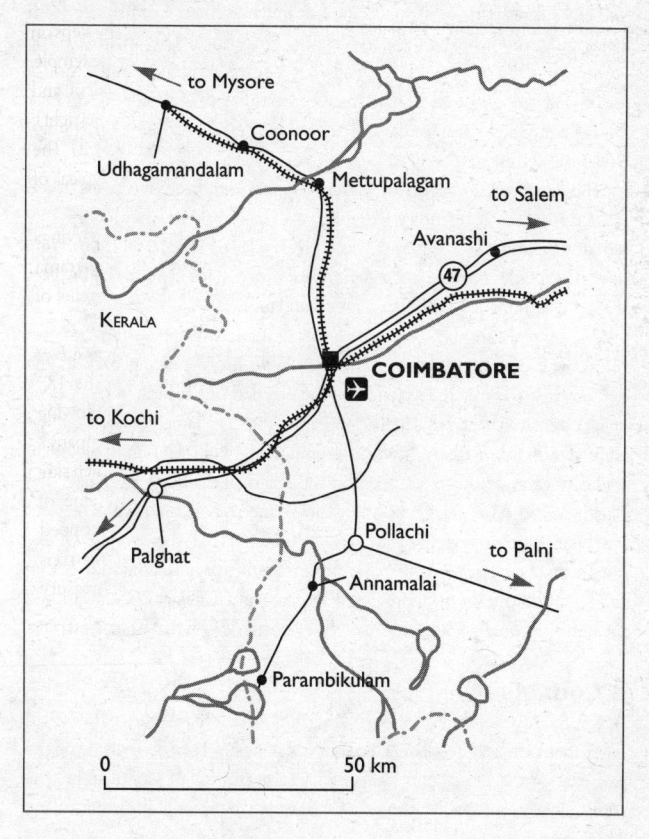

Coimbatore owes much of its economic importance to its location immediately east of Palghat, the broadest pass in the Western Ghats between Tamil Nadu and Kerala. While the city itself [A] preserves only a few features of historical interest, it serves as the gateway to the Nilgiri Hills, among the highest in Southern India, with its British period hill stations of Coonoor [B] and Udhagamandalam [C]. A stay at either is recommended.

Unlike other parts of Tamil Nadu, the Coimbatore area has few religious monument, an exception being the temple at Avanashi [D]. This is reached as a half-day excursion from Coimbatore, with the option of continuing on to Salem [42].

A. COIMBATORE

The city's forested mountain setting has not prevented Coimbatore from developing into a major industrial centre. Since the 1930s hydro-electric power from the nearby Pykara Falls has boosted cotton manufacturing; textile mills are scattered all over the city. Coimbatore is also of importance for agricultural development, and serves as the home of an Agricultural College and Research Institute.

The *Botanical Gardens*, on the western edge of Coimbatore, were established at the turn of the 20th century. Extending over some 300 ha., they incorporate formal plantations of roses and a recently developed section with flowering trees. The nearby *Museum of the Agricultural College* (closed Sundays) displays seeds, fibres, minerals, rocks, implements and tools.

The only historical monument of note in the Coimbatore area is at *Perur*, 6 km. west of the city centre. The *Patteshvara Temple*, dating back to the 14th century, was much developed by the Nayakas of Madurai [44A], before being extensively renovated in the 19th century. A stone lamp pole, some 11 m. high, stands immediately inside the entrance gopura. Carvings of Indian soldiers bearing muskets are seen on the pillars of the outer mandapa. The Nandi placed on an axis with the main shrine is associated with the saint Sundarar, who is supposed to have actually visited the temple. Three-dimensional figures adorn the columns in the mandapa leading to the main shrine. Among the deities represented here are Shiva dancing on the dwarf, and the same god holding out the skin of the elephant demon that he has just slain.

B. COONOOR

At 1,858 m. above sea level, this is the second highest hill station in the Nilgiri Hills, after Udhagamandalam. Coonoor lies at the head of a deep ravine on the east side of the Dodabetta Range, 85 km. northwest of Coimbatore. The climate here is noticeably warmer and less wet than that at Udhagamandalam, 13 km. distant.

Sim's Park, the chief attraction of Coonoor, was founded in the middle of the 19th century. Spreading across a ravine, the park is laid out as a botanical garden, with a large variety of trees and plants, including huge tree ferns, giant rhododendrons and more than 300 varieties of roses. The *Pasteur Institute* (open Saturdays), opposite the main gate, established in 1907, conducts research into rabies and polio vaccines. The Silkwork Rearing Station is situated next door. Nearby *All Saints Church* was consecrated in 1872. This bold basalt building has steep gables and a corner tower topped with a gallery and steeple.

Numerous excursions are possible from Coonoor. Lamb's Rock, 6 km. away, offers panoramas of the coffee and tea plantations covering the lower slopes of the Nilgiri Hills, with the plains of Coimbatore beyond. Catherine's Falls can be viewed from Dolphin's Nose, 10 km. distant. The ruins of a fort used by Tipu Sultan at Droog, 13 km. away, will require a walk of 3 km. from the nearest road.

Wellington, 3 km. above Coonoor, was established in 1852 as a military cantonment. It still serves as the headquarters of the 250-year-old Madras Regiment.

C. UDHAGAMANDALAM

This celebrated hill station, with its numerous vestiges of the British period, is still affectionately known as Ootacamund, or simply as Ooty. It is situated at 2,240 m. above sea level, at which elevation the Nilgiri Hills form a high plateau, with grassy rolling slopes planted with imported eucalyptus and conifers. Heavy rain and mist are characteristic of the winter season. This landscape is the original habitat of the Todas, an indigenous tribal people who tend herds of shaggy buffalo. The Todas live in barrel-vaulted thatched houses, and worship in similarly constructed conical shaped temples, which function like dairies. Many Todas have now converted to Christianity.

In 1799 the East India Company annexed the Nilgiri Hills, together with their Toda population, from Tipu Sultan. However, it was not until 1818 that Udhagamandalam was identified as a desirable location by two young assistants of John Sullivan, the collector of Coimbatore. Within a few years a bridle path was completed to the new hill station, and by 1823 Sullivan had completed his stone house on land purchased from the Todas. This encouraged the settlement of other Europeans, who were attracted by the cool climate and the possibility of cultivating European fruits, vegetables and trees. In 1861 Udhagamandalam, which by this time had been Anglicised to Ootacamund, began to function as the summer capital of the Madras Presidency. Governors and their retinues flocked to the resort, followed by other Europeans and even princely personalities. The active life of the station included a lively programme of sporting events. Tea was introduced by a French botanist, M. Perrotett; coffee was a later import. The popularity of the resort has continued to increase, and it is now the largest hill station in Tamil Nadu.

The main town of Udhagamandalam lies between the lake and the botanical gardens, two of the town's main attractions. The 2.5 km. long lake covers an area of more than 25 ha., with the famous 'toy' railway line running along one bank; rowing boats are for hire. *St Thomas's Church* of 1870, on the east bank of the lake, is a modest structure with a low steep roof. The adjoining cemetery has a large pillar surmounted by a cross, marking the grave of William Patrick Adam, a governor of Madras, who died in 1881. Fernhill Palace, just south of the lake, was built in 1842 as a holiday retreat for the Mysore ruler. It is now a hotel.

Two main bazaar streets proceed in parallel formation from the railway station until they unite on Commercial Road. To the south is the Racecourse, site of the most active equestrian club in Tamil Nadu, dating back to 1894. The bazaar terminates at *Charing Cross*, a major intersection marked by a cast-iron fountain. A short distance further along stands Sullivan's stone house, now the residence of the principal of the Government Art College, which has its campus opposite.

A road running perpendicular to Commercial Road leads to *St Stephen's Church*. On the way it passes the red brick *Nilgiri Library* of 1885, designed by Robert Fellowes Chisholm. Its lofty reading room is lit by five arched windows with a tall Neo-Gothic window at the end. The nearby *District and Sessions Court* is contained in a red brick range, with a steeply pitched corrugated-iron roof, and a slender clock tower capped with a spire. It was built in 1873 as a private school.

St Stephen's Church, one of Udhagamandalam's most important landmarks, was consecrated in 1831 by the Bishop of Calcutta, and was named in honour of Stephen Lushington, then Governor of Madras. The building has a long narrow nave flanked by windows, separated by buttresses that protrude as steeples above the battlemented parapet. A quartet of similar steeples crowns the massive square tower. The church is entered through an arcaded porch. The timbers used in its roof are said to have been pillaged from Tipu Sultan's palace at Srirangapattana [15C]. The cemetery which climbs up the hill behind is filled with graves, many of them of children.

A short distance beyond St Stephen's Church stands the exclusive *Ootacamund Club*. A drive lined with conifers leads to the main building, erected in 1830 by Sir William Rumbold as his private residence. Among his guests in 1834 were Lord William Bentinck, who suppressed the practice of sati, and Thomas Babington Macauley, who wrote the Indian Penal Code. The club was convened in 1843 and still maintains its British traditions. The walls are hung with hunting trophies and portraits of British and Indian worthies. The game of snooker is said to have been invented in the billiards room here; the rules, dated 1881, are posted on the wall. The Ooty Hunt, which still rides to hounds in pursuit of jackals, is the club's other major claim to fame. A short distance nearby stands the *Savoy Hotel*, originally intended as a school for the Church Mission Society.

Ootacamund Club, Udhagamandalam.

Among the other sights of interest in Udhagamandalam are the *Botanical Gardens*, 2 km. northeast of the station, established in 1848. Over 20 ha. are planted with more than 1,000 varieties of plants, shrubs and trees, including orchids, ferns, alpines and medicinal plants, among beautiful lawns, lily ponds and glass houses. The annual Flower Show is a popular event in May. The half-timbered gateway to *Raj Bhavan*, formerly Government House, is superbly sited on Dodabetta Ridge at the top of the gardens. The mansion, which stands in its own well maintained grounds, was built in an Italianate style in 1880 for the Duke of Buckingham when he was Governor of Madras (permission required to visit). A typical Toda village, or mund, with thatched wooden houses is seen nearby.

Udhagamandalam spreads over a number of hills, many of which are now built up. Dodabetta, Big Mountain, which rises to 2,637 m., east of the town, is still comparatively bare. The valley of the Nilgiri Mountains contain a large number of lakes and reservoirs, including Marlimund Lake, 5 km. distant. Kalhatti Falls, which drop some 400 m., are located 12 km. north. Mukerti Peak is a spectacular lookout on the western edge of the Nilgiris, gazing down into Kerala from a perpendicular rock face some 2,000 m. deep. The peak forms part of the Nilgiri Tahr Sanctuary, noted for its wild buffalo.

D. AVANASHI

This town, 40 km. northeast of Coimbatore, takes its name from the *Avanishvara Temple*. Founded in the 13th century, the monument was substantially renovated in the 18th century under the patronage of the Wodeyars of Mysore [15A], who were responsible for erecting the gopuras in 1756. A colossal Nandi is placed on axis with the main sanctuary. The nearby carvings of two alligators, each shown disgorging a child, refer to the legend of the saint Sundarar, who interceded with Shiva for the life of a child who had been swallowed by an alligator. A shrine to the saint is included in the complex.

44. Madurai

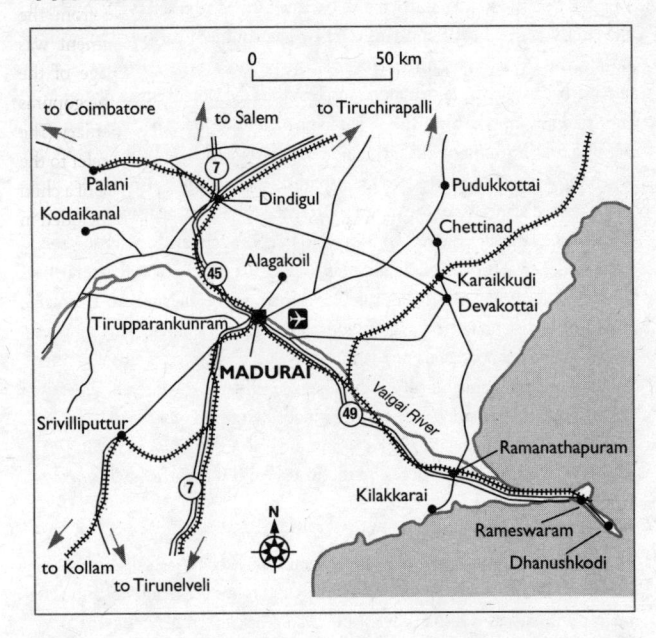

This city [A] is celebrated for its great temple, one of the largest in Southern India and without doubt one of the most vibrant. The complex is a testimony to the wealth and patronage of the Madurai Nayakas in the 16th-17th centuries, who were responsible for building the palace in Madurai, as well as the religious monuments at nearby Tirupparankunram [B] and Alagarkoil [C]. Two days should be reserved for visiting these sights.

A journey northwest of Madurai may take in the fort at Dindigul [D] and the hill temple at Palani [E], but additional time will be required to reach the hill station of Kodaikanal [F], which is recommended for an overnight stay.

The twin temples at Srivilliputtur [G], south of Madurai, may be visited on the way to Tirunelveli [45].

An excursion to the Setupati palace at Ramanathapuram [H], the port of Kilakkarai [I] and the sacred island of Rameswaram [J], southeast of Madurai, can be achieved in a single long day.

A tour of the mansions of Chettinad region [K] makes an unusual day trip from Madurai, with the option of spending a night in the area or continuing on to Tiruchipalli [41A].

A. Madurai

Located near the south bank of the Vaigai River, this city served as the capital of the Pandyas, the most important rulers in the southern part of Tamil Nadu during the 7th-13th centuries. However, no vestiges of the Pandya period survive, because of the destruction caused by the Delhi forces which conquered the Madurai kingdom in 1323. The city thereupon became the centre of Muslim rule in Southern India. The sultanate of Madurai lasted only until 1378, when the city was absorbed into the empire of Vijayanagara [20B-C]. Because of the great distance from the capital in Karnataka, the Vijayanagara governors, known as Nayakas, enjoyed considerable freedom, gradually asserting their independence. By the second half of the 16th century they ruled with freely over the former territories of the Pandyas. Of the many powerful Nayakas, Tirumala (1623-60) is celebrated for his ambitious building programmes, many supplied with his personal portraits. The Madurai Nayakas came into conflict with their counterparts in Thanjavur [40A] and Gingee [39F], but managed to resist the Mughal and Maratha invasions that extinguished these other lines. The last Nayakas were taken up with battles against the Nawabs of Arcot [38B]. In 1763 the city came under the control of the British, and was garrisoned for some years afterwards.

The centre of Madurai is dominated by the *Minakshi Sundareshvara Temple*, founded by the Pandyas, but entirely rebuilt in later times. Almost all the Madurai Nayakas, together with their wives and ministers, made donations to the monument; as a result, the temple is an amalgam of different structures dating from the 17th-18th centuries. This is even true of the twin shrines to Sundareshvara, a form of Shiva, and Minakshi, the guardian goddess of Madurai and the protective deity of its ruling house. The temple calendar is replete with ceremonies and celebrations, the most important being the 12-day festival in April-May. This commemorates the coronation of Minakshi and her marriage to Shiva. The climax of this event is the great chariot festival that takes place in the broad streets that run around the outer walls of the complex.

The temple is contained by high walls that create a vast enclosure, some 254 by 238 m. This is entered in the middle of each side by *Gopuras* that soar above the houses of the city. The gates are exceptional for their towers with elongated proportions and curved profiles, which achieve a dramatic sweep upwards; that on the south is the tallest, attaining a height of approximately 55 m. The lower granite portions of the gopuras have moulded basements and double tiers of moulded basements and pilastered walls. Carvings here are confined to miniature animals and figures at the base of the wall pilasters. The brick towers above have openings in the middle of the long sides to admit light to the hollow chambers at each level. The openings immediately above the eaves sheltering the passageways are distinguished by pairs of stone colonettes. The upper storeys are crowded with plaster figures of divinities, celestial beings, guardians and animal mounts, all painted in brilliant colours. Polychrome monster masks with protruding eyes and horns embellish the arched ends of the barrel-vaulted roofs.

Most visitors enter the Minakshi Sundareshvara complex through the *Ashta Shakti Mandapa*, or Hall of Eight Goddesses. Projecting outwards from the enclosure walls to the south of the east gopura, this porch was erected by two of Tirumala Nayaka's queens. Eight goddesses and two male donor figures are carved onto the columns; modern paintings cover the brick vault above. A doorway flanked by sculptures of Ganesha and Subrahmanya leads into the *Minakshi Nayaka Mandapa*, a spacious mandapa crowded with shops and stores. This hall was erected in 1707 by Shanmugan Minakshi, chief minister of Vijayaranga Chokkanatha II (1706-32). Its piers have lion brackets carrying suspended beams. At the far end (west) of this corridor is a doorway surrounded by a brass frame covered with oil lamps. This towered gateway is on axis with the Minakshi shrine at the core of the monument.

The corridor beyond the gateway is flanked by superb column sculptures of dancing men, attendant maidens, and Shiva as Bhikshatanamurti. This leads to the courtyard of the *Potramarai Kulam*, or Golden Lily Tank. This rectangular stepped reservoir has a brass-clad lamp column in the middle and colonnades on four sides. Carvings on the columns in the middle of the north side depict royal figures. The walls of the colonnade on the north and east are covered with murals. These represent the 64 legendary deeds that Shiva performed in and around Madurai. Large lotus medallions are painted onto the ceiling of the colonnade. One composition, showing the marriage of Minakshi and Shiva, adorns the ceiling of a small pavilion that projects over the water on the west side of the tank. The hall beyond is known as the *Pancha Pandava Mandapa*, after the heroes of the Mahabharata epic that are sculpted in full relief on the columns lining its central north-south aisle. Dating from the late 17th century, the hall and its carvings precede the *Minakshi Shrine*, which stands in its own compound, together with subsidiary shrines (only Hindus admitted). The bedchamber in the northeast corner is where the processional image of Sundareshvara is brought each night, having been transported in a palanquin from the god's own sanctuary elsewhere in the complex.

A small gopura at the north end of the Pancha Pandava Mandapa marks the entry into the colonnaded enclosure that surrounds the *Sundareshvara Shrine* on four sides. Fish emblems on the columns here are considered emblems of Minakshi. A large Ganapati image is positioned opposite the gopura just noticed. Entry to the main Shiva shrine, which also stands in its own walled compound, is through a small gate on the east flanked by guardian figures (only Hindus admitted). Immediately in front (east) of the gate is the *Kambattadi Mandapa*, an imposing hall with a seated Nandi within a pavilion, and an altar and gilded flagpole in the middle. These features are surrounded by eight massive, composite piers carved with outsized images of Natesha, Virabhadra, Kali and other deities, as well as the marriage scene of Minakshi and Sundareshvara together with Vishnu, who is here considered the brother of the bride.

A gopura on the east side of the hall leads to the *Viravasantaraya Mandapa*, an addition of Vijayaranga Chokkanatha. More than 75 m. long, this immense corridor lined with piers leading to the outermost east gopura of the complex is usually filled with merchants and pilgrims. To the south is the wooden roofed Kalyana Mandapa, where the ritual marriage of Minakshi and Sundareshvara is celebrated at festival time. The extensive thousand-columned hall to the north now serves as the *Temple Art Museum*. The frontal (south) supports are carved with animals and figures in almost three dimensions, including a mounted warrior, dancing bearded man, and gypsy woman. The corner supports are concealed by clusters of cut-out colonettes. A corridor lined with deities, attendants and yalis leads to an impressive bronze icon of dancing Shiva installed on the raised dais at the north end of the hall. Stone carvings, bronzes, ivories and metal ritual objects form part of the museum display. Also exhibited are instructive copies of the murals from the colonnade that surrounds the Portramarai Kulam.

Exiting the temple through the great gopura on the east side of the complex visitors should proceed to the *Pudu Mandapa*, on the opposite side of the street. Built in 1635 by Tirumala Nayaka, this hall now accommodates the tailors of Madurai, all busy with their sewing machines in the peripheral corridor. The columns at the east and west ends of the Pudu Mandapa have sculpted riders on magnificent animals rearing outwards. Large, three-dimensional icons of Kali (south) and Natesha (north) mark the ends of the front (west) corridor. Here, too, can be seen the marriage scene of Minakshi and Sundareshvara in the company of Vishnu. The side aisle have lofty ceilings carried on brackets fashioned as seated yalis. The interior of the Pudu Mandapa (ask for the key) opens up into a large space lined with columns carved with robust royal figures that portray all of the Nayaka kings up to Tirumala. Each ruler is accompanied by family members and ministers. A small pavilion with slender polished black stone columns and a wooden roof stands freely at the western end of the interior.

A short distance further west east stand the lowest storeys of Tirumala's unfinished *Raya Gopura*. This colossal gate is more than twice the dimensions of the other gopuras of the temple. The door jambs, some 15 m. high, have finely carved scrollwork.

The Minakshi Sundareshvara temple is not the only Hindu monument worth visiting in Madurai. A short distance southwest of the complex, near the bus stand, is the *Kudal Alagar Perumal Temple*, the principal Vaishnava sanctuary in the city. This late 16th century temple represents the Nayaka style at its finest. It is entered through a gopura on the east, which gives access to a corridor with a spacious north-south aisle. Yalis are carved onto the central quartet of piers. The main shrine is approached through two mandapas. The outer hall has a porch with staircases on the north and south flanked by animal balustrades, and a small Garuda shrine on the east. The Vishnu shrine that forms the nucleus of the complex consists of three superimposed chambers of diminishing size. From bottom to top they house seated, standing and reclining images of the god. (This scheme recalls that of the Vaikuntha Perumal temple at Kanchipuram [37E].) The outer walls are raised on an elaborate basement with varying sequences of mouldings. Slender pilasters with differently shaped shafts have miniature yalis at the base. High-relief towers cap single pilasters standing in pots. Perforated screens with graceful designs, including one with figures in entwining stalks (south) admit light to the passageway within. The steeply pyramidal tower that rises above is capped by a hemispherical roof. A shrine to Vishnu's consort, Lakshmi, stands in its own compound south of the main temple.

On the other side of the street from the entrance to the Alagar Perumal temple stands the *Anglican Cathedral*, consecrated in 1881. This austere Neo-Gothic building, designed by Robert Fellowes Chisholm, has an unplastered tower devoid of any steeple. Nearby is the *Kazimar Mosque*, regarded as the main place of prayer for Muslims of the city. This 14th century structure dates back to the period of the Madurai sultans. Its simple colonnaded prayer hall is preceded by a porch, now obscured by an extension on the east.

One km. southeast of the Minakshi Sundareshvara temple stands the *Nayaka Palace*. Though associated with Tirumala Nayaka, this served as the headquarters for most of Madurai's rulers. Only portions of the extensive complex survive; even so, they are impressive for the monumental scale of the interior spaces and the exuberance of the plaster decoration, much of it restored in the 19th century. A doorway in the east wall of the complex leads to a rectangular court, surrounded by colonnades with massive circular shafts, more than 12 m. high. Animal brackets above the peripheral supports are sheltered by curving eaves. Interior colonnades carry broad arches with pointed and lobed profiles. The throne hall at the western end of the court is roofed with pyramidal domes and shallow vaults, some elevated on a clerestory with small windows to admit light. An enlarged octagonal dome rises some 21 m. over the central chamber. A doorway in the northwest corner gives access to the dance hall. Its double-height space is bridged by transverse arches carrying a pointed vault. The lobes of the arches are richly encrusted with plaster animals and birds in scrollwork and flame-like tufts. Stone sculptures from various sites in the vicinity have been assembled here by the Tamil Nadu Department of Archaeology. A second colonnaded court with a domed chamber adjoined the hall at one end, but has now mostly collapsed.

A short distance from the Nayaka Palace stands *St Mary's Cathedral*. This early 20th century Neo-Gothic edifice has an interior with a stone ribbed pointed vault and some stained glass.

Nayaka Palace, Madurai.

Other important Nayaka period features in Madurai include the *Teppakulam*, at the eastern fringe of the city near the Vaigai River. Created by Tirumala in 1636, this great tank was intended as a setting for festivals in which sacred images were floated in illuminated barges. These rites continue to this day, each January-February. The square reservoir has steps, flanked by animal and bird balustrades leading down to the water in the middle of each side. A pavilion with a pyramidal tower occupies an island in the middle, with similar but smaller pavilions at the four corners.

Monuments associated with the Madurai sultans stand in a walled compound outside the old city, on the opposite bank of the Vaigai. The *Tomb of Alauddin and Shamsuddin*, two of the 14th century rulers, consists of a domed chamber surrounded by a colonnade, originally open but later filled in, topped with curving eaves and a battlemented parapet. The adjacent mosque is notable for the tapering octagonal minarets on either side of the flat roofed prayer hall. The nearby octagonal tomb of Bara Mastan Sada, a local Sufi saint, is a 16th century structure.

A short distance from the sultanate monuments just noticed is the *Gandhi Memorial Museum*. This is housed in the Tamukkam, a 17th century Nayaka pleasure pavilion from where animal fights were once viewed. Extended by the British in the 19th century, the building was used for a time as a courthouse. Its domed upper level now accommodates an extensive display documenting the history of the Freedom Movement and the life of the Mahatma.

B. Tirupparankunram

This small town, 6 km. southwest of Madurai, is known for its sacred hill, which rises 345 km. above sea level. Cut into the side of this granite outcrop hill is a Pandya period cave temple, dated 773. This serves as the nucleus of the large-scaled Murugan temple located at the southern end of the main street of Tirupparankunram. The cave temple is reached only after passing through an ascending sequence of mandapas linked by multiple fights of stairs, all additions of the 17th-18th centuries.

The *Murugam Temple* is approached from the north through an outer mandapa, the peripheral columns of which are adorned with sculpted riders on horses, and yalis with elephant snouts, all brightly painted. The central space of the hall is lined with additional animals; the ceiling above shows a painting of Subrahmanya. A large gopura on the south side of the mandapa, with an impressive pyramidal tower rising above the roof, marks the entrance into a great inner mandapa (only Hindus admitted). Flights of steps climb to an upper mandapa accommodating sculptures of Nandi and the peacock, the latter associated with Subrahmanya. A doorway on the west leads to a large outdoor tank. Further steps on the south ascend to a smaller mandapa at the highest level. This is built up to the original cave temple. Nayaka patronage is evident in the portraits of Tirumala and other courtly donors carved onto the column shafts.

The *Cave Temple* itself consists of a central shrine, with Pandya period carvings of Durga flanked by Ganapati (right) and Subrahmanya (left), and lateral shrines housing a Shiva linga (right) and a Vishnu image (left).

Subrahmanya, popularly known as Murugan, has been singled out for particular veneration, since it is to this deity that the whole complex is dedicated. A subsidiary shrine to Shanmuga, a six-headed form of Subrahmanya, is seen to the east of the principal sanctuary. A 14-day festival held here in March-April celebrates the victory of Subrahmanya over the demon Suran, and his coronation and subsequent marriage to Devayani.

Further historical features are situated on the summit of the hill that rises above the town. The *Dargah of Sikandar Shah* contains the tomb of the last Madurai sultan, who took refuge here, but in 1378 lost his life fighting the Vijayanagara army. In time Sikandar Shah came to be revered as a pious saint and the tomb is now a popular pilgrimage spot for both Muslims and Hindus. The steep path to the dargah begins southwest of the town. Halfway up are a number of graves, believed to be those of Sikandar Shah's soldiers slain in battle. The saint himself is buried in a simple grave, under a large rock which juts out of the ground. The small domed chamber built over the rock was added in the 17th-18th century. The flat-roofed halls in front are 15th century structures.

C. ALAGARKOIL

This imposing Vaishnava complex at Alagarkoil, 12 km. north of Madurai, is built up to the base if a forested hill. The *Alagar Perumal Temple* is dedicated to a form of Vishnu known as Kallalagar. This deity is considered the brother of Minakshi, and is an important participant in the marriage festival that takes place at Madurai in April-May each year. The Alagarkoil complex is approached from the south through dilapidated compounds. A mandapa beside the road is of interest for the elegant carvings of donor figures, including a gracefully posed Nayaka queen. The outer enclosure of the temple has a large unfinished gopura in the middle of the south walls, now picturesquely overgrown. It recalls the similarly uncompleted project of Tirumala Nayaka at Madurai. Visitors generally enter through a nearby break in the walls, from where they make their way towards the principal gopura on the east. This gate has double sets of walls with bold projections and miniature yalis at the base of the pilasters, as in the gopuras at Madurai, with which it is contemporary. A seven-storeyed tower rises above.

The enclosure within is of interest for the mandapa with three-dimensional figures and animals on the piers lining the central aisle. They show incarnations of Vishnu, such as Trivikrama, Narasimha and Krishna, as well as Garuda, Hanuman and yalis; donors are positioned on the two columns at the east end. Another large gopura provides access to the innermost enclosure (only Hindus admitted). A mandapa with piers decorated with lions and lotus brackets stands immediately within. Here, too, is a small part-circular shrine that houses an image of Garuda gazing inwards to the main sanctuary. This stands in its own rectangle of walls, entered through a single doorway on the east.

At the core of the complex is a small 12th century circular shrine, a rare example of Pandya architecture. The walls are raised on a frieze of boldly modelled yalis. The wall pilasters alternate with perforated stone windows, overhung by curved eaves. The hemispherical roof above has been renovated and gilded. A colonnade on three sides has its rear walls covered with murals, showing Vaishnava shrines at other sites. The Lakshmi shrine, on the south side of the innermost enclosure, is a later structure.

Visitors to the Alagar Perumal temple should not neglect the *Vasanta Mandapa* that stands outside the complex, to the south. This small square structure has an internal pavilion sheltering a dais used for ceremonies at the time of the spring festival. Ramayana paintings dating from the 18th century cover the ceiling and upper parts of the walls. The scenes are arranged in narrow strips, with Tamil labels on black bands. On the ceiling of the central pavilion they proceed in a clockwise direction, beginning with the sacrifice of Dasharatha and the birth of Rama and his three brothers, to the exploits of the youthful Rama and the departure of the wedding parties. The large panel in the middle shows Vishnu with Lakshmi and Bhudevi.

D. Dindigul

This city, 64 km. north of Madurai on NH45, is renowned for its great *Rock Fort*, which rises some 90 m. above the surrounding plain. This citadel was developed in the 17th century as an outpost of the Madurai Nayakas, guarding the pass between their domains and Coimbatore [43A]. In the 18th century it was contested by the Marathas and the Wodeyars, and then successively occupied by Haidar Ali and the British. The fort was much improved by Saiyad Sahib, a relative of Tipu Sultan and governor of Dindigul in 1784-90. It was further strengthened by the British after they captured it permanently in 1792.

Dindigul's bare rock presents a forbidding wedge of granite, approximately 400 m. long by 300 m. wide. Stone walls with openings for canon run around the crest. A flight of more than 600 shallow steps, hewn into the stone at the thin edge of the rock ascends to a single gate. This is defended by a barbican and a long passageway with a turn. A Persian inscription is incised onto the lintel. West of the gate are several structures, possibly prisons, with barrel vaults sunk below ground level. Two magazines with steeply pitched roofs of British construction are located above. A large building nearby may have served as officers' quarters. A small abandoned goddess temple crowns the summit of the rock.

The cemetery, which has many British tombs dating from the early 19th century, is located opposite the end of the rock, facing the steps.

E. PALANI

Located 57 km. west of Dindigul, this is perhaps the most famous of all the mountain shrines of the god Subrahmanya, also known as Murugan, and is the destination of a mass pilgrimage every January-February. The town of Palani is charmingly situated on the edge of the great Vyapuri tank, with distant views of the bold cliffs of the Palani Hills beyond. On the east side of the tank is *Shivagiri*, a hill that rises steeply 148 m. above the plain. A flight of approximately 660 steps, on which devotees have cut their names and footprints, winds past lesser shrines and subsidiary structures until it arrives at the summit, where the main *Subrahmanya Temple* is located. The complex is dedicated to Subrahmanya as Dandayudhapani, Bearer of the Staff. Curiously, the image the god venerated in the sanctuary is neither of stone or metal, but is composed of nine different kinds of poisonous substances resembling wax. The temple marks the spot where Murugan retired in anger after having been tricked by his brother Ganapati of the fruit symbolising Shiva's approval.

The east facing Dandayudhapani sanctuary is surrounded by colonnades on three sides. The squat tower above is encrusted with plaster sculptures and topped by a hemispherical roof. The goddess shrine, immediately south, is capped by a similarly squat tower.

From Palani it is possible to continue to Coimbatore, 108 km. northwest.

F. KODAIKANAL

This popular hill resort is easily reached from Madurai, 120 km. to the southwest. Kodaikanal occupies a natural wooded basin in the Palani Hills, 2,133 m. above sea level. Steep escarpments offer dramatic panoramas to the north and southwest.

Kodaikanal was first developed by members of the American Mission of Madurai, who chose this location in 1845 as a retreat from the plains. The station grew steadily, and by the end of the 19th century there were more than 2,000 inhabitants, mostly members of the Mission and British civil servants. A prominent figure at this time was Sir Vere Henry Levinge, who was responsible for building the dam that creates Kodaikanal Lake. The difficult ascent from the plain was eased in 1916 with the completion of a motorable road.

Kodaikanal Lake, covering 24 ha. in a star formation, is surrounded by wooded slopes; boating is popular and fishing in permitted. The Boat Club and the Levinge Memorial overlook the water. Bryant Park, on the east side of the lake, is noted for its flowers, hybrids and grafts. A horticultural show is held here in May. The International School and other educational institutions are located near the small bazaar, north of the lake. At the end of the main bazaar street is *Union Church*, previously the American Church, with a somewhat severe stone tower rising over the main entrance. Here begins Coaker's Walk, with glorious views of the 2,440 m. high, volcano-like peak of Perumal, 11 km. distant. The walk ends at the *Church of St Peter of* 1884, notable for its stained glass, and the small telescope house.

The so-called *Biscuit-Tin Church* stands in a wooded hill south of the lake. A granite obelisk nearby marks the site of the first American Mission Church. British and American graves lie overgrown in the adjacent cemetery. A popular walk from here leads to Bear Shola, 1.5 km. northwest of the lake.

The *Shenbaganur Museum*, 1.5 km. northeast of the lake, is maintained by Sacred Heart College, a theological seminary founded in 1895. It houses a small but interesting collection of local flora and fauna. Archaeological artefacts include pottery fragments with varying designs brought from prehistoric burial sites in the vicinity. Chettiar Park, 500 m. beyond the museum, is much visited because of the nearby Kurunji Anadavar temple.

Other features of interest at Kodaikanal are located further away. Some 3 km. west of the lake is the *Solar Astro-Physical Observatory*, established in 1898 at an altitude of 2,347 m. Pillar Rocks, 7 km. southwest of the lake, is a striking viewpoint, with three granite formations more than 120 m. high.

G. Srivilliputtur

This town, 74 km. southwest of Madurai, is celebrated for its twin *Vatapatrashayi* and *Andal Temples*. The latter monument is dedicated to the female saint who attained renown for her devotional compositions honouring Vishnu. It is, however, the Vatapatrashayi temple, consecrated to Vishnu, that dominates Srivilliputtur. Its 63 m. high gopura, reputedly the tallest in Southern India, represents the climax of the gopura form as developed by the Madurai Nayakas in the 17th century. It serves today as the official emblem for the state of Tamil Nadu.

The two-storeyed mandapa in front (east) of the main shrine of the Vatapatrashayi temple is notable for its timber vault, roofing the upper level. Carvings of different deities are seen on the angled struts. A smaller mandapa with yalis sculpted onto granite piers leads to the rectangular shrine, in which Vishnu is venerated in his reclining form as Ranganatha. This small structure is capped by a vaulted roof with arched ends. A subsidiary shrine in the southwest corner of the outer enclosure enshrines an unusual bronze image of triple-faced Vishnu, and a seated image of Narasimha in yoga posture.

The adjacent Andal temple is also entered from the east, through a lesser gopura. This stands at the end of a long colonnade with a broad central aisle flanked by piers with leaping yalis, inclining inwards. The enlarged heads of the beasts have fierce expressions and long manes. The gopura gives access to two concentric enclosures, mostly packed with corridors and colonnades. The main temple is entered through a porch with side entrance, the corner piers being concealed by clusters of cut-out colonettes. This leads to a mandapa, in the middle of which stands a small swing pavilion, its columns and canopy encased in brass. Column carvings of Tirumala Nayaka and his brother are also covered in metal. The shrine beyond accommodates an image of Ranganatha flanked by images of Andal and Garuda.

H. RAMANATHAPURAM

Previously known as Ramnad, this town lies 117 km. southeast of Madurai on NH49. Ramanathapuram rose to prominence at the end of the 17th century as the headquarters of the Setupatis, a line of local rulers who began their careers under the Madurai Nayakas. The Setupatis derived much of the prestige and income from control of the isthmus leading to Rameswaram Island. In the course of the 18th century the Setupatis were involved in the struggles against the British and the Nawabs of Arcot, but succumbed to the East India Company's forces in 1772. Ramanathapuram surrendered in 1792, thereby bringing the Setupati line to an end.

The *Setupati Palace*, in the west part of the town, was first established by Kilavan (1674-1710), though little of his period survives. The complex is surrounded by a high stone wall, with the main entrance on the west. This gate is an ornate structure with turrets and a small dome. *Ramalinga Vilasa*, on the north side of the complex, is the most interesting feature. Its east facade presents arcades at two levels, capped with a long vault; domical towers are seen at either end. Paintings almost entirely cloak the interior walls of the audience hall, antechamber and private apartments within, the last arranged on two levels at the rear of the building. The clear linework and vivid tones of red, ochre and blue are typical of the 18th century pictorial style developed in Tamil Nadu. Episodes from the Ramayana, Mahabharata and Bhagavata Purana are arranged in horizontal bands. The depictions of linga and goddess shrines refer to different holy spots within the Setupati kingdom. Royal topics also appear. The murals in the audience hall show formal receptions with seated Setupati kings, one of whom is specified as Muttu Vijaya Raghunatha Tevan (1710-28). Battle scenes include lines of animated soldiers brandishing weapons, and even a British officer firing a canon. One item of curiosity within the audience hall is a square stone pedestal on which the Setupatis were crowned.

The walls and arches of the sleeping chamber of the Setupati Palace are also adorned with paintings, especially of the king: standing with his women, who hold mirrors, fans and standards; listening to an exposition of sacred texts; sitting in a European chair, holding the holy sceptre of the family goddess, Rajarajeshvari; reclining on a cushion in full military attire, holding a long sword; being entertained by female dancers and singers; receiving gifts from

European envoys; lifting up his bow as part of a hunting expedition, while embracing his favourite consort.

The small north facing Rajarajeshvari shrine stands within its own compound immediately south of Ramalinga Vilasa.

Another monument within Ramanathapuram is *Christ Church*. This was built in 1799 as a Catholic place of worship by Manuel Martinez, a Portuguese military officer, who was buried here in 1810. It is now used for Protestant services. Its gabled facade has unusual corner pinnacles. The windows are fitted with stained glass.

I. KILAKKARAI

This port on the Gulf of Mannar lies 16 km. southwest of Ramanathapuram. Because the coastline here is steadily emerging from the sea, the land is dotted with maritime fossils, to a height of 5 m. Kilakkarai was once famous as a centre for pearl diving and fishing for conch shells. The lucrative commerce in these products attracted foreign visitors, the Dutch gaining a concession from the Setupatis to set up a trading post here in 1759. The ruins of the factory that they established can still be seen. A Catholic church stands nearby.

The town has a large Muslim population, many of whom are traders. Pearls and conches may still be purchased here, the latter fashioned into bangles, rings, lamps and other items. The most important place of prayer is the *Jami Mosque*. This incorporates the tombs of Sitakathi Markayar and Sathakkathulla Appa, two renowned holy figures.

J. RAMESWARAM

Almost 50 km. long and little more than 12 km. wide, this sacred island forms a sandy spit that protrudes away from the coast of Tamil Nadu towards Sri Lanka. That Rameswaram Island was connected to the mainland in times past is indicated by the submerged blocks of a Causeway that can still be seen from the modern bridge that now serves as a link with Ramanathapuram, 55 km. distant.

Rameswaram is identified with several important episodes in the Ramayana epic. The Ramanatha temple, in the middle of the island, marks the spot where Rama worshipped Shiva after returning from his successful battle in Lanka. Having killed Ravana, Rama wished to purify himself by making offerings to Shiva's linga. This emblem is the chief object of worship within the innermost sanctuary. Devotees generally bathe in the sea at nearby Agni Tirtha before entering the temple, where they hasten to be sprayed with water from 22 wells, known as tirthas, within the complex. Dripping wet, they then visit the twin linga shrines and the goddess shrine that form the ritual core of the temple.

Founded during the Pandya era, the *Ramanatha Temple* dates mainly from the 17th-18th century Setupati period. The complex is contained within a rectangle of walls with gopuras in the middle of three sides. The gates on the north and south remain unfinished, and stonework is much eroded by the salt air; the gate on the west is topped by a pyramidal tower. The main entrance from the east is through two doors in the outer walls, one aligned with the Ramalingeshvara shrine, the other with the Parvati shrine, both within the third, innermost enclosure. Both doors give access to mandapas that project outwards from the walls. They lead to a spacious corridor that proceeds around four sides of the second enclosure. The corridor is exceptional for its great length, 220 m. on the north and south, with receding perspectives of piers. The columns, raised on a continuous plinth, are adorned with scrollwork and lotus designs enhanced with plasterwork; pendant lotus brackets above rest on crouching yalis. Portraits of the Setupatis and their ministers adorn the central piers in the east corridor. Painted medallions adorn the ceilings throughout.

The west corridor is interrupted by another one that runs from the west gopura to the second enclosure wall. The piers here are carved with royal figures, warriors, maidens and rearing animals. Subsidiary shrines, dating partly from the 12th century, can be seen near the intersection of the two corridors. These small structures have simply moulded basements, pilastered walls, and towers crowned with hemispherical roofs. A large square tank is situated nearby.

The entrance to the second enclosure from the east is through the largest gopura of the series. This leads via a second door into the third enclosure, which is divided into three compounds. That on the east contains a Nandi pavilion and a square bathing pond. The north compound is where the Ramalingeshvara and Vishvanatha shrines are located. The former is preceded by mandapa with columns carved with effigies of the Ramanathapuram rulers and their ministers. The Parvati shrine stands in a separate compound to the south. Its attached mandapa has portraits and attendant maidens sculpted on the column shafts.

Rameswaram Island also has other sacred spots. *Gandhamadana Hill*, crowned by a small shrine containing the stone relief footprints of Rama, lies 3 km. northwest of the Ramanatha temple. *Dhanushkodi*, at the extreme tip of the island, 18 km. distant, is where Vibhashana, Ravana's brother surrendered to Rama. Though this bathing spot was washed away in the cyclonic storm of 1964, the small Kodandarama temple here survives intact.

K. Chettinad

This region northeast of Madurai is associated with the wealthy Chettiar merchant community. The somewhat arid territory is dotted with small settlements, with *Grand Houses* laid out in regular streets. These residences are notable for their intricately carved woodwork, the finest to be seen anywhere in Tamil Nadu. Many of the houses date from the late 19th and early 20th centuries, at which time the Chettiars had become prosperous merchants and financiers in Madras, Burma and Malaya. Much of the wood with which these houses was in fact imported teak. Curiously, most of these houses are not lived in permanently, being used only for family reunions and celebrations. This, however, does not prevent some houses from being beautifully maintained.

The typical Chettinad mansion, as seen in *Devakottai, Karaikkudi* and *Kandakuthan*, some 90 km. from Madurai, or 70 km. north of Ramanathapuram, is fronted with a European styled masonry facade, embellished with colonnades, arcaded storeys and corner towers. Most houses are entered through verandahs, with circular wooden columns on stone bases, and brackets ornately carved with pendant lotuses. Wooden doorways are elaborate compositions, with intricately worked jambs and lintels, often with upper panels filled with images of Ganesha, or Lakshmi with elephants. Angled struts cut into the semblance of horses with riders, yalis, birds and makaras support overhangs with pendant brass lotus buds. Interiors of houses are laid out in a sequence of courts surrounded by colonnades, generally with smaller rooms leading to the kitchen and service areas at the rear.

One of the most imposing examples of domestic architecture in Chettinad is the palace at *Kanadukatan*, a modest village 11 km. north of Karaikkudi. Home of the descendants of the most prominent family in the region, this mansion conforms to the scheme just described, However, it is fronted by a two-storeyed reception hall immediately inside the front door. This grand room is paved in marble, and lit by clerestory windows, as well as by imported glass chandeliers suspended from the timber vault.

45. Tirunelveli

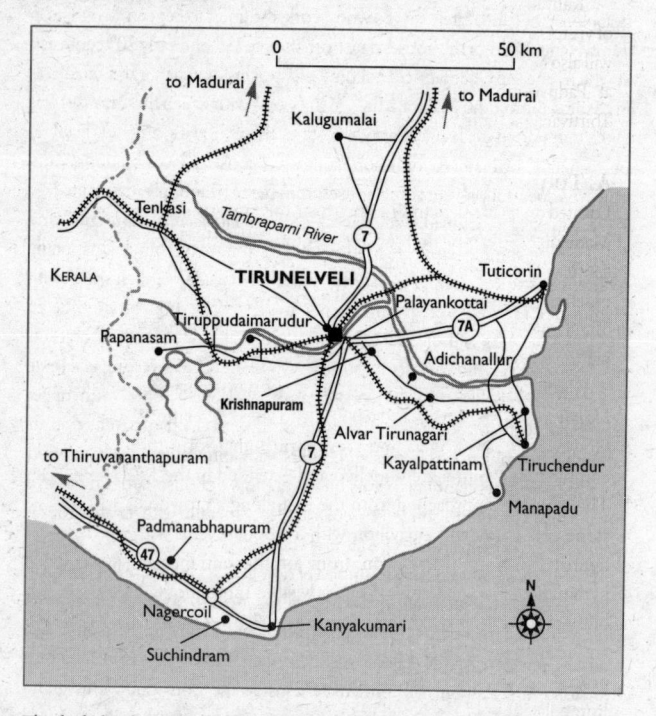

The lush landscape of the Tambraparni River Valley provides a delightful setting for a host of historical sites in the extreme south of Tamil Nadu.

While a few hours should be sufficient to visit the great religious monument in Tirunelveli [A], the largest city in this area, a full day will be required to reach the temples at Krishnapuram [B], Alvar Tirunagari [D] and Tiruchendur [E], with a diversion to the Iron Age site at Adichanallur [C]. All of these are located along the road running east from Tirunelveli.

Additional time will have to be reserved for the Christian and Muslim places of worship at the small settlements of Manapadu [F] and Kayalpattinam [G] on the Gulf of Mannar. The largest port on this coast, Tuticorin [H], is of lesser interest.

A journey from Tirunelveli north towards Madurai [44] can take in the early rock-cut monument at Kalugumalai [I].

The waterfalls and shrines near Tenkasi [J] and Papanasam [L] are located west of Tirunelveli. A stop on the way is recommended at Tiruppudaimarudur [K] in order to inspect the remarkable murals. Keep a full day for these sights.

Kanyakumari [M], at the southern tip of Tamil Nadu, attracts a multitude of visitors. An overnight stay permits ocean views of both sunrise and sunset. It will also facilitate an excursion to the temple at Suchindram [N] and the palace at Padmanabhapuram [O], both of which may be visited en route to Thiruvananthapuram in Kerala [46], 52 km. to the west on NH47.

A. TIRUNELVELI

Located on the bank of the Tambraparni, this city was much developed by the Madurai Nayakas in the 16th-17th centuries. By the beginning of the 18th century, Tirunelveli was under the control of a line of local chiefs, who were much engaged in struggles with the rulers of the adjacent Travancore kingdom. The Tirunelveli chiefs eventually succumbed to the Nawabs of Arcot [38B], but the city was ceded to the British in 1797.

Tirunelveli preserves a large and important religious monument, the *Nellaiyappa Temple*, which dates back to the 13th century Pandya period. However, the twin Shiva and Devi shrines that form the nucleus of this complex were entirely remodelled and extended in the 17th-18th centuries. The temple is approached from the east along a crowded street. An open stone colonnade and a pavilion with a wooden vault with carved bracket figures stand immediately in front of the entrance gopura. The tall pyramidal tower that rises above is visible throughout the city. An altar, brass-clad lamp post and gigantic Nandi surrounded by massive piers are arranged in a line immediately inside the gate. Spacious corridors proceed around the first enclosure; major gopuras mark the four sides. Immediately west of the Nandi is a porch with frontal piers carved with three-dimensional figures of Virabhadra, Karna and Arjuna, overhung by deeply curved eaves. A gopura with wooden doors leads to the second enclosure (only Hindus admitted).

The linga shrine beyond is entered through a raised porch with side steps flanked by elephant balustrades. Columns here have clusters of slender colonettes, with up to 48 cut-out elements at the corners. A great bell also hangs here. Guardian figures with clubs flank the entrance to the mandapa that precedes the shrine. Shiva is not the only god worshipped here; a large image of reclining Vishnu is located in the corridor immediately north. To the northeast is a second linga shrine, set beneath the level of the floor, with a small tower, possibly dating back to the Pandya era. A small Devi shrine occupies the south side of the same enclosure. An unusual square structure near the northwest corner of the enclosure has wooden screens and a metal-clad pyramidal roof; carvings adorn the timber struts and brackets. A Somaskanda shrine at the southwest corner is partly obscured by a modern plaster tableau of Kailasa, Shiva's mountain home.

The colonnade that proceeds around the first enclosure of the Nellaiyappa temple has already been noted. On the west this passes by a long hall with yali piers, in which an icon of Subrahmanya is venerated. Donor sculptures portraying the Tirunelveli chiefs are seen in the south colonnade.

The gopura on this side leads directly to the adjacent *Ambal Temple*. A corridor set at a slight angle has piers sculpted with almost three-dimensional representations of Rama and Lakshmana in the company of Sugriva and Hanuman. These figures are flanked by yalis with enlarged monster heads. The corridor leads past a square tank surrounded by colonnades. A lamp post, altar and Nandi pavilion are aligned with the doorway of the goddess sanctuary. Turning east, towards the entrance gopura, it is necessary to pass through a long mandapa with yali piers lining the central aisle. As in the adjacent Nellaiyappa temple, the east gopura is fronted by a wooden vaulted entrance structure with carved brackets.

Christian evangelists were active in Tirunelveli from the end of the 18th century. The headquarters of the Church Missionary Society in Tamil Nadu is at *Palayankottai*, 3 km. east of the city, also the site of a demolished fort. *Trinity Church*, the Society's principal place of worship, was erected in 1826. Its handsome Neo-Classical tower is surmounted by a tall spire that attains an overall height of 35 m. The Jesuit Mission also maintains a presence in Palayankottai; their Church of St Francis Xavier was completed in 1863.

B. KRISHNAPURAM

The *Venkatachala Temple* in this small village, 13 km. east of Palayankottai, is renowned for its remarkable 16th-17th century sculptures. The monument is entered on the east through a gopura of standard design, with carved wooden doors. The gate is preceded by a mandapa with a raised dais at one end. The Virappa Nayaka Mandapa, immediately to the right inside the first enclosure, is named after one of the Madurai kings. Its front six piers have smoothly rounded figures carved almost in three dimensions of (left to right) female dancer, tribal man, Karna, Arjuna, tribal woman, and female dancer; mounted warriors appear on the sides of two of the piers. A long colonnade proceeds west towards the doorway that gives access to the second enclosure of the temple. The mandapa beyond has a central aisle flanked by yalis alternating with vigorously posed figures of attendants, Virabhadra, Rati, and dancing ascetic (north row); Virabhadra, Manmatha, and Bhima (south row); and guardians with clubs (west row). The sanctuary at the end houses Vishnu with consorts. Twin Lakshmi shrines occupy the two west corners of the enclosure.

C. ADICHANALLUR

This *Iron Age Site*, 14 km. east of Krishnapuram, on the south bank of the Tambrapani, just off the road leading to Tiruchendur, is worth visiting for the prehistoric burials that have been unearthed here. Sepulchral urns of thick red earthenware, up to 1 m. in diameter, are found all over the site, especially on a long piece of high ground overlooking the river, where about 40 ha. have been fenced off for protection. The urns are accommodated in rock-cut cavities, with bands of uncut rock in between. When cleared, these chambers revealed the bones and skulls of the dead, as well as an abundance of other remains. More than 1,000 iron weapons, implements and ornaments were collected here, including swords, spears, arrows, axes, adzes, hammers, chisels, rings, bangles and lamps, as well as a few gold items. Most of these artefacts have been removed to the Government Museum, Chennai [36D].

D. ALVAR TIRUNAGARI

This small town, 31 km. east of Tirunelveli, marks the birthplace of Nammalvar in about the 9th century. This figure holds a high position among the Vaishnava saints of Tamil Nadu, and it was in his honour that the *Adinatha Temple* was founded here in the 13th century. Most of the buildings incorporated into this extensive monument are, however, no earlier than the 16th-17th centuries. The principal gopura on the east is approached through a long colonnade standing outside the walls. Another similar colonnade occupies the space between the first and second gopuras. The two mandapas that abut the colonnade on the north show yalis and energetic figures on the columns. A similarly adorned mandapa on the north has an elaborate porch with slender colonettes grouped around the column shafts; heroes and female dancers embellish the internal supports.

The second enclosure of the Adinatha temple, entered through lesser gopuras on the east and north, is filled with colonnades, halls and subshrines. The mandapa leading to the focal Vishnu sanctuary incorporates a small Garuda shrine, brass-clad flagpole and altar. Another shrine, on the north, is consecrated to Nammalvar. The columns on its entrance porch are sculpted with lively heroes and dancing maidens. A small open court at a higher level to one side has a tamarind tree growing freely in the middle; Nammalavar is believed to have meditated under its spreading branches. Two small shrines in the west part of the enclosure are dedicated to Lakshmi and Bhudevi.

E. TIRUCHENDUR

Built on a rocky promontory extending into the Gulf of Mannar, the *Subrahmanya Temple* at this seaside town, 51 km. east of Tirunelveli, is a popular place of pilgrimage. While references to the temple date back to the 9th century, the corrosive effects of the sea air are such that the monument was substantially renewed at the turn of the 20th century; the shrine was reconsecrated in 1941.

The temple is entered on the west through the lofty Mela Gopura. Its nine-storeyed, pyramidal tower, which reaches a height of 45 m., is a prominent landmark visible from the ocean. The tower is covered with plaster figures, some showing scenes from the life of the saint Manikkavachakar. The bell fixed into the topmost storey was presented by a British official. The other entrance to the monument is from the south, via the Shanmuga Vilasa, an imposing modern structure with four corridors meeting at a central hall, some 15 m. square. Together with the Mela Gopura, this structure gives access to the outer rectangular enclosure of the temple. This is partly occupied by a colonnade that runs along the perimeter walls on four sides. Additional doorways are positioned on the north, but there is no access form the seaside, on the east.

The Vasanta Mandapa, on the west side of the corridor, displays portraits of saintly personalities who assisted in the reconstruction of the monument. A small subshrine dedicated to Vishnu is incorporated into the north corridor. The ritual core of the temple consists of a pair of shrines, each with a pyramidal tower capped by a hemispherical roof. The Subrahmanya shrine, which faces east towards a lesser gopura in the second set of walls, has a stone image of the god placed next to a small linga cut out of a natural boulder. The south facing Shanmuga shrine accommodates metal icons of six-headed Subrahmanya together with consorts.

Rock-cut shrines and natural carvings of Subrahmanya dot the shoreline near the temple. A sanctuary with an image of Dattatreya is seen 200 m. to the north. Two square wells, one inside the other, curiously filled with different tasting waters, are found about the same distance to the south.

F. MANAPADU

This predominantly Roman Catholic village stands on the arid shore of the Gulf of Mannar, 18 km. south of Tiruchendur. Manapadu was one of the first places to be visited by St Francis Xavier in 1542, when he initiated missionary activity on what was then called the Fishery Coast. A grotto on the seaward face of a cliff is pointed out as the spot where the saint lived and prayed. Close to the sea is the *Church of the Holy Cross*, founded in 1581. This possesses what is believed to be a fragment of the True Cross of Jerusalem. The public display of this relic each September attracts thousands of pilgrims.

G. KAYALPATTINAM

This small port on the Gulf of Mannar, 11 km. north of Tiruchendur, near the mouth of the Tambraparni River, is inhabited almost exclusively by Muslims. Local accounts claim that the inhabitants of Kayalpattinam are descended from immigrants who came from Arabia in Pandya times. This suggestion is supported by the obviously foreign dress and customs of the local population, as well as the religious monuments that date back to the 14th century.

The *Al-Kabir Mosque* of 1337, in the middle of the town, has a large prayer hall divided by columns into long aisles, with an arched mihrab projecting away from the west wall. A central space in the middle, defined by 12 piers, is roofed with a large dome, an addition of the 18th century. The *Al-Saghir Mosque* opposite is simpler and plainer. Several graves in the adjoining tomb chamber, known as the Shrine of the Seven Martyrs, bear 15th century dates.

The nearby *Qadiriya Mosque* of 1871 is of greater architectural merit. Its colonnaded court is surrounded by chambers for students. The remarkable circular prayer hall of the Mahlara Mosque forms part of the complex. Four external buttresses rise as tapering octagonal minarets, crowned with domical tops. The pointed dome that roofs the chamber within is more than 12 m. in diameter.

Rettaikulampalli, at the north end of the town, is a mosque with 18th century piers lining the central aisle. Other mosques, such as the Marakkayarpalli and Appapapalli, have diminutive rectangular tombs roofed with pyramidal vaults that enshrine the graves of 17th-18th century saints.

H. TUTICORIN

This port, 52 km. east of Tirunelveli via NH7A, or 30 km. north of Tiruchendur, is the busiest in Tamil Nadu after Chennai, its chief exports being cotton and rice. Until recently Tuticorin was also the chief departure point for overnight passenger ferries to Sri Lanka. In past times the port was celebrated as the centre for pearl fishing. Tuticorin was originally settled by the Portuguese in 1540, but it was captured in 1658 by the Dutch, and remained in their possession until it was ceded to the British in 1824.

The two small temples in Tutucorin are of little architectural interest, unlike the Christian places of worship. In spite of its name, the *English Church* was founded in 1750 by the Dutch East India Company. The 'VOC' monogram of the Company appears on the plastered gable over the entrance. Monuments in the adjacent cemetery include a lofty obelisk with corner urns and an inscription of 1824. The Roman Catholic church dedicated to Our Lady of the Snows, at the south end of the beach, dates from the 17th century.

I. Kalugumalai

The monolithic temple at Kalugumalai, Hill of the Vulture, about 50 km. north of Tirunelveli, partly via NH7, is a rare example of Pandya architecture. The *Vattuvan Kovil* is hewn out of a massive outcrop of granite, facing east through a cleft towards the village beneath. Begun in the 8th century, the temple was never completed beyond its pyramidal tower, capped with an octagonal domical roof. The tower is adorned with friezes of dwarfs beneath the eaves, and fully modelled Nandis at the corners. Gracefully posed seated images of Dakshinamurti (south), Narasimha (west), Brahma (north), and Shiva with Uma (east) are seen in the middle of each side. The arch-shaped motifs are embellished with delicately incised foliage and jewelled garlands. The attached hall remains an unshaped block of granite.

Rows of *Standing Jinas* are carved onto the flank of the main rock, indicating that the monument also served as a Jain place of worship. Ambika between a lion and dancer are seen to one side. A crowned king kneels in front of a Tirthankara, shown larger than human size. Another Tirthankara is seated on a lion throne, surrounded by attendants.

J. Tenkasi

Nestling picturesquely at the base of the Western Ghats, 52 km. northwest of Tirunelveli, Tenkasi was the home of a line of local Pandya chiefs in the 15th-16th centuries. It later came under the sway of the Madurai Nayakas. The town is dominated by the *Vishvanatha Temple*, entered on the east through an immense gopura, the tower of which has only recently been completed. Carvings on the jambs within the passageway are finely finished; the columns in the side chambers show Shiva with the wives of the sages, Rama with Lakshmana, and Kali. The columned structure that stands outside the gopura serves as a market.

The first inner enclosure of the temple is occupied by a large mandapa. The piers lining the central aisle have 2 m. high figures of Shiva dancing, Rati and Bhikshatanamurti (north row); and Kali, Krishna, Manmatha and Virabhadra (south row). These remarkable, three-dimensional sculptures belong to the 17th century. At the west of the hall is a second smaller mandapa that leads to the second enclosure. The principal linga shrine has its outer walls adorned with pilastered niches that frame icons of Dakshinamurti (south), Shiva (west), and Brahma (north). Colonnades surrounding the shrine on four sides incorporate sets of Nayanmars on the south, sanctuaries of Vijayaka and Subrahmanya at the two western corners, a small cistern on the north, and a jack-fruit tree at the northeast corner.

A shrine to Subrahmanya, standing freely south of the outer enclosure, has ornate basement mouldings, pilastered walls, and overhanging eaves. The 12 columned pavilion in front has piers with leaping yalis at the corners, a pair of guardian figures on the west, and legendary heroes elsewhere. The Devi shrine stands in its own compound further south.

The resort of *Kuttalam* lies 5 km. south of Tenkasi. Though little higher that 150 m. above sea level, the site enjoys a refreshing climate; for this reason it was developed as a sanatorium by the British. The sacred waterfall here takes its name from the nearby Kuttalanatha temple.

K. Tiruppudaimarudur

This small village, 25 km. west of Tirunelveli, is home to the *Narumbanatha Temple*, charmingly sited on the south bank of the Tambraparni River. The monument is notable for the remarkable paintings and wooden sculptures in the upper storeys of the second east gopura. Successive chambers within the hollow brick tower are reached by ladder-like steps. The intricately carved timber columns with ornate brackets carry ceilings with lotus panels. The plaster walls are covered with murals with animated black linework and bright colours; the red and green backgrounds do not quite meet the linework, leaving a curious white band around the figures.

A large variety of legends and narratives is illustrated here. Rama and Hanuman, and Rama battling with Ravana, appear either side of the west window in the first upper chamber. The story of Arjuna fighting Shiva as the hunter is seen nearby; also the legend of Sambandar converting the Pandya king. The second chamber is furnished with depictions of Narasimha and Nataraja. Other compositions here show battle scenes, receptions with parades of horses and elephants, and even a ship transporting warriors. The columns have carvings of Virabhadra and yalis. Yet further wooden sculptures are seen in the third upper chamber. Paintings at this level portray the avataras of Vishnu, Vishnu reclining on the serpent, and Rama seated in the company of Hanuman. Murals in the fourth chamber, at the topmost level, illustrate Krishna, Bhairava, and a set of lingas.

A covered space links the second and third gopuras of the Narumbanatha temple. The interior of the third enclosure is filled with mandapas and colonnades. These give access to twin shrines dedicated to Shiva and Devi. Doorways in the west side of the enclosure lead down to the river bank, where there is a delightful assortment of shrines and bathing ghats.

L. Papanasam

The natural beauty of this spot, 47 km. west of Tirunelveli, is enhanced by the *Waterfall by* which the Tambraparni descends from the Western Ghats to the plains. The water drops about 100 m. over an almost sheer wall of rock, flanked by forested hills. The cascade is imbued with great sanctity, since the water here is believed to wash away all human sins. The unassuming *Temple of Papavinaseshvara*, about 1 km. downstream, has broad flights of steps descending to the river. Nearby cotton mills, in operation since the late 19th century, are worked by water power.

M. KANYAKUMARI

Previously known as Cape Comorin, this rocky promontory at the southern tip of the Indian peninsular, 83 km. south of Tirunelveli, marks the point where the waters of the Bay of Bengal and the Arabian Sea mingle with the Indian Ocean. Kanyakumari takes its name from Kumari, the goddess who protects India's shores. Pilgrims come here to bathe in a rocky ocean pool near the *Kumari Temple*. The monument is entered through a small porch that leads to three concentric enclosures, with the goddess sanctuary at the core (only Hindus admitted). This dates from about the 18th century, but has been much remodelled since.

The *Gandhi Memorial*, west of the temple, is where Mahatma's ashes were exposed before being immersed in the ocean. Its painted concrete tower, capped with a ribbed circular element, derives from the temple architecture of Orissa. The *Vivekananda Memorial*, perched on a rocky islet 250 m. southeast of the promontory, is accessible by ferry. This revivalist structure, supposedly incorporating all the different styles of Indian architecture, dates from 1970. It commemorates the Bengali religious leader and philosopher, who lived at Kanyakumari from 1892 as a simple monk and devotee of the goddess, swimming out to the islet and sitting there in deep meditation. In later years he founded the Ramakrishna Mission in Chennai.

N. SUCHINDRAM

This village, 13 km. west of Kanyakumari, is dominated by the *Sthanumalaya Temple*, picturesquely sited on the south bank of a large square tank. The east entrance to the complex is preceded by a colonnade, the central columns of which are sculpted with sages and rearing yalis. The passageway of the gopura beyond is flanked by demonic figures, and smaller panels of Natesha and Trivikrama, with paintings depicting events from the Ramayana epic and local legends above. The interior of the temple is dominated by two focal shrines: the one to the north accommodates the Sthanumalaya linga, representing the triad of Shiva, Brahma and Vishnu; the one to the south houses an image of Vishnu. These small, unadorned structures date back to the 13th century, but the remainder of the monument is assigned to the 17th-18th centuries, when the region was contested by the Madurai Nayakas and Travancore rulers.

Devotees approaching the linga shrine, aligned with gopura already noted, pass by a small pavilion with a dais in the middle. The corner columns have almost three-dimensional images of Manmatha and Rati (east), and Karna and Arjuna (west). A flagpole and a large seated Nandi in plaster covered brickwork are located to the west. A small pavilion, sheltering an image of Garuda, stands immediately south, on axis with the Vishnu shrine. Its columns have portraits of Nayaka donors and their queens. To the west is a mandapa with sculpted piers defining two aisles leading to the main shrines. The ceiling is painted with floral designs. Friezes on the supporting beams illustrate episodes from the Ramayana and Krishna legends.

A spacious corridor runs around four sides of the perimeter walls of the temple. Large brackets and crouching lions support the flat ceiling. A small west facing linga shrine, near the southwest corner of the colonnade, is elevated on a granite boulder covered with inscriptions. The Murugan shrine, next to the north arm of the corridor, is preceded on the east by the Alankara Mandapa, with ornate carvings on the central aisle. Clusters of colonettes here frame carvings of royal figures, including a portrait of Martanda Varma of Thiruvananthapuram. The Chitra Sabha, in the northeast corner, has sculptures of heroes in the company of Venugopala and Bhikshatanamurti. The aisle leads to a small Natesha shrine.

O. PADMANABHAPURAM

In the 16th-18th centuries the palace at Padmanbhapuram, 35 km. northwest of Kanyakumari, served as the headquarters of the rulers of the kingdom of Tiruvittankur, better known to Europeans as Travancore. For much of this period the site was known as Kalkulam, however Martanda Varma (1729-58) renamed it Padmanabhapuram, City of the Lotus Born, in honour of Padmanabha, guardian deity of the Travancore kings, worshipped in the temple at Tiruvananthapuram [46A]. This ruler was responsible for renovating the palace, and much of the present complex dates from his era. After 1750, when the capital was shifted to Thiruvananthapuram, Padmnabhapuram was to reduced to a minor royal residence. It survives today as the principal example of Kerala royal architecture, even though it is now located in Tamil Nadu.

Padmanabhapuram Palace (closed Mondays) is laid out in a sequence of four walled compounds, creating a transition from public to private zones, connected by simple doorways. The complex consists of individual structures linked by a maze of corridors, colonnades, verandahs and courts. The timber columns, beams and louvred screens are typical, are is the sloping roofs clad in terracotta tiles.

The principal entrance to the complex, from the west, is through an outer court reserved for public ceremonies. The *Padipura*, or main gate, displays an ornamented gabled roof. The *Pumukham* on the upper level of a two-storeyed building in the second court is an audience hall, with circular wooden columns and angled timber screens. To the north is the dance hall, known as the *Navaratri Mandapa*, after the festival celebrated here. The polished blackened plaster floor reflects the female attendants carved onto the granite piers. The central aisle leads to a small shrine dedicated to Sarasvati. Among the detached carvings displayed in the surrounding colonnades are several 12th century stone images, and wooden figures from a temple chariot.

The third court marks the beginning of the private zone of the palace. Here stands the *Upparika Malika* of 1749, a masonry tower that soars above the sloping tiled roofs of the adjacent buildings. Its four chambers, arranged one above the other, connected by steep steps, serve as a treasury, royal sleeping room, royal meditation room, and shrine room, the last with an empty bed for Padmanabha. Cots dating from the 18th century, intended for the king and for the god, have decorated head panels incorporating coats-of-arms of the Dutch East India Company. Wooden balconies with angled screens project outwards from the upper levels; louvred shutters permitted the ruler to discreetly survey the activities in the court below. The walls of the shrine room at the top of the Upparika Malika are covered with brightly toned murals. These splendid examples of Kerala pictorial art are devoted exclusively to mythological topics. Padmanabha appears on the end walls, the god reclining on the coils of the cosmic serpent, with multiple hoods rearing over his head. Compositions on the north wall depict (from left to right): a linga with eyes being worshipped by women; Ganesha above, and Natesha with sages beneath; Shasta above, and Krishna below; and Vishnu with consorts. The south wall shows (from left to right): Lakshmi, and Krishna playing the flute; Rama and Sita above, and Durga beneath; Vishnu on Garuda; Shiva and Parvati above, and Vishnu beneath; and a linga with eyes.

Residences of other members of the royal family are located nearby. The Lakshmi Vilasam and Pilamuttu Kottaram were reserved for courtly women. The queen mother's apartment, the *Thai Kottaram*, is one of the oldest parts of the complex. Its chambers are arranged around a small internal court with a shallow pool in the middle. The upper level has wooden screens overhung by a sloping tiled roof. Nearby stands the *Homapura*, a building for ritual use, with its own stepped tank, and the *Uttupura*, which has two long dining halls, one above the other, used for feeding priests on special occasions; each hall has a central row of columns.

The fourth court of Padmnabhapuram palace occupies the easternmost zone. Additional dining rooms and apartments are disposed around *Kalkulam*, a reservoir reached by a flight of steps. The *Indra Vilasam*, incorporating a residence and audience hall, in the extreme northeast corner of the complex, is partly built in a Neo-Classical style. It faces a garden, now sadly neglected. The offices at the north end of this compound are accessible from the street that runs outside the palace walls.

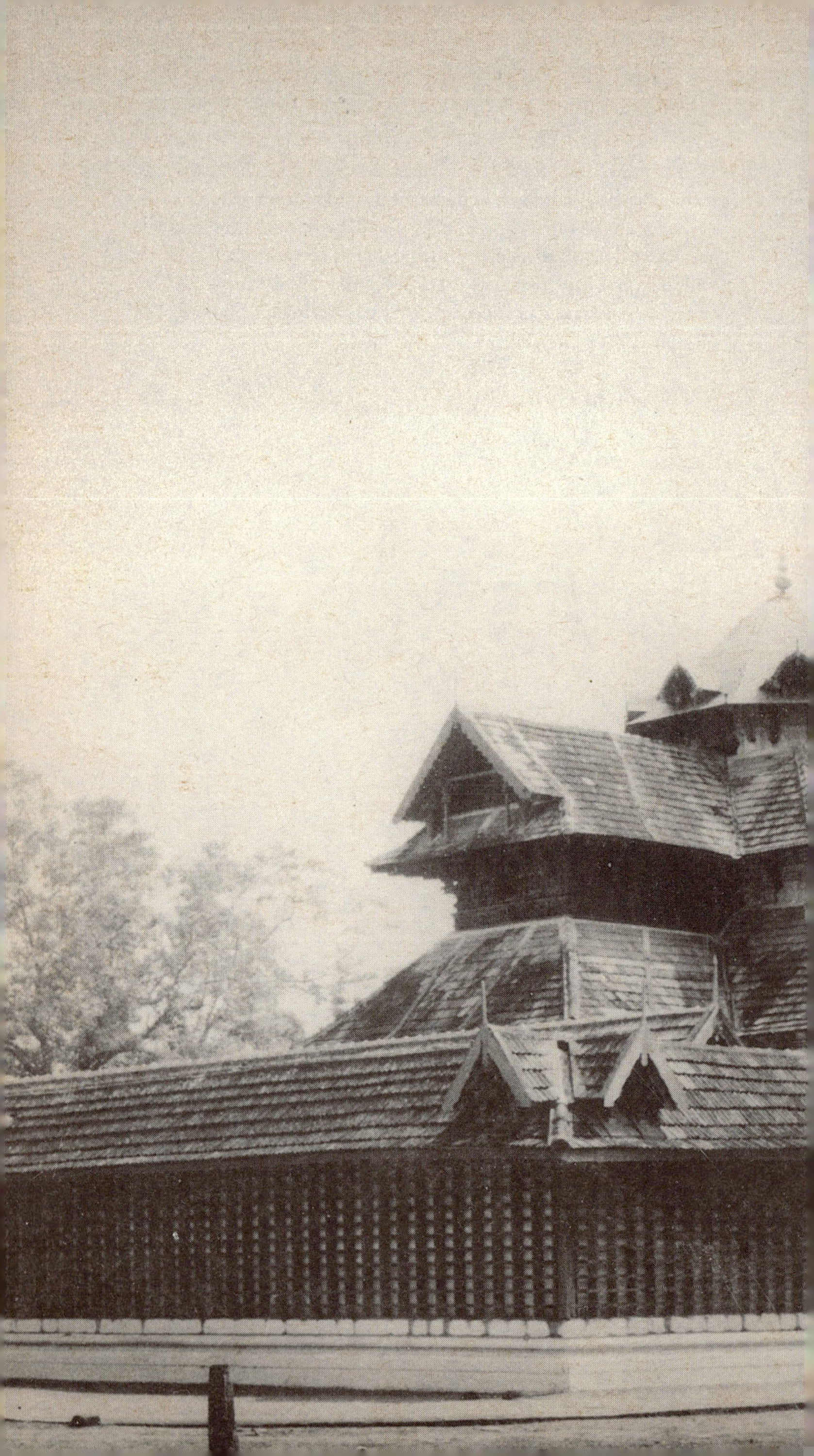

Mahadeva Temple, Peruvanam

KERALA

Kerala

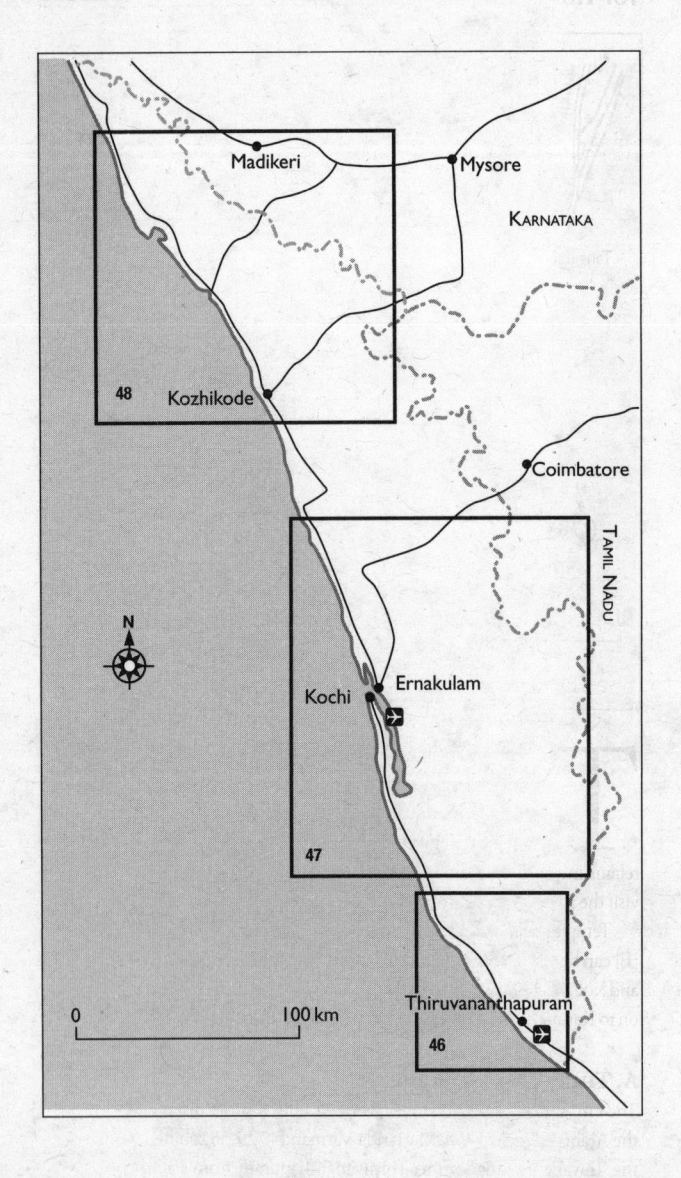

46. Thiruvananthapuram

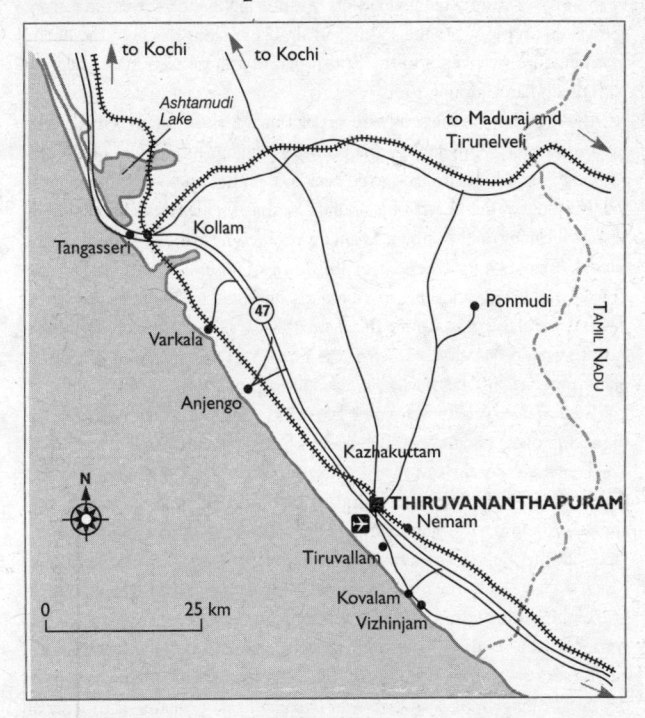

The current spelling of Thiruvananthapuram revives the indigenous form for Trivandrum, the name by which the city is still familiar. Once the headquarters of the rulers of Travancore and now the capital of Kerala, Thiruvananthapuram is a delightful city that retains much of its traditional charm. A half-day tour is recommended [A] to visit the palace, temple and museum.

Temples at Nemam [B], Tiruvallam [C], Vizhinjam [D] and Kazhakuttam [E] can be reached as short side trips. An excursion to Anjengo [F], Vakala [G] and Kollam [H] may be completed in a single day, with the option of continuing on to Kayankulam [47N], Alappuzha [47B] and Kochi [47A], all along NH47.

A. Thiruvananthapuram

The city spreads agreeably over wooded hills, a short distance inland from the Arabian Sea. In 1750, Martanda Varman (1729-58) shifted the capital of the Travancore kingdom to Thiruvananthapuram from Padmnabhapuram

[45O], 52 km. southwest. Under this ruler and his successor, Rama Varma (1758-98), Travancore attained its greatest influence, extending from Kanyakumari [45M] to the south, and almost as far as Kochi to the north. The kingdom survived into the British period as a princely state, merging with the Indian Union in 1956.

The royal zone in the southern part of Thiruvananthapuram is marked by the Padmanahaswamy temple, the principal religious monument of the city. Although records for this shrine go back to the 10th century, the temple was totally rebuilt at the orders of Martanda Varma. The deity worshipped here, Vishnu reclining on the serpent Ananta, gives its name to the city, which means Sacred Ananta's City. The cult of this form of Vishnu was central to the Travancore kings, and the monument continues to be managed by a descendant of the royal family. This figure still leads the procession during the Arat festival in March-April, when the image of Padmanabha is carried to Shanmuga beach, to be ritually bathed in the ocean.

The *Padmanabhaswamy Temple* is laid out as a vast square, with entrances in the middle of each side. Gates on three sides have tiled gabled roofs in the typical Kerala manner. But the east gate, the largest, is a Tamil styled gopura, with two tiers of granite walls topped by a squatly proportioned pyramidal tower. This consists of four diminishing storeys roofed with a long barrel vault; gilded pot finials line the ridge. The gopura is approached through a long colonnade, close to which is a large tank. The mandapa immediately inside (only Hindus admitted) has columns with portrait sculptures, one supposedly depicting the architect. The corridors to the north and south form part of a free-standing colonnade that runs around four sides of the temple enclosure. Its piers are enlivened with female devotees bearing lamps. Mandapas with 16 columns are located at each corner of the colonnade. An additional mandapa in front (east) of the entrance to the inner enclosure has lofty piers with three-dimensional carvings of Shiva dancing, Bhairava, Krishna, and the Pandava heroes. A greater array of sculpted divinities appears in the Kalasekhara Mandapa to the south, where each figure is framed by a miniature pavilion with cut-out colonettes. A Krishna shrine, near the northwest corner of the colonnade, stands in a small compound.

The inner enclosure of the Padmanabhaswamy temple is contained with a double line of masonry walls and timber screens. The main shrine within accommodates a large icon of reclining Vishnu, fashioned out of brightly painted plasterwork. The head, navel and feet of the god are viewed through a row of three doorways. The outer walls of the shrine have pilastered projections covered with murals depicting different aspects of Vishnu and his consorts. Tiers of wooden gables covered with copper sheets rise above. A large wooden hall in front shelters devotees; its ceiling has square lotus panels with miniature celestials and nagas serving as brackets.

Several features of interest are seen near the approach road that leads to the east gate of the Padmanabhaswamy temple. The *Kuchira Malika* is a traditional wooden residence with a polished floor and sloping tiled roofs. The *Mettanmani* nearby is a curious tower, with a mechanical clock. Various structures that once formed part of the 18th century *Royal Palace* are located southwest of the temple. The combination of Neo-Classical features with indigenous tiled roofs is characteristic. Portions of the laterite walls of the fort laid out by Martanda Varma can still be seen to the west.

Mahatma Gandhi Road, the principal route running north through the middle of Thiruvananthapuram, passes by the Secretariat of 1939, and the Victoria Jubilee Town Hall. The *Public Library* opposite, founded in 1829, is the oldest in Southern India. Palayam Junction is marked by the formidable Neo-Gothic bulk of the city's main Latin Catholic church. The nearby *Christ Church*, also in the Neo-Gothic style, was erected in 1859 by Anglican missionaries. The building has generous side windows and two-stage tower over the arcaded porch. At the northern extremity of Mahatma Gandhi Road is an attractively planted public park, in which stands the city's main cultural institutions.

The *Art Museum* (closed Mondays), originally the Napier Museum, is an unusual structure of considerable charm, designed by Robert Fellowes Chisholm in 1872. It successfully fuses the wooden balconies, timber screens, tiered tiled roofs and ornate gables typical of the Kerala tradition with Neo-Gothic elements, such as polychrome brickwork, arcaded ranges and towers with slender pinnacles. The collection of metal, stone and wooden sculptures exhibited here comes from various sites in the vicinity. The bronzes dating from the 9th century Chera period are the earliest metal images from this part of Kerala; the smoothly modelled standing Vishnu with inlaid gold eyes is particularly fine. Small, well detailed icons from the 17th-18th centuries include images of Narasimha, Virabhadra, and Vishnu on Garuda. A seated figure of Sashta, the head surrounded by a halo of hair, is perhaps the most interesting of these later metal images. Brass lamps fashioned as miniature female figures are also on display. An impressive set of wooden bracket figures comes from the 17th century temples at Kulathapuzha. They include a remarkable image of Durga standing on the buffalo, one foot pressed down on the animal's head. The lower part of a chariot covered with carvings, and a small wooden pavilion are also on display.

The adjacent *Sri Chitra Art Gallery* (closed Mondays) houses a collection of Indian paintings, including Mughal and Rajput miniatures. There are notable examples of Kerala's most famous artist, Ravi Varma, and an assemblage of early 20th century Bengali paintings. Many of these oils attempt to fuse indigenous themes of Indian culture with European techniques and styles. The

Museum of Natural History and the Childrens' Museum stand next door. The sprawling Botanical Gardens, with their wealth of plant life, and the Zoo and Aquarium, are attractively set in wooded hilly parkland to the north. Towards the east of the Botanical Gardens stands the *Kanakunna Palace* (permission required to visit). This is one of many early 20th century royal residences scattered around the city. Its sprawling arcades survey landscaped grounds.

B. NEMAM

This village, 7 km. south of Thiruvananthapuram, just off NH47, is of interest for the *Niramankara Temple* (only Hindus admitted), best known today for its Vishnu image, enshrined in a subsidiary modern structure. This magnificent icon, one of the finest in Kerala, is a fully sculpted, four-armed figure dressed in elaborate costume and jewellery. The temple itself, usually dated to the 14th century, is now ruined and abandoned, but is worth examining, since it reveals the interior arrangement of a typical Kerala styled structure. A small square linga sanctuary at the core of the temple contained by pilastered masonry walls is topped with an octagonal-domed roof. The surrounding eight columns once supported timbers for the conical roof. The sanctuary and columns are contained in a circle of outer walls, complete with moulded basement, pilastered niches, and overhanging eaves.

C. TIRUVALLAM

This small settlement, 8 km. south of Thiruvananthapuram, on the road to Kovalam, is of interest for the triple-shrined *Parashurameshvara Temple*. The complex is entered on the north through a traditional structure with sloping tiled roofs (only Hindus admitted). Three small, north-facing sanctuaries of different shapes stand in the middle of the inner enclosure: a part-circular Brahma shrine on axis with the entrance; a small square Vishnu shrine; and a circular Shiva shrine encasing a square sanctuary with a conical, metal-clad roof. The basement and walls of the Brahma shrine are assigned to the 13th century; they have pilastered projections alternating with niches headed by pediments framing miniature divinities. The circular brick and plaster tower above is topped with a hemispherical roof. The other shrines, including a rectangular, west facing Matsya sanctuary, are additions of the 16th-17th centuries.

D. VIZHINJAM

This seaside village, 18 km. south of Thiruvananthapuram, was a former Dutch and British factory, of which nothing can now be seen. Two mosques overlook the beach: the *Moienuddin Pillai* has a traditional prayer hall with twin minarets; a larger new prayer hall is built an international Islamic style.

Some of the earliest architectural remains in Kerala, dating back to the 9th-10th centuries, are seen nearby. The *Shiva Shrine* (only Hindus admitted) is a small square sanctuary, with a low tower capped by a square, dome-like roof in plaster covered brickwork. The adjacent *Bhagavati Shrine* (only Hindus admitted) is rectangular in layout, but lacks its original brick tower. Sculptures placed here include an icon of Kaumari. A modest rock-cut shrine a short distance east, though unfinished, has graceful reliefs of Shiva as the hunter, holding the bow, and dancing together with Parvati.

E. KAZHAKUTTAM

This town, 10 km. north of Thiruvananthapuram, is of interest for the Mahadeva Temple, which dates back to the 9th century. The outer enclosure is entered through a main gate with characteristic gabled roofs on the east (only Hindus admitted). Here stand a number of subsidiary shrines with different shaped roofs, dedicated to Ganapati, Krishna, Vishnu and Shasta, the last with an apsidal-ended plan. The focal sanctuary at the core of the inner enclosure of the temple has a square linga chamber surrounded by a passageway. The outer masonry walls have pilastered projections, with doors in the middle of three sides flanked by niches framing window-like panels. The pilasters carry rounded eaves with carved animals on top, and a parapet of ornamental roof forms with barrel-vaulted elements in the middle. Angled timber struts fashioned as deities and attendants are fitted between the roof elements. The second storey of the sanctuary repeats this scheme, but at a reduced scale. Both storeys are partly concealed by sloping tiled roofs, the upper roof forming a pyramid with dormer windows in the middle of each side. A later pavilion, also with a pyramidal roof, is built up against the east entrance to the linga shrine.

F. ANJENGO

This small port, 30 km. north of Thiruvananthapuram, was occupied by the Portuguese in the 16th century. A modest church from this period still survives. The English arrived in 1684, establishing their own factory and warehouse. These have now vanished, leaving only the crumbling laterite *Fort* that protected the trading post. The English cemetery nearby preserves a number of tombs dating from the 18th century.

G. VARKALA

A charming coastal resort, 45 km. north of Thiruvananthapuram on NH47, Varkala is also known for its curative mineral springs. The *Janardana Temple*, built up to a rocky eminence overlooking the ocean, has records going back to the 13th century. The European bell inside the main gate is said to have been presented by a Dutch sea captain in the 17th century. The shrine (only Hindus admitted) is approached through a mandapa with granite columns in the Tamil manner, with three-dimensional figures of Nataraja, Bhikshatanamurti, Manmatha and Rati.

At *Sivagiri*, 3 km. east, is a matha founded by Narayana Guru (1855-1920). This celebrated social reformer is revered for his dictum: 'One Caste, One Religion, One God for Man.'

H. KOLLAM

Formerly known as Quilon, this lively industrial city, 72 km. north of Thiruvananthapuram, occupies a narrow strip of land between the Arabian Sea and Ashtamudi Lake, the southern point of Kerala's inland lagoon, and the beginning of an intricate network of backwaters. Kollam is intimately connected with Kerala's history, giving its name to the era by which the Malayali calendar begins, traditionally fixed at 825.

Through the centuries Kollam has always been known as Kerala's premier port. Annals of the Tang dynasty record the visit of Chinese merchants in the 7th-8th centuries. Marco Polo, landing here in 1293, referred it as Koilum. The Portuguese established a factory and fort here in 1503, but were evicted in 1653 by the Dutch, who maintained a post here until 1741, when Kollam was captured by the Thiruvananthapuram army. Thereafter, the city served as the second capital of the Travancore kingdom. British forces were stationed here from 1795 onwards.

The oldest building still standing in Kollam is the 15th century *Ganapati Temple* (only Hindus admitted). This is situated in Tamarakulam, opposite Old Tobacco Godown. The temple comprises a square sanctuary with pilastered walls capped by a brick and plaster, dome-like roof. Unlike most other temples in Kerala, there is no sloping tiled roof. Such a roof does occur, however, in the open pavilion that stands in front (west). The pavilion is raised on a stone basement with animal balustrades flanking access steps. The *Rameshvara Temple* nearby, though thoroughly renovated, preserves a moulded basement dating from the 14th century.

Kollam is reputedly the oldest Catholic diocese in Southern India. Friar Jordanus was consecrated bishop by Pope John XXII in 1328, though he probably died before assuming his Episcopal functions. The *Cathedral*, no earlier than the 18th century, has a Baroque styled facade divided into three stages by pilastered elements capped with vase-like pinnacles. The central bays are flanked by double side volutes. Another interesting Christian monument is the *Syrian Church*, founded in 1519, but much rebuilt in later times. This small edifice has an unpretentious gabled front. Unusual 18th century murals of saints cover the inner sanctuary walls: they include Mar Aproth and Mar Sapor in the central panels, with the Madonna, St John, St Peter and St Thomas at the sides. St George slaying the dragon is seen on the left wall.

Valiakada Arikade, Kollam's largest and most important mosque, was thoroughly renovated in 1962. Unsightly concrete balconies and corner minarets conceal the prayer hall, which is roofed in traditional fashion with sloping tiles on a timber framework. Janakappuram Palli, close to the beach, is an older mosque, but has also been rebuilt.

The *Travellers' Bungalow*, on the bank of Ashtamudi Lake, north of Kollam, was once the home of the British Resident (permission required to visit). Its period charm is enhanced by the collection of military prints and Chinese porcelain.

Tangasseri, 3 km. west of Kollam, was a trading post associated with the Portuguese and Dutch, both of whom were involved in the construction of *Fort Thomas*. The sloping laterite walls with round corner towers of this citadel can still be seen. The East India Company installed a factory at Tangasseri in 1683, trading successfully until 1782, when it was challenged by the forces of Haidar Ali of Srirangapattana [15C]. Two European cemeteries are located nearby.

47. Kochi

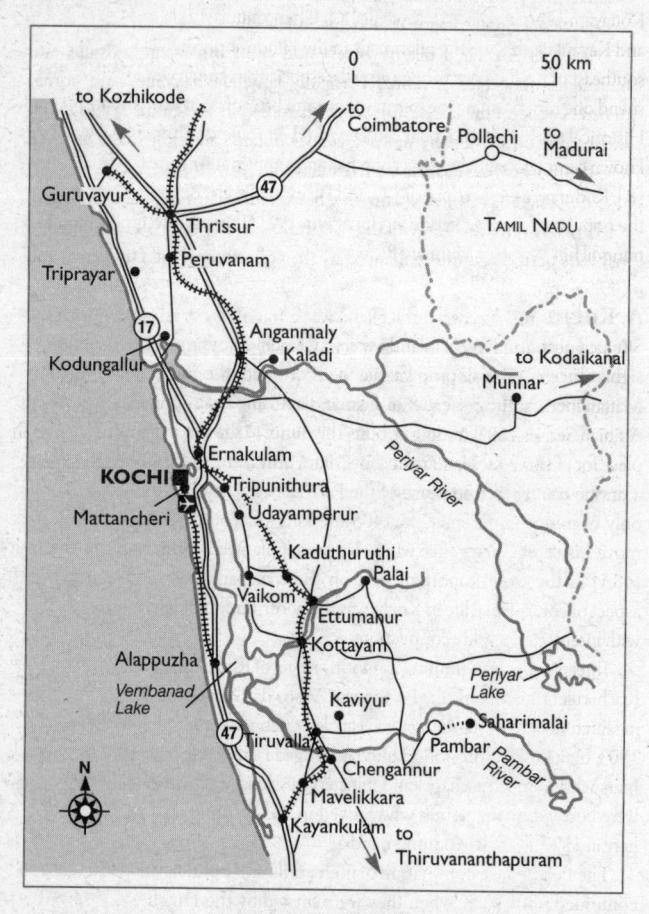

Still widely known by its former name of Cochin, this port city represents the historical and commercial hub of central Kerala. The densely populated region around Kochi is home to peoples of different religions, which explains the profusion of temples, churches, mosques and even synagogues.

Most visitors will wish to begin this itinerary with a tour of Kochi itself [A], for which at least half a day should be set aside. An attractive excursion by the backwaters to Alappuzha [B], to the south, will require a full day.

Travelling by road south from Kochi, it is possible to pass through towns with interesting and varied historical monuments, such as Tripunithura [C],

Udayamperur [D], Vaikom [E], Kaduthuruthi [F], Ettumanur [G], Palai [H], Kottayam [I], Tiruvalla [J], Kaviyur [K], Chengannur [L], Mavelikkara [M] and Kayankulam [N]. The pilgrimage to the Hindu shrine at Sabarimalai [O], southeast of Kochi, attracts huge crowds, especially in January. Many devotees spend one night making the journey there and back on foot from the car park. Historical sites north of Kochi can be visited en route to Thrissur [V], a well known centre. They include the churches and temples at Angamaly [Q], Kaladi [R], Kodungallur [S], Triprayar [T] and Peruvanam [U]. Beyond Thrissur lies the popular pilgrimage shrine at Guruvayur [W]. There is also the attractive, tranquil hill station of Munnar [P].

A. Kochi

Situated on a magnificent inland waterway, Kochi enjoys a unique mercantile significance. The area known as the Fort and the nearby quarter of Mattancheri occupy the tip of a long peninsula that runs between the Arabian Sea and an extensive lagoon. The outlet to the sea, a natural meeting place for ocean vessels and river crafts, dates only from 1341, when there was a drastic change in the course of the Periyar River. Prior to this, Kochi was only of minor importance. In 1405 the king of central Kerala decided to move his capital here, after which Kochi supplanted Kozhikode (Calicut) [48A] as the most important port on the Malabar Coast. An interesting aspect of commercial life in Kochi was the contribution of Jewish merchants with international trade connections.

Threats from the Samutiri (Zamorin) rulers of Kozhikode encouraged the Kochi rulers to welcome the Portuguese. Vasco da Gama landed here in 1500, in search of pepper, returning two years later. Albuquerque spent time here in 1503, obtaining permission to build a fortified factory. He brought with him friars who founded a chapel and initiated missionary activities. These efforts were boosted by the Jesuits, who arrived in 1524, setting up a printing press here in 1577, the first in Southern India.

The Portuguese domination of mercantile and political affairs in Kochi continued until 1663, when they were ousted by the Dutch, much to the benefit of the local Jews, who had been prosecuted by the Portuguese. The Dutch remained throughout the 18th century, continuing to trade here even after Haidar Ali of Srirangapattana [15C] captured the port in 1773. With the fall of Holland to Napoleon in 1795, the British seized the Indian Dutch possessions, and Kochi passed into British hands where it remained until Independence.

Kochi remains one of the premier ports of Southern India. Its harbour, much developed in the 1930s, enjoys a reputation for ship repair. Ernakulam, on the mainland, is a busy city with a large range of engineering facilities.

The tour of Kochi described here begins in the *Fort*, reached most conveniently from other parts of the city by ferry. The town retains much of its traditional character, with narrow streets lined with old warehouses stocked with grains and spices, as well as with traditional mansions set in walled gardens. Of the ramparts that once protected the Fort, however, nothing now remains.

The *Church of St Francis* is located at the northern end of the Fort, within sight of the Chinese fishing nets beside the water's edge. Reputed to be the oldest European Christian place of worship in Southern India, the church occupies the site of the 1503 wooden chapel, later rebuilt in masonry. Vasco da Gama was buried here in 1524, but his body was conveyed to Portugal 14 years later. (The site of the original grave is pointed out within the nave, to the north.) The Dutch renovated the church, using it for Protestant services; its sombre facade with volutes dates mostly from their era. The church was further remodelled by the British in 1887. The interior is of little merit, other than the memorials set into the walls and floor, the earliest of which being the tomb of Simao de Miranda dated 1524 (left wall, inside the entrance). Additional graves from the Dutch and British periods are see in the adjacent cemetery.

A short distance to the south is the *Basilica of Santa Cruz*. This Catholic place of worship dates back to Portuguese times, but the original building of 1557 was demolished by the British in 1795, at which time it was used as a warehouse. The present basilica, which dates from 1904, has a handsome Neo-Classical facade. The finest features of the interior are the carved wooden pulpit and the stucco altar. The house of the Catholic bishop next door accommodates the small Padroado Museum (permission required to visit) of Kochi's ecclesiastical history.

Mattancheri, 2 km. southeast of the Church of St Francis, is worth visiting for its palace and nearby synagogue. The *Dutch Palace* was built in 1557 for Kerala Varma, the ruler of Kochi, in exchange for trading rights, but then totally rebuilt by the Dutch in 1663, hence its name. The exterior is European in character, with sloping masonry walls and round-headed windows and doors; the angled tiled roof and wooden balconies are, however, typically Kerala in style. The palace is entered by a flight of steps leading to a portico on the south. This gives access to a suite of public rooms on the upper level. They look down onto an inner court, within which stands a small shrine dedicated to Bhagavati, the protective goddess of the Kochi royal family. The rooms serve as a setting for a display of regal memorabilia, including ceremonial robes, headdresses, weapons, palanquins and furniture. It is, however, for its murals that the palace is best known. They constitute one of the most important (and accessible, to non-Hindus) series of wall paintings in Kerala. Their crowded and animated compositions and varied colour schemes, with vivid orange, red, green and deep blue tones, suggest several phases of work, spanning the 17th-19th centuries,

The king's bed chamber occupies the southwest corner of the palace. Its walls are covered with scenes from the Ramayana, which relate the story in considerable detail (English labels provided). The epic begins (east wall) with the fire sacrifice of Rishyashringa, the devotions of Dasharatha, and the birth of Rama and his three brothers (left panel). The story is interrupted with two depictions of Krishna (central panel), before continuing with Vishvamitra meeting Dasharatha, Rama killing Tataka, the sacrifice of Vishvamitra, Rama liberating Ahalya, Rama breaking Shiva's bow, the marriage of Rama and Sita, and Rama tying the string of Parashurama's bow (right panel). The narrative continues (south wall) with Dasharatha appointing Rama as his heir, Rama leaving for the forest, the meeting of Bharata and Rama, and Lakshmana disfiguring Suparnaka (left panel); Rama and Sita in the forest, Rama killing the golden deer, Ravana's abduction of Sita, and Jatayu's attempt to intercept Ravana (right panel). Further scenes (west wall) show the meeting of Rama with Sugriva, Rama shooting the arrow through seven palm trees, the fight of Vali and Sugriva (left panel); Rama giving the ring to Hanuman, Hanuman leaping through the air with the mountain of sacred herbs, Hanuman entering Lanka, Ravana attempting to woo Sita, Rama performing penance, the building of the stone bridge, and battles between Ravana and Sugriva, Rama and Kumbhakarna, and Rama and Ravana, and his fire ordeal of Sita (central panel); Rama returning to Ayodhya, and the reception at the palace with attendants holding lamps (right panel).

Another important series of paintings in the Dutch Palace is found in the upper room to the right of the entrance, reached by a steep staircase. Among these compositions are Lakshmi seated on the lotus, sleeping Vishnu, Shiva with Parvati, the coronation of Rama, and Shiva as kirata, the hunter. The adjacent chamber has a single panel portraying Vishnu seated on the serpent.

Narrow steps descend to a series of rooms at the lower (ground) level of the palace. The murals here are quite different in style. The first chamber has unfinished paintings with faint, but delicate ochre lines, showing the marriage of Shiva and Shiva accompanied by courtly maidens. The second chamber has large panels with figures enhanced by deep shading, indicating European artistic influence in the 19th century. Here are portrayed Parvati, Shiva and Mohini, Krishna lifting Govardhana Hill, and the same deity in reclining position, attended by women.

Immediately south of the Dutch Palace, standing in a walled compound, is a small Krishna temple (only Hindus admitted). Its circular sanctuary is topped with a smoothly conical roof.

The *Synagogue* (closed Saturdays) in Mattancheri is the finest Jewish place of prayer in Southern India. It stands at the end of a small lane, a short distance from the palace. After their expulsion from Kodungallur in 1568, the Jewish community of central Kerala shifted to Kochi, where they founded a synagogue. This was destroyed by the Portuguese in 1662, but restored in 1664. The present building is mostly the result of the reconstruction by Ezekial Rahabi in 1761, reflecting the community's new found wealth under the Dutch.

Synagogue, Kochi.

Though the Jewish community of Kochi is virtually extinct, the synagogue is well maintained. It presents an unadorned masonry exterior with simple window openings, capped by a tiled roof. The corner tower, an addition of

1767, has clock faces on four sides with different scripts: Malayalam on the north (facing towards the palace), Hebrew, Roman and Arabic. The floor of the prayer hall is enlivened with blue and white tiles from Canton, showing willow patterns and other motifs. Wooden benches line the walls; the central prayer stand has a gleaming brass balustrade. The tabernacle, set into the rear wall, framed by ornate wooden Corinthian colonettes, houses three Torah scrolls, kept in gilded and embossed metal cases. Ornate glass chandeliers hang from the ceiling. Among the documents displayed in a side chamber is a copper-plate record from Kodungallur, recording a grant by Bhaskara Ravi Varman (962-1020), confirming the antiquity of Kerala's Jewish community. The cemetery nearby has many tombstones with Hebrew script.

The old Muslim quarter of Kochi is located a short distance south of Mattancheri. The *Safai Jami Mosque*, known locally as Chembattapalli, is built in traditional style. Its double sloping roofs, covered in terracotta tiles (below) and copper sheets (above), are carried on a timber framework. The entrance chamber has a coffered wooden ceiling. Carved panels over the doorways have Arabic inscriptions, that above the north door mentions the date 1520, but this probably only refers to the masonry structure of the prayer hall. The hall is of interest for the carved wooden pulpit, and the mihrab headed by a painted lobed arch. A ladder in the entrance chamber provides access to an upper level surrounded by angled louvred screens. Among the other Muslim monuments in this part of Kochi is the shrine of Shaykh Zainuddin. Its tiled gabled roof shelters a triangular panel filled with Arabic script.

Most visitors to Kochi will enjoy the ferry rides across the splendid natural harbour. One historical feature stands on Vypeen Island, immediately north of the Chinese nets in the Fort. Dating from 1605, *Our Lady of Hope* is built on the site of a church founded in 1560. This was the principal Catholic church during the Dutch era. Its Portuguese origins, however, are evident from the gabled facade and Baroque styled doorway. The screen within was removed from the Church of St Francis.

Palm fringed *Bolgatty Island*, in the northern part of the harbour, enjoys an idyllic location and serene atmosphere. The *Palace Hotel* incorporates a spacious bungalow erected in 1744 by the Dutch; it served as the home of the British Resident at Kochi after 1799. The original building preserves much of its period character, with verandahs and overhanging roofs. The *Customs House* on *Willingdon Island* opposite, surveys the impressive panorama of Kochi's busy port. Just south of the bridge from here to Ernakulam is the *Church of St Peter and St Paul*. The altarpiece within is finely worked.

Ernakulam, on the east side of the harbour, does not benefit from the historical prestige or charm of Kochi and Mattancheri. Among the few buildings of interest in the middle of the city is the *Shiva Temple* (only Hindus admitted). This is entered on the east through a gabled porch, in front of which stands a brass-clad, lamp column. The *Parishah Thambura Museum* nearby (closed Mondays) occupies a darbar hall with typical Kerala woodwork. Here are displayed sculptures, coins and oil paintings by Ravi Varma and other Kerala artists, formerly in the royal collection.

B. ALAPPUZHA

Formerly called Alleppey, this port lies between Kochi, 56 km. to the north, and Kollam [46H], 84 km. to the south, connected to both by NH47, as well as by inland waterways. Alappuzha dates from the period of the Travancore rulers, who annexed this part of Kerala in the middle of the 18th century. After 1762, the port was vigorously developed by Kesava Pillai, the Prime Minister of Travancore, who constructed warehouses and invited merchants from other parts of the country to settle here. His vigorous programme of shipbuilding encouraged trade with Mumbai and Kolkata.

Alappuzha derives its wealth from tea, rubber, pepper and other highland products, which are shipped via a network of rivers and canals to Vembanad Lake. The city occupies a narrow strip of land between the lake and the ocean, traversed by Canals that connect the two bodies of water. Numerous bridges cross these canals, lending a distinctive character to the city. Alappuzha is today one of the world's chief suppliers of coir mats and matting.

Other than the bulky lighthouse of 1862, the beams of which are visible for 25 km. out to sea, there are few buildings of merit. The city is of greater interest for the colourful water carnival, culminating in the famous snakeboat race, with up to 100 oarsmen in each boat, which takes place on Independence Day each August.

Tamboli, 4 km. north of Alappuzha, has at least one historical monument. This is the *Catholic Church* with a remarkable Baroque styled interior of the 17th century. The altar on the right side of the nave has a painted wooden crucifix set against painted panels depicting the Virgin Mary, Mary Magdalen, and St John in the company of soldiers. The altar opposite is intricate carved and gilded. The Virgin holding the Infant Christ, which forms the focus of the principal altar at the end of the nave, is said to have been imported from Europe.

C. TRIPUNITHURA

This town, 12 km. south of Ernakulam, served for a time as a residence of the Kochi rulers and their nobles, as can be seen from the many imposing mansions that line the streets. One of these, in the middle of Tripunithura, has been opened to the public as the *Hill Palace Museum* (closed Mondays). It displays regalia and arms, as well as paintings and sculptures from the royal collection. The nearby *Purnathrayisha Temple* was rebuilt in a traditional style after a fire in

1920. The west gate, which survived the fire, has a finely sculpted ceiling. The circular sanctuary within (only Hindus admitted) has curving masonry walls entirely covered in brass sheets embossed with images of diverse divinities. The *Church of St Mary* on the main road is a Jacobite Syrian place of worship. Its charming Baroque styled facade is enhanced by an octagonal bell tower.

D. UDAYAMPERUR

This small settlement, 6 km. south of Tripunithura, is celebrated for its *Roman Catholic Church* of 1510. This was the venue of the Synod of Diamper, convened by Archbishop Alexis de Menenzes in 1599, who attempted to compel the Syrian church of Kerala to accept Roman obedience, while at the same time preserving its unique Syriac history. The building itself is a modest structure, with a sombre facade flanked by curved volutes. The mortal remains of a local ruler who embraced Christianity are preserved here. The granite cross that stands in front may date back to pre-European times.

E. VAIKOM

The sprawling town of Vaikom, 14 km. south of Udayamperur, a total of 32 km. south of Ernakulam, is prominent in the recent history of Kerala. Here took place the famous sathygraha movement of 1925, in which Mahatma Gandhi participated. This led to the opening of temple roads to people of all castes.

The *Vaikkathappan Temple* (only Hindus admitted) is contained in a spacious rectangular enclosure, with gates in the middle of four sides; only that on the east is roofed with sloping tiles. Brass-clad lamp columns flank the path leading to the east entrance in the second enclosure. The entrance is preceded by a monumental hall, with granite piers showing cut-out colonettes and crouching yali brackets in the typical Tamil manner. The peripheral supports are sculpted with rearing yalis and fierce guardian figures. The enclosure walls have an outer line of timber screens, supplied with brass lamps and wooden yali brackets carrying a tiled roof; dormer windows mark the corners. The inner line of stone contains the colonnade that runs around the enclosure within. The linga shrine that stands freely in the middle of the enclosure is an elliptical masonry structure, the only example of this shape in Kerala architecture.

The shrine walls are raised on a moulded masonry basement. A spout emerging from the north side is supported on a carving of a demonic guardian brandishing a club. The walls display pilastered niches, into which wooden windows have been inserted. Paintings entirely cover the walls; originating in the 17th century they have recently been reworked. Among the major compositions are Shiva dancing in the company of the gods, Vishnu riding on Garuda, Bhairava, and Rama battling with Ravana. Sculpted guardians brandishing clubs and trampling on serpents are repeated several times. Projecting timber brackets above carry the overhang of the conical roof. Sheathed in copper, the roof is capped with a gilded pot finial. A small square hall sheltering a seated Nandi is located in front (east) of the linga shrine. Its carved stone columns support a wooden ceiling, sheltered by a pyramidal, metal clad roof.

A smaller, but equally artistic religious monument is located at *Udayanapuram*, 2 km. north of Vaikom. The *Peruntirukkoil* (only Hindus admitted) consists of a circular linga sanctuary, the outer walls of which have wooden screens set in pilastered niches. Carved guardian figures flank the doorway on the east. Wall paintings portray various divinities, including Parvati with infant Ganesha, and Garuda supporting Vishnu's consorts on outstretched wings. Wooden struts beneath the roof overhang are fashioned as heroes and hunters, in illustration of Arjuna's fight with Shiva disguised as the hunter.

F. KADUTHURUTHI

This long established Christian centre, 14 km. south of Vaikom, is celebrated for its Syrian Catholic churches. The oldest is the *Church of St Mary*, rebuilt in 1599 immediately after the Synod of Diamper. This date is recorded on the 10 m. high monolithic cross that stands outside the church. The cross is raised on an elaborate stone platform adorned with miniature figures of Virgin Mary and Infant Jesus, together with hunters, fighters and dancers.

The three-storeyed facade of the church is conceived in the Baroque manner, recently repainted in pale blue, pink and yellow. Pairs of Corinthian colonettes flank a round-headed doorway with triangular pediment; above is a niche housing a statue of the Virgin. Imaginative reliefs enliven the facade: fish-tailed humans bearing boats on their heads, with peacocks above, are seen on the second stage; angels appear on the third stage in the company of the Virgin, with fierce monsters in three-quarter circles at either side. Mary surmounted by the Holy Trinity fills the medallion beneath the cross that crowns the whole composition. Further reliefs on the rear wall of the church show hunting scenes, including an armed male accompanied by a dog, shooting a stag.

Epitaphs with Persian crosses are fixed into the walls inside the church. Here can be seen a circular granite font, probably dating from the 15th-16th centuries; its sides are embellished with scrollwork and miniature figures. The glory of the interior is, however, the brilliantly gilded wooden altar, one of the most elaborate in Kerala, dating from the 18th century. Fully sculpted saints occupy Neo-Classical niches arranged around a sunburst medallion of the Holy Ghost, capped with a small spire. The Virgin with Christ and God the Father are painted on the topmost panel. Luxuriant volutes filled with musicians are surrounded by carved angels, those at either side being dressed in Portuguese costume. Modern paintings adorn the barrel-vaulted ceiling.

At *Muttuchira*, 1.5 km. south of Kaduthuruthi, stands the *Forane Church of the Holy Ghost*, outside which is another ancient stone cross. The five-bayed facade of the church has windows with grilles at the upper level, flanked by volutes. The exuberantly carved and gilded altar of the interior focuses on a central sunburst, with an expressive three-dimensional Crucifix above. The composition is topped with a scene of the Coronation of Mary, surrounded by volutes filled with angels. Smaller, but equally ornate side altars of the church contain brightly painted figures of the Virgin, the Pieta, and the Christ Child. The church is overlooked on one side by a five-stage octagonal tower, with a gabled tiled roof topped with a large cross.

G. ETTUMANUR

The *Mahadeva Temple* at Ettumanur stands on the main road, 19 km. south of Kaduthuruthi, a total of 60 km. south of Ernakulam. This grandly conceived shrine goes back to the 12th century, but was entirely remodelled in 1542. The monument is entered from the west through a traditional structure with wooden columns. This supports a sloping tiled roof in two tiers, with a carving of Yoga Narasimha in the central gable. Vividly toned, crowded paintings on the inner walls of the gate show Padmnabha, the form of Vishnu reclining on the serpent (right), and multi-armed Nataraja surrounded by admiring celestials (left). These compositions are among the finest examples of Kerala temple murals accessible to non-Hindus. A path leads past a brass-clad lamp post to the porch that gives access to the inner enclosure (only Hindus admitted). A porch with a stone altar and an ornate metal lamp is contained within wooden screens, sheltered by a low roof. Similar screens running around the stone walls of the enclosure have dormer windows at the corners.

The circular linga shrine of the Mahadeva temple that stands in the middle of the inner enclosure has a conical roof sheathed in copper tiles. The walls consist of intricately carved wooden screens framed by friezes of warriors, musicians, sages and animals. In between are brightly painted wooden panels carved with deities in the company of attendants: Vishnu and consorts, Rama and Sita, Ganesha and consort, Krishna, Nataraja, and Surya. Angled struts carrying the roof overhang are sculpted as female dancers and characters from the story of Arjuna and Shiva as disguised as kirata, the hunter. Small stone guardians are placed either side of the four doorway leading to the shrine; the access steps are flanked by balustrades.

Immediately in front (west) of the shrine stands an open square hall topped with a pyramidal roof, also covered in metal tiles. Stone columns within support wooden brackets and beams; the ceiling has 25 lotus panels surrounded by miniature deities. The hall accommodates two Nandis, one of stone, the other of brass.

H. PALAI

This small town, 16 km. east of Ettumanur, is one of the headquarters of the Syrian Catholic church. Close to the new cathedral stands its predecessor of 1502, the *Cathedral of St Thomas*, one of the grandest churches in Kerala. The building preserves it traditional character, with sloping tiled roofs and a central squat tower, with a pyramidal roof. These features are concealed by the monumental five-bayed facade. Three stages of the central bay are framed by pairs of Corinthian colonettes, topped with volutes and a cross. The bays are enlivened with relief figures of angels, two of which flank a statue of St Thomas set into a niche in the third stage. Other saintly figures occupy niches in the second stage of the intermediate bays. Two sets of fanned volutes serve as the transition to the end bays.

The interior of the church is dominated by magnificent gilded altars set into the rear wall. The central altar is placed within a recessed bay roofed by a coffered barrel vault, enhanced with painted woodwork. This shows the Apostle and five other saintly figures in two tiers of Baroque styled niches. The Coronation of the Virgin painted on the topmost panel, surrounded by a sunburst ending in fanciful volutes, is flanked by fully carved angels in Portuguese costume, holding garlands. The side altars, dedicated to the Virgin (right) and a king holding an orb and sceptre (left), are smaller but equally ornate. They are accompanied by painted angels and pediments with sunburst motifs. Another artistic feature of the interior is the carved wooden pulpit with a curving floral festoon at its base, A small pavilion with a pyramidal tiled roof nearby is used by musicians.

Other than the cathedral just described and several lesser churches, there are two important temples in Palai, one in the middle of the town, the other on the Minachil River. The latter, recently consecrated (only Hindus admitted), has an unusual curving masonry tower, inspired by Northern Indian models. Worshippers view the focal linga through doorways on four sides.

I. KOTTAYAM

This city, 11 km. south of Palai, a total of 72 km. south of Ernakulam, lies on the bank of the Minachil River, a navigable waterway connected with Vembanad Lake. Practically all the hill produce of central Kerala passes through Kottayam, from where it is shipped to Alappuzha and Kochi. The economic importance of the city is matched by its religious significance as one of the principal headquarters of the Orthodox Syrian and Latin Catholic communities.

Puthenangadi, one of Kottayam's northern suburbs, preserves many Orthodox Syrian churches. *Valliyapalli*, the oldest, was founded in 1550, but in its present form dates only from 1588. It crowns the top of a small hill overlooking the river. An interesting, pre-European period arched block is set into the gate leading to the church. This is adorned with carvings of a bird and a cross, with leaves at either side. The church itself is a plain structure with a square tower at one corner, entered from a side arcade. A gleaming altar stands in front of oil paintings on the rear wall. A stone relief of a cross surrounded by early styled script is seen above a side altar, on the right. (This resembles the inscribed panel displayed in the church on St Thomas Mount in Chennai [36I].)

Cheriapalli is another Orthodox Syrian church at Puthenangadi. Founded in 1579 and dedicated to St Mary, the church was restored in 1993. Its handsome Baroque facade, complete with fan volutes and pinnacles, is partly concealed behind a later porch. The entrance on the west is bridged by an arched block sculpted with a cross, flanked by figures and peacocks. The interior is of interest for the painted panels, narrating the life of the Virgin, on the walls beside the main altar. Figures and floral motifs are painted onto the stone barrel vault above.

Remnants of the residence of the Chenganassy rulers are seen in *Thazhathangadi*, an outlying suburb of Kottayam. These kings had one of their capitals at Kottayam, before being overrun by Travancore in the middle of the 18th century. The *Mosque* nearby is a traditional structure, with tiers of sloping tiled roofs sheltering the double-storeyed prayer hall. The building is entered on the east through a porch with a decorated gable displaying carved colonettes and struts.

J. TIRUVALLA

This town, 27 km. south of Kottayam, is home to the *Vallabha Temple*, one of the largest Hindu complexes in central Kerala. Inscriptions on the monument go back to the 12th century, but the present building is probably no earlier than the 17th century. The temple is approached from the east by a long and wide flight of steps. These lead by way of a large open structure into the spacious outer enclosure. Here stands a unique building with triple tiers of diminishing gables, with projecting porches on four sides at the lowest level. Rising through the roof is a 16 m. high column of black granite, supporting a gilded image of kneeling Garuda. Vishnu's eagle mount gazes west towards the gate leading into the inner enclosure (only Hindus admitted). This imposing structure has tiers of tiled roofs and ornate gables filled with carved wooden struts. Carvings cloak the ceiling of the screened inner chamber.

The circular Vishnu shrine that stands freely in the middle of the temple enclosure has a conical roof cloaked in copper tiles. The pilastered walls of the shrine are raised on a masonry basement. Stone balustrades flanking the steps on the east are carved with images of Shiva as Dakshinamurti and Yogeshvara, suggesting that they were not intended for this Vaishnava sanctuary. A standing yaksha bears a stone spout on the north. The open square hall immediately in front (east) has a pyramidal roof. The wooden ceiling inside preserves a panel of Vishnu surrounded by 24 petals, each containing a different emanation of the god. The supporting beams are embellished with intricately carved Ramayana scenes and other narrative friezes.

Tiruvalla is the headquarters of the Mar Thomites, a reformed, Protestant influenced offshoot of the Catholic Syrian church, in communion with Anglicans. *St John's Cathedral* is a modern building designed by Laurie Baker, a British architect who lived and worked in Kerala. Its drum-shaped shrine with a conical roof is inspired by indigenous temple forms.

K. KAVIYUR

Some of the finest carved woodwork in Kerala is to be seen in the *Mahadeva Temple* in this small town, 7 km. east of Tiruvalla. The main entrance to the temple is from the east, through a modest gate with a double tier of sloping roofs (only Hindus admitted). A sacred tree with naga stones set around its base is seen to the right. The path towards the inner enclosure is marked by a brass-clad lamp post with miniature deities at its base. The gate consists of two successive porches roofed with an ornate frontal gable; this shows a linga flanked by guardians, with elephants beneath. Chambers within the porch have wooden ceilings divided into square bays. They are surrounded by intricately worked miniature brackets carved as Rama and other characters from the Ramayana, supported on elephant torsos. Beneath are diminutive scenes from the Ramayana and other epics, arranged in continuous rows, carried by small figures headed by snake hoods.

The inner enclosure of the Mahadeva temple is surrounded by colonnades, bounded by the usual combination of wooden screens and stone walls. The circular linga shrine within, approached by four doorways, is roofed with a smooth cone of copper tiles, topped by a gilded finial. The roof shelters the wooden panels and screens that create the curving walls of the shrine. These are almost entirely covered with delicate, but vigorous carvings. The screens are divided into square perforations, with the central and side panels occupied by miniature divinities. The intermediate uprights are carved with pairs of fierce guardians, either side of the doorways, as well as full sets of Vishnu's avataras and of the dikpalas, and a scene of Shiva with ascetics. Among the accessory themes found here is the story of the rescue of Gajendra, showing the elephant trapped in the lotus pond (beneath), and the appearance of Vishnu, and the elephant paying homage to the god (above) (southwest quadrant). Large icons of Natesha (left) and Trivikrama (right) are painted on the recessed masonry walls either side of the east doorway to the linga chamber.

Other fine carvings are seen on the ceiling of the square hall that stands immediately in front (east). The nine-panelled composition here shows Yogeshvara Shiva surrounded by the dikpalas.

A small *Cave Temple*, set into the west face of a granite hill 1.5 km. north of Kaviyur is the best preserved monument in Kerala of the 8th-9th century Chera period. The interior consists of a small chamber with a monolithic linga, preceded by a columned verandah. Fully rounded figures carved onto the walls show a chieftain with folded arms, possibly a donor, a bearded sage, Ganesha, and a guardian leading on a large club.

L. CHENGANNUR

Numerous temples and churches dot this sprawling town, 10 km. south of Tiruvalla. The *Narasimha Temple* at *Chathankulangana*, in the western part of *Chengannur*, is of outstanding interest for its exquisite wood carving dating from the 17th-18th centuries. The outer gate to the temple is a colonnaded structure, with double tiers of sloping tiled roofs, facing the main street on the north. The entrance porch to the second enclosure, however, is from the east. A lamp post stands in front, with a large tank beyond. The porch leads to the second enclosure (only Hindu men and boys admitted), inside which stands the square sanctuary with its copper-tiled, pyramidal roof, topped by a gilded finial.

The west facing masonry chamber, housing an image of Narasimha, is completely encased by wooden screens with geometric designs, with friezes of animals beneath. Small panels at the sides of the screens are filled with diverse figures: for example, Krishna in the tree, hiding the clothes of the gopis (north wall, left); monkeys building the stone bridge to Lanka (east wall, right); Padmanabha accompanied by sages and Vishnu's avataras (east wall, left); and Vishnu rescuing Gajendra (west wall, right). Intermediate uprights are also treated sculpturally; they show figures holding clubs guarding the doorways in the middle of four sides, as well as demonic Narasimha, seated Yoga Narasimha (west wall); Krishna killing the horse demon (north wall); Krishna killing the bull, Ganesha (east wall); and a maiden with a mirror (south wall). Friezes run along the beams at the top of the screens. Among the topics depicted here are the forest episodes from the Ramayana (north wall), and the churning of the ocean (south wall). The small square pavilion in front, also with a pyramidal roof, is devoid of carvings.

One Christian place of worship in Chengannur is also of artistic interest. The *Church of St Thomas* consists of a long nave roofed with a double tier of sloping tiles. The main entrance is concealed within a porch with an ornate frontal gable. The door panels here are elaborately carved with leafy designs, and a composition showing the visit of the Three Magi. The rear portion of the nave is marked by a square tower with a pyramidal roof. The interior of the church has an unusual sculpted relief of a hunting scene, dating from the 15th-16th century, set into the walls. Another relic from the same era is the stone baptismal font; its base is enlivened with a floral frieze. A monolithic cross on a high steeply plinth stands in the compound outside.

M. MAVELIKKARA

This town, 14 km. south of Tiruvalla, was the site of various battles between the Travancore and Kayankulam rulers in the early 18th century. Remains of the square laterite Fort, with bastions on each side, dating from this time can still be made out. A curiosity of Mavelikkara is the Statue of Buddha, discovered in 1936 in the fields outside the town, and subsequently set up as an object of worship by local people who installed it in a modern shrine. Dating from the 9th-10th century, the image confirms that Buddhism was once prevalent in Kerala. The image shows the Master seated in lotus posture, the eyes closed in meditation.

The *Mahadeva Temple* at *Kandiyur*, 2 k.m north of Mavelikkara, is of interest for its unusual stone carvings dating from the 16th-17th century. The linga shrine stands in a shaded compound with entrances on four sides (only Hindus admitted). The east entrance is an elaborate, gable roofed structure. The shrine walls, raised on a high plinth, are divided into bays by pilasters and niches, enlivened with small panels showing mythological scenes, sculpted in a manner resembling woodwork. A roof with double sloping tiers with copper tiles rises above. Steps leading to the east doorway have ornate balustrades carved with dancing scenes. The open hall in front (east) has 16 columns supporting a pyramidal roof.

N. KAYANKULAM

This town lies on NH47, 48 km. south of Alappuzha, or 28 km. south of Tiruvalla. Kayankulam served as the capital of a local line of rulers, who struggled against Travancore until they were vanquished in 1746. The principal attraction here is the *Krishnapuram Palace*, 2 km. south of the town. The complex is attributed to Ramayya Dalwa, ruler of northern Travancore under Rama Varma (1758-98). Together with Padmanbahapuram [45O], it is the best preserved example of Kerala royal architecture.

The palace (closed Mondays) stands in a rectangular enclosure, entered through a small gate on the east. This leads to a garden overlooked by a pillared verandah. The main building has a tiered roof of sloping tiles, ending in gables with carved wooden rafters. Balconies with inclined slats on curving brackets project outwards. The interior of the complex consists of rooms disposed either side of a central corridor. This ends in a balconied chamber that overlooks a square pool on the west side of the palace. Small interior courts have floor recesses for collecting rainwater. One chamber to the left of the corridor has a large, vividly coloured mural on the rear (east) wall. This depicts Vishnu riding on Garuda, in the company of gods and attendant women: a small panel of Balakrishna is seen beneath. Steps nearby descend to a room at a lower level, provided with side seating. From here it is possible to enter the pool. Copies of Ramayana murals are displayed in one of the balconied rooms on the upper level. They depict Rama, the death of an ogress, Rama with Lakshmana, and Hanuman with monkey warriors.

NH47 continues to Kollam [46H], 36 km. south.

O. SABARIMALAI

This remote site in dense forest, lies 120 km. southeast of Ernakulam, or 182 km. north of Thiruvananthapuram [46A], both routes by way of Kottayam. The most convenient starting point for the journey is the parking area at Pamba, from where there is a 5 km. climb up a well maintained path.

Sabarimalai is famous through Southern India for the *Ayyappa Temple*, with stands at about 900 m. elevation in the rugged terrain of the Western Ghats. Ayyappa, also known as Shasta, is a child deity believed to be the offspring of Shiva and Vishnu disguised as the goddess Mohini. He is looked upon as the guardian of mountainous tracts, and is famous for the ability to grant boons.

In spite of the arduous journey, the concourse of pilgrims to Sabarimalai is steadily increasing. In order to prepare for pilgrimage, the Ayyappas, as they the devotees call themselves, observe rigorous fasting and penance for 41 days during the Mandalam festival in November-December; they dress only in black or blue, and leave their hair uncut. In this regime they are under the direction of older, more experienced gurus. Only boys and men may visit Ayyappa's shrine, though girls and old women are also permitted (as well as non-Hindus). The sanctuary is open for about four months, during April, one day in May-June, and late August-early September; the final ceremonies of the Mandala festival take place on 14 January, after which the shrine is closed.

The temple itself is a modest structure, out of all proportion to the crowds that visit. The final 18 steps of the path in front of the entrance are believed to be especially sacred, and are clad in metal. The temple dates only from the 1940s, being built after a fire destroyed the original. The innermost sanctuary is a small square structure with a pyramidal tiled roof, within which the seated image of the infant god is housed.

P. MUNNAR

The route running east from Ernakulam passes through a variety of landscapes, before arriving at this delightful Hill Station, at an altitude of 1,524 m. Located 224 km. distant from Ernakulam, the resort owes its birth to planters, who were responsible for the tea, coffee and cardamom estates in the vicinity. Recreational life for residents in the rambling settlement that forms the centre of Munnar focuses on the *High Range Club*, which proudly preserves its British period traditions. The men's bar is decorated with hunting trophies, especially bison heads and elephant tusks. The Protestant church of 1911 and its adjacent cemetery occupy a hill above. Fine panoramas of the surrounding Annamalai Hills may be had from Lockhart Gap, 20 km. southeast, on the road to Kumily. Expeditions can be arranged to Anaimudi, 12 km. north of Munnar; at 2,694 m. this is the highest peak in Southern India,.

The road from Munnar continues to Kodaikanal in Tamil Nadu [44F], 92 km. east.

Q. ANGAMALY

This town, 32 km. north of Ernakulam on NH47, has a large Christian population, as is demonstrated by the many places of worship dating from the 17th-18th centuries. *St George's Church*, for example, has a simple Baroque facade, the upper stage with three openings surrounded by triangular pediments, with a single round-headed doorway beneath. The stone cross to one side is elevated on a finely detailed base. *St Mary's Church* is of interest for the murals on the side walls of the nave. The scenes include the Last Judgement (left), and a vivid illustration of hell, crowded with tortured figures (right). A composition showing Christ commanding St Thomas to visit India is located near the side altar.

Another Christian place of worship of artistic interest is seen at *Kanjoor*, 3 km. east of Angamaly. *St Mary's* is a traditional structure, with a central tower rising above a gabled roof. The Baroque styled facade is partly hidden by a modern porch; the outer walls are covered with curious murals illustrating the defeat of Tipu Sultan of Srirangapattana [15C]. The ornate west facade is divided into bays by pairs of columns. The topmost pedimented stage contains a niche occupied by a statue of Mary. The carved wooden doors set within a broad arch serve as the principal entrance to the church. Murals adorn the side walls of the chancel.

R. KALADI

This historic village, 11 km. east of Angamaly on the north bank of the Periyar River, was the birthplace of Shankacharya, the great Hindu philosopher and teacher (788-820). The site has been revived for worship, and is now a popular place of pilgrimage. The two shrines next to the river, erected in 1910, have identical, polygonal-shaped pyramidal towers. One is dedicated to Shankacharya as Dakshinamurti, the teaching form of Shiva, the other to Saradamba, the protective goddess of the sage.

A more recent building is the *International Temple*, which enshrines a life-size marble statue of the philosopher, and has a splendid library. Beside the road nearby stands the recently completed, 45 m. tall *Kirthi Sthamba Mandapam*. This nine-stage, octagonal tower commemorates Shankacharya's life and work in words, symbols and pictures.

S. KODUNGALLUR

Formerly called Cranganore, this small town just off NH17, 51 km. north of Ernakulam, faces the lagoon near the mouth of the Periyar River, and can be reached directly by boat from Kochi.

Archaeologists have identified Kodungallur as Muziris, mentioned by Pliny the Elder in the 1st century CE as the premier port on the Malabar Coast, celebrated for its exports of spices to Alexandria and Oman. Roman coins found in the area confirm this identification. This site was also of local importance in later times. Emigrating Jews, Christians and Muslims alike claim Kodungallur as the place of their first settlement in Kerala.

Kodungallur figures repeatedly in the wars between the Kochi and Kozhikode rulers. The town also attracted the attention of European traders. The Portuguese sacked the town in 1504; 30 years later, they built a watchtower on the river bank to control pepper exports. The Dutch captured Kodungallur in 1662, and held it until the forces of Tipu Sultan arrived in 1790. A few years later it passed into the hands of the British, by which time the Periyar had silted up and international trade had come to an end.

According to local legend, St Thomas is believed to have landed on the island of Malankara, near the village of *Pallipuram*, 5 km. south of Kodungallur. The *Church of St Thomas* here is supposed to have been founded by the Apostle after he landed here in AD 52. As it stands today, the building is no earlier than the 17th century. It houses a relic set in an ornate meal casket, venerated as a bone of St Thomas, transferred here from San Thomé in Tamil Nadu [36G].

The Kodungallur area also preserves several fine Hindu monuments. The *Mahadeva Temple* at *Thiruvanchikulam* is entered on the east through a gate roofed with triple sloping tiers. The central gable has carvings of guardian figures, with Lakshmi and elephants beneath. This leads past a multi-stage, metal lamp on a tortoise base and a brass-clad lamp column to the porch that marks the entrance to the second enclosure (only Hindus admitted). Carved figures of Rama and Lakshmana, together with Hanuman and Sugriva, appear on the frontal gable. The interior of the porch has a stone altar surrounded by wooden screens. Brahma and the dikpalas appear in the panels of the wooden ceiling above.

Immediately inside the temple enclosure stands the open hall, sheltering a stone Nandi. The stone columns have bulbous fluted capitals; maidens bearing lamps adorn the corner supports. The columns support the angled beams of the pyramidal roof, their projecting ends sheathed in embossed metal caps. The ceiling within repeats the Brahma and dikpala theme of the porch; naga figures and celestials are seen beneath. The main linga shrine is a square masonry structure with pilastered wall projections, repeated at a diminishing scale on the upper level before being roofed with angled tiles. Stone guardian figures flank the doorway on the east. Paintings on the Saptamatrika shrine, to the south, include a Mahabharata battle scene.

The *Krishna Temple* at *Thirukkalasekharapuram*, only a short distance from Thiruvanchikulam, is of particular architectural interest since it is one of the few religious monuments in Kerala that preserves its original 10th-11th century features. In spite of its name, the deity enshrined within the central square sanctuary is a four-armed Vishnu (only Hindus admitted). Two sets of passageways surround the sanctuary on four sides. Raised on a high but plain plinth, the outer walls have pilastered projections alternating with niches. These frame sculptures of two-armed figures of Dakshnamurti, Arjuna and guardians. The niches are headed with elaborate pediments of eaves and miniature towers.

The roof of the Krishna temple rises in two tiers of sloping tiles, the upper part forming a pyramid. The square hall, which adjoins the sanctuary on the east, is also roofed with tiles. The main unit stands in the middle of a colonnaded enclosure. Subshrines in the outer enclosure are dedicated to different deities. The Govardhana shrine has delicate carvings of dancers and musicians on the balustrades flanking the access steps. The plinth exhibits a frieze of well formed yalis.

The most popular shrine in Kondungallur is the *Kurumba Devi Temple*, consecrated to Bhagavati, the potent eight-armed goddess who presides over smallpox and cholera. The festival held here in February attracts large crowds of worshippers. The present temple is a modern structure of traditional design, with several unusual features. A small chamber adjoining the sanctuary on the west houses the Saptamatrikas. Another chamber on the east, lacking any openings and supposedly built around a prehistoric megalith, can only be reached by means of an underground passageway. A unique, 4 m. high stone figure of a guardian holding a mace, dated to the 17th century, stands within the temple enclosure (only Hindus admitted).

T. TRIPRAYAR

The *Rama Temple* in this small village, 20 km. north of Kodungallur, just off NH17, is enchantingly situated on the Triprayar River. A portico shelters the landing stage used by devotees arriving by boat. The complex is contained within a square enclosure, surrounded by colonnades (only Hindus admitted). At the core of the complex stands a circular sanctuary with doorways on four sides, and a copper-tiled conical roof. The outer walls are raised on a moulded basement with an inscription belonging to the 11th century the paintings covering the walls, however, are no earlier than the 18th century. They have escaped retouching, and are among the finest examples of Kerala mural art. Executed in a glowing yellow and ochre tones, they illustrate Vishnu with consorts, Ramayana battle episodes, the story of Narasimha, and other

Vaishnava topics. Intricately worked wooden figures on elephant brackets and angled beneath the roof overhang. They show Rama with Lakshmana and Ravana; Ravana in his aerial chariot; Narasimha; and celestial maidens and sages. The pyramidal roofed hall in front of the sanctuary has a wooden ceiling divided into panels occupied by Brahma and the dikpalas.

U. PERUVANAM

This village, 10 km. east of Triprayar, 9 km. south of Thrissur, is renowned for the *Mahadeva Temple*, one of the most imposing Hindu monuments in Kerala. The temple stands in a quadrangular enclosure defined by timber screens and stone walls. Two entrances (only Hindus admitted) in the long columned hall flanking the walls on the west are marked by small stone altars outside. The south entrance is aligned with the Madattiplappan shrine; the north entrance with the Irattayyappa shrine. These two west facing shrines, both dedicated to Shiva, are built in contrasting styles.

The *Madattiplappan Shrine* is a square masonry structure that rises in four storeys, each with pilastered wall projections capped by bold, arch-like motifs. The lowest level is solid; worshippers have to climb a steep flight of steps to reach the porch and linga sanctuary surrounded by a double passageway at the second level. Both this level and that above are partly concealed by angled tiled roofs carried on wooden struts. The struts in the middle of three sides are carved with vigorous images of Maheshvara (south), triple-headed Shiva (east), and Vishnu (north). The topmost storey is crowned by an octagonal roof with small gables on each face, achieving a total height of 21.5 m. above the pavement.

The adjacent *Irattayyappa Shrine* is a circular structure containing a small square sanctuary with two lingas. The roof rises in a smooth, metal-sheathed cone capped by a pot finial. The walls have pilastered projections covered with paintings, now somewhat faded. Angled wooden struts beneath the roof overhang are fashioned as figures, many of which illustrate the story of Arjuna fighting Shiva disguised as kirata, the hunter; Garuda also appears here. Stone guardians flank the doorway on the west. The square pavilion that stands in front is roofed with a pyramid of metal tiles. Rows of miniature figures and animals adorn the wooden beams inside.

A stone structure identified as a treasury stands in between the two shrines. An inscription on its base records the renovation of the temple by one of the Kochi rulers in 1758.

V. THRISSUR

Known also as Trissur or Trichur, this city lies 69 km. north of Ernakulam on NH47. Thrissur became a second capital for the Kochi kingdom during the 16th century, when the Portuguese presence was dominant. The city was occupied by the Zamorin of Kozhikode in 1750-60, and then by Haidar Ali and Tipu Sultan in 1776-90. It was, however, reclaimed by the Kochi rulers, who resided here intermittently during the 19th century.

Thrissur is built around a low hill crowned by the *Vadakkunnatha Temple*, one of the largest in Kerala. The Puram festival, held here in April-May, is a spectacular event attracting huge crowds, with magnificent fireworks and processions of richly caparisoned elephants. The temple dates back to the 9th century, but was substantially remodelled in the 16th-17th centuries. The complex is contained within a spacious rectangle of walls, entered through grandiose gateways in the middle of each side. The gateways follow a standard scheme, with double or triple tiers of sloping tiled roofs rising on pilastered masonry walls. The path from the main gate on the west passes by stone altars and metal lamps. On the left stands the Kuttambalam, which is a hall used for theatrical and dance performances. This timber structure has angled screens and an impressive tiled roof. Its interior has an independent pavilion with 16 stone columns, some with intricately carved shafts. They carry a wooden ceiling divided into nine squares, with Shiva appearing out of the linga occupying the central square; miniature figural brackets are seen beneath.

The inner enclosure of the Vadakkunnatha temple is entered through triple entrances on the west (only Hindus admitted). These pass through timber screens and stone walls linked by colonnades. The entrances are aligned with three west-facing shrines that stand freely in the middle of the enclosure. An additional entrance on the north is flanked by walls adorned with paintings.

Vadakkunnatha Temple, Thrissur.

The *Vadakkunnatha Shrine* (north) consists of a linga sanctuary contained within a circle of masonry walls. The walls are raised on a moulded basement, with a spout protruding on the north, carried on a sculpted kneeling figure. Stone guardians flank the west doorway. The pilastered walls are overhung by a low conical roof sheathed in copper tiles. The hall in front is capped with the usual pyramidal roof. Immediately south stands a rectangular masonry sanctuary dedicated to Ganesha. To the south stands the circular *Shankara Narayana Shrine*, which is smaller but more finely finished than the Vadakkunnatha. The murals here mostly date from the 18th century. They include large representations of Nataraja and Padmanabha, as well as Dakshinamurti and Ganesha. Intricately carved wooden struts depict various divinities on elephant torsos, including Garuda with pointed wings. The conical roof above rises in two stages. The *Rama Shrine* (south) is a square masonry structure with pilastered walls, also covered with murals. Carved struts are placed beneath double tiers of sloping roofs, with dormer windows in the upper tier. A small east-facing sanctuary stands in an extension on the north side of the temple enclosure. Paintings here show Krishna playing the flute and other topics.

In the eastern part of Thrissur stands the *Archaeological Museum* (closed Mondays), worth visiting for its fine collection of artifacts. They include pottery from megalithic sites near Guruvaryur, 1st-2nd century CE Roman pottery, and 14th-15th century Persian and Chinese ceramic fragments from Kodungallur. Stone sculptures, hero stones and bronze figurines, some going back to the 12th century, are also on display, as are instructive models of temples, and copies of mural paintings in the Dutch Palace at Mattancheri.

The *State Museum*, next door, presents a large range of costumes, weapons, brass utensils and stone epigraphs. The finest items are in the adjacent *Art Museum* (both closed Mondays). They include a superb pair of 17th century bronze guardian figures, with encrusted costumes and headdresses, and a contemporary image of Devi standing within an ornate frame. Hanging bronze lamps have been assembled in the upstairs gallery. Some are fashioned as model shrines, complete with temple-like roofs; others have pairs of divinities set in ornate frames. Large metal vessels, ivories and paintings on glass are also exhibited.

Thrissur is headquarters of a small community of Nestorian Christians. The *Church of St Mary*, much rebuilt in the 19th century, has a Baroque facade partly hidden by a modern entrance structure. The interior is of interest for its extraordinary wooden pulpit, supported on a long stalk issuing from the mouth of a black lion, the symbolism of which remains obscure. More impressive is the Catholic *Church of Our Lady of Dolours*, built in an exuberant Neo-Gothic manner, with corner belfries topped with ornate octagonal steeples. A similarly decorated dome rises over the crossing of the transepts. The vast interior is one of the largest for any church in Southern India. Fine altars are seen at the end of the nave.

NH47 makes a turn at Thrissur, continuing to Coimbatore [43A] via Palghat, 109 km. northeast. The road running north from Thrissur meets up with NH17, and proceeds to Kozhikode, 125 km. north.

W. Guruvayur

Together with Sabarimalai, this is the most popular Hindu pilgrimage destination in Kerala. Guruvayur lies 29 km. north of Thrisssur, a total of approximately 100 km. north of Ernakulam, a short distance off NH17. The deity worshipped in the Krishna temple here is conceived as an infant engaged in childish pranks, taking unconcealed delight in sweets and the good things of life. The importance of the monument in the 16th-17th centuries is indicated by the many grants made to the temple by local rulers, including the Zamorins of Kozhikode. Tipu Sultan plundered Guruvayur in 1789, but the main image was buried for safety.

The *Krishna Temple* is approached along a wide street lined with shops. A 36 m. high flag post, encased in gilded brass, stands in front of the main gate on the east side of the complex (only Hindus admitted). The stone columns of its porch are carved with heads of elephants and bulls. The interior walls are covered with murals depicting Arjuna's adventures in the Mahabharata epic. The roof above has two sloping tiers. The focal sanctuary within the inner enclosure has been much altered by modern renovations after a recent fire. It consists of a small square structure with a double-tiered, pyramidal roof sheathed in copper. The cult divinity enshrined here is a standing figure of Krishna holding a conch, discus, mace and lotus. The image is bathed in the large tank to the north of the complex during ten days of ceremonies in February-March. The Ekdashi festival attracts large crowds in November-December.

4 km. east of Guruvayur, at *Punnathoor Kotta*, is an old mansion with an exquisitely carved doorway. The elephants associated with the Krishna temple are kept in a compound here.

The region immediately east of Guruvayur is rich in prehistoric remains, dating back at least 2,000 years. Sites near *Chovannur* and *Porkala* villages, both within 10 km. of Guruvayur, preserve diverse *Megalithic Monuments*, such as stone burial pits covered with hood stones, hat stones raised on four pieces of stone, dolmens and menhirs. Pottery fragments discovered by the excavators here have been removed to the Archaeological Museum in Thrissur.

48. Kozhikode

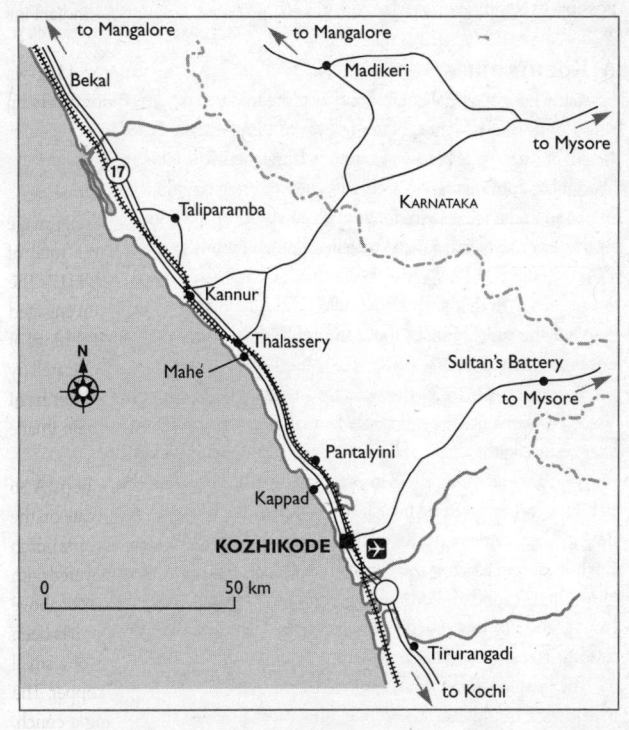

Northern Kerala narrows to a coastal strip, lined with glorious beaches and dotted with historical towns and forts, flanked for much of its length by a wooded plateau. This rises almost 1,000 m. above sea level, and is home to extensive tea, coffee, pepper and areca nut estates. The Muslim presence is noticeable, and there are many mosques to be seen here, the finest being in Kozhikode [A]. Allow a half day to visit the sights of the city, capital of the Zamorins. The journey inland through the Western Ghats, passing by Sultan's Battery [B], can be extended as far as Madikeri [16] or Mysore [15] in Karnataka.

Most visitors will not be able to resist the coastal scenery. An excursion south of Kozhikode is easily made to Tirurangadi [C], to inspect the mosque and shrine there. A full-day trip north can take in the mosques at Pantalyini [D], the French and British vestiges at Mahé [E] and Thalassery [F], and the fort, mosque and churches of Kannur [G]. Additional time will be required to reach the temples Taliparamba [H].

From the citadel at Bekal [I], at the northern extremity of Kerala, it is possible to continue on to Mangalore [17A].

A. Kozhikode

Formerly known as Calicut, this city was the traditional home of the Samutri rulers of northern Kerala, better known to Europeans as the Zamorins. The wealth of Kozhikode has always attracted foreigners. The Chinese were the first to establish commercial contacts with the city, bringing gold, silver, copper and silks, and exchanging them for pepper, cinnamon, ginger and woven cottons. By the time the North African traveller Ibn Battuta spent time in Kozhikode in 1342-47, the Muslims were the dominant commercial class, many having arrived from Arabia and the Middle East. This mainly émigré community enjoyed the protection of the Zamorins, whose army they equipped with imported arms and horses.

The arrival of the Portuguese threatened Arab commercial supremacy. Vasco da Gama made his first safe landfall near Kozhikode on 20 May 1498, after rounding the Cape of Good Hope, but he was not welcomed. Even so, one year after attacking the Zamorins in 1513 the Portuguese were permitted to built a fortified trading post at the mouth of the Kallai River. But unable to defend their settlement, they left in 1525. Other Europeans followed: the English erected a factory here in 1667, the French in 1703, and the Danish in 1752. In 1766, Kozhikode was occupied by Haidar Ali of Srirangapattana [15C]. The city was ceded to the British in 1792, and thereafter became the headquarters of the Malabar District.

The bustling, traditional commercial character of Kozhikode is still much in evidence. In addition to tea, coffee and spices, timber is the primary industry. The city is also a centre for the export of the light cotton textiles called calicos, after the former name of the city. Warehouses line the narrow crowded streets that run down to the port, which lacks any natural harbour. Today, as in the past, large boats have to anchor off shore, and goods transferred to smaller craft. The 33.5 m. high lighthouse was erected in 1847.

The centre of Kozhikode is marked by *Mananchira*, a large tank with a park to its north. Several Christian places of worship are located nearby. The *Catholic Church*, dating from the 18th century, has an altar with the Crucifixion and an image of the Virgin. The *Basel Mission Church*, now the local headquarters of the Church of South India, was established in the middle of the 19th century. Its unadorned facade is dominated by a lofty square tower with a pointed steeple in the German style.

The *Tali Temple*, the largest and most important Hindu monument in Kozhikode, is situated 1.5 km. east of *Mananchira*. The complex is approached from the east through a gate roofed with sloping tiled roofs. The path passes between minor shrines dedicated to Krishna (north) and Narasimha (south), both standing in their own walled compounds. An altar and a brass-clad lamp post are located in front (east) of the columned hall that serves as the entrance to the inner enclosure (only Hindus admitted). The carved and painted wooden ceiling over the central passageway shows Brahma surrounded by the dikpalas.

The inner enclosure of the temple is contained within double lines of wooden screens and masonry walls. The main shrine that stands here consists of a square linga sanctuary and attached antechamber. Both have pilastered walls with niches raised on a high basement. Animals are carved on the eaves and parapet elements above, with angled wooden struts positioned beneath the overhanging roof. The walls of the antechamber rise in a second stage, capped with a pyramidal tiled roof. The antechamber walls display unusual stone sculptures of Sarasvati, Vishnu, Shiva, Bhagavati and Rama with Hanuman. The square hall that stands in front (east) has stone columns concealed by wooden screens, with corner brackets fashioned as yalis eating foliage. The ceiling within is carved with rows of miniature figures and animals.

Kozhikode's mosques are of particular architectural significance, since they preserve their traditional multi-tiered, sloping tiled roofs. The finest examples are seen in the Mappila quarter near the port. *Mithqalpalli*, the largest mosque, takes its name from its founder, Nakhuda Mithqali, a local trader during the time of Ibn Battuta. Only the stepped plinth dates from the 14th century; the remainder of the building was reconstructed after the mosque was burnt down by the Portuguese in 1510. The prayer hall is divided into bays by timber columns, and approached through a later antechamber and ablutions area. Both hall and antechamber are contained within a double line of plastered masonry walls, marked by alternating openings and niches with round-headed arches. The narrow space between these walls is occupied by the mihrab in the middle of the west wall. Steps ascend to an upper level, until recently used as a school. The building is capped with an imposing triple-stage roof, each tier carried on angled beams and rafters concealed by wooden screens. The roofs terminate in decorated gables on the east side only. Three brass pots line the roof ridge.

A short distance south, beside a large tank known as Kuttichira, stands the *Jami Mosque* of the city. Though the foundation date of this communal place of prayer is unknown, an inscription inside mentions a restoration of 1481. The mosque is raised on a stepped plinth and is contained by masonry walls. The prayer hall and antechamber both have steps ascending to the upper level. The entrance porch, in the middle of the east side, is a multi-storeyed structure with angled roofs and a prominent gable filled with colonettes and rafters. Wooden beams carry the decorated coffered ceiling within the prayer hall. The beams are adorned with a frieze of foliation and a long Arabic inscription that mentions a renovation to the mosque in the 17th century. Lotus medallions occupy the central panels of the ceiling. The 1481 epigraph is cut into a wooden lintel inserted between the walls of the antechamber.

Micchandipalli, another mosque, is located nearby. The original prayer hall can easily be made out, with additions on the east. Two inscriptions, one a bilingual record in Arabic and Malayalam, mentioning renovations belonging to the 14th-16th centuries. The mosque stands on a 1.5 m. high plinth. The semicircular mihrab in the rear walls in an arched niche. Similar arches mark openings in the outer walls, but these are cut out of stone slabs. The decorated wooden beams carry a coffered ceiling resembling that of the Jami mosque. The double-tiered sloping roof has an elaborate frontal gable, but the timber screens beneath the upper tier have been replaced by plaster walls.

Smaller mosques in the vicinity are also worthy of notice. *Allahrapalli* and *Idrispalli* both display double tiers of sloping roofs with decorated frontal gables. They contrast with the *Tomb of Sayyid Abdullah*, immediately in front (east) of the Idrispalli mosque. This marks the burial place of a saint who died here in 1771. The building, however, may be earlier. It consists of a small domed chamber with plain outer walls; the corners are topped by small finials.

5 km. east of Kozhikode, on East Hill, is the *Pazhassiraja Museum* (closed Mondays). This has a worthwhile collection of local arts and crafts, metal and wooden sculptures, coins and other antiquities. The display also includes models of different prehistoric monuments found in the area. The *Art Gallery* next door has an excellent assemblage of paintings by Keralan artists, especially Ravi Varma, as well as of wooden and ivory carvings. A separate section, the *Krishna Menon Museum*, houses personal memorabilia of V.K. Krishna Menon, a locally born political leader who became a prominent minister under Jawaharlal Nehru.

B. SULTAN'S BATTERY

In about 1780 Tipu Sultan erected a small *Fort* at this site strategically located in the Western Ghats, 67 km. east of Kozhikode, on the main road leading from Mysore down to the Arabian Sea. The British captured the fort in 1805, reducing it to ruins. Only traces of overgrown laterite walls remain.

6 km. southwest of Sultan's Battery, on the western slopes of Edakkal Hills, is a natural 'cleft' with enigmatic *Relief Carvings* of figures and symbols. Though the meaning of these signs remains unknown they appear to predate nearby inscriptions of the 12th-13th centuries.

C. TIRURANGADI

This town, 36 km. south of Kozhikode on NH17, occupies the south bank of the Kadalundi River. Tirurangadi was active in the struggles against the Portuguese, and also successfully resisted an attempt by the Zamorins to capture it in the 1740s. A fierce engagement between the British and the forces of Haidar Ali took place here in 1780, followed ten years later by a decisive victory over Tipu Sultan's troops. The town returned to prominence in August 1921, when it was the centre of the Mappila revolt against British authority.

The town is worth visiting for two monuments. The *Jami Mosque*, built on a wooded hill overlooking the Kadalundi, preserves its traditional character. It consists of two superimposed masonry walls with tiled overhangs, carrying a wooden structure with timber slats sheltered by a sloping tiled roof with a frontal gable. Four pot finials line the roof ridge. The *Shrine of Sayyid Alawi* at *Mambram*, directly opposite, on the north bank of the river, marks the last resting place of an influential local Muslim teacher. The shrine is a rectangular building with a dome raised on a circular drum unusually concealed within a conical roof at one end. Tombs in the ground-floor hall beneath the dome include that of Sayyid Alawi, who died in 1843, his uncle, and other relations. The adjacent hall is used for sermons and public readings.

D. Pantalyini

This small town, 25 km. north of Kozhikode, just off NH17, is a place of historical importance, being linked with the Zamorins, who maintained a residence here. Pantalyini has a *Jami Mosque* that enjoys a reputation similar to that of the mosque at Kodungallur [47S], supposedly erected by the 7th century Arab missionary, Malik bin Dinar. However, the present building is entirely remodelled and shows no evidence of its early history.

A local curiosity is to be seen on a rock near the seashore, 3 km. west of the town. This is believed to be the outline of the *Footprint of Adam* as he landed in India on his way to Sri Lanka, where there is a similar footprint at the summit of the mountain known as Adam's Peak.

8 km. south of Pantalyini, at *Kappad*, is a modern memorial pillar that marks Vasco da Gama's first landing spot in Southern India.

E. Mahé

This former French enclave, no larger than 7.5 sq. km., now part of the Union Territory of Puducherry [39A], is situated 62 km. north of Kozhikode on NH17. Originally known as Mayyali, the small port of Mahé took its name from Mahé de La Bourdonnais, who occupied it for the French East India Company in 1721. It thereupon became the principal trading post on the Malabar Coast. Mahé suffered from the vicissitudes of the Franco-British rivalry, and was occupied by the British in 1761-65 and 1779-85, and then again in 1793-1817, during the Napoleonic wars.

Mahé overlooks a wide estuary of a coast river that affords shelter to ocean going vessels. This water-seaside location and the European character of some of the buildings, including the former French Residency, lend the town a certain charm. A reminder of the French presence is the cast-iron monument, erected in 1889, with an inscription recording that 100 years earlier, the French Republic granted the people of Mahé full rights of French citizenship. The whitewashed Church of St Therese d'Avila presents a dignified Baroque facade.

F. THALASSERY

In about 1683 the East India Company began operations at this attractive coastal town, previously known as Tellichery, 6 km. south of Mahé, trading primarily in pepper and cardamom. The *Fort*, begun in 1708, is built of massive laterite blocks laid out in the form of a square. A lighthouse on the ramparts looks out towards the surf breaking on the reefs. An overgrown cemetery on the landward side is all that remains of the English presence. Traditional warehouses and residences, many of them belonging to Mappila traders, cluster around the fort. Some were used by Portuguese refugees during the invasion of Haidar Ali. Here, too, stands the *Odothipalli*, a traditional styled mosque, founded in the 17th-18th century. Its copper clad roof rises in two sloping tiers, separated by screens with timber slats. A small octagonal turret crowns the frontal gable of the upper tier, while three gilded pot finials are arranged along the ridge behind. The *Jami Mosque* in the town has recently been rebuilt in a Neo-Mughal manner. Its imposing arched portal is flanked by domed pavilions.

Among the Christian buildings of Thalassery is *St Joseph's Church*. Its Baroque facade, flanked by squat towers with corner pilasters, dates from the 19th century, but the monolithic cross standing at the rear is much earlier. The Church of St Peter is a modern structure, with domed pavilions raised on corner towers.

G. KANNUR

Formerly called Cannanore, this historical port, 22 km north of Thalassery, or 92 km. north of Kozhikode on NH17, was the seat of the Ali Rajas. These rulers constituted the only Muslim royal house in Kerala, and were noted by Ibn Battuta as being among the most powerful on the Malabar Coast. It was one of the Ali Rajas that gave the Portuguese permission to build Fort St Angelo in 1505. The Dutch captured the fort in 1663, but sold it back to the Ali Rajas in 1772, by which time these rulers had formed an alliance with Tipu Sultan, offering vigorous resistance to the British. The fort was eventually captured in 1783, after which it housed the largest British garrison in Malabar District.

Fort St Angelo occupies a delightful site on a rocky promontory jutting into the ocean, northwest of the town. It is a massive triangular structure of laterite, with strong flanking bastions surrounded by water on two sides, and a dry ditch on the landward side. The ramparts are in a fairly good state of preservation, even though parts have fallen into the sea. A few obsolete guns are still to be seen lying around. Dungeons, once used as a jail, and the magazine still survive. A small lighthouse has been erected inside the fort. The remains of the British military Cantonment are located nearby. Other vestiges of the British include the *Church of St John*, of 1811. This simple tiled roof structure has steep gables and a frontal verandah. The *Jami Mosque* in the old town, south of the fort, is of interest for its double-storeyed prayer hall roofed with sloping tiles. It is flanked by a pair of octagonal minarets with internal staircases, both recent additions.

The *Palace of the Adil Rajas* is a charming ensemble of modest whitewashed buildings with characteristic tiled roofs. The interiors are traditional, with wooden floors and ceilings, and shuttered windows. The complex includes a small mosque.

From Kannur it is possible to drive directly to Mysore, 91 km. northeast.

H. TALIPARAMBA

This town, 22 km. north of Kannur, is celebrated for its two temples, among the finest in north Kerala. Both monuments date back to the 9th century, but were substantially renovated in the 16th-17th centuries. The *Rajarajeshvara Temple* is entered on the east through a dilapidated, unfinished gate. A Nandi pavilion and an intricately carved stone altar line the path to the main entrance (only Hindus admitted). This is reached only after passing through the wooden screen that surrounds the outer walls of the inner enclosure. The entrance has a sloping tiled roof with ornamented gables. The carved wooden ceiling over the passageway shows the Navagrahas with Surya in the middle, and rows of elephants and playful dwarfs beneath. An unusual wooden female figure, 1.5 m. high, is placed to the right of the passageway.

The main linga shrine inside the temple enclosure is a large square structure, with a double passageway surrounding the central passageway. The outer walls, which are divided into pilastered bays, rise in two stages, each sheltered by a sloping tiled roof; the upper roof forms a pyramid. Finely sculpted wooden struts are placed beneath the roof overhangs. Those at the corners are fashioned as yalis on elephants. Deities appear at the lower level: Dakshinamurti (south), Narasimha (west), and Parameshvara (north). The figures of warriors at the upper level form part of the story of Arjuna's battle with Shiva disguised as kirata, the hunter. Similar struts are seen in the square pavilion that stands in front (east). The internal four corners of this structure are of turned wood.

1.5 km. south of the centre of Taliparamba, at *Trichambaram*, stands the *Krishna Temple*, the second important Hindu monument of the town. Steps lead past a small pond with a small Shiva shrine standing in the middle A gabled roofed entrance porch on the east gives access to the enclosure (only

Hindus admitted). Here stand the square, double-storeyed shrine, of the same type as the Rajarajeshvara temple. The walls here, however, are more deeply articulated, with secondary niches marking the projections, and wooden window screens inserted into the recesses. Traces of paintings can still be made out. Friezes of yalis and makaras surmount the curved eaves. Angled wooden struts, with yalis at the corners, appear at both levels, together with maidens and couples below, and deities above. Similar yalis appear at the corners of the pavilion that stands in front (east). The ceiling inside is carried on beams with intricately worked friezes illustrating the Krishna story.

I. Bekal

The largest and best preserved coastal fort in northern Kerala is situated on the outskirts of this town, 77 km. north of Kannur on NH17. Bekal was founded by Shivappa Nayaka of Nagar [19F] in the middle of the 17th century, and remained one of the principal Nayaka strongholds of the coastal region until it was seized by Haidar Ali in 1763. The fort passed into the hands of the British in 1792, together with the other Kerala dominions of Tipu Sultan.

Bekal Fort consists of an irregular quadrangle built up to the sands of the Arabian Sea. The laterite ramparts, with sloping walls and round bastions, are still intact, as are the battlements, which display wide embrasures for gun emplacements. Only a few isolated structures stand within the open ground inside the fort. They include a rectangular building with a curved vault, possibly a powder magazine.

NH17 continues to Mangalore, 60 km. to the north.

Glossary

Mostly restricted to Indian names and terms.

Abdul Razzaq: 15th century Persian traveller
Abdul Wahad Khan: 17th century Adil Shahi commander
Abdullah: 17th century Adil Shahi ruler
Achaleshvara: name of Shiva
acharya: saint
Achyutaraya: 16th century Tuluva emperor
Adi Keshava: name of Vishnu
Adil Shahi: 16th-17th century dynasty of Karnataka ruling from Bijapur
Adinatha: first of the 24 Tirthankaras
Adinatha: name of Vishnu worshipped at Alvar Tirunagari
Adivaraha: Varaha
Afaqi: newcomer to the Deccan
Afzal Khan: 17th century Adil Shahi commander
Agastishvara: name of Shiva
Agastya: legendary sage
Aghoreshvara: fierce form of Shiva
Agni: god of fire, one of the dikpalas
Ahalya: woman liberated by Rama in the Ramayana
Ahilyabai: 18th century Holkar queen
Ahmad: 15th century Bahmani ruler; 15th-16th century Nizam Shahi ruler
Airavateshvara: name of Shiva
Akbar: 16th century Mughal emperor
Akhilandeshvari: name of Devi
Alagar Perumal: name of Vishnu worshipped at Alagarkoil
alam: Shia ceremonial standard
Alara: hero of the Samkhapala Jataka

Alauddin: 14th century Madurai ruler; 16th century Imad Shahi ruler
Ali: 16th century and 17th century Adil Shahi rulers; 17th century Baridi ruler
Ali Raja: 14th-18th century dynasty of north Kerala, ruling from Kannur
Alvar: Vaishnava saint
Amareshvara: name of Shiva worshipped at Amaravati
Ambal: Devi
Ambaranatha: name of Shiva worshipped at Amarnath
Ambika: Jain mother goddess
Ammaiyar: female Shaiva saint at Karaikal
Amman, Ammanavara: goddess
Amriteshvara: name of Shiva
Ananta: serpent mount of Vishnu
Anantashayana: Vishnu reclining on Ananta
Ananteshvara: name of Vishnu
Andal: poetess, worshipper of Vishnu
Andhaka: demon killed by Shiva
Angre: 17th-19th century naval commanders based at Alibag
anicut: irrigation canal
Anjaneya: name of Hanuman
ankusha: elephant goad
Appar: one of the Nayanmars
Aravidu: 16th-17th century dynasty of Andhra Pradesh and Tamil Nadu, ruling from Penukonda and Chandragiri
Ardhanarishvara: Shiva and Parvati joined
Arjuna: hero of the Mahabharata
Arunchaleshvara: fiery linga worshipped at Tiruvannamalai
Asaf Jahi: 18th-20th century dynasty of Andhra Pradesh and Maharashtra, ruling from Hyderabad, known as the Nizams
Ashoka: 3rd century BCE Maurya ruler
ashram: religious and spiritual centre
ashurkhana: congregational hall of Shia Muslims used at Muharram
Atmanatha: invisible form of Shiva worshipped at Avudayarkoil
Aurangzeb: 17th-18th century Mughal emperor
Aurobindo: 20th century teacher at Puducherry
Avalokiteshvara: a Bodhisattva
Avanishvara: name of Shiva
avatara: incarnation of Vishnu
Ayyappa: son of Shiva and Mohini worshipped at Sabarimalai
Azam Shah: 17th century Mughal noble

Baba Musafir: 17th century Sufi saint at Aurangabad

Babulnath: name of Krishna worshipped in Mumbai
badgir: wind tower
bagh: garden
Bahadur Shah: 16th century ruler of Gujarat
Bahmani: 14th-15th century dynasty of Karnataka, Maharashtra and Andhra Pradesh ruling from Gulbarga and Bidar
Bahubali: son of the first Tirthankara
bala hisar, bala kila: citadel
Baladeva: name of Shiva worshipped at Parel
Balaji Bajirao: 18th century Peshwa ruler
Balaji Vishvanath: 18th century Peshwa ruler
Balakrishna: infant Krishna
Ballala: 13th century Hoysala ruler
Banashankari: name of Devi
Banganga: Rama's magical bow
baradari: pavilion
Baridi: 16th century dynasty of Karnataka ruling from Bidar
basti: Jain temple
bauri: reservoir
bazaar: market
Bedar: 17th-19th century rulers of Shorapur
Begum Rabia Durani: wife of Aurangzeb buried at Aurangabad
Bhagavata Purana: story of Krishna
Bhagavati: fierce aspect of Devi
Bhairava, Bhairaveshvara: fearful aspect of Shiva
Bhairavi: fierce aspect of Devi
Bhaktavatsaleshvara: name of Shiva
bhakti: fervent devotion to a Hindu deity
Bharata: brother of Rama in the Ramayana
Bharata Mata: goddess personifying the Indian nation, worshipped at Daulatabad
Bhavani: form of Durga worshipped at Tuljapur
Bhave, Vinoba: 20th century social reformer
Bhikshatanamurti: Shiva as the naked ascetic
Bhima: mighty Pandava hero in the Mahabharata
Bhimalingeshvara: name of Shiva
Bhoganandishvara: name of Shiva worshipped at Nandi
Bhonsale: 18th-19th century dynasty of northern Maharashtra, ruling from Nagpur
Bhringi: attendant of Shiva
Bhu, Bhudevi: consort of Vishnu

bhuta: spirit
Bhutanatha: name of Shiva
Bhuvaneshvari: name of Parvati
Bhuvaraha: Varaha rescuing Bhu
bidri: inlaid metalwork manufactured in Bidar
Bimbisara: 6th century BCE ruler of Northern India, contemporary of Buddha
bodhi: tree of enlightenment
Bodhisattva: Buddhist saviour
Brahma: creator god
Brahmalingeshvara: name of Shiva
Brahmapurishvara: name of Shiva
Brihadambal: name of Devi
Brihadishvara: name of Shiva
Brihadnayaki: name of Parvati
Buddha: founder of Buddhism in the 6th-5th centuries BCE; later worshipped as a divinity
Bukka: 14th century Sangama ruler
Burhan: 16th century Nizam Shahi ruler; 16th century Imad Shahi ruler

chaitya: vaulted Buddhist shrine, horseshoe-arch
Chakrapani: name of Vishnu
Chakreshvara: name of Shiva
Chalukya: see Early Chalukya and Late Chalukya
Champeyya: serpent hero of Jataka story
Chamunda: terrifying form of Devi
Chamundara: 10th century Ganga commander
Chamundeshvari: goddess worshipped at Mysore
Chand Bibi: 16th-17th century Nizam Shahi queen
Chandra: moon god
Chandesha, Chandeshvara: devotee of Shiva
Chadragupta: royal devotee of Bahubali
Chandralamba: name of Devi
Chandramauleshvara: name of Shiva
Candranatha, Chandranatheshvara, Chandraprabha: one of the Tirthankaras
Chandrashekhara: name of Shiva
Chandreshwar: name of Shiva worshipped on Chandranatha Hill
Changla Vateshvara: name of Shiva
char kaman: four arches
char minar: four minarets
chaturmukha: four-faced
Chenchu: tribal people of the Eastern Ghats

Chennakeshava: name of Vishnu
Cheraman Peruman: one of the Nayanmars
cheruvu: lake
Chhaddanta: elephant hero of a Jataka story
Chhatrapati: title of Maratha rulers; name of the 18th-19th century Maratha dynasty ruling from Satara
chhatri: Hindu memorial
Chikka Deva Raja: 17th century Wodeyar ruler
Chinna Bomma: 16th century Aravidu ruler
Chintala: tamarind tree
Chishti: Sufi order
Chola: 9th-13th century dynasty of Tamil Nadu ruling from Thanjavur and Gangaikondacholapuram
Cholishvara: name of Shiva

dad mahal: hall of justice
daitya: demon
Dakhni: Muslim nobles of the Deccan; local form of Persian
Dakshinamurti: Shiva as the teacher
Dandayudhapani: name of Subrahmanya worshipped at Palani
Dantidurga: 8th century Rashtrakuta ruler
darbar: formal audience
dargah: Muslim shrine, saintly grave
darshana: auspicious gaze
darush shifa: hospital
darwaza: gate
Dasara: royal festival
Dasharatha: father of Rama in the Ramayana
Dashavatara: ten incarnations of Vishnu
Dattatreya: emanation of Vishnu
Daud Khan: 17th-18th century Mughal commander
Devadatta: cousin of Buddha
Devaraya: 15th century Sangama ruler
Devayani: wife of Subrahmanya
Devi: consort of Shiva
dharma chakra: wheel of the law; emblem of Buddha's teachings
Dharmaraja: eldest of the Pandava brothers
Digambara: Jain sect
dikpalas: guardian deities of the eight directions
Dilawar Khan: 17th century Nizam Shahi commander
Diwan: prime minister

diwan-i am: public audience hall
Doddashankanna: 16th century Nayaka ruler of Ikkeri
Doddeshvara: name of Shiva
Draupadi: wife of the Pandava brothers
Durga: powerful goddess created by the gods to kill Mahisha
Dvarkadishvara: name of Krishna

Early Chalukya: 6th-8th century dynasty of Karnataka, Maharashtra and Andhra Pradesh, ruling from Badami
Eastern Chalukya: 9th-10th century dynasty of Andhra Pradesh
Ekadashi: Hindu festival
Ekakeshvara: name of Shiva
Ekambaranatha, Ekambareshvara: name of Shiva worshipped at Kanchipuram
Ekanatheshvara: name of Shiva
Eknath Maharaj: 16th century Hindu teacher saint
Ekoji: 17th century Maratha ruler of Thanjavur

Fathullah: 15th-16th century Imad Shahi ruler
Faruqi: 14th-16th century dynasty of Khandesh in northern Maharashtra, ruling from Thalner and Burhanpur in Madhya Pradesh
Firuz Shah: 14th century Tughluq ruler

gadigge: memorial shrine
gagan mahal: sky(-reaching) pavilion
Gajendra: elephant rescued by Vishnu
Galaganatha: name of Shiva
gana: dwarf attendant of Shiva
Ganapati, Ganesha: lord of the ganas; popular elephant-headed deity, son of Shiva
Ganapatideva: 13th century Kakatiya ruler
gandabherunda: double-headed eagle, royal emblem
Ganga: 9th-11th century dynasty of southern Karnataka ruling from Talkad
Ganga: goddess personifying the Ganges
Gangadhareshvara: name of Shiva when bearing the impact of Ganga's descent to earth
Garuda: eagle mount of Vishnu
Gautama: family name of Buddha
Gesu Daraz: 14th-15th century Sufi teacher at Gulbarga
ghat: bathing place, mountain range
Ghrishneshvara: jyotirlinga worshipped at Ellora

giri: hill
Gobind Singh: tenth Sikh Guru
Gokarneshvara: name of Shiva
Golingeshvara: name of Shiva
Gommateshvara: name of Bahubali
Gond: rulers of the Nagpur region
Gondeshvara: name of Shiva worshipped at Sinnar
gopi: milkmaid companion of Krishna
Gopinatha: name of Krishna
gopura: towered temple gateway
Govardhana: mountain lifted by Krishna to shield the herds from Indra's storm
Govinda Dikshita: 17th century prime minister of the Nayakas of Thanjavur
Govindaraja: name of Krishna
Gowda: 16th-17th century of southern Karnataka ruling from Bengaluru
gudi: temple
gumbad, gumbaz: dome, domed tomb
guru: teacher
Guru Granth: holy book of the Sikhs

Haidar Ali: 18th century usurper of the Wodeyar throne
Hamid Qadir Wali: 15th-16th century Muslim saint at Nagore
hammam: steam bath
Hanuman: monkey hero in the Ramayana
Harihara, Harihareshvara: Shiva and Vishnu joined
Harishena: 5th century Vakataka ruler
Hariti: consort of Panchika
Harsha: 7th century ruler of Northern India
Hayat Baksh Begum: 17th century Qutb Shahi queen
Hazara Rama: thousand Ramas
Hazrat: title of Muslim saint
Hidimbeshvara: name of Shiva
Hiranyakashipu: demon killed by Narasimha
Holkar: 18th-19th century Maratha dynasty of Madhya Pradesh ruling from Indore
Hoysala: 11th-14th century dynasty of Karnataka ruling from Halebid
Hoysaleshvara: name of Shiva worshipped at Halebid
hundi: treasury
Hussain: 16th century Nizam Shahi ruler

Ibn Battuta: 14th century North African traveller in India
Ibrahim: 16th century Qutb Shahi ruler; 16th-17th century Adil Shahi ruler

idgah: outdoor mosque used at festival times
Ikshvaku: 2nd-4th century dynasty of Andhra Pradesh ruling from Nagarjunakonda
Imad Shahi: 16th dynasty of Berar in northern Maharashtra ruling from Achalpur
Indra: lord of the heavens; one of the dikpalas
Irattayyappa: Ayyappa
Iravataneshvara: name of Shiva
Ishvara: Shiva

Jagadishvar: name of Shiva worshipped at Raigad
Jalakanteshvara: name of Shiva worshipped at Vellore
Jambukeshvara: name of Shiva worshipped at Tiruvannakoil
Jambulinga: name of Shiva
Jami mosque: congregational (Friday) mosque
Janardana: name of Vishnu
Jataka: folk tale, narrative of one of the former lives of Buddha
Jatayu: vulture who attacked Ravana in the Ramayana
Jeejeebhoy, Jamsetjee: 19th century Parsi businessman and philanthropist
Jehangir: 17th century Mughal emperor
Jijibai: mother of Shivaji
Jina: Tirthankara
Jnanaprasumbha: name of Parvati
Jvaraheshvara: name of Shiva
Jyeshtha: Shakti
jyotirlinga: luminous linga of light, worshipped at Bhimshankar, Trimbak, Ellora, Srisailam and Rameswaram

Kadamba: 11th-13th century dynasty of Goa and western Karnataka
Kailasa: mountain home of Shiva
Kailasanatha: name of Shiva
Kakatiya: 12th-14th century dynasty of Andhra Pradesh ruling from Warangal
Kala: name of Vishnu
Kala Rama: name of Rama worshipped at Nasik
Kalachuri: 5th-6th century dynasty of western Maharashtra
Kalahastishvara: name of Shiva worshipped at Sri Kalahasti
Kalambal: name of Devi
kalamkari: printing and dyeing textile technique
Kali: goddess of death
kali masjid: black mosque
Kalidasa: 5th century Sanskrit poet and dramatist

Kaliya: serpent demon subdued by Krishna
Kalleshvara: name of Shiva
kalyana mandapa: marriage hall
Kama: god of love
Kamakshi: name of Parvati worshipped at Kanchipuram
Kameshvara: name of Shiva
Kampahareshvara: name of Shiva
Kanhoji: 17th and 19th century Angre rulers
Kannagi: heroine of a Tamil story
Kannappa: Shaiva saint at Sri Kalahasti
Kapaleshvara: name of Shiva
Kapardishvara: name of Shiva
Kapoteshvara: name of Shiva
Karna: hero of the Mahabharata
Karttikeya: warrior son of Shiva, also known as Kumara and Subrahmanya
Kashivishvanatha, Kashivishveshvara: name of Shiva worshipped at Kashi (Varanasi)
Kaumari: consort of Kumari
Kayarohana: name of Shiva
Kedareshvara: name of Shiva
Kempe: 17th century Gowda ruler
Keshava: name of Krishna
Khalji: 14th century dynasty of Northern India ruling from Delhi
Khan Jahan Bahadur: 17th century Mughal governor
Khandoba: form of Shiva worshipped at Jejuri
khazana: treasury
kila: fort
Kilavan: 17th-18th century Setupati ruler
kirata: forest hunter; disguise of Shiva when fighting Arjuna
Kodandarama: Rama with the bow
koil: temple
Koran: holy book of Muslims
Koranganatha: name of Shiva
kota: fort
kovil: temple
Krishna: incarnation of Vishnu; separate cult deity of Hinduism
Krishna: 8th century Rashtrakuta ruler
Krishna Menon: 20th century political figure
Krishnadevaraya: 16th century Tuluva emperor
Krishnaraja: 19th-20th century Wodeyar rulers
Kshatrapa: 2nd-4th century dynasty of western Maharashtra and Gujarat

Kubera: chief of the yakshas, one of the dikpalas
Kudal Alagar: name of Vishnu worshipped at Madurai
Kufic: early Arabic script
kulam: pool
Kulottunga: 12th-13th century Chola ruler
Kumara: name of Subrahmanya
Kumari: name of Durga worshipped at Kanyakumari
Kumbha Mela: river festival at Nasik
Kumbharkarna: brother of Ravana in the Ramayana
Kumbheshvara: name of Shiva worshipped at Kumbakonam
kund: well, pool
Kurmanatha: tortoise avatara of Vishnu worshipped at Srikurman
kuttambalam: performance hall in Kerala temples

Ladle Sahib: 14th century Sufi saint at Aland
Lajja Gauri: squatting goddess with a lotus head
Lakshmana: brother of Rama
Lakshmi: goddess of prosperity, consort of Vishnu
Lakulisha: yogic aspect of Shiva
Lanka: island home of Ravana in the Ramayana
Lankeshvara: name of Shiva worshipped at Ellora
Late Chalukya: 10th-12th century dynasty of northern Karnataka ruling from Basavakalyan
lena: cave
linga: phallic emblem representing Shiva
Lingayat: Shaiva sect
Lokeshvara: name of a Bodhisattva
lungi: men's cloth

Madha, Madhavaraya: name of Vishnu
Madhava: 12th century Vaishnava philosopher
Madhukeshvara: name of Shiva
madrasa: Muslim theological college
Madur Qadiri: 17th century Adil Shahi governor
maha chaitya: great stupa
Mahabaleshvara: name of Shiva at Mahabaleshwar
Mahabharata: epic story of the war between the Pandavas and Kauravas
Mahadeva: name of Shiva
Mahajanaka: royal hero of a Jataka story
Mahakali: name of Kali
Mahakapi: monkey hero of a Jataka story

Mahakuteshvara: name of Shiva
mahal: pavilion, hall
Mahalakshmi: Lakshmi
Mahalinga: name of Shiva
Mahalrao: 18th century Holkar ruler
Mahamakam: bathing festival at Kumbakonam
Mahanandishvara: name of Shiva
Mahanavami: annual festival at Vijayanagara
Mahavira: last of the 24 Tirthankaras
Mahayana: Great Vehicle, school of Buddhism
Mahboob Ali Khan Bahadur: sixth Nizam of Hyderabad
Mahendravarman: 7th and 8th century Pallava rulers
Maheshvara: name of Shiva
Mahisha: buffalo demon killed by Durga
Mahishamardini, Mahishasuramardini: Durga
Mahlasa: female aspect of Vishnu worshipped at Mardol
Mahmud Gawan: 15th Bahmani prime minister
Mahodsadha: hero of a Jataka story
Maitreya: future Bodhisattva
makara: aquatic monster
Makhdum Ali Mahimi: 15th century Muslim saint buried at Mahim
Malik Ambar: 16th-17th century Nizam Shahi prime minister and general
Malik bin Dina: 7th century Arab missionary
Malik Kafur: 14th century Tughluq commander
Malik Raja: 14th century Faruqi ruler
Malik Rihan: 17th century Adil Shahi governor
Malika Jahan: 16th century Adil Shahi queen
Malleshvara: name of Shiva
Mallikarjuna: name of Shiva worshipped at Srisailam
Mamalla: 7th century Pallava ruler
mandapa: columned hall
Mandhatu: royal hero of a Jataka story
mandir: temple, hall
Manguesh: name of Shiva worshipped at Manguesh
Manikanteshvara: name of Shiva
Manikkavachakkar: Shaiva saint at Avudaiyarkoil
Manjunatha: name of Shiva worshipped at Mangalore
Manjushri: a Bodhisattva
Manmatha: name of Kama
Mappila: Muslim trading community of northern Kerala
maqbara: Muslim tomb

Mara: temptor of Buddha
Maratha: 17th-18th century dynasty of Maharashtra ruling from Raigad and Satara; 17th-19th century dynasty of Tamil Nadu ruling from Thanjavur
Marghabandhu: name of Shiva worshipped at Vrinchipuram
Markandeya: devotee rescued by Shiva from Yama
Martanda Varma: 18th century Travancore ruler
Marubhuta: previous birth of Parshvanatha
Matangeshvara: name of Shiva
matha: Hindu religious institution
Matiposaka: youthful hero of a Jataka story
matrikas: the mothers
Matrimandir: Hall of the Mother at Auroville
Maurya: 4th-2nd century BCE dynasty of Northern India; 5th-6th century CE dynasty on the Konkan coast of Maharashtra
Maya: mother of Buddha
mihrab: prayer niche in a mosque
mimbar: stepped pulpit in a mosque
Minakshi: goddess worshipped at Madurai
minar: minaret, tower in a mosque for calling the faithful to prayer
Mir Akbar Ali Khan Sikandar: 18th century Asaf Jahi ruler
Mir Osman Ali Khan: seventh Nizam of Hyderabad
Miran Mubarak: 15th century Faruqi ruler
Mohini: female form of Vishnu
Moro Pingle: 17th century Maratha commander
Muchalinga: serpent which protected Buddha
Muchukunda: Shaiva saint
Muchukundeshvara: name of Shiva
Mughal: 16th-18th century dynasty of Northern India ruling for a time at Aurangabad
Muhammad: Prophet, and founder of Islam
Muhammad: 17th century Adil Shahi ruler; 17th century Qutb Shahi ruler
Muhammad Ali: 18th century Wallajah ruler
Muhammad Mayshakha: 14th century saint at Holkonda
Muhammad Quli: 16th-17th century Qutb Shahi ruler
Muhamad Shah: 14th century Tughluq ruler; 18th century Mughal ruler
Muharram: Shia festival commemorating the martyrdom of Imam Husayn
Mukambika: name of goddess worshipped at Kollur
Mukteshvara: name of Shiva
Mukunayanar: Shaiva saint
Mumbadevi: name of goddess worshipped in Mumbai
mundu: men's cloth

Munishvara: name of Shiva
Murugan: name of Subrahmanya in Tamil Nadu
Murtaza: 16th century Nizam Shahi ruler
muslin: fine cotton cloth
Muttu Vijaya Raghunatha Teva: 18th century Setupati ruler

naga: cobra
Nagakumara: royal hero of a Jain legend
Naganatha, Nagesha, Nageshvara: name of Shiva
Nameshvara: name of Shiva Nana Phadnavis, 18th century Maratha prime minister
Nammalvar: Vaishnava saint at Alvar Tirunagari
Nanda: cousin of Buddha
Nandi: bull mount of Shiva
Nandikeshvara: name of a bhuta in the form of a bull
Nandivarman: 8th century Pallava ruler
Nanjundeshvara: name of Shiva worshipped at Nanjangud
Naroji, Dadabhai: 19th-20th century Indian member of British Parliament
Narada: celestial musician
Narashankara: name of Shiva
Narasimha: man-lion avatara of Vishnu
Narasimha: 13th century Hoysala ruler; 15th century Saluva ruler
Narayana: name of Vishnu
Narayana Guru: 19th-20th century religious reformer
Narumbunatha: name of Shiva
Nataraja, Natesha: Shiva as lord of the dance
Navagrahas: nine planetary deities
Navalinga: nine lingas
Navaratri: Dasara festival
Nawab: title of the 18th century dynasties of southern Andhra Pradesh ruling from of Arcot and Cuddapah; title of Wallajah rulers
Nayaka: 16th century commanders under the Tuluva rulers; 16th-17th century dynasties of Karnataka ruling from Keladi, Ikkeri and Chitradurga; 16th-17th centuries dynasties of Tamil Nadu ruling from Gingee, Thanjavur and Madurai
Nayanamar: Shaiva saint
Nellaiayappa: name of Shiva worshipped at Tirunelveli
Neminatha: one of the Tirthankaras
Nilakanteshvara: name of Shiva
Nirmankara: name of Shiva
nirvana: enlightenment

Nityeshvara: name of Shiva
Nizam: title of Asaf Jahi rulers of Hyderabad
Nizam Ali Khan: 18th century Asaf Jahi ruler
Nizam Shahi: 16th century dynasty of Maharashtra ruling from Ahmadnagar
Nizamul Mulk: 18th century Mughal governor, first Asaf Jahai ruler
Nolamba: 9th-11th century dynasty of Karnataka and Andhra Pradesh ruling from Hemavati
nritya sabha: dance hall

Olakkanatha: name of Shiva
Omkareshvara: name of Shiva

Padmanabha: reclining form of Vishnu worshipped at Thiruvananthapuram
Padmapani: name of Avalokiteshvara
Padmavati: name of Lakshmi
Pahari school: paintings from the Himalayan valleys
Paigah: 19th-20th century nobles under the Asaf Jahis
Pallava: 4th-9th century dynasty of Tamil Nadu ruling from Kanchipuram
palli: old mosque or church in Kerala
Pampa: goddess worshipped at Hampi
panchaganga: five rivers
panchalinga: five lingas
Panchalingeshvara: Shiva as five lingas
Panchanandishvara: name of Shiva
Panchatantra: folk tales with animal and bird heroes
panchayatana: group of five shrines
Panchika: chief of the yakshas
Pandavas: five brothers in the Mahabharata
Pandya: 7th-13th century dynasty of Tamil Nadu ruling from Madurai
Papanatha: name of Shiva
Papavinaseshvara: name of Shiva worshipped at Papanasam
Parameshvara: name of Shiva
Parashurama: avatara of Vishnu of Rama holding the axe
Parashurameshvara: name of Shiva
Parinirvana: death of Buddha
Parshvanatha: second last of the 24 Tirthankaras
Parsi: Zoroastrian
Parthasarathi: consort of Krishna worshipped at Triplicaine
Parvati: consort of Shiva
pata: painted cloth scroll
Pataleshvara: name of Shiva

Patanjali: mythical philosopher
Pattabhirama: Ram crowned
Patteshvara: name of Shiva
Perumal: name of Vishnu
Peshwa: 18th century prime ministers of the Marathas ruling from Pune
Pramanatheshvara: name of Shiva
Prataparudra: 13th-14th century Kakatiya ruler
Pratapsinh: 19th century Maratha ruler of Satara
puja: rite of worship
pujari: Brahmin priest
Pulakeshin: 6th and 7th century Early Chalukya rulers
Pundalika: devotee of Vitthoba
Puranas: compendia of Hindu mythological stories
Purna: convert of Buddha
Purundevi Tayar: consort of Varadaraja

Qasim: 15th-16th century Baridi ruler
Quli Qutb al-Mulk: 16th century Qutb Shahi ruler
Qutb Shahi, 16th-17th century dynasty of Andhra Pradesh ruling from
    Golconda and Hyderabad
Qutbuddin Mubarak: 14th century Khalji ruler

Radha: consort of Krishna
Raghoji: 19th century Angre ruler
Raghuji: 18th century Bhonsale ruler
Raghunatha: name of Rama
Raghunatha: 17th century Thanjavur Nayaka ruler
Raghurajeshvari: name of Parvati
Raja: 17th century Wodeyar ruler
Rajagopala: name of Krishna
Rajamalla: 10th century Ganga ruler
Rajaraja: 10th-11th century Chola ruler
Rajarajeshvara: name of Shiva
Rajarajeshvari: name of Parvati
Rajaram: 18th century Maratha ruler
Rajasimha: 8th century Pallava ruler
Rajendra: 11th century Chola ruler
Rama: incarnation of Vishnu and hero of the Ramayana
Rama Varma: 18th century Travancore ruler
Ramakrishna: mission established by Vivikenanda

Ramalingeshvara, Ramanatha: name of Shiva worshipped by Rama at Rameswaram
Ramana Maharishi: 20th century teacher at Tiruvannamalai
Ramanuja: 11th-12th century Vaishnava philosopher
Ramaraya: 16th century Tuluva commander
Ramaswami: Rama
Ramayana: epic story of Rama
Rameshvara: name of Shiva worshipped by Rama at Rameswaram
Ranganatha: reclining form of Vishnu
Ranganayaka: name of Vishnu
rangin mahal: coloured pavilion
Rashtrakuta: 8th-10th century dynasty of Maharashtra, Karnataka and Andhra Pradesh
Raste: 18th century Maratha family at Wai
ratha: chariot, temple model
Rati: consort of Rama
rauza: Muslim funerary complex
Ravana: demon king of Sri Lanka, opponent of Rama in the Ramayana
Ravi Varma: 20th century artist
raya: king
Readymoney: nickname of Courasji Jehangir, 19th century Parsi businessman and philanthropist
Recherla Rudra: 13th century Kakatiya commander
Reddi: 15th-16th century dynasty of eastern Andhra Pradesh ruling from Kondavidu
Rishabhadeva: first of the 24 Tirthankaras
Rishyashringa: deer-headed sage in the Ramayana
Rudradeva: 12th century Kakatiya ruler
Rudramadevi: 13th century Kakatiya queen
Rukmini: wife of Krishna
Rumi Khan: 16th century Nizam Shahi commander

sabha: hall
Sadashiva: 16th century Tuluva ruler; 16th century Nayaka ruler at Keladi
Sadat Ullah Khan: 18th century ruler of Arcot
sahasra linga: linga with 1,008 miniature lingas
Sai Baba: 19th-20th century teacher at Shirdi
Salabat Khan: 16th century Nizam Shahi prime minister
Salar Jung: 20th century prime minister of the Nizams of Hyderabad
Saluva: 15th-16th century dynasty ruling from Vijayanagara
Sama: hero of a Jataka story

samadhi: Hindu memorial, tomb of a Hindu saint
Sambandar: Shaiva saint
Sambhaji: 17th century Maratha ruler
Samkhapala: serpent hero of a Jataka story
Samutiri: 16th-17th century dynasty of north Kerala ruling from Kozhikode, known also as the Zamorins
Sangama: 14th-15th century dynasty of Karnataka, Andhra Pradesh and Tamil Nadu ruling from Vijayanagara
Sangameshvara: name of Shiva
Saptakoteshvara: name of Shiva worshipped at Naroa
Saptamatrikas: the seven matrikas
sarai: rest house
Sarangapani: name of Vishnu worshipped at Kumbakonam
Sarasvati: river goddess, also consort of Brahma
sarovar: lake, pond
Sassoon: 19th-20th century Jewish business family
Satavahana: 2nd century BCE–3rd century CE dynasty of Maharashtra, northern Karnataka and northern Andhra Pradesh ruling from Paithan
Serfoji: 19th century Thanjavur Maratha ruler
Setupati: 17th-18th century dynasty of Tamil Nadu ruling from Ramanathapuram
Sevappa: 16th century Thanjavur Nayaka ruler
Shachi: consort of Indra
shah: royal title
Shah Abdul Faid: 15th century Muslim saint at Bidar
Shah Jahan: 17th century Mughal emperor
Shahji: 17th century Maratha commander under the Adil Shahis; father of Shivaji
Shahu: 18th century Maratha ruler
Shaiva: belonging to the cult of Shiva
Shaka: 1st-2nd century dynasty of Western India
Shakti: female divinity, sometimes associated with Shiva
Shakyamuni: title of Buddha
Shankara: name of Shiva
Shankara, Shankaracharya: 8th-9th century Shaiva philosopher
Shanmuga: name of Subrahmanya
Shantadurga: name of Durga worshipped at Quelem
Shantinatha, Shantishvara: Tirthankara
Sharabheshvara: composite animal form of Shiva
Shasta: name of Ayyappa
shaykh: title of a Muslim saint

Shaykh Burhanuddin Gharib: Sufi saint at Khuldabad
Shaykh Zaynuddin Shirazi: Sufi saint at Khuldabad
Shesha: serpent mount of Vishnu
Sheshayi: name of Vishnu
Shia: Muslim creed
Shilaharas: 11th-12th century dynasty of southern Maharashtra ruling from Kolhapur
shilakhana: armoury
Shinde: 18th-19th century Maratha dynasty of Madhya Pradesh ruling from Gwalior
Shitab Khan: 15th-16th century Bahmani governor
Shiva: principal cult deity of Hinduism
Shiva Purana: collection of stories about Shiva
Shivaganga: tank of Shiva
Shivaji: 17th century Maratha ruler crowned at Raigad; 19th century Maratha ruler of Kolhapur
Shivakamasundari: Shiva's consort worshipped at Chidambaram
Shivappa: 17th century Nayaka ruler at Nagar
Shivarajeshvar: name of Shiva, identified with Shivaji, worshipped at Sindhudurg
Shivaratri: Shaiva festival in February-March
Shravanakumara: youthful hero of a story in the Ramayana
Shri, Shridevi: name of Lakshmi
Shrirama: Rama
siddha, siddhara: saint
Siddhartha: personal name of Buddha
Siddheshvara: name of Shiva
Sidi: 16th-17th century Abyssinian admirals based at Janjira
Sikandar Shah: 14th century Madurai ruler
Simhala: princely hero of a Jataka story
Sirajuddin Junaydi: 14th century saint at Gulbarga
Siriyala: one of the Nayanmars
Sirul Khan: 18th century Sidi ruler
Sita: wife of Rama
Skanda: name of Subrahmanya
Somanatha: 13th century Hoysala general
Somanatheshvara: name of Shiva
Somaskanda: Shiva with Parvati and Skanda
Someshvara: name of Shiva
Srinivasa: name of Venkateshvara
Sthanumalaya: Shiva and Vishnu worshipped at Suchindram

stupa: hemispherical funerary mound symbolising Buddha's teachings
Subrahmanya: son of Shiva and Parvati
Sufi: mystical Islamic sect
Sugriva: rightful monkey king in the Ramayana
Sundara: Shaiva saint
Sundaravarda: name of Vishnu
Sundareshvara: name of Shiva worshipped at Madurai
Sunni: orthodox Muslim creed
Suparnaka: female demon in the Ramayana
Surya: sun god
Sutasoma: lioness heroine of a Jataka story
svastika, swastika: auspicious cross-shaped emblem
swami: lord
Swaminatha: name of Murugan

Tagore, Abandrinath: 20th century artist
Tajuddin Firuz: 14th-15th century Bahmani ruler
takht mahal: throne chamber
Talagirishvara: name of Shiva
talao: lake, pond
Tata: Parsi business family
Tataka: female demon killed by Rama in the Ramayana
Tara: consort of Avalokiteshvara
teppakulam: great tank
Tilak, Lokmana: 19th-20th century social reformer
Timmaraja: 17th century Wodeyar ruler
Tipu Sultan: 18th century ruler based at Srirangapattana
tirtha: river crossing, holy spot
Tirthankara: Jain saviour
Tirukameshvara: name of Shiva
Tirumala: 17th century Madurai Nayaka ruler
Tiruvengalanatha: name of Venkateshvara
Toda,: tribal people of the Nilgiri Hills
Tondaiman: 17th-18th century dynasty of Tamil Nadu ruling from Pudukkottai
Trailokyanatha: name of Rama
Travancore: 17th-19th century kingdom of southern Kerala
Trikuteshvara: Shiva as triple lingas
Trimbakeshvar: jyotirlinga worshipped at Trimbak
Trimurti: trio of Brahma, Vishnu and Shiva
Tripurantaka: Shiva as destroyer of the demon of the triple cities
Trivikrama: avatara of Vishnu pacing out the universe in three giant steps

Tughluq: 14th-16th century dynasty of Northern India ruling from Delhi and Daulatabad
Tuluva: 16th century dynasty of Karnataka, Andhra Pradesh and Tamil Nadu ruling from Vijayanagara
Tumburu: celestial musician
Tyagaraja: name of Shiva worshipped at Tiruvarur; 18th century musician who lived at Tiruvaiyaru

Ucchalingamma: name of Devi
Uma: name of Parvati
Umamaheshvara: Shiva with Parvati
Upamanyu: one of the Nayanmars
Urs: festival commemorating the death anniversary of a Muslim saint

Vadakkunnatha: name of Shiva worshipped at Thrissur
Vaidyeshvara: Vaidyanatha, name of Shiva
Vaikkathappan: name of Shiva worshipped at Vaikom
Vaikuntha: heavenly abode of Vishnu
Vaishnava: belonging to the cult of Vishnu
Vakataka: 4th-5th century dynasty of Maharashtra ruling from Nandivardhana near Ramtek
Vali: wicked monkey king in the Ramayana
Vallabha: name of Vishnu worshipped at Tiruvalla
Valmikinatha: name of Shiva
Vamana: dwarf avatara of Vishnu
Varadaraja: name of Vishnu worshipped at Kanchipuram
Varaha: boar avatara of Vishnu
Varaha Deva: 5th century feudatory of the Vakatakas
Vardhamana: one of the Tirthankaras
Varuna: god of the ocean, one of the dikpalas
Vasanta: spring festival
Vatapatrashayi: name of Vishnu
Vayu: god of wind, one of the dikpalas
Vedagirishvara: name of Shiva
Vedanta: philosophy derived from the Vedas
Vedas: ancient scriptures of Hinduism
Venkatachala: name of Vishnu
Venakatadri Nayadu: 18th century Asaf Jahai governor
Venkatadri Nayaka: 17th century Aravidu governor
Venkatapatideva: 16th-17th century Aravidu ruler
Venkatappa: 17th century Ikkeri Nayaka ruler

Venkataramana, Venkateshvara: name of Vishnu worshipped at Tirumala
Venugopala: Krishna playing the flute
Vessantara: princely hero of a Jataka story
Vidhurapandita: royal hero of a Jataka story
Vidyaranya: pontiff worshipped at Sringeri
Vidyashankara: see Shankara
vihara: Buddhist monastery
Vijayaditya: 8th century Early Chalukya ruler
Vijayaraghava: 17th century Thanjavur Nayaka ruler
Vijayaranga Chokkanatha: 18th century Thanjavur Nayaka ruler
Vikramaditya: 8th century Early Chalukya ruler
vilasa, vilasam: palace or hall
Vinayaka: name of Ganapati
Virabhadra: fierce form of Shiva
Virattaneshvara: name of Shiva
Virupaksha: name of Shiva worshipped at Hampi
Vishnu: principal cult deity of Hinduism
Vishnukundin: 5th-6th century dynasty of eastern Andhra Pradesh
Vishnupad: footprint of Vishnu
Vishnuvardhana: 12th century Hoysala ruler
Vishvakarma: mythical architect of the gods
Vishvamitra: teacher of Rama in the Ramayana
Vishvanatha, Vishveshvara: name of Shiva
Vishvarupa: cosmic form of Vishnu with multiple heads
Vitthala, Vitthoba: name of Vishnu worshipped at Pandharpur
Vivekananda: 20th century teacher and philosopher
Vriddhagirishvara: name of Shiva worshipped at Vriddhachalam

wada: palace, mansion
Wadiya: 19th-20th century Parsi business family
Walkeshwar: name of Shiva worshipped at Mumbai
Wallajah: 18th century dynasty of northern Tamil Nadu ruling from Arcot
Wodeyar: 17th-19th century dynasty of southern Karnataka ruling from
    Mysore

Yadava: 11th-14th century dynasty of Maharashtra ruling from Devagiri
yagna, fire sacrifice
yaksha: earth spirit, guardian
yali: leonine beast
Yama: god of death, one of the dikpalas
Yamuna: goddess personifying the Jumna river

Yellamma: guardian folk goddess
yoga: mental and physical discipline
Yogeshvara: Shiva as a yogi
Yogeshvari: name of Durga
yogi: practitioner of yoga
yoni: female sexual emblem
Yusuf Adil Khan: 16th century Adil Shahi ruler
yupa: pillar in the middle of a stupa

Zamorin: see Samutiri
zenana: women's quarters
Zulficar Khan: 17th-18th century Mughal commander

Index

AP, Andhra Pradesh
Ka, Karnataka
Ke, Kerala
Ma, Maharashtra
Pu, Puducherry
TN, Tamil Nadu

Achalpur (Ma), 10D
Adichannallur (TN), 45C
Adoni (AP), 32H
Adyar (TN), 36H
Afzalpur (Ka), 23D
Agassaim (Goa), 11F
Aguada (Goa), 12A
Ahmadnagar (Ma) 6A-B
Ahobilam (AP), 32F
Aihole (Ka), 22E
Ajanta (Ma), 5F
Alargakoil (TN), 44C
Alampur (AP), 32B
Aland (Ka), 24C
Alappuzha (Ke), 47B
Alibag (Ma), 2G
Alleppy, see Alappuzha
Alvar Tirunagari (TN), 45D
Amaravati (AP), 29K
Amarnath (Ma), 2J
Ambajogai (Ma), 9E
Amritpur (Ka), 19I

Anantapur (AP), 33
Anegondi (Ka), 20D
Angamaly (kE), 47Q
Anjengo (Ke), 46F
Antarvedi (AP), 30D
Anwa (Ma), 5I
Aralaguppe (Ka), 18F
Arcot (TN), 38B
Arikamedu (Pu), 39B
Arsikere (Ka), 18E
Ashtur (Ka), 25B
Aurangabad (Ma), 5A-B
Auroville (Pu), 39C
Avanashi (TN), 43D
Avudaiyarkoil (TN), 41H

Badami (Ka), 22A
Bagali (Ka), 20H
Balligave (Ka), 19D
Banashankari (Ka), 22B
Banavasi (Ka), 19E
Bandora (Goa), 11J
Bandra (Ma), 1H
Bangalore, (see Bengaluru) (Ma), 14A-B
Bapatla (AP), 29J
Barkur (Ka), 17H
Basavakalyan (Ka), 25D
Basavanagudi (Ka), 14A

Bassein, see Vasai
Bedsa (Ma), 3E
Bekal (Ke), 48I
Belgaum (Ka), 21A
Belur (Ka), 18A
Bengaluru (Ka), 14A-B
Bhadrachalam (AP), 28E
Bhairavakonda (AP), 34E
Bhaja (Ma), 3D
Bhatkal (Ka), 17K
Bheemunipatnam (AP), 31D
Bhimarayanagudi (Ka), 24F
Bhimavaran (AP), 30C
Bhimshankar (Ma), 3G
Bhongir (AP), 27D
Bidar (Ka), 25A-B
Bijapur (Ka), 23A
Bikkavolu (AP), 30E
Bolarum (AP), 26D
Bolgatty Island (Ke), 47A
Bombay, see Mumbai
Brahmagiri (Ka), 20L
Brindavan Gardens (Ka), 15A
Byculla (Ma), 1H

Cabo da Rama (Goa), 13H
Cabo Raj Niwas (Goa), 11C
Calangute (Goa), 12C
Calicut, see Kozhikode
Cannanore, see Kannur
Chamundi Hill (Ka), 15B
Chandor (Goa), 13F
Chandragiri (AP), 35C
Chandranatha Hill (Goa), 13G
Chandrapura (Goa), 13F
Chandravalli (Ka), 20K
Chapora (Goa), 12D
Chathankulangana (Ke), 47L
Chaul (Ma), 2H
Chebrolu (AP), 29I
Chengalpattu (TN), 37C
Chengam (TN), 38F

Chengannur (Ke), 47L
Chennai (TN), 36A-I
Chepauk (TN), 36F
Cherzala (AP), 29N
Chettinad (TN), 44K
Chidambaram (TN), 39H
Chikalda (Ma), 10E
Chikmagalur (Ka),18
Chitradurga (Ka), 20K
Chovannur (Ke), 47W
Cochin, see Kochi
Coimbatore (TN), 43A
Colaba (Ma), 1F
Colva (Goa), 13B
Coonoor (TN), 43B
Courtorim (Goa), 13E
Cranganore, see Kodungullur
Cuddapah (AP), 34A

Dabhol (Ma), 7E
Dambal (Ka), 21D
Darasuram (TN), 40F
Dattatreya Pitha (Ka), 18D
Daulatabad (Ma), 5C
Degamve (Ka), 21B
Devaganga (Ka), 19F
Devagiri (Ma), 5C
Devakottai (TN), 44K
Dhanushkodi (TN), 44J
Dharmasthala (Ka), 17G
Dindigul (TN), 44D
Dodda Gaddavahalli (Ka), 18C
Dowleshwaram (AP), 30A
Drakasharam (AP), 30F

Elephanta (Ma), 2A
Ellora (Ma), 5E
Ernakulam (Ke), 47A
Ettumanur (Ke), 47G

Firuzabad (Ka), 24D

Gadag (Ka), 21C
Gandikota (AP), 34C
Gangaikondacholapuram (TN), 40J
Gavilgad (Ma), 10E
Ghanapur (AP), 28D
Ghantasala (AP), 29E
Ghatotkacha (Ma), 5H
Gingee (TN), 39F
Goa Velha (Goa), 11E
Gogi (Ka), 24E
Gokarna (Ka), 17L
Golconda (AP), 26E-F
Goli (AP), 29L
Gooty (AP), 33A
Gorantla (AP), 33E
Gudimallam (AP), 35E
Guindy (TN), 36I
Gulbarga (Ka), 24A
Guntupalle (AP), 30B
Guntur (AP), 29H
Guruvayur (Ke), 47W

Halebid (Ka), 18B
Hampi (Ka), 20B
Hanamkonda (AP), 28B
Harihar (Ka), 20J
Hemavati (AP), 33G
Hire Benekal (Ka), 20B
Holkonda (Ka), 24B
Hospet (Ka), 20A
Hubli (Ka), 21
Hyderabad (AP), 26A-C

Ikkeri (Ka), 19C
Ittagi (Ka), 20G

Jagannathapuram (AP), 30I
Jaggayyapeta (AP), 29C
Jalasangi (Ka), 25C
Jalna (Ma), 5J
Janjira (Ma), 2I
Jejuri (Ma), 3K

Jhodge (Ma), 4E
Jogeshwari (Ma), 2C
Junnar (Ma), 3H

Kaduthuruthi (Ke), 47F
Kakinada (AP), 30I
Kaladi (Ke), 47R
Kalugumalai (TN), 45I
Kamalapura (Ka), 20C
Kambadahalli (Ka), 15I
Kanchipuram (TN), 37E
Kandakuthan (TN), 44K
Kandiyur (Ke), 47M
Kanganahalli (Ka), 24G
Kanheri (Ma), 2D
Kanjoor (Ke), 47Q
Kannur (Ke), 48G
Kanyakumari (TN), 45M
Kappad (Ke), 48D
Karaikal (Pu), 40P
Karaikkudi (TN), 44K
Karkala (Ka), 17D
Karla (Ma), 3C
Karvan (AP), 26F
Kavaledurga (Ka), 19G
Kaviyur (Ke), 47K
Kayalapattinam (TN), 45G
Kayankulam (Ke), 47N
Kazhakuttam (Ke), 46E
Keladi (Ka), 19B
Khed (Ma), 3F
Khuldabad (Ma), 5D
Kilaiyur (TN), 40C
Kilakkarai (TN), 44I
Kochi (Ke), 47A
Kodaikanal (TN), 44F
Kodumbalur (TN), 41D
Kodungallur (Ke), 47S
Koilkonda (AP), 27A
Kolaba (Ma), 2G
Kolar (Ka), 14G
Kolhapur (Ma), 8A

Kollam (Ke), 46H
Kollur (Ka), 17J
Kondapalli (AP), 29B
Kondavidu (AP), 29M
Kondvite (Ma), 2B
Korle (Ma), 2H
Kottayam (Ke), 47I
Kozhikode (Ke), 48A
Krishnapuram (TN), 45B
Kudaveli (AP), 32B
Kukkanur (Ka), 20F
Kumatgi (Ka), 23C
Kumbakonam (TN) 40G
Kurnool (AP), 32A
Kurudumale (Ka), 14H
Kuruvatti (Ka), 20I
Kuttalam (TN) 45J

Lakkundi (Ka), 21E
Lakshmeshwar (Ke), 21F
Lepakshi (AP), 33F
Lohagad (Ma), 3D
Lonar (Ma), 5K

Machilipatnam (AP), 29D
Madikeri (Ka), 16A
Madras, see Chennai
Madurai (TN), 44A
Mahabaleshwar (Ma), 7A
Mahakuta (Ka), 22C
Mahanandi (AP), 32D
Mahé (Pu), 48E
Mahim (Ma), 1H
Mahuli (Ma), 7H
Malabar Hill (Ma), 1G
Maligaimedu (TN), 40J
Maliyabad (Ka), 20N
Malvan (Ma), 8D
Mamallapuram (TN), 37A
Manapadu (TN), 45F
Mandagapattu (TN), 39E
Mangalagiri (AP), 29G

Mangalore (Ka), 17A
Mangapuram (AP), 35D
Manguesh (Goa), 11G
Manipal (Ka), 17B
Mannargudi (TN), 40K
Mardol (Goa), 11H
Margao (Goa), 13A
Maski (Ka), 20M
Matheran (Ma), 2K
Mattancheri (Ke), 47A
Mavelikkara (Ke), 47M
Medak (AP), 27C
Mekkekattu (Ka), 17I
Melkote (Ka), 15G
Mogalrajapuram (AP), 29A
Moira (Goa), 12E
Motupalle (AP), 29J
Mounts of St Thomas (TN), 36I
Mudabidri (Ka), 17C
Mudgal (Ka), 20O
Mukhalingam (Ka), 31H
Mumbai (Ma), 1A-H
Munnar (Ke), 47P
Muttuchira (Ke), 47F
Mylapore (TN), 36G
Mysore (Ka), 15A

Nagalapuram (AP), 35H
Nagapattinam (TN), 40M
Nagar (Ka), 19F
Nagarjuna Sagar (AP), 27H
Nagarjunakonda (AP), 27H
Nagore (TN), 40O
Nagpur (Ma), 10A
Nagulpad (AP), 27G
Naldurg (Ma), 9B
Namakkal (YN), 42D
Nanded (Ma), 9F
Nandi (Ka), 14F
Nandikandi (AP), 27B
Nandivardhana (Ma), 10B
Nanjangud (Ka), 15F

Naraspur (AP), 30D
Narayanavanam (AP), 35G
Narnala (Ma), 10F
Naroa (Goa), 12F
Narttamalai (TN), 41F
Nasik (Ma), 4A
Nellitoppu (Pu), 39A
Nemam (Ke), 46B

Old Goa (Goa), 11B
Ootacamund, see Udhagamandalam

Padmagad (Ma), 8D
Padmanabhapuram (TN), 45O
Paithan (Ma), 5L
Palai (Ke), 47H
Palampet (AP), 28C
Palani (TN), 44E
Palayankottai (TN), 45A
Pallipuram (Ke), 47S
Panagal (AP), 27E
Panaji (Goa), 11A
Panamalai (TN), 39G
Pandharpur (Ma), 9H
Pandu Lena (Ma), 4B
Panhala (Ma), 8B
Panjim, see Panaji
Pantalyini (Ke), 48D
Papanasam (TN), 45L
Parel (Ma), 1H
Parenda (Ma), 9G
Parnasala (AP), 28F
Pattadakal (Ka), 22D
Pavnar (Ma), 10C
Penukonda (AP), 33D
Pernem (Goa), 12G
Perur (TN), 43A
Peruvanam (Ke), 47U
Pilar (Goa), 11E
Pillalamarri (AP), 27F
Pitalkhora (Ma), 5G
Ponda (Goa), 11L

Pondicherry, see Puducherry
Poompuhar (TN), 40R
Poona, see Pune
Porkala (Ke), 47W
Prabal (Ma), 2K
Pratapgad (Ma), 7B
Puducherry (Pu), 39A
Pudukkottai (TN), 41G
Pulicat (TN), 37H
Pullamangai (TN), 40D
Pune (Ma), 3A-B
Punjai (TN), 40S
Purandhar (Ma), 3J
Pushpagiri (AP), 34B
Puthenangadi (Ke), 47I

Quelem (Goa), 11K
Quilon, see Kollam

Rachol (Goa), 13D
Raichur (Ka), 20N
Raigad (Ma), 7C
Rajahmundry (AP), 3O
Rajgad (Ma), 3M
Rajgurunagar, see Khed
Rajpuri (Ma), 2I
Ramanathapuram (TN), 44H
Ramatirtham (AP), 31E
Rameswaram (TN), 44J
Ramnad, see Ramanathapuram
Ramtek (Ma), 10B
Ranipetta (TN), 38B
Reis Magos (Goa), 12B
Revdanda (Ma), 2H

Sabarimalai (Ke), 47O
Salem (TN), 42
Salihundram (AP), 31F
Saluvankuppam (TN), 37A
Samalkot (AP), 30H
San Thomé (TN), 36G
Sancoale (Goa), 13C

Index

577

Sankaram (AP), 31C
Sankaridurg (TN) 42B
Sannathi (Ka), 24G
Santan (Goa) 11D
Sasvad (Ma), 3I
Satara (Ma), 7G
Satyavolu (AP), 32E
Savoi Verem (Goa), 11M
Secunderabad (AP), 26D
Sevagram (Ma), 10C
Shimoga (Ka), 19A
Shirdi (Ma), 6C
Shivaganga (Ka), 14C
Shivneri (Ma), 3F
Sholapur (Ma), 9A
Shorapur (Ka), 24H
Sibi (Ka), 14D
Simhachalam (AP), 31B
Sindhudurg (Ma), 8D
Singavaram (TN), 39F
Sinhagad (Ma), 3L
Sinnar (Ma), 4D
Sira (Ka), 14E
Sirwal (Ka), 24G
Sittanavasanal (TN), 41E
Sivagiri (Ke), 46G
Somapalem (AP), 33C
Somnathpur (Ka), 15D
Sopara (Ma), 2F
Sravana Belgola (Ka), 15H
Sri Kalahasti (AP), 35F
Srikurman (AP), 31G
Srimushnam (TN), 39I
Sringeri (Ka), 19H
Srinivasanallur (TN), 41C
Sriperumbudur (TN), 37D
Srirangam (TN), 41B
Srirangapattana (Ka), 15C
Srisailam (AP), 32C
Srivilliputtur (TN), 44G
Suchindram (TN), 45N
Sultan's Battery (Ke), 48B

Suvarnadurg (Ma), 7D
Swamimalai (TN), 40E

Tadpatri (AP), 33B
Talakaveri (Ka), 16B
Taliparamba (Ke), 48H
Talkad (Ka), 15E
Tambdi Surla (Goa), 11N
Tamboli (Ke), 47B
Tangasseri (Ke), 46H
Tanjore, see Thanjavur
Tarangambadi (TN), 40Q
Tellicherry, see Thalassery
Tenkasi (TN), 45J
Ter (Ma), 9D
Terakol (Goa), 12H
Thalassery (Ke), 48F
Thalner (Ma), 4F
Thanjavur (TN), 40A
Thazhathanangadi (Ke), 47I
Thirukkalasekharapuram (Ke), 47S
Thiruvananthapuram (Ke), 46A
Thiruvanchikulam (Ke), 47S
Thrissur (Ke), 47V
Tiruchendur (TN), 45E
Tiruchengodu (TN), 42C
Tiruchirapalli (TN), 41A
Tirugokarna (TN), 41G
Tirukkalakkundram (TN), 37B
Tirumala (AP), 35B
Tirumalai (TN), 38D
Tirumangalakuddi (TN), 40I
Tirunelveli (TN), 45A
Tiruparuttikunram (TN), 37E
Tirupati (AP), 35A
Tirupparankunram (TN), 44B
Tiruppudaimarudur (TN), 45K
Tirurangadi (Ke), 48C
Tiruttani (TN), 37G
Tiruvaiyaru (TN), 40B
Tiruvalanjuli (TN), 40E
Tiruvalla (Ke), 47J

Tiruvallam (Ke), 46C
Tiruvannakoil (TN), 41B
Tiruvannamalai (TN), 38E
Tiruvarur (TN), 40L
Tiruvidaimaradur (TN), 40H
Tranquebar, see Tarangambadi
Tribhuvanam (TN), 40H
Trichambaram (Ke), 48H
Trichinopoly, see Tiruchirapalli
Trichur, see Thrissur
Trimbak (Ma), 4C
Trimulgherry (AP), 26D
Triplicaine (TN), 36F
Triprayar (Ke), 47T
Tripunithura (Ke), 47C
Trivandrum, see
 Thiruvananthapuram
Tuljapur (Ma), 9C
Tuticorin (TN), 45H

Udayagiri (AP), 34D
Udayamperur (Ke), 47D
Udayanapuram (Ke), 47E
Udhagamandalam (TN), 43C
Udupi (Ka), 17B
Ulsoor (Ka), 14A
Undavalli (AP), 29F
Uttiramerur (TN), 37F

Vaikom (Ke), 47E
Vallam (TN), 37C
Varkala (Ke), 46G
Vasai (Ma), 2E
Velanganni (TN), 40N
Velinga (Goa), 11I
Vellore (TN), 38A
Venur (Ka), 17E
Vijayadurg (Ma), 8C
Vijayanagara, see Hampi
Vijayapuri, see Nagarjuna Sagar
Vijayawada (AP), 29A
Villianur (Pu), 39D

Visakhapatnam (AP), 31A
Vishalgarh (Ma), 2K
Vishapur (Ma), 3D
Vittal (Ka), 17F
Vizhinjam (Ke), 46D
Vontimitta (AP), 34F
Vriddhachalam (TN), 39J
Vrinchipuram (TN), 38C

Wai (Ma), 7F
Waltair (AP), 31A
Warangal (AP), 28A
Wardha (Ma), 10C
Wellington (TN), 43B
Willingdon Island (Ke), 47A

Yaganti (AP) 32G
Yanon (Po), 30G
Yercaud (TN), 42A